PRAISE FOR CHRISTIAN CARYL'S
STRANGE REBELS

Shortlisted for the 2013 Cundill Prize in Historical Literature

"Christian Caryl's *Strange Rebels* argues convincingly that the problems of the 21st century were all hatched in 1979, and looks particularly at the move away from secularism and the welfare state."—Andrew Solomon, *New York Times Book Review*

"By amalgamating distinct geographic areas and seemingly disparate historical forces, Caryl uncovers new and vivid questions. . . . A virtuoso of connection, Caryl joins Poland and Afghanistan into a single cold war narrative. . . . These patterns and claims challenge the current journalistic obsessions with economic statistics and with social media's promise to gild the motors of globalization. Caryl brings forward a fierce contest over ideas, religious beliefs, and methods of government. The twenty-first century has not escaped from the age of ideology bequeathed to it by the twentieth century."—*The New Republic*

"[Caryl] makes a strong, sweeping case that the year ushered in, as his subtitle puts it, the birth of the twenty-first century."—*New Yorker*

"[An] engrossing new book. . . . A well-written and thorough work of history." —*New York Times Book Review*

"[A] riveting account. . . . [Caryl] is to be applauded."—*The Guardian*

"A provocative and vivid portrait.... One of the great virtues of Caryl's book is that it invites reflections about the role of contingency and inevitability in recent world history."—*Sunday Times* (London)

"*Strange Rebels* ... is carefully researched, broad in scope and smoothly written. Whether or not we agree that the 21st century began in 1979, or share Caryl's views as to the nature of that beginning and of the century thus far, he is undoubtedly correct that we could not possibly begin to understand the world we now live in without understanding what took place during that eventful year."—*Chicago Tribune*

"The reader comes away convinced that the forces set in motion, for good and for ill, in 1979 set the stage for the world we see today, in ways that were hard to see at the time."—*Wall Street Journal*

"A book about what happens when the world stops co-operating with ideological categories and they lose their explanatory power. It is also an extended demonstration of the law of unintended consequences."—*The Guardian*

"A welcome addition to a growing bibliography on the remarkable rise and astonishing success of the neoliberal credo in the last 30 years.... Nuanced and balanced ... *Strange Rebels* is a fine book which is bound to generate long overdue discussion on the reasons why 1979 continues to loom so large."—*Prospect*

"Readers old enough to recall 1979 will come away from this book viewing that year as much more than just a miserable one for America; those too young to remember 1979 will gain new understanding of the only world they've known—and of why history matters."—*Pittsburgh Post Tribune*

"Christian Caryl is a journalist of the old school.... His book demonstrates the breadth of his experience in journalism. A riveting read, it is interspersed with gripping anecdotes and an admirable attention to detail. Its main thesis—that our current world would be unimaginable without the unique concatenation of world events that occurred in a very short period of time in 1979—is both novel and compelling."—*National Interest*

"Caryl unites his extensive travels with keen analysis, arguing that 1979 was a hinge moment in the history of the twentieth century, one that continues to exert profound effects upon both Europe and the United States. The resulting work is beautifully written and, to borrow a phrase from the late Robert Bork, an intellectual feast. . . . [A] marvelous book. . . . In his book, then, Caryl has staged his own rebellion against humdrum writing and conventional analysis. It is a profound accomplishment."
—*The Washington Monthly*

"Caryl captures something important. . . . In the year 1979, a great many lies were exposed."—Charles Moore, author of *Margaret Thatcher*, writing in the *Telegraph*

"A pleasure to read . . . *Strange Rebels* teaches an imperishable lesson: never underestimate the power of reaction."—*Literary Review*

"Caryl displays an impressive facility with Western, Soviet, Chinese, and Islamic political traditions and circumstances, and he manages to present a relatively coherent and unified view of world affairs."—*Publishers Weekly*

"A highly focused work. . . . As ably shown by Caryl, the events of this cataclysmic year would continue to bear fruit for years to come. An astute assessment of the efforts of a group of historic newsmakers."—*Kirkus*

"At the end of the 20th century, two coiled forces, religion and markets, sprung onto the world stage. From China's reforms to Margaret Thatcher's rise to Ayatollah Khomeini's revolution, they all began in 1979 and have been shaping international life ever since. Christian Caryl tells the story of that pivotal year—and its consequences—with intelligence, grace and lucidity."—Fareed Zakaria

"If you haven't thought much about the year 1979, it's time you should. In this provocative work of scholarship and reporting, Christian Caryl argues that this was the year when a counter-revolution—led by Margaret Thatcher, John Paul II, Ayatollah Khomeini, and Deng Xiaoping—changed the course of history. After reading this book you won't think the same way about the 20th century again."—Anne Applebaum, author of *Iron Curtain: The Crushing of Eastern Europe, 1944–1956*

"Christian Caryl's book is eloquent, elegant, and persuasive. It makes a connection that is obvious once he points it out—about the transformations in the Middle East, central and east Asia, and Europe from West to East whose after-effects shape our politics, culture, and economy even now. After reading this book, I will always think differently about developments in Iran, Afghanistan, China, and elsewhere because of the connections Caryl has drawn out. This is a very valuable and readable work combining the best elements of history and high-end contemporary reportage."
—James Fallows, author of *China Airborne*

"We knew something was happening in 1979. And now, thanks to Christian Caryl, we know what it was. A hands-on reporter with global experience, Caryl follows the common thread running through the seemingly unrelated upheavals in Britain, Poland, Iran, Afghanistan, and China that year, revealing a powerful revolutionary traditionalism that continues to shape the world we live in today. An eye-opening and deeply sobering book."—Mark Lilla, author of *The Stillborn God: Religion, Politics, and the Modern West*

"One of the books I am most proud to have on my bookshelf, it uses one pivotal year to explain so much of where we are as a deeply troubled planet. The chapter on Afghanistan is worth the price of admission alone."—Gary Shteyngart, author of *Absurdistan*

Strange Rebels

STRANGE REBELS

1979 AND THE BIRTH OF THE 21ST CENTURY

CHRISTIAN CARYL

BASIC BOOKS
A MEMBER OF THE PERSEUS BOOKS GROUP
New York

Books published by Basic Books are available at special discounts for bulk purchases in the United States by corporations, institutions, and other organizations. For more information, please contact the Special Markets Department at the Perseus Books Group, 2300 Chestnut Street, Suite 200, Philadelphia, PA 19103, or call (800) 810-4145, ext. 5000, or e-mail special.markets@perseusbooks.com.

Designed by Timm Bryson

Library of Congress Cataloging-in-Publication Data
Caryl, Christian.
Strange rebels : 1979 and the birth of the 21st century / Christian Caryl.
pages cm
Includes bibliographical references and index.
ISBN 978-0-465-01838-3 (hardcover)—ISBN 978-0-465-03335-5 (e-book) 1.
History, Modern—1945–1989. 2. World politics—1975–1985. I. Title.
D849.C374 2013
909.82'7—dc23
2012048264
ISBN (paperback): 978-0-465-06567-7
ISBN (e-book): 978-0-465-06564-6

10 9 8 7 6 5 4 3 2

In memoriam: Leonard Caryl, Joan Greene,
and Henry Greene—the best parents a boy could have

CONTENTS

PROLOGUE: THE GREAT BACKLASH

History has a way of playing tricks. As events unfold around us, we interpret what we see through the prism of precedent, and then are amazed when it turns out that our actions never play out the same way twice. We speak confidently about "the lessons of the past" as if the messy cosmos of human affairs could be reduced to the order of a classroom.

Rarely has the past proven a more deceptive guide to the future than at the end of the eighth decade of the twentieth century. If you take a certain pleasure in seeing the experts confounded and the pundits dismayed, then 1979 is sure to hold your interest.

In January of that year, the shah of Iran got on a plane and left his country, never to return. He had been on the throne for thirty-seven years. He was toppled by a wave of rebellion that brought millions of protesters onto the streets of Iranian cities. The crowds they formed were some of the biggest humankind has ever witnessed, before or since. Yet just a few years earlier, well-informed observers had been hailing Iran as a miracle of modernization and praising the shah for the brilliance of his economic reforms. His hold over Iranian society was deemed unshakable; after all, he presided over one of the world's biggest armies, not to mention a brutally effective secret police. But now his subjects were taking to the streets, declaring their eagerness to die for the cause of an elderly Shiite legal scholar living in Parisian exile.

Most outsiders couldn't fathom what was happening in Iran. Decades earlier the German philosopher Hannah Arendt had assured her readers that revolutions—France in 1789, Russia in 1917—were, by definition, the products of secular modernizers. So what was one to make of the Iranian masses chanting religious slogans?

Surely, the very phrase *Islamic Revolution* was a contradiction in terms. Many Westerners and Iranians alike responded by denying the phenomenon altogether, concluding that it was all a smoke screen for a "real" revolution engineered by the forces of the Left, who had to be using religion to camouflage their real intentions. Others compared Khomeini to Gandhi, another leader who had employed the rhetoric of faith in an anti-imperialist struggle. Events soon demonstrated just how misplaced this analogy was.

Jimmy Carter, who was US president at the time, had a simpler analysis. Khomeini, according to him, was simply "crazy."[1] This was a view that, in its sheer desperation, speaks volumes about the difficulties facing outsiders who were struggling to comprehend the events in Iran. Khomeini was not insane (though he might have been willing to assert that he was sometimes "drunk with the presence of God," since he was a man steeped in Sufi poetic traditions). He was, in fact, a shrewd and methodical man who, in his approach to politics, repeatedly displayed a sharp sense of pragmatism.

Khomeini was no improviser. He had spent years shaping his vision of a future Iran, one in which Shia clerics would run the government and exercise supervision over virtually every aspect of society. But the road to that goal turned out to be a complicated one. Although the Quran offers a comprehensive ethical and political blueprint for society, it offers little practical detail on the ins and outs of administering a modern nation-state. For all its philosophical and poetic richness, the Holy Book of Islam has little to say about the specifics of monetary policy, exchange rates, or agricultural subsidies. So the course of the Iranian revolution ricocheted through abstruse scriptural debates, outbursts of violence, and the constraints of the possible—a history that bequeathed to the new Islamic Republic a range of eccentric political arrangements that make it a strikingly unpredictable place to this day. It should come as little wonder that Khomeini found the path to be so tortuous. In this respect, the "Islamic Revolution" was untraveled territory not only to outsiders, but also to its founders.

The upheaval in Iran had an explosive effect on the rest of the Islamic world. This was most apparent in Afghanistan, its neighbor to the east. Here, too, the decision makers in both Washington and Moscow initially overlooked the impact of religion. When the doddering Soviet leader Leonid Brezhnev and his Politburo colleagues decided to send their troops across the border on Christmas Day 1979 to quash a revolt against the country's recently installed communist regime, Western observers instinctively recalled earlier episodes of the Cold War. Moscow's grab for Kabul, they said, was simply a repetition of earlier interventions in Hungary in 1956 or Czechoslovakia in 1968, when Russian tanks had crushed local anti-Communist rebellions. Officials in Washington immediately assumed that the Russians were seizing an opportunity to make an aggressive thrust toward the strategically vital Persian Gulf. The old men in the Kremlin actually had more modest motives: they were desperate to shore up the crumbling twenty-month-old Communist regime, which had succeeded in the course of its brief life in alienating just about everyone in the country. The KGB even suspected the Afghan Communist leader, Moscow's own client, of hatching covert plans to court the West.

But both Washington and Moscow failed to predict the forces that the invasion would unleash. Here, too, the insurgent power of revivalist Islam took observers by surprise. Some commentators, recalling Afghanistan's history of resistance to foreign invaders, speculated that fanatical Muslims would prove a match for the Russians. But what loomed in their minds was the image of the romantic tribal fighters who had given the British Empire such difficulties in the nineteenth century. What no one foresaw was how the odd fusion of Islam and late-twentieth-century revolutionary politics—a formula whose mostly Sunni version in Afghanistan had much in common with the fervor stirred up by Khomeini's Shiite followers—would combust into a strange new kind of global religious conflict. It is true that the Afghan revolt against Communist rule initially took the form of a traditional tribal uprising. But events soon demonstrated the power of the odd new phenomenon known as "Islamism." Within the space of just a few years, this religious insurgency would supplant Marxism and secular nationalism as the dominant opposition ideology of the Middle East.

This revivalist spirit was not restricted to the world of Islam. There were Westerners, too, who believed that it was time for religion to reassert itself against the onslaught of secularization. In October 1978, the College of Cardinals that had come together in Rome to elect a pope had jolted the world by settling upon a Pole, Karol Wojtyła, the archbishop of Kraków. The new pontiff, who chose the name "John Paul II," was a virtual unknown even to the faithful in St. Peter's Square who had assembled to hear the outcome of the election. News commentators and Vatican officials mispronounced his name. Their confusion was understandable. He was the first non-Italian to become bishop of Rome since the Dutchman Adrian VI was chosen for the job 457 years earlier.

But it was the politics of the Cold War that really made Wojtyła's selection momentous. As a priest who came from behind the Iron Curtain, he had spent his entire career confronting the political and spiritual challenge of Communism. Just seven months after his election, in June 1979, the new pope proceeded to demonstrate his transformative potential by embarking on a pastoral visit to his

Polish homeland that shook Communist rule in East Central Europe to its very foundations. Here, too, it would take time for all the ramifications of this event to reveal themselves—perhaps because no one suspected that it would catalyze a campaign of nonviolent moral and cultural resistance to a twentieth-century totalitarian regime. For all his determination to undermine Marxism-Leninism, the pope himself could not foresee how his efforts would hasten the collapse of the Soviet empire within his own lifetime. "On being elected pope, John Paul II did not believe that the day was close at hand when communism would lose," as George Weigel, his most sympathetic biographer, notes.[2]

Margaret Thatcher's election as British prime minister in May 1979 marked another radical caesura. It wasn't just that she was the first woman to hold the nation's highest elected office; her significance went far beyond the mundane fact of her gender. If the pope and the Islamists stood for the rising assertiveness of religion, the ascendancy of Thatcher signaled a new shift with equally profound global implications: she was a missionary of markets, zealously determined to dismantle socialism and restore the values of entrepreneurship and self-reliance among her compatriots.[3] At the beginning of her term in office, her views on economic policy were so unconventional that they made her part of the minority within her own cabinet. Indeed, it was Thatcher's battles with her fellow Conservatives, as much as with her opponents on the Left, that shaped the free-market agenda that would soon alter her country and the world.

She was, at the time, just possibly the last person in British politics that anyone would have tapped to become the most influential premier of the twentieth century since Winston Churchill. But it is hard to blame those who did not guess what was to come. In 1979 Thatcher herself did not yet dare to use the word *privatization*, a recent coinage that just a few years later would figure prominently in the global market revolution that she helped to unleash.

Markets also played a prominent role in a less conspicuous shift that was under way at the same time in the world's most populous country. At the end of 1978, the septuagenarian Chinese Communist Party leader Deng Xiaoping heaved himself into the top job, and in the months that followed he and his comrades introduced a series of economic reforms that ultimately changed the country beyond all recognition. Emulating other East Asian success stories like Singapore, Hong Kong, and Taiwan, party leaders laid the groundwork for "Special Economic Zones" that would invite in foreign capital and technology. They allowed private entrepreneurs to found small companies and opened up the country to an influx of information from the outside world. And in the all-important countryside, where the overwhelming majority of Chinese still lived, Deng and his colleagues began to allow the dissolution of the collective farms set up by Mao Zedong and permitted the peasantry to return to their old system of family farming.

No one really grasped the full magnitude of what Deng had in mind. No Communist regime, after all, had ever succeeded in reforming itself. The incomprehension had much to do with the fact that Deng, who carefully deployed Maoist slogans in support of his restructuring program, remained a sincere believer in the primacy of Communist Party rule. In the spring of 1979, he even moved to quash a nascent prodemocracy movement that he had initially used to outmaneuver his political rivals. All this obscured the details of a grand political and economic experiment that has left a profound mark on both China and the world.

Today, without thinking much about it, we tend to measure China's success against the leading industrialized countries of the West. As the reforms began to get off the ground in 1979, however, the comparisons that most observers drew were with Yugoslavia, Hungary, or even East Germany (the latter still considered a paragon of socialist productivity). During an official visit to Tokyo in 1978, Deng bewildered his Japanese hosts with an offhand remark about a territorial dispute the two sides had agreed to shelve: "And beyond ten or twenty years, who knows what kind of system China will have?" The Japanese thought that he must be joking. Today we know that he wasn't.[4]

These five stories—rich in event and grand personalities—would be worth telling in themselves. But do they really have that much to do with each other? Surely, Britain's first female prime minister has nothing in common with Iranian Shiism's leading militant cleric. And what could possibly unite the bishop of Rome, the budding Islamists of Afghanistan, and the leader of the Chinese Communist Party? The fact that they lived through the same historical inflection point, one might argue, does not mean that their stories are linked. Coincidence is not correlation.

In fact, though, they have much more in common than at first meets the eye. The forces unleashed in 1979 marked the beginning of the end of the great socialist utopias that had dominated so much of the twentieth century. These five stories—the Iranian Revolution, the start of the Afghan jihad, Thatcher's election victory, the pope's first Polish pilgrimage, and the launch of China's economic reforms—deflected the course of history in a radically new direction. It was in 1979 that the twin forces of markets and religion, discounted for so long, came back with a vengeance.

Not all of the historical figures whose fates converged that year necessarily thought of themselves as conservatives, and none of them tried to turn back the clock to some hallowed status quo ante. This is precisely because they were all reacting,

in their own ways, to a long period of revolutionary fervor that expressed itself
in movements ranging from social democracy to Maoism—and it is striking that
they were all variously denounced by their enemies on the Left as "reactionaries,"
"obscurantists," "feudalists," "counterrevolutionaries," or "capitalist roaders" who
aimed above all to defy the march of progress.

There was a grain of truth to these accusations. The protagonists of 1979 were,
in their own ways, participants in a great backlash against revolutionary overreach.
Deng Xiaoping rejected the excesses of Mao's Cultural Revolution in favor of pragmatic economic development—a move that, despite Deng's disclaimers, entailed a
gradual restoration of capitalist institutions. Khomeini's vision of an Islamic state
was fueled by his violent repudiation of the shah's state-led modernization program
(known as the "White Revolution") as well as the Marxist ideas that dominated
Iran's powerful leftist opposition movements. (The shah, indeed, denounced the
Shiite clerics as the "black reaction" in contrast to the "red reaction" of the Marxists.) Afghanistan's Islamic insurgents took up arms against the Moscow-sponsored
government in Kabul. John Paul II used Christian faith as the basis for a moral crusade against the godless materialism of the Soviet system. And Margaret Thatcher
aimed to roll back the social democratic consensus that had taken hold in Great
Britain after World War II.

At the same time, it was easy to underestimate just how much these leaders
had actually absorbed from their opponents on the utopian Left. A conservative
can be defined as someone who wants to defend or restore the old order; a
counterrevolutionary, by contrast, is a conservative who has learned from the
revolution. John Paul II, who had spent most of his adult life under the Communist
system, knew the Marxist classics intimately and devoted considerable intellectual
and pastoral effort to countering their arguments—knowledge that helped him
to shape his program of moral and cultural resistance. (It also left him with an
intense interest in the politics of the working class that informed his patronage of
the Solidarity movement—as well as feeding a deep skepticism about Western-
style capitalism.) Khomeini and his clerical allies appropriated Marxist rhetoric and
ideas wherever they could, forging a new brand of religious militancy that railed
against colonialism and inequality; socialist notions of nationalization and state
management later played a large role in the Islamist government's postrevolutionary
economic policy. (One historian describes the resulting synthesis as "revolutionary
traditionalism.")[5] Afghanistan's jihadists borrowed from the Communist playbook
by building revolutionary political parties and comprehensive ideological systems to
go with them. Margaret Thatcher, who studied at Oxford when Marxism was the

reigning political fashion, fused her conservative instincts with a most unconservative penchant for crusading rhetoric, ideological aggression, and programmatic litmus tests. It was precisely for this reason that many of the Conservative Party comrades-in-arms who accompanied her into government in 1979 questioned just how "conservative" she really was. As for Deng Xiaoping, he insisted on maintaining the institutional supremacy of the Communist Party even as he charted a course away from central planning and toward state capitalism. Cold War historian Odd Arne Westad describes Deng's reform program as "a counterrevolution in economics and political orientation the likes of which the world had never seen."[6]

It was entirely in keeping with this spirit that Thatcher proudly reported to a Conservative Party rally in April 1979 that her political opponents had dubbed her a reactionary. "Well," she declared, "there's a lot to react against!"[7] It was, indeed, precisely this peculiar spirit of defiance that gave the year its transformative power. The decisions of these leaders decisively defined the world in which we live—one in which communist and socialist thought has faded, markets dominate economic thinking, and politicized religion looms large. Like it or not, we of the twenty-first century still live in the shadow of 1979.

1

Malaise

The 1970s have long been overshadowed by the decade that came before them. For the countries of the West, the 1960s were a period of intense social change and grand political theater, of revolutions practiced and proclaimed. By comparison, the years that followed looked—at least superficially—more like an era of transition, a muddled in-between time of dead ends and thwarted utopias, of disillusionment and drift. (One of the first histories of the 1970s, published just two years after the end of the decade, was appropriately entitled *It Seemed Like Nothing Happened*.) For Americans, the 1970s evoke the scandal of Watergate and the defeat in Vietnam. For Western Europeans, the period conjures up an ebbing of ideological passions that saw so many disappointed sixties radicals turn their backs on revolutionary politics, while a far smaller minority embraced the quixotic life of "urban guerrillas" (as the left-wing terrorists in Germany or Italy were sometimes called).

With the passage of time, though, the 1970s begin to appear less like a sideshow and more like the main event. In the United States, a recent surge of interest in the period has brought a fundamental reappraisal of its impact. In one (conservative) view, it was only in the 1970s that the radical notions advanced by the 1960s cultural and political elites translated into a broad social upheaval. The antiauthoritarianism of the sixties activists translated into a pervasive loss of faith in leaders, institutions, and ideals across classes. Watergate and the lost war in Vietnam fueled an unprecedented political cynicism. Drug use proliferated, crime rates soared, and racial tensions intensified. The lofty aspirations of John Kennedy's Camelot and Lyndon Johnson's Great Society gave way to a debilitating sense of chaos and disorder.[1]

Other students of the period focus on the collapse of economic expectations. For much of the West, the 1970s marked the end of a long period of extraordinary economic growth. Virtually all the countries of Western Europe as well as the United States experienced an enormous surge in prosperity for the first thirty years after the end of World War II. (The French, indeed, refer to this period as *les trente glorieuses*, "the glorious three decades.") Americans, in particular, watched productivity increase steadily from year to year, as did wages and consumption. Everyone benefited: factory workers saw their standard of living rise just as precipitously as that of their bosses. For the first time, even manual laborers could afford washing machines, vacations to faraway places, or college educations for their kids. This upward trajectory of wealth and opportunity continued through the 1960s and just beyond. It was in the seventies that this "Age of Compression"—so named for the steady increase in income equality that was one of its features—finally ground to a halt.[2]

There was one particular event that contributed to this revision of economic expectations. In 1973 the Arab-dominated Organization of Petroleum Exporting Countries (OPEC) responded to Washington's decision to supply the Israeli forces in the Yom Kippur war by cutting off oil exports to the United States and other Western countries viewed as supporters of the Jewish state; the resulting surge in prices affected even the countries that were not directly targeted by the embargo. The result was the deepest economic slump since the Great Depression. Long lines formed at gasoline stations throughout the developed world. Officials in the United States beseeched consumers to go without Christmas lights over the holiday season; gas rationing was introduced. Suddenly, those optimistic assumptions about enduring growth no longer seemed to apply.

The energy crisis had a devastating economic effect, but perhaps its most enduring impact was psychological. Macroeconomic orthodoxy held that inflation tended to stimulate economic activity, so slow growth and high unemployment were assumed to be at odds with high price levels. Central banks in the United States, Europe, and Japan jointly cut interest rates, desperately hoping to stimulate a recovery. But nothing happened. Investment and employment failed to respond—yet inflation, already high before the "oil shock," now began to climb. "Stagflation," as this new phenomenon was called, defied all expert prognoses. The experts in Washington, and in the other capitals of the Western world, no longer appeared as the guarantors of prosperity.

In some ways, the first energy crisis merely exacerbated shifts that were already under way. The impact of the Arab oil embargo on the economies of the West was so devastating in part because the rules that had governed the postwar order were already in flux. At the end of World War II, the Americans and their allies had collaborated to create the Bretton Woods system, which laid out a framework for the global economy in the form of a system of loosely fixed exchange rates. Bretton Woods remained in place for thirty-six years. It established the US dollar as the pole around which everything revolved. By 1971, however, the United States faced a looming balance-of-payments crisis brought on by the costs of the Vietnam War and by its growing trade deficits with rising economic powerhouses like West Germany and Japan. The Nixon administration attacked the problem by announcing that the dollar would no longer be directly convertible to gold. The system of stable exchange rates was over, and the world economy would never be quite so predictable again. It is no coincidence that the seventies became the moment for the first anguished ruminations on what was then called "interdependence." (The word *globalization*, which soon replaced it, earned its first mention in an article in the *New York Times* in 1974.)[3]

Other less visible forces were pushing the world toward interconnectedness. The Americans and the Western Europeans had long benefited from their privileged positions as the pioneers of advanced technological know-how and management; throughout the twentieth century, steady industrialization offered big productivity gains as labor shifted from agriculture to factories. But by the 1970s, these advantages were gradually eroded by the spread of manufacturing expertise around the world.[4] It was in the seventies, arguably, that the West first began to realize that it had no monopoly on the fruits of development. The astonishing postwar success of Japan set the path for the newly industrializing "tigers" of East Asia (Taiwan, Singapore, South Korea, and Hong Kong). The two biggest Latin American economies, Brazil and Mexico, posted tigerlike annual growth rates of 7.5 percent during the 1970s. Growth in all of these countries built on their success as exporters, especially in manufacturing. By 1979, these six countries—the four East Asians plus the two Latin American giants—were supplying 40 percent of the West's clothing imports; some of them were already moving into consumer electronics and shipbuilding. All this demonstrated that new players were perfectly capable of challenging the economic primacy of the established capitalist countries.[5]

Technology played a crucial role in these transformations, too. American sociologist Daniel Bell coined the term *postindustrial society* in the 1960s, but his readers had to wait a few years to appreciate what he meant by it. The seventies brought a forward leap in the development of semiconductors and microprocessors and ushered in an era that would see computers move from the preserve of governments and big corporations to small businesses and even individuals. The cost of satellite communications now dropped to a level that enabled widespread use—with dramatic effects on the spread of news and the speed of global financial transactions. Consider the extent to which the twenty-first century remains in the thrall of technological innovations that were born in the 1970s: e-mail, the bar code, the MRI, the pocket calculator, and the personal computer.

Apple and Microsoft were both founded in the 1970s. In the years before, most people had thought of computers as monstrous machines affordable only by big bureaucratic organizations. The seventies changed all that for good. From then on, it was no longer the belching smokestacks of the huge Ford factories in Michigan's River Rouge that symbolized industrial prowess. The world that was coming into being would be a messier, more volatile place, one in which an elegant idea could end up counting for more than an army of assembly-line workers. In the new US economy, corporations could easily relocate factories to lower-cost venues overseas, services and finance played an increasingly prominent role, and the once-enormous political power of unions was beginning to flag. This shift in the balance of economic forces meant, among other things, that the rewards of economic progress would no longer be spread quite so widely as before. The year 1979 marked the moment when income inequality in the United States began to increase for the first time since 1945—the beginning of a trend that has continued to the present day.

Of all the Western economies that were buffeted by these trends, none of them suffered quite so badly as Great Britain. The OPEC oil embargo dented growth figures everywhere, but the United Kingdom proved especially vulnerable.

Some of the problems had their roots in the political and economic system that Britain had built in the wake of World War II. In the general election of 1945, British voters had given overwhelming approval to the Labour Party's ambitious plans for the creation of a far-reaching welfare state. Under Prime Minister Clement Attlee, the Labourites soon made good on their word. They established the National Health Service and comprehensive systems for pensions and unemployment insurance. They also nationalized key sectors of the economy, from coal to railroads, and firmly embraced Keynesian macroeconomic policies. Even when the Labour government lost power in 1951, the new Conservative government made no challenge to the reforms implemented by its predecessor, thus attesting to their enduring popularity with the public. Thus was born what came to be known as the "postwar consensus," the bedrock of British politics until the end of the 1970s.

The postwar consensus endured because it worked—at least for the first few decades. The British economy grew steadily through the 1950s and 1960s, widely spreading the benefits of expanding national wealth. But by the 1970s, the bloom was off. Rising global competition had revealed the structural rigidities of Britain's social-democratic system. The oil shock hit at a moment when traditional British manufacturing industries were already affected by painful decline. Once-proud working-class cities had turned into landscapes of blight, factory ruins defaced with graffiti. In the 1970s, the British economy tottered from one crisis to another. In 1974, in the wake of the Arab oil embargo, Conservative prime minister Edward Heath was forced to introduce electricity rationing and a three-day workweek. Unemployment surged and productivity sagged. British business seemed to have lost its way. Entrepreneurs fled punishing tax rates for more hospitable climes. Strikes punctuated the national news with benumbing regularity; the trade unions repeatedly demonstrated their enormous political power, contributing mightily to the fall of Heath's government in 1974.

These were the problems that confronted James Callaghan as he assumed the office of prime minister two years later. His Labour Party had won the 1974 election under the leadership of Harold Wilson, who returned to Number Ten Downing Street after an earlier stint as prime minister. But Labour's margin of victory in the election was narrow, and the best that Wilson could do was to form a minority government with his party in the lead. His administration soon foundered as it struggled to deal with the aftereffects of the energy crisis and the intensifying demands from the unions, his party's most powerful constituency. By the time Callaghan stepped in to take the beleaguered Wilson's place, inflation had reached a staggering 25 percent. Outside investors lost confidence that the British government would ever regain control over its finances, and the pound became so anemic that London found itself facing a full-blown balance-of-payments crisis. Put simply, the British state had run out of the foreign exchange it needed to pay for imports. Bills were coming due that the United Kingdom was not in a position to pay.

To his credit, Callaghan did not soft-pedal the causes. He inherited stewardship of the economy at a moment when the old sureties were crumbling. His chancellor of the Exchequer, Denis Healey, declared that Britain couldn't go on spending

its way out of crises. Callaghan's son-in-law, an influential journalist by the
name of Peter Jay, had even become a convert to the economic school known as
"monetarism," which deemed strict control of the money supply to be the only
remedy for inflation. This flew in the face of the Keynesian principles of Britain's
postwar consensus, which placed a premium on combating unemployment through
government spending. The speech that Callaghan gave at the 1976 Labour Party
conference, authored by Jay, turned into something of a elegy for Britain's postwar
economic system:

> For too long this country—all of us, yes this conference too—has been ready
> to settle for borrowing money abroad to maintain our standards of life,
> instead of grappling with the fundamental problems of British industry. . . .
> [T]he cozy world we were told would go on forever, where full employment
> would be guaranteed . . . that cozy world is now gone. . . . We used to think we
> could spend our way out of a recession and increase employment by cutting
> taxes and boosting government spending. I tell you in all candor that that
> option no longer exists, and that insofar as it ever did exist, it only worked
> on each occasion since the war by injecting a bigger dose of inflation into the
> economy followed by a higher level of unemployment as the next step.[6]

Finally, in November 1976, the United Kingdom was forced to ask the International Monetary Fund (IMF) for a $3.9 billion loan to tide it over through the crisis.
The conditions included brutal spending cuts and across-the-board austerity measures.[7] Back in 1945, the United Kingdom had been America's partner in creating
the international economic system that had brought the IMF to life. Now London
was calling on the fund for help in an existential crisis. It was the first time that
one of the world's developed countries had ever asked for IMF support. (Nothing
comparable would happen again until 2008, when Iceland was forced to follow suit
during the global financial crisis.)[8]

This was a humiliation of epochal proportions. A country that had been at the
heart of the Western economic and political system found itself reduced to the status of a banana republic. Callaghan diagnosed the problems but was unable to come
up with a remedy. Something always seemed to get in the way: the resistance of the
unions, the global economic climate, the accustomed way of doing things. The old
ideas no longer worked—that much was clear. But where were the new ones? Britain was waiting for something to give.

There were, of course, countries that benefited from the oil shock. First and foremost among them was the Imperial State of Iran, one of America's key Cold War allies in the Middle East. Nevertheless, the shah of Iran, Mohammad Reza Pahlavi, welcomed the cash that poured into his coffers as a result of the OPEC embargo. He had ambitious plans for the remaking of Iranian society, and changes on the scale he envisioned certainly did not come cheap.

Ten years earlier, in 1963, he had inaugurated the grand reform scheme that he called the "White Revolution." The idea of a revolution led by a reigning monarch might have seemed odd, but there was a certain logic to it under Iranian conditions. The shah knew that his country urgently needed modernization, but it had to be pursued without endangering his own rule. And the main threat to that rule, as he saw it, came from the Left. In 1953, an American-assisted coup had saved his throne by toppling Mohammed Mossadeq, a leftist-nationalist prime minister who had achieved immense popularity among Iranians through his efforts to nationalize the British-controlled oil industry. The shah knew that Far Left ideas enjoyed broad currency among Iran's intensely politicized intellectuals and that the country's deep class divides and entrenched poverty made it vulnerable to the lure of revolution. Though he had banned the powerful communist party, the Tudeh, in 1949, it was still enough of a force to lend vital support to Mossadeq in his nationalization campaign in the years that followed. After Mossadeq's arrest, the shah responded by cracking down even harder on the communists. Thousands of their activists vanished behind bars, and the party never quite regained its former strength.

The White Revolution represented the other major component of the shah's response to the communist challenge. Having crushed their organization, he would now selectively steal their ideas. On paper, at least, the shah's program sounded as though it had been lifted from a Marxist-Leninist manifesto: sweeping land reform, state-sponsored literacy campaigns, nationalization of forests, the awarding of company shares to the workers. In practice, of course, many of these positive-sounding measures were undermined by corruption, nepotism, and bad planning—in other words, by the very nature of the regime they were supposed to be changing for the better.

Yet the White Revolution, fueled by rising oil revenues, did succeed on many fronts. By the beginning of the 1970s, Iran boasted an educational system that was the envy of its neighbors, a broad array of showcase industries, and the most powerful military in the Middle East. Many countries in the nonaligned world regarded it as a model of successful authoritarian development—something like China in the early twenty-first century. (Iran's economic growth rates at the time were similarly dazzling.) Still, the achievements of the shah's rush to modernity brought a whole host of new problems. The reforms jolted Iranian society. Migrants lured by the promise of factory jobs poured from the countryside into sprawling urban shanty-towns. Accelerated economic change undermined the positions of traditional elites like the once-powerful bazaar merchants. And the proliferation of educational opportunity, as positive as it was, raised unfulfillable expectations: the system produced graduates faster than the economy created jobs.

The shah's policies were also calculated to anger one particularly influential interest group: the Shiite religious establishment. For hundreds of years, these scholars and clerics had proudly cultivated a sense of independence from the state. This didn't stop them from doing business with it, or even accepting its favors, but they were careful to maintain control over their own institutions—above all the *hawza*, the prestigious Shiite seminaries, and the wealthy religious foundations. Whereas the shah's father, the strong-willed Reza Shah, had railed against the clergy, and had once even physically attacked seminarians, his son had generally left the Shiite establishment to itself, muting resistance to his policies.

The White Revolution, however, was hardly calculated to meet with their approbation. Its embrace of Western ways posed a threat to the religious elite. The expansion of modern schools and universities offered overpowering competition to traditional educational institutions dominated by the clergy. Secular courts grew more important than those based on Islamic law. Reforms encouraged women to study, to work, and to scorn the veil.

The most prominent critic of these policies was an outspoken Shiite legal scholar named Ruhollah Khomeini, who denounced the launch of the White Revolution for measures that he deemed un-Islamic, such as its extension of suffrage to women in 1963. He was particularly incensed by the shah's dependence on the United States and his closeness to Israel, which Khomeini regarded as the foremost enemy of Islam. Khomeini persuaded other senior religious scholars to join him in urging voters to boycott a referendum on the shah's modernization plans. The shah responded by ordering Khomeini's arrest in the seminary town of Qom, triggering three days of rioting by thousands of seminarians. The security forces quelled the protests at the cost of dozens of lives. Khomeini was later released, but after delivering another jeremiad against the regime in 1964, he was finally deported. The shah and his entourage presumed that this would put a stop to Khomeini's influence within Iran.

They were wrong. In 1971, when the shah staged a lavish celebration to commemorate the twenty-five-hundredth anniversary of the founding of the Iranian monarchy, Khomeini issued a blistering condemnation of the shah's extravagance from his exile in Iraq. Based in the Shiite holy city of An Najaf, Khomeini received a steady stream of zealous young clerics-in-waiting eager to absorb his message that a return to Islam was the only solution for what ailed their country. Some of these clerics later found themselves under arrest as well—but prison, as is so often the case, proved to be a productive learning experience in its own right. The shah had continued his crackdown on leftist dissidents, and imprisonment brought the men of religion together with them on equal terms. Their Marxist cell mates engaged the Shiite clerics in vigorous polemics, debates that would prove unexpectedly useful in the context of subsequent events.

Meanwhile, a new generation of Iranian thinkers was exploring ways to counter the onslaught of Westernization and to assert a distinctly Iranian political identity. A writer named Jalal Al-e Ahmad chastised his compatriots for their humiliating desire to ape the ways of the West and urged them to find a way back to their own culture. Politician Mehdi Bazargan and religious scholar Ayatollah Mahmoud Taleqani speculated about how to bring economic policy in harmony with the teachings of the Quran. Sociologist Ali Shariati devised an idiosyncratic fusion of Marxist economics and the Islamic concern for social justice. He succeeded in melding his passion for revolution with what he saw as the original militant mission of the Prophet.

Neither the shah nor his opponents on the Far Left recognized just how potent these new ideological explorations would prove. Pahlavi and the communists were united in their failure to understand the reactive power of Islam scorned.

The masters of the Kremlin had little reason to worry about the obscure maneuverings of Shiite scholars. The global geopolitical situation in the seventies offered Moscow many opportunities, and Soviet leaders were eager to seize them. The same oil-price hikes that hit the Western economies so hard were a boon for the USSR, one of the world's leading petroleum producers. At a time when the West was deeply demoralized by its declining economic fortunes, the Soviets moved to press their advantage. Their greatest successes came in the developing world, where the process of postwar decolonization was approaching its climax.

The epochal American defeat in Vietnam was the high-water mark of Soviet global ambitions. The North Vietnamese capture of Saigon in 1975 conclusively established Moscow's presence in Southeast Asia. The new pan-Vietnamese communist government immediately granted the USSR full basing rights at Cam Ranh Bay, the superb deepwater port that the Americans had turned into a state-of-the-art logistics terminal. The Kremlin had already established a key strategic foothold in South Yemen, right at the entrance of the all-important Persian Gulf, after a Marxist government had seized power there at the beginning of the decade. Moscow was cultivating close relations with the regimes in Iraq and Algeria. In Ethiopia, a communist military junta called the Derg seized power in 1974, anchoring Soviet power in the Horn of Africa. The Kremlin and its Cuban allies supported a Marxist-Leninist revolutionary party in the bitter civil war in Angola. The USSR maintained a close alliance with South Africa's African National Congress and a host of other revolutionary movements around the continent. Moscow also supported many leftist groups in Latin America.

But despite this upward trend, the Soviets did suffer just enough setbacks to keep them nervous. The Kremlin offered ample support to Chile's Marxist president Salvador Allende, but he was toppled by an American-supported right-wing coup three years after he came to power—one of the few clear strategic setbacks suffered by the Soviets during the 1970s. Another was the decision by Egyptian president Anwar Sadat to switch allegiance to the Americans after years of receiving Soviet assistance. The memory of that betrayal would haunt the Politburo in Moscow for years to come.

The Sadat precedent had particularly far-reaching consequences in Afghanistan. Throughout the 1960s, Kabul found itself the object of the two superpowers' intense rivalry. Afghanistan occupied a geopolitical crossroads, right on the USSR's southern border and north of the Persian Gulf, home to the energy resources that kept Western economies humming. Afghanistan was flanked by two important US allies, Iran and Pakistan, yet it had close historical ties to the Soviet Union, which had been the first country to recognize its independence in 1919. All this made it a focus of Cold War competition—something that the Afghans were able to leverage to their own benefit, at least for a while. The Americans and the Soviets spent hundreds of millions of dollars in their efforts to vie for influence. Washington sent in countless Peace Corps volunteers to offer assistance with agriculture or to teach in schools. Moscow built factories and roads and brought thousands of Afghans to the Soviet Union to learn engineering or medicine. And Afghanistan needed as much of this aid as it could get. It was one of the poorest countries in the region, hampered, among other things, by a weak state that had never managed to overcome the ethnic and geographic rifts that fragmented the country.

By the early 1970s, though, Moscow could begin to feel satisfied with its efforts. The Americans already had stronger regional allies in Iran and Pakistan, and policy makers in Washington were throttling back their assistance to Kabul. As American efforts waned, the Russians stepped up their own efforts to gain well-placed friends among the Afghan elite. The number of Afghan notables who had studied in the USSR or otherwise directly benefited from Kremlin largesse increased. Most important, the Soviets brought thousands of Afghan soldiers to train in the USSR. The Afghan military was probably the most powerful institution in the country, and one of the very few with national reach. Many of the trainees returned home convinced that Moscow's way, with its radical creed of social reorganization, offered the best path for overcoming their own country's backwardness.

Oddly enough, there were even some supporters for this view among the Afghan aristocracy. One of them was Mohammed Daoud Khan, who served as prime minister from 1953 to 1963 under King Zahir Shah (who also happened to be his cousin and brother-in-law). Daoud was a modernizing autocrat rather than a communist. A stint in Europe in his youth had sharpened his awareness of the technological superiority of the West; his long career in the military had given him a deep-seated respect for the realities of power of home. He harbored the conviction that the only hope for his country lay in a secular, modernizing despotism that would wrench it out of its medieval stagnation into the twentieth century. For Daoud, like so many Third World autocrats, Marxism-Leninism was attractive less as an ideology per se than as a blueprint for ruthless national mobilization. In just a few decades, the Bolsheviks had seemingly thrust their backward, overwhelmingly agrarian society into the ranks of the world's industrialized nations; surely, that was worth emulating. There were also more personal reasons for Daoud's interest. A wily intriguer, Daoud understood that Soviet backing—including the support of the many Kremlin sympathizers among Afghan military officers and intellectuals—could provide him with a secure base for taking power.

In 1973, Daoud put his plans into action. He launched a bloodless coup that enabled him to seize control of the government while Zahir Shah was away on an Italian vacation. But instead of proclaiming himself king in his cousin's place, Daoud abolished the monarchy altogether. He declared Afghanistan to be a republic with himself as its president. He received crucial support for his takeover from the homegrown communist party, the People's Democratic Party of Afghanistan (PDPA), whose members recalled his tilt toward Moscow during his term as prime minister under the deposed king.

Daoud soon demonstrated, however, that he was unwilling to let Afghanistan become just another East-bloc satellite. Although he was happy to continue receiving as much Soviet aid as he could get, he also signaled that he was determined to retain Afghanistan's formal status as a "nonaligned country," one that had no official alliances with either of the main parties of the Cold War. He maintained cordial relations with the Americans and expanded Afghanistan's ties with the countries of the Islamic world, especially Iran, Saudi Arabia, Egypt, and Pakistan. During his term as prime minister, he had soured Kabul's relations with Islamabad through his support for Pashtun nationalism, aggravating the Pakistanis, who had a large Pashtun population on their own side of the border to worry about; that he was willing to soften his policies as president demonstrated his determination to avoid the trap of excessive dependence on the Soviets. The Afghan communists looked on this hedging strategy with skepticism; they felt that salvation could only come from closer ties with Moscow.

But Daoud was also unpopular with many conservative elements in this deeply traditional society. He wanted to build a strong activist state in a country where officialdom's writ had never extended far beyond the capital. He wanted equal rights and educational opportunity for women. And, in keeping with the overwhelming majority of the other nationalist rulers who ruled in the Middle East and South Asia at this time, he wanted to structure Afghan society along secular lines. This meant the gradual removal of Islamic scholars and clerics from the educational and justice systems. Needless to say, not everyone was happy about this. But the mullahs and rural notables, fragmented and backward, proved ill-equipped to formulate an adequate response to Daoud's policies. (In contrast to Iran, Afghanistan had no monolithic and powerful religious institutions that could pose a credible counterweight to the power of the government.) Ironically, it was the rising intelligentsia, emerging from the state-sponsored schools and universities of the new Afghanistan, who would figure out how to fight back more effectively.

It took time for this growing discontent among the faithful to find an effective form of resistance. In 1975, a group of Islamic radicals tried to overthrow Daoud in a dilettantish coup attempt. His security forces made short work of the rebels. The president could be forgiven for failing to realize that these misguided enthusiasts—an odd mix of religious scholars and university students—would one day come to dominate the political life of his country. They styled themselves as a new kind of political movement that they called the "Islamic Society" (Jamiat-e Islami), organized according to the same cell structure used by underground communist groups. (Like the Iranians, they had learned much from the Marxists.) For the moment, though, that was little help to the militants. Most of them disappeared into Daoud's jails or execution cellars; the rest fled to Pakistan.

But for Daoud, this was merely a blip along the way. He pushed ahead with his modernization plans. In 1977, he created his own "National Revolutionary Party" and declared that the Republic of Afghanistan was thenceforth a one-party state.

He knew perfectly well that there was no room in such a state for a communist party beholden to the wishes of the Kremlin. One day, he knew, a showdown would come. Little did he know that it would pave the way for a renewed competition between the Cold War superpowers—and for the ascendance of a new Islamic insurgency.

Ultimately, though, the superpower rivalries in the Third World were a sideshow. The crux of Cold War tensions lay in Europe—and, more precisely, in Central Europe. This meant Germany and, along with it, Poland.

Stationed in East Germany was a 400,000-man Soviet army, heavy with tanks, that formed the core of the Warsaw Pact's forces in Europe. Together with the armies from the USSR's satellites, the East-bloc force far outnumbered NATO's conventional forces. The Kremlin had poured the cash from its oil boom into building a world-class navy and modernizing its nuclear arsenal with the latest submarines, intercontinental ballistic missiles, and long-range bombers.

By the 1970s, both sides in the Cold War had reached the point where their nuclear forces were capable of destroying the world many times over, and it was above all this destructive potential that persuaded both sides to launch the era of détente, a concept that became one of the watchwords of the decade. Détente assumed that both sides—the Soviet bloc and its American-led rivals—were to remain fixtures on the international scene for the foreseeable future. Few experts at the time took seriously the possibility that the USSR might just collapse.

Marxism, it should be remembered, was not just an academic theory about historical truth; its adherents believed that they held the key to superior economic management as well. Communist central planners claimed for themselves the mantle of science and efficiency, knowledge that was supposed to grant them an edge over the messy spontaneity of markets. According to one widely held interpretation, American capitalism had demonstrated its essential weakness in the world economic slowdown of the 1930s, only to be pulled out of its doldrums by the extensive state intervention of the New Deal and the centralized planning of the war years that followed. "A Russian seeing the growth of the Communist empire over the past 15 years would not naturally come to the conclusion that its system of political organization was basically wrong," wrote Henry Kissinger in 1960. "If the issue was simply the relative capacity to promote economic development, the outcome is foreordained [in favor of communism]." Kissinger would later become one of the authors of détente.[9] But there were many others who thought similarly. Economist John Kenneth Galbraith wrote a book predicting that the rise of Western multinational corporations and Eastern bureaucratic socialism would end in a hybrid that combined in the strengths of both—an idea that came to be known as "convergence theory."[10]

In reality, of course, the Soviet colossus stood on clay feet. The intimidating might of the Warsaw Pact came at a crippling cost. Peacetime Soviet defense expenditures reached their peak in the 1970s. By some estimates, Moscow was spending up to a quarter of its gross domestic product on the military—a burden that no country, however well endowed with natural resources, can sustain indefinitely. The USSR and its satellites, committed to an economics of secretive autarky, largely walled themselves off from the rest of the world, and it was hard to know precisely what was going on behind that wall. But many planners and economists inside the East bloc were well aware that their system was falling behind.

Central planning had functioned relatively well at the stage when managers needed big factories to produce goods identified as crucial to further industrialization. In the 1930s and 1940s, the Soviets had astounded the world by leapfrogging their way into the smokestack era, studding their enormous empire with steel plants and giant dams. For a few decades into the postwar period, they kept up the pace, rapidly rebuilding the European territories that had been leveled by the Nazi invaders. But by the early 1970s, the boom in investment was petering out. Productivity stalled. Consumer goods and many basic foodstuffs, especially meat and fruit, had never been plentiful in a system where planners gave priority to heavy industry, but now the scarcities became critical. Some historians argue that the West and the East were facing different forms of the same "post-Fordist" crisis: what was to be done with the coal mines and the giant factories that had outlived their usefulness in the new global environment?[11] The countries of the West, to varying degrees, ultimately opted to let market forces sort it all out. But the Russians, wedded to an ideological vision of the primacy of heavy industry, had a much harder time coming up with a workable solution. At a time when the pace of innovation was picking up in the rest of the global economy, the tight control over information practiced by communist governments was becoming a critical handicap. The shift to a computerized, knowledge-driven economy was hard enough for the West. For the communist world, it proved almost insurmountable.

Nor was this merely an economic problem. Just as central planning failed to keep up with the volatile demands of globalization, so, too, the ideological hegemony of Marxism-Leninism stifled the moral and spiritual development of East-bloc populations. Every citizen of the Soviet empire lived the daily contradiction between the triumphant pronouncements of official propaganda—tirelessly and uniformly repeated in schools, workplaces, and the official media—and the shortages, bottlenecks, and petty corruption of real life. In Stalin's day, the discrepancies had been overlaid by the exercise of state terror and the demands of everyday survival. By the time of Brezhnev's dotage in the 1970s, these more immediate constraints had given way to apathy, cynicism, and squalor. Those who lived through the period dubbed it the "time of stagnation." It was a label that evoked a psychological crisis as well as an economic one. Some responded to the void with drink; alcoholism soared. A select few questioned the rationale behind the party's monopoly over history, culture, and the search for meaning. It is no accident that the 1970s were the decade of Aleksandr Solzhenitsyn and Andrey Sakharov. They may have spoken only for a minority—just as did the sixties counterculture radicals or the civil rights activists in the United States. But what they had to say resonated for society as a whole.

This contradiction between public orthodoxy and private skepsis was at its strongest, perhaps, in Poland. Communist rule in Poland, since its establishment in 1944, had a rocky history. Some Poles had managed to continue armed resistance to the Soviet-installed government well into the 1950s. Every few years, it seemed, Poles took to the streets to protest the communist system. In 1956, workers rioted in the central city of Poznan. In 1968 students took to the streets, inspired by the Prague Spring in neighboring Czechoslovakia and the youth revolts in Western Europe. In 1970, workers in factories and shipyards along the Baltic seacoast went on strike and marched through cities. All of these public protests were suppressed by force.

Some of the worst violence took place in 1970, when at least three dozen workers were killed and some one thousand others wounded during an operation involving thousands of heavily armed troops. The reigning party leader, Władysław Gomułka, had sparked the unrest by sharply hiking food prices. He was now forced into retirement as punishment for his error. Gomułka, who had lived for years in Moscow, was a classic slogan-intoning apparatchik. The man who replaced him as communist party leader, Edward Gierek, seemed to offer something different. Gierek—who had studied for a while in Belgium and even spoke a bit of French— was a natty dresser and a self-confessed technocrat who felt equally at home meeting with workers and foreign dignitaries. As soon as he assumed power, he headed off to Gdańsk to apologize to the workers there for the bloodshed and to promise a fresh beginning. Then he embarked on a series of "consultations" with various social groups to demonstrate his democratic credentials. German chancellor Helmut Schmidt and French president Valéry Giscard d'Estaing pronounced Gierek a man they could do business with and took every opportunity to sing his praises.

Gierek differed from Gomułka in economic policy, too. Gomułka, like many traditional Stalinists, had praised the values of economic self-sufficiency, but Gierek saw nothing wrong with expanding foreign trade. Gierek believed, in fact, that co-operating with the West might even offer a way out of an economic impasse that failed to provide Poles with adequate supplies of meat, milk, or housing. As he saw it, his government didn't need to make fundamental changes to the existing system of central planning; instead, it could borrow money from Western banks to modernize the economy. The resulting growth would enable repayment of the loans, Poles would have more consumer goods, and everyone would be happy.

And for a while, it seemed to work. In the first half of the 1970s, Poland posted growth rates of 10 percent per year. The number of private cars in Poland rose from 450,000 in 1970 to more than 2 million by the end of the decade.[12] An opinion poll in 1975—yes, there was such a thing, even in communist Poland—found that some three-quarters of the population judged that their living standards had been rising.[13]

Poles were happy that life seemed to be improving. Yet this still did not mean that they accepted the official view of communism as the best of all possible systems. This skepticism was something that they had in common with many other citizens in the communist bloc. But there was one particularly striking thing that set Poles apart, and that was their loyalty to the Roman Catholic Church. For centuries—even when their nation had been divided up among more powerful European empires—the Poles had linked their national identity with the church, and this pact continued even in the People's Republic of Poland.

The party had done everything it could to efface its rival from the hearts and minds of Poles. In 1953, the Polish primate, Stefan Cardinal Wyszyński, who had managed to maintain important church prerogatives at the very height of Stalinist persecution, went to jail rather than bend to the dictates of the Politburo. When he emerged three years later, he enjoyed a moral prestige that few party functionaries could have challenged and firmly established the church as a credible spiritual alternative to official Marxism-Leninism.

For whatever reason, Poles kept going to church. The communists inaugurated officially sanctioned name-giving rituals for newborns—but people kept asking priests to baptize their babies. The party offered benefits for teens who participated in communist coming-of-age ceremonies—but parents continued getting their children confirmed. The state promoted civil wedding services—but couples kept tying the knot in churches instead. In 1975, despite decades of antichurch propaganda, 77 percent of Poles surveyed declared that they regularly participated in religious activities. The most active group of churchgoers were workers (about 90 percent).[14]

For intellectuals, the church offered the possibility of regular immersion in a competing narrative, one that was not couched in the language of historical materialism. Children who attended Catholic Sunday schools learned about a system of morality that contrasted with state utilitarianism. Those who read Catholic books and regularly attended mass absorbed a Christian eschatology that stood at odds with the dictatorship of the proletariat; along the way, too, they sometimes picked up a historical narrative about their own country that had little in common with official communist myths about the triumph of the working class. By the late 1970s, the Catholic weekly *Tygodnik Powszechny* (General Weekly) had a circulation of forty thousand (compared to three hundred thousand for the party's official equivalent).[15] The Catholic University of Lublin was the country's only nonstate institution of higher education.

By the second half of the 1970s, the optimism of the early Gierek period was evaporating. The government was having trouble finding the hard currency to service its growing foreign debt, and its only choice was to squeeze domestic producers harder to make up the shortfall. A new round of price hikes in 1976 triggered strikes and protests in the industrial city of Radom. Gierek rescinded the increases within twenty-four hours, but the upheaval had an interesting side effect. A new civil society began to emerge. One of the dissident groups perceived a growing but inchoate potential for working-class protest. What if the intellectuals started helping strikers with political and legal advice? The new organization called itself KOR, the Polish acronym for "Workers' Defense Committee."

The assertiveness of these new activists spooked Gierek's Politburo. Western leaders wanted to see their East-bloc counterparts observe the niceties of respect for human rights, and Gierek, eager to preserve the flow of foreign credit, accordingly ordered his secret police, the Służba Bezpieczeństwa (Security Service, known by its abbreviation as the SB), to tolerate a certain degree of dissident activity—a policy wryly referred to by its beneficiaries as "repressive tolerance."

The tolerance was not always in evidence. On May 7, 1977, a young university student named Stanisław Pyjas, a member of KOR, was found dead in a Kraków alleyway. He had been murdered. His classmates took the opportunity to stage public demonstrations against the killing and call for an investigation. Even workers and peasants from the area joined in—testimony to the increasing effectiveness of KOR's efforts.[16] The students who organized it all called themselves the "Student Solidarity Committee." The priest who chose to preside over the funeral mass for Pyjas was none other than the archbishop of Kraków himself, Karol Józef Cardinal

Wojtyła, the man who would later be known as John Paul II. Pyjas, he said, had "fallen victim to the authorities' hatred of the democracy movement among the students."[17] He openly supported the protests.

It was a bad moment for Gierek. In July, eager to avoid being censured by the West, he announced an amnesty for some KOR members (though the secret police continued to harry the group, albeit less visibly). The activists returned to the work of building ties among themselves, the workers, and the Roman Catholic Church, thus laying the groundwork for a concerted opposition to the regime. In retrospect, this can be seen as a crucial precondition for what was to follow.[18] But it certainly didn't look that way at the time. The socialist system, after all, had weathered far more serious challenges in the past.

Matters looked radically different in another part of the communist world. While the leaders of the USSR found themselves confronting the symptoms of stagnation at home, the People's Republic of China faced the opposite problem. The Chinese entered the 1970s in a state of upheaval.

In 1966, Chinese Communist Party (CCP) leader Mao Zedong had launched the Great Proletarian Cultural Revolution. In 1960, prompted by Nikita Khrushchev's anti-Stalinization policies, Mao had broken off relations with Moscow, denouncing the Soviets as "revisionists" and declaring, even more provocatively, that the Kremlin had embraced "state capitalism" (an allusion to Khrushchev's tentative efforts to loosen central planning).

The Russians had also roused Mao's ire by criticizing his utopian plans for the wholesale introduction of communal agriculture at the end of the 1950s, the so-called Great Leap Forward. The disruptions caused by this hasty attempt to reengineer Chinese agriculture resulted in nationwide famines that ultimately killed some 45 million Chinese from 1958 to 1961. For Mao, Moscow's attacks on his policies were further proof that the Soviets were backsliding, exemplified by an ossified, bureaucratic mind-set that amounted to a wholesale rejection of Stalin's revolutionary achievements. Mao insisted that China set itself apart by embracing the principle of "continuing revolution," renewing itself through repeated assaults on the remnants of the privileged classes. As Mao saw it, his views were under attack at home as well. Even though he still stood at the center of an all-encompassing personality cult, he saw many enemies among his own comrades at the top of the party. There was no question that the catastrophe of the Great Leap had cost him some political capital within the leadership; in the wake of the great famine, some of his high-ranking colleagues—most notably Liu Shaoqi, chairman of the People's Republic, and Deng

Xiaoping, CCP general secretary—had modified some of Mao's most foolhardy reforms, thus ameliorating the crisis. This was something that Mao was not prepared
to forgive, and he was eager to unleash a purge that would enable him to get the
upper hand on his domestic opponents. His already rampant paranoia was reinforced by Khrushchev's downfall in 1964, the victim of an internal Kremlin coup. If
the Soviet leader's enemies could band together to take him down, what was to stop
Mao from meeting a similar fate?[19]

The Cultural Revolution was his attempt to regain the initiative. Seventeen years
of tough communist rule had left society seething with resentment, and through a
carefully orchestrated effort Mao now directed these pent-up frustrations against the
party establishment and anyone else who could be labeled an enemy of change. Urged
on by Mao and his allies, mobs of radical young students and workers, organized
into detachments known as "Red Guards," began to launch assaults against officials,
intellectuals, or anyone with alleged connections to the "bourgeoisie" or nefarious
foreign powers. Between 1966 and 1976, millions of people were tortured, killed,
or driven to suicide on the slightest of pretexts. Countless cultural artifacts and
cultural monuments were destroyed as part of a frenzied campaign to vilify the past.

Many of the victims were tried-and-true Communists. Mao skillfully directed
the vicious passions of the Cultural Revolution against his own foes within the
party. The ranks of the purged reached to the highest levels of the state. Liu Shaoqi,
who had become chairman of the party in 1959, was arrested and tortured, finally
dying from abuse in 1969. Millions of others were denounced in humiliating mass
"self-criticism" sessions, thrown into jail or labor camps, or sent off to farms or factories in remote places.

They were soon followed into exile by many of the authors of their misfortune.
It didn't take long for the violence of the early stages of the Cultural Revolution to
descend into armed anarchy, as competing detachments of Red Guards began bat-
tling each other in obscure doctrinal feuds. (The fighting was anything but trivial,
though; in some cases, even tanks and artillery were involved.) Mao soon realized
that enough was enough and called out the army to restore order. The government
shut down the universities, and millions of radical students were dispatched to the
impoverished countryside to discover the joys of honest manual labor. Many never
returned.

The ascendancy of the army also meant the rise of its leader, Marshal Lin Biao,
who for a time in the early 1970s became Mao's official successor. (It was Lin who
published the *Little Red Book* of canonical Mao quotations, driving Mao's personality cult to new heights.) But then Lin fell into disfavor and fled the country after

an alleged attempt to seize power. The precise circumstances of the incident remain obscure; Lin died when his underfueled plane crashed in Mongolia. Though the sloganeering continued, the chaos of the Cultural Revolution gradually ebbed. But the damage it had caused endured for years. Education and scholarship were stunted by the assaults on "counterrevolutionary" science, technology, and culture.

By the mid-1970s, some of the survivors were beginning to trickle back. Those at the highest ranks of the party knew that Mao was dying and that his era was at an end. But no one knew what would come next.

2

Dragon Year

In the early hours of July 28, 1976, deep beneath the industrial city of Tangshan in northeastern China, a slab of the earth's crust slipped out of place. The jolt that resulted lasted only fifteen seconds, but it was enough to scar the mind of a generation. Many of the city's 1.6 million residents, still half-asleep, died as their homes, mostly shoddy brick apartment buildings, collapsed around them. The bewildered survivors, many of them seriously hurt, stumbled into the darkness. The quake destroyed hospitals and blocked roads, preventing emergency teams from reaching the hardest-hit areas, in some cases for days. Thousands of the wounded died before help reached them. The death toll announced by the government came to 250,000; the real figure was probably much higher. (Experts now say that the casualties of the quake may have been three times higher than the official number.) It was the deadliest earthquake of the twentieth century, but unless you happen to be Chinese, chances are that you have never heard of it. The reasons for its obscurity have little to do with geology and everything to do with politics.[1]

The earthquake made itself felt far beyond the city limits of Tangshan. Even in Beijing, about a hundred miles away, residents awoke in terror as walls and ceilings gave way. People milled in the streets, refusing to go back inside their homes. Some moved their beds into their courtyards, too scared to sleep indoors; soon, as if to compound the general misery, it began to rain, forcing many of them back inside. One particularly enterprising family of Beijingers, after camping outside in their courtyard for a few nights, decided to build a makeshift earthquake shelter inside their home. They gathered together all the tables they could find, lined them up, and covered them with the wooden frames and planks from their beds; mattresses went on the floor underneath. Now, it seemed, they could sleep without fear.

But there was a problem with the patriarch of the family, age seventy-one: "He had the typical old man's enlarged prostate gland, which meant that he had to get up several times during the night to urinate," his daughter later recalled in a memoir. "The shelter was low and bending was difficult. That wasn't so bad, but he sometimes bumped his head."[2] He would just have to cope. This was only the latest in a series of misfortunes. Just a few months earlier, he had been one of the most powerful people in China—but then he had been felled by his enemies, stripped of his positions and dispatched into political limbo. His future, and that of the family that depended on him, was unclear. There was no way for them to know how long the situation would last.

The old man's name was Deng Xiaoping. Over the previous decade, his life had described a bewildering trajectory. By the middle of the 1960s, he had attained a lofty position as general secretary of the Chinese Communist Party, just below Mao Zedong, the party's giant, and Liu Shaoqi, China's head of state. The onset of the Cultural Revolution changed everything. Liu was abruptly purged and died not long afterward of prolonged torture and medical neglect. Deng, too, found himself a victim of the savage capriciousness of Mao, the man he had so long revered. With stunning rapidity, Deng fell from the summit of government into humiliation and obscurity. In 1969 he and his wife were dispatched to a provincial tractor-repair shop, where they spent the next four years. Though Deng managed to escape the humiliations and torture visited upon so many others, his period in internal exile was not easy. His family members endured many privations. At one point, his older son jumped out of a top-floor window to escape rampaging Red Guards and was crippled for life in the fall.

Countless other Chinese had lived through similar horrors during the Cultural Revolution; many of the survivors had experienced stories even more convoluted than Deng's. But by the mid-1970s, as the Cultural Revolution faded, a decade of violence and upheaval was giving way to pervasive exhaustion and disillusionment. In this light, perhaps, it was understandable that many Chinese saw the Tangshan earthquake not merely as a natural disaster but also as a portent of serious change. The year 1976, as everyone knew, was the Dragon Year—a moment in the Chinese zodiac that is pregnant with the possibility of epochal transformation, and perhaps calamity as well. (In Chinese history, indeed, those two things frequently go together.)

The earthquake was not the only omen. A few months earlier, in January, the nation had witnessed the death of Premier Zhou Enlai, an urbane party grandee whose passing triggered a surprising surge of public grief. Not everyone was quite so sad to see him go. The people who had benefited the most from the Cultural Revolution—above all Mao's wife, Jiang Qing, and her political allies—hated Zhou, who did not share their radical zeal. Taking their cue from Mao, who had become increasingly hostile toward his colleague over the years, they ensured that the funeral observances were kept to a minimum. But many Chinese deemed this an insult to the memory of the man. As they saw it, this was someone who had worked to contain the worst excesses of the Cultural Revolution, and for that he deserved their thanks. People around the country expressed their loyalty to Zhou in wall posters and commemorative bouquets—often openly defying official instructions against public displays of sympathy for the dead premier.

Deng, who had returned from internal exile in 1973, just three years earlier, had done his best to carry on Zhou's course, which prioritized practical economic development over revolutionary sentiment. Jiang and her friends accused Deng of masterminding the popular expressions of mourning for Zhou and succeeded in persuading Mao—who, old and ailing, was getting more paranoid and ill-natured by the day—to remove him from his day-to-day work at the top of the government.

Just a few weeks later, public opinion caught the leadership off guard by reasserting itself once again. In early April, many Chinese seized upon the Qing Ming Festival, China's traditional day of mourning, to make up for the party's failure to pay the necessary respect to Zhou. In Beijing alone, close to 2 million people visited Tiananmen Square to show their respect for the dead premier. Party leaders ordered the police to move in and clear the square of the vast pile of flowers and wreaths left by the mourners. When mourners gathered in the square again on April 5, they were outraged to discover that their tributes to Zhou had been cleared away. Anger gave way to public demonstrations. Soon tens of thousands of people were rioting in the heart of the capital.

Jiang and other acolytes of the Cultural Revolution denounced the mourners as enemies of the state and called out the troops, who cleared the streets with considerable bloodshed. Many demonstrators were injured; it is not clear whether any were killed. Jiang and her three main allies—soon to be known as the "Gang of Four"[3]—now saw an opportunity to finish off Deng, whom they viewed as their primary enemy. Mao had brought him back from exile precisely because he saw Deng as a skilled manager and problem solver. As Mao saw it, the Cultural Revolution had achieved his intended goal of jolting society out of its lethargy, and he now acknowledged that it was time to restore a degree of stability after years of economic turbulence. Mao still valued Deng's administrative expertise, and he knew that this small yet tough man was just the person he needed to reinstill a sense of discipline.

He also knew that Deng's comeback would balance the growing power of the radical faction surrounding his own wife, whom he correctly suspected of maneuvering to seize the reins after his death.

But by the time of Deng's dismissal, Mao, now eighty-one, was seriously ill, plagued by the symptoms of what appears to have been amyotrophic lateral sclerosis (Lou Gehrig's disease). Barely capable of speech, he was reduced to communicating by means of cryptic remarks scrawled on notepads; often the only person who could decipher them was the comely young woman who now served as his constant companion. His poor condition was clearly visible during his last public appearance in late May 1976, when he received the visiting Pakistani prime minister, Zulfikar Ali Bhutto. Photos of the meeting, which showed Mao's head lolling on the back of his armchair, made it clear to everyone that the Great Helmsman could not go on for long.

Mao's fragility made it all too easy for Jiang and her faction to pin the blame for the Qing Ming protests on Deng. They accused him of orchestrating the "counter-revolutionary" demonstrations in the heart of the capital to further his own subversive political agenda. The ailing Mao finally gave in to their demands, and Deng was formally purged from the leadership. Yet the Chairman still held back from the final blow. He allowed Deng to retain his party membership, a move that allowed at least the possibility of yet another comeback in the future. For all that had happened, Mao still had great respect for Deng's toughness and abilities. (In 1954, in a meeting with Khrushchev, he had once drawn the Russian's attention to Deng, saying, "See that little man there? He is highly intelligent and has a great future ahead of him.")[4]

A few years earlier, as he was maneuvering to return to Beijing, Deng had sent Mao two obsequious letters in which he assumed responsibility for his past "errors" and respectfully requested to be returned to proper party work. But now, in 1976, Deng refused to offer even a hint of apology to his persecutors. This was not the time to recant. Deng still had many powerful friends in the upper ranks of the party, and they would be looking to him as their standard-bearer in the months to come. Deng and his allies settled down to bide their time.

In early July came yet another major event: the demise of Marshal Zhu De, a titanic figure widely regarded as the military mind behind the Communist victory in the twenty-three-year-long civil war, when, at the end of the 1940s, they had finally defeated the Nationalist armies of Chiang Kai-shek, driving him into ignominious exile on the island of Taiwan. Zhu was a man of immense prestige and rocklike stolidity. If giants like him could fall, anything was possible.

This, then, was the situation when the Tangshan earthquake struck. It rattled the members of the gang, already anxious about the impending loss of their patron, Mao. They knew all too well that Deng's demotion did not mean his final defeat. For months after Deng's downfall, Jiang and her friends kept up a drumbeat of demonizing propaganda, exhorting their compatriots to "criticize Deng." In the wake of the earthquake, they even unleashed a media campaign, warning, a bit too loudly, against the misuse of Tangshan relief efforts by their number-one political foe: "Be alert to Deng Xiaoping's criminal attempt to exploit earthquake phobia to suppress revolution," ran one of the slogans. The Gang allegedly took the campaign one surreal step further by declaring: "The earthquake in Tangshan affected only one million people, of whom only a few hundred thousand died. It's nothing compared to the criticism of Deng, which is a matter of eight hundred million people."[5]

Her efforts proved in vain. The Dragon Year of 1976 soon made good on its promise. In September Mao himself finally died. The man who had orchestrated the founding of the People's Republic—its father, its presiding genius, its mercurial god—was gone. Within weeks, the man he had designated as his successor, a colorless apparatchik by the name of Hua Guofeng, moved to arrest the Gang of Four, forestalling the threat of a Far Left coup within the CCP leadership and bringing the Cultural Revolution to an end. A few months after that, Hua welcomed Deng back into active political life. Deng Xiaoping was finally back for good, and he would remain in power long enough to send his country in a completely different direction.

It was not immediately apparent that Deng had his own plans for China. After Hua allowed him to return, in July 1977, Deng initially assumed a job as vice premier, responsible mainly for foreign affairs—a position that seemed to pose little threat to Hua, who was, after all, Mao's anointed successor. Most Chinese didn't even notice that the little man was back until state television happened to linger over his image in the stands at a soccer match. A month later, Deng turned seventy-three. The doddering Leonid Brezhnev, the man who already embodied the senescence of Russian Marxism-Leninism, was two years younger than this veteran of the Chinese Communist Party. Deng could be forgiven for a certain amount of impatience. He had a lot of catching up to do.

D eng was born in 1904, the son of a landlord in the densely populated inland province of Sichuan, a place whose people were known for their stubborn pragmatism. His father, who had enjoyed the benefits of a university education, belonged to the local secret society. His son came of age during a period of intense political ferment. After the collapse of imperial rule in 1911, China became a republic. But the exalted expectations of the revolutionaries who had brought it about remained unfulfilled. Central control proved tenuous. China succumbed to coup, countercoup, fragmentation, feuding. In 1919, still a teen, Deng participated in the May Fourth Movement, when students around China demonstrated against Western and Japanese encroachment on Chinese national sovereignty.

Deng proved a talented student, and his father soon spotted a unique opportunity to make the best of his son's skills. A group of prominent Chinese who strongly believed that China could become strong by mastering Western knowledge and technology set up a work-study program in France. Deng—at age fifteen, the youngest in his group of eighty-four students—set sail for Marseille in 1920. Badly mismanaged by its organizers, the program turned out to offer somewhat less than it advertised. The Chinese students, who were parceled out to factories as cheap labor with little chance to study French, quickly discovered they were essentially on their own. But Deng soon demonstrated his own knack for getting by. Moving from one factory to another, he managed to earn just enough to eat. His experience as an unskilled laborer exposed him to some of the worst ills of the modern industrial work environment and undoubtedly contributed to his deepening sympathy for the Communist cause.

France introduced Deng to three of his lifelong enthusiasms: soccer, croissants, and Communism. The Chinese Communist Party was established in China in 1921. Just two years later, Deng participated in one of the first meetings of its European branch in France. His interest in Marx probably had as much to do with his friends as his political interests. One who took an interest in him was Zhou Enlai, an older Chinese student who had come to France on a different program and would become one of his most important political patrons in the years to come. With Zhou's patronage, Deng became the editor of *Red Light*, the Communist Party newspaper in France, and quickly demonstrated his abilities as a political operator and organizer. But then, in January 1926, Deng's involvement in a Communist demonstration brought him to the attention of the French authorities. He managed to leave the country one day before the police showed up to arrest him. By the time they arrived at his apartment he was on his way to Moscow.

There he attended Sun Yat-sen University. The university, named after China's most revered revolutionary, had been set up by the Soviets to train future Chinese leaders. Starting in the early 1920s, Moscow had pushed the Chinese Communists into a close collaboration with Sun's Nationalist Party (KMT), based on the two groups' common aim of defeating warlordism and reunifying China under a single government. In 1923 the Soviets even ordered a merger of the two parties in which the Nationalists remained the senior partner. The Kremlin's policy reflected Stalin's skepticism about the viability of the Chinese Communist movement, which remained small.

Deng spent a year in Russia, learning the fundamentals of revolutionary politics, before he finally received an assignment to assist Communist Party organizers back home. In 1927 he returned to China, where, after some misadventures, he made his way to party headquarters in Shanghai.

He arrived at a critical moment. This marriage of convenience between the Communists and the Nationalists had held for the better part of a decade. But then, in 1925, Sun Yat-sen died. The man who emerged from the resulting succession struggle was General Chiang Kai-shek, commander in chief of the KMT army (and the father of one of Deng's Moscow classmates). Chiang's main rival was a leading member of the left wing of the KMT, and in 1927, as soon as Chiang had the chance, he struck out against his perceived enemies, who included the Communists. In Shanghai, where their headquarters was located, he unleashed a bloody purge that came to be known as the "White Terror." This effectively marked the beginning of twenty-three years of civil war between the Nationalists and the Communists. It was a conflict that would profoundly shape Deng's outlook, reinforcing his devotion to the Communist cause even as it gave him a wealth of practical political and military leadership experience. Along the way, it would also link his fate closely to Mao's.

Deng managed to escape the Shanghai bloodletting and join the Communist peasant armies then being organized in the countryside—some of them under a shrewd party functionary named Mao Zedong. In 1929 the party sent Deng to the western province of Guangxi to represent the Communists in an alliance with some local warlords. Deng spent a year there until KMT troops succeeded in crushing the movement. The pro-Communist army was destroyed, and Deng left his troops and made his way back to Shanghai, where the Communists were gradually rebuilding their organization. His party superiors were not happy with his decision to leave his troops, and for a while he remained under a cloud. But at least he had had an experience of hands-on military command.[6]

His troubles did not end there, though. During his studies in Moscow, he had met a young woman and married her. Now, shortly after his return to Shanghai, she died in the hospital during childbirth; their infant daughter died as well. The Hobbesian world of the Chinese civil war left little time for private grief, and Deng was not particularly sentimental to begin with. No sooner was this personal tragedy

over than the party center was sending him on his next assignment. It took him
to the Jiangxi Soviet, the Communist haven in the Southeast where Mao and his
peasant army had succeeded in creating a mountain stronghold that was holding
out against the Nationalists. Deng was deeply impressed when he saw what Mao
had achieved. Deng, after all, knew from his own disheartening experience just how
hard it was to set up a viable base area.[7] This was just the beginning of a long professional relationship between the two men.

The history of the Chinese Communist Party during the civil war is a tale of intrigue and intricate factional maneuverings. Different groups within the party vied
for supremacy, and there was a period in the early 1930s when being associated
with Mao was not necessarily a plus. Party headquarters accused Mao of exceeding his authority, and Deng—now characterized as a leader of the "Mao faction" in
the party—was accused of "defeatism" and purged. He was harshly criticized and
stripped of his post; he may have been imprisoned for a while. Not long before, he
had married for a second time. But now, as the party leadership ratcheted up the
pressure, his second wife publicly renounced him, demanded a divorce, and then
quickly married another man. Deng, who had previously enjoyed a reputation as
a talkative extrovert, withdrew into himself. For the rest of his life, he would be
known as someone who was careful with his words.[8]

As good Communists learn early, however, history waits for no man. In 1934
Nationalist pressure finally forced Mao to abandon his Jiangxi stronghold, and the
Communist forces resolved to set off for another base on the other side of the country. It was this trek that would later become known as the "Long March." It took
them more than six thousand miles, wandering over much of western China on their
way to a Communist refuge in the far northwestern part of the country. The journey
took them through some of China's most formidable terrain: mountains, swamps,
and deserts. Nationalist troops harried them along the way. Illness and hunger
took an additional toll. The Communists began their trek with eighty-six thousand
troops and ended it a year later with ten thousand. In objective terms, it doesn't seem
like much of a victory, but the fact that anyone had survived at all counted as an
achievement. The party's mythmakers stylized the march into an epochal triumph.

It certainly marked an important watershed. It was in the course of the Long
March that Mao succeeded in besting his opponents within the party and became
its undisputed leader—a development that boosted the career of Deng, now regarded as one of Mao's most loyal deputies. During the march, Deng had the job
of overseeing the party's propaganda effort, though the difficulties of the trip gave

him scant opportunity to show off his talents. A few months into the journey, he contracted typhoid and nearly died.

But he did make it to the end, and in 1937 he was ready when the Japanese invasion of China gave him his next chance to make a mark. The armies of Imperial Japan had begun their push into Chinese territory six years earlier, taking advantage of the power vacuum resulting from the seemingly endless fighting among Communists, Nationalists, and warlords to assert control over the resource-rich northeastern region of Manchuria. In 1937 Japanese forces seized upon a pretext to advance far into the Chinese interior. By the end of the year, they had occupied Shanghai and the capital of Nanjing.

Once again, albeit begrudgingly, the CCP and the Nationalists joined forces to combat the common foe. As part of a new effort to expel the invaders, Deng was dispatched to an important job in the Eighth Route Army, a Communist force based in the interior province of Shaanxi. Deng became the political commissar of the most powerful unit in the army, the 129th Division, commanded by his fellow Sichuanese Liu Bocheng, a talented strategist with a gift for command. Liu, who had lost an eye during an earlier campaign, had ample combat experience from the warlord era and had also studied in the Soviet Union.

The two turned out to be a highly effective team. For the rest of the war, they showed themselves to be one of the most effective Communist units in the field. Deng's hands-on knowledge of the business of war would prove enormously beneficial decades down the road, when his close relationships with top generals would stand him in good stead. But running the 129th Division also provided valuable lessons in civilian administration. For eight years, Deng and Liu controlled a large swath of territory centered on Taihang Mountain in eastern Shaanxi, and they bore responsibility for making sure that the local population, whose support was crucial to the continued existence of the base, was able to maintain a reasonable standard of living. Deng followed the usual Communist practice of killing or imprisoning the landlords and dividing up the land among the peasants. Yet unlike some other leaders, he eschewed radical Marxist doctrine in favor of giving farmers incentives to produce. "People should be taxed according to the average production of recent years and any amount exceeding that average should entirely belong to the producer," Deng declared.[9]

Deng did find time, in 1939, to head back to Mao's headquarters in far-off Yanan to marry a young university-educated activist named Zhuo Lin. (Like Deng, she came from a relatively well-to-do family; her father was a prosperous pork merchant.) This time the marriage stuck. The two remained together for fifty-eight years and had five children. They were married in front of Mao's cave in Yanan—as visible an example of solid Chinese Communist pedigree as you could get.

As the war with Japan drew to a close in the 1940s, Mao's old feud with Chiang Kai-shek and the KMT came back out into the open. Deng was now the highest Communist Party official in a key northeastern region of the country, and the forces he and Liu commanded played a crucial role in the decisive phase of the civil war, the Huai Hai Campaign of 1948–1949. The Central Plains Army of Deng and Liu formed the core of an overall Communist force that numbered half a million men opposing a larger and much better-equipped Nationalist army. By the end of the campaign, Deng had risen to become the political commissar for the army. He earned a reputation as a ruthless, hard-charging leader. He wanted results, and he was not overly worried about the casualty rate needed to achieve them. The climactic battles of the Huai Hai Campaign, which caused hundreds of thousands of Nationalist casualties, effectively finished Chiang's armies as a fighting force. KMT resistance collapsed; Chiang fled to Taiwan. From then on, it was a rout.

In 1949 Mao's forces moved into Beijing, which the Communists declared to be the capital of the new People's Republic of China. Deng's impressive military record over the years positioned him for a swift rise now that Communist power was firmly established on the mainland. He assumed responsibility for governing the southwestern region of the country, including the especially unruly Guangdong Province, which had been a heartland of Nationalist support during the civil war. He rose to the occasion, and in 1955 he joined the Politburo Standing Committee and assumed the rank of general secretary of the party's Central Committee. In 1956 he gave one of the two main reports at that year's important party congress; the other was delivered by chairman-in-waiting Liu Shaoqi, the man who would soon become one of his main political allies.

As the party's leading expert on foreign relations, Deng traveled to Moscow in 1956 for what would be one of the great turning points in twentieth-century history. This was when Khrushchev gave his "Secret Speech" to the Twentieth Congress of the Communist Party of the Soviet Union. In the speech—officially titled "On the Cult of Personality and Its Consequences"—Khrushchev presented a startling indictment of Stalin and his rule, including details of the Great Terror (though dwelling specifically only on its victims among the Bolsheviks) and Lenin's suspicions about the man who became his successor. The Chinese delegation was not allowed to attend the actual speech but, like other foreign Communist Parties present for the Congress, received a copy of it the next day. The speech was a terrible shock for party stalwarts, both Soviet and foreign. For devoted Communists, Stalin had been something akin to a demigod, the leader whose own infallibility was ensured by the perfection of Marxist doctrine. To see him dethroned in this way by the current Soviet leader was traumatic. Some of those who got wind of the speech committed suicide, and the Polish party chief died of a heart attack shortly after being apprised of the speech's contents.

Deng's reaction seems to have been entirely clearheaded: he immediately understood its profound systemic implications—and the implicit challenge it posed to Mao, an unrepentant Stalinist. His report to Beijing was correspondingly critical, and in the years to come Khrushchev's de-Stalinizing policies would become a major factor in the deepening split between the USSR and Communist China. The Chinese accused Khrushchev and his Kremlin of debilitating "revisionism" and aspiring to seize the mantle of leadership in the Communist world. Just as importantly, perhaps, Deng would retain for the rest of his life a vivid image of the destabilizing effect that questioning the legacy of a longtime party leader could have—a point that informed his thinking when it came time to address Communist China's approach to reform at the end of the 1970s.

In the wake of Khrushchev's speech, Mao—intensely paranoid even in the best of times—resolved to safeguard against any potential de-Stalinizing tendencies in China. In 1957 he unleashed a vicious purge (the so-called Anti-Rightist Campaign) of critical intellectuals that ultimately sent hundreds of thousands of people to jails, concentration camps, or internal exile. Deng proved his fealty by running the campaign. It was only in 1960 that Deng finally dared to distance himself from the chairman, delicately addressing "problems in Mao's thinking."[10] (This was just after the calamity of the Great Leap Forward, when Mao was probably more vulnerable politically than at just about any other time in his career.)

Now, allying himself with the newly ascendant Liu Shaoqi, Deng began to suggest that it was time for China to consolidate after the long years of upheaval and tend to the efficiency of production and the task of raising living standards. In 1961, during a speech to a party assembly, he uttered his famous aphorism: "I don't care if it's a black cat or white cat. It's a good cat if it catches mice."[11] It was a line that opened him up to the inevitable accusation of infidelity to revolutionary ideals, but Deng dismissed the charge with aplomb: "If they tell you you're a capitalist roader, it means you're doing a good job," he remarked.[12] This stubbornness came in handy during the trials of the Cultural Revolution that were about to follow.

By the mid-1960s, Deng, like other Chinese Community Party leaders, had emerged from a chastening school. His experience in the civil war had hardened him, reinforcing his belief in the essential rightness of Communist Party leadership. It gave him crucial on-the-job experience in military command as well as a web of valuable personal contacts, bolstered by a sense of shared adversity. It also taught him a great deal about political intrigue. From his master, Mao, he had learned the importance of controlling the terms of the debate if he wished to gain the upper hand over his enemies. At the same time, his stint as the de facto commander in chief of Taihang Mountain had provided him with a real-world laboratory in which he learned the virtues of pragmatic adaptation to complex political realities.

In the 1950s, then, Khrushchev's "Secret Speech" had shown Deng the threats posed by uncontrolled political liberalization, while the disaster of the Great Leap Forward had revealed for all to see the drawbacks of belief in Mao's infallibility. For Deng, these two lessons were not contradictory; they were, in fact, equally crucial to his evolving administrative philosophy, which viewed the maintenance of political stability as a crucial precondition for much-needed economic reform and experimentation.

In the years ahead, it was Deng's ruthless self-confidence, steeled in the long years of infighting and war, that would prove decisive. Winston Lord, a former US ambassador to China, recalled him this way:

> He was four foot ten, but he dominated the room. His feet barely touched the floor. He was a chain smoker. He used the spittoon freely. He was very skillful in his meetings . . . [He] would get off a few pithy one-liners to dominate the international media, to get the themes across he wanted to make sure the world heard, then in a meeting he would draw out his interlocutor first, and then with seeming casualness, segue into two or three topics that he was determined to make points on.
>
> He was very straightforward. He didn't use elusive symbols and allegories like Mao, and he didn't have the elegance of [Zhou Enlai]. He was very practical. He could be self-deprecating about himself and about China, which of course reflected the fact that he had serene confidence in both.[13]

The word *practical* crops up in accounts of Deng's life with benumbing frequency, and with good reason. This was a man who had mastered the art of survival. Now, as he assumed all the trappings of power, it was time to see what he could achieve with the time he had left.

3

"A Wild but Welcoming State of Anarchy"

I n the early twenty-first century, we tend to think of Afghanistan as a place cursed by eternal warfare, an endlessly bleeding wound in the global body politic. What we tend to overlook is that this view is a recent invention, one conditioned by the country's recent past. In the 1970s, before war broke out, the image of Afghanistan was starkly different—more Bali or Bhutan than geopolitical trouble spot. These were the years of the "Hippie Trail," when self-designated "world travelers" piled into used Volkswagen vans and embarked on a path of self-discovery that led from Istanbul to Katmandu.

Afghanistan was not the end of the road, but it was certainly one of the high points. "Herat [on the border with Iran] was the first real destination on the hippie trail," one traveler recalls. "The paranoia of oppressive control in Turkey and Iran was left behind for a wilder but welcoming state of anarchy."[1] Afghans seemed to love foreigners. You could always find someone who was willing to take time off for a friendly chat—or for a shared sampling of the fine local hashish. Everyone seemed to be smoking it. And the prices were hard to beat. Yes, of course, this was the result of local impoverishment. But surely the best thing you could do to remedy that was to spend your own money.

In Kabul you could stay at Sigi's Hotel, a landmark on the trail. Since the dollar or the D-mark went such a long way in 1970s Afghanistan, you could easily linger for weeks, getting high, feasting on cheap kebab, or venturing out to the fantastic archaeological sites that dotted the city and its environs. (True hippies especially enjoyed communing with the giant Buddhas carved out of a hillside in Bamiyan, a day's drive away from the capital.) Then, when the time was ready, you could continue the journey all the way to Nepal, the El Dorado for recreational drug users. Still, trail adventurers later recalled their sojourns in Afghanistan—easygoing, soporific Afghanistan—with particular fondness.

But they weren't the only ones. The Westerners who actually lived in Afghanistan in the 1970s, on their tours of duty with the Peace Corps or European-sponsored development projects, loved the place for its laid-back exoticism. If you needed a bit of modern luxury, all you had to do was pop over to one of the foreigners' clubs, which offered all the amenities, or pay a visit to the Hotel Intercontinental for a dip in its fine pool. And crime was minimal. An American high school student whose father was doing a stint at the University of Kabul thought nothing of riding alone on the bus to Peshawar, across the border in Pakistan, for the weekend.[2]

Such views were not entirely illusory. As the 1970s dawned, Afghanistan was unquestionably poor and backward, but it seemed to be making remarkable progress in its efforts to embrace modern life. In the 1971 edition of her guidebook to Kabul, the American author Nancy Hatch Dupree bemoaned the difficulties of tracking the attractions of a city in which "change is rampant." But she was determined to document the many charms that remained—like the Khyber Restaurant on the first floor of the Finance Ministry in Pashtunistan Square: "It is a popular meeting place in Kabul, especially during the summer when sidewalk tables set under gay umbrellas beckon weary sightseers. The Ariana Cinema next to the restaurant shows foreign pictures in many different languages." There were magnificent museums and countless historical sites—all of them catering to the influx of foreign tourists: "Rounding the curve on Mohammad Jan Khan Wat, one notes many modern stores and small hotels which have sprung up in the last few years to attract the ever-increasing number of visitors to Kabul." There was also the Nejat School for Boys, which "will soon shift to ultra-modern quarters currently nearing completion on the road to the airport, across from the area hotel." (More and more of Kabul's schools, as she noted, were going coed.) Dupree also pointed out the Kabul Zoo, which received some of its animals from its sister institution in the West German city of Cologne. There were the bazaars where you could purchase yarn or lentils or the garlands of paper flowers that were used to decorate cars during weddings and the shops where you could buy lapis lazuli or dried fruits or karakul skins, "for which Afghanistan is justly famous."

One of the most conspicuous features of Afghanistan's tentative modernization was the prominent role of outside sponsors. On the outskirts of Kabul, Dupree noted the construction of the Mikrorayon, "a series of high-rise apartments being constructed with assistance from the Soviet Union."[3] For years Afghanistan had been playing both sides in the Cold War. As part of their strategic rivalry in Asia, both the Soviets and the Americans were willing to contribute significant amounts of aid in return for Kabul's friendship. The trick with "nonalignment," as this policy was known, was keeping one's balance.

And for a long time, it worked just fine. Afghanistan dispatched students to the United States on Fulbright scholarships for business degrees; others headed off to the USSR to study the technical professions. Foreign aid poured in. The Americans helped build dams and schools, West Germans trained the police force, and the Russians laid out natural gas pipelines and power plants. Development money also helped the Afghans to jump-start locally run businesses, like textile factories. And some of the funds were also used to build up the institutions of government. Every year, it seemed, Kabul erected yet another ministry building in the brutalist concrete style that was supposed to signify enlightened modernity. Each month brought a new announcement about some new agreement on technical assistance or foreign investment. The country was moving ahead. Peace reigned. The last serious uprising against the government had taken place in 1929.[4]

What the foreigners tended to overlook, however, was the extent to which their own presence reflected the weakness of the Afghan state, which remained critically dependent on aid from outsiders and had little motive for change as long as the money from its patrons kept flowing in. Both the Americans and the Soviets were happy to buy influence in the strategically important country. From 1956 to 1973, foreign grants and loans made up 80 percent of the country's spending on investment and development. Afghanistan was also heavily dependent on the export of agricultural products and natural resources, including, eventually, natural gas, most of which went to the USSR, which had also supplied virtually all of the engineering know-how and facilities for the nascent industry. One of Afghanistan's biggest export hits consisted of the skins of those karakul sheep mentioned by Dupree, which were prized by hatmakers around the world. Still, taken together, these weren't exactly the ingredients of a robust modern economy. In the early 1960s, indeed, 80 percent of all taxes came from exports. By the 1970s, taxes from domestic sources, mainly on land and livestock, accounted for less than 2 percent of government revenues. A survey of fifty developing countries from this period showed that only one—Nepal—had a poorer record than Afghanistan's when it came to collecting taxes from the citizenry.[5]

Afghanistan in the 1970s thus offered a textbook example of what the economists like to call a "rentier state"—one that lives by exploiting the advantages of
good fortune (natural resources or favorable strategic position) rather than capital-
izing on the talents and skills of its people. There were deep-seated historical reasons for this. Afghan rulers had long governed according to a somewhat minimalist
philosophy, dictated, to some extent, by the country's bewildering ethnic diversity
and its fantastically rugged terrain. Roads were few and far between. The high
mountains and deep valleys fragmented the population, exacerbating differences
of language and custom. When the Soviets finally completed the Salang Tunnel in
1964, the world's highest traffic tunnel at the time, they supplied the missing link to
a road that connected the northern and southern halves of the country for the first
time in its history. The Americans, meanwhile, had already built the first east-west
highway, from Kabul to Kandahar. This new infrastructure transformed Afghanistan's economy and dramatically simplified the government's ability to communicate
with the interior.

Even so, the average Afghan's dealings with Kabul remained shallow and infrequent. The primary function of the local administration was less to provide people
with public services, few of which were available in the countryside to begin with,
than to prevent them from organizing opposition. Most people correspondingly
regarded officials as a remote and somewhat unnecessary presence, better avoided
than engaged. American anthropologist Thomas Barfield, who conducted field research in Afghanistan in the mid-1970s, noted that, for most Afghans in the countryside, "government" meant not a concept but a place, namely, the local government
compound. "On passing out its front gate, and particularly after leaving the road
that led to it,'government' ended," he wrote.[6] (And this, in turn, helps to explain why
literacy rates in the country were so shockingly low. In the 1970s, only 10 percent of
the population could read or write—and only 2 percent of women.)[7]

The real power in most communities came from traditional leaders, usually
tribal notables or landowners. The local khan might provide jobs, adjudicate disputes, or allocate resources (especially water, that scarce but vital commodity for
this overwhelmingly rural population), and his authority rippled through the intricate networks of kinship that structured most of society. The leader's followers
judged his legitimacy in part according to his success at distributing wealth. In the
old days, that might have meant the booty from battle, but in the 1960s and 1970s,
this often translated into access to a cushy government job or a place in the university in Kabul. Afghanistan is often described rather loosely as a "tribal society," but
the reality is more complex, given the fantastic ethnic and social diversity of the

place. The word Afghans use for the defining characteristic of their society is *qawm*, which can refer not only to networks of blood relationships but also to linguistic, religious, and geographical traits that shape the group to which an individual belongs.[8] A Turkic-speaking Uzbek might define himself above all by the dialect that he speaks, a Persian-speaking Tajik by the district that he hails from, a Pashtun by his tribal affiliation.

If anything could be said to unite them all, it is religion. Virtually all Afghans are Muslims, most of them Sunnis. (The most prominent exception are the Hazaras, an ethnic group, descended from the Mongols, who happen to be Shiites.) Even in the 1960s and '70s, observers often remarked upon the simple piety of the people in Afghanistan. All activity stopped whenever the call to prayer sounded from the local mosque. References to God and the Prophet punctuated everyday speech. Public figures were expected to invoke the supremacy of the Almighty at every turn.

Yet this did not mean that religion and politics seamlessly overlapped. Throughout their history, Afghans had known rule by kings, not religious leaders. Village mullahs, who performed a variety of religious services in exchange for fees, were often regarded as corrupt or buffoonish, the butt of jokes rather than figures of respect.[9] There were, of course, some religious figures who enjoyed privileged status—Islamic scholars, perhaps, or *pirs*, Sufi spiritual leaders. But none of these individuals had any clearly defined institutional power over the others. The diffuse quality of Afghan Islam was also a product of practices that many other Sunni Muslims would have regarded as heterodox—such as the veneration of saints, whose graves, beflagged and decorated, were treated as holy places. In Iran, the Shiite religious elite presided over a clearly defined hierarchy, which greatly increased the power of the clerics. In Afghanistan, there were no central religious institutions to speak of. Islam was flat, localized, and fragmented.

Yet the mystical bent of Afghan Islam did not mean that it was passive. On many occasions in the past, the Sufi brotherhoods had provided surprisingly resilient networks for armed resistance to unjust rulers or foreign invaders. But by the 1970s, Islamic institutions seemed to have lost most of their power to offer coherent opposition to the increasingly powerful central state.

King Zahir Shah, on the throne since 1933, saw little reason to put this to the test. He had little cause to challenge the religious establishment; in 1959, for example, veiling was declared to be voluntary within the city limits of Kabul—a concession to the modern world that excited little response from religious authorities.[10] But this relaxed status quo changed dramatically in 1973, when he was overthrown by his cousin, an intensely ambitious ex-general and former prime minister named Mohammed Daoud Khan. Daoud made his move while the king was receiving medical treatment in Italy. The coup went off without a hitch; no blood was spilled. Daoud declared a republic with himself at the helm. His program had two main planks. First, like so many other Third World leaders at the time, he was eager to lift his country onto the bandwagon of twentieth-century modernization. His second signature cause was "Pashtunistan," code for unifying the millions of Afghan ethnic Pashtuns with the millions who lived on the other side of the border in neighboring Pakistan. The Pakistani government, which understandably rejected such talk, broke off relations.

Both of these factors—Daoud's desire to speed up industrialization and his estrangement from one of his country's most important trading partners—motivated him to edge closer to Moscow. This was also a way to boost his domestic standing with the modernists, since the Soviets had many sympathizers in Afghanistan by now. Their political home was the People's Democratic Party of Afghanistan, the indigenous Communist Party, formed in 1965. It was an unruly organization, with most of its members falling into two mutually hostile factions, the moderate Parcham ("Banner") and the radical Khalq ("the Masses"). The two groups essentially went their separate ways two years after the party was formed (though the split was never made public).

Still, the PDPA remained a force to be reckoned with. Daoud, a firm believer in state control over the economy, had great respect for the Soviet Union's achievements, and he did what he could to bring PDPA leaders into the fold. Parchamis had even helped him pull off his coup. Once it was over, Daoud asked their leader, Babrak Karmal, to join the new government, but Karmal declined. Under the king, he had made a career out of giving rousing speeches in the Afghan parliament, assailing the forces of feudalism and backwardness. Now Daoud had closed parliament down, and Karmal and his comrades reasoned that it was better for them to remain on the outside, offering tactical support to Daoud whenever that made sense. But there was no reason to tie their cart too closely to his. Daoud himself had demonstrated how easy it was to topple a government. Surely, they reasoned, their own chance to follow suit could not be far off.

History, after all, was on their side. Wherever the Afghan Communists looked—Africa, Central America, Southeast Asia—Moscow's allies appeared to be surging ahead. To be sure, the appeal of Marxism-Leninism was waning in the developed world, where leftist ideology was splintering into a kaleidoscope of options: Social Democracy, Trotskyism, Eurocommunism, Maoism, the New Left, the Extra-Parliamentary Opposition. But such examples held limited relevance to would-be modernizers in the Third World. To the elites in the poor countries, the key to Marxism's attraction lay in its ability to mobilize backward societies. To them, the history of the Soviet Union showed how a relatively small bunch of zealous Communists had transformed a land of illiterate peasants into a mighty industrial power in the course of a few years. What Afghan Communists saw in the USSR was exactly what they wanted for Afghanistan: big factories, hard-topped roads and hydroelectric dams, widespread literacy, and modern military equipment. As Stalin had noted, "You can't make an omelet without breaking eggs." The adherents of material progress could not hope to make things better without destroying the forces that stood in the way: the big capitalists, the feudal landowners, the mullahs, the priests.

So the Afghan Communists welcomed the rousing talk of militant social reform and armed anti-imperialism that was so essential to the Soviet revolutionary program. A country like Afghanistan, they reasoned, could be changed only by decisiveness and force. What the United States and its liberal Western allies offered by comparison was a Band-Aid on a suppurating wound. Sometimes you had to stir people out of their torpor, smash the old order. Didn't those Westerners understand that gradual economic reform and incremental progress toward democracy would take millennia in a place like Afghanistan? That the feudalists would never give up power willingly?

Some of the PDPA radicals knew the United States from firsthand experience. Nur Mohammed Taraki, the leader of the Khalq group, had worked for a while at the Afghanistan Embassy in Washington. Another Khalq member, Hafizullah Amin, had earned a master's degree in education at the teachers college of Columbia University in New York. The Americans themselves delivered an additional argument for the Communist propaganda about the superiority of the Soviet model. US assistance to Afghanistan had peaked in the 1960s, as Washington tried to counter Moscow's rising influence. But the Americans gradually decided to concentrate their efforts on other, more powerful, allies in the region, Iran and Pakistan. Afghanistan didn't really seem like it was worth the investment.

So Soviet influence steadily grew, though the Communists were no threat to Daoud at first. The challenges to his budding dictatorship came from other quarters. An urbane, Western-educated secularist who favored women's rights and government control of education and the courts, he had little sympathy for Islam. He managed to buy off many of the members of the Islamic religious establishment, who were used to receiving favors from the state in return for their support, but a group of young religious hotheads were still causing problems. In the late 1960s, some enthusiastic young Muslims, taking their cue from Communist practice, had decided to form their own semiclandestine political organization, which they named the "Muslim Youth Organization." Some of them went well beyond the usual religious platitudes by agitating for the creation of an "Islamic state" in which sharia (Quranic law) would reign supreme and the government would be in the hands of people who followed the example of the Prophet. Upon taking power, Daoud had thrown some of their organizers in jail. The rest had fled to Pakistan.

Then, in 1975, they tried to organize a dilettantish coup that went awry almost as soon as it began. Few in the society at large paid attention, and Daoud suppressed it easily. The activists who fell into his hands, including several key leaders, were summarily shot, shattering the movement. The survivors returned to Pakistan, where they could expect sympathy from a Pakistani government that was eager to take revenge on Daoud for his Pashtun irredentism. But the religious establishment back at home—the village mullahs, the religious scholars, and the Sufi notables who were all tightly bound into the status quo—didn't lift a finger in the rebels' defense. And why should they have? The Islamists, after all, had come to their cause through the universities, not the madrassas, and thus had few ties with the ulama, the religious establishment.

By now Daoud felt himself safe enough to set his own course. In 1975, he created his own political party and declared all competitors illegal. He started purging the army and the security services of Communists. And he began to show other signs of easing away from Moscow's suffocating embrace. He removed Soviet advisers from military units and sent them home. He put Pashtunistan on the back burner and worked to repair his relations with Pakistan. And he began promoting ties with other countries in the Muslim world, courting Egypt as well as oil-rich Iran and Saudi Arabia. The Islamic world welcomed Daoud's initiatives. The Soviets (and their Afghan proxies) watched these shifts with growing dismay.

In the final analysis, though, Afghanistan was still a bit player. If someone had asked you, in the middle of the 1970s, to name a country that would have an impact on the world's affairs in the decades to come, Afghanistan would have been near the bottom of the list—perhaps along with Bangladesh and Bolivia and some of the more obscure African countries. It was just too poor, too underdeveloped. Someone like Mohammed Daoud was probably its best bet: an enlightened dictator, secular, "progressive," with a clear vision for the future. Little did he and his supporters realize that the way of life they represented would soon become extinct.

4

The Emperor as
Revolutionary

When Daoud tried to turn Afghanistan into a one-party state in 1975, he was not doing anything original. He was following advice given to him by a neighboring ruler who had achieved remarkable success in his efforts to wrench another deeply traditional and underdeveloped Islamic country into the modern age. This was the Head of the Warriors, the Light of the Aryans, the King of Kings, Shah Mohammad Reza Pahlavi of Iran.

Iran, in 1977, was one of the world's great economic success stories. When the shah ascended the throne back in 1941, at age twenty-one, his country had been an economic and political dwarf. Indeed, the shah owed his crown to the two outside powers, Great Britain and the Soviet Union, that had invaded the country and deposed his father, Reza Pahlavi, for what they deemed to be his friendliness toward Nazi Germany.

In the 1940s, Iran was a feudal backwater where the central government could barely collect taxes. Three decades later, it was an industrial powerhouse with a strong, centralized state. Its growth rates—averaging 9 to 10 percent for the decade between 1963 and 1973—were astonishing. It boasted modern communications networks and health care systems, car factories, and hydropower dams. Literacy was expanding. Iranian universities were filled with upwardly mobile youth—almost as many women as men—and thousands of others were studying overseas, all aspiring to join the ranks of the ever-expanding middle class. Iran's military was the envy of the Middle East, well trained and armed with the latest weaponry. And it was all the achievement—or so you thought if you were an aspiring despot like Afghanistan's Mohammed Daoud—of a single wise leader.

The shah's rule had started off in uncertainty. The Allied invasion plunged Iran into chaos—but also freed up its political development. The departure of the shah's domineering father, who had been known to administer personal beatings to his political opponents, ushered in an era of ferment. Political parties came out into the open to fight parliamentary elections; opinions proliferated in the media.

The end of the 1940s saw the rise of Mohammed Mossadeq, the reformist prime minister who rode to power on a wave of populist demands. Mossadeq fused moderate socialism and anticolonial nationalism into a program with broad electoral appeal. He made himself immensely popular by nationalizing the British-dominated oil industry in 1951. The British, who had built the Iranian oil industry, were accustomed to keeping the lion's share of the revenues to themselves—a fact well known to the impoverished Iranian citizens who were left to suffer the consequences of their country's underdevelopment. Because the shah was so dependent on outside powers, Mossadeq's move undermined the very foundations of the Iranian monarchy. In 1953, prodded by the British, the US Central Intelligence Agency collaborated with a camarilla of royalist schemers and disaffected generals to topple Mossadeq's government. From now on, firm in the knowledge that he enjoyed the patronage of the world's most powerful country, the shah managed to reassert his control over the political system, rolling back the constitutional limits to his rule and establishing a ruthlessly effective secret police, the SAVAK (which received training from the United States and Israel).

After the fall of Mossadeq, the Americans and the British agreed with the Iranian government on a more equitable sharing of revenues from the sale of Iranian oil. The shah's authoritarian instincts coexisted with a strong desire to modernize his country, and now he had the resources to make it happen. The shah's father had instilled in him a great admiration for Mustafa Kemal Atatürk, who created the new Republic of Turkey from the ruins of the Ottoman Empire in the wake of World War I. Atatürk was a ruthless modernizer, a secularist and a fan of all things Western who forced Turks to wear Western clothes, embraced European-style educational and political institutions, and imposed the Latin alphabet on the Turkish language (written until then in Perso-Arabic script). The young Mohammad Reza Shah wanted to follow suit, but he wanted to do it in a way that would respond to Iran's unique conditions and at the same time cement his reputation as a monarch in step with modern times. He also wanted to steal some thunder from Iran's powerful

Communist Party, the Tudeh, as well as respond to insistent demands for reform from the new Kennedy administration in Washington.

In 1963, the shah launched the White Revolution, his far-reaching plan to re-engineer Iranian society. He aimed to borrow the Left's ideas about social justice and equality while implementing them without revolutionary violence or class warfare. The centerpiece of the White Revolution was a land-reform plan that broke up many of the big inherited landholdings and parceled them out to former tenant farmers. It also included a national literacy campaign, introduced suffrage for women, and nationalized forests, pasturelands, and water resources. Other legislation privatized state-owned enterprises and allowed workers to earn shares in the companies where they worked.

The White Revolution remains a source of huge controversy even today. Its supporters say that it essentially succeeded in its aim of breaking down some of the structural barriers that held Iran back and creating a base for modern economic development. Its critics—including many of those who hold power in today's Islamic Republic—say that its reforms were primarily cosmetic and delivered on few of its promises. What is indisputable about the White Revolution is that it left hardly any aspect of political or economic life in the country untouched. It shook the social landscape. Traditional landholding families gave up farming and moved into finance and manufacturing, spurring industrialization. Peasants who received their own land aspired to new, middle-class lives. And millions of other rural Iranians began to head into the cities, which beckoned with jobs in factories and services. Urbanization, which utterly transformed the face of the twentieth century, was off to a roaring start in Iran. The impending oil boom of the 1970s would turbocharge it.

The shah himself was a contradictory figure. A playboy in his youth, he retained until the end of his days his fondness for beautiful women and flashy cars. Yet he was also intelligent, a hard worker with a strong sense of duty. Like his father, he spent considerable amounts of energy trying to check the power of the Shiite religious establishment, but he also harbored a personal brand of deep, almost mystical belief in Islam. At some moments he gave way to vacillation or crippling paranoia, while at others he displayed considerable political astuteness. He relentlessly pushed for greater economic performance, even as he indulged in the traditional prerogatives of a monarch who regarded the entire country as his personal property, amassing enormous wealth and tolerating highly visible corruption among his relatives and courtiers.

The shah continued to fear the power of Iran's Communists, by now driven deep underground by wave after wave of SAVAK-engineered repression. He had launched the White Revolution in recognition of the urgent need to co-opt the

Left's demands for radical reform. For years Iran was home to one of the Middle East's most powerful Communist Parties, the Tudeh, and he and his courtiers were well aware of its ability to exploit social tensions. In 1949 the shah barely escaped an attempt on his life, and the young gunman was identified as a member of the Tudeh (though historians have since disputed the accuracy of this claim). The shah unleashed a huge police action against the Communists that did considerable damage. But he also knew that the party could be eliminated for good only by addressing the political conditions that sustained it. The White Revolution, as historians have sometimes said, was designed above all to head off a Red one.

In this, at least, it succeeded. But the costs were high. In reality, the reforms—almost always imposed from above with little feedback from below—were ill-conceived and erratically implemented. The Polish journalist Ryszard Kapuściński wrote a vivid account of the Iranian Revolution in which he observed: "Development is a treacherous river, as everyone who plunges into its currents knows."[1] He was right. The Iranian regime's uncritical admirers overlooked the destructive effects of the shah's reforms.

For one thing, he did not really trust private initiative. Instead, he followed the reigning economic orthodoxy laid down by the postwar theorists of "development economics" and reinforced by the lending policies of the World Bank. It was a model heavy on state intervention, which suited the shah's centralizing proclivities just fine. He believed in planning rather than markets, protection rather than openness to trade. One of the core tenets of the approach was "import substitution." Rather than pay for goods produced outside of the country, the Iranian government pushed the creation of indigenous manufacturing, in fields ranging from electronics to helicopters. While this created jobs and promoted the growth of a domestic technical class, these new industries—usually state monopolies that were protected from external competition by high tariffs—turned out to be inefficient. The hidden costs of this sort of development were high, and so these projects tended to become a drag on the economy in times of crisis.

One reform effort in 1972 offered a good illustration of the sorts of political disruptions that could result from breakneck modernization. The shah's planners decided to introduce the Western-style mass production of bread. Iranian consumers generally preferred the traditional bread that was baked fresh each morning in the ovens of the local bazaar—but no one asked them. Some six thousand bakery workers lost their jobs (though the planners had assumed that the number would be even higher). Shoemakers were hit by a similar shift, almost overnight, to automated manufacturing. Such measures were part of the government's broader effort to encourage a rational economy of modern supermarkets and department stores, one in which the bazaars and long-established guilds no longer played the influential role to which they were accustomed. This eroded the shah's support among the more tradition-minded members of the middle class—who expressed their growing opposition by building ties to the dissident clergy.[2]

If the shah had hoped that undermining these traditional estates would bolster his own rule, events soon showed that he was sadly mistaken. The speed and intensity of their country's transformation left Iranians reeling. The displaced rural folk who crowded into the new suburban shantytowns found themselves in a strange new landscape filled with seductive distractions. Many lost their way. Social vices like prostitution, drug addiction, and alcoholism were rampant. Parental authority broke down, as children succumbed to delinquency or decadence. Others reacted by clinging even more defiantly to their Shiite faith, the one source of identity that tended to survive the move from village to city more or less intact. If you needed advice on how to find your way in this topsy-turvy world, the local mosque was often the best place to look. Urbanization thus had the paradoxical effect of fueling a revival of traditional religion. One scholar has compared this dynamic in the shah's Iran with England's Industrial Revolution, when members of the new urban middle class reinvented religious practice by turning to John Wesley and his socially activist Methodist movement.[3]

Even those who directly benefited from the opportunities afforded by the shah's modernization program could not escape the feeling of alienation. Farman Farmaian, a pioneering social worker who received her degree in the United States, understood perfectly well that her likelihood of receiving an education would have been almost zero had she been born just a few years earlier than she was. Yet she could not help feeling dismay as she watched what was happening. In her book *Daughter of Persia* (1992) she supplies a vivid snapshot of the 1970s:

> An almost delirious admiration for things Western had seized the country. Everywhere in North Teheran one saw liquor stores, fancy international hotels, and signs advertising Gucci clothes or Kentucky Fried Chicken, as well as Western movie theaters and discos where young people could dance and drink on Thursday nights until all hours. Everyone, especially the young, was avid for European or American clothes, films, music.
>
> Such developments might not have seemed disturbing in the West, but in our country, propriety and filial obedience provided the glue that held families together, and hence society itself. Many people felt that we were

not only trying to catch up with the West, but to become the West, while
an entire older generation of parents, even among Persians of my class,
was shocked and outraged at what these Western ways were doing to their
children, culture, and what Iranians considered moral behavior. . . . Even the
poor immigrants in the Tehran shantytowns, who deeply disapproved of the
garish billboards and—to us—risqué cinema posters displaying the faces and
limbs of Western movie actresses, craved Pepsi-Cola and Levi's.[4]

The most famous chronicler of this queasy sensibility was Jalal Al-i Ahmad,
an Iranian writer who coined his own word for it. He called it *gharbzadegi,* usually
translated as "westoxification" or "occidentosis." His immensely influential book, *Occidentosis: A Plague from the West* (1962), portrayed Iran as a unique society under
assault from the alienating "machine culture" of the industrialized West. As he saw
it, his country was coming under the control of forces it could not really understand
or command: "If we define occidentosis," he wrote, "as the aggregate of events in
the life, culture, civilization, and mode of thought of a people having no supporting
tradition, no historical continuity, no gradient of transformation, but having only
what the machine brings them, it is clear that we are such a people."[5]

The shah's Iran experienced all the contradictions of what the French sociologist
Émile Durkheim called "crises of prosperity."[6] Perhaps the most fundamental paradox involved education. The enormous surge in university enrollment in the 1960s
and 1970s meant that educational institutions were churning out graduates faster
than the economy could generate jobs for them. Masses of underemployed young
male intellectuals are a reservoir of instability for any society that is undergoing a
tumultuous shift from one sort of social order to another. Needless to say, it was
clear even to those who did not have the benefit of university degrees that they lived
in a society plagued by profound inequality and social stratification. But it was the
educated who tended to ruminate about the causes and felt challenged to come up
with possible remedies.

The problem was that the shah had closed off every possible avenue for political
expression. The crackdowns on the Communists continued. In 1951, as Mossadeq
pressed for nationalization, the Tudeh, long since driven underground by the secret
police, revealed astonishing resilience by organizing big public demonstrations in
support of his government. This unnerved the shah and his entourage, reinforcing
their paranoia about Communism's hidden strength—and prompting SAVAK to
keep its operations focused on the Tudeh for decades after the party became essentially moribund. After the 1953 coup, the shah also outlawed Mossadeq's National

Front, choking off the option of moderate secular nationalism. The exile of Khomeini and the imprisonment of other recalcitrant clerics muzzled the religious establishment. By the 1960s, only two political parties remained—and both were fakes, staffed by the shah's followers to provide a democratic facade.

Still, some young Iranians concluded that adopting leftist ideologies merely meant exchanging one brand of imported Western intellectual tyranny for a different one. So they set out in search of solutions closer to home. In this search they were gradually influenced by an array of thinkers who combined the old ideas of the Left with new ideas about anticolonialism and national self-awareness. The liberation struggle in Algeria, where Muslim socialists were fighting a war of independence against the French, was particularly resonant. Pan-Arabism and Baathism, which shaped political discourse throughout much of the Middle East in the 1950s and 1960s, showed how socialist ideas could be melded with radical nationalism, but they held limited appeal for Iranians, who tended historically to define themselves in contrast to the mostly Sunni Arabs.

It was perhaps inevitable that many educated Iranians in search of a potent but distinctive alternative to the shah's regime would turn to Islam. For centuries the Iranian religious establishment had served as a latent source of opposition to the overweening power of the state. In 1890, leaders of the Shiite ulama, the hierarchy of religious scholars, had instigated a highly effective protest against a tobacco concession that the shah had awarded to Great Britain. Desperate to thwart growing foreign control over the Iranian economy, the most important religious authority, Mirza Hasan Shirazi, issued a fatwa, a legal ruling, prohibiting the use of tobacco, which was a highly popular commodity at the time. Overnight Iranians ceased consuming it, rendering the British concession virtually worthless. Two years later the shah repealed the privileges he had granted the British, in the process acknowledging the power of the clergy to influence Iran's political agenda.

That power was on display again in 1906, when the clergy and the rising middle class combined forces in a revolt based on demands for a constitutional order with an elected parliament at its heart. The Iranians got their parliament, but the revolt collapsed when key clerics decided that secular democrats were assuming too much power in the new system. The Constitutional Revolution then devolved into a long interregnum of anarchy that ended only with the rise to power of Reza Shah, the ruthless soldier who seized power and founded the Pahlavi dynasty. Reza Shah, highly focused in his dictatorial ambitions, understood the mobilizing potential of the Shia religious establishment all too well and saw undermining it as one of his major tasks.

Reza Shah's secularizing tendencies worried many of the leading clerics. Yet the dominant religious authorities during the early years of his son's rule—especially Grand Ayatollah Hossein Tabatabai Borujerdi, effectively the leader of Iran's Muslims from 1947 to 1961—were quietists who preferred to maintain their distance from day-to-day politics. The younger generation respected his wishes while Borujerdi remained alive, but after his death one of them emerged into public view as a harsh critic of the shah's policies, openly articulating the objections that many other clerics were unwilling to utter aloud.

This was Ayatollah Ruhollah Khomeini, who, in March 1963, "publicly accused the Shah of violating his oath to defend Islam and the Constitution."[7] Khomeini assailed the White Revolution for what he saw as its cavalier regard for established mores. By extending the franchise to women, Khomeini said, the shah's reforms were promoting the "spread of prostitution." He also objected strongly to measures that would make it possible for non-Muslims to hold appointments as judges.

But what he objected to most of all was the shah's dependence on the United States and his willingness to pursue close relations with Israel. In one of his speeches, alluding to the fact that Iran had formally recognized the government of Israel, Khomeini wondered aloud whether the shah was actually a "Jew" and an "infidel." The shah's secret police, the infamous SAVAK, arrested Khomeini. The security forces had already cracked down on religious students in the seminary town of Qom a few weeks earlier when they gathered to protest government approval for the opening of liquor stores there. Now the students rioted again. Dozens were killed.

Other leading clerics, though not quite as aggressive as Khomeini, shared his disapproval of the White Revolution; Grand Ayatollah Borujerdi, before his death, had issued several fatwas condemning aspects of the shah's reform program. After the riots in Qom, leading clerics worried that the shah was preparing to have Khomeini executed, and one of their most prestigious members, Grand Ayatollah Mohamed Kazem Shariatmadari, moved to have the title of "Grand Ayatollah" given to Khomeini as a preemptive measure. (Their reasoning was that the shah would never dare to end the life of one of the country's highest-ranking clerics.) The shah backed down and released Khomeini. In 1964, Khomeini delivered another scorching reproach of the shah over a planned agreement for the stationing of US forces in Iran, which many Iranians regarded as a violation of their country's sovereignty. Khomeini was arrested again.

By now his religious colleagues had tired of their tug-of-war with the shah, and there was little protest when the government sent Khomeini into exile. Most of the religious scholars saw their primary role as helping the faithful to navigate the tremendous moral and social confusion generated by the shah's program. They did what they could to push back against plans to create a state-approved "Religion Corps" that would push an officially sanctioned view of Islam, and they resisted, to the extent that they could, the steady erosion of their moral authority. The shah was just as determined to keep them in their place. For the time being, the overwhelming majority of religious scholars saw no reason to engage in outright opposition.

The oil money was flooding in. The economy was booming. Few challengers dared to speak openly against the monarchy. And so, in 1971, the shah decided it was time to celebrate. Given the scale of his presumptive success, he saw no reason to stint. Years earlier his advisers had brought up the idea of organizing a public ceremony to showcase Mohammad Reza Shah's achievements. Now the revenue from Iran's energy windfall made it possible for those plans to be realized in the most lavish possible fashion. The festivities needed a suitably grandiose occasion, and so the shah decided that they should commemorate the twenty-five-hundredth anniversary of the founding of the Persian monarchy, staring with the rule of King Cyrus the Great. The event began in October 1971, when the shah formally paid his respects at the tomb of Cyrus. The religious establishment of the country noted that their secularizing monarch was choosing to portray Iran's pagan past as the real source of national glory. It was a vision that left little space for the role of Shiite Islam.

Most of the celebration took place nearby on the grounds of the ancient Achaemenid capital of Persepolis, where the organizers had erected a city of lavishly appointed tents to house the six hundred invited guests, who included sixty heads of royalty and heads of state. For the chief designer the shah hired the man who had redecorated the White House for Jacqueline Kennedy. The visitors, who were ferried between the site and the airport by a fleet of Mercedes-Benz limousines, watched a lavish son et lumière show against the backdrop of the ruins that included a procession by seventeen hundred Iranian army soldiers dressed in period costumes. Then the partygoers indulged in a six-hour feast catered by Maxim's of Paris. The guests included Emperor Haile Selassie of Ethiopia and Soviet president Nikolay Podgorny, US vice president Spiro Agnew, and Yugoslavia's Josip Broz Tito, the Duke of Edinburgh and Imelda Marcos of the Philippines, Spain's Prince Juan Carlos and the Congolese president, Joseph Mobutu. It was, arguably, the jet-set event of the century—notwithstanding the abject poverty on display in villages just a few miles away from the site of the festivities. And no one paid much attention when that radical cleric, Khomeini, issued his own jeremiad against the event from his exile in Iraq.

The *New York Times* estimated that the total bill for the event came to around $100 million, though that probably involves a considerable amount of guesswork.[8] Aware of the sensitivity of the subject, the shah forbade any discussion of the costs. He was, however, undoubtedly in a position to pay the bill. Oil revenues hit $885 million the year of the Persepolis celebration. The next year they doubled. In 1974 they reached $4.6 billion—and then soared to $17.8 billion in 1975. With little apparent consideration of the effects, government officials doubled the amount allocated to the shah's Fifth Development Plan, raising it to $63 billion.[9] Iranian growth went up by 30.3 percent in 1973–1974 and 42 percent in 1974–1975.[10] Unsurprisingly, inflation shot up. The economy overheated. Lines of ships formed outside Iranian port facilities that did not have the capacity to unload all the goods that had been purchased.

Nineteen seventy-five was also the year that the shah decided to complete his country's political transformation. Though he was ostensibly an ally of the United States, Mohammad Reza Pahlavi often expressed his contempt for what he saw as the indiscipline and moral laxity of the liberal democracies. Though a staunch anti-Communist, he believed in central planning and the Soviet Union's apparent success in mobilizing resources for the common good. Having spent decades curtailing the opportunities for political expression of his subjects, he now moved to bring that process to its logical culmination by declaring Iran to be a one-party state. From now on, everyone had to be a dues-paying member of his Rastakhiz (Resurgence) Party. "Those who believe in the Iranian Constitution, the Monarchical regime, and the principles of the White Revolution, must join the new party," he announced. "Those who do not believe in these principles are traitors who must either go to prison or leave the country."[11] It was precisely this brand of centralizing arrogance that Mohammed Daoud and many other leaders found so worthy of emulation.

They were mistaken. Politically and economically, the shah's regime had attained the apogee of hubris. From here the initiative would pass to others.

5

Tory Insurrectionists

By the summer of 1978 Prime Minister James Callaghan appeared to have weathered the worst. The trauma of 1976, when Britain had been forced to go cap in hand to the International Monetary Fund, was fading from memory. Callaghan and his team had managed to make moderate cuts in spending and hold inflation at manageable levels. The economy was picking up, and if Callaghan could sustain the positive trend, he had a good chance of winning the next election.

But there was a catch: these achievements were contingent on good relations with the unions. A former union official himself, Callaghan had plenty of credibility with the labor movement's leaders, and he had put this capital to use by pressing them to moderate their pay demands. This was in keeping with Keynesian orthodoxy, which dictated that the best way of fighting inflation was the control of wages and prices, an approach known as "incomes policy." In July 1978 it was time to negotiate a new deal. Union leaders felt that their previous forbearance entitled them to a reward. The government recommended a raise of 5 percent. The Trades Unions Confederation rejected it.

Desperate to keep inflation at bay, Callaghan tried to bring the unions to heel by denying government contracts to companies whose workers refused to go along. But the unions had had enough. The first unraveling came in September, when 57,000 workers at Ford Motor Company's British subsidiary voted to go on strike. In late November, company management finally capitulated, granting its workers a pay increase well above the limit that Number Ten Downing Street had recommended.

Callaghan and his government protested, but that was about all they could do. Other unions decided that it was time to join in.

The floodgates opened. The public-sector unions announced that they, too, wanted higher pay. Next the nurses joined the strike, followed by hospital support staff. Emergency rooms closed their doors to all but the most dire cases. Callaghan was forced to dispatch substitute workers from the armed forces to keep basic services going. Garbage men went on strike, and uncollected trash began to pile up around British cities. Bread rationing was declared when bakers stopped work. A work stoppage by truck drivers triggered shortages of food and gasoline. On January 22 the unions announced a nationwide "Day of Action" that was observed by 1.5 million workers; a whole range of institutions, from schools to airports, shut their doors. The United Kingdom had not seen the likes of it since the General Strike of 1926. The misery was magnified by a bitterly cold winter that buried many parts of the country in wet snow. In Liverpool even the grave diggers stopped work. The city council actually considered, for a while, burying the dead at sea.[1]

It was a prodigious mess, but if anyone could deal with it, surely it was Callaghan. No one else could boast a comparable range of experience. Before taking up residence in Number Ten Downing Street, Callaghan had served as chancellor of the Exchequer, foreign secretary, and home secretary, which made him the only British politician to have held all four of the great offices of state. He had a smooth, jovial manner and an easy pragmatism that endeared him to both ruling-class and ordinary voters. His personal popularity was immense.

But while the prime minister well understood that Britain could not continue on its current path, he had no clear alternative to offer. He was, after all, the Labour leader. The unions dominated his party. What's more, the characteristics that had served him so well on his rise now boomeranged against him. His cheery sense of absolute self-belief had earned him the label "Sunny Jim," and his unflappability was a key ingredient of his personal popularity. On January 10, 1979, this trait was on full display as he returned to London from a summit meeting of the leading industrial powers held on the island of Guadeloupe. It was bad enough for his image that Callaghan had been basking in the Caribbean sunshine at a time when his countrymen were slogging their way through mountains of garbage. Greeting journalists at the airport, Callaghan brushed off their questions about the dark national mood: "I promise if you look at it from the outside . . . I don't think other people in the world would share the view that there is mounting chaos." It was a remark that made him appear fatally disconnected. The next day's edition of the tabloid the *Sun* ran a damning headline: "Crisis? What Crisis?"

Callaghan never actually said those words. But the accusation stuck—precisely because his optimism appeared at such odds with the images that dominated the evening news. For nonunionized Britons, the "Winter of Discontent," as the months of strikes were soon dubbed, was more than just another episode in a long history of industrial unrest. It was not just that sidewalks were vanishing under piles of garbage or that coffins were going unburied. Strikers and the police clashed in pitched battles that evoked nightmarish visions of anarchy. The promise of the late-nineteenth-century labor movement—the brotherhood of man and the rights of the oppressed—had devolved into a kind of storm-trooper anomie. Twice before in the course of the decade, the unions—with the all-powerful miners in the vanguard—had toppled governments. Now that recent history appeared to be repeating itself, with a vengeance. It all reinforced the widespread notion that Britain had entered a period of crippling decline.

There was one small consolation for Callaghan: he had little to fear from the leader of the opposition. Her name was Margaret Thatcher. She had ascended to the leadership of the Conservative Party four years earlier after launching a surprise challenge to Edward Heath, the former prime minister in whose cabinet she had served for four years until his defeat in 1974. She had been in charge of the Ministry of Education, where one of her modest reforms—canceling free milk in school lunches—earned her the nickname "Margaret Thatcher, Milk Snatcher." (Never mind that she had actually increased the budget for her department during her stint.) In professional terms, this scarcely compared with Callaghan's experience as a holder of all four of the great offices of state.

She represented, as far as Callaghan and his advisers could see, a sort of ideological dead end. She talked, almost like an American, about "free markets" and the virtues of capitalism. She preached the need to tighten the money supply and choke off inflation—all fine and good, but the unions would never allow it, as they were now demonstrating. She even talked quite aggressively about the need to discipline the labor movement: "The unions have unique power and unique power requires unique responsibility," she declared in one of her duels with Callaghan in the House of Commons. "That responsibility has not been forthcoming. That is the reason for the position in which the country finds itself today—about which there can be no dispute."[2] This was tough talk, but few professional politicians took it seriously—even within her own shadow cabinet. What could she possibly do about the unions that hadn't been tried before?

And then there was the fact of her gender. Callaghan was a practiced debater in the Commons, and a certain condescension came through whenever the two of them sparred. Where he was genial, she was earnest. Where he was smooth, she was grating, sometimes even a bit shrill. What could you expect, really, from a woman? At one point, when Thatcher chastised him for his "avuncular condescension," Callaghan replied that he found it hard to imagine her as his niece.[3]

The Winter of Discontent took its toll. As the early months of 1979 gave way to spring, it no longer looked as if Callaghan could count on an economic upturn to counter the prevailing gloom. But his advisers took some consolation from the polls. They showed that Thatcher's personal approval ratings still lagged behind Callaghan's. By the time the election came, they reasoned, Sunny Jim could rely on the power of his charm to best the joyless Milk Snatcher.

Callaghan's personal popularity was not the only obstacle that Thatcher faced in 1979. She was also confronting the inertia of a well-entrenched political and economic consensus that had reigned since the end of World War II—a consensus that included wide swaths of her own party. In the 1940s, tired of their country's class conflicts and minimal social protections, Britons had begun to dream of a radical break with the past. It was a dream that first assumed concrete form in a book published under the stewardship of an economist and civil servant named William Beveridge in 1942. The Beveridge Report, as it came to be known, was an instant best-seller. People lined up all night to purchase a copy. It was translated into twenty-two languages, and British airmen dropped copies of it on occupied Europe.[4] At the end of the war, two copies of the text, translated into German, were found in Hitler's underground bunker in Berlin.[5]

The report was an extremely unlikely candidate for popular success. It was an official publication that bore the notably drab title of *Report of the Inter-Departmental Committee on Social Insurance and Allied Services.* But no matter. The Beveridge Report fired the public imagination because it provided the blueprint for a reorganization of the British state that would eliminate poverty, hunger, and sickness.

"Now, when the war is abolishing landmarks of every kind, is the opportunity for using experience in a clear field," the report declared. "A revolutionary moment in the world's history is a time for revolutions, not for patching." What the report proposed, however, was a distinctly British kind of revolution: a bureaucratic transformation of the state. It declared that full employment should be the goal of economic policy. It proposed the creation of comprehensive public pensions and unemployment insurance. It laid out the basis for a national health insurance system. And it argued for a broad expansion of public education at all levels.

We have no record of how the young Margaret Thatcher regarded the report. But it is entirely possible that, like so many of her young Conservative contemporaries, she accepted its conclusions. The privations of the Great Depression and the war compelled even many staunch Tories to recognize that the country needed a more extensive welfare state. Even Churchill welcomed the report—within limits. As a young Liberal politician, he had been something of a social reformer, and had even cooperated with Beveridge on some proposals in the years before World War I.[6] Now, in a 1943 speech titled "After the War," he promised that the government would do its best to implement many of the key provisions of the report—including a "broadening field for State ownership and enterprise" and "national compulsory insurance for all classes for all purposes from the cradle to the grave." But he also warned against saddling the government with too many ambitious obligations that might break the budget and said that any plans for implementing the Beveridge proposals would have to wait until the first postwar elections.[7]

The result of the general election of 1945 was not what Churchill had expected. Churchill's Conservatives were buried by a Labour Party landslide. It was the party of Clement Attlee that had campaigned most aggressively on a Beveridge platform, and his newly formed government announced to the British public that it would use the mandate given it by the electorate to move the country forward to the "New Jerusalem" of a comprehensive welfare state. Attlee himself had worked in the slums of East London as a young man, and the experience had left him with a profound sense of the need for wide-ranging social protections.

It took the Labour government just a few short years to implement a raft of social welfare policies that transformed British society. The Labourites established child subsidies, expanded a range of social insurance programs, built vast new tracts of public housing, imposed far-reaching rent controls, and launched a comprehensive program of state-run, single-payer health care (the National Health Service). It all proved enormously popular.

Labour's economic policies were even more far-reaching. "It is doubtful whether we have ever, except in war, used the whole of our productive capacity," the Labour election manifesto proclaimed. "This must be corrected." Attlee and his cabinet set out to do this through a series of measures that transformed British capitalism. They nationalized the "commanding heights" of the economy: coal, oil and gas, communications, railroads, iron, and steel.[8] They instituted management boards to oversee the new publicly owned industries. And they put into place a wide-ranging system of price controls and regulations. By 1951 about 20 percent of the British economy was under public ownership.

This was revolutionary, even if it didn't quite add up to a revolution. Many aspects of capitalism continued to coexist with these reforms. The Labourites borrowed some of their most consequential policies from the thinking of an economist who had transformed economic theory between the wars precisely as part of his effort to save capitalism from its own weaknesses. This was John Maynard Keynes. A lifelong member of the Liberal Party, Keynes was far from being a socialist. But he had posited that classical economics tended to understate the possibility of market failure. Real markets did not always balance out perfectly, he argued. In some cases, supply and demand could achieve equilibrium without creating full employment. Governments could pick up the slack by stimulating demand through increased spending during economic slowdowns.[9]

Keynesian prescriptions had picked up many adherents throughout the Anglo-Saxon world since the great deflationary crisis of the Great Depression. The policies he proposed seemed to offer a tool for overcoming the problem of the destructive boom-and-bust cycles that seemed to plague capitalist economies. The Labour government of 1945, which touted its belief in "rational" economic decision making, was ready to follow suit. The centerpiece of Attlee's New Jerusalem was "freedom from want," which meant, in practical terms, full employment. Keynes had argued that the best way to sustain full employment was through government spending—even if it led to temporary budget deficits.

Churchill had contributed to his Conservative Party's defeat in the 1945 election by expressing skepticism about the degree of state control that a Beveridge-style reform program would entail. In so doing, he alienated not only many members of the electorate but also quite a few Tories as well—especially younger ones. By the time the Conservatives returned to power in 1951, many members of the party had to concede that the reforms of the Labour era were deeply entrenched in the public mind. The Conservatives offered a few modest corrections but left most of the Attlee-era edifice in place. The generation of Conservative leaders, embodied by the centrist R. A. Butler, acknowledged the virtues of the mixed economy. Conservatives argued that their greater business expertise would enable them to manage it better. But they did not challenge the fundamental assumptions of the Labour model. A consensus of sorts, often called "the postwar settlement," had been achieved.

There were good reasons the postwar settlement proved so durable. First, it accurately reflected the spirit of the times. Soviet planning—its apparent success in speedy industrialization with zero unemployment in the 1930s as well as its astonishing performance in marshaling resources against the Nazis during the war—had many admirers in Great Britain; the immense human costs of this achievement had received far less notice. America's New Deal experiments with government intervention and an expanded social welfare state also found considerable resonance in Britain, whose leaders had responded to the Great Depression mostly by muddling through. And finally, the UK's own experience with government planning of the economy during the war had been remarkably positive. It demonstrated that shrewd government management could "squeeze much more production out of the industrial machine than its capitalist owners had done before the war."[10]

Second, the postwar consensus worked—at least for a while. Indicators of health and social welfare climbed sharply during the immediate postwar period. Wartime rationing took longer to eliminate, but in the 1950s and early 1960s, the British economy grew steadily. Broad swaths of society that had been left out of earlier upswings now tasted the benefits of prosperity. The same Britons who had suffered through the turmoil of the 1920s and 1930s now enjoyed a notably far higher standard of living, cushioned by the state against the threats of disability, job loss, or sudden illness. Jobs were plentiful. The Keynesian magic seemed to work. When the economy began to slow, you could stimulate demand through fiscal "fine-tuning," adjusting government spending and taxation to promote full employment. And if these policies led to inflation, it was to be controlled by regulating wages and prices (known as "incomes policy").[11]

In the 1960s and 1970s, however, a darker side of the postwar consensus began to show through. Inflation proved naggingly persistent. Government attempts to tame it through incomes policy found increasingly little traction; indeed, it began to look as though each round of wage hikes was actually exacerbating the problem. Financing the welfare state was becoming an increasingly onerous burden. Income tax rates had reached levels that were driving entrepreneurs out of the country. By the third decade after the war, faith in the near omnipotence of economic policy makers was beginning to wane.

In 1970, with the Conservatives in opposition again, party leader Edward Heath convened his shadow cabinet in a hotel in the London suburb of Selsdon. The program that emerged from the meeting betrayed a strong free-market bent, arguing strongly for curtailing government intervention in the economy, putting the fight against inflation at the center of monetary policy, and cutting back on the power of organized labor. Prime Minister Harold Wilson dubbed the Conservative mentality behind the document "Selsdon Man." (The allusion to "Piltdown Man" was intended to evoke the allegedly antediluvian quality of the Conservative program.) To everyone's surprise, however, the Conservatives won the election; the electorate did not appear to find the ideas from Selsdon quite as frightening as Wilson did.

But the Heath government soon discovered the limits of its mandate. The powerful trade unions, now enshrined at the very heart of British economic policy, soon grew restive. As unemployment ticked upward, Heath abandoned the Selsdon principles. He launched a new round of monetary expansion, restored controls over incomes and prices, widened industrial subsidies, and put plans for union reform on the back burner. He even nationalized Rolls-Royce. Finding an alternative to the postwar consensus was proving a challenge.

Though few dared to criticize it publicly, Heath's "U-turn," as it became known, profoundly disillusioned some of the members of his cabinet. One of them was his young secretary of state for education and science, Margaret Thatcher. She was, perhaps, the most unusual member of Heath's team. She fulfilled very few of the typical attributes of a leading Tory at the time. She was of solidly middle-class origins. She attended a girls' grammar school outside her hometown rather than one of the posh private boarding schools for boys that still turned out England's highborn leaders. She had not served in the army. She attended Oxford, but she was unable to join the Oxford Union, that training school of future politicians, since it was closed to female students. Nor was she a member of any of the famous London clubs that were frequented by an upper-class clientele that included many leading Conservatives. These establishments, too, were off-limits to her gender.

These peculiar circumstances explain a great deal about Margaret Thatcher, but they do not explain everything. We should be wary of biographies that rely excessively on social determinism. People are not only the products of their surroundings. Other Chinese men of Deng Xiaoping's generation emerged from environments comparable to his, but that didn't necessarily turn them into leaders of the Chinese Communist Party. Unlike Khomeini, most Shiite clerics did not end up challenging the shah and engineering revolution.

What circumstances can do, though, is give peculiar shape to the predilections we were born with, and it is easy to imagine how Thatcher's upbringing contributed to the politician she was to become. She was born Margaret Roberts in the Midlands town of Grantham in 1925. Her father, Alfred—by her own testimony the central influence in her life—raised his two daughters in an atmosphere of strong discipline and clearly articulated values. He was a shop owner—the owner of two shops, to be precise—and an active participant in city government. (For all his traditionalism, however, he was not a Conservative; he was a Liberal who seems to have believed firmly in the postwar principles of the mixed economy.)

He was also a devout Methodist who insisted that his family attend church up to four times on a single Sunday and regarded public dances as deplorable frivolities. By the 1930s English Methodism had lost some of the socially activist spirit that had made it such an influential force in nineteenth-century Britain, especially as far as the creation of the Labour Party was concerned.[12] But the ethics of activism that alderman Alfred Roberts transmitted to his daughter Margaret certainly retained a strong whiff of John Wesley's original brand of antiestablishment revivalism. Wesley developed Methodism as a way of bringing God back into the lives of those who experienced the poverty and social turmoil of the Industrial Revolution and whose spiritual needs, as he saw it, were neglected by the entrenched Church of England. Like modern evangelical movements, Methodism emphasized a direct and individual relationship to Christ; the path to salvation did not lie through official institutions or trust in elites. Though Wesley preached strongly against greed, his teachings also contained a strain of individual self-improvement that has to have impressed itself on the ambitious young Margaret Roberts—as this excerpt from a Wesley sermon might suggest:

> These cautions and restrictions being observed, it is the bounden duty of all who are engaged in worldly business to observe that first and great rule of Christian wisdom with respect to money, "Gain all you can." Gain all you can by honest industry. Use all possible diligence in your calling. Lose no time. If you understand yourself and your relation to God and man, you know you have none to spare. . . . If you understand your particular calling as you ought, you will have no time that hangs upon your hands. Every business will afford some employment sufficient for every day and every hour. That wherein you are placed, if you follow it in earnest, will leave you no leisure for silly, unprofitable diversions.[13]

Church of England stalwarts derided what they saw as the unseemly fanaticism of the Methodists: there was something distastefully effervescent about all those public displays of godly fervor, all that preaching in open fields and the insistence on charity as an everyday reality. Wesley was fond of quoting Galatians 4:18: "It is always good to be zealously affected in a good thing."[14] One can easily imagine Alfred Roberts making the same arguments to his daughter. "Never do things because other people do them," he told her. "Make up your own mind what you are going to do and persuade people to do things your way."[15]

The message of gritty self-sufficiency undoubtedly resonated amid the deprivations of a small English town during the Depression. But Thatcher's value system was affected most dramatically, as was the case with most of her generation, by the experience of the Second World War. She had done well enough in school that she managed to earn a scholarship to Oxford, and she arrived at Somerville College when the war was already well under way. The sense of patriotism and political ferment that reigned there at the time dovetailed with her natural inclinations. Many of the students were off in the war, and those who remained spent a good deal of their time debating the postwar political order. Marxism was a dominant intellectual current at wartime Oxford, but Roberts certainly did not find it amenable. She was already defining herself as a Tory, though the party was in the midst of an agonized redefinition triggered by the disaster of the Depression and the rising popularity of Beveridge-style plans for the future. Since the Oxford Union was closed to women, Roberts cut her political teeth in the Oxford University Conservative Association. (She became its head in 1946.) True to her no-nonsense mind, she eschewed the liberal arts in favor of hard science, choosing chemistry as her major. (When she was later asked about her status as Britain's first female prime minister, she would say that she preferred to be remembered as the first scientist who won the office.)

At Oxford, Thatcher did not make a name for herself as a radical enthusiast of the values that would later be associated with her name. The Toryism of the time was very much under the sway of the period's progressive mainstream. Just before the 1945 election, Oxford's student conservatives published a paper declaring that "Liberal Capitalism is as dead as Aristocratic Feudalism," and welcoming "a state without privilege where each shall enrich himself through the enrichment of all."[16] No one can recall Margaret Roberts taking up a stand that radically differed from this stance. She later claimed to have read Friedrich von Hayek's *Road to Serfdom* during her last year at Oxford. If so, it had little visible effect on her public positions.

But she was eager to make her mark. Upon her graduation she got a job as a chemist with a food company, where she worked on the development of cake frostings and pie fillings. This position, however, was merely a placeholder for someone of her ambitions. The Conservative Party, to which she remained loyal, was eager to field more female candidates, and she soon got her chance to campaign for a seat in Parliament. She lost on her first try for Parliament in 1950 (as the youngest Conservative woman candidate), and the next year as well. But she was certainly noticed.

She met Denis Thatcher in 1949, at her induction as a Tory candidate for Parliament. They married two years later. For her it meant a step up the social ladder. Her new husband, who had served with distinction during the war, ran a chemical company that had been founded by his grandfather. With his support she set out to study law, and in 1953 she qualified for the bar. It was also the year that she gave birth to twins, which actually made it harder for her to get a candidacy. Several local party associations rejected her on the rationale, more or less openly expressed, that a young mother would find it harder to campaign. Finally, in 1958, circumstance conspired to give her the chance to campaign for the seat from Finchley, a northern suburb of London that usually voted for Tories with comfortable majorities. In 1959 she won with a comfortable majority, a seat that she would retain for the next thirty-three years. In 1961 Prime Minister Harold Macmillan gave the young striver a job in the Ministry of Pensions. In 1965 she and her parliamentary colleague Keith Joseph had suggested encouraging private alternatives to the National Health Service and state pensions as a way of reducing taxes—a modest position, by today's terms, but one that stamped them at the time as staunch conservatives.

In the 1960s some Conservatives were already articulating a program of opposition to the reigning wisdom. One of them was Enoch Powell, a Tory stalwart who railed against socialism in terms that came close to the apocalyptic. Some of his ideas would become mainstream in the 1980s, but in the 1960s, as one commentator notes, his philosophy was regarded as "extreme."[17] Powell believed that the solution to all economic problems, great and small, could be found in the market. Competition within the private sector, rather than the close collaboration of business and state, was the source of lasting growth. In 1964 he even came out in favor of "denationalizing" the postal system and the state telecommunications monopoly— an idea far ahead of its time. Powell regarded inflation as an unmitigated evil, the scourge of productivity rather than the somewhat regrettable side effect of a worthy effort to manage demand. Luckily, there was a simple remedy: slow down the government printing presses. Powell believed that the most effective way to combat the state's pernicious intervention in the workings of the market was to exercise tight control of the money supply.

Unfortunately, Powell also happened to profess radical views on the even more delicate subject of immigration and race. In 1968, he gave a soon-to-be notorious speech—dubbed "Rivers of Blood" for its near-apocalyptic rhetoric—in which he declared that the influx of immigrants from the former colonies would, if unchecked, lead to the collapse of British society. It effectively ended his political career.

Yet his airing of free-market ideas, summarily dismissed by most of the political elite, resonated within the party. Thatcher—a member of the new shadow cabinet under the Conservative leader of the opposition, Ted Heath—was one of them. By now she was avidly consuming the publications of the Institute of Economic Affairs and steeping herself in the works of Hayek (whom she later claimed to have begun reading during her Oxford days). Her positions in the cabinet—first as the future minister responsible for the energy industries, then for transportation—confronted her directly with the issue of state ownership of strategic segments of the economy. Under Heath's leadership, the Tories pledged to stop any further nationalizations—but that was as far as it went. In the late 1960s, the notion of actually returning state-owned industries to the private sector was regarded as wildly outlandish.

Unlike Powell, whose radical economic ideas were way ahead of his time, Thatcher always remained a practical politician, acutely conscious of the gap between idealism and political reality. Her career climb was going smoothly, and she was not prepared to jeopardize it at this early stage. Heath, the party leader, was a firm believer in the reigning mixed-economy consensus, and as a future minister, she took care not to depart too far from his line. Heath was a gifted politician, a man who had risen from circumstances even more humble than Thatcher's (his father was a carpenter, his mother a maid) to gain admission to Oxford's Balliol College in 1935. His travels around Europe as a student in the 1930s, including an alarming visit to Nazi Germany, made him a foe of appeasement—at the time a choice decidedly at odds with majority views in the Conservative Party. After 1945, however, he wholeheartedly embraced the "postwar settlement." He believed firmly in the principle of state intervention in the economy, though perhaps not as actively as some Labourites. In Heath's vision, it was "partnership" between an active, entrepreneurial private sector and the government that reigned supreme.[18] This was, at the time, a solidly establishment view. In 1968, when Heath scolded a few lonely Conservatives who had dared to express sympathy with some of Powell's economic ideas, he was praised by the *Times* for exercising "plain common sense."[19]

Thatcher knew that the Conservatives had a good chance of winning the next election, so she was not about to declare herself a rebel. Yet Powell's iconoclasm clearly resonated with her, and that same year—in 1968—she made a small but discernible step toward defining a distinct political identity. Addressing the meeting of a Conservative policy group in the seaside resort of Blackpool, she set out markers that clearly identified her as a member of the party's incipient free-market camp. She expressed doubts about the virtues of state intervention and declared herself firmly in favor of rigorous control of the money supply. But none of this deviated too drastically from conservative rhetoric. She said little, for example, about privatizing those parts of the economy that were already under state control.

In retrospect, though, it was not her policy prescriptions that made the speech striking. It was, instead, a first distinct flash of the missionary zeal that one day became such a clear mark of the authentic Thatcher. It is important to remember that Thatcher's arguments in favor of free enterprise were never only about economic efficiency. She believed, with Hayek, that state intervention in the economy limited the scope for individual freedom. As she explained to her Blackpool audience, giving markets the room to operate was a moral imperative, and not just a matter of sound administration: "It is good to recall how our freedom has been gained in this country—not by great abstract campaigns but through the objections of ordinary men and women to having their money taken from them by the State. In the early days people banded together and said to the Government, 'You shall not take our money before you have redressed our grievances.' It was their money . . . which was the source of their independence against the government."[20] There was nothing wrong with people wanting to earn more money, she continued. But they should also be expected to contribute to society as a whole. She strongly rejected an uncritical embrace of materialism, declaring at one point, "Money is not an end unto itself."

It was this fundamentally moral impulse that drove her, in the climax of the speech, to an explicit rejection of the hallowed principle of consensus. Consensus, she declared, should not be viewed as an end unto itself; consensus could also be viewed as "an attempt to satisfy people holding no particular views about anything." Much more essential was to have "a philosophy and policy which because they are good appeal to sufficient people to secure a majority. . . . No great party can survive except on the basis of firm beliefs about what it wants to do. It is not enough to have reluctant support. We want people's enthusiasm as well."[21]

As Thatcher biographer John Campbell observes, "More than anything else it was this crusading spirit which was Mrs. Thatcher's unique contribution to the anti-collectivist counter-revolution which ultimately bore her name." It was other thinkers—eccentric fellow politicians such as Powell and her friend Keith Joseph and the scholars at the conservative Institute for Economic Affairs—who elaborated the policy ideas that animated her reign in office. What Thatcher brought to the mix was the ferocious zeal with which she pursued the realization of these political aims. British politics in the three decades before her arrival on the scene was dominated by consensus. Thatcher, by contrast, believed in the value of polarization; she had a penchant for defining herself as a rebel and a revolutionary. The conventional political wisdom, in her view, needed to be demolished, and if this required a certain degree of aggression, so be it. It was characteristic of her mind-set that her ire sometimes focused on the doubters within her own party as well as her opponents in the others.[22]

Thatcher and Joseph took comfort from the result of the surprise Conservative victory in the 1970 election. Some pollsters suggested that Powell's diversions from orthodoxy—and in particular his controversial remarks about the need to limit immigration—had actually drawn many working-class voters to the Conservatives (a feat that Thatcher would later strive to repeat, on her own terms, in 1979). The 1970 Conservative Party meeting in Selsdon that resulted in the markedly free-enterprise policy document so derided by Harold Wilson may have also played a role.

Thatcher joined the new government as the secretary of state for education and science. Although she did manage during her term to boost the budget for schooling, she failed to make much headway on her declared objective of curbing the growth of comprehensive schools (which are supposed to take in all pupils regardless of their previous academic achievements). In keeping with her strong beliefs in competition and personal responsibility, she preferred the more traditional grammar schools, regarding comprehensives as a classic example of left-wing egalitarianism that held back talented pupils. The problem was that comprehensives were just too popular with the public. (And Thatcher, ever the realist, ended up inaugurating a record number of them on her watch.) This was not the last time she would have to square her views with tricky political facts.

If the economic liberals in the party had hoped that their ideas would guide Heath's actions as prime minister, they were soon disabused by the notorious "U-turn." Though Thatcher publicly supported her leader, she clearly felt little personal investment in his policies. She later complained that her role in the government was primarily to act as the "statutory woman" who was consulted in the event of any issue likely to matter to the female electorate. In any event, she had little opportunity to push for implementation of the 1970 Conservative manifesto in the cabinet, and few paid attention when she did. Her disillusionment reflected a broader dissatisfaction with Heath that soon made itself felt among many other Tories.

In the event, Heath's government did not survive the general election of 1974. The defeat triggered considerable soul-searching among Conservatives. Heath himself saw little reason for second thoughts and made it clear that he intended to continue leading the party in opposition. But not all of his colleagues agreed. Keith Joseph, who had served as Heath's secretary of state for social services, had undergone a conversion to the free-market gospel and launched a series of speeches in which he proposed a radically different direction for the party that presaged much of what would later come to be known as "Thatcherism." He soon become a lodestar for Heath's right-wing critics. But Joseph—a nervous character with a marked self-questioning strain to his personality—followed in Powell's self-destructive path by holding a speech in which he warned against rising teen pregnancies in terms that evoked early-twentieth-century theories of eugenics. His bid for the leadership of the party was over before it really began.

Thatcher decided to pick up the gauntlet. She was an unlikely candidate for the leadership, even with Heath in a relatively vulnerable state after his election defeat. A parliamentary veteran named Airey Neave managed her campaign for the leadership (after having asked three other prominent party right-wingers, including Joseph, to go after Heath). Shrewdly assessing that Heath's camp did not take her challenge seriously, Neave aggressively wooed party backbenchers disgruntled by Heath's imperious style of government, driving home that Thatcher was the candidate of genuine change. It proved exactly the right approach for a deeply demoralized party. To his astonishment, Heath lost the first ballot to Thatcher. He resigned immediately. But he never got over his resentment toward the woman who, he felt, had behaved disloyally.

Thatcher, however, had a memory of her own. In April 1979, when that year's general election was drawing to its close, an anxious aide pressed her to let Heath join her at a press conference to appeal to wavering voters. Thatcher categorically refused. The old paragon of "consensus" remained on the back benches, an impotent symbol of the old order, throughout Thatcher's eleven years as prime minister.[23]

6

A Dream of Redemption

To non-Catholics, the procedure for choosing a new bishop of Rome has always been something of a curiosity. By the late twentieth century, when many Westerners increasingly seemed to be dismissing religion as mere superstition, papal elections seemed to hark back to an outmoded world. The cardinals who participated in the conclave resided temporarily in the Sistine Chapel, made their deliberations in absolute secrecy, and revealed the outcome with a puff of smoke. While the process entailed plenty of drama, the person chosen at the end was usually more of an anticlimax. Popes were always male, and usually elderly and Italian as well.

And then, in the fall of 1978, John Paul I died of an apparent heart attack after a mere thirty-three days as pontiff. The conclave that formed to choose his successor was almost identical to the one that had picked him. The shock of his sudden death made the College of Cardinals reassess the inscrutable will of the Almighty. Perhaps, some of them wondered, this was a sign. Perhaps they were being urged to make a dramatic break with the past, to take a leap of faith. The most likely candidate, another in a long line of well-established Italians, suddenly encountered reservations. The other favored candidate was unable to muster enough votes for a challenge. The members of the conclave found themselves considering an improbable way out of the impasse.

On October 16, 1978, a puff of white smoke emerged from the Sistine Chapel chimney. When Pericle Cardinal Felici stepped out onto the balcony of St. Peter's

Basilica to announce the choice of a new pontiff, the crowds grew confused. *Carolum?* Who was Carol? Felici continued: "Cardinalem Woi-ty-wa." A young American newscaster stumbled over the peculiar name: *Wojtyła.* Who was that? A foreigner, someone said. "E il Polacco," someone said. "It's the Pole!"[1] Then, at 7:42 p.m., the new pope emerged into view, charming them with his accented Italian as he commiserated with them over the loss of his predecessor. It was in his honor that the Polish pope, the first non-Italian to assume the post in 456 years, chose the same regnal name as his predecessor.

Age fifty-eight at the moment of his election, John Paul II was the youngest pope in well over a century. As a correspondent from *Time* put it, the College of Cardinals had "done not merely the unexpected but the nearly unthinkable." They had chosen a pontiff from behind the Iron Curtain.

Many Poles did not believe the first rumors. Finally, a special announcement on television brought confirmation: some thought they detected a note of pride in the newsreader's voice—distinctly unlike the bland tones with which he announced the usual record harvests or steel production figures. In Kraków, where Karol Józef Wojtyła had spent most of his life as a priest, the news spread fast. The British journalist Mary Craig, who was there, records how joyous crowds filled the streets to celebrate the news:

> No one went to bed that night. Young and old stayed in the Rynek Glowny, the historic market place which many say is the most beautiful in Europe, with its enchanting medieval Cloth Hall (the Sukiennice), and the splendid Gothic and Renaissance churches which surround it. "The drawing-room," they call it in Cracow, and in the daytime it is ablaze with flower stalls and a-flutter with pigeons, while the townsfolk gather in groups under the arches of the Sukiennice. This evening the square was floodlit, and all night long the crowd swayed and seethed, making emotional impromptu speeches, singing religious and national songs (often one and the same), reverting again and again to what often seems like an alternative national anthem—"*Sto lat, sto lat, niech zyje zyje nam*"—the Polish equivalent of "For he's a jolly good fellow."[2]

The new pontiff's election was cause for joy in those quarters that still saw an intimate connection between Catholicism and the long struggle for national sovereignty. For precisely the same reasons, Polish Communist Party officials were quick to comprehend the magnitude of the challenge that the new situation in the Vatican presented to them. Party chief Edward Gierek couldn't help himself when he heard the news, exclaiming, "Oh, my God!" One of his aides, hearing about the spontaneous celebrations in Kraków, stated that "he would prefer to deal with a different nation."[3]

If anything, the leaders of the Soviet Union—a country whose official ideology was grounded on strict allegiance to atheistic "historical materialism"—reacted to the news with even greater anxiety. As good students of history, they knew how religion had served in the past as a force for the mobilization of Polish national feeling, and they understood that a revival of such sentiments could easily direct itself against the Kremlin. The KGB station chief in Warsaw quickly dispatched a character study of the new pontiff to his masters in Moscow. The contents of the memo had been supplied by the SB, the KGB's Polish sister service:

> Wojtyła holds extreme anti-communist views. Without openly opposing the Socialist system, he has criticized the way in which the state agencies of the Polish People's Republic have functioned, making the following accusations: that the basic human rights of Polish citizens are restricted; that there is an unacceptable exploitation of the workers, whom "the Catholic Church must protect against the workers' government"; that the activities of the Catholic Church are restricted and Catholics treated as second-class citizens; that an extensive campaign is being conducted to convert society to atheism and impose an alien ideology on the people; that the Catholic Church is denied its proper cultural role, thereby depriving Polish culture of its national treasures.[4]

Yuri Andropov, the head of the KGB, immediately dispatched a cable to his *rezident* in Warsaw that berated the man for allowing this debacle to happen. To his credit, the KGB officer wrote back to his boss that Andropov might be better advised to direct his ire to the station chief in Rome.

Ultimately, however, Andropov and his Polish comrades were unsure about precisely how John Paul II would choose to approach relations with his home country's rulers and the rest of the Communist world.

His past offered some useful clues. Few other world leaders could claim the same degree of familiarity with the excesses of twentieth-century totalitarianism—in both its National Socialist and Soviet flavors—as Karol Wojtyła. He had studied for the priesthood in an underground seminary during the Nazi occupation, then came of age as a priest during the most brutal period of postwar Stalinism. From the very beginning, his religious vocation was bound up with the challenge of defending spiritual values against the overweening state.

Wojtyła was born in the small town of Wadowice in 1920. His father, who had risen to the rank of captain in the Austro-Hungarian Army, was a fervent Catholic. Karol, the youngest of his two sons, inherited his piety—which offered vital consolation during a tragic family history. The Wojtyłas had much experience with death in the family. Karol's mother, Emilia, died in childbirth when he was nine. Her daughter, who would have been her third child, was stillborn. Karol's older brother, Edward, died two years later from scarlet fever, which he had caught from his patients while he was working in a hospital during an epidemic of the disease. So Karol spent his formative years living alone with his father, who instilled in his son a deep attachment to the teachings of the church.

From an early age Karol showed both an avocation for sports as well as a passion for poetry and the theater. In 1938 he and his father moved from Wadowice to Kraków so that Karol could enter Jagiellonian University, an institution that dates back to the fourteenth century. He studied languages and literature.

Karol's second year at university was preempted by the start of World War II and the German invasion. The university, like all others in Poland, was shut down. To avoid being deported to Germany, Wojtyła took up a series of manual jobs, working in a stone quarry and a chemical factory. His work immersed him in the life of the Polish working class and also gave him many opportunities to witness firsthand the brutalities of German occupation. In 1941 his father died, leaving Karol orphaned and alone. "I was not at my mother's death, I was not at my brother's death, I was not at my father's death," he later told a biographer. "At twenty, I had already lost all the people I loved."[5] His father had already instilled in him a strong personal faith, and now the loss of his loved ones, experienced against the background of war and general deprivation, drove Wojtyła into an even deeper exploration of his relationship with Christ, which helped him to make sense of the reality of human suffering. His belief acquired an additional dimension from Jan Tyranowski, a lay mystic who helped show the way toward a more immediate experience of the divine.

Even before his father's death, the young Wojtyła's deeply felt faith had led him to wonder about the possibility of pursuing a vocation within the church. It was a question that assumed greater intensity against the backdrop of the German occupation. The Nazis, who were determined to eradicate all the sources of Polish national selfhood, soon began a campaign to destroy the Polish church. They dispatched priests to concentration camps or had them summarily shot for activities deemed hostile to the occupation. So Wojtyła joined an underground seminary run by Adam Stefan Cardinal Sapieha, a formative influence on the future pope and an extraordinary figure in the long history of Polish Catholicism. As the head of the church in German-occupied Poland, Sapieha gained fame for his uncompromising stance. When Hans Frank, the head of the Nazi occupation government, invited himself to dinner, the archbishop of Kraków served him black bread (partly made from acorns), jam made from beets, and ersatz coffee, served on the elegant silver service of the cardinal. Sapieha explained to his guest that this was all the food that he could offer according to the rations set by the Nazis.[6]

Wojtyła continued his studies through the hazards of wartime. He would later be credited with helping to protect many Polish Jews from the Nazis. In February 1944, a German truck ran him over—but officers in the truck jumped out and brought him to the hospital. In the wake of the second Warsaw Uprising in 1944, he evaded a Gestapo search by hiding behind a door when they came to the house where he was living. He spent the rest of the war in hiding in the archbishop's palace. After the Germans abandoned the city in January 1945, he helped save a teenage Jewish girl named Edith Zierer who had escaped from a nearby concentration camp.

In 1946 he was finally ordained as a priest and soon earned popularity for the openness of his pastoral approach. He was deeply involved in the lives of his parishioners. He did not believe in restricting his faith to the confines of church, often accompanying members of his congregation on camping trips or ski outings. In public they developed the habit of referring to him as *wujek,* "uncle," to avoid the unwanted attention that the word *father* might have earned from the authorities. He was not your usual priest. In a sharp departure from the stuffy practice of the times, he even counseled his parishioners on the joys of sex—within the bounds of marriage, needless to say. (He later put his thoughts on the subject into a book, *Love and Responsibility,* published in 1960.)

When the war was over, the new Communist rulers of Poland were not more favorably disposed toward the church than the Nazis had been. The Soviet forces who had occupied half of Poland in September 1939, after the Molotov-Ribbentrop Pact, had arrested and shot many priests. Now the Polish government installed by Moscow did whatever it could to beat back the power of the church. The authorities accused priests of everything from sedition to violations of tax law, mocked them in the media, or threw them in jail. But somehow Wojtyła managed to navigate these treacherous waters. He succeeded not only in anchoring himself firmly in the hearts of his congregation but also in maintaining a demanding schedule of academic work, studying for his doctorate in philosophy at the Catholic University of Lublin, the only nonstate university allowed by the authorities in the People's Republic of Poland. In 1958, when he became the youngest bishop in the country at age thirty-eight, the Polish secret police opened up its first permanent file on him.[7]

In the first decades after World War II, the leaders of the Roman Catholic Church faced harsh choices as they surveyed the geography of the faith. Millions of believers now lived behind the Iron Curtain, under the rule of Communist governments that had little tolerance for religion, however strongly they insisted the opposite. Officially, East-bloc regimes subscribed to full religious freedom; in reality, they viewed organized religion with intense suspicion, since its existence implied institutional alternatives to the official atheism that undergirded Marxist-Leninist doctrine.

Relations between the Vatican and the Soviet government had never been good. In the first phase of the Cold War, relations between Moscow and the Holy See were mutually hostile. The Yalta agreement, which granted the USSR control of Eastern Europe, had dramatically expanded the number of Catholics under Communist control, and in the 1940s and '50s, Stalin's minions had done their best to crush the church by persecuting priests and harassing churchgoers.

But by the early 1960s, both sides saw reason for compromise. The Kremlin wanted to advertise a spirit of tolerance, and the church was worried that continued confrontation could lead to the complete destruction of the Catholic communities who lived within the Soviet empire. So in the early 1960s Agostino Cardinal Casaroli, as cardinal secretary of state of the Holy See, signed agreements on mutual diplomatic recognition with Hungary and Yugoslavia—the first step in the Vatican's version of what would later come to be known as *Ostpolitik*. He was striving to do the same with Poland. His reasoning was understandable enough: the Soviet Union was not going anywhere, and a deal would give the Vatican at least some sort of diplomatic leverage for protecting Catholic rights.

The leaders of the Polish church tended to be skeptical about the extent to which the Soviets could be expected to honor the terms of any such agreement. They believed, based on their own experience of the Communist system, that the best way to defend the community of believers was by insisting on their rights to worship as they pleased. There could be no compromise on this essential point. Wojtyła agreed. But his philosophical investigations increasingly led him to a conclusion that the church had not always defended human rights as aggressively as it should have:

namely, that the teachings of Christ demanded that the church defend the rights of all human beings, not just those who happened to be Catholic. The integrity of the individual stood at the core of Christian ethics. To be sure, there could be no real freedom without freedom for the church. But neither was it possible to imagine a free church in an unfree society. Of course, one might have argued that such questions were moot in a country as tightly controlled as the People's Republic of Poland. Wojtyła, however, was not willing to concede the point.

As a rule, the management of world affairs tends to demand certain mental skills and crowd out others. Intense ambition, shrewdness, and focused practicality tend to outweigh gifts of contemplation, poetic language, or metaphysical abstraction. A capacious memory—a characteristic common to Thatcher and Deng—goes a long way. Most presidents and prime ministers are monoglot; in rare cases they might know a second language, but usually little more than that. And you will rarely see them consuming philosophy or exploring noncanonical art.

John Paul II was such a dramatic exception to this rule precisely because he did not set out to be a politician. He became a priest because he wanted to serve God. He never lost sight of that fundamental calling until the end of his days; it was the onlookers, especially non-Catholics, who tended to look at him as a statesman. Even as he hobnobbed with the presidents and the general secretaries, it was never quite possible to deny his otherness.

It was partly his range of experience that made him unique. There were very few twentieth-century heads of state who had been on the receiving end of both Nazism and Stalinism. But it was also a peculiar combination of intellect and accessibility that made Wojtyła extraordinary. This was a pope who bantered with his flock in a dozen languages. As a young man he acted in experimental theater productions of a type that probably would have left Margaret Thatcher sniffing in scorn, and he continued to write poetry well into his old age. At the same time—thanks to his long immersion in the daily affairs of the parishioners to whom he devoted so many years—he never lost his touch with the joys of ordinary life and the reality of everyday suffering.

He was also a professional academic philosopher. Wojtyła actually earned two doctorates—the first, in theology, in 1948 (after two years of study in Rome) and the second, in philosophy, in 1954.[8] He wrote his second doctoral dissertation on the German thinker Max Scheler, who extended the teachings of the great pioneer of phenomenology, Edmund Husserl, into a discourse that placed love at the center of moral action. Phenomenology, which seeks to root insights about the world in the fact of human experience, can be rather forbidding stuff. But in Scheler's emphasis on the authenticity and primacy of individual experience, Wojtyła found a powerful tool to combat what he saw as the crisis of twentieth-century ethics, which had undercut the centrality of moral choice. His work led him to the conclusion that the philosophy of the Enlightenment had, at its worst, spawned materialist ideologies that ran roughshod over individual freedom and responsibility, and in so doing opened the way to totalitarianism.

Wojtyła's interest in personalism emerged, of course, directly from his own confrontation with the radically depersonalizing (and secularizing) ideologies of Nazism and Stalinism. His radical insistence on the rights and responsibilities of the individual thus represented an important step toward a philosophical stance that directly challenged the central claims of these systems. For the Marxist-Leninists who ruled Poland at the time he was writing, Wojtyła's writings could only be regarded as profoundly counterrevolutionary. Little did they suspect that his philosophical explorations were indeed preparing the ground for a fundamental challenge to their ideological hegemony.

Scheler had found a way to make a critique that avoided the solipsism and pure subjectivity of other defenders of individuality, and Wojtyła would develop a similar line of thought in his work *Person and Act,* which he intended to be the authoritative statement of his own inquiry but never quite managed to complete (though a version of it was finally published, in Polish, in 1969). In the book, which combines traditional Thomist ethics with a stark new phenomenological sensibility, Wojtyła argues that human subjectivity is defined precisely through its dialogue with society. There is an irreducible specificity and uniqueness to each individual—yet no human being can exist in isolation. Individuality is defined by social interaction. By the same token, the exploitation or violation of the dignity of an individual's rights represents a repudiation of the most fundamental principle that binds society together. There should be no contradiction between the interests of the collective and the individuals who make it up. A society cannot be free if some of its members are not.

The secret police could not fail to notice such heresy. While the SB continued to keep Wojtyła under surveillance, there was little that they could do to silence him as long as he enjoyed the protection of the church establishment. And, indeed, his brilliance did not go unnoticed in Rome, either.

In 1960, shortly after his appointment as archbishop of Kraków, Wojtyła received a letter from the commission that was organizing the recently summoned Second Vatican Council called by the new pope, John XXIII. The letter asked for his recommendations about the agenda. He responded with an impassioned plea for a council that would directly confront the ethical emergency of twentieth-century society. The church, he wrote, should formulate a renewed emphasis on Christian humanism that placed the inviolability of the individual human being at its center. It was an emphasis that emerged from a philosophical and theological trend known as "personalism," which aspired to counter the mechanistic schemes of modern thought that subordinated the fates and choices of individuals to the dictates of history, economics, national identity, or realpolitik. His experience as a priest in a society that denied freedom of confession had made Wojtyła particularly sensitive to the need for a clear statement of the centrality of human rights.

Vatican II proved a watershed in the life of the newly anointed bishop, Wojtyła. Though often portrayed as a doctrinal conservative, John Paul II is perhaps better seen as a somewhat idiosyncratic traditionalist with a decidedly vernacular sensibility. He strongly believed that the church needed to renew and revive the message of the Gospel in order to resist the dehumanizing tendencies of modern culture—a threat he saw as much in the rampant modernizing capitalism of the West as in the atheistic materialism of the East. Bishop Wojtyła became a member of the committee that composed *Gaudium et Spes* (Joy and Hope),[9] one of the key documents of the Second Vatican Council promulgated in 1965, and his own thinking finds intriguing reflection in it: "This council lays stress on reverence for man.... [T]here is a growing awareness of the exalted dignity proper to the human person, since he stands above all things, and his rights and duties are universal and inviolable." One sentence in the document strikingly expresses the paradox that had already preoccupied Wojtyła in his earlier writings: "Man . . . cannot fully find himself except through a sincere gift of himself."

Wojtyła's beliefs in the primacy of individual freedom governed his behavior toward the state as his responsibilities grew. In 1964 Pope Paul VI appointed him archbishop of Kraków, the position that had been held before him by the charismatic Sapieha. Kraków is both the cultural and the spiritual center of Poland, the home of many of the country's greatest artists, thinkers, and priests, and Wojtyła engaged in a rich and multilayered dialogue with the city and its residents for forty years of his life. He was well acquainted with its workers, its intellectuals, its university students. In 1967 he was created cardinal. His new status necessarily brought him into direct confrontation with a state that brooked no rivals to its spiritual hegemony. It was a job that required less in the way of theological subtlety than practical political guile. In his relations with the Communist Party, Wojtyła focused from the very beginning on a strategy of holding and broadening the space available to the church in the public sphere. Every year, for example, he dueled with the party hierarchy over the city's traditional Corpus Christi procession. Over the years the functionaries had worked to restrict the procession, which followed the Stations of the Cross around the city's most prominent religious landmarks, to a barely visible minimum. Wojtyła fought back, marshaling the support of his parishioners in a variety of maneuvers to win back as much symbolic terrain as possible.[10]

The most famous duel with the powers that be, however, focused on the suburb of Nowa Huta, a Communist "model town" built around the Lenin Steelworks. From start to finish the steel town was conceived as a showcase of socialist values—right down to the thousands of indistinguishable apartments in rows of modular high-rise apartment buildings. The party's planners, however, did not trouble to include a church. Why would the enlightened working class need a place of worship? The workers, and the diocese of Kraków, came up with their own solution to the oversight: they would build it themselves. The workers contributed their own labor, donating their spare time to the construction. Wojtyła leveraged his prestige and political astuteness. When the bureaucracy proved reluctant to issue the necessary permits, the archbishop took to conducting Christmas midnight mass under an open sky at the spot where the Church of the Ark was to be built, attracting thousands of worshipers who gave the lie to the official party propaganda that the "masses" had turned their backs on the church. Wojtyła broke ground at the construction site of the church in 1967. Ten years later he was finally able to celebrate mass in the finished building.

Wojtyła also lent his support to a beleaguered Catholic youth organization called Light and Life, organized by Father Franciszek Blachnicki. Blachnicki's group had evolved out of another of his initiatives called Oasis, which organized Catholic summer camps for teens as an alternative to the system of activities promoted by the party youth organizations. Blachnicki believed that the most effective way to counter Communist spiritual hegemony was precisely by carving out preserves where people could develop their own alternative values. He called it "living in the truth." "If enough Poles 'plucked up the courage to live by the truth and unmask lies,' Blachnicki insisted, 'we would already be a free society.'"[11] Blachnicki's camps were subject to a range of official harassment—permits denied, fines issued against landowners who hosted the events—but the now archbishop Wojtyła persisted in lending whatever support he could.

For Wojtyła, his dealings with the world of politics were an inescapable yet ultimately incidental function of his job as a priest. In a society where the official ideology claims supremacy over every aspect of citizens' lives, however, any attempt to promote an alternate view of existence—whether aesthetic, moral, or spiritual—inevitably acquires a political dimension. And though Wojtyła was prepared to acknowledge the practical political reality of Communist rule, he was consistently unwilling to concede its claimed monopoly on truth—a point he made clear at every step. This was not lost on the Communist Party. In 1973, we now know, the secret police, the SB, considered prosecuting Wojtyła for three of his sermons—based on a paragraph of the criminal code that specified jail terms of one to ten years for seditious statements.[12] In 1976 and 1977, Wojtyła's contacts with Polish dissidents—especially Bohdan Cywiński, one of the founders of KOR—were also carefully documented by the SB's informers.

This, then, was the man Poles gathered to celebrate in November 1978. British journalist Mary Craig, who had already experienced how Krakówites reacted to his election, now watched as they experienced his inauguration. The receptionists at the city's main hotel for foreigners, asked whether they could point the way to a television, demurred. Then a passing waiter whispered to Craig that there was a set in the common area on the fourth floor, if she and her companion didn't mind walking up. In this unlikely location they found a crowd of spellbound Poles watching a black-and-white television, barely audible, encased in a glass box. Someone went to complain about the sound and returned with a hotel official carrying a huge bunch of keys. Finally, the official managed to open the box and turn up the volume.

The ceremony in Rome had already started. The onlookers in Kraków watched as the cardinals lined up to pay homage to the new pontiff. One of the first was the venerable Stefan Cardinal Wyszyński, who just a few days before had been Wojtyła's boss:

> The old man knelt to make his obeisance, ready to kiss not only the hand of the Pontiff but also his feet. Wojtyła acted swiftly to forestall him. Gently pulling the old Cardinal to his feet, he embraced him three times, in the Polish fashion, and kissed his hand. In the Dom Turysty there was a sudden explosion of coughing and shuffling and chairs were shifted this way and that, in a bid to escape the intolerable emotion aroused by the scene. The men standing near me looked at the ceiling, then inserted a finger beneath their spectacles to brush away the tears.[13]

The reaction of the audience attested to the intense feelings that this new pope could unleash. They were not inherently political emotions, but they rarely followed the paths of acceptable sentiment charted out by the party. A commentator from Polish State TV, carried away by the range of nationalities in St. Peter's Square, suddenly remarked: "We may belong to different nations yet we are all children of the same God." As Craig aptly observed, it was "an unremarkable comment elsewhere perhaps, but on the State Television service of a People's Republic . . ."[14]

A few weeks later the pope made his first official outside visit outside of the Vatican, to the city of Assisi. Someone in the crowd cried out, "Don't forget the Church of Silence!" The remark was a reference to the Catholic Church in Eastern Europe. John Paul II replied, "It's not a Church of Silence anymore because it speaks with my voice."[15]

The new pontiff—a vigorous and cosmopolitan man—made it clear from early on that he intended to minister to the world, and Vatican officials barely had time to get used to their new boss's presence before he set off on his first trip.

On January 26, 1979, the new pope flew to Mexico for his first overseas pilgrimage. For much of the twentieth century, Mexico had been governed by a secular revolutionary movement with a history of violent anticlericalism. In the 1920s, Mexican priests had been actively persecuted, many of them shot. At the time of the pope's visit, the church still faced a number of official restrictions, and the Mexican government had no diplomatic relations with the Vatican. The Mexican president, José López Portillo, issued the invitation to the pope with the proviso that he would not be welcomed as a head of state.

Yet López Portillo was there to greet him at the airport, having understood that it was politically expedient to do so. Mexicans were thrilled to greet John Paul II. More than a million of them lined the roads to cheer the pontiff during his visit. When he and his aides left the country, they looked down to see the light from countless mirrors held aloft to reflect the sun's rays at his departing plane. It was a remarkable dress rehearsal for an even bigger trip the pope was planning, to another country where the faith of ordinary people stood at odds with a government's program of militant secularism.

The term *Liberation Theology* was invented by the Peruvian priest and theologian Gustavo Gutiérrez Merino in 1971. Merino would be accused of swapping out theological terms with political ones and of reducing a spiritual teaching to a materialist social theory. One of the most famous of the liberation theologians was Ernesto Cardenal, the Nicaraguan priest and poet who in July 1979 became the minister of culture in the new Sandinista government that took power in Managua after toppling dictator Anastasio Somoza Debayle.

"We cannot be Christian and materialist," John Paul had once said. "We cannot be believer and atheist."[16] Now he used his Mexico trip to drive the point home. He seized the occasion of his address to the bishops for an uncompromising restatement of church doctrine. The Gospel, he said, could not be reduced to a set of social or political precepts, however well intentioned; the message of the Catholic Church was one of eternal salvation, and to choose it was to make a choice of cosmic and eternal dimensions. Violent revolution and class warfare could not be reconciled with church teaching—not least because they always ran the risk of violating the rights of one group of people while exalting those of another. The next day the pope celebrated mass with representatives of Mexico's indigenous peoples, whose long history of suffering served to drive home the point that the struggle for justice was an integral part of the church's mission. He conceded the point that Catholic institutions had sometimes allied themselves with the forces of dictatorship and oppression and went on to stress that, whenever the church took sides, it should always strive to take the side of justice.

These were not tactical compromises, made for the sake of calming his critics in the Liberation Theology camp. Christian humanism, and the inviolability of the individual, remained at the core of his thinking. In March he addressed these issues in his first encyclical. Entitled *Redemptor Hominis* (Redeemer of Man), it offered one of the clearest statements of his personalist philosophy. It is a text that displays a profound anxiety about the rising threat posed to individual human rights by various collectivist systems, including totalitarianism, imperialism, and colonialism:

> If human rights are violated in time of peace, this is particularly painful and from the point of view of progress it represents an incomprehensible manifestation of activity directed against man, which can in no way be reconciled with any program that describes itself as "humanistic." . . .
>
> If, in spite of these premises, human rights are being violated in various ways, if in practice we see before us concentration camps, violence, torture, terrorism, and discrimination in many forms, this must then be the consequence of the other premises, undermining and often almost annihilating the effectiveness of the humanistic premises of these modern programs and systems. This necessarily imposes the duty to submit these programs to continual revision from the point of view of the objective and inviolable rights of man.[17]

Redemptor Hominis is first and foremost a statement of religious doctrine, but it is also a crucial addition to the long and deepening discourse on human rights that has also been one of the twentieth century's great gifts to mankind. But John Paul II was not content to make his contribution in words alone. He was also planning to take a public stand in defense of the principles he held dear. And what better place to do it than in his own homeland?

John Paul II had begun to think about making a pilgrimage to Poland within days of becoming pope. The coming year of 1979 offered a perfect occasion for a visit. It was the nine hundredth anniversary of the martyrdom of Poland's greatest saint, Stanisław Szczepanowski. He was the Polish equivalent of Thomas à Becket, a man who stood up to the highest power in the land in the name of his faith. In 1072 Szczepanowski became the bishop of the city of Kraków. What we know of him is blurred by legend, but it is clear that he must have been a man of strong will and stubborn principles. He soon became embroiled in a feud with the king of Poland, a brutal character by the name of Bolesław the Bold. (As is so often the case in history, the nickname "bold" was really a euphemism for "psychopathic.") Bolesław refused to put up with the churchman's challenge to his authority, and he demanded the death of Stanisław. But no one would carry out the order, so Bolesław did the deed himself. He is said to have cut the bishop down while he was conducting a mass. Few of the king's deeply Catholic subjects were willing to countenance the killing, and Bolesław soon lost his hold on power. Stanisław, on the other hand, quickly achieved sainthood as one of Poland's greatest martyrs.

Though many of the details of Stanisław's death remain mysterious, one thing we do know for certain is that it happened in 1079. A thousand years might seem like a long time to most of us, but the particulars of the story—the principled stand of a bishop of Kraków laying bare the moral bankruptcy of untrammeled state power—gave it unnerving relevance to Poland's situation in 1979. The Communists certainly thought so, in any case.

So the announcement that John Paul II intended to return to Poland to celebrate the nine hundredth anniversary of Stanisław's martyrdom sent a shiver of dread through the ranks of the United Polish Workers' Party. "The cause of the bishop's death was a conflict with the king," one internal party memorandum noted in late 1978. "We see no sense in invoking the memory of the bishop's head and the royal sword, because they symbolize the sharpness of church clashes with the government. We are for cooperation and create favorable conditions for this."[18]

The Russians did not need to understand this particular historical backstory to see the potential for trouble if the pope were to return home. Leonid Brezhnev phoned Gierek to persuade him to cancel the visit. "How could I not receive a Polish pope," Gierek answered, "when the majority of my countrymen are Catholics?" Brezhnev countered by recommending, somewhat bizarrely, that the pope declare himself indisposed. Gierek, presumably gritting his teeth, replied that John Paul II was clearly determined to make the trip. "Well, do what you want, so long as you and your party don't regret it later," Brezhnev said—and hung up.[19]

In October 1978, the Polish Episcopate invited John Paul II to visit Poland to commemorate Stanisław's death. A few days later, a Communist Party spokesman responded that, while such a visit would undoubtedly be welcomed by the pope's compatriots, the exact timing depended on unspecified "circumstances" that necessitated detailed discussions.[20] The party was so nervous about the Saint Stanisław issue that it censored a reference to him in the Polish version of the pope's new Christmas address just as it was about to be published.[21]

Elaborate negotiations ensued. This exhaustive back-and-forth over the details of John Paul's itinerary might have seemed absurd to outsiders. In fact, though, what these preparations show is just how anxiously the authorities reacted to the prospect of a visit by the new pontiff. For the government in Warsaw, the homecoming of this one man was a terrifying prospect. The talks continued into the new year.

7

The Imam

As Khomeini settled into his exile in France in the fall of 1978, the unrest was spreading back at home. Unprecedented mass demonstrations filled the streets of Iranian cities. Voices from across the political spectrum openly demanded change, both gradual and revolutionary. Leftist guerrillas engaged in battles with government security forces. The shah's regime had never faced a challenge of such proportions before.

All this kindled utopian expectations among the revolutionaries who had gathered in Neauphle-le-Château. Yet the ayatollah remained imperturbable. He continued his daily prayers without interruption, making his obeisance to God in a tent especially erected on the grounds. He received an endless file of visitors, advisers, and petitioners. His supporters marveled at his supernatural equanimity, his simplicity, his unchanging steadiness. Everyone could see that he lived a life of uncompromising modesty; he owned almost nothing in the way of material possessions, and he ate no more than the plainest of meals. His granite sense of remove alienated many of his Western observers. A British correspondent noted that the ayatollah did not deign to shake his hand and that Khomeini's gaze remained fixed on some faraway point during their conversation.[1] Iranians tended to see this otherworldliness as a virtue, evidence of a genuine spirituality that refused to lose itself in the messy trivialities of daily existence.

It is one of the great ironies of the Iranian Revolution that the precise course it took depended crucially on the political acumen and personal instincts of this one

man. Khomeini's supporters might argue that God had provided well; he had chosen the ayatollah as the medium through which he was determined to act. If we do
not accept this belief, however, it is hard to escape a sense of profound contingency.
Without the presence of Khomeini, the revolution in Iran would have assumed a
fundamentally different form. "In fact, Khomeini is to the Islamic Revolution what
Lenin was to the Bolshevik, Mao to the Chinese, and Castro to the Cuban revolutions," writes historian Ervand Abrahamian, who goes on to note that the ayatollah
had such a powerful impact on the course of events precisely because of his aura
of purity and principle. Most Iranian politicians were calculating intriguers looking for an angle. Khomeini, by contrast, had spent long years in the loneliness of
exile for the sake of his principles. As Abrahamian notes, he lived a life of ostenta-
tious simplicity, more akin to a medieval mystic than a 1970s activist. He rejected
compromise and refused to maneuver for the advantage of his family; indeed, he
famously stated that he would have his own children executed if they acted against
the laws of God. Most notably of all, perhaps, he was ostentatiously incorruptible.
Even once he had assumed the position of supreme leader, he insisted on living a life
of minimal material comfort.[2]

Westerners did not know what to make of Khomeini. The leaders of contemporary revolutions were supposed to be flamboyant, strident, perhaps even promiscu-
ous or a bit messy—like Mao or Che or the student activists in Paris or Frankfurt
in the 1960s. Perhaps the closest comparison was to be found in earlier paragons
of revolutionary idealism like Robespierre or Lenin, ascetic fanatics whose lives
were entirely devoted to the cause. But the zeal of these men derived from a quasi-
scientific view of history that prescribed the inevitability of social transformation.
They were aggressively secular materialists—exactly the sort of personality that
had shaped the idea of modern revolution, and was, correspondingly, regarded as
almost inseparable from it.

Nothing remotely like that applied, of course, to this white-bearded religious
scholar, shrouded in the black robes and turban of his calling, who so deftly dodged
the journalists' questions about the nature of the future Iranian state. That same
dark gaze that so disconcerted Khomeini's non-Iranian interviewers resonated with
his compatriots, who knew him to be a lifelong student of *erfan*, the Shiite mystical
tradition that emphasized the immediacy of the divine and the dismissal of this-
worldly passions. The imam, as some were beginning to call him, spoke an idiom of
sacrifice and justice that galvanized the people back at home. They parsed the voice
issuing from black-market cassettes or illicit shortwave broadcasts for clues about
what was to come.

Had an objective biography of the ayatollah been available at the time, it would have revealed a great deal. It was his peculiar personal circumstances and his inclinations that made Khomeini into a revolutionary; he certainly did not come into the world as one. He was born in 1902 in Khomein, a small provincial town that seemed to owe more to the sixteenth century than the twentieth. Modern technology had little impact on life there; the same big landowning families who had dominated the social and political life of the community for generations remained firmly in control. The central government was remote; the state was weak. The only other figures capable of exercising competing influence were the members of the religious establishment.

Khomeini's father, Mostafa, came from a long line of illustrious clergymen, and he enjoyed a reputation as a lover of justice. In March 1903, his father announced that he was going to the local governor's office to raise a formal complaint about the behavior of several local khans (nobles) who were known for their harassment and exploitation of the locals. But the men killed Mostafa before he could get there. His son Ruhollah was four months and twenty-two days old.[3] We can only speculate, of course, about the extent to which his father's murder shaped the mature Khomeini's attitudes toward the society in which he lived. But it is certainly striking how many revolutionaries and political extremists have experienced violence directly in their own lives.[4]

From an early age, it was clear that Ruhollah would stay with the family vocation. He began his studies of the Quran as soon as he learned to read and soon showed that he had a prodigious memory and remarkable analytical skills. His temperament was mild—he showed little inclination to rebellion. He followed the prescribed path toward his calling as a religious scholar with patience and obedience. But he did experience a major shock when his mother died in his early teens, during a cholera epidemic that struck Iran during the First World War. He was now an orphan.

Khomeini may have originally intended to complete his studies at the great Shiite seminary in the Iraqi city of Najaf—the same place to which he would later be exiled for his resistance to the shah. But the end of World War I brought with it the collapse of the Ottoman Empire, and Najaf was caught up in the unrest that accompanied the turbulent birth of the new state of Iraq. So Khomeini opted to stay in Iran, enrolling at a seminary in the city of Arak. In 1922 he was invited to attend the newly opened Faiziyeh Seminary in Qom, which would soon become the most prestigious center of religious learning in Iran.[5]

He proved himself an exemplary student in Qom. Yet it was here that he began to diverge somewhat from the path of convention. While pressing ahead with his prescribed studies in logic and jurisprudence (including a solid grounding in tax law), he also began to explore the esoteric teachings of *erfan*, the rich but demanding tradition of Shiite mysticism. The word *erfan* literally means "gnosis" (occult knowledge), and it promises, to those capable of mastering its mysteries, a direct experience of communion with God. Most budding religious scholars steered clear of such heterodox territory, but once the young Khomeini discovered a willing instructor, he immersed himself in the subject.

Because the religious authorities regarded *erfan* with a certain degree of suspicion, Khomeini's teacher, Ayatollah Mohammed Ali Shahabadi, conducted his classes in the subject at home and always confined his students to a small but select group. There they discussed the canonical works of the Shiite mystics. Borrowing from the Neoplatonists, some of these Shiite thinkers ascribed to the essential unity of all creation and dismissed the complexities of visible reality as illusory. But it was possible, through discipline and study, to achieve an immediate and personal experience of this underlying divinity. As was so often the case in other mystical traditions, *erfan* taught that an individual seeker could achieve union with the godhead directly, without the help of priests or other intermediaries. A regime of spiritual discipline enabled the practitioner to bypass the deceptive information of the senses and the attachments of the individual soul. The adept who mastered these techniques could achieve "divine wisdom and the status of sainthood."[6] In one version of this teaching that had a particularly profound effect on Khomeini, someone who has developed the mystical training to appreciate the oneness of God behind all things can be considered a "perfect man"—a status that enables him to become an imam, the leader of a just and virtuous community.

The secrets of *erfan*—not unlike the Sunni mystical tradition of Sufism with which they can be compared—thus have potentially far-reaching political implications. The traditions in which Khomeini was immersed had their intellectual roots in the Greek philosophers, particularly Plato and his descendants, who dreamed of a perfect community in which enlightened scholar-rulers would transcend the messiness of this-worldly politics. The Greeks imagined this polity to be based on philosophy, not religion. But the Muslim theorists of government who emulated them later easily translated this vision into Islamic terms. The Prophet Mohammed was the earthly leader of the first perfect community. The tricky part was how to continue it once he was gone. This was an issue of considerable complexity, and the twentieth century was now challenging Muslims to figure out new answers to it.

In practical terms, a Shiite cleric of Khomeini's generation faced two fundamental choices about politics. One was to follow the example of the quietist clerics, who essentially believed that the clergy should leave politics to the politicians. The other position was represented by two of Khomeini's personal heroes. The first was Sheikh Fazlollah Nuri, a Shiite clergyman who had initially backed the Constitutional Revolution and had then rejected it when the revolutionaries had moved toward the creation of secular political institutions that undermined clerical power. Nuri was ultimately hanged by his enemies—an episode viewed by Khomeini as an instructive example of the sorts of betrayals of which secular revolutionaries were capable.

Khomeini only knew about Nuri through stories. But his second hero was someone whose public example he had followed for much of his youth. This was a Shiite notable named Seyyed Hassan Modarres, who persistently and publicly criticized the powers that be—above all Reza Shah, that fierce secularizer and founder of the Pahlavi dynasty. Modarres opposed Reza Shah's assumption of dictatorial powers and ended up spending much of his life in jail as a result. The shah finally had him killed in prison in 1937. But during Modarres's life, he offered the young Khomeini a compelling model for how a principled religious scholar could exercise moral force in the political arena. During the 1920s Khomeini often cut classes at the seminary in order to hear Modarres speak at the Iranian parliament. There, among other things, Modarres conducted master classes in parliamentary theatrics, dishing out one fearless tongue-lashing after another as he lectured the most powerful man in the nation on the imperatives of Islamic law and the constraints of the constitution.[7] Khomeini still managed to find time to graduate. In 1936 he received his permission to act as a *mujtahid*, an expert on Islamic jurisprudence. He was unusually young to receive such a distinction.

The 1940s were a difficult time for Iran's religious elite—just as they were for the country as a whole. The new leader in Qom, Grand Ayatollah Hossein Tabatabai Borujerdi, was, like his predecessor, a quietist, and he was reluctant to challenge the new shah directly. The Allied invasion of Iran and the period of political volatility that followed confronted the clerics with difficult choices, and they wanted to tread carefully.

Khomeini, however, was gradually losing his reservations. He watched the arrogant maneuverings of the infidel foreigners, the British and the Russians, with mounting fury. The young shah, as he saw it, was only too happy to serve as their pawn. In 1943 he published a book entitled *Kashf-i Asrar* (The Revealing of Secrets) that contained a withering assault on the secularizing tendencies of the shah, who wanted to continue the Westernization program inaugurated by his father. The word *kashf*, literally "unveiling," came straight from the Sufi lexicon: it alluded to the process of stripping away deceptive appearances from the true face of the divine. For the first time Khomeini issued a plea for a virtuous "Islamic government" to be run along divine guidelines: "Government," he wrote, "can only be legitimate when it accepts the rule of God and the rule of God means the implementation of the Shari'a." And he specified that a truly Islamic government should ban any writing "against the law and religion . . . and hang those responsible for such nonsense."[8] Yet for all the invective he unleashed at the shah, he still stopped short of calling for the complete abolition of the monarchy.[9] And Khomeini saved some of his harshest insults for his fellow clerics, whom he accused of cowardice when it came to standing up for the rights of their estate. His book did not win him a mass following, but some of his younger colleagues, who shared Khomeini's concern about the direction the country was taking, took note.

During the 1950s the attitudes of the religious scholars remained divided. Some of them, like Modarres, supported Mossadeq's plans to nationalize the oil industry and effectively curtail the shah's powers. Others, like Ayatollah Abol-Ghasem Mostafavi Kashani, ended up siding with the coup plotters who put an end to Mossadeq's ascendancy and revitalized the rule of the shah. This divided religious establishment—some of them wooed by the shah with money and favors—was in no position to act as an alternate power center.

In 1961, Grand Ayatollah Borujerdi died. This gave his pupil Khomeini the freedom to act as he saw fit. He now had no reason to hold back from public attacks against the shah. The shah had not helped matters by acclaiming an ayatollah in Iraq as the preeminent spiritual leader of Iran's Shiites—a transparent attempt to undermine the authority of politically minded clerics back in Iran like Khomeini and his older (and somewhat more cautious) colleague Ayatollah Mohamed Kazem Shariatmadari. Khomeini was ready.

In October 1962 the cabinet passed a law that allowed Iranians to vote for representatives to local councils. The new law gave the vote to women and no longer required Islam as a condition for holding office. Khomeini immediately made an announcement denouncing the bill as the "first step toward the abolition of Islam." It was all part of a Zionist plot, he said, to destroy the family and spread prostitution.[10] It wasn't just the local councils law, though. The shah had already announced the first stage of a national land reform—the early stages of the White

Revolution—and the clerics were worried that the measure could threaten the financial independence of the religious endowments that owned large amounts of land around the country. The shah's plans to introduce a Soviet-style "Literacy Corps" also instilled anxiety in the clerics, who wondered whether this was a covert secularization measure designed to undercut the traditionally dominant role of religious scholars as village teachers.[11]

In reaction to the storm of protest, the prime minister ultimately rescinded the local councils law—at least for the time being. But land reform went ahead. In January 1963 the shah put land reform and five other measures on the ballot in a nationwide referendum. Though the 99.9 percent "yes" vote was clearly fraudulent, the clergy did not dare to issue religious rulings against the land reform, recognizing its popularity. The shah deepened the insult by referring to the clerics as the "black reaction."[12]

In March 1963 Khomeini fired back with sermons accusing the government of plotting to destroy the religious classes in the interest of nefarious foreign interests. The shah's patience snapped. He ordered a raid on the Faiziyeh seminary in Qom. At least one student was killed and dozens injured. Khomeini assailed the government for its assault and assured the shah that "I will never bow my head to your tyranny." On June 3—during the holy month of Moharram, when Shiites celebrate the self-sacrifice of their greatest martyr in intensely emotional rituals—Khomeini held a famous speech at the Faiziyeh in which he settled accounts with the shah. Once again he accused the shah of acting as a proxy for Israel. Once again he denounced the shah in witheringly personal terms, addressing him as "you unfortunate wretch." On June 5, the security forces arrived at Khomeini's house and arrested him. Demonstrations erupted in Qom and other cities around Iran. Martial law had to be declared. Hundreds of people were killed. It was the worst unrest in Iran since the fall of Mossadeq a decade earlier.[13]

Some within the government apparently considered sending Khomeini to the executioner. But Shariatmadari ensured his safety by awarding him the title of "grand ayatollah" (since the constitution prevented anyone of that exalted rank from capital punishment). In 1964 Khomeini was finally released after ten months in prison—just in time to wade into yet another political fray. This time the issue was the new status-of-forces law the shah had signed with Washington. The law gave wide-ranging immunity to US forces stationed on Iranian soil—precisely the sort of cause that still tends to inflame popular opinion in countries already concerned about overweening US influence in their domestic affairs. "If the men of religion had influence," Khomeini declared, "it would not be possible for the nation to be at one moment the prisoner of England, at the next, the prisoner of America. . . . If the men of religion had influence, governments could not do whatever they pleased, totally to the detriment of our nation."[14]

The government arrested him again. This time, however, Khomeini was immediately expelled from the country. He was sent first to Turkey, where he lived for the better part of a year with the family of a Turkish government official before receiving permission to move to the holy city of Najaf in Iraq. Unlike 1963, however, his arrest and exile prompted little reaction from the religious establishment or the public at large. Land reform had won the government a certain degree of credit among the populace, and the senior clergy felt that they had taken enough risks in his defense.[15] Khomeini's departure from Iran in 1964 seemingly marked the end of his political career. He would spend the next thirteen years in Iraqi exile.

Khomeini took it all in stride. His strength of belief was extraordinary, if not eerie. Most of the Iranians who met him were deeply impressed by his otherworldliness and his powers of self-control. A story made the rounds about the death of Khomeini's infant daughter. While Khomeini's wife was pulling her hair in grief, Khomeini remained outwardly unmoved: "God gave me this gift, and God has taken it away." Khomeini's son noted that his father believed himself to have an especially intimate and privileged relationship with God.[16] For a man with such a cosmic view of existence, a few years in exile from his home country was a triviality, a minor inconvenience.

Yet exile did change him in one respect: it radicalized him. This might seem hard to imagine, given the intensity of his pre-1964 invective against the shah. But even amid his most scurrilous attacks, Khomeini had never called into question the monarchy itself. He had insisted that the government observe sharia law. He had demanded a greater role for the ulama in appointing the shah, and at one point in 1963 he even asked the government to grant the religious authorities a say over education and a "few hours of radio time" each week.[17]

Now his views began to change.[18] Exile forced him, perhaps, to confront the real balance of forces. This was not the timid, financially weak Iranian monarchy of the nineteenth-century Tobacco Protest. This was a strong, twentieth-century state with all the means of political control that went along with that: an all-encompassing secret police; a government-run educational system; official media, including television networks that reached into every cranny of society; state-of-the-art communications; an increasingly modern economy that threatened to rationalize away traditional interest groups; a well-equipped military; and the full political and economic support of the United States, the world's most powerful country, and its allies. Even the religious authorities were now cowed into submission, as the sub-dued reaction to his exile had shown. And the secular intellectuals of the National Front and the leftist parties—they might criticize the shah, but they had no moral fiber. As for the Communists, they were atheists, but there were things that could be learned from them: political organization, planning, building resilient networks.

As the 1960s went on, Khomeini gradually became persuaded that the modern Iranian state could not be persuaded to change its ways. It would have to be cap-tured. And the only way to do this was through revolution. *Revolution* was a word that, by now, had already become something of a religion in its own right for many young Iranians (even if the word was still anathema to most religious scholars). But even as Khomeini received and taught a steady flow of students from his homeland, he was also deepening his familiarity with the wider world of Islamic revivalism. By now a full-fledged "model of emulation" (*marja-e taqlid*) to Shiites around the Middle East, Khomeini was entitled to receive religious taxes contributed by his followers, and he began to put these funds to a variety of political uses (including support for the Palestine Liberation Organization, whose cause he held especially dear to his heart). He continued to digest the works of the modern Islamist thinkers and met members of the Muslim Brotherhood from around the Sunni world. All this helped to sharpen his awareness of how a genuinely Islamic state should look.

He was also building a political organization of his own, a covert network of young religious radicals. Known as the Combatant Clergy Association, it was based on a growing cadre of young clerics attracted by his principled stand against the shah. They came to Iraq to attend his lectures, absorbed his teachings, and then returned to Iran to distribute funding, advice, and cassette recordings of his ser-mons. They sought coalitions with those who had borne the brunt of the shah's transformation of Iranian society, like the *bazaaris* and the dislocated denizens of the shantytowns.

Not everyone among the senior clerics shared Khomeini's views. Most of them dismissed his theory of the Islamic state, regarding it as unorthodox. So a great deal of his polemical work in this period was directed at fellow members of the religious establishment. Throughout the years of exile, Khomeini kept up a steady drumbeat of pronouncements keyed to major political and religious events, and he carefully aimed them not only at general public opinion but also at the ulama. Shame was one of the most powerful weapons in his arsenal. In 1971, when Khomeini issued a tirade against the shah's celebration of the twenty-five-hundreth anniversary of the monarchy, he reserved special contempt for fellow members of the religious class. Millions of Iranians were starving as the shah lavished the nation's wealth on his senseless projects; when university students (including women) protested, the security forces attacked them viciously. Yet the religious elite, Khomeini acidly observed, had nothing to say:

> Are we not to speak out about these chronic ailments that afflict us? Not to say a single word about all these disasters? Is it incompatible with our position as religious scholars to speak out? . . . How is that now, when it is the turn of the present generation of religious scholars to speak out, we invent excuses and say that it is "incompatible" with our status to speak out? . . . If the 'ulama of Qum, Mashhad, Tabriz, Isfahan, Shiraz and the other cities in Iran were to protest collectively today against this scandalous festival, to condemn these extravagances that are destroying the people and the nation, be assured that results would be forthcoming.[19]

By this time Khomeini's relationship with Grand Ayatollah Shariatmadari, his ally back in 1963, was giving way to outright rivalry.[20] Shariatmadari did not see the point in outright challenges to the power of the shah; it was better, he believed, for the religious establishment to remain united if it hoped to survive the onslaught of the state.

This position became increasingly hard to maintain as the economic and social contradictions of the shah's modernization program intensified. The younger clerics were increasingly demanding a principled stand from the ulama. Aside from Khomeini, the only other leading religious scholar the young radicals took seriously was Ayatollah Mahmoud Taleqani, who had joined with Mehdi Bazargan in 1961 to form the Iran Freedom Movement. Taleqani, who spent much of the 1960s and 1970s in jail, would later join forces with Khomeini during the revolution.

Many Iranians had never heard of Khomeini before 1978; the riots of 1964 were part of the past. But for those in the know, he had already acquired a unique status. They began referring to him as "the imam"—a provocative break with Shiite tradition. True, the Lebanese Shiite leader Musa Sadr had been hailed that way by his followers starting in the 1960s—but they were Arabic speakers, and the word has a different connotation in Arabic, where it is a title of respect attached to anyone who leads the daily prayers. For Shiites, by contrast, it refers to the twelve spiritual and religious successors of the Prophet Mohammed, a line that begins with Ali ibn Abu Talib and ends with Mohammed al-Mahdi, the imam of the ages who will one day reemerge from occultation to inaugurate a new age of perfect justice. It is a term that is redolent with exalted emotion and apocalyptic yearning, and now, for the first time in centuries, Iranian Shiites were using it to refer to a living person.[21]

This, too, was a form of revolution. For centuries Shiite legal scholars had been expected to climb the ladder of their religious vocation through patient scholarship and teaching, laboriously building reputations and followings through the force of pious example and scholarly devotion. But now the acolytes of Khomeini were putting him above the rest—and they were doing it on the basis of his political engagement, not his religious credentials.

In the fall of 1977, the crowds who gathered at a Teheran mosque to commemorate the death of Khomeini's son Mostafa hailed their leader as the "imam." According to a report by SAVAK, several other ayatollahs in Qom refused to participate in the mourning ceremonies, saying that they regarded Khomeini's exaltation as an "insult." But soon the revolution would no longer allow them the luxury of nonparticipation.[22]

8

With a Gun in the Hand

In the capital of Afghanistan, the day of April 27, 1978, dawned cool and clear. Through the morning the staffers at Radio Kabul, the national Afghan broadcaster, stuck to their normal routine. Then, shortly before noon, a colleague asked Akbar Ayazi to read the midday news bulletin; for some reason his friend, who was supposed to do the job, preferred to pass. He promised the twenty-two-year-old Ayazi that he'd treat him to a kebab at a place around the corner in return for the favor.

As Ayazi read the bulletin, he found himself suppressing a growing sense of dismay. The news was ominous. The first item announced that the government of President Mohammed Daoud had placed all the leaders of the Communist Party under arrest.

It was immediately clear that Daoud's move could have catastrophic consequences—for he was doing no less than embarking on a showdown with the world's Communist superpower. For years Afghanistan had stood in the shadow of the Soviet Union. Leaders in the Kremlin, eager to counter America's influence in Iran and Pakistan throughout the 1970s, had responded by boosting their assistance to Afghanistan in every way they could think of. The Soviets poured in billions of dollars in aid. They built Afghanistan's industry, paved its roads, and purchased its oil and gas. They invited thousands of Afghans to study in the USSR. They supplied the Afghan military with tanks and planes and artillery and filled its ranks with Soviet advisers. And now the president of the country was throwing their friends in jail.

Despite his youth, Ayazi had already seen enough of Afghanistan's factional politics to understand the potential for serious conflict. In Kandahar, where he grew up, his father was the principal of a local high school. Early in the 1970s the student body had begun to fragment into competing blocs. No sooner had the school's young Communists formed a discussion group than militant Muslims responded with a cell of their own. Ayazi's father, a secularist liberal who disagreed with both tendencies, had banned all activism from the school grounds, earning him the enmity of both camps. Just for good measure he had also forbidden his son to get involved in politics until he was mature enough to make informed choices.

The tensions in Ayazi's high school reflected what was happening in the country at large. President Mohammed Daoud Khan had originally sympathized with the Communists. In 1973 he had overthrown King Zahir Shah, his own cousin, and declared a republic with himself at the helm. The People's Democratic Party of Afghanistan, the local version of the Communist Party, had helped him overthrow the king. But as the years went by, Daoud grew wary of his allies and maneuvered to avoid becoming an outright client of the USSR. He sought improved relations with the Muslim Middle East and particularly with Iran, America's main regional ally.

The Kremlin viewed these efforts with a growing degree of alarm, and they transferred their dissatisfaction to their Communist allies inside Afghanistan. PDPA leaders grew increasingly vocal in their criticisms of Daoud's policies. As a result, by the spring of 1978, Daoud's friends on the Left were beginning to make him nervous. Tensions between the president and the Communists rose. In April one of the senior leaders of the PDPA was shot dead by two assassins who appeared at the door of his home. Who orchestrated the killing remains unclear to this day, but there is no dispute about the consequences. The Communists, scenting a government plot, railed against the government and staged a big protest march through downtown Kabul. Daoud hesitated for a few days, then rounded up the leaders of the PDPA. It was a declaration of war.

As he read the announcement of the arrests, Ayazi suspected that the Communists might attempt to fight back. Little did he know how quickly he would be proved right. As he and his friend walked out of the radio station, they were startled to see a tank lumber into the courtyard. Confused, the two men ran into the street—just in time to see more tanks heading toward them. As Ayazi watched, one of the tanks swiveled its turret and fired a shell into the nearby presidential palace. Soviet-made MiG fighter jets swirled overhead. Ayazi rushed off to warn his mother, who was working in another part of the city, and bring her home to safety, where they sheltered as the fighting continued.

The gunfire and the confusion went on for another twenty-four hours. By the end the Communists and their allies were able to celebrate their triumph. With surprising ease they had succeeded, in less than a day, in routing the government. Daoud and most of his family were dead, gunned down in the palace, where they had held out until the end against the rebels. The commander of the tank that fired that first shot became the new minister of defense.

When Ayazi returned to work, he discovered that he was out of a job. It turned out that most of his colleagues at the radio station, who were now proudly sporting red armbands, had been covert members of the Communist Party. Ayazi was not, and the new order no longer required his services. He was fired.

Officially, supreme power in the state now resided with the PDPA and its leader, a former writer by the name of Nur Mohammed Taraki. The new government immediately launched a public relations campaign lauding his modest origins, his grand plans, and his extraordinary talents. Afghans learned that the new ruling party, the heroic vanguard of workers and peasants, was solidly behind the man who was now described as the "great leader," united like no organization before it in the country's history. The future was bright, and Afghans were heading straight for it.

It was all facade. The new rulers grandly dubbed their seizure of power the "April Revolution," but it was actually a classic palace coup that had been orchestrated by a Taraki aide named Hafizullah Amin. While the other PDPA leaders languished in prison, Amin, for some mysterious reason, had drawn only house arrest. Perhaps Daoud regarded him as a relatively harmless junior. It was a fatal mistake.

Over the next few months, Amin would prove to be the most relentless schemer in the PDPA, combining thrusting ambition with an easy if somewhat reptilian charm. Unbeknownst to Daoud or even the other Communist leaders, Amin had spent years patiently honeycombing the Afghan military with his supporters, often building on the proto-Communist inclinations of officers who had received much of their training in the Soviet Union. When Daoud made his move against the PDPA, Amin was ready and took advantage of his lax detention to send his armed followers into the field against the president. Once he had heaved Taraki into power, Amin positioned himself as the older man's most loyal acolyte—the substitute son of the childless leader who had sacrificed his entire life to the cause of the party. None of this, as events would show, altered the fact that the son was really the more powerful of the two and that his feelings toward his father figure were fueled more by Freudian resentment than filial piety.

As for the party's unity, this was the biggest lie of all. Far from the monolithic structures of so many Communist Parties elsewhere, the fractiousness of the PDPA was an open secret. It was actually two parties bolted together, a coalition of necessity that reflected the ethnic and sectarian fault lines that ran through Afghan society.

From their beginnings, back in the 1960s, Afghan Communists had tended to gravitate around two poles. One was the group known as Parcham (meaning "Banner"), led by the imperious Babrak Karmal, a general's son who never quite lost the aura of his privileged upbringing.

Karmal and his followers believed that Afghanistan was too backward to fit the orthodox Marxist template of a prerevolutionary society, and even as they railed against the ruling classes, it was clear that their view of social transformation was essentially a gradualist one. While the Parchamis included in their number many Pashtuns, Afghanistan's largest ethnic group, their membership drew heavily on the other ethnicities—Tajiks, Uzbeks, and Hazaras—who tended to communicate in the Afghan lingua franca of Dari (the local version of Persian). Though Karmal liked to claim descent from a rough-hewn Pashtun clan in order to broaden his appeal, his family actually came from an urban, Persian-speaking milieu.

Taraki and Amin both belonged to the PDPA's other faction, known as Khalq ("the People" or "the Masses"). Khalq's ethnic basis was narrower than Parcham's: Khalqis were overwhelmingly Pashtuns, and more often than not they hailed from a particular subset of the Pashtuns. Taraki and Amin were both members of a particular Pashtun tribal confederation, the Ghilzais, that had long chafed under the domination of more powerful Pashtun groups—and especially the Durranis, the dynasty that had dominated Afghanistan for centuries, right up until the Communist coup. (Both Daoud and Zahir Shah were Durranis.) The Khalqis tended to be far less vested in the existing system of ruling elites, and this helps to explain the radicalism that dominated their thinking.

Khalqis were, above all, dutiful Leninists. Like so many other would-be Third World modernizers, they detested their country's backwardness, and they believed that the only reasonable cure was to frog-march it into the twentieth century by brute force, if need be. To be sure, Afghanistan didn't really have a proletariat, and though many aspects of its agricultural system appeared backward and traditional, most peasants actually owned their own land. But no matter. There was one institution that could still serve as a revolutionary vanguard, and that was the army. For years the military had been one of the few structures in the country—along with the monarchy and a steadily expanding state educational system—that managed to coalesce the notoriously unruly Afghans around a sense of shared national destiny.

The military was one Afghan institution that offered opportunities for advancement even to those who weren't part of the traditional elites. And the upper ranks were filled with officers who had studied in the Soviet Union, which offered them a clear example of a primitive rural society that the Communists had mobilized into a modern industrial power.

The ideological differences between Parcham and Khalq were just part of the problem. There were also intense personal feuds at work. Karmal, the Persian-speaking patrician, despised Taraki and Amin as upstarts, and they were happy to return the favor. In the old, prerevolutionary parliament, Amin had been famous for his easy joshing with his opponents among the religious conservatives, who gave their atheist colleague the joking nickname of "Satan."[1] Karmal, a formidable orator once imprisoned for five years by the king, had emerged to become a political heavyweight courted even by Daoud himself, and he cultivated a self-regard that alienated just about everyone. As the new Communist regime got under way, Amin couldn't help reminding the Parchamis that they had spent the "revolution" cringing in prison while the Khalqis got on with the job. The Parchamis, in turn, regarded the Khalqis as bumbling zealots who needed a bit of adult supervision.

The Afghan public at large knew little of this, of course. What they saw instead were slogans, revolutionary parades, and a burgeoning personality cult centered on Taraki. There is little doubt that the vast majority of Afghans—most of whom had no access to television or newspapers—regarded all this with bemusement, apprehension, or apathy. But the state almost immediately denied them the luxury of disengagement. Within weeks of seizing power, the new revolutionary government announced a series of far-reaching edicts that would tip Afghan society into a maelstrom from which it is still struggling to recover.

Decree Number One proclaimed land reform. The proclaimed intent was to uproot the supposedly feudal underpinnings of Afghan society, stripping power from traditional landlords and canceling unfair lending arrangements that had kept millions of people indentured to local power brokers. The political aim was to give the majority of Afghans—who overwhelmingly lived in the countryside—a reason to love the new government. A flurry of other new reform measures followed. A literacy campaign taught the benighted how to read and write. Women received full civic rights. It was a program that bore a striking resemblance to the shah's White Revolution.

It all sounded wonderful, on paper. The problem was that this blizzard of reforms, and especially the realities of their implementation, bore little or no relation to the society they were intended to change. Of course, everyone believed in the goal of literacy, but the catch was that the government had little in the way of resources to accomplish the task of educating the rural poor. So it relied, as Communist regimes so often had in the past, on a mixture of mobilization and brute force to fill the gap. Zealous young schoolteachers dispatched to the villages, invariably without proper textbooks or teaching materials, often ended up haranguing the locals on their backwardness. What particularly inflamed the locals was the newcomers' insistence that women should take part in the courses, in classrooms that mingled both sexes. Mobs drove the arrogant outsiders away. In some cases the do-gooders then returned with escorts of government troops, and literacy classes then proceeded at bayonet point.

The land-reform program similarly ignored the complex skeins of social relations that bound Afghans together in the countryside in a million site-specific ways. Given its extreme topography, hybrid civilizations, and ethnic and social pluralism, Afghanistan has never been a country about which useful generalizations can be made. But this is precisely what the land reform of 1978 entailed. It attempted to impose a one-size-fits-all template on a messy array of situations. It is true that Afghan landlords acted as exploiters—but they were also important organizational centers of society who played religious or social roles as well as economic ones. And there were massive problems with implementation as well. Plots of land awarded to previously landless peasants could not be cultivated without money for seed and fertilizer—yet the reforms had failed to provide for supporting changes in the financial system, like the creation of agricultural banks. Instead, they stripped away traditional sources of finance without replacing them with new ones.

What all of this showed, of course, was that the April Revolution (as the new government referred to the coup against Daoud) failed to root itself in Afghan society. Its leaders essentially admitted as much. Taraki's official speeches stressed that the April Revolution was advancing a dramatically new theory of Marxist revolution—one driven by a progressive, antifeudal military elite rather than an industrial working class or a militant peasantry. (Afghanistan had no industrial class to speak of, and the peasantry was largely quiescent.) Marx would have probably interpreted this view as a form of "Bonapartism." The keepers of the faith in Moscow—people like the Kremlin's chief ideologue, Mikhail Suslov—ought to have regarded this as a perversion of orthodox Marxist-Leninism. But by this point they had spent so many years trying to stir up Third World revolutions in places with little or no signs of "proletarian consciousness" that they don't seem to have noticed.

In the developing world, indeed, the word *revolution* had long since devolved into code for just this sort of brute-force modernization. Starting in 1975, the Cambodian Maoist offshoot known as the Khmer Rouge adopted a bizarre amalgam of Communism, primitivist nostalgia, and militant ethnonationalism that involved driving all city dwellers into the countryside, where they would be forcibly reeducated at the hands of zealous revolutionaries. (In practice this meant that you could be killed for wearing a pair of glasses.) An estimated 2 million people died. The Communist military junta that seized power in Ethiopia unleashed a Red Terror in 1977 that took a half-million lives. The rhetoric as well as the actions in both cases represented ominous precedents for Afghanistan.[2]

What stood out for many Afghans was, simply enough, that the new government consisted of Communists, and Communism, by definition, is an atheistic ideology. Though Taraki and his ministers never tired of proclaiming their respect for Afghanistan's Islamic society, their actions consistently undercut that message. One of the new government's first actions was to change the Afghan flag from the black, red, and green tricolor that had survived from the monarchy into Daoud's republic (in slightly modified form) with a new design in basic red, that unmistakable signature of revolutionary intentions. This was deeply offensive to those Afghans who regarded the removal of the color of Islam (green) as a clear indication that the Communists were planning to reduce the role of religion in public life. The slogans and imagery at PDPA demonstrations included virtually no religious references, and the demonstrators often included women as well as men, which incensed conservatives. As political violence increased, the PDPA buried its deceased members in secular ceremonies and sometimes left the bodies of its opponents in the field without following the Islamic customs that dictated burial within a certain period.

The plotters of the coup against Daoud also sowed the seeds of future problems with their Soviet patrons. Far from instigating the coup, as many in the West assumed, the men in the Kremlin had been caught completely off guard by the news—they learned of Daoud's overthrow from a Reuters report.[3] They were nonplussed. No one had warned them what was afoot, and initially they were not entirely sure they approved. Moscow had been happy enough with the situation under Daoud. But the Soviet leadership nonetheless responded positively to Taraki's initial requests for additional aid and advisers. Daoud's overtures to the West in his last years had unsettled Brezhnev and his entourage, so the news of the coup seemed, at first, to offer reassurance that the new government would safeguard Soviet interests on the Hindu Kush. Taraki's rhetoric did little to disappoint them. He increasingly larded his speeches with references to the example of the Great October Socialist Revolution and praised the Soviet Union's selfless efforts toward the betterment of his country.

But Taraki's talk had an opposite effect at home. Afghans did not like to hear their leaders kowtowing to other countries. While many appreciated the aid that they had received from the Russians over the years, there were limits to their gratitude.

Everyone knew that atheism was part of the Soviet Union's official creed. Many Afghans, indeed, had personal memories of the 1920s and '30s, when the Soviet government had brutally suppressed an Islamic guerrilla movement in what later became the central Asian republics of Uzbekistan and Tajikistan. Many refugees from that campaign had fled across the border to the south and settled in ethnically congenial parts of Afghanistan, bringing with them a residual memory of heroic Muslims in revolt against atheist Russian rule. Afghans were quick to recall this poisonous legacy as Soviet involvement in their country's affairs increased.

In June 1978, two months after the coup, Afghan government police in the remote Pech Valley, in the province of Kunar, arrested two local tribal elders, men who enjoyed considerable respect in the community. The reasons for the arrest remain unclear to this day: some say that the men were detained for opposing government policy, but other accounts suggest that the officials doing the arresting were abusing their power to settle a personal grievance. What we do know is the effect that the arrest had on the locals. As the jeep carrying the prisoners passed through the small town of Ningalam, an old woman cried out, "Is there no man among you? Two of our men are being taken away." Someone in the crowd opened fire on the vehicle, killing an officer and two soldiers. The very next day the army invaded the town with tanks and artillery. According to local accounts, government forces set fire to the houses. They even burned the local mosque and the Qurans inside it.[4]

Out of these desultory origins was born the first uprising against the Communist government. The stream of disturbing decrees from Kabul stirred talk of heathen practices that would soon be extended to the entire countryside. It was said that officials of the new government had told people to abandon the Quran and study the books of Marx and Lenin instead and had instructed children in school to spy on their parents. Communist officials openly drank, smoked hashish, and paid for the services of prostitutes. And, as with the Ningalam arrests, they insulted tribal leaders, figures held in high esteem by local clans. The Communists said that women were equal to men and that all the received institutions of marriage, like the bride price, would be eliminated—perhaps even marriage itself.[5]

The arrest of the two elders, and the government retaliation that ensued, provided the spark. Locals gathered up their weapons and attacked the town, driving out the government troops. But they were able to hold it for only a few days before they were forced to withdraw. For months the rebellion remained fragmented and diffuse. That changed in January 1979, when one of the local tribal notables, a man named Samiullah Safi, returned home to the valley from a long sojourn in Kabul. He had served for a while as a deputy in parliament, where he had opposed Daoud's increasingly authoritarian reform program. After the April coup, Hafizullah Amin, apparently seeing him as a potentially weighty ally in a notoriously fractious part of the country, had even tried to bring him over to the side of the Khalq. But now, disgusted by the government's apparent contempt for Islam, Safi was returning home to take up the flag of revolt.

A few days after his return, he brought together a group of local leaders—who represented both his own Safi tribe (who were ethnically Pashtun) as well as the neighboring Nuristani people (who belonged to their own distinct ethnicity)—for a traditional conference. They agreed on the need to rise up against the government and organized an attack on a nearby district headquarters. It was the signal for a broad revolt that quickly seized the entire region. The *lashkar,* or tribal army, that materialized soon numbered, by their own estimates, fifteen to twenty thousand people.[6] The leaders of the rebellion formed assemblies, or *jirgas,* representing the areas liberated from the control of the Communist government. The assemblies, protected by small detachments of armed men, moved down the valley, contacting villages still under ostensible government control, to persuade them to join the revolt. Sometimes the emissaries were fired upon by government troops, but more often than not the locals quickly declared their willingness to resist the government. The rebels were willing to accept the risks of this approach because they knew that maintaining tribal unity was paramount. Otherwise the government would play on long-established tribal feuds to divide the opposition.

One of the men who fought with the Nuristanis, starting in late 1978, was not a member of any of the local tribes. He was an ethnic Tajik from the Panjshir Valley, a place—though not that distant geographically—that was culturally and linguistically remote to the people of Nuristan. His name was Ahmed Shah Massoud, and he stood for an entirely new kind of Afghan jihad. The son of a high-ranking military officer, he was a gifted student with a good mind for math. He had received an elite education at the French high school in Kabul before going on to study engineering at the Kabul Polytechnic Institute. An obsessive consumer of literature and a natural leader—the kind of kid who ordered his friends around during their games—he had dreamed of embarking on a military career.

But then, as so often happens, his life was derailed by politics. Massoud, a man with a strong religious upbringing, soon found himself joining like-minded classmates in their fights against left-wing student groups. The contempt the two camps felt for each other spilled over into full-scale battles on the campus of Kabul University, just around the corner from Massoud's institute, throughout the early 1970s.

Massoud was soon radicalized by the rivalry. He often walked over to the university campus to listen to lectures by Burhanuddin Rabbani and Abdul Rab Rasul

Sayyaf, two Afghan religious scholars who had had the privilege to study at al-Azhar University in Cairo, the most prestigious religious university in the Sunni Islamic world. In Egypt the two men had also imbibed the Islamist ideas of the Muslim Brotherhood, which they subsequently set upon importing to their homeland. It was to that end that Rabbani founded his Jamiat-e Islami, the "Islamic Society," which set as its goal the establishment of an Islamic state in Afghanistan. The avowed secularist Daoud viewed the group as a natural foe and unleashed his secret police against its leadership.

In 1975 the Jamiat leaders decided to strike back by launching an uprising against Daoud's government.[7] Massoud, then age twenty-two, took on the job of fomenting an armed rebellion in the Panjshir Valley, his home district. The disastrous failure of the uprising—which ended in the execution and imprisonment of dozens of its activists—forced him to flee to Pakistan, where some of the movement's leaders had found refuge. The abortive revolt also triggered a split among Afghanistan's Islamists. A former Kabul University engineering student, a firebrand named Gulbuddin Hekmatyar, denounced Rabbani's leadership and established his own organization, which he called Hezb-e Islami ("the Party of God"). Massoud stuck with Rabbani and spent his time in Pakistani exile reading Persian classical literature and absorbing the classic works of guerrilla warfare, including Che Guevara, Mao Zedong, and Régis Debray.[8] He also followed the reports from home of Daoud's growing repression of the Islamist movement and the electrifying news of the Communist takeover. The stories of the new government's campaign to crush Islam and implement its ideas by force deepened Massoud's determination to fight back.

The revelation that the Nuristanis had revolted against Communist rule galvanized Massoud. He headed there, several colleagues and a French journalist in tow, to fight for several weeks at the side of the rebels. The tight-knit Nuristanis showed how a determined guerrilla force, motivated by faith and exploiting the difficult terrain, could fight back against to drive out government forces. The guerrillas managed to retain a hold over some of the territory they freed from the Communists for months. Massoud watched and learned.

The Nuristanis were surprised to see him. Afghans had little sense of themselves as citizens of a wider state. When they rebelled, they usually did so as representatives of tribes or villages. But Massoud brought a larger view, one influenced by the gathering agitation in the global Islamic community in the 1970s. As a student of Rabbani and Sayyaf, he knew about the burgeoning Islamist movement in Egypt and other faraway corners of the Muslim world. Islam could no longer be regarded as "merely" a faith, something innately separate from politics. The new Islamists were reminding believers that their religion offered an answer to all of life's questions, that it was better at addressing the problems of modern life than Marxism or liberal democracy. Meanwhile, the astonishing success of the revolution in Iran had demonstrated that Muslims united by their faith could defy an oppressive local government even when it enjoyed the direct support of the world's most powerful country.

Few in the West were paying much attention. Foreign-policy experts still viewed the world, understandably, through the lens of Cold War conflict. Even the Arab-Israeli conflict, which pitted mostly Soviet allies against the US-sponsored Jewish state, fitted neatly into the template. The Israeli political elite was still dominated by secular Zionists, and their Arab enemies—especially the Palestinians—adhered to this-worldly ideologies of their own. The Palestine Liberation Organization and its offshoots consisted of revolutionary Marxists. Even the Baath Party dictatorships in Syria and Iraq had little time for religion—and this made them all the more intelligible to Western observers. Very few people in the international elite suspected that Islam was capable of posing a fundamental challenge to the global order—and certainly not in a place as backward and marginal as Afghanistan.

What happened next was extraordinary, even in light of Afghanistan's long history of organized resistance to central authority. What outsiders often miss is that Afghan revolts tended historically to be highly specific affairs: a particular group in a particular place rises up against a perceived affront and fights until its demands are met or an acceptable balance of power in Kabul is restored. But by late 1978 this was already beginning to change. The tribal revolt in the Pech Valley quickly found imitators all around the country. Afghans of a wide variety of ethnic and social origins rose up against the government, and most of them took issue with the very nature of the regime.

Most of the anti-government feeling in the countryside was spontaneous and poorly organized, following age-old fault lines of tribe and tradition. But increasingly the rebels were being encouraged by young holy warriors like Massoud, people who had been educated at a university—just like the Marxists—to serve as doctors and engineers of a future, more modern Afghanistan. These young men know about the wider world; some of them even spoke foreign languages. But what they shared with their Shiite counterparts across the border in Iran was the belief that Islam had all the answers—and especially when it came to problems with twentieth-century politics. These new radicals did not want to see Afghanistan transformed into a republic that merely gave lip service to Islamic beliefs; nor did they want to see it revert to monarchy, a system they, like Khomeini—regarded as un-Islamic. These young Islamic revolutionaries in Afghanistan wanted to see Islam capture the state, just as they had in Iran. They were about to get their chance.

9

The Prophet's Proletariat

Enthusiasm for the Islamic revolution extended beyond the border of the Islamic world. In October 1978 an Iranian student named Mohsen Sazegara drove to O'Hare International Airport in Chicago and boarded a flight for Paris. Three years earlier Sazegara had enrolled at the Illinois Institute of Technology to study mechanical engineering. Like thousands of other Iranians who had traveled overseas to study in the same period, he had expected that he would be staying put in the United States until he completed his degree. He didn't have the money to travel back and forth between Chicago and Tehran.

But now the demands of politics were reshaping his agenda. The day before his flight, Sazegara had received a phone call from Ebrahim Yazdi, a Texas-educated Iranian lawyer and political activist. Yazdi, one of the leaders of a revolutionary organization called the Iran Freedom Movement, had traveled to Iraq to act as a political adviser to a Shiite religious scholar who was living there in exile after making a name for himself as a merciless critic of the shah. The cleric, Ayatollah Ruhollah Khomeini, had been living outside of Iran for thirteen years. He had spent the first year of his banishment in Turkey, then moved to Najaf in Iraq, a center of Shiite culture and learning. But now, due to a rising tide of unrest in Iran, the shah had grown nervous about Khomeini's relative proximity, and the Iranian government had prevailed upon the Iraqi leaders to expel him.

At first Khomeini and his aides had tried to go to Kuwait, but at the border the Kuwaiti authorities had refused them entry. Now they had settled upon Paris as the Ayatollah's new place of exile. From there, the theory went, it would be easier to generate attention from the world's media as the struggle against the shah shifted into high gear. "We need you to come and join us," Yazdi beckoned Sazegara from Paris. This was what Sazegara had been waiting for. At age twenty-four he was already a fully credentialed member of the revolutionary movement.

He was so eager to get to the airport that he left behind most of his belongings. He made the transatlantic trip with eight dollars in cash. He had borrowed the money for his plane ticket—two hundred and fifty dollars—from a doctor in Chicago, an Iranian immigrant to the United States who was sympathetic to the cause Sazegara represented. A member of Khomeini's entourage met him at Orly Airport and drove him to the Paris suburb of Neauphle-le-Château, where the ayatollah and his fellow activists were setting up a political headquarters that gradually took on the look of a government in exile. It was getting cold, and Sazegara soon found himself regretting that, in his hurry to leave Chicago, he had forgotten to bring along a winter coat. A friend scrounged an old German Army jacket for him.[1]

Sazegara and his comrades-in-arms would not be deterred by the elements. Some of the other Iranians in Paris refused to eat three square meals a day out of solidarity with their compatriots who were still suffering under the tyranny back home; some of them ended up suffering from a vitamin deficiency. In their ardor to topple the shah, they were continuing a long tradition of revolutionary idealism that would have been instantly recognizable to the French who had agitated against Louis XVI in 1789 or the Russians who had overthrown the Romanov dynasty in 1917. Like their European forerunners, these Iranians had elevated the notion of "revolution" to a kind of religion in itself, an all-encompassing ideal that transcended mere politics. And like many of their contemporaries in the Third World, they spoke obsessively about the need to defeat the evils of "imperialism" and "colonialism" by mobilizing the "oppressed masses" to rise up against the accursed monarchy.

Yet there was one thing that set these Iranians apart: they prayed. Five times a day they gathered together in a large tent set up on the grounds, prostrated themselves in the direction of Mecca, and paid obeisance to the Creator of All the Worlds. The man they had followed to this unlikely place, Ayatollah Ruhollah Khomeini, was not a labor leader or a radical lawyer or a rabble-rousing young agitator with a thing for the opposite sex. He was a sere, elderly man who went about in the traditional black robes and turban of a *marja-i-taqlid*, a Shiite legal scholar who had devoted his life to the pursuit of the holy and the pure and had achieved the status of an exemplar of piety to be emulated by the faithful. Now, here in his Parisian suburb, he was doing something that no one of his kind had ever done in the nine centuries since Iran had adopted Islam. He was engineering the overthrow of Shah Mohammad

Reza Pahlavi, the monarch who had ruled the country for the past thirty-seven years. And not only that: Khomeini was calling for the end of the monarchy itself. He was putting himself on the side of revolution.

The notion of revolutionary transformation had been familiar to Iranians since the Constitutional Revolution in 1906 had bequeathed to the country the outlines of a constitutional monarchy. The shahs who followed honored it mostly in the breach. For years after that, giving life to the framework established in 1906 remained an honorable political goal but little more. In the early 1950s, the nationalist leader Mohammed Mossadeq demanded that the monarch respect the constitutional constraints on his power. He refrained, however, from calling for the shah's overthrow.

In the years following the anti-Mossadeq coup, it was mainly the Communists and their allies on the Left who kept alive the demand for all-out revolution—even though their Soviet patrons sometimes advised them to moderate their tactics for reasons of expediency. *Revolution*, after all, was a word that evoked the great political struggles led by socialist parties. It is true that the Arabic word—*enqelab*, meaning "overthrow"—also occurs in the Quran, where it refers to the fate that must befall unjust rulers. But it was still not a term that Shiite clerics made a habit of using.

The 1970s, however, were a period of profound political change in Iran, and much of the change drew its energy from the universities. During the 1970s, the number of students enrolled in them reached 175,000, double the figure in the 1960s. The young men and women who emerged from these institutions expected that their degrees would pave their way into the growing middle class. Yet despite the economic boom, not all of them were able to find jobs upon graduation, which transformed many of them into a volatile class-in-waiting. In any country, the experience of a university education is almost always a catalyst for those with ambition or a penchant for activism, but under the shah the path to any genuine political participation was closed. As historian Said Amir Arjomand points out, the would-be members of the middle class who dreamed of "national sovereignty and popular democratic government" had no legal avenues for pursuing their aims.[2] Their goals and their means for achieving them changed accordingly, shifting from critical engagement with the authorities to calls for wholesale transformation of the existing system.

So it should come as no surprise that Sazegara and his contemporaries aspired to a life as professional revolutionaries. By the time he came of age, various theories of violent emancipation were percolating in the minds of his contemporaries, and the universities had become the focus of discontent. Some of those who engineered the revolution were older than Sazegara, but many of those who actually made it happen—who organized the demonstrations, marched in the streets, crafted the slogans, and took the fight to the shah's security forces—were his contemporaries. They were both beneficiaries and victims of Iran's headlong rush to modernization. The Iran of the late 1970s was a society of the young. It was also a place of violent contradictions, evolving values, tumultuous modernity coexisting with old ways. The rules that governed this society—or at least so it seemed to many of those who inhabited it—came from somewhere else, and they coexisted uneasily with everyday life (like the wholesale introduction of modern capitalist distribution systems in a country where such tasks had earlier been the prerogative of the bazaar).

Quite a few of these students, like Sazegara, traveled overseas to study in the universities of the West, where they were expected to absorb the technological and economic know-how of the modern world while somehow remaining immune to the ideological and political ferment that was washing through the campuses of Europe and North America in the 1960s and 1970s. In the dormitories where Iranian students clustered, they were free to trade in ideas that were regarded as pure sedition back home. Some of them absorbed the rhetoric and theater of the student revolutionaries in their host countries, but others found themselves rejecting Western ways and rediscovering the virtues of native traditions they had neglected back at home. "We don't want Western civilization," went the rallying cry. "We want our own traditions." What was self-evident in Iran became a political and cultural statement in the alien West. Sazegara recalls one young Iranian woman who became a devout Muslim during her stay in the United States and began wearing the chador, the head scarf. Her secular father was shocked when he met her at the airport in Iran: "I thought I was sending you to America, not to Qom."

This embrace of religion was not a statement in favor of the status quo. If you shared the view that Islam was under assault by the shah's reforms and the influx of foreign customs, then taking up the chador became a gesture laden with radical significance. Many of the young intellectuals, indeed, rediscovered Islam through their political engagement, not the other way around. This was precisely Sazegara's story. His father was a solidly middle-class shopkeeper who had little interest in religion. He regarded the clergy as reactionary and corrupt. Sazegara's mother, on the other hand, stuck to traditional belief. There were seven children in the house, and the constant philosophical and political discussions made it feel, Sazegara says, "like a university dormitory." Throughout his school years Sazegara consumed every book he could get his hands on—including critics of organized religion like Bertrand Russell.

Yet the arguments of the rationalists had the opposite effect on him, and, still in high school, he began to feel the pull of Islam. It was, he says, part a search for ultimate meaning in a society that seemed awash in materialism, part political statement. Shia Islam, after all, was the authentic essence of Iranian culture and tradition, a perfect vehicle for rejecting the tyranny of alien ideas. He began to pray. His more secular brothers and sisters made fun of him. Did religion really fit in the modern world? Wasn't Islam a dead end?[3]

I t was easy to lose your way in this swirling, bewildering, unevenly evolving Iran. The Shiite mystery play in the local bazaar was just a short walk away from the cinema where they were showing the latest film by Jean-Luc Godard. The geographical distance might be short, but psychologically it was huge. Iranians needed a special sort of mental daring, a particular eagerness to embark on an imaginative quest, to bridge such gaps. Few were capable or willing.

The thinker who did it to the most dramatic effect was a nervous, perennially distracted, prematurely balding scholar from a village near the holy city of Mashad, not far from the border with Afghanistan. His name was Ali Shariati. He was born in 1933 into a family with a long tradition of scholarly devotion to Islam, even though few of its members actually ended up attending seminary. His father was a pious Muslim who taught Islamic history to high school students and impressed upon his son from an early age the imperative of faith.[4] But as Shariati came of age, his questing mind soon confronted the bustling paradoxes of mid-twentieth-century Iran, and his faith took an idiosyncratic turn, which was perhaps to be expected of a man with an equally intense passion for Sufi poetry and Marxist theory.

He took his degree in foreign languages (Arabic and French) from Mashad University in 1958. His first long literary work was a translation of an Arabic text about Abu Zarr, one of the Prophet Muhammad's earliest and most illustrious companions. Shariati became so fixated on the figure of Abu Zarr that he soon wrote a tract of his own exploring the man's life and legend. In Shariati's telling, Abu Zarr was a man of stark egalitarianism who accepted unconditionally Allah's demand that the faithful must provide succor to the weak. Abu Zarr later opposed the third caliph, Osman, for permitting the rise of a privileged class and allowing the social stratification of the previously egalitarian Muslim society.[5] Shariati went so far as to describe Abu Zarr as the "first socialist."

Islam, in other words, had invented true socialism long before Karl Marx or his ilk. Shariati had managed to contrive a model of radical social justice that took nothing from the West—a neat solution to the problem of cultural alienation. The

Iranians who aspired to mimic European-style leftism had failed to realize, Shariati suggested, that Islam had actually solved the problem back in the seventh century. The Quran had proclaimed that the future belonged to the *mostazafin*, the oppressed of the earth, long before anyone had considered the revolutionary potential of the proletariat. Abu Zarr represented the socialist spirit in its most authentic form. True Islam drew its force from a radical emphasis on justice; it was not a creed that defended the status quo. It was a revolutionary religion. The figure of Abu Zarr, as an embodiment of this insight, never let Shariati go.

In 1959 Shariati won a state scholarship to study in France, thus becoming one of the growing army of young Iranians to venture abroad in search of fresh intellectual stimuli. He arrived in Paris at a moment when the culture of the radical Left was already in full bloom. The revolution in Algeria was in full swing, and the proclamations of the Islamic Marxist insurrectionists fascinated Shariati and his fellow Iranians.[6] He immersed himself in the works of Jean-Paul Sartre, Che Guevara, Mao, and the North Vietnamese military strategist General Giap—all the while continuing with his reading of his favorite mystic poets. He took part in radical student politics and embarked on an enthusiastic correspondence with Frantz Fanon, the *tiers-mondiste* theorist and publicist for the Algerian cause who counseled would-be revolutionaries from the developing world to find insurrectionist programs that fitted their local identities. As Fanon saw it, the colonial powers imposed their will on oppressed populations in part by imposing imported ideologies upon them. In this indictment Shariati experienced the shock of self-recognition. One of the most influential books he wrote after his return from Paris bore the suggestive title *Return to Oneself.* Where Shariati differed with the atheist Fanon was in his assessment of the centrality of religion. Iranians, Shariati argued, should understand that their inherited Shiite Muslim culture was not a barrier to modernity, as the shah and the European leftists so often asserted. Islam, in fact, was the original path to a revolution that would end in a perfect, classless society unified in adoration of the One God. Marx, by comparison, was a pale Johnny-come-lately.

Shariati was by no means the first thinker to fuse Islam and revolution. By now many young Iranians were familiar with the works of early-twentieth-century Muslim activists like Hussein al-Banna, the founder of the Muslim Brotherhood, and Abul Ala Mawdudi, the Pakistani Islamist who had popularized the notion of an "Islamic state." The Islamist reformers of the early twentieth century had rejected the image of an Islam mired in premodern superstition and tried to reclaim their faith for the modern age. Islam, they argued, was just as "progressive" as any of the fashionable ideologies like Marxism or revolutionary nationalism, but it also held out the promise of transcending materialism and returning man to the consoling unity of the divine.

Such ideas were spreading even among the younger generation in the seminary town of Qom, where the radical cleric Khomeini gave his incendiary speeches against the shah in 1963. To be a religious scholar required fluency and Arabic, and since Iran had more than its share of religious scholars, there were plenty of qualified linguists to ensure that the Islamist debates now under way in the broader Muslim world entered the Iranian mental universe. So, for example, an eager young student named Ali Khamenei—later to achieve fame by succeeding Khomeini as the supreme leader of postrevolutionary Iran—translated two books by the influential Egyptian Islamist Sayyid Qutb from Arabic into Farsi.[7] Still, few of these Sunni thinkers went quite as far as Shariati, who sometimes seemed uncertain whether he was a Marxist masquerading as a believer or a Muslim enthralled by revolution. (It's worth noting that, throughout his life, Shariati hid behind fictional alter egos and literary labyrinths, and his teachings bristled with startling metaphors and nested enigmas.)

By the 1970s, members of the Iranian religious establishment were increasingly becoming engaged in the intense political debates that were now under way. Some clerics—including, but not exclusive to, the followers of Khomeini—had gone public with criticisms of the shah's policies and were rewarded with lengthy prison terms. There they had plenty of time to engage in polemics with their Marxist cell mates, and the experience proved useful in the effort to fashion a more contemporary idiom for the cause of Islam.

Some younger members of the clergy, sensitive to the spread of leftist ideas, set out to establish Shiism's revolutionary credentials in the minds of the younger generation. A key figure in this effort was a cleric and philosophy professor named Morteza Motahhari, a strong supporter of Khomeini. Seeing the need for a new kind of educational institution that would bring Islam into the lives of ordinary young Iranians who might otherwise be lost to the faith, he and a group of collaborators solicited funds from wealthy donors and established the Hosseiniye Ershad in 1963.[8] They envisioned it as a place where scholars could give lectures to lay audiences about the contemporary relevance of Islam.

In the 1970s, Motahhari and his collaborators noticed that Shariati's lectures at the University of Mashad—circulating in the form of bootleg cassettes or Xerox samizdat—were proving an unlikely hit among young Iranians, who were transfixed by his melding of revolution and Islam. So the sponsors of Ershad, knowing that Shariati had already encountered problems at his university because of the controversial subject matter of his teachings, invited him to Tehran to speak at their institute. His presentations were mobbed.

Like quite a few other Muslim political theorists of the twentieth century, Shariati never offered much detail about how his Islamic revolution would look once it became a reality. He seems to have thought of Islam as a kind of "permanent revolution," a never-ending process of spiritual challenge. In those cases where he explicitly addressed the character of a future "Islamic state," the vision he outlined was emphatically egalitarian and collectivist. He did not trust democracy or elections and imagined that the future Islamic polity would be led by a caste of pious citizens who were qualified in the ways of government but free of the taint of personal ambition. He rejected theocracy. He was suspicious of the Shiite religious authorities, whom he denounced as *akhunds*, paragons of the ossified, institutional Islam that he regarded as a perversion of the true faith. This did not endear him to members of Iran's religious establishment. But it was hard for them to reject Shariati out of hand. The motivating effect of his lectures—despite his contempt for punctuality, his clotted ambiguities, and his remarkable absentmindedness—was astonishing. Some of his listeners absorbed his teachings and headed straight off to the mountains to join the new breed of guerrillas who preached the violent overthrow of the shah in the name of "Islamic Marxism." Shariati talked a lot about martyrdom. He frequently cited the example of Imam Hussein, the paragon martyr of Shiism, as the exemplar of the politically conscious Muslim who was prepared to sacrifice his life in the name of the revolutionary cause.

The shah's secret police finally responded to his lecture-room provocations. Shariati was arrested in 1973 and endured several months of intensive SAVAK interrogation (though his leading biographer, Ali Rahnema, notes that there is no evidence that Shariati was subjected to physical torture).[9] After his emergence from prison Shariati continued to publish his ideas, but the pressure from constant surveillance and intimidation by the secret police took its toll. In early 1977 he decided to quit Iran for Britain. A few months later, on June 22, 1977, Shariati died of a heart attack in Southampton. There were the usual theories about SAVAK involvement in his death, but it seems more likely that he was simply worn down by the stresses of his vocation.

There were many other intellectuals theorizing about radical change in the Iran of this period. Others were already debating the dialectic or ruminating about "Islamic economics" or looking for ways to reconcile constitutionalism with the demands of sharia. Some of these Islamist intellectuals—like Mehdi Bazargan, a former Mossadeq prime minister who went on to found the Iranian Freedom Party,

Sazegara's political home—would serve in the early phase of the Islamic Republic and leave behind enormously influential legacies. But none of them had an impact comparable to Shariati's. It was his specific achievement to combine intellectual fireworks and idealism with a persuasive and emotional call to political action. It was his lectures that inspired the guerrillas and the radicals who launched Iran's Islamic Revolution. He had planted the seed. Others would nurture it and bring it to fruition.

10

Truth from Facts

Winter comes early in Beijing. By mid-November 1978, freezing winds were already sweeping through the capital, the air thick with diesel exhaust, smoke from countless coal stoves, and yellow dust from the deserts of Mongolia and the Loess Plateau. In the gathering gloom, 219 top-ranking members of the Chinese Communist Party, all wearing identical round-collared Mao suits in gray or blue, converged on a spot just outside of the Forbidden City.[1] Owned, operated, and closely guarded by the People's Liberation Army, the Jingxi Hotel promised just the degree of seclusion necessary for a sensitive discussion about the fate of the world's most populous country. It would be decades before ordinary Chinese, much less curious foreigners, learned the details of the meeting that took place there.

For years, party conferences had been occasions for the participants to compete in singing the praises of their hallowed leader, Chairman Mao Zedong. He was the unassailable lodestar of Chinese Communism, the man who had led the party since the Long March and crafted the strategy that brought it to victory in 1949. Lenin and Stalin rolled into one, he stood at the center of an elaborate cult of personality. To an extent, perhaps, this was justified, since he truly was a strategist without parallel, a gifted intriguer who always managed to end up on top. As a hardened survivor and the architect of years of pitiless struggle—on battlefields, in remote guerrilla camps, or in the warren of government buildings in central Beijing—he reacted swiftly to any sign of criticism or dissent. He had dispatched his foes, real or imagined, by the millions. None of this was calculated to foster an atmosphere of lively debate.

Now, in his absence, the tone was about to change. The ostensible purpose of the 1978 Central Party Work Conference was to set a course for economic policy in the post-Mao era. Ostensibly, its participants were supposed to be doing routine organizational work, preparing the agenda for a subsequent meeting, the thrillingly entitled Third Plenum of the Eleventh Central Committee of the Chinese Communist Party. Today it is the Third Plenum that is usually cited as the official turning point of China's post-Maoist development. We now know, however, that it was actually the preliminary work conference, held in the seclusion of the Jingxi Hotel, where the crucial battles were fought. It was here that two political camps, whose latent differences had gradually emerged into the open in the years after Mao's death, came to grips over competing visions of China's future.

The conference began with Hua Guofeng ensconced as Chinese Communist Party chairman. In office for just two years after Mao's departure, Hua had already accumulated an impressive array of titles and powers. In the last weeks of his life, Mao had personally designated Hua as his successor, and the leader's blessing was a sure formula for success in a system where everything revolved around him.

Hua was a creature of the Cultural Revolution. In 1966, as it began, Hua had been a middle-ranking functionary. But as the purges gathered speed, and as many in the senior ranks of the party watched their careers and their lives fall apart, he had capitalized on the sudden opportunities for upward mobility, scrupulously negotiating every tortuous political switchback of the era, always managing to position himself as the most loyal of Maoists. Yet he also managed to avoid associating himself too closely with the Gang of Four—which weighed in his favor as the Cultural Revolution came to an end. Mao had chosen Hua both as a way of protecting his own political legacy (since Hua was unlikely to reverse his policies) and as a way of creating a counterbalance against his wife, Jiang Qing (whose push for power was becoming increasingly clear with each passing day). "With you in charge, I am at ease"—these were the words with which Mao had supposedly declared Hua to be his political heir in 1976.

In the wake of Mao's death, the colorless Hua surprised everyone with a sudden show of initiative. Allying himself with two established party elders, Army Marshal Ye Jianying and veteran functionary Li Xiannian, Hua engineered the arrest of the Gang of Four. It was a startling gambit even by the Byzantine standards of twentieth-century Communist conspiracies. Hua had started by splitting off one of the Gang's key allies, a man by the name of Wang Dongxing, who had risen with the

Gang's help to become the head of the party's Praetorian Guard, the 8341 Special Regiment, which provided for the security of top officials. Hua and Wang arranged for two of the Gang's leaders to be called to a special session of the Politburo. They were arrested at gunpoint as they stepped into the room. Jiang Qing, Mao's widow and the Gang's leader, was taken into custody in her bedroom; one of her personal servants is said to have spat on her as she was led away. Under orders from Hua, the People's Liberation Army quickly moved to disarm the heavily armed militias and the powerful media machine that Jiang's faction had built up over the years. The Cultural Revolution was finally coming to an end.

Yet what was Hua offering in its place? This was not immediately clear. Hua certainly understood that the country could no longer afford permanent revolution. Adopting a strategy originally envisioned by Zhou Enlai, he declared that China should push ahead with "the Four Modernizations" (science and technology, industry, national defense, and agriculture). He moved to restore the economy's animal spirits by ordering a huge surge of investment in industry and agriculture. Like Gierek in Poland, Hua seemed to believe that part of the solution involved taking big foreign loans for flagship projects; also like Gierek, he seemed to have few concrete ideas about how these loans would be paid back.

Hua's program did result in tangible growth. But it also led to big budget deficits and scandalous waste, since it failed to tackle many of the serious problems of management and organization bequeathed by Maoist excess. Hua had the right idea, but he was still, in essence, relying on mobilization and slogans rather than substantive economic policy. Some of his critics belittled the program as another Great Leap Forward, a utopian exercise with little practical foundation. Hua, for example, urged a rapid increase in the output of steel, which duly materialized. But to what end? What, precisely, was the underlying economic strategy?

Hua had eliminated the Gang of Four. He tried to revive the economy. But he seemed hesitant to put an end to the broader legacy of the Cultural Revolution. In February 1977, a few months after Mao's death, Hua's supporters published a statement containing a conspicuous quote: "We will resolutely uphold whatever policy and decisions Chairman Mao made, and unswervingly follow whatever instructions Chairman Mao gave." This credo came to be known as the "the two whatevers," and its adherents, "the Whateverists." Like many factional nicknames, this one contained a large grain of truth. Hua's legitimacy stemmed from the fact that he was Mao's chosen successor. That counted for a lot. But it also limited his freedom of maneuver. He could not chip away at the memory of the Great Helmsman without undermining himself.

As soon became clear, Hua's position was not impregnable. Almost from the moment that he assumed office, party power brokers—including Ye and Li, the two men who had helped Hua best the Gang—began pushing for the return of their high-ranking comrades who had been purged in the years before Mao's death. The most prominent survivor of this group, of course, was Deng Xiaoping.

Hua was aware of the potential challenge and moved quickly to forestall it. In March 1977, he admonished delegates at a key party meeting: "Criticizing Deng and attacking the rightist reversal of verdicts were decided by our Great Leader Chairman Mao Zedong. It is necessary to carry out these criticisms." Just to make sure everyone got the point, he compared Deng with Khrushchev, the "arch-revisionist" whose attempts at cautious political liberalization in the USSR had made him a bogeyman among the Chinese.[2]

But Hua was not lucky in his choice of opponents. Deng, though still on the outside, was a man of considerable resources. His previous stint in power from 1974 to 1976 had been short, but he had still managed to put his administrative skills on ample display. In those two years he had implemented policies that healed some of the economic damage from the Cultural Revolution—in one case even ordering troops to seize a crucial railway terminal that was in the hands of a volatile faction of Red Guards.[3] He had also commissioned a trio of noteworthy articles—dubbed "The Three Poisonous Weeds" by the Gang of Four—that argued unabashedly for the primacy of professional expertise over revolutionary enthusiasm. In doing so, Deng had deftly laid out the terms of debate for the next stage of the post-Mao era. And, perhaps most important of all, he still had many powerful friends. He stood for the party elders who had suffered in the Cultural Revolution. This was a large group of people, many of them with illustrious backgrounds, and all of them had axes to grind. Hua could not ignore them—especially when figures with the august status of Le and Yi insisted that he bring them back into the fold.

Hua tried to put off a decision on Deng's rehabilitation as long as he could, but more and more members of the old guard were returning to political life, and they stepped up the pressure for their comrade's return. In 1976, Hua sent emissaries to Deng who were supposed to sound out his positions and request that Deng publicly embrace the Cultural Revolution. Deng refused. He declined to offer any apologies for his past or to offer any guarantees about the future. He would return to power on his own terms—and, unlike Hua, he would not allow himself to be tied to Mao's policy mistakes. Hua was soon forced to concede the point. The first the Chinese saw of Deng after his post-Tiananmen downfall was at the famous soccer match in

July 1977, when the cameras lingered over the diminutive former leader as he sat in the stands. The spectators in the stadium gave him a big ovation.

In the ensuing months Deng spent his time quietly cementing his position, nudging his allies forward into key posts, and pushing hard for the rehabilitation of still more high-ranking victims of Maoist extremism. Deng was calling in a lifetime's worth of chits. Hua, relatively obscure until Mao had singled him out for the top job, had little in the way of comparable leverage. His only hope was to marshal the support of others like himself, those who had benefited from the rapid turnover of the Cultural Revolution.

The party leadership revealed few signs of conflict to the outside world. The Whateverists maintained an orthodox Maoist tone in the media, which was to be expected, considering that Cultural Revolutionaries still occupied many of the key positions. Yet a great deal was going on behind the placid facade. Those who wanted to roll back the legacy of ultra-Maoism were poising themselves for a challenge.

A totalitarian system like Mao's China offered little opportunity for the overt display of competing political agendas. Rival groups within the leading circles tended to advance their agendas with the help of subtle signals, floating trial balloons, marshaling bureaucratic support, or smoking out enemies. Impending feuds or major policy shifts could be signaled through recondite slogans or obscure cultural debates. (For example, Mao's acolytes had launched the Cultural Revolution by attacking a play, *Hai Rui Dismissed from Office*, that they declared to be an assault on Mao and the revolutionary principles he embodied.) To outsiders, the distinctions involved in such maneuverings could be utterly bewildering, if not absurd. But, as the Chinese knew only too well from personal experience, even the most arcane debates could have profound, if not lethal, effects.

And so it was that many took note when, in May 1978, the prominent national newspaper *Guangming Daily* published an article with the innocuous title "Practice Is the Sole Criterion for Judging Truth." The piece was quickly picked up by a series of other publications, including the leading army newspaper. The title sounds dull enough, but it went off like a bomb. The article, collectively authored by a team of academics working under the direction of rising party reformer Hu Yaobang, argued that Communist ideology was not the only yardstick for determining what was true. If Marxism was indeed a scientific theory, as it claimed to be, its findings ought to be tested through experiment: apply them to reality and see if they worked. Marx had said that the social and political prescriptions derived from his theory had to be subjected to constant empirical testing to make sure that they coincided with the dictates of historical materialism. And just to be sure that everyone got the point, the authors of the article undergirded their argument with a slogan from Mao himself—the one they used as the article's title.[4]

They were, in short, using Mao's own words to undermine the central Maoist postulate of the Cultural Revolution, namely, the idea that the imperative of "revolution" overrode all else, including professional expertise, scientific knowledge, or economic efficiency. To many Chinese, the article's paean to pragmatism sounded like a healthy dose of common sense after years of hysteria. Yet this was exactly what the Whateverists did not want to allow. After all, during the Cultural Revolution, Mao and his adepts had followed a rather different principle: for them it was revolutionary zeal, directed against the entrenched establishment, that had become the decisive litmus test for the correctness of policy. It was this same mind-set that had led to the persecution of countless engineers, managers, scholars, and scientists on the grounds of insufficient "class consciousness"—with devastating consequences for the Chinese economy.

Prioritizing "practice," as the authors of the new article demanded, thus represented an implicit challenge to those who considered themselves to be the keepers of the chairman's flame. If this new argument won the day, unwavering loyalty to Maoist slogans would no longer be the deciding factor in career advancement or political struggle. Professional skill, managerial competence, or scholarly acumen would come to the forefront.

Deng, who does not appear to have been directly involved in the publication of that article, was quick to see its uses in his reckoning with Hua. Since his return to the center of party life, Deng had already been putting a different Mao quote at the center of his speeches: "Seek truth from facts." This, of course, was a dig at Hua and his adherents, who continued to stress that truth was whatever Mao had said it was. Among the things that Deng had learned from his long years of involvement in party intrigues was the importance of defining the terms of debate.[5] He now set out to deploy his "good," pragmatic Mao against the "bad," doctrinaire one of the Cultural Revolutionaries. Would the party cling to the Mao celebrated by the Gang of Four, inflexible, rigid, and dogmatic? Or would Chinese Communists reach back to the earlier version of Mao that was now held up high by Deng and his friends—a Mao who had (allegedly) celebrated the virtues of practicality and sober realism?

In truth, of course, the rather abstruse debate now under way between the Whateverists and the reformers who became known as the "Practice Faction" was less about philosophical semantics than about power. The pragmatists around Deng did not want to discard Mao altogether. Many of them still believed in the revolution that had brought them to power, if not its more recent excesses. They were haunted by the example of Khrushchev, who had (as they saw it) fatally undermined the Soviet Communist Party by discarding Stalin. They concluded that rejecting Mao completely was out of the question: even those whose criticisms of his policies ran deep feared the destabilizing effects of an all-too-hasty reckoning with the recent past. Most members of the Practice Faction wanted to retain Mao's image as the father of the revolution, the ultimate, quasi-divine source of party legitimacy, while discarding the more radical side of his thought that stood in the way of a prosperous and productive China. These two new slogans—"Seek truth from facts" and "Practice is the sole criterion for judging truth"—became the rallying cry of those who, like Deng, wanted to see China prosperous and productive rather than pure and poor.[6] As Deng traveled about the country, speaking to local party gatherings and hobnobbing with old associates, he made it clear that China could not hope to move forward unless it put economics before ideology. While the party should continue to treat Mao with the respect due his real achievements, it was time to drop the "key link" of class struggle and to focus on raising living standards. China could not become strong as long as it was backward.

This, then, was how things stood in late 1978 as the delegates to the Central Party Work Conference crowded into the gloomy conference rooms of the Jingxi Hotel. Everyone there was aware of the stakes. Some of the conference participants had benefited from the Cultural Revolution, rising to take the places of the purged. Others had been on the receiving end of the same turmoil, forced to wear dunce caps as they were paraded through the streets before jeering mobs or banished to the far ends of the country, beaten, or tortured. Some of them had only recently been rehabilitated. It was hard to imagine how the experiences of both groups could be reconciled within the same party.

The delegates in attendance also faced pressing problems within wider Chinese society. Mao's death, the arrest of the Gang of Four, and the effective end of the Cultural Revolution had released enormous pent-up tensions in the country at large. To begin with, there were the students. Mao had come to regard traditional institutions of learning as a major source of the traditionalism he wanted to destroy, and in the early years of the Cultural Revolution he had shut down the universities. Many of the students joined the militant Red Guards, in which capacity they tormented those deemed to be "counterrevolutionary." A few years later, in an effort to counter the spreading anarchy, Mao had many of the Red Guard units disbanded and dispatched their members to the countryside. Some, caught up in the utopian fervor of the moment, had even gone willingly. This was only logical. The Red Guards had celebrated heroes of militant ignorance, like the schoolboy who handed in an empty exam paper rather than submit to the bourgeois testing standards of his reactionary teachers. For ten years Chinese higher education had ground to a halt.

But by 1977 and 1978, hungry and disillusioned, the students—of whom seventeen million had been dispatched to the countryside—were beginning to return to the cities. One of Deng's first tasks after reassuming his post under Hua was to jump-start China's entire university system. In the fall of 1977 the government announced that university entrance examinations would be held once again. Young Chinese thrilled to the news. Deng managed to revive entrance examinations, push would-be students through, and reopen the universities and institutes that very fall (although with delays). It was a remarkable feat. Even so, the fact remained that there were simply not enough places for all of them. Some of the rusticated students were too old and no longer saw the point. They demanded work. But there were no jobs to give them. Some economists have estimated that effective unemployment in the years following Mao's death approached 25 percent.

Some of these frustrated youths turned, predictably enough, to delinquency. The Cultural Revolution had imbued the younger generation with a spirit of violent rebellion that proved hard to stamp out entirely. Meanwhile, millions of prisoners were being released from concentration camps and rural exile. Not all of them had been punished for political reasons; many of those freed were genuine criminals. Crime rates soared. Discontented workers, frustrated by low living standards and chaotic management, staged strikes or expressed passive resistance through shoddy work. The army and police were constantly on the move, stamping out brush fires of discontent.

Most of these malcontents were incapable of articulating their demands. But someone was prepared to do it for them. In September 1978, the editors of a magazine called *China Youth*, which had been prohibited from publishing during the Cultural Revolution, decided to relaunch it. They decided to mark its return in style by publishing some poems commemorating the Tiananmen Incident of 1976. Party censors intervened and thwarted the editors from going ahead with their plans. The frustrated literati refused to give up, so they resorted to a time-honored technique of Chinese mass communication: the *dazibao*, or "big-character poster." They decided to print the poems in poster form and paste them up in a public place. They needed a venue where a big audience was ensured, so they opted for a spot that other unrecognized writers had been using for a few months. This was a long stretch of brick wall under a row of leafless sycamore trees next to a bus depot in Xidan, a spot in downtown Beijing, just a few blocks from the Jingxi Hotel, that tens of thousands of commuters passed through every day.[7]

China Youth's decision to use the site dramatically boosted its notoriety. Crowds of readers quickly formed. To everyone's surprise, the authorities declined to interfere. Posters proliferated. Soon people were coming from all over China to take a look. Crowds gathered, eager to experience the heady atmosphere of a place where a myriad of views competed for attention.

This was Xidan Democracy Wall. Young Chinese described it as their version of Speaker's Corner in London's Hyde Park. For a few weeks in the winter of 1978–1979, it would become a key strategic asset in the battle for China's soul.

At some point in late November, a poster appeared on the wall criticizing Mao by name. No one could recall such a thing ever happening before. The author of the poster, who called himself Work Permit Number 0538 (and gave the address of the motor repair shop where he worked), wrote: "In 1976 after the Tiananmen Incident, the Gang of Four made use of the prestige and power of Chairman Mao's mistaken judgment on class struggle and launched an all-out attack on the cause of revolution in China." During the Cultural Revolution, one man had been sentenced to fifteen years in a labor camp for absentmindedly scratching his back with a copy of the *Little Red Book* during a mass meeting. Now everyone waited to see what would happen to the author of this shocking text. Would he be shot? Surely, at least, the poster itself would be torn down. But two days later it was still there.[8]

The posters that followed pushed the boundaries even further. One wondered how the all-knowing Mao had failed to notice that his own wife, Jiang Qing, was actually a "traitor." Another called on the party leadership to observe the rule of law. Another demanded the rehabilitation of party leaders who had been purged by Mao in the early 1960s. Not all of the provocations were political. "Why can't the national economy catch up with the one in Taiwan?" one poster asked. "How can the United States, a capitalist country only 200 years old, be the most developed in the world?"[9]

By now the wall was besieged by visitors, day and night. People read, expostulated, and listened "with an openness unprecedented in the history of the People's Republic." Some visitors spoke their messages through bullhorns. The foreign correspondents and diplomats who came to see what was going on found themselves besieged by curious locals. During the years of the Cultural Revolution, ordinary Chinese had done whatever they could to avoid even the most cursory contact with citizens of other countries. Now, liberated by the air of candor around the wall, they peppered the foreigners with questions. Roger Garside, a Chinese-speaking British diplomat who wrote one of the most vivid accounts of the early reform period in China, recalled the scene:

> They bombarded me with questions on democracy and human rights: "Can you really criticize your Prime Minister? Who owns the newspapers in Britain? How do they decide their editorial policy? How is the BBC controlled? How are elections organized?"
>
> Some were by no means ignorant but wanted to check out the information they had acquired one way or another; others were simply thirsty for knowledge.[10]

In Garside's description, Democracy Wall functioned like a sort of proto-Internet: posters with derivative content were quickly papered over, while those that had something new or powerful to say were left uncovered. Readers wrote comments on some of the posters with ballpoint pens; when a popular one was torn by accident, visitors quickly glued it back together. Some of the texts were written on scraps of paper torn from notebooks, while others were composed on sheets of paper three feet high with brush and ink. Some authors used paper in pink or green to attract attention.[11]

Garside listened in as a group of Chinese interrogated an Australian visitor to the wall about his views on the state of human rights in China:

> His circumspect answer was greeted with obvious disappointment, so he turned the questioning around and asked the young men what they wanted for China. One of them replied: "A prosperous nation, with a strong army [fu-guo qiang-bing]."
>
> "What do you others think?" asked the Australian. "Do you agree or disagree?"
>
> "Agree! Agree!" other voices called out. As I heard this exchange I could not help wondering where the ideal of Communism fitted in. What we were hearing was the nationalist strain to which Zhou Enlai's Four Modernization formulation appealed so strongly.[12]

As this exchange suggested, something important was shifting in Chinese political discourse. Some were already thinking beyond the narrow parameters of Maoist ideology. The question was precisely how much latitude the Communist Party's leaders were prepared to allow.

The importance of Democracy Wall was not limited to its role as a proving ground for new ideas. It also had eminently practical effects on the looming power struggle in the upper ranks of the Communist Party. Even as the writers at the wall dismantled one taboo after another, they were notably reluctant to say anything negative about Deng. Criticism focused on those who had engineered the Cultural Revolution and still clung to the doctrine of Mao's infallibility. One poster, for example, attacked the "feudal fascist despots" who were behind the suppression of the 1976 Tiananmen protests—and then went on to eulogize Deng as the "living Zhou Enlai."[13] It is extremely hard to determine the extent to which such sentiments reflected genuine public opinion at the time. What is clear is that Deng was perfectly positioned to take advantage of them.

D eng was not physically present as the Central Party Work Conference opened in Beijing on November 10, 1978; he was traveling in Southeast Asia. It was Hua, in his capacity as the top leader, who gave a keynote speech urging delegates to push ahead with the Four Modernizations; it was time, he said, to focus on economic development, above all in agriculture. But the spirit of Democracy Wall, and the many criticisms of the party's course that had emerged there, had already shown that the public mood was changing. Sensing a shift within the party as well, Hua refrained from his usual invocation of the "two whatevers."[14]

Many of the delegates quickly made it clear that they were not going to leave it at that. Members of the Practice Faction showed that they were more interested in addressing simmering political issues than trading platitudes about farming. In speech after speech, they assailed the "two whatevers." Many officials who had been victimized during the Cultural Revolution were still awaiting rehabilitation, they declared, and their verdicts had to be reversed. The delegates at the conference had been divided into six groups. One of them, representing the southern coastal regions of the country, declared their unanimous support for "Practice is the sole criterion for judging truth." It was obvious that Hua had lost control over the agenda of the meeting. By the second day of the conference, Marshal Ye—whose status as the party's senior soldier made him a key power broker—was warning Hua to pay attention to the critics.[15]

Conference participants did manage to address the biggest economic problem that faced them. One of Hua's deputies, Vice Premier Ji Dengkui, gave a speech that

frankly acknowledged the dire state of China's 700 million farmers, who made up
the overwhelming majority of the country's citizens. In not so many words, Ji acknowledged that the twists and turns of official policy during the Cultural Revolution had left farmers unsettled and confused. He proposed a few technical remedies:
increasing the supply of seeds and fertilizer, boosting the volume of agricultural
credits, and significantly raising the price the state paid farmers for their grain.[16]

Ji's speech did mark a departure from the sterile sloganeering of the Cultural
Revolution era. Even so, party policy remained detached from the brutal realities of
rural life. There was no way you could improve the prospects for China's economy
without bettering the lot of its peasants. Yet at the end of the 1970s, the countryside
remained mired in poverty, a hollow landscape haunted by ghosts and famine. The
legacy of the Great Leap Forward was still tangible. In the early 1960s, in the wake
of the titanic famine caused by the Great Leap, Deng Xiaoping and his then-mentor,
Liu Shaoqi, had tried to stimulate agricultural productivity by allowing some peasants to return to the prerevolutionary practice of family farming. The onset of the
Cultural Revolution (which had cost Liu his life) put an end to these experiments.

Wherever possible, though, the peasants seized opportunities to work the system. The incentives were greatest in the regions that had been hit hardest by the
Great Leap. In the late 1970s there were rural areas—especially in the provinces of
Anhui, Sichuan, and Guizhou—where many people still lived under the threat of
starvation. Very quietly, some of them began to make deals with local officials, who
were only too eager to improve their own living standards. Farmers paid bribes for
the privilege of cultivating extra plots on vacant lots, raising animals on the side, or
keeping surplus produce for their own use. "Give enough to the state and to the collective and the rest to ourselves" was one of their slogans.[17]

Here and there, officials embraced the principle of agricultural reform. One of
them was Zhao Ziyang, the newly appointed head of Sichuan Province (the lush
southern region where Deng had grown up). In 1962, Zhao had actually moved
to disband the people's communes there—a policy that had landed him in deep
trouble early in the Cultural Revolution. By 1978, worried that famine was looming in remote corners of the province, he was already moving to lift restrictions on
private farming for some of the hardest-hit areas. In Anhui Province, on the other
side of the country, another provincial party chief, Wan Li, was considering similar
measures to prevent a recurrence of starvation. At the Central Party Work Conference, Wan justified his efforts by pointing out that his province's per-capita grain
production had yet to reach the level of 1955.[18]

So the notion of reintroducing the early 1960s principle of farming by household (*baochan daohu*) was clearly on the minds of the delegates. Farmers needed incentives in order to get agriculture going again—but this implied discarding one of Mao's most treasured policies, the nationwide collectivization campaign of the Great Leap, when he had forced farmers together into "people's communes." Mao had reacted with indignation to any suggestion of a return to family farming, a policy he regarded as a scandalous, "counterrevolutionary" heresy.

Nor was anyone quite yet ready to take that fateful step in November 1978. Yet Hu Yaobang—the same official who had orchestrated the publication of "Practice Is the Sole Criterion for Judging Truth"—nonetheless made a report at the Work Conference that ventured into this delicate territory. It was time, he said, to take measures that would awaken the private initiative of the farmers. Those who heard or read his speech understood immediately what he had in mind. Yu Guangyuan, a Deng associate who chronicled his own experiences as a participant in the conference, recalled it this way: "Hu Yaobang spelled out his views so fully that I realized that he was speaking of the necessity of 'bao chan dao hu,' fixing farm output quotas down to each household. Although he did not yet use the expression precisely, it was as if—with a light poke of the finger through a thin piece of window paper— the four characters would appear.... He maintained that once the farmers' initiative was aroused, China had enormous potential for increasing agricultural production." Given the times, merely implying the need for such a policy was an act of extraordinary boldness. But Hu's sally was as far as anyone could go for the moment—at least officially.[19]

Indeed, it is notable that the Central Party Work Conference failed to bring any concrete progress in the specific policy realm, agriculture, that it was intended to address. Mao had been dead for two years, but his ghost still loomed large in the minds of his heirs. It was becoming increasingly clear that they could move ahead only by putting his spirit to rest. That was the challenge that they now faced.

At the previous round of high-level party gatherings in the spring of 1977, Whateverist orthodoxy had held fast. But a lot had changed by November 1978. The unresolved social legacy of the Cultural Revolution—the economic devastation, the rise in crime and hunger, the discontent of the students, and the general sense of disillusionment—had spilled out into the streets. Democracy Wall was giving critics a public voice. The trickle of senior Communist functionaries returning from banishment was starting to reshape sentiment within the party as well.

It took only a few days for all the pent-up frustration to explode into the open at the conference. In speech after speech, delegates assailed Hua and his fellow leaders for moving too slowly on the rehabilitation of the party members who had suffered during the Cultural Revolution.

On November 12, two days in, party heavyweight Chen Yun took to the lectern. Chen was a veteran Communist and economic expert who enjoyed wide respect for his granite-like probity. Now he surprised everyone by issuing a ringing condemnation of the leadership's current course. He demanded that the party reverse its negative judgments on five groups of people who had, in his opinion, suffered unjust condemnation during the era of Mao's reign. One of the cases he cited dated back to 1937.

But the most sensitive topic he broached was also the most recent: the Tiananmen Incident of April 1976. As the Central Party Work Conference began, Hua and his Maoist allies had persisted in defining the pro-Zhou demonstrations of two years earlier as a "counterrevolutionary movement." Now Chen insisted that those who had suffered in the 1976 crackdown should be cleared of the charges against them and that the Tiananmen upheaval "should be treated as a popular mass movement."[20]

Chen's speech galvanized his listeners. Many of them had long looked askance at the party's suppression of the Tiananmen demonstrators, who were, after all, expressing their reverence for Zhou Enlai. Chen's taboo-breaking remarks had the added effect of implicating two of the most powerful people at the top: Hua and former Mao bodyguard Wang Dongxing (the one who had helped Hua neutralize the Gang). Both men had played a crucial role in organizing the 1976 crackdown— along with the Gang of Four, who were now behind bars. Speakers in each of the six working groups seconded Chen's demands. Just in case Hua and Wang had not grasped the extent of their defeat, the leading Beijing newspaper followed up the next day by publishing an announcement from the Beijing party chapter that unilaterally declared the Tiananmen protests to be "revolutionary" (a synonym for "good" in partyspeak). The text of the announcement was quickly republished in a number of other media—effectively issuing a public rebuke to two of the most senior leaders in the country.[21]

To everyone's surprise, Hua reversed himself with barely a murmur. A few days later he allowed himself to be photographed signing the title page of a collection of poems praising the 1976 demonstrators. Wang, the leading Politburo stalwart of ultra-Maoist sloganeering, was not quite so flexible. Just days before, Wang's position had appeared impregnable. Wang was not only a Politburo member, a vice chairman of the Central Committee, and the head of the party's elite security detail. He was also in charge of the effort to edit the collected works of Mao's writings and speeches, a position that—in a society where Mao's words exerted totemic force— imbued the person who held it with an aura of sanctity. It was no surprise that Wang had bitterly resisted demands for further rehabilitations.

Nonetheless, the speakers at the conference gathered up their courage and began to assail Wang by name. Virtually no one came to his defense. By the end of the session, the chastened vice chairman was forced to present a "self-criticism" acknowledging all of his past political sins. Wang's foes would have to wait a few weeks more, until the Third Plenum, for his formal resignation. But it was at the Party Work Conference that they did the essential work of demolishing his standing.

In short, a great deal had already happened by the time Deng finally arrived, four days after the start of the Central Party Work Conference, on November 14. He had kept track of the conference proceedings during his travels, so he was not entirely surprised by the changed political landscape that greeted him upon his arrival. The precipitous downturn in the fortunes of Hua and Wang transformed the balance of power in the upper ranks of the leadership. Marshal Ye, the man who had presided over this startling twist, greeted Deng by informing him that it was time for him to step into the breach by assuming the job as top leader. Deng accepted. Within the next few days he met with the members of the Politburo Standing Committee, the tiny group of senior party leaders who actually the ran the country, to sketch out his vision for the country's future course. From now on, he told them, it was imperative that China pursue the goal of modernization. This could be done only by maintaining domestic stability, and that meant retaining Mao Zedong and his thought as the country's unifying symbol. Deng made it clear to the other leaders he had no intention of repeating Khrushchev's mistake of hasty political liberalization. But Deng also made it clear that many of Mao's specific policies would need to be reversed. The other members of the Politburo signed off, enshrining Deng's principles as the party line.

Deng did not tell his fellow Politburo members everything that he had in mind, however. For weeks before the Party Work Conference, he had been thinking about the remarks he was supposed to deliver at its end (as well as the public speech he was set to give during the more public plenum that followed). One of the men he asked for help was his confidant Yu Guangyuan, an experienced party ideology

expert who also attended the conference as a delegate.[22] Yu's notes on their preparatory sessions provide vivid insight into Deng's thinking as he began to conceive of
the policies that would launch China into the modern era.

Sometime earlier Deng had astonished Yu with the comment that "we must work
in the spirit of Meiji Japan and Peter the Great."[23] It was in the Meiji period that the
Japanese ruling class had made the strategic decision to embrace Western technology
and know-how to catapult their country into the modern world—not unlike Peter
the Great's decision to transform Russia into a great power by adopting European
ways in the early eighteenth century. Deng's ideological boldness in his choice of
these two examples is striking. Mao and the Cultural Revolution radicals had violently disowned the notion that the People's Republic of China had anything to learn
from the outside world; any functionary in the 1960s who had cited positive lessons
from the experiences of imperial Japan or czarist Russia would have opened himself
to instant censure as a "revisionist." (It also says something about his frank assessment of China's development that he chose to cite eighteenth-century Russia and
late-nineteenth-century Japan as relevant models.) Of course, Deng's remarks in this
case were not for public consumption. But his temerity was remarkable nonetheless.

Deng was also interested in more contemporary examples of successful modernization. As he told Yu, his travels to Japan and Singapore had made a powerful
impression: "In Singapore, whoever has 1,500 Singaporean dollars is entitled to buy
an apartment. A five-room apartment with a floor space of about 70 square meters
costs a worker six months' wages and can be bought on installments. In Japan, in the
units giving fairly high bonuses, bonuses are equivalent to six months of a worker's
wages and are enough to buy a car. Rent in Singapore amounts to 15 percent of a
worker's monthly wages, and in Europe, one third."[24]

He noted sarcastically that the Chinese Communist Party was still trying to
motivate workers through "socialist competitions" (the Communist equivalent of
those "worker-of-the-month" campaigns in businesses in the West). This, he said,
was ridiculous. In the countries he had visited, workers got rewards in cash if they
performed better—a practice that was obviously highly motivating.[25]

Deng had drawn other conclusions from his travels around the region. Chinese
bureaucracy had become top-heavy, he told Yu, and decision-making authority
needed to be shifted down to lower levels and away from the center. In some cases, he
added provocatively, this might even take the form of local elections. Power within
the party had to be diffused to prevent the recurrence of a Mao-style personality
cult; collective leadership was imperative. (For all his strength of personality, Deng

did much more to incorporate the views of his colleagues into the decision-making process in the years to come than the imperious Mao.) Another of his observations was even more radical. "We should not be afraid of chaos caused by reliance on the market," he told Yu. "We should accept a certain degree of regulation by the market." Economic decision making was a matter of adjusting the balance between supply and demand.[26]

In another major departure from orthodoxy, Deng also took aim at the egalitarianism that had stood squarely at the center of Maoist policies. It was all right, Deng told him, for some people or regions to become "better off" faster than others; to do otherwise would be to suppress initiative, creativity, and a healthy measure of competition. This, Deng explained, was a crucial point: "We should permit some people to achieve prosperity sooner than others, with the percentage of rural people who are prosperous first reaching five percent, rising to 10 percent, and increasing further to 20 percent. The percentage of urban people who are prosperous can stay at 20 percent. . . . Only this way shall we have a market, which itself will enable us to open up new industries. We must oppose egalitarianism. Whoever fares well will set a good example for his or her close neighbors to follow."[27]

It is worth pointing out that Deng was broaching these ideas ten years after the Soviet leadership had abandoned the cautious decentralizing reforms of Nikita Khrushchev. In November 1978 the government of Leonid Brezhnev was two years into its Tenth Five-Year Plan, which doggedly maintained the supremacy of central planning even as it implicitly acknowledged that the USSR was falling behind in technological innovation. (Among other things, the plan provided for large purchases of information technology from the West.) Soviet prime minister Aleksey Kosygin was crafting a new set of directives for the following year that actually concentrated more decision-making power in ministries. The "reforms," implemented in July 1979, expressly rejected the modest freedoms granted to enterprises by the Hungarians in their economic experiments.[28]

Of course, the speech that Deng ended up giving at the end of the Central Party Work Conference was nowhere near as radical as the thoughts he was sharing privately with Yu. But his remarks, which he delivered on December 13, were still sufficiently dramatic to signal the beginning of a new era of potentially far-reaching reforms. Deng spoke of the need to "emancipate our minds" and to "seek truth from facts." He talked about encouraging the masses "to offer criticisms" and stated that "the thing to be feared most is silence." One should not, of course, overstate the extent of his tolerance of free speech; Deng was still a senior leader of the

Communist Party, after all, and his willingness to tolerate an exchange of opinions would prove quite limited even for those inside the party. But the shift in tone was still conspicuous.

It was on the economic front, though, that the distinctness of Deng's vision came through most clearly. "Initiative cannot be aroused without economic means," he told his listeners. "A small number of advanced people might respond to moral appeal, but such an approach can only be used for a short time." And he spoke with real passion of the imperative to pursue modernization through advances in science, technology, and modern management. Such generalities might sound banal to modern audiences, but to his listeners in the Jingxi Hotel, they represented a bracing rejection of Maoist zealotry.

By the end of the Central Party Work Conference, it was clear that Deng's reformist faction had bested the defenders of Maoist-style "class warfare." But Deng did not want the outside world to think that the party leadership was divided, so he and his associates made sure to keep some changes in the dark. Wang Dongxing was the only figure in the upper ranks of the party who was forced to make a quick departure. Hua emerged from the conference with his titles intact—though it would be just a few short years until he was pushed out of the leadership altogether. Chen Yun, the tough old Communist veteran who had called for the new policy on the Tiananmen Incident, and Hu Yaobang, the other Deng speechwriter and muscular advocate of reform, both joined the Politburo, where they became key personalities in the coalition that saw through the early phase of economic reforms.

As for Deng, his title as vice premier, officially the number-three position in the hierarchy, remained unchanged. But titles did not necessarily mean that much in the murky world of the Chinese Communist Party. What mattered was power, and Deng was the one who now held more of it than anyone else. His status had been explicitly acknowledged by the Politburo, and his personal authority—bolstered by the respect of his many allies in the top ranks, and especially by his close military ties dating back to the civil war—ensured that he never lost it.

At the conference itself there was one small outward signal that revealed something of the shift that had taken place. According to Communist Party protocol, it was the privilege of the country's top leader to end a major party function like the Work Conference with a concluding summary. But this time the honor was given to no one. Hua was not entrusted with the task of providing the wrap-up, while Deng's speech was not elevated to that state.[29] That was fine by him.

Even today most Chinese are accustomed to thinking of the Third Plenum, the much bigger and more formal meeting in December 1978 that followed immediately after the Work Conference, as the start of the reform era. The communiqué that was issued at the end of the Third Plenum does indeed display ample evidence of the victory of Deng's reform faction. The text, carefully prepared by a party committee, specified that, starting in the next year (1979), the work of the party would thenceforth focus on "socialist modernization" (code for economic reform). The statement went on to criticize excessive bureaucracy and overcentralization and explicitly encouraged shifting authority away from central planners and dispersing it among lower-level managers and officials. It even promised farmers greater latitude in using private plots and pursuing side businesses (though there was still no talk of family farming).

The communiqué most certainly did not condemn Chairman Mao, though it did speak delicately of "shortcomings and errors" that he might have made.[30] The chairman was still the party's God. But he was also dead, and his remaining acolytes held new views about the substance of his teachings. From now on the party's leaders would interpret his Word according to their own convenience.

11

The Blood of the Martyrs

For most countries, 1979 dawned in a fog of uncertainty. News of the party plenum in December 1978 gave many Chinese an inkling that positive changes were on the way, but no one knew for sure how far-reaching the reforms would be or how quickly they would come. Britons, for the moment, remained mired in the frustrations of the Winter of Discontent; an end to the strikes was not in sight. The simmering rebellion in Afghanistan posed little in the way of a systemic challenge to the government. The election of John Paul II suggested the possibility of a shift in Vatican policy toward the East bloc, but the Communist authorities in Warsaw had yet to issue a response to the new pope's request for permission to visit his homeland.

In Iran there was no ambiguity. The opposition's long wait was coming to an end. The regime was fighting for its life. Cordite, tear gas, and the smoke from burning tires laced the air of Iran's big cities. By January 1979, demonstrations had become a daily occurrence. Security forces and antigovernment guerrillas engaged in firefights. The only question now was how long the shah would manage to hold on.

Everyone disagrees about when the Iranian Revolution began. Some historians argue that it really got under way with the guerrilla campaigns waged by the left-wing Islamist groups who took their inspiration from Shariati's teachings in the 1970s. Others point to the economic slump of 1976 that followed the astronomical oil prices of the year before. Desperate to bring the economy back under control, the Iranian government tried to throttle back the rate of growth. The shah's planners cut credit and froze prices. The bazaar merchants, already hit hard by earlier reforms, now found themselves at the receiving end of an "antispeculation campaign" that landed many of them in jail. (The corruption at the higher reaches of government and in the entourage of the shah remained untouched, of course.) The boom came to a screeching halt. Firms went bankrupt. Employees lost their jobs. All of it fueled anger with the government.

Some pinpoint the liberalization measures the shah cautiously implemented in 1977 in response to the human rights rhetoric of newly elected US president Jimmy Carter. Carter had entered office pledging to make human rights a central criterion in Washington's relationship with its allies, and, at least in the case of the shah, he was as good as his word.

The shah's relations with previous administrations had been straightforward. Richard Nixon had viewed Iran as America's proxy in the Persian Gulf and had shown little inclination to involve himself in the country's internal affairs. Gerald Ford had followed suit. But Carter's arrival in the White House, and his disapproving rhetoric about the limits of freedom in Iran, disconcerted the shah. The Iranian ruler was highly sensitive to the slightest shifts in US policy; it was the Americans, after all, who had helped to put him back on his throne in 1953 when all had seemed lost. So he was quick to offer concessions.

He released some political prisoners and made it known that human rights organizations would thenceforth be allowed to operate (within limits). Activists quickly took advantage of the chink of freedom to establish high-profile campaigns. New political groups formed, and lawyers and writers signed declarations criticizing the government. A series of poetry readings late in 1977 sponsored by the West German cultural institute in Tehran sparked a series of public demonstrations that showcased the dissatisfaction of the middle-class intellectuals.[1] For the moment, most of the religious establishment held its fire. The main exceptions were Grand Ayatollah Shariatmadari, a politically active cleric who forged contacts with the moderate Islamist opposition groups, and Ayatollah Taleqani, a co-founder of the Iran Freedom Movement of Mehdi Bazargan. Shariatmadari, a cleric who had built up a powerful political organization among his followers, had grown critical of the White Revolution's program of secularization and its encroachments on clerical power. Taleqani, who was strongly influenced by leftist thinking on economic justice, had lent his voice to Bazargan's program of a "progressive" nationalism with a strong admixture of Islamic values. Yet most of the main clerics, still strongly influenced by quietism, were reluctant to enter the political fray.

This changed in October 1977. That month Khomeini's eldest son died of an apparent heart attack, and thousands of the ayatollah's supporters took to the streets to denounce the shah and his minions, whom they blamed for the death. Forty days later, when Islamic ritual dictated an additional mourning ceremony, they demonstrated again. Suddenly, Khomeini, largely forgotten until then, was back in the public eye. The shah vacillated, searching for a proper response. Then, in January 1978, one of Iran's leading newspapers, *Ettalat*, published a long commentary denouncing Khomeini as a British agent, a sexual deviant, and a leader of the "black reaction," the obscurantists who opposed the shah's "progressive" reforms. (The shah's camp always referred to the Communists as the "red reaction.") By now Khomeini, still ensconced in his Iraqi exile, was a full-fledged *marja-e taqlid*, "a source of emulation" for millions of Shiites around the world. So this kind of insult could not go unanswered. The day after the article's appearance, students in the seminary at Qom, the center of Iran's spiritual life, told local merchants to shut down the bazaar. Then they filled the streets, their chants mocking the king who had dared to defame their hero. "We demand the return of Ayatollah Khomeini," they chanted.[2] The security forces opened fire. Dozens of students were killed. The next day Khomeini published a statement calling for more demonstrations and congratulating the "progressive clergy" for finally standing up to the shah and the American infidels. (This was, in part, a calculated nudge aimed at the quietists; Khomeini was trying to urge the fence-sitters among the senior clergy to join the cause.)

Forty days later, on February 18, the deaths of the students in Qom were commemorated with more demonstrations. Bazaars and universities shut down. Protesters attacked police stations and hotels, anything that evoked the shah's authority or foreign cultural contamination. Thousands of protesters took to the streets in Tabriz. More demonstrators were shot, their deaths marked in another forty days. The traditional rhythms of Shiite mourning had become an accelerant of modern revolution.[3] Violence surged again on March 29.

In May, however, Ayatollah Shariatmadari called for calm—and this time the protesters listened to him rather than Khomeini. Many observers concluded that the shah was regaining the upper hand. The government had tried to placate the religious opposition by cracking down on some of the most offensive manifestations of un-Islamic behavior, such as erotic cinemas and liquor stores. The shah's officials tried to initiate talks with the largest of the myriad opposition groups that were now emerging into the open. Most of them were demanding a return to the constitutional framework defined in 1906. None of the major parties was calling for the overthrow of the monarchy—much less the establishment of an Islamic Republic.[4] In early June, Prime Minister Jamshid Amouzegar declared, "The crisis is over."[5]

Some of the revolutionaries were not ready to give up. In July 1978, Mehdi Bazargan sent Khomeini a memorandum on tactics. Bazargan, a bearded, bespectacled intellectual who had served as oil minister under Mossadeq and had written extensively on the theory of "Islamic economics," was an experienced political professional. The shah was promising free elections to placate the opposition, and Bazargan advised accepting the offer. While agreeing that the shah should go, Bazargan suggested that it might be worth allowing the institution of the monarchy to continue. He stressed playing by the rules of the still-extant constitution, which— at least on paper—limited the authority of the sovereign and provided for expansive democratic representation. He proposed that Khomeini moderate his attacks on American "imperialism," since the new Iran would still be reliant on help from the United States and the other Western countries. And he also counseled against "a clerical monopoly of the leadership of the movement," since the ulama lacked adequate political experience.[6]

Khomeini, still in his Iraqi exile, did not take the advice. He maintained his attacks on the shah and the Americans and continued to stress that Islam was the guiding force of the revolution. "The whole nation, throughout Iran, cries out: 'We want an Islamic Republic,'" he wrote. The monarchy needed to be eliminated, and the constitution for the new state should be "the law of Islam," which he described, in a characteristic nod to leftist jargon, as "the most progressive of laws."[7] Yet when he was asked to explain what he meant by the evocative phrase *Islamic Republic*, he refused to be drawn, saying merely that the details would be provided in the future.

The relative respite of the summer proved deceptive. Near the end of August, a movie theater in the hardscrabble oil town of Abadan, the Cinema Rex, went up in flames. More than four hundred people died. Who was behind the attack has never been conclusively established. It is possible that hard-line Islamists, some of whom denounced movies for religious reasons, were behind the arson. The film being shown in the theater at the time, however, assailed the regime, and that prompted many Iranians to believe that SAVAK had started the fire as a way of intimidating the opposition. The fire proved an extraordinarily polarizing event. Many members of the middle class—their loyalty to the shah already dented by his erratic economic policies and contempt for individual rights—parted ways with him for good. This marked the point when the movement against the shah began to spread from Khomeinist and Marxist militants to a broader revolt that had its roots in the shah's harsh authoritarian politics.

The Pahlavi dynasty now entered its death spiral. Under American pressure, the shah swung back to a harder line, empowering the military to crack down on the protests. In early September, as a religious holiday began, crowds chanting pro-Khomeini slogans filled the streets of Iran. The government declared martial law—but many Iranians were unaware of the announcement. The next day, on September 8, a crowd of up to twenty thousand gathered in Jaleh Square in the center of Tehran, in unintentional defiance of the state of emergency. Troops opened fire on the massed demonstrators; helicopter gunships machine-gunned the stragglers. The streets ran red with blood. Hundreds, perhaps thousands, were killed. After "Black Friday," as it came to be known, there was no way for the monarchy to redeem itself.

By now the shah had prevailed upon the Iraqi government to expel Khomeini, but this proved a Pyrrhic victory. Khomeini's arrival in Paris quickly revealed its advantages as a headquarters. He was now even better positioned to propagate the revolution's message. He gave hundreds of interviews to reporters from around the world. Iranians from all walks of life made pilgrimages to Neauphle-le-Château, and a cross-section of illustrious visitors paid their obeisance to the man whose portrait was now replacing the shah's as the most ubiquitous in Iran. A crowd of well-wishers from the homeland gathered outside the police barricades, and whenever Khomeini appeared, they broke into ecstatic cries, hailing him as "the imam." Sometimes the faintest hint of a smile played over his face, but aside from that, he maintained his distinctive air of otherworldliness, never betraying a sign of his emotions.

In Iran itself the demonstrations continued, growing larger by the week. Strikes rippled out across the country. In September the oil workers stopped work—a final crippling shock to the economy, which ground to a halt as oil revenues tapered off. Collective emotions ratcheted up again in December with the start of the holy month of Moharram, when Shiites commemorate the martyrdom of Imam Hossein. Iranian sociologist Sattareh Farmaian, who wrote one of the most vivid memoirs of the revolution, recalled how Khomeini urged Iranians to emulate Hossein by sacrificing their lives:

> Crowds large and small filled the streets, angry men and black-veiled women with waving fists and bulging eyes. Neighborhood organizers and the "beards" [pro-Khomeini activists] kept the protestors disciplined, but it was impossible to near a crowd without fearing that it might turn into a lynch mob. To set foot in the city was like getting caught in a slow-moving cyclone. A million people would move along Shahreza Avenue, the main artery across

the city, stretching from one side of Tehran to the other, carrying banners and shouting slogans, a thick, black, living river. On every street one saw shuttered, empty, burned-out stores, broken pavements, flashing police lights, overturned cars and trucks. The smells of burning buildings and rubber tires, billowing smoke, and tear gas pervaded the chilly air.[8]

On Ashura, the climactic day of Moharram, Ayatollah Taleqani and National Front leader Karim Sanjabi led a demonstration of 2 million people through Tehran. By now the most effective slogan in the protesters' repertoire was this one: "Brothers in the army: Why are you killing your brothers?" When young conscripts heard it, they often broke into tears, threw away their guns, and joined the demonstrators.

Iranians now faced a winter of political uncertainty, rampant violence, and shortages of food and fuel. The exiles in Neauphle-le-Château were feeling the cold, too. The ayatollah stuck to his rigorous schedule of prayer despite the complexities involved in remote-controlling a revolution. Throughout the year Khomeini had remained in constant contact with his network of supporters inside Iran. The state-of-the-art telephone switching system recently installed in Iran by the Americans was a major source of logistical support, enabling easy long-distance calls from Paris to anywhere inside the country. His speeches and statements, duplicated with the help of Xerox copiers, were smuggled in by the thousands. The cassette tape—cheap and portable—carried his sermons into the most remote corners of Iran.

The backbone of Khomeini's network consisted of his former students, united by their teacher's activist vision of Islam, and leaders from the firmly traditional caste of bazaar merchants (*bazaari*), who tended to be both deeply pious and profoundly skeptical of the culture of technocratic capitalism promoted by the shah's reforms. The network financed its work both with donations from the *bazaaris* as well as with the traditional religious tax that Khomeini's followers were duty bound to contribute to him. He had empowered one of his favorite students, Morteza Motahhari, to collect these funds and disburse them in accordance with the needs of the movement. Khomeini had already designated a group of other young clerics, including Motahhari, to act on his behalf in Tehran.

When he met with Bazargan in late October 1978, Khomeini asked him and his colleague Ebrahim Yazdi—the man who had asked Mohsen Sazegara to come to Paris from Chicago—to draw up a list of people who could advise him, acting as a sort of shadow government. The final group of eighteen that Bazargan and Yazdi came up with included members of Khomeini's band of young activists as well as a cadre from Bazargan's moderate Islamist Party, plus a sprinkling of bazaar merchants and ex-security officials who had fallen out with the shah's regime. They formed the core of what came to be known as the Revolutionary Council, which would become one of the most important institutions in Iran after the fall of the monarchy.[9]

The formation of the Revolutionary Council was a clear indicator that the religious opposition to the shah was planning to take power. But Khomeini and his entourage chose not to advertise the fact. In public Khomeini was still careful with his views. He took every occasion to express his respect for democratic institutions, the vote, and freedom of the press. When asked what he meant by the enticing phrase *Islamic Republic*, he responded that it would be "a republic as you have in France." Khomeini continued to make reassuring signals to the leftist groups, who, with their guns and radical ideas, still formed an important part of the militant resistance to the government. He made a point of saying that the new state would allow even Communists all the freedoms they wished as long as they pledged to stay within the law. Once he returned to Iran, he said, he would settle back down in Qom, hinting that he would leave the governing of the country to the politicians.

Where he remained uncompromising was in his attitude toward the shah, who by now had been forced to acknowledge that his power was slipping away. It was clear that there was no longer any way to contain the protests or the strikes. Parts of the economy were grinding to a halt. The Americans, who had no clear policy on how to respond to the crisis, had been sending contradictory signals, sometimes urging the shah to pursue a harder line, sometimes pushing him to make concessions. But as the new year dawned, they made it clear that he no longer enjoyed their support. The shah had nowhere else to turn.

His departure now appeared increasingly like a foregone conclusion. On January 3 came the news that the shah had appointed Shapour Bakhtiar, one of the leading figures of the National Front, as the new prime minister. The shah empowered Bakhtiar to prepare the way for a transitional government. Though his own party disowned him for accepting the appointment, Bakhtiar, a moderate, believed that it was the last hope for deflecting a full-fledged revolution and easing Iran into a democratic system. He amnestied political prisoners, abolished SAVAK, and eliminated censorship—all measures that, at this late stage, probably sped up the course of the revolution. He dispatched an emissary to Paris to consult with Khomeini, asking for a grace period in which to hold elections for a constituent assembly. Khomeini—cleaving to his role as revolutionary maximalist—denounced Bakhtiar as a collaborator and refused to have anything to do with him.

On January 16, parliament in Tehran gave a vote of confidence to the new Bakhtiar government. Mohammad Reza Pahlavi had been waiting for the news.

His options were exhausted. He and his family drove to the airport, boarded a plane, and flew out of Tehran. Officially, he and his family were leaving Iran only for a "vacation." But the truth quickly dawned on the populace.

The streets of Tehran suddenly fell quiet. For four months, Sattareh Farmaian noted, the city had been awash with the sounds of raucous demonstrations, gun battles, and car horns—so the abrupt onset of silence was disconcerting. Around one o'clock in the afternoon, the mood changed again. Farmaian heard shouting. The young soldiers standing watch in the streets began to jump up and down, hugging each other in joy. Some burst into tears. The manager of the restaurant where Farmaian was sitting turned up his radio so that everyone could hear the news. It had finally happened. The shah had left the country.[10]

Jubilant demonstrators toppled statues of the shah or cut his picture out of banknotes. Images of Khomeini replaced them. Demonstrators stuffed carnations in the barrels of soldiers' guns. In Neauphle-le-Château, the ayatollah maintained his usual unruffled demeanor. "God is great," he said when told the news. Then he walked across the street to give reporters his reaction. "The departure is not the final victory," he said. "It is the preface to our victory. I am congratulating the brave people of Iran for this victory. We must consider that this victory will not only mean the abdication of this dynasty but also the end of foreign domination, and this is more important even than the eradication of the Pahlavi dynasty."[11]

The activists around Khomeini now faced a tricky decision. The shah was gone. The power vacuum inside Iran was deepening by the day. If the ayatollah was to return to Iran, this was the time. But how to proceed? After several fits and starts, it was finally decided that Khomeini would fly back to Iran on February 1. But at the last minute, Bakhtiar's government announced that the plane would not be allowed to land.

So the ayatollah's aides opted for an insurance policy. They chartered an Air France Boeing 747 and packed it with Western journalists: the army would surely think twice about shooting down a French airliner filled with representatives of the world's media. As the Boeing neared the Iranian border, one of Khomeini's men unnerved the reporters with an announcement: "We have received news that the plane will be shot down as soon we enter Iranian airspace." It was a false alarm.[12]

One minor incident on the plane threw an intriguing light on Khomeini's attitude toward the revolution. An American reporter on the plane conducted a brief interview with the ayatollah. "How do you feel about returning to your homeland?" he asked. "Nothing," Khomeini replied. "I don't feel anything." Nationalist Iranians opposed to the revolution would later cite this exchange as evidence of Khomeini's lack of patriotism. But for his supporters, it was merely further evidence of his intense spirituality. This was a man whose primary duty in life was service to God.

No one shot at the plane. The 747 landed without problems and taxied to a stop. Khomeini's companions argued about who would help him down the stairs to the tarmac: everyone was aware of the political benefits accruing to the person who appeared in what was sure to be an iconic image. In the spirit of compromise, the honor was finally delegated to an Air France steward. Frenzied crowds swarmed around the airport as the ayatollah's feet touched Iranian soil once again. Khomeini and his entourage could barely make it through the terminal building because of the hysterical mob; at one point his turban was knocked off. From the airport Khomeini headed straight to Behesht Zahra cemetery, where he aimed to commemorate the martyrs of the revolution. The crowds that lined the road numbered in the millions. The revolution had a new slogan: *Shah raft, Imam amad*—"The Shah has gone, the Imam has come."[13]

To some extent, every revolution is an exercise in political improvisation, and this was also true of the first Islamic revolution. Secular theorists like Marx and Montesquieu had at least given their followers a set of eminently practical notions about the workings of government. But someone striving to establish the rule of Islam in a 1970s nation-state had many blanks to fill in. Khomeini's medium-term plan was simple enough. He would avail himself of the services of the nonreligious groups that favored the revolution as long as they were useful—and then he would eliminate them. He knew he wanted theocracy—but how, precisely, to get there? Khomeini had presented his own theory of clerical rule, known as "guardianship of the jurisprudent," back in Najaf in 1970. Now he had to translate it into practice.

His idea was the fruit of a long evolution. In his first book on religion and its relationship to society, *The Revealing of Secrets* (1944), Khomeini had pilloried the corruption and excesses of the shah's regime. Yet he had stopped short of calling for the abolition of the monarchy, admonishing the shah to follow clerical guidance and heed the demands of Islamic justice. A ruler who did not govern in line with the precepts of sharia ran the risk of losing all legitimacy—but Islamic government could, theoretically, be provided by a king who governed in a genuinely Islamic spirit. Some scholars say that this was merely a tactical concession by Khomeini, who was not yet ready to alienate his clerical colleagues by openly calling for revolution. The argument is not entirely convincing. Khomeini's early book hardly comes across as an exercise in political tact, since he was anything but subtle when it came to heaping vituperation on the monarch. It seems much more likely that he was still developing his ideas about the precise nature of Islamic rule.[14]

Whatever the reason, by the late 1960s Khomeini's ideas on the proper form of Islamic government had crystallized. In Najaf in 1970, he held a series of lectures that gave coherent shape to his political ideas. His followers soon collected his talks into a book that came to be known most widely under the title *Hokumat-i Islami* (Islamic Government), though it is sometimes referred to by the Persian phrase for the doctrine that Khomeini placed at the core of his theory: *velayat-e faqih*, meaning "guardianship of the jurist." In it Khomeini develops an elaborate argument about who should govern in a future Islamic state. In so doing, he builds upon a discourse that evolved in the nineteenth century to address the fundamental dilemma of Shiite governance.

Twelver Shiites, who make up the overwhelming majority of Iranians, believe that the legitimacy bestowed upon the Prophet by his divine revelation was transferred, upon his death, to his cousin and son-in-law Ali bin Ali Talib, the first of the twelve imams to hold rightful leadership over the community of Muslims. The last of the twelve, Muhammad al-Mahdi, went into "occultation," withdrawing himself from the view of mortals, in AD 874, and according to prophesy he will not return until the moment when temporal history comes to an end. This, of course, poses the question of how Muslims are to be governed in the meantime. The traditional answer has been, essentially, that existing political rulers are not legitimate but tolerated and that they must be held to account for their actions by the ulama and the people.

In his 1970 lectures, Khomeini—in what one commentator calls "a bold innovation in the history of Shiism"[15]—elaborates a radically different argument. Contrary to what its title might suggest, *Islamic Government* is not really a book about governance. It is, rather, very much about legitimacy. Khomeini sets out to address the question, "Who is qualified to rule?" The answer is clear: the clerics, people with proper training in matters of Islamic jurisprudence and its application. Yes, Khomeini says, it is true that the last imam is absent. But we can scarcely conclude from this fact that God wanted the rule of the community of believers to be left to chance. To the contrary, the Quran makes it eminently clear that religion and politics are not separate; they are part of a single, unified realm. Governing must be left to those who have an impeccable sense of justice and are the most thoroughly schooled in the tenets of Islamic law. This can only be the jurisprudents, the religious scholars, the *fuqaha*.

Monarchy, Khomeini explains, is actually inimical to Islam. The Prophet had only contempt for kings, and it is the primal Muslim community led by Muhammad that provides a model for the sort of state organization in which Islam can find full and proper development. What worked for the seventh century remained valid for the twentieth. The laws of Islam retain their validity until the end of history. Islam, Khomeini says, has provided everything that is needed for the modern state as well.

If you are a proper Muslim, in fact, you have no choice. If you are confronted by an evil government, revolution is not only advisable but obligatory. "We have no choice," Khomeini wrote, "but to shun wicked governments, or governments that give rise to wickedness, and to overthrow governments who are traitorous, wicked, cruel and tyrannical."[16] If oppressive rulers refuse to acknowledge the just demands of the Islamic opposition, this means that they have engaged in "armed aggression against the Muslims and acquired the status of a rebellious group." Muslims then have the duty of conducting holy war against the rulers until they succeed in achieving a society that conforms to Islamic principles.[17]

The fact that Khomeini felt compelled to lay out this argument in such detail implies that there are those within the clerical establishment who needed to be convinced. Khomeini's reading was not one that enjoyed universal approbation even within the community of Shia legal scholars. These lectures were aimed at bringing listeners around to a new vision that implied a revision of many long-held views about the extent to which the reigning authorities had a right to rule.

While *Islamic Government* has much to say about the justification for a future Islamic state, it offers little detail about the precise nature of that state. The phrase *Islamic Republic* does not occur anywhere in the text. In fact, there is virtually no discussion of specific institutions at all. The book is silent on topics like constitutions, elections, or political parties—all concepts that would figure prominently in the course of the revolution. Contrary to what a Western reader might expect from its title, Khomeini's book is not a tract about statecraft. Somewhat like a utopian socialist, Khomeini apparently believed that the state would wither away of its own accord once the proper kind of rule was established. In a casual aside to an interviewer, Khomeini once observed that he could run Iran with the help of two clerks if need be; God had already provided the necessary guidance. He was also known to have expressed the view that Islamic tribunals, unhindered by the niceties of Western law and bureaucracy, could settle the vast backlog of cases in the shah's court system in a matter of a few days.[18] At one point Khomeini even dismissed the need for a parliament, since the Quran and the scriptural traditions had already provided for all the laws that were needed. It was merely a matter of carrying them out.[19]

Many people—from liberal intellectuals to Communist Party agitators—had worked to undermine the shah's throne. But when the collapse of the monarchy finally came, few of them had clear ideas of what to do next. Khomeini was different. Like Lenin in Petrograd sixty-one years earlier, he knew the ultimate goal that he wanted to achieve, though he allowed himself considerable tactical flexibility along the way. He went straight to work.

The Revolutionary Council officially started work on January 12, though its precise composition was revealed only much later. Immediately upon his return to Tehran, Khomeini set up his headquarters in an Islamic girls school that the council had been using as its base. Suddenly, the modest building, long overshadowed by the nearby parliament and the huge central mosque, became the center of political gravity in a country of 35 million people. It rapidly turned into an object of pilgrimage for Khomeini's followers—who arrived bearing food, medicine, and countless petitions—and a source of terror for his foes.

The executions of political opponents started in the days immediately following the ayatollah's return. A firing squad operating under Revolutionary Council orders dispatched SAVAK officials and leading generals on the roof of the school. This marked the start of a new phase of violence. Until this moment, the overwhelming majority of those who had died in the revolution had been victims of the state. From now on it was the revolutionaries themselves who did most of the killing—sometimes among themselves. This type of bloodletting would prove hard to control.

Khomeini had originally intended to postpone his return until a provisional government, free from any ties to the shah, could be appointed, but that plan had been overridden by fears that the military might seize power.[20] So now he set about creating his own. On February 4 he appointed Bazargan prime minister, with responsibility for the army, police, and civil service. There were now two people in Iran who held this office: the other was Bakhtiar, who still governed according to the existing constitution and refused to give way. But real power was draining away from him by the hour.

The military itself, one of the few of the shah's institutions to have survived the revolutionary turmoil unscathed, now began to fragment as well. In the course of the preceding months, many lower-ranking officers and enlisted men had transferred their sympathies to the revolution. The unavoidable confrontation came on

February 10. At a military base in Tehran, junior officers who sympathized with the revolution got into a gun battle with the Imperial Guard, the elite force of the shah's army. Reinforcements from left-wing militias, the Fedayeen-e Khalq ("the People's Strugglers") and the Mujahideen-e Khalq ("the People's Mujahideen"), rushed to the scene. Neither group, it should noted, took its orders from Khomeini; they were loyal to the "revolution." The revolutionaries won—and then proceeded to march on other bases where royalist forces were still holding out. Around midday on February 11, the army proclaimed its "neutrality"—a euphemism for capitulation. This meant that there was no one left to defend Bakhtiar's government. The revolution had triumphed. Bakhtiar left Iran in April, never to return.[21]

Iran's 35 million people were now under the control of a revolutionary government. But what sort of government was it, precisely? The Bazargan cabinet did not appear particularly radical. He and his cabinet, which included no clerics, essentially wanted a secular, parliamentary state. One of the most important tasks Khomeini had entrusted it with was the passing of a referendum on the future form of government, to be followed by the drafting of a constitution and its submission to a constituent assembly. The precise timetable for these events remained unclear. For the moment, Bazargan accordingly announced, the 1906 constitution would remain in effect—minus the monarchy—until a substitute was approved. After all, the prime minister declared, Iranian society still needed some sort of ground rules. In speeches he depicted himself as a "delicate passenger car" that traveled on a "smooth asphalted road," in stark contrast with Khomeini, the "bulldozer" of the revolution. Bazargan's respect for the rule of law undoubtedly endeared him to nervous members of the middle and upper classes, but it was not necessarily the thing that died-in-the-wool revolutionaries—lusting for blood, power, or justice—wanted to hear. "Those who imagine the revolution continues are mistaken," Bazargan's press spokesman told the public. "The revolution is over. The era of reconstruction has begun."[22] It soon turned out that Khomeini had his own views on the matter.

Revolutionary government in Iran actually predated the formation of Bazargan's cabinet. For months, extending well back into 1978, Islamists and other activists around the country had been forming *komitehs* (revolutionary committees) that coordinated protests, arranged supplies of food and fuel to neighborhoods, or stockpiled weapons. There were *komitehs* on the scale of a city block; others controlled major cities, some as early as December 1978. Students of history noted a striking antecedent: the Russian word *soviet*, meaning "council," was used for the local groups formed by workers and soldiers after the overthrow of the czar in March 1917. Some of the *komitehs* had similar origins, and there were leftists who tried to refashion them as workers' councils—an effort doomed as Khomeini's support-ers gained the upper hand.[23] But most of the *komitehs* were organized by religious activists, often with a local mosque at their center. There were some one thousand of them in Tehran alone. They often indulged in the practice of arbitrary justice, sometimes erecting checkpoints that aimed to screen out whatever they deemed as seditious or "anti-Islamic behavior." (There were cases of people shot for playing chess, which was associated with the reign of the shah.)[24]

Thus ensued the Iranian version of a situation common to many revolutions: dual government. The revolution had spawned two parallel structures of authority. Since each claimed superior legitimacy, rivalry was inevitable. The *komitehs* paid little attention to the edicts issuing from Bazargan's provisional government. While Bazargan's cabinet consisted primarily of moderate oppositionists, the *komitehs* consisted largely of religious radicals who were eager to see Islamic law applied on the ground. They tended to follow the lead of the Revolutionary Council, whose members increasingly had very different ideas from the government's about the di-rection the revolution should take. The council was now dominated by clerics, since Bazargan's secular allies had moved over to his cabinet. While Bazargan's cabinet continued to churn out laws and decrees, the council increasingly exercised its will through the *komitehs* and the revolutionary tribunals that were springing up around the country.

For the moment, Khomeini did little to bring clarity to the situation. He was dissatisfied with the secularizing tendencies of Bazargan's cabinet, but he had to be cautious. Secular political groups were trumpeting their own visions of the future. The left-wing parties—as they had demonstrated during the confrontation with the Imperial Guard—had powerful militias that remained a force to be reckoned with. And there were also challenges from Iran's many ethnic minorities, who now began to foment separatist rebellions.[25] Under these conditions, establishment of a system of rule by the religious elite was anything but ensured.

On top of all this, Khomeini's theory of Islamic government had yet to meet with wide acceptance among the rest of the religious establishment. There were quietist clerics, like Ayatollah Khorasani, who rejected the entire premise of theocratic rule: the business of government, this camp argued, should be left to the politicians. Oth-ers, like Ayatollah Shariatmadari, approved of greater clerical involvement in gov-ernment, but insisted on the maintenance of democratic freedoms. Shariatmadari's Islamic People's Republican Party, with a solid base in Tabriz, Iran's second-largest city, was also a force to be reckoned with; his movement had tens of thousands of followers who were fiercely loyal to their leader and who could be sent into the streets on short notice if the occasion demanded. Meanwhile, Ayatollah Taleqani continued to side with Bazargan's Freedom Movement.

The referendum on the nature of the postrevolutionary state was set for the end of March. On March 1, four weeks before, Khomeini laid down an important marker: he warned against using the modifier *democratic* for the new republic. The only proper adjective, he said, was *Islamic*. Finally, as Bazargan had promised, Iranians went to the polls to express their preference. On March 30–31, the revolutionary government asked voters to answer yes or no to a simple query: "Should the monarchy be replaced by an Islamic Republic?" No one knew precisely what was meant by the term. But the voters—at least those who participated—liked the sound of it, and 98.2 percent of them said yes.[26] With this, the march toward clerical rule passed its first crucial watershed.

Iran, however, was not at peace with itself. Chaos reigned. The shah was gone, but as the months went by it became clear that the central issue of who would hold power in the state had still not been conclusively resolved. There were many groups vying for their share of power. In March the Kurds and Turkmens rose up in separatist revolts. The Tudeh Party was back in business, its armed wing roaming the streets, its leaflets coursing through the universities. Students battled each other over obscure doctrinal questions, and more and more of them gravitated toward the various armed groups: the leftist Fedayeen-e Khalq or the Mujahideen-e Khalq, or the new pro-Khomeini organization that was known simply as "the Party of God": Hezbollah. The Hezbollahis were the storm troopers of *velayat-e faqih*. They attacked opposing demonstrations, swooped down on displays of ostensibly "anti-Islamic" behavior, and torched the offices of newspapers and political parties whose thinking they disagreed with. In some cases, particular localities had their own Islamist guerrilla groups.

All this was deeply worrying to Ayatollah Taleqani. Like his friend Bazargan, he was worried that the rise of the *komitehs*, the revolutionary courts, and Hezbollah was undermining the democratic freedoms achieved in the revolution and paving the way toward theocracy. (Though Taleqani—long one of Khomeini's most important allies—was a cleric himself, that didn't mean that he wanted his colleagues to seize power.) Increasingly, it appeared as though Khomeini was not only denying support to the government he had placed in power but also enabling activities that undermined its work. In April, Taleqani issued a public warning against a "return to despotism." Thousands of his supporters, mostly "progressive Islamists" of a pro-Shariati coloration, took to the streets, chanting their ayatollah's praises and denouncing "reactionaries"—meaning Khomeini and his entourage.

This was a serious matter. The chain-smoking Taleqani was the revolution's second-most popular figure and, for a time, the chairman of the Revolutionary Council (a fact that became known only after his death). He was closely allied with Bazargan and enjoyed the backing of the People's Mujahideen, the Mujahideen-e Khalq, who had lent him their support because of his opposition to clerical rule. If Bazargan ever had a chance to thwart the slide toward theocracy, this would have been it. But he failed to respond decisively. Pro-Khomeini forces arrested two of Taleqani's sons; then Khomeini called Taleqani to Qom (where Khomeini was now ensconced) and forced him to recant. Taleqani, publicly humiliated, was hardly heard from again. (In September he died under mysterious circumstances.)

A key aspect of the growing struggle between the provisional government and the Revolutionary Council was control over the security forces. In late April, one of the moderate ayatollahs and the chief of the regular national police announced a plan to integrate four thousand members of the various revolutionary militias into the regular police force. This would have given a significant boost to the provisional government's ability to crack down on the chaos in the streets. But on May 1, 1979, Ayatollah Morteza Motahhari—the loyalist who had run Khomeini's network of supporters inside Iran as well as helping to establish Hosseiniye Ershad, the site of Shariati's most famous lectures—was killed by an assassin. For Khomeini, this was not only a profound personal shock (since Motahhari had been one of his most promising students). He also saw the attack as a direct assault on the clergy. The revolution was under siege, and the army, still staffed by officers appointed by the old regime, could not be relied upon to defend it.

In the week after Motahhari's death, Khomeini entrusted Ebrahim Yazdi with the job of melding the various armed groups into a new force to be called the "Corps of the Guardians of the Islamic Revolution."[27] From here on the Revolutionary Guard became the armed avant-garde of the nascent Islamic state. It was designed to provide a counterweight to the traditional military, which was ideologically suspect, and assumed responsibility for defending the revolution against those deemed to be its enemies by Khomeini and his followers. Its institutional partner in this task was the Islamic Republican Party (IRP), a new political organization created by the hard-line clerics to advance the Khomeinist agenda amid the rough-and-tumble of Iranian politics. The creation of the Revolutionary Guard was another watershed on the march toward theocracy.

By contrast, the draft constitution that Bazargan finally presented in June was surprisingly moderate. It abolished the monarchy and replaced the shah with an elected president according to the French model. It did not give any special role to the clergy. It provided for a Council of Guardians who were supposed to guarantee that laws conformed with the principles of Islam. Only a minority of the guardians would be clerics.[28] Khomeini approved most of the draft, though he did add provisions that restricted women from becoming judges or assuming the office of the president. (They did, however, have the right to vote and to sit in parliament—entirely contrary to Khomeini's position back in 1963, when he had made female enfranchisement the cornerstone of his resistance to the White Revolution.)

Why did Khomeini approve the draft even though it did not enshrine an Islamic government? It's not entirely clear, but the best answer seems to be that he felt that it was as far as he could go for the moment. Perhaps he felt that the political situation was still too fluid to make a push for full-fledged theocracy. If so, such fears were entirely justified by the public reaction to Bazargan's constitution. To Khomeini's consternation, it touched off a frenzy of debate. At this stage revolutionary Iran still offered considerable freedom of discourse, and every party and civic group weighed in. Secular leftists, drawing on a wealth of legal opinions from various professional and human rights groups, proposed an alternate vision that made parliament supreme, guaranteed an independent judiciary, and enshrined broad human rights (including full rights for women). They pressed home their demands with a flurry of demonstrations and editorials. Most of these secular moderates were skeptical of private property and favored policies that promoted equality. They came out strongly in favor of broad nationalization and social justice. But they tended to oppose plans for a strong presidency, which, in their view, opened the way toward dictatorship. In fact, there was a remarkable degree of consensus among this secular bloc.[29]

But the tide was already running against the moderates. They could talk as much as they wanted; it was the institutions and groups under Khomeini's sway that increasingly commanded real power in Iran. Jolted by the flood of criticism, Khomeini now decided it was time to push back on his plans for clerical rule. In July, in an acknowledgment of political realities, the beleaguered Bazargan accepted the appointment of four clerics to the provisional government.[30] One part of the dual state established in the wake of the revolution's triumph was now giving way to another. Back in 1917, Lenin had used the *soviets* to topple the moderate provisional government in postrevolutionary Russia and to impose his radical political agenda. Now Khomeini was using the *komitehs* and the other Islamist institutions to undercut Bazargan's government and to give flesh to his theocratic vision.

Subsequent events underlined Bazargan's powerlessness. He had shown little inclination to limit freedom of opinion. But in August, at Khomeini's urging, the government introduced a new set of restrictive press laws that banned criticism of the Islamic Republic.[31] The office of the moderate left-wing newspaper *Ayandegan*, accused of taking money from Israel and SAVAK, was attacked by Hezbollah thugs; then the paper was shut down altogether. It was only the first. Dozens of other newspapers, including the two largest in Iran, were closed in the weeks that followed. Hezbollahis also staged raids on the headquarters of the Tudeh Party and the two main left-wing militia groups.[32]

The focus of political struggle now shifted to the constituent assembly. In August, Iranians voted for the seventy-three members of the Assembly of Experts, who were to be entrusted with the job of drawing up the constitution for the Islamic Republic.[33] Fifty-five of those chosen were clerics. This was more than enough to dominate the proceedings; by now, after all, Khomeini effectively controlled all the key levers of power in the country, including the press. They convened on August 18. Khomeini, addressing the delegates, warned them that the constitution must be "100 percent Islamic." Khomeini's old rival Ayatollah Shariatmadari, who was now becoming one of the foremost critics of the new order, had urged postponement, arguing that it would be better to stick to the 1906 constitution for the moment. But he was easily overridden. Public debate continued for the next few weeks. But that was enough to show Khomeini and his entourage that there was no serious opposition to their plans for a state run according to the principles that he had mapped out in *Islamic Government*. So the clerical party proceeded to draw up a constitution that enshrined Khomeini's *velayat-e faqih*, the "guardianship of the jurist," as its guiding principle.[34]

In 1918, Lenin had sent in the troops to dissolve a democratically elected constituent assembly that didn't follow his plan for Communist government. Ayatollah Khomeini, by contrast, succeeded in controlling the drafting process from within. From now on it was the clerics who shared his vision who would define the ground rules for the state to come. Still, though the momentum was clearly on Khomeini's side, the new order was not yet complete. A few significant pockets of opposition remained. But events would soon come to the clerics' aid.

12

The Lady

The labor unrest of the Winter of Discontent gradually ebbed as wage deals were made to placate the unions. But the damage had been done. Inflation was starting to rise again. Prime Minister Callaghan's reputation as the man who could bring the unions to reason had been demolished. And now a new threat arose to his government from an entirely different quarter.

Among the many other problems facing the United Kingdom during the 1970s was a sharp rise in nationalist sentiment in Northern Ireland, Wales, and Scotland. In 1978, Callaghan tried to mollify the advocates of Scottish independence by promising them greater powers of self-administration, to be vested in a Scottish legislature. The act was supposed to be confirmed by a referendum, which was held on March 1, 1979. But earlier, as the law creating the new legislature passed through the British Parliament, a Labour parliamentarian opposed to the devolution of powers had tacked on a condition setting a higher bar for approval. As a result, the referendum didn't pass, even though most of the Scots who participated had voted yes. Angry Scottish nationalists in the House of Commons, who felt they'd been betrayed by Callaghan's government, vowed revenge. There were only a few of them in the House of Commons, but the government was by now so unpopular, and enjoyed such a perilous margin of support, that they felt they could do some real damage. They tabled a no-confidence vote.

The leader of the opposition immediately spotted an opportunity to bring down the government. Ironically, Margaret Thatcher and her fellow Conservatives were fiercely opposed to Scottish devolution. But this was a classic case of "the enemy of my enemy is my friend." The Liberal Party, which had lent its support to Callaghan's government for a while, had followed the changing electoral winds and shifted back to opposition. The Labour Party had also lost two by-elections on March 1, shaving its majority even further. Thatcher decided that it was worth the gamble. She put down her own no-confidence motion, which took precedence over the one initiated by the Scottish nationalists, on March 28. If the motion passed, Callaghan would be forced to call a fresh election.

The day of the vote has been described as one of the most dramatic moments in British parliamentary history. The catering staff was on strike, so members of Parliament had to bring their lunches with them. The party whips, charged with marshaling the votes, engaged in frantic maneuvering. One Labour member was dying of a heart ailment in a Yorkshire hospital, and for a while the prime minister considered bringing him down to Westminster in an ambulance; Callaghan ultimately decided against it. Thatcher struggled to maintain her composure. As the vote count proceeded, she and her Tory colleagues agonized over the outcome. For a while they thought that they had lost. But then the tally was announced: Ayes, 311. Noes, 310. It was the first no-confidence motion lost by a British government since 1925. At that moment, as Thatcher rather extravagantly recalls in her memoirs, "James Callaghan's Labour Government, the last Labour Government and perhaps the last ever, fell from office." In a sense she was right. Labour would take the helm of government again, many years later, but by then it would be a party completely transformed— not least by the success of the counterrevolution she was about to launch.

W hen the election finally came, Norman Tebbit was ready for it. By the spring of 1979 he had already served two terms in Parliament. A staunch Tory, Tebbit represented the London suburb of Chingford. This was not the sort of affluent, traditionally minded area that would have counted as typical Conservative territory. Tebbit's voters were what he described as "aspirational working class"— skilled laborers who were skeptical about the leaders of their own unions and increasingly viewed high taxes, inflation, and government regulation as curbs on their upward mobility. On top of that, many of them commuted to jobs in London, so they had been hit hard by the transportation strikes of the Winter of Discontent— "a game changer," Tebbit calls it, that aggravated an already widespread sense of anger at the disproportionate power of the unions. His voters also had plenty of firsthand stories to tell about abuses of power by union leaders (who, for example, might bring in outside workers during strike votes to ensure that they got the result they wanted). As Tebbit canvassed his district, he uncovered an intense sense of frustration with the symptoms of British decline. His tough rhetoric on the need to rein in organized labor resonated with voters.

For Tebbit, there was no mistaking the signs of a building desire for drastic change among his constituents, and Margaret Thatcher, he believed, was the perfect politician to take advantage of such sentiments. Despite his relatively low position in the Conservative Party's parliamentary ranks, Tebbit was uniquely qualified to make such an assessment. Long known within the party as a staunch right-winger, Tebbit had joined forces with Thatcher early on. In 1975 he had served as a member of the team (led by the brilliant political strategist Airey Neave) that had engineered her election as leader of the party. Since then Tebbit had belonged to a small group that helped to prep Thatcher for parliamentary debates, a job that gave him ample insight into her way of doing things. It was his immense respect for her that yielded one of the best laugh lines in his 1979 stump speech. Thatcher was one of the most talented leaders in Westminster, he assured his election-rally listeners. As a matter of fact, he would add, "She's the best man among them."[1]

The election of 1979 marked a watershed moment in British politics. This is not to say that everything about the vote was black-and-white. It is, for example, indeed true—as many contemporary historians are wont to point out—that Thatcher was careful to avoid making her proposals sound too radical and that the Conservative manifesto (the party program) included little in the way of detailed policies for change. It is true that she might have faced a much different political landscape if Callaghan had called for a general election back in the early fall of 1978 (as some of his advisers had counseled), before the Winter of Discontent had left British voters conclusively disgusted with the direction of the country. And it is even true that her personal popularity rating remained well below Callaghan's right up to the end.

Yet despite these qualifiers, there can be no mistaking the fact that Thatcher used the election of 1979 to offer a fundamental break with the way the country had been governed. Voters saw that she was offering a dramatically new approach to dealing with the unions, and it was also clear to them that she was proposing a new set of policies on management of the economy. She pledged change to an electorate that was deeply disillusioned with the status quo—and she did this less through election documents than through her own speeches and campaign appearances. Along the way she also departed decisively from the received wisdom on British electioneering. The message here was, at least in part, the medium—Margaret Thatcher herself.

Conservative leaders before her had focused their campaigns on the classic Tory electorate—those members of the middle and upper classes living in the more affluent parts of the country. Thatcher and her advisers, however, set out to target voter categories long neglected by Conservative campaigners. She made a point, for example, of specifically wooing skilled laborers of the type that Tebbit was courting in his home district. Known in the mysterious argot of British pollsters as "C2s," these workers had long been considered automatic Labour voters. Thatcher disagreed. She believed that many union members resented the undemocratic ways and the cynical tactics of their leaders, and she surmised that many working-class voters would be correspondingly receptive to her calls for greater constraints on union power. She also felt that upwardly mobile workers would welcome her proposals to allow the tenants of public housing to buy their homes. She reasoned that many C2s were also tired of inflation and runaway spending. This was why she staged her first big election rally in the traditional Labour stronghold of Cardiff in Wales. "Labour, the self proclaimed party of compassion, has betrayed those for whom it promised to care," she told her audience. "So in this campaign we'll not only extend and consolidate Conservative support, we'll carry the fight right into what were once the castles and strongholds of Labour, and in many places we'll win."[2]

Her campaign tactics were equally novel. She shunned the traditional Conservative support network in the broadsheet newspapers and favored instead the tabloids and daytime TV—an approach that allowed her to tap into a new electorate in the embattled middle classes who felt threatened by the growing power of the state and the unions and also allowed her to avoid probing questions about policy specifics. She made aggressive use of television, whereupon she was accused (comical as it might seem to a modern audience) of the egregious sin of importing "American-style campaigning" to Britain. She proved very effective at exploiting the medium—especially once her adviser Gordon Reece prevailed upon her to lower her voice, an adjustment that lent her gravitas and authority.

This might seem trivial, but it was especially important in light of Callaghan's magisterial efforts to use her gender against her. It was not so much what he said as how he said it; he was a master at sardonically implying that whatever the leader of the opposition said was made even sillier by the fact that it was being said by a woman. She countered this by doing what she had always done to beat so many male competitors before: she worked harder, sleeping just a few hours a night as she relentlessly studied her briefing papers and learned her lines. At the same time, she turned her gender to her own advantage by slipping, when she chose to, into the role of a commonsensical housewife, hoisting sample grocery bags to drive home the corrosive effects of runaway prices on the ordinary household budget. Nor was she afraid to give interviews to women's magazines in which she shared recipes and stressed her fussy mastery of good housekeeping. Not only did this help to draw in female voters, but it also underlined her point that the economic remedies she was proposing were less a matter of abstract theories than of the everyday ethos of thrift and moderation on which many British households prided themselves.

Thatcher and her team found other ways to make the argument that Britain needed a change of course. In 1978, casting around for a new approach to her campaign, she had hired two young budding advertisers, Maurice Saatchi and Charles Saatchi, to come up with fresh ideas. They produced the famous poster depicting a long queue of people winding around the slogan LABOUR ISN'T WORKING. Once you saw the image, it was a hard thought to get out of your head. The tagline nicely bundled several strands of disappointment. Callaghan's economic policies were supposed to be aimed at producing full employment, but jobs were becoming scarce. He claimed that his close ties with the unions were supposed to enable good labor relations—but the Winter of Discontent showed that his government had delivered only chaos and dysfunction.

Callaghan's strategy was to depict Thatcher as an unbalanced radical whose extremist experiments would damage the gradual restoration of British economic fortunes that he claimed was already under way. Thatcher, in response, was careful not to be too specific with her promises. The 1979 Conservative election manifesto began by declaring that "the balance of our society has been increasingly tilted in favor of the State at the expense of individual freedom" and warned that "this may be the last chance we have to reverse that process." The Tories pledged to fight back by cutting spending and tightening the money supply. The manifesto promised moderate curbs on union power, such as wider use of secret ballots and a law to prevent the spread of closed-shop rules (which imposed union membership on all the employees of a particular company). It vowed to reduce tax burdens and to prevent the government from taking over still more industries (the only hint of privatization was a mention of selling some shares in recently nationalized companies back to their employees). It also included calls for law and order and a strong national defense. It was a clear contrast to the programs offered by Labour and the Liberals, but it was hardly the stuff of revolution. The election campaign showed her to be a cautious, calculating, and eminently practical campaigner. She knew what she had to do.

In the end it all worked to her advantage. Voters wanted change; they merely had to be persuaded to take the chance. Thatcher was ready to help them. In 1968 Richard Nixon had decided to play on the discontent of conservative southern Democrats in an effort to woo them into voting Republican. Now the British Conservative

Party tried something similar, launching an unprecedented campaign to persuade Labour voters that their party no longer stood for their values. Many were ready to listen. In the final days of the campaign, Thatcher spoke stirringly of a "world-wide revolt against big government, excessive taxation and bureaucracy," of an era "drawing to a close."[3] Little did she know that, at about the same time, Callaghan had reached a similar conclusion. He confided to one of his aides that they were witnessing "a sea change" in politics, an epochal shift of a kind that comes along once in a generation—and this time "it is for Mrs. Thatcher." But this, of course, was a private thought. In public, he showed no lack of resolve.

She was an odd phenomenon in so many ways, this Thatcher. She ran a party that still bore the imprint of her predecessor as party leader, Edward Heath. The Conservative election manifesto in 1979 did not differ conspicuously from the program on which the party had campaigned under Heath in 1970. Most of the members of her shadow cabinet had served in comparable positions under Heath. The voters still didn't really know her, and she did not spend much time lingering over her own biography. She never managed to raise her personal popularity to the level of Callaghan's; indeed, the gap was increasing as the election neared.

Her image makers were all too aware of the problem. As election day neared, they did their best to keep her voice off the airwaves. They also staged photo opportunities carefully designed to make her look as unthreatening as possible—perhaps most famously when she traveled to a farm and hefted a newborn calf for the photographers. Though Thatcher later became famous for her domineering manner, during the 1979 campaign she was happy to yield to the advice of her handlers. In stark contrast to Keith Joseph, her volatile mentor, Thatcher never forgot for a moment that she was above all a politician. And not only did she know how to play the game, but she was determined to be better at it than anyone else.

But she was, of course, hardly a typical Tory politician. Her gender was not the only thing that made her unique. It was also her unapologetic commitment to the ideals of freedom. In her last major speech before the election, in her constituency in the London suburb of Finchley, she made her priorities unmistakably clear. "Of course it has been about prices and jobs and standard of living and all the economic things, but this election is about even more than the cost of the shopping basket," she told her audience. "It really is about our fundamental freedoms and the future of our whole way of life in this country." She stressed the need to end the long erosion of personal freedom, to halt the breakneck growth of the state. "Ladies and gentlemen, we are not prepared to accept decline for Britain as inevitable. We wish to change it and we will shall change it!" She cited the long list of former Labour grandees who had recently gone public with their denunciation of the Labour Party and once again ran through the Conservative blueprint for containing inflation, cutting taxes, restraining union power, and restoring the preconditions for an "enterprise society." And she wound it up by returning to her favorite theme. "Much of politics is fought about what you might call the economic factors or the material factors, and sometimes too little attention is given to the moral factors," she told her audience. "But you know, in the end, it's the moral factors which decide the status and pride of a nation." And that "moral case," she informed them, "is on the side of the free society." The choice that Britain now faced was one between a freer state that ensured personal liberties and economic initiative—or the one envisioned by Labour, where the state played an ever-increasing role. This was not the voice of Britain's postwar consensus. This was something verifiably new.[4]

The ideas that Thatcher broached in her 1979 campaign speeches promised change to British voters precisely because few British politicians before her had spoken with such ringing conviction about the challenge to freedom posed by a growing state. But the ideas themselves, as Thatcher well knew, had been around for some time.

In 1947, two years after Britain's march to New Jerusalem began, a group of thirty-six thinkers—economists, historians, journalists, and philosophers—met at a Swiss resort to discuss the fate of Western society. They were all devotees of classical liberal economics, and they were united by a fear that freedom was under threat. The source of that threat was the spirit of collectivism that they saw in the beginnings of the British welfare state, the prevalence of socialist thinking, and the onset of the Keynesian economic revolution. The man who had convened them was an Austrian economist, Friedrich von Hayek, who taught at the London School of Economics (LSE). (He knew Keynes well. During the war, when Hayek was lecturing at Cambridge, he had shared fire-warden duties with his celebrated counterpart.) Hayek was particularly worried about the way that his academic colleagues had provided intellectual support for wartime planning that concentrated economic decision making in the state. A few years earlier he had published a book called *The Road to Serfdom*, an articulate polemic about the perils of liberty in a world where planners increasingly reigned. Most of those in the British establishment dismissed the book's ideas. (That did not stop it from becoming a surprise best-seller in the United States.)

Most of the men—and they were, in fact, all men—who came together to form the Mont Pèlerin Society (named after the resort where they met) drew their intellectual sustenance from three particular universities: the London School of Economics, the University of Chicago, and the University of Vienna. It was these three universities that would deliver many of the crucial theoretical and academic underpinnings for the liberal counterrevolution the new society hoped to unleash. Among the men present were Milton Friedman, Ludwig von Mises, and Karl Popper—each of whom would help to reshape twentieth-century discourse about political liberty and market economics in the decades to come. Hayek opened the meeting with an address in which he asserted that "a great intellectual task must be performed" if the ideals of liberty were to be revived. That task, he said, involved "both purging traditional liberal theory of certain accidental accretions which have become attached to it in the course of time, and also facing up to some real problems which an over-simplified liberalism has shirked or which have become apparent only since it has turned into a stationary and rigid creed."[5]

The participants passed a broad manifesto pledging to defend the values of an open society, combat the encroachments of totalitarianism, and search for ways to guarantee a stable and peaceful international order. Its statement of aims concluded with the assurance that the group rejected "propaganda" and had no intention of establishing a new orthodoxy to replace the ones it denounced. The drafters also denied any particular partisan affiliation. Their object, they said, was "solely, by facilitating the exchange of views among minds inspired by certain ideals and broad conceptions held in common, to contribute to the preservation and improvement of the free society."[6]

This might have seemed like a decidedly modest agenda. But the attendees at the conference felt themselves to be intellectual outcasts. In the postwar United States, the principles of New Deal interventionism and wartime bureaucratic management still reigned supreme. Hayek loved to tell a story about West Germany's top economic bureaucrat, Ludwig Erhard, who had decided in 1948 to free all prices and production controls overnight, thereby unleashing the postwar economic miracle. Academic economists throughout the English-speaking world pooh-poohed the decision. According to Hayek, Erhard had received a phone call from Lucius Clay, the US general in charge of administering still-occupied Germany, who informed him that "'my advisers tell me you are making a great mistake.' Erhard replied, 'So my advisers are also telling me.'"[7] In fact, of course, the radical reforms launched by Erhard had placed Germany on the path to an extraordinary economic revival.

It struck the Pèlerins as ironic that Britain, given its role as the birthplace of classical liberalism, was the place where their ideological crusade against statism faced its biggest uphill climb. Labour's cradle-to-grave welfare state was sweeping all before it; the younger generation in the Conservative Party, led by R. A. Butler, believed that the Tories should yield to the spirit of the times.

Among those who disagreed was a British businessman who proved to be a key personality in this struggle. He was not a particularly distinguished academic, nor was he a notably adept politician. He was, instead, a hybrid of the two, and his name was Anthony Fisher.

Much later Milton Friedman would refer to him as "the single most important person in the development of Thatcherism." While Hayek and his scholarly colleagues appreciated the "seminal importance of ideas," in the words of journalist Richard Cockett, it was the businessman Fisher who figured out the most effective means for spreading those ideas far beyond the precincts of academe.[8]

Fisher brought to this effort his remarkable skills as an entrepreneur. After earning a degree in engineering at Trinity College, Cambridge, he had shown a knack for business by opening his own car rental company in the late 1930s. During the war he made a name for himself with inventions for the Royal Air Force, and once it was over he went back into business—this time, oddly enough, in farming, at which he became a tremendous success. Like many others, he was deeply impressed by Hayek's *Road to Serfdom*, and a few years after the war's end he sought out the author for advice. Fisher wanted to contribute to the fight against socialism. Hayek advised him to forget about a career in politics. What was needed, he said, was a "scholarly research organization" that could argue the case for free-market economics and disseminate its conclusions to the broadest possible audience.[9]

In 1955, Fisher, with the help of some like-minded colleagues, founded the Institute for Economic Affairs. In its structure and its mission, the IEA was explicitly modeled after the Fabian Society. Founded in 1884, the Fabian Society was the brainchild of early British socialists who wanted to make the country more receptive to their ideas. As part of their effort, they had recruited wealthy patrons to sponsor professors at the LSE, who propagated the group's moderate socialist thinking among the nation's elites. "Socialism was spread in this way and it is time we reversed the process," Fisher wrote to one of his colleagues.[10]

Fisher was content to be the institute's author and patron, but he did not want to be responsible for its day-to-day management. He needed a director, and he soon found the perfect man in Ralph Harris, who had worked briefly for the Conservative Party's think tank before taking a job as a lecturer in political economy at the University of St. Andrews in Scotland. Harris had flirted briefly with politics, having campaigned for the Conservative Party candidate in the elections in 1951 and 1955, but Fisher insisted that he abandon his Conservative affiliation when he joined the IEA, since Fisher believed that the institute's work would be more effective if it stayed clear of overt party ties. (The desire to preserve the institute's charitable status presumably had something to do with it as well.)

Fisher, understanding that what the Communists referred to as "propaganda and agitation" stood at the center of the IEA's mission, attributed great importance to the institute's publishing effort, so he did not stint when it came to finding a suitable figure to run it. The man he found was Arthur Seldon. Like Harris, Seldon was of working-class origins, but in contrast to the IEA director, he had started off his political life, during his East End upbringing during the Great Depression, as a convinced socialist. (In this respect, and like quite a few of the other intellectual progenitors of Thatcherism, his ideological evolution presaged that of the American neoconservatives who emerged in the Reagan era and its aftermath. Many of them, too, had started off as members of the dogmatic Left before finding their way to the Republicans.) Seldon had undergone his own conversion when he began reading Hayek and other liberal thinkers at the LSE just before the war.[11]

Harris and Seldon took pride in embracing the unfashionable. One of the institute's earliest pamphlets was a strident defense of the value of advertising at a time when the industry was under attack for allegedly misleading consumers. The provocation was entirely calculated. Harris and Seldon knew that they would not be able to make their mark without challenging orthodoxy head-on. Another early project was a pamphlet on pensions that attacked the notion of a comprehensive state system of social insurance for the elderly right at the moment when Labour was introducing just such a system. The IEA tried to keep its works relatively short and inexpensive to ensure the widest possible distribution. Throughout the 1960s and 1970s, the IEA's authors became known among the cognoscenti for a steady stream of works on trade-union reform and monetary stability. Hayek and Friedman both wrote on these subjects. One of Friedman's most notorious works bore the revealing title *The Counter-Revolution in Monetary Theory*. It was a line of thinking that would soon come into its own as the horrors of stagflation became clear.[12]

There were other voices challenging the consensus, to be sure. Enoch Powell was one. But his political self-immolation with the "Rivers of Blood" speech had only reinforced the popular image of free marketeers as cranks who were out of step with the times. What the market proselytes needed was intellectual credibility, and the IEA supplied it. Increasing numbers of young academics, policy makers, and politicians began beating a path to the IEA's door. But the IEA's growing impact was such that even some on the Left were forced to acknowledge it. In 1968, David Collard of the Fabian Society published an analysis that shockingly conceded the intellectual coherence of the "New Right" exemplified by the IEA theoreticians.[13]

Margaret Thatcher joined their number rather late in the game; it was only in 1971, during her stint as a junior minister in Heath's government, that she first cited one of the institute's papers on education in a parliamentary debate. In the 1960s she appears to have focused more on building her Tory Party career than exploring fresh policy ideas. It was the profound disillusionment of the Heath U-turn, and the attendant realization that believers in the free market needed to articulate a persuasive case for their views, that finally convinced her, later in the 1970s, to seek out the work of the IEA. Before any notion of "Thatcherism" emerged, the IEA had already articulated a body of ideas that encompassed the major themes of Thatcher's prime ministership.

One of the IEA's biggest admirers was a rising Conservative Party star by the name of Keith Joseph. Despite the IEA's ties to individual Conservatives, the institute's directors had always insisted on remaining unaffiliated with any of the major British political parties—leaving an opening for the creation of another organization that would specifically supply Tory policy makers with ideas. Joseph, who had served with Thatcher in the Heath government, became increasingly dissatisfied with the British situation in the 1970s, and he vowed to mix things up. He found his opportunity in 1974, when Heath, now leader of the opposition once again, entrusted Joseph with the creation of a new Conservative Party think tank. Joseph took him at his word. He quickly turned the Center for Policy Studies into a place that aimed to challenge consensus politics—including those who defended it within his own party. Joseph saw the CPS as an arsenal of ideas for a future conservative revolution, happily subverting the received notion of the think tank as natural left-wing territory. "What Britain needs is more millionaires and more bankrupts," Joseph famously declared.[14] This was provocation of the first sort, and Joseph and his followers knew it. Yet they spread the word with the insurgent zeal of the student disciples of Mao and Che (from whom, evidently, they had learned a thing or two about the seductions of revolutionary style). He chose Alfred Sherman, a recovering socialist, as its first director. The IEA had tried to keep above the political fray. The CPS had no such scruples. Joseph was eager to assault the status quo, and he was happy to take on his own party in the process.[15] This desire only intensified after his own bid for leadership collapsed—opening the way for his ally Thatcher to gain election as the party's new leader. (She was, incidentally, one of the cofounders of the CPS.)

Joseph firmly believed in the power of ideology. "A gun is certainly powerful," he told the Tory party conference in 1976, "but who controls the man with the gun? A man with an idea."[16] And Joseph was good at expressing what he believed. One of his most forceful programmatic exercises came in April 1976, in a famous lecture he gave at the CPS. It was called "Monetarism Is Not Enough":

> We were as a country in a transitional stage from world industrial primacy, and our need was in fact to adjust to new realities. The technological decline of our old staple industries, now having to face fierce competition from other countries, was not sufficiently offset by the growth of our new industries, particularly as depression and protection dramatically cut world trade. The response of government, industry, trades unions, advisers was to move rather to work-sharing cartels, rationalization and restrictive trade oligopolies than to modernization and competition.
>
> In short, they tried to thwart change rather than smooth a path for it.[17]

The proper remedy, he said, was not just to impose limits on the monetary supply in accordance with the theory some called "monetarism"—a view that was gradually winning favor even among some Labourites, like Callaghan's son-in-law Peter Jay, who did some work for the IEA—but to pursue a whole suite of measures that would get the government out of the business of economic micromanagement and restore space for entrepreneurship and commercial innovation. "Risk-taking has little appeal these days: the upward potential is small: the downward risk is almost unlimited," Joseph noted. In a passage that sounded the death knell for years of Keynesian "fine-tuning" in Britain, he showed how rising government spending crowded out private investment and boosted inflation. While the resulting high taxes, dense regulation, and rising costs drove private firms out of business, public companies simply relied on the government to come to their aid—thus fueling even more spending and upward pressure on prices. The "inflationary spiral" that Joseph described came to be known as the "ratchet effect," and it offered up a devastatingly convincing picture of Britain's economic situation.

It was a vision that Thatcher undoubtedly shared. It is true enough that her understanding of academic economics was limited (but this applies to many politicians). Her economic thinking emerged organically from her firmly held notions of patriotism, thrift, and individual responsibility. But this should not be taken to mean that she lacked any deeper interest in economic ideas. After the fall of the Heath government, she avidly consumed the work produced by Joseph's CPS, and she actively solicited its recommendations (and those of the IEA) during her time as leader of the opposition. Along the way she rediscovered the work of Hayek, whom she had first read during the war, and became a convert to the monetarist theories of Milton Friedman, who rejected Keynes with a decisiveness that was just beginning to resonate among the English-speaking political elite. These were the main purveyors of what came to be known as the "market revolution" of the 1980s and 1990s—although, of course, their works actually constituted a reaction to the ideas of the socialists and the "Keynesian Revolution."

Again, this body of thought was not new. But instead of asking what thinkers like Hayek and Friedman gave to Thatcher, we might be better off turning the question around: what did she do for their ideas? The answer soon revealed itself. What Thatcher contributed to the cause of the free marketeers was the unstinting force of her convictions. Ordinary politicians had programs. The grocer's daughter had a mission.

13

Thrice Banished,
Thrice Restored

Throughout the 1970s the United States and China had been negotiating, on and off, about opening formal diplomatic relations between the two countries. The process had started with Henry Kissinger's secret trip to Beijing in 1971, and President Nixon's historic visit to China the following year firmly established a common agenda. But both countries soon found themselves slogging through periods of pronounced domestic turmoil. Watergate derailed Nixon's presidency and led to an era of uncertainty in US politics. In China, Mao's senescence and death, followed by the arrest of the Gang of Four and the rise of Hua, similarly diverted the political elite from sealing a deal with the Americans.

The Sino-American rapprochement arose from a shared desire to counter the Soviet Union's growing geopolitical ambitions, a problem that assumed increasing urgency as the decade wore on. By 1977 the worried Chinese, anxious about the growing Soviet role in Vietnam after the US defeat, began pushing the Americans to restart the talks on diplomatic normalization. The new American president, Jimmy Carter, was at first preoccupied with pursuing his predecessors' policy of détente with the USSR. But soon he was able to dispatch his own national security adviser, the tough-minded Zbigniew Brzezinski, to work out the foundations of a deal that would finally allow Beijing and Washington to exchange ambassadors.

The major stumbling block was the status of Taiwan. Though the Carter administration was willing to acknowledge the People's Republic as the sole government of China, the Americans made clear, just as the two sides were about to go public with the normalization announcement, that they were determined to go on selling arms to Taiwan. Chinese negotiators had somehow failed to understand this point, and the Americans' last-minute clarification threw Deng into a rage. But he elected to go ahead with the deal anyway. The People's Republic of China and the United States of America agreed to establish formal diplomatic relations as of January 1, 1979. Nixon had made several visits to Beijing, and protocol suggested that it was time for the Chinese to return the honor. And so, four weeks into the new year, fresh from his Third Plenum triumph, Deng set off on his state visit to the United States.

On January 28 he arrived in Washington, accompanied by a delegation of twenty senior officials. He was received with all the honors befitting a full-fledged head of state. Hua, his putative superior, stayed at home. Deng's agenda was appropriately ambitious. His visit extended over eight days and took him across the entire country. Deng and his wife spent the first three days in Washington, where his schedule included three meetings with President Carter—in itself a mark of the significance afforded to the new relationship, since Carter rarely granted foreign visitors more than two meetings. Deng and his wife stayed in Blair House, which White House staff had carefully equipped with spittoons (an acknowledgment of the vice premier's legendary spitting habit). The first evening featured a gala performance at the Kennedy Center and a state dinner at the White House. The guests included former president Richard Nixon, whom Deng had expressly invited out of respect for his efforts to renew diplomatic ties between the two countries. (Some liberal Democrats considered declining the invitation, but relented when they were told that they would not have to sit at the same table with the villain of Watergate.)

It was a trip rich in odd cultural juxtapositions, but the most surreal moment came when actress Shirley MacLaine, seated at Deng's table during the state dinner in the White House, gushed to him about her last trip to China. MacLaine, an enthusiastic supporter of New Left causes, had chosen the waning years of the Cultural Revolution to shoot a documentary about the wonders of Chinese socialism. She told Deng how she and her friends had been taken to visit a rural commune. There they ran into a professor who was plowing a field. How wise the party had been, he told the Americans, to send him and his fellow academics to the countryside to learn the true ways of the people. MacLaine thought this was marvelous.

Deng looked at her scornfully and said, "He was lying." Professors, he told her, should be teaching university classes, not planting crops.

Deng had always been a man with little tolerance for pleasantries, and he proved it again in his meetings with the US president. He wasted little time in confirming to Carter what US intelligence experts, armed with satellite reconnaissance data, had already been suspecting: China was preparing to send its army into Vietnam. For years tensions between the two countries had been rising, fueled primarily by Hanoi's increasingly cozy relations with the Soviet Union. By giving the Soviet Navy privileged access to Cam Ranh Bay, the Vietnamese had tipped the regional strategic balance, as the Chinese saw it, into Moscow's favor. Beijing was also worried about the Vietnamese Communist government's expressed intention to establish a Communist "Indochinese Federation" with Hanoi at the helm. Here, too, the Soviets would clearly be the ultimate beneficiary. It was incumbent upon China to "teach Vietnam a lesson," Deng declared.[1] The Chinese troops would not stay for long on Vietnamese territory, he told Carter. Once the Vietnamese had been "punished," the Chinese troops would pull out. His American interlocutors refrained from endorsing the invasion plans, but they also made it clear that they would not condemn Beijing if it did so. That, indeed, was just what Deng wanted to hear. (Later, as a demonstration of their goodwill, the Americans would even share some of their intelligence with the Chinese.)

The rest of the visit said a great deal about the various motives behind China's new friendship with the United States. The possibility of American investment in China's economy loomed large. At every possible occasion the vice premier repeated his country's earnest desire for modern technology and management know-how. Deng visited Coca-Cola headquarters in Atlanta, where he took a good, thorough look at a modern, highly automated production facility. He also took a tour of a Ford car-assembly plant with Henry Ford II as his guide. The itinerary also included a call on Boeing headquarters in Seattle. (China had already ordered three Boeing 747s from the company.) At the Lyndon B. Johnson Space Center in Houston, Deng was given a chance to try out a flight simulator that enabled him to practice flying a space shuttle—an experience he enjoyed so much that it proved difficult to pry him away. He and his party comrades also attended a rodeo in a small Texas town, where Deng, attired in his usual dark-gray Mao suit, happily donned a cowboy hat for the cameras. He turned out to be a natural at public relations. During one of his meetings with members of the US Congress, lawmakers asked Deng whether he was prepared to allow Chinese the freedom to travel. "Oh, that's easy," Deng replied. "How many do you want? Ten million? Fifteen million?" That effectively ended the discussion.[2] A bit unexpectedly, the tiny Deng—"blunt, outgoing and humorous," as one reporter wrote—proved something of a hit with the US public.[3]

To be sure, there were also reminders that the relationship between Communist China and the liberal democracy of the United States still faced plenty of obstacles. One commentator in the *Washington Post* informed his readers that current US investment projects in China—like a plan to build six new Intercontinental hotels or a big US Steel plant for processing iron ore—would almost certainly run into problems with the top-heavy Chinese bureaucracy or the mutual incomprehension between Chinese workers and their US managers. "This may dampen the enthusiasm of American businesses eyeing the China market, an enthusiasm even leading promoters of China trade here think has gone too far."[4]

Officials in Deng's entourage had other problems on their minds. Taiwanese extremists, angry that the United States was forsaking their country in favor of the People's Republic, were said to have hired snipers to shoot Deng during the visit. A Ku Klux Klan member actually attempted to attack Deng in Houston, but Secret Service agents succeeded in tackling him first. And there was even an attack— somewhat more symbolic in nature—by members of a self-described Maoist group based in the United States, who vandalized the Chinese Liaison Office in Washington, the embryonic embassy. They broke windows and splashed white paint across the front of the building, all to underpin their denunciation of Deng as a "capitalist roader" who was selling out China's real interests.[5]

This last bit of political theater reflected a more ominous reality. For all the upbeat atmospherics, Deng's program still had plenty of bitter enemies back at home. And this, perhaps, was the even more important subtext of his American journey: it was carefully designed to build momentum for the reforms to come. Each stage of his itinerary was exhaustively covered by the Chinese media, who conveyed every detail to an audience of hundreds of millions of people. The Chinese heard radio broadcasts about factories where industrial robots already worked with humans at the assembly line and machines that could make you believe that you were flying. Those lucky few with access to TV sets—still a rare commodity in preform China—saw images of skyscrapers and glistening shopping centers and highways filled with cars that were apparently (astounding as it seemed) mostly owned by ordinary Americans.

By the time Deng embarked on his American visit, he was already unusually well traveled for a Chinese politician (even disregarding his youthful years in France and the Soviet Union). In 1974 he had attended the United Nations session in New York, and then, after his return to power in the wake of Mao's death, he had taken a series of other trips around East Asia, including one to Southeast Asia and one to Japan. (It was these visits that had such a profound impact on his thinking in the run-up to the Central Party Work Conference.) All of these journeys had brought tangible benefits—including vital industrial investments from the Japanese as well as useful advice on the advantages of authoritarian capitalism from Singaporean prime minister Lee Kwan Yew. His visits to Singapore and Japan had also yielded plenty of favorable coverage in the media back home. But none of these trips had quite the impact of the one he took to America. It is one thing to hear about the advantages of an open economy; it is another to see them. Deng's trip to the United States brought the potential benefits of modernization into the homes of ordinary Chinese. As for Deng himself, he later told his colleagues that his experiences in America had kept him awake for several nights after returning home. How could China possibly catch up?[26]

The triumph of Deng's visit added to the growing political momentum in favor of change. In January, while Deng was still away, a crowd of high-ranking guests gathered in the Great Hall of the People. There was no mistaking the sense of euphoria. It was January 1979, the first time in fifteen years that the Communist Party elite had gathered to mark the beginning of the Chinese Lunar New Year. The Cultural Revolutionaries had banned the Spring Festival (the most important Chinese holiday, analogous, perhaps, to Christmas in the West) as a vestige of out-moded tradition. But now Mao was gone, and many of the guests were celebrating their return from oblivion. The widow of Liu Shaoqi, the former head of state who had been tortured to death by Red Guards, rubbed elbows with a once-disgraced vice premier who, like her, had been banished from public view for years. Peng Zhen, the former Beijing mayor who had been savagely vilified and abused at the start of the Cultural Revolution, announced that he was ready to return to work after a decade of exile in the countryside. All of them offered ritual praise to Hua Guofeng, but they knew whom they really had to thank for their political resurrection.

These people were Deng Xiaoping's past. Like them he had emerged from the ruins of the old imperial order to pledge himself to the Communist ideal, one that had little prospect of success in the beginning. Like them he had weathered the horrors of the Long March, when the Communist guerrilla army had staged its epic escape from the Nationalist armies of Chiang Kai-shek in 1934. Like them he had endured the humiliations of the Cultural Revolution and reemerged to release the

country from Mao's ideological straitjacket. Like them he was responsible for countless lives destroyed in political intrigues or on the battlefields of the wars against
Japan and Chiang. And, like them, he had navigated his way through countless
moral compromises along the way. The ex-Beijing mayor Peng, for example, had
been one of Deng's allies until he became one of the first senior officials to fall from
grace in 1965–1966. Deng had disavowed him—the kind of betrayal committed by
many others during those harrowing years. (Indeed, the path of the Cultural Revolution had been so tortuous that individual stories often fused the roles of victim
and perpetrator.) Still, Peng would prove to be a crucial supporter of Deng and the
economic reform program in the years ahead.[7] Contradictions ran deeply through
all the biographies of these party survivors.

Yet, almost miraculously, most of them continued to remain deeply loyal to the
Communist Party. They shared Deng's belief that it was only the party that could
lead China forward to modernization. After all, they had not brought the revolution to its fruition in 1949 only to relinquish power. They wanted to tame Mao's
legacy, not to eliminate it altogether. They wanted to repair the injustices committed under his rule—which they viewed primarily in terms of the damage he had
done to the party itself.

But many ordinary Chinese did not necessarily see things this way. Discontent
ran deeply through the countryside, where the material situation of the peasantry
had improved little since the early 1960s, after the Great Leap Forward had devastated their way of life and plunged the countryside into starvation. Workers, exhausted by a decade of sloganeering, raucous campaigns, and sometimes even open
warfare, also remained impoverished. The students now flooding back to the cities
jostled for precious spots in the universities and institutes, where academic life was
still in the process of returning to normal.

The most obvious public sign of the festering contradictions of Chinese society
was the presence of the petitioners. For months, hundreds of thousands of people
had been appearing in the cities to ask redress for the suffering they had endured
during the revolutionary caprice and mob rule of the previous decade. Like other
Communist societies, the People's Republic had an institutionalized process for
handling petitions. But the offices designed to cope with demands for rehabilitation or the restoration of property found themselves overwhelmed. Petitioners who
found themselves unable to find a receptive audience in their hometowns often traveled hundreds or thousands of miles—sometimes on foot—to seek better treatment in Beijing. Some of them even pressed their demands with public demonstrations. The British diplomat Roger Garside, perhaps the best foreign observer of
this period in China, encountered a group of these justice seekers freshly arrived

from the countryside in central Beijing. Their clothes ragged and patched, their faces sunburned nearly black, the elderly petitioners evoked all too vividly the dire poverty that the "New China" was supposed to have eliminated for good after the Communist takeover in 1949. Garside described another group he encountered in January 1979 as the "angriest group of people" he had ever met.[8] It was easy to understand why. Officials at the lower levels usually had little in the way of reparations to offer, or were ill-inclined to satisfy demands for justice that might cast a poor light on the party. And all too few of the petitioners who made the trip were able to find satisfaction in Beijing, either.

Deng's focus on raising living standards certainly offered one way of addressing the general yearning for change. But some of his policies cut in a different direction. During his visit to the United States, Deng had warned President Carter that China was preparing a "punitive strike" against Vietnam, which, in the Chinese view, had grown a bit too self-assured in its role as Moscow's proxy in Southeast Asia. (Among their other offenses, the Vietnamese had invaded Cambodia in December 1978, bringing down the Chinese-supported regime of the Khmer Rouge, which had just completed one of the century's most horrific genocides against its own people.) On February 17, 1979, Deng made good on his threat. Two hundred thousand Chinese troops crossed the border into Vietnam, confident that they would quickly inflict a humiliating defeat on the uppity Vietnamese Communist Party. Instead, the result was a shocking humiliation for the People's Liberation Army, and the first serious political setback for Deng since his ascent to the summit of the political hierarchy. In the first two weeks of the war, the Chinese force managed to penetrate only twenty-five miles into Vietnamese territory. The commanders of the People's Liberation Army needed just one month to decide that they had had enough. They pulled back to the border, destroying everything they could along the way. In those four weeks, according to one Western analysis, twenty-six thousand Chinese soldiers were killed and tens of thousands of others wounded.[9] Both sides in the conflict declared victory. In reality, it was an utterly pointless exercise for all concerned.

Needless to say, the official party media maintained strict discipline on the subject, trumpeting China's achievements and ignoring the problems. But for once, those who disagreed with the government's foreign policy had a forum to air their concerns. The writers at Democracy Wall were quick to pick up on the theme. The text of one poster criticized the leaders of a "big country like China" for "striking a little child like Vietnam."[10] This was not the sort of open challenge to his authority that Deng was prepared to tolerate.

Among the voices demanding change at Democracy Wall was a stocky young man who worked as an electrician at the Beijing Zoo. This was a former Red Guard by the name of Wei Jingsheng. During the Cultural Revolution, he had enthusiastically embraced Mao's call to overturn the established order. His revolutionary enthusiasm launched him on a prolonged journey deep into the interior, where he saw first-hand the extraordinary poverty and backwardness of rural China. He witnessed the famine conditions that still plagued the peasantry years after the end of the Great Leap. He heard about the injustices committed against farmers and workers by party activists who claimed to hold their best interests at heart. The experience changed him forever. After Mao's death, as the memory of utopian hysteria ebbed away, Wei returned to the capital a deeply disillusioned man. On December 5, 1978, he posted a text at Xidan Democracy Wall that presented the conclusions he had drawn.

Its title was "The Fifth Modernization," a reference to the "Four Modernizations" that were now being held high by Deng and other reformers eager to prioritize economic development over ideology. Wei began by observing that popular opinion strongly approved of Deng's new emphasis on pragmatism: "The people expected him to review the past and lead them to a realistic future with a 'seeking truth from facts' approach." Yet, he noted, the party's willingness to correct or revise Maoist ideology only went so far. The fundamental principle of Communist Party rule in China brooked no modification. It was merely being clothed in new slogans—"the Four Modernizations"—that offered no substantive change. Wei advised his compatriots to cease believing in the "political swindlers" and urged them to start trusting their own judgment. "We have been tempered in the Cultural Revolution and cannot be that ignorant now," he wrote. "Let us find out for ourselves what should be done."

What was needed, he said, was not the sort of limited reform proposed by Deng and the other party elders. Wei wanted something he called "true democracy," which he defined as the right of the people to choose their own representatives. The Americans, the Japanese, and the French all had the political power to run their own leaders out of office. In China, by contrast, anyone daring enough to make critical remarks about the deceased Chairman Mao could expect to end up in jail. This was not the way it should be: "We want to be masters of our own destiny. We need no gods or emperors. We do not believe in the existence of any savior. We want to be masters of the world and not instruments used by autocrats to carry out their wild ambitions. We want a modern lifestyle and democracy for the people. Freedom and happiness are our sole objectives in accomplishing modernization. Without this fifth modernization all others are merely another promise."[11]

Many of the earlier Democracy Wall writers had assailed Mao or the Gang of Four without challenging the precepts of Communist rule itself. Wei was different. He dared to question the very basis of the system. His principled stand soon brought him in contact with other liberal dissidents, and together they began to publish a new magazine called *Explorations*, in which they pushed the boundaries even further with pieces that exposed the caprice and injustice of one-party rule. They were not alone in this. They were merely the vanguard of a broader movement that seized upon the new opportunities for expression to demand greater freedom.

On January 27, 1979, before his departure for the United States, Deng had given a speech that had seemed to acknowledge the necessity of deeper reforms. He had acknowledged the failures of socialism and even declared that China should emulate the "bourgeois countries" in their practice of democracy. "We should find a way to let people feel that they are masters of the country." (Tellingly enough, this speech was not included in his *Selected Works*.)[12]

Yet within just a few weeks, his public stance shifted dramatically. We do not, of course, know what was going on inside Deng's head. But judging by the way events developed, it is reasonable to conclude that this shift had less to do with the evolution of his beliefs than with a coolheaded assessment of his own political position. Deng was happy to tolerate a certain degree of public questioning as long as it undermined his opponents. But now the Gang of Four was behind bars, the radicals had been defeated, and Hua had been pushed aside. There was no longer any reason for Deng to allow pluralism—and especially not when it called into question the very foundations of the People's Republic. The public criticisms of the war in Vietnam by dissidents like Wei proved the last straw.

Responding to signals of an impending crackdown, Wei proceeded to burn his bridges. On March 25, 1979, he published an essay titled "Do We Want Democracy or New Dictatorship?" The title said it all: the text directly challenged Deng's new ascendancy. Wei was arrested three days after his poster appeared. Police tore down the text. Tellingly, the authorities charged him with passing military secrets about the brief war with Vietnam to foreigners—a clear indication that this episode had become a neuralgic point for the leadership. When Wei appeared in court later in the year, the state prosecutor accused him of acting as the "running dog of Vietnam."[13] He would remain in prison for another fifteen years.

The wall's glory days were over. At the end of March, Beijing city authorities finally cracked down. Police banned further posters and directed would-be writers to a new site far on the outskirts of the city (where, of course, no one would see what they wrote). A wave of arrests swept up other government critics. At least one official publication was banned. The petitioners also felt the heat. Even as the party pushed ahead with the immense job of righting some of the most obvious injustices, the security forces implemented their own solution. Leaders of the biggest groups of petitioners disappeared into prisons and labor camps.[13]

As always, Deng understood that simply unleashing the men with the guns was not enough. He needed to explain away his own reversal on the value of "bourgeois" democracy, and the party needed an ideological underpinning for its tightening of the screws. The reasons for ending the political thaw, which some had already dubbed the "Beijing Spring," had to be made explicit and unmistakable. In a major speech on March 30, 1979, Deng proceeded to elucidate what he called "the four basic principles" (in symbolic equilibrium with the "Four Modernizations"). Every party member, he urged, should uphold "the socialist road," "the dictatorship of the proletariat," "the leadership of the Communist Party," and "Marxism-Leninism and Mao Zedong Thought." It was only by sticking to these ground rules, he told his audience, that the country's leadership could ensure the stability needed to push ahead with necessary economic reforms. Deng did not need to do much to evoke the ancient Chinese fear of "chaos"; the terrors of the Cultural Revolution were still all too present to his audience. He spent much of his text assailing the temerity of the democratic dissidents who challenged the party's right to rule.

Deng had never been a liberal democrat to begin with. But his experiences since 1966 had merely reinforced this tendency. For him and many other party members of his generation, the word *democracy*—often invoked by Mao and the radical students who had worshiped him—evoked the mob rule of the Cultural Revolution as much as anything else. Deng had no intention of ceding control to the streets, and that message comes through with brutal directness in the speech, which is noteworthy for the ferocity with which it assails the new generation of dissidents. Deng mentioned by name the Chinese Human Rights League, a group that incited his ire by calling upon President Carter to "show concern" for human rights in China. The new paramount leader of the Chinese Communist Party was having none of it. "What kind of democracy do the Chinese people need today?" Deng asked. "It can only be socialist democracy, people's democracy, and not bourgeois democracy, individualist democracy."[15]

But he did not forget to proffer a carrot. Once again stressing his fidelity to the "Four Modernizations," Deng made sure to signal that economic reform would continue unabated. Those who wanted to challenge the regime directly now fell silent. But at the same time, a certain measure of liberalization persisted. The reopening of educational institutions continued. A huge rehabilitation effort, engineered largely by Hu Yaobang (the reformer who had left his stamp on the Central Party Work Conference), cleared the charges against countless victims of the Cultural

Revolution. And the party restored "citizens' rights" to some ten million people who, as the children of landlords or rich peasants, had borne the brunt of official discrimination due to their class origins through most of Mao's reign. Deng saw no contradiction between his toleration of mainstream intellectuals and his harsh treatment of the democracy movement. "Intellectuals, especially members of the established intelligentsia, posed no political threat to the regime," notes historian Maurice Meisner. "They had no organizations of their own beyond those under the firm control of the party."[16]

Deng was determined to maintain his own freedom of maneuver. Economic and administrative reforms would continue. But the Beijing Spring was over.

14

The Evangelist

In most of Britain, the day of the general election dawned cool and overcast. As voters walked to their polling stations, some of them noticed the front page of the *Sun*, prominently displayed at the front of the newsstands. The tabloid, owned by press baron Rupert Murdoch, had long exulted in its status as the preferred reading of the working class; no one, it was considered, commanded the affections of the traditional Labour voter like the *Sun*. (This, indeed, was the same newspaper that had once dubbed Margaret Thatcher "the Milk Snatcher.")[1] So its editorial message on this day, splashed across the front page, was all the more shocking: "Vote Tory this time. It's the only way to stop the rot." The members of the print workers' union at the paper did their best to sabotage the day's edition, even cutting parts of the text they didn't agree with. The editors still managed to get it out, though a bit late.[2]

It was apparent, by the end of the five-week election campaign, that Thatcher's message of change had resonated with her audience. Callaghan had acknowledged this widespread desire and tried to present himself as the candidate who would ensure that change came in a "controlled" way, without the chaos that, according to him, the Tories' radical "free-market" approach was sure to bring. But the humiliations of the Winter of Discontent were still fresh, and many voters now saw "Sunny Jim" above all as the man who had allowed the unions to roll over his government. These disillusioned Britons were willing to take a chance on someone truly new.

Many of those who cast their ballots for Thatcher that day were voting against a lifetime of political habit. The famously left-wing playwright Harold Pinter, vexed by "union selfishness," cast his vote for Thatcher, as did his wife, the writer Lady Antonia Fraser. The theater director Peter Hall, who had voted for Labour since the 1950s, struggled with conflicting feelings, but ultimately opted for the Conservatives with his vote as well, noting in his diary that "we have to have change." Journalist Stephen Fay also voted for the Tories for the first time "because he felt we needed a corrective."[3]

But it was not only the traditionally left-of-center intellectuals who found it in their hearts to make the change. So, too, did a remarkable number of skilled workers, the legendary "C2s" of the statisticians. In some parts of the industrial Southeast (including the city that was home to the giant Ford plant that had played such an important role during the unrest of the fall), up to 13 percent of the traditional Labour electorate switched to the Tories. Even among members of the unions, there was substantial support for Thatcher's positions: 51 percent thought that the Conservatives had the best tax policies, and a shocking 37 percent even believed that Thatcher's party had the best approach to combating unemployment. Meanwhile, support for the Liberal Party, the political home of centrists, evaporated—an indication that Britons, at least on this day, were willing to vote for a more sharply defined alternative.[4]

In the afternoon Callaghan called his key aide, Bernard Donoughue, and gave him the bad news: "Mrs. Thatcher [will] be in No. 10 as Prime Minister tomorrow. So we must be out by 3:30 PM." The polling stations were scheduled to close at 10 p.m., but preliminary counts and exit polls were already showing the scale of Callaghan's defeat. The Conservative Party won 44 percent of the vote, translating into a parliamentary majority of forty-three seats. Thatcher's strategy of aggressively targeting Labour voters had paid off dramatically: the 5.2 percent swing from Labour to Conservative was the largest in any election since 1945.

But this was not the only ingredient of her triumph. Simon Heffer, a recent Cambridge graduate who was working in a pub at the time of the 1979 election, represented yet another important segment of the pro-Thatcher vote: a rising new generation of Conservatives who rejected the clubbiness of the postwar party and wanted to see a new, meritocratic Britain. On the night of the election, he attended a Tory victory party with several of his university friends, and as they watched the returns come in on the BBC, they exulted in the palpable sense of a watershed. "It was as if we had been dragged into the modern era, and that prehistoric world where the country was governed by unelected trade unions was over."[5]

On the afternoon of May 4, Thatcher paid the traditional visit to the queen in Buckingham Palace. When she descended the stairs, she was met, according to tradition, by the principal private secretary to the prime minister—in this case, Kenneth Stowe, who had accompanied Callaghan to the palace when he had left Number Ten Downing Street earlier in the day. Now he escorted Thatcher back to the prime minister's residence. There, standing in front of the TV cameras, she recited an uplifting quote attributed to Saint Francis of Assisi: "Where there is discord, may we bring harmony. Where there is error, may we bring truth. Where there is doubt, may we bring faith. And where there is despair, may we bring hope."

In fact—though few picked up on it at the time—the prayer was of solidly nineteenth-century origins. But no matter. The passage had been chosen for her by her chief speechwriter, Ronnie Millar. Thatcher was not especially keen on it at first. Still, it was her first public statement as prime minister, and as such it was subjected to copious analysis. Most of the commentators focused on her call for harmony, which few of them took seriously. As her biographer John Campbell noted, no one paid particular attention to the middle lines of the quatrain, which neatly summed up her sense of her own mission. Saint Francis, after all, was a reformer whose deeply held beliefs infused a radical program of social renewal. As another observer put it at the time, she was the first "political evangelist" of any stripe to enter Number Ten since 1945.[6]

The ambiguity of the quote—invoking both consensus and polarization—nicely summed up the political reality in which Thatcher found herself. She had fought the election by forcefully promising change, yet she had done so on a platform that was vague on the details. This was no accident. The Margaret Thatcher we envision when he hear her name today did not emerge in all of her glory from the general election of 1979. She was an evangelist, to be sure, but she was also an eminently practical politician, and she understood perfectly well that she could not unduly try the patience of her voters. Nonetheless, there was no mistaking the decisiveness with which she moved ahead.

The situation the new government faced was dire. Britain in 1979 was a country that had been "collectivized" to an extraordinary degree. Nearly a third of the 25 million Britons who had jobs worked in the public sector. The civil service was roughly twice the size it had been in 1939. Nearly half of the people working in manufacturing were employed by nationalized industries. Public-sector corporations had enormous debts, and the government was pouring subsidies into the industries it controlled. Most of that cash was being spent on declining businesses like coal (which was producing a third less than in 1938 despite the injection of public funds) and the railways (which were offering one-half as many miles of service as in 1938). In the private sector, two huge union organizations had an almost unchallenged say over policy—even though the number of working days lost to strikes was eight times higher than in the years before World War II. Meanwhile, inflation had drastically eroded the value of the pound sterling. One pound in 1980 had one-twentieth the purchasing power of the same amount of currency in 1938. Prices had risen by an average of 13 percent over 1978–1979 and showed no sign of slowing.[7]

Thatcher had been waiting in the wings for four years, enough time for her to devise a blueprint for what she wanted to do. When the time came, she was ready, and she got down to work with noteworthy speed. She needed all of two days to assemble her new government—a remarkable achievement considering the modest resources of the British prime minister's office (especially when compared with the enormous apparatus that stands behind every US president). She had always made a point of working harder than anyone else around her, and she continued that ethos as prime minister, sleeping as little as four hours a night. That left plenty of time for her to stoke her bottomless appetite for briefing books and memoranda. Her mastery of homework was a lifelong point of pride.

It was also a weapon of control. She was determined to know the subject matter of government better than any and all of her ministers. As for the professional bureaucrats of the British civil service, Thatcher regarded them as suspect from the start. They were, she believed, sly defenders of the entrenched status quo, and she was not going to let them get the better of her. She believed that career civil servants would always find ways to undermine directives from the political leadership; she was convinced, among other things, that resistance from left-leaning officials had been a major cause of Heath's downfall, and she was determined not to tolerate it. From the very beginning of her stint at Number Ten, she looked for ways to supersede or bypass the bureaucrats wherever she could. She paid surprise visits to the ministries, and she carefully noted who was likely to go along with her program and who was not. Over time she came to realize that most of these highly professional government officials were willing to implement the course that she set, and she gradually relaxed. Still, from the very beginning she began to make a habit of appointing special political advisers to help her formulate policy on particular issues. And within the cabinet itself, she took care to appoint her own loyalists to the most important economic positions.

Perhaps her most significant appointment was the one she did not make. The minister with the most direct responsibility for the British economy is the chancellor of the Exchequer, and many onlookers assumed that her natural choice for this position was Keith Joseph. He was, after all, her avowed mentor on economic issues. It was Joseph who had first dared to challenge Heath for the leadership in

1975, and it was Joseph who had done the most to lay the groundwork for an intel-
lectually credible challenge to the reigning mixed-economy consensus. Yet many of
Joseph's colleagues—not to mention Thatcher herself—had harbored doubts about
his steadiness ever since the gaffe that had ended his ministerial ambitions. In the
event she passed him over for the big job. She chose him instead as the secretary
of state for industry, where he was to supervise the state-owned corporations, the
commanding heights of the British economy. "To put Joseph in charge of the one
Whitehall department whose whole purpose was to pursue active government industrial policies was the political equivalent of putting a monk in charge of a whore-
house," one commentator wrote at the time.[8] As it happened, Joseph's reputation
as a crusader for the free market was little in evidence during his term—further
confirmation, to his doubters, that he was more of a talker than a doer. The first
year of the Thatcher government brought only a few cautious measures to expose
the nationalized industries to greater market competition; a few shares were sold in
some of the companies. Joseph gained notoriety primarily for his efforts to win even
greater allocations of budget funds for his charges.

It was, instead, Geoffrey Howe that Thatcher picked to be her chancellor of the
Exchequer. It was a revealing choice. Howe boasted nothing of Joseph's oratorical
flair. The famously caustic Labour politician Denis Healey memorably compared
listening to Howe in the House of Commons to "being savaged by a dead sheep."
But Thatcher was not looking for flashiness. For years Howe had been quietly carving out a name for himself as a student of monetarist theory and market-oriented
policies. His somewhat pedestrian exterior concealed a spirit of remarkable tenac-
ity. On the surface he seemed to have little of Thatcher's combativeness, but he was,
in fact, impossible to dislodge on an issue once he had made up his mind. True to
form, he was to prove one of the most persistent of Thatcher's ministers, remaining
in the cabinet almost until the end of her administration.

Shepherded by an anxious prime minister, Howe now set to work devising the
new government's first budget. The scheduling of the election left him just a few
weeks for the task. Thatcher was determined to use the 1979 budget as the occasion for a stark declaration of her policy priorities for the economy. In the event, the
supposedly plodding Howe proved that his instincts were even more radical than
hers. His budget not only proposed dramatic cuts in income tax and public spending and a considerable tightening of the money supply—all principles laid out in
the election manifesto—but also ushered in the dismantling of exchange controls.
There could be no clearer statement of the new government's commitment to the
workings of the market. But it was a highly risky move. The turbulence that had

plagued the British economy in the preceding years had not inspired great confidence in foreign investors. The removal of controls could potentially spark a run on the pound sterling—a horrendous prospect for a newly inducted prime minister. In her memoirs Thatcher claimed to be on board with Howe's move from the start. In fact, as Howe later recalled, she needed considerable persuading.

The budget that Howe revealed to the nation in June 1979 thus made for a radical departure. It slashed the rate of income tax for top earners from a punitive 83 percent to 60, and took the basic rate from 33 percent to 30. It unveiled the first steps toward the elimination of exchange controls. (The chancellor waited until later in the year to abolish them altogether.) Howe also announced deep cuts in public spending—though he boosted funding for the military and the police, in line with Thatcher's election pledges. That meant that some revenues would still have to be increased, and Howe did it by raising taxes on consumption. The budget accordingly provided for a sharp rise in value-added tax, which now rose to 15 percent. This point also gave Thatcher cause for nervousness. As she was perfectly aware, the hike in VAT would add several percentage points to retail prices, thus contributing to inflationary pressures.

This was not the only factor that looked likely to undermine price stability. In its final months the Callaghan government had agreed on substantial pay hikes for public-sector unions, and during her campaign Thatcher had agreed to respect her predecessor's pledges. Just as expected, inflation rose. The consumer price index jumped from 11 percent in the summer to 20 percent by the end of 1979.

Thatcher and Howe believed that they knew the solution. It was Milton Friedman who had declared—with bracing but controversial clarity—that "inflation is always and everywhere a monetary phenomenon." In the view of Friedman and other monetarists, the notion that governments could tame inflation by demand-side methods, like tinkering with wage and price controls, was utterly illusory. The acolytes of monetarism insisted instead that government's task was to ensure price stability by restraining the supply of money in circulation—or, to use the more populist formulation, to slow down the rate at which government printing presses were turning out banknotes. Thatcher's team was not breaking entirely new ground here. Key members of the Callaghan government's economic team—above all his own chancellor, Denis Healey—had already accepted the basic monetarist premise. So, too, had the directors of the Bundesbank, the central bank that had presided over West Germany's economic miracle (and thus represented a prominent foreign model for the Thatcherites). And in the United States that autumn of 1979, the new chief of the Federal Reserve, Paul Volcker, launched a tight money policy also aimed at tamping down his country's high rate of inflation.

But no one went about it with quite the same single-mindedness as the new government in London. Howe pledged to squeeze the money supply a few percentage points beyond what Healey had done, and he backed it up by raising interest rates from 12 percent to 14 percent. In June, he raised them again, from 14 to 17 percent—the largest one-day hike in British history. This amounted to a serious austerity program. Unemployment, exacerbated by the cuts in government spending, continued to climb. This was, perhaps, a bit more determination than the commercial class had counted on from the new prime minister. British business associations—noting continuing threats from the unions, Thatcher's pledges of monetary restraint, and the generally dim prospects for global growth—predicted a rash of bankruptcies. After reaching a euphoric high upon her election, the British stock market plummeted in the first few months after Thatcher took office.[9]

Thatcher, however, was determined to push ahead. The critics who attacked monetarism as an exercise in scholasticism were missing the point. For all her attention to political ideas, Thatcher was not interested in doctrine for the sake of doctrine. She drew her motivation from values, a firmly held set of moral principles; policy was just a way of putting them into action. The distinction is important. Shirley Robin Letwin, one of Thatcher's most persuasive apologists, argues that the key to understanding Thatcher is not ideology but a core ideal. For her, Thatcherism is a practical approach to achieving certain political ends in the specific historical context of Britain at the end of the 1970s. Thatcherism, she argues, was above all an effort to promote certain "vigorous virtues." It aimed to restore the primacy of the individual by nurturing a sense of personal choice and responsibility and to revive the family's role as the basic unit of society, and it aspired to achieve these goals without resorting to active government intervention. It was this political agenda, she writes, that explained the distinctive style of government that characterized the Thatcher administration. In her pursuit of these "vigorous virtues," Thatcher inevitably assumed a role as the "leader of a crusade," a "continuous revolution."[10]

In this reading, the Thatcherites were drawn to monetarism not because they had particular views on the technicalities of the monetary supply but because the monetarists stipulated that direct government management of the economy through the control of prices, wages, dividends, or foreign exchange was inefficient and wrong. Thatcher's supporters often made the point, in later years, that she herself never

approved of the conceit of "Thatcherism." It is true that did not see herself as the
progenitor of an economic theory. What she aspired to do above all else was to
restore to Britons a sense of individual agency, to create an environment that rewarded entrepreneurial risk and self-sufficiency and did away with the notion that
government could be relied upon to meet all needs. In economic policy, this translated into the assumption that it was not the business of government to microman-
age economic activity. Privatization was consistent with this view. So, too, was her
consistent opposition to any form of wage and price controls.[11] This was an instinct
that she first revealed, with bracing clarity, in 1979. When Thatcher took office, the
British government had a long-established mechanism that held down prices on a
number of retail goods. It was clear that lifting the controls would fuel already gal-
loping inflation. But she quickly moved ahead to dismantle them.

Thatcher regarded economics as the realm in which the most decisive battles
would be fought, and it was above all for her economic policies that she is remembered. Cutting taxes, reducing public spending, curtailing the money supply, and
lifting controls on foreign exchange were all measures that she began in 1979, thus
making a clear break with the principles of the postwar consensus and laying the
groundwork for even more crucial reforms that were to come later.

Needless to say, there were other matters that demanded her attention during
her first year in office. Quite a lot of her time went to the problem of Northern Ireland, where the situation had steadily deteriorated throughout the 1970s. In August
1979 things took a dramatic turn for the worse. That was the month the Provisional
Irish Republican Army managed to assassinate Lord Mountbatten, the last viceroy
of India, by blowing up his boat during a vacation on the Irish coast. The same day
the IRA staged a carefully engineered ambush outside of the Northern Irish town
of Warrenpoint that took the lives of eighteen British soldiers—the largest loss
suffered in a single incident by British security forces during the Troubles. The two
attacks presaged a long and bitter struggle with Irish Republicans that would run
straight through the Thatcher era. She responded by ratcheting up British military
action against the IRA—a tough and resolute policy that was sure to invite retaliation from the Nationalists, and did, years down the road.

The most immediate foreign policy issue to be resolved was the problem of Rho-
desia, where the minority white population was struggling to cling to power in the
face of an armed struggle conducted by several revolutionary anticolonial movements. In the end, despite a certain degree of resistance from those within her own
party who maintained ties with the white settlers, Thatcher managed to find an elegant diplomatic solution that allowed Britain to divorce itself from the colony and
ensured majority rule. Her success was attributed, in part, to a highly effective (and

photogenic) goodwill gesture: her dance with Zambian president Kenneth Kaunda at a meeting of the Commonwealth countries aimed at addressing the question of Rhodesian independence. The commentators at home greeted this triumph as evidence that she was a far more practical politician than her uncompromising manner might otherwise suggest.

If they thought that they had figured her out, however, she soon moved to confound them. In November 1979 she attended her first European Economic Community (EEC) summit meeting in Dublin. There she presented the other heads of state with a demand that no other British leader had made before her in such categorical terms. For some time it had been clear that the United Kingdom was paying more into the European budget than it took out. Contrary to existing EEC policy, Thatcher now informed her colleagues that Britain wanted the extra money back. They agreed to consider the matter and resolved to move on to other points on the agenda. Thatcher, having made the point, then continued to make it, for hours. German chancellor Helmut Schmidt and French president Valéry Giscard d'Estaing, who were accustomed to having their way at European get-togethers, displayed their disapproval. Schmidt ostentatiously began to leaf through his newspaper. Giscard d'Estaing pretended to fall asleep. Thatcher went on. Giscard d'Estaing ordered his driver to rev the car engine outside the windows of the summit venue. Still Thatcher continued. No one had seen anything like it. Giscard d'Estaing later stated publicly that the summit, completely overshadowed by this single issue, had been on the brink of collapse several times.

Thatcher was unrepentant. "I left our partners in no doubt that my room for maneuver was limited, but I did not feel it right to refuse to make this further effort," she later told parliamentarians. "We should get more, and it is worth while going on negotiating to get more, particularly as a number of countries in the Council of Ministers were trying very hard to help us achieve a better result." Down the road European leaders ultimately granted Britain a rebate far beyond what the Foreign Office had considered possible. But it came at the cost of considerable damage to Britain's reputation as a reliable player on the European stage—doubts that lingered for the rest of Thatcher's term in office and beyond.

Of the many pressing issues that Margaret Thatcher faced in her first year, however, there was one that she had to handle with particular care. This was the weighty question of trade-union power. The Winter of Discontent and the shift in public attitudes toward the unions that it helped to bring about had been a crucial factor in the Conservative electoral win. Yet Thatcher moved relatively cautiously on this front at first.

She had good reasons for opting to proceed with care. Tackling the unions was not among her immediate priorities. Cutting taxes, adopting new monetary targets, and abolishing exchange controls took precedence—partly because they were relatively easy to do. No one's interests were directly threatened, and no legislation was immediately required.

As Thatcher understood perfectly well, moreover, her administration needed time to prepare the ground. The unions were formidable opponents, and they were deeply rooted in British political life. Here again her own experience as a minister under Heath proved a useful legacy. He had made no advance preparations to deal with the miners' strike that finished off his government. This was a mistake she would not repeat. She made a conscious choice to refrain from confronting the unions all too directly at first. Instead, she moved ahead incrementally, starting with small reforms that chipped away at the rules that made it far too easy for union leaders to launch strikes (sometimes even absent a clear mandate from their members).

But there was also a narrower reason for her hesitation, and it had to do with the dynamics of her own political organization. Thatcher had won the 1979 election as the head of a deeply divided party. Despite her victory in the 1975 leadership fight, the rest of the Conservative Party elite had remained little changed from the days of Heath. Thatcher and her like-minded colleagues remained a minority in her shadow cabinet, whose membership largely overlapped with the ministerial team that had governed from 1970 to 1974. Many of these shadow ministers were Tory heavyweights, backed by powerful constituencies and decidedly loyal, if not to Heath himself, then to the brand of consensus politics that he had seemed to embody.

In public Thatcher spoke in ringing tones of the need for a "conviction cabinet" that mirrored her own evangelical political style:

> If you're going to do the things you want to do—and I'm only in politics to do things—you've got to have a togetherness and unity in your Cabinet. There are two ways of making a Cabinet. One way is to have in it people who represent all the different viewpoints within the party, within the broad philosophy. The other way is to have in it only the people who want to go in the direction in which every instinct tells me we have to go. Clearly, steadily, firmly, with resolution. We've got to go in an agreed and clear direction.[12]

The reality was starkly different, and in private her tone reflected that. In a small gathering in Number Ten she once referred to herself dramatically as "the rebel head of an establishment government."[13] This was perhaps not quite as strange as it sounded; at least one observer of the British political system argues that prime ministers must behave like rebels within their cabinets while projecting unity to the outside.[14] But Thatcher, it turned out, had to work much harder than many prime ministers to have her way.

Journalist Hugo Young observes that Thatcher's 1979 government team manifested less "togetherness" than any other postwar cabinet.[15] This had many reasons. One of them, at least partly, was the matter of her gender. (Conservative grandees were not the only ones guilty of lingering chauvinism, of course. On her first visit to NATO headquarters in Brussels, journalists considered it entirely legitimate to ask, "What are you going to do with your handbag?")[16] Her team was dominated by pillars of the establishment, just the sort of people one might expect to find in a Conservative Party government—and this also meant that they were men. Six of her ministers were alumni of the Guards, the senior regiment of the British Army, and six were alumni of Eton. Universities other than Cambridge and Oxford barely figured in the mix. On this score, at least, the grocer's daughter could claim a degree of commonality—but only up to a point. Although she was a natural politician, her social origins certainly did not predestine her to be a member of the ruling class. Politically, only six out of the twenty-two could be considered her allies. As later became known, only one of them had actually voted for her on the first secret ballot in the leadership contest in 1975.[17] She had beaten Heath because she marshaled the most credible challenge to his leadership—not because everyone agreed with her views.[18]

As leader of the opposition she had succeeded, to a considerable degree, in papering over some of the resulting divisions. Policy toward the unions was a case in point. In late 1977 two of Thatcher's stalwarts, John Hoskyns and Norman Strauss, presented the party leaders with a memorandum titled "Stepping Stones." In their paper the authors made a passionate case that confronting the unions had to be the centerpiece of any serious strategy to reverse Britain's economic decline. Rather than sticking to the consensus view that dictated compromise with the unions, Hoskyns and Strauss insisted that it was time for the Conservatives to pursue a long-term strategy of identifying organized labor as an obstacle to prosperity. This was too much for the Heathites. Thatcher had chosen one of them, party grandee James Prior, to serve as the shadow cabinet's point man on industrial relations precisely because his reputation as a compromiser would mollify labor leaders. While Prior agreed in principle that union powers needed to be reduced, in practice he favored a characteristically Heathite course of accommodation. He pronounced "Stepping

Stones" a provocation that could sabotage the party's prospects of winning the next election if its contents became known. He prevailed upon Thatcher to keep it out of the public eye. (Party chairman Peter Thorneycroft, who later proved himself a devoted monetarist, actually demanded that every existing copy be burned.) But "Stepping Stones" remained enormously influential within her administration—especially after the Winter of Discontent shifted the boundaries of public tolerance for union behavior. This divide returned when the Conservatives began drawing up their manifesto for the 1979 election. Thatcher, confident that voters were ready for a change, proposed several specific reforms (including a law against secondary picketing and a ban on strikes by public-sector workers). But she met with stiff resistance from the moderates, and the language of the manifesto was watered down accordingly.[19]

During Thatcher's first term in office, indeed, it was above all the split within her own party that most vividly expressed the challenge she faced. The aim of the Thatcherite counterrevolution was to dismantle the postwar consensus, and no one embodied this better than the Heathites within her own cabinet. A nineteenth-century term was revived to express the distinction: the Thatcherites were the "dries," like the arch-conservatives of the Victorian era, while the centrists came to be known as the "wets," evoking a political pedigree that went back to the One-Nation Tories of Disraeli, who insisted that Conservatives should pursue policies that addressed national interests rather than sectional ones. Prior, in this scheme, functioned as the "chief wet" of Thatcher's first cabinet. As her secretary for employment, he was the only one of the moderates to hold an economic office. His centrist stalwarts included the eloquent Ian Gilmour, whose later book, *Dancing with Dogma*, provides perhaps the best elucidation of the moderates' views. Another, the aristocrat Peter Carrington, served as her foreign minister, while Willie Whitelaw, popular among the party rank-and-file, became her home secretary and deputy prime minister.

The wets revolted against both the style and the substance of Thatcher's new order. There was, to begin with, her habit of browbeating her colleagues—an approach that applied to her allies as well as her enemies. Though she was famously kind to her personal staff, her attitude toward the members of her cabinet was relentless. She harangued them like schoolboys. Even her longtime friend Keith Joseph came to dread his sessions with her; before heading off to meet her, he would tell his staff "to send two ambulances at 3 o'clock." Whitelaw told a confidant that, for the first time in his life, politics had ceased to be "fun."[20] "Fun," of course, was a very poor description of what Thatcher was about. Her domineering manner grated on her middle-aged male colleagues who, thanks to their traditionalist upbringings, were accustomed to deference from the women in their lives. James Prior was writing only partly in jest when he confessed in his memoir that "I found [Thatcher's bossiness] very difficult to stomach and this form of male chauvinism was obviously one of my failings."[21]

She made things worse with her habit of filling the key economic posts in her cabinet with like-minded allies while reserving the less important positions for the moderates. Her tendency to rely on ad hoc groups of advisers and loyalists also alienated the wets. Though it was not widely known at the time, for the first years of her administration she breakfasted regularly with a small group of trusted political aides who shared her views. These unofficial meetings played a major role in shaping policy.

There was little time left over for the objections of dissenters like Prior, who cast himself as the lonely voice of reason amid the clamor of right-wing fanatics. "I was telling her all the time that we should take things steadily, and not believe that we could solve all the problems by draconian legislation," wrote Prior.[22] The announcement of Howe's budget dispelled any illusions that the views of Prior and other wets would receive a fair hearing. The night before the budget was announced, Prior was having dinner with a leading union official, who asked about the rumors of an impending hike in VAT. Prior reassured him that no one was considering such madness.[23] All the greater, then, his embarrassment the next morning:

> It was really an enormous shock to me that the budget which Geoffrey produced the month after the election of 1979 was so extreme. It was then that I realized that Margaret, Geoffrey and Keith really had got the bit between their teeth and were not going to pay attention to the rest of us at all if they could possibly help it. That first budget also brought it home to me that I was really on a hiding to nothing from the very beginning, as the only economic Minister who was not of the monetarist right.[24]

Monetarism, for the wets, amounted to a doctrinaire rejection of "pragmatic" economic policy. Gilmour later published an eloquent denunciation of the "*sans culottes* of the monetarist revolution" embodied by Thatcher and her ilk. "British Conservatism is not an '-ism,'" he sneered. "It is . . . not a system of ideas. It is not an ideology or a doctrine." The wets derided the monetarists' obsession with precise money-supply targets. Prior and his colleagues also pointed out that the combination of the high pound and the new government's policies of austerity would have devastating effects on British industry, which was, certainly at first, the case. Prior sneered at treasury monetarists in his memoir as impractical ideologues whose ideas about economics came from books and lecture rooms rather than contact with business realities: "None of them had any experience of running a whelk stall, let alone a decent-sized company. Their attitude to manufacturing industry bordered on the contemptuous."[25]

None of this had much effect on Thatcher's determination to push ahead with her change of economic course. Still, Prior was somewhat more successful when it came to the government's policies on organized labor. Prior did agree to outlaw secondary picketing, but Thatcher wanted to make good on her promises in the election manifesto by cutting welfare benefits for strikers and banning secondary strikes as well. Howe proclaimed that Prior's bill was just the beginning of a longer process to bring the unions back under control, provoking equally public disagreement from Prior. This marked the beginning of what one observer described as "open war" between the two sides.[26] And that was essentially the way it remained until Thatcher began to purge them from her cabinet two years later. But she had, at least, started down the path that ultimately led to her successful challenge to union power in the miners' strike of 1984–1985.

The wets fought their corner as best they could. They scored many valid points but never quite won the argument. In their own defense, much later they pointed to the self-destructive behavior of the unions, the ineptitude of the Labour opposition, and a rightward shift in public opinion abetted by Rupert Murdoch's conservative press as factors that undermined their chances.[27] There is truth to this. There is a sense in which the wets simply found themselves on the wrong side of history. For the present-day student of politics, reading the memoirs of Prior and his like-minded colleagues is to breathe the air of a vanished age—a bit like perusing the memoirs of the aristocrats who fled revolutionary France or the liberal democrats exiled from Russia by the Bolsheviks. For better or worse, the Conservative opponents of Margaret Thatcher palpably belong to a vanished world.

Of course, one can argue that the battles of 1979 gave little indication of the revolutionary scale of what was yet to come: the epic confrontation with the coal miners, the financial deregulation of the "Big Bang," the far-reaching sell-off of state-owned corporations. Indeed, the word *privatization*, taken up by Joseph and his followers, was just on the verge of widespread acceptance, an evolution that underlined just how entrenched statist assumptions had become. (Thatcher originally preferred the less provocative *denationalization*, but it proved too unwieldy.) In 1979, though, Thatcher and her supporters spoke only of "selling shares" in the nationalized industries. There was little talk, at the time, of returning them entirely to the private sector.

All true enough. Yet it was precisely her triumph in the 1979 general election that made the rest of her reforms possible. Her victory marked a decisive break with the postwar consensus and the principles that underlay it. Margaret Thatcher was the first British politician since 1945 to declare that the drift toward socialism had to be stopped and who won a clear majority after campaigning on just this basis. Her electoral win was not a random one-off; to a large extent it reflected a fundamental shift in British thinking. Public opinion surveys from the 1970s showed, for example, a striking rise in the belief that high taxes stifled entrepreneurship and job growth.[28] A Gallup poll in 1979 showed that 77 percent of Britons surveyed favored some privatization of nationalized industries—an increase of 18 percent over the previous decade.[29] A 1976 survey revealed that a majority of Britons believed that unions were a major factor in the country's economic decline, and 74 percent believed that British unions had far too much power—a figure that rose to 82 percent by the year of Thatcher's election. All these data help to explain why the 1979 election indeed amounted to a watershed. "Even if what was achieved in the short term was limited," writes journalist Simon Jenkins, "there was no question that 1979 was a revolutionary moment."[30]

For the thirty-four years before her rise to power, Britons had accepted a particular model for how British society ought to be run. In 1979 few understood that Thatcher's upset was opening the way for eighteen straight years of Conservative rule and a fundamental reordering of the British political landscape. The consensus was over.

15

Eleven Million People

The negotiations between the Vatican and the Communist government in
Warsaw had continued throughout the winter, through John Paul II's visit
to Mexico and into the weeks that followed.[1] Finally, in February 1979, the Polish
United Workers' Party announced its decision: John Paul II was invited to return to
his homeland. The government did what it could to make the best of a bad situation.
The pontiff would not, it turned out, be allowed to commemorate the anniversary
of the martyrdom of Saint Stanisław in May. Instead, he was invited to make his
trip in June, a date that officialdom regarded as somewhat less provocative.

This, however, was a face-saving exercise. The reality was that the newly elected
Polish pope's return to his home country represented an absolutely fundamental
challenge to the official Communist version of life in the People's Republic. According to this official picture, the socialist system was the best of all possible worlds,
every material and spiritual problem had been solved, and the church represented
the old, backward order, a pack of superstitions and obscurantism, that enlightened
Communist rule had long since rendered irrelevant. Intellectuals did not need religion because they were too smart for it; workers did not need it because they already lived in a workers' paradise. This was the image reinforced at every stage, from
cradle to grave, by all the official institutions of the Communist state.

It was self-evident to the majority of Poles that John Paul's visit was likely to
defy this alternate reality in just about every way that mattered. The mere fact of
a Polish pope evoked a national pride that stood in stark contrast to the spirit of

"proletarian internationalism" that the Communist regime constantly tried to instill in the people as a substitute. And this particular pope, as the former members of his Kraków flock recalled so well, was a figure of enormous intellectual gifts and human warmth who had a natural rapport with people from just about every section of society. He was, in short, the very embodiment of the qualities that were supposed to be reserved, in the official view, to the Communist avant-garde.

"The pope's trip to Poland was such a unique event that it didn't matter what the official media said or didn't say," recalls Catholic priest Adam Boniecki. "Everybody knew what to think about it."[2] Boniecki was working as a journalist at the Catholic weekly paper *Tygodnik Powszechny*, and shortly after John Paul II's election, the new pontiff had chosen him to come to Rome to edit the Polish edition of the Vatican newspaper, *L'Osservatore Romano*. But the Communist authorities hesitated for months to issue Boniecki a passport, ensuring that he was still around to witness the events before and during John Paul II's pilgrimage. Boniecki didn't mind about the postponement of his departure. He and his colleagues were in a state of "exultation" in the months that followed their compatriot's assent to the head of the Holy See.

For Boniecki and many others, it was already clear that John Paul II's election had "torn through the Iron Curtain." No expert knowledge of Eastern Europe was needed to understand that the pope's visit to his homeland represented a profound challenge to the Communist system there, and the world's interest in the pope's impending visit was correspondingly intense. Reporters from all over the world descended on *Tygodnik Powszechny*'s editorial offices, desperate for inside information about the new pope and his biography. At the same time, as it became clear that the government was intent on minimizing its own involvement with the pope during his trip, churchgoers all over the country began mobilizing. They welcomed the chance to organize the pilgrimage. In a world where everything was monopolized by the state, John Paul II's admirers happily seized upon the chance to show that they, too, could manage a national event.

For its part, the Communist Party resorted to its characteristic coping strategy. It had two primary instruments: the security services and the propaganda apparatus. The Polish secret police, the SB, and its Politburo masters created a special operation called LATO '79. (*Lato* means "summer.") As archbishop of Kraków, Wojtyła had already spent nearly twenty years as the focus of a considerable intelligence-gathering effort by the SB as well as, intermittently, the KGB, the East German Stasi, and other East-bloc secret services. LATO '79 drew most of its operational intelligence from seven moles who had served in the archbishop's immediate entourage over the years. They included both priests and laymen; one of them, code-named JUREK, was a member of the church organizing committee. Every possible measure to limit the effects of the pope's visit was considered. Tens of thousands of police would be deployed in the course of the nine days. The SB informants who were involved in trip planning were advised, for example, to express worries about safety wherever possible (in the hope that this calculated disinformation would reduce the number of pilgrims). No effort was spared. In the event, 480 SB agents were deployed during the four days the pope spent in Kraków during the visit.

Presumably because a large number of East German Catholics also expressed a desire to see the pope, the East German secret police, the Stasi, deployed hundreds of its own agents to cover the event. The East Germans even set up a special headquarters post on the Polish border to coordinate their operations. The famous Stasi master spy Markus Wolf had planted his own mole inside the Vatican, a German Benedictine monk whose identity was not even known to the Stasi man in charge of the operation.[3]

The apparatchiks were especially intent on managing the media coverage. In the weeks leading up to the visit, official media issued a stream of warnings. People should stay away from the pope's events, the government urged: chaos and hysteria were sure to reign, and spectators could almost certainly count on being trampled to death. Foreign reporters were charged exorbitant accreditation fees, which excited a great deal of angry complaint and undoubtedly boosted the country's desperately needed hard-currency reserves. But it doesn't seem to have kept many journalists away. Domestic reporters were easier to deal with. The party issued reams of carefully considered guidelines and talking points. TV cameramen attended special training sessions. Their instructors told them to avoid shots of large crowds. Instead, they were supposed to point their cameras toward the sky while leaving a few people at the bottom of the frame. Shots of elderly people, nuns, and priests were to be preferred; young people, families, and laypeople should be avoided. The idea was to make it appear as though the pope's supporters were a marginal, backward bunch, and certainly nothing like a cross-section of society.[4]

Meanwhile, the party was taking no chances. In the weeks before John Paul II's arrival, the Polish police arrested 150 dissidents—including Adam Michnik and Jacek Kuron, one of the founders of KOR. (A few weeks earlier a gang of toughs had attacked Kuron on the street and beaten him badly. No one was charged in the assault—a fact that suggested the complicity of the security services.) Another one of those detained was a Catholic activist named Kazimierz Switon, who was sentenced to a year in jail for the peculiar crime of attempting to set up an independent trade union.[5] This was an intolerable offense in a country that claimed to be run with the interests of the workers at its heart. Surely, the dictatorship of the proletariat obviated the need for any new labor movements outside of the state.

But appearances were deceptive. In fact, by the end of the 1970s, the essential schizophrenia of life was firmly established. Publicly, officially, there was the Poland of Communist Party rule: a place of grandiose slogans, lockstep marches, and central planning. This nation coexisted with an alternative Poland defined by opposition-organized "flying universities," underground publications from dissident groups like KOR, and the parallel moral universe embodied by the Catholic Church, long linked with the struggle to assert Polish nationhood. Poles of this era had grown up in a society were life was split into two parallel realms, the public and the private, each with its own versions of language and history. As in so many other authoritarian states, citizens of the People's Republic of Poland learned from early on to parrot their allegiance to official ideology in public while keeping their real opinions to themselves and their families.[6] Communist rule depended on ensuring that people persisted in paying public tribute to the official version of truth, thus preventing them from seeing how many of them actually rejected it. But what would happen when they were allowed to make their private feelings manifest, on a mass scale?

Even before his return, it was clear that John Paul II's visit was going to be an extraordinary event. There were the special trains arriving every few minutes at Warsaw's stations, crammed with pilgrims. There was the sudden ubiquity of church orderlies, immediately identifiable by their yellow hats, who had the job of managing the expected crowds—a task that would have normally been left to the security forces of the state. There was the presence of Czech, Hungarian, and East German visitors who had made the journey to Poland to share in an experience of genuine fraternal significance that had nothing to do with proletarian internationalism. There were the word-of-mouth reports that Ukrainians, Belarusian, and Lithuanians—Catholic believers in parts of the Soviet Union adjacent to Poland—were moving closer to the border in order to catch TV or radio broadcasts of the visit.

At 10:02 on the morning of June 2, 1979, John Paul's chartered Al Italia flight landed at the Warsaw Airport and taxied to its berth adorned with the flags of the Holy See and the People's Republic of Poland.[7] At the bottom of the gangway, the pontiff knelt and kissed the ground—a gesture that became a trademark for him in the years of travel that followed. He was met by the country's president and a high-ranking official visiting committee; he was, after all, a head of state. Then he stepped into a truck that had been converted into a mobile viewing stand, painted in the yellow and white colors of the Holy See and adorned with the emblems of the Vatican and Poland. As he entered Warsaw, it became apparent that hundreds of thousands of Poles and foreign visitors had gathered to welcome him. Multitudes lined the streets. (The Polish government itself was compelled to provide two thousand buses to transport the six hundred thousand people who were expected to arrive overnight.)

An enormous cross had been erected in the center of Victory Square—the heart of a country where the public display of Christian symbols had been officially discouraged for the previous forty years. There the pope celebrated an open-air mass with an estimated one million congregants.[8] His homily was an event that remained in the minds of those who experienced it decades later. John Paul II invoked the memory of the great martyr Stanisław, the man who had put the good news of Christ above the dictates of the king, and elucidated the theme of Christian redemption as the central key to understanding the human drama. And he spoke of Poland's unique historical experience of suffering, describing it as "the land of a particularly responsible witness." Christ, he explained, "cannot be kept out of the history of man in any part of the globe, at any longitude or latitude of geography." People in the congregation began to clap, and the applause swelled and spread. John Paul II had to wait for several minutes before he could go on:

> We no longer understand ourselves. It is impossible without Christ to understand this nation with its past so full of splendor and also of terrible difficulties. . . .
>
>   And I cry—I who am a Son of the land of Poland and who am also Pope John Paul II—I cry from all the depths of this Millennium, I cry on the vigil of Pentecost:
>
>   Let your Spirit descend.
>
>   Let your Spirit descend and renew the face of the earth, the face of this land.[9]

A cheer rose from a million throats, an enormous cathartic outpouring. Some of those present interpreted the pope's call to the Holy Spirit as a call to individual action—a call to live life as it should be lived.[10] The pope's audience consisted of people who had spent the previous three decades concealing their private sentiments while being forced to parrot allegiance to official ideology. They had spent much of their lives watching television broadcasts or attending public rallies where the only language to be heard was the ponderous idiom of Marxism-Leninism. And now, suddenly, they found themselves at a public event where the speaker was expressing heartfelt beliefs in words of poignant immediacy.

A Canadian journalist later recalled what happened next:

> The crowd began to croon hymns. "Christ conquers, Christ rules," they sang as yellow-and-white papal flags were unfurled—and some a lot more daring. Close by, a thin young man began furiously waving a banner proclaiming (in Polish) "Freedom, Independence, Human Rights!"
>
> It was startling. My first reaction was worry for the safety of the young man. I looked around for the public-security goons who, surely, would soon knock down his banner and cart him away.

Yet nothing happened. The man waved his banner and no one intervened. The crowd continued to serenade their pope for another eight minutes, as he stood in front of his giant cross. The reporter realized that he was witnessing one of those extraordinary moments. "Suddenly, the fear was gone," he wrote. "Eastern Europe was beating its way back to civilization."[11]

Each step of the pope's itinerary had been chosen to illuminate a particular theme. The next day, in the ancient cathedral city of Gniezno, the pope broached a topic that was bound to upset the Communist rulers in Moscow as well as Warsaw. As a pope from Poland—a Slavic pope—he was, he suggested, uniquely qualified to address the issue of "the spiritual unity of Christian Europe." He called attention to a banner held up in front of the church by visitors from Czechoslovakia: "Remember, Father, your Czech children." He assured them he would: "We cannot fail to hear also . . . other Slavic languages" as well as our own, the pope said. And, he added, "these languages cannot fail to be heard especially by the first Slav pope. Perhaps this is why Christ has chosen him . . . in order that he might introduce into the communion the words and the languages that still sound strange to the ear accustomed to Romance, Germanic, English and Celtic tongues."[12] It was a message that resonated among the Christians of Eastern Europe who did not have the luxury of Poland's stubbornly powerful Catholic tradition. The new pope was making good on his promise to promote the cause of the "Church of Silence." And that church's members did not only inhabit the countries of East Central Europe, many citizens of which—from Hungary, Czechoslovakia, and East Germany—were mingling with the Poles in the crowd that heard his words. John Paul's homily clearly also had the much-oppressed Christians of the Soviet Union in mind—above all his fellow Catholics in Ukraine and the Baltic republic of Lithuania. This was the first time since the start of the Cold War that a pontiff had addressed their plight so directly, thus vividly illuminating the dire lack of religious freedom throughout the East bloc (and not only for Christians).

Tuesday, June 5, was the day that he dwelled upon another taboo subject: the bond between Polish national identity and the Catholic Church. In the pilgrimage town of Częstochowa, he spoke from an altar built on the ramparts of the Jasna Góra Monastery, home of the Black Madonna, the holy icon reputed to have saved Poland from a Swedish invasion in the seventeenth century. Given his surroundings, it is no surprise, perhaps, that John Paul's homily became even more emotional than before. His audience responded exultantly, repeatedly interrupting him with applause and singing. ("To judge by the pope's reception by ordinary Poles, he does not require saints' anniversaries to boost his crowd," noted a reporter from the *Economist*, alluding to the pope's original plan to commemorate the martyrdom of Saint Stanisław, which Poles had observed the previous month.)[13] This time the topics of his sermon acquired a more directly political character, as he argued the case for "the rights of each nation" with startling frankness. Among them he included the "rights to existence and self-determination, to its own culture and the many forms of developing it"—a clear reference to the oppressive cost of Soviet rule in Eastern Europe: "We know from our own country's history what has been the cost to us of the infraction, the violation and the denial of those inalienable rights. Let us therefore pray with greater enthusiasm for *lasting reconciliation between the nations of Europe and the world*. May this be the fruit of recognition of and real respect for the rights of each nation."[14]

After the mass he held a private meeting with seventy Polish bishops. The Vatican press office issued advance copies of his speech, then withdrew them, then reissued them without additional comment. Someone in the papal entourage was evidently feeling anxiety about possible diplomatic fallout from the pope's remarks. Such fear was not entirely unjustified. John Paul II had chosen to indict the Communist regime's handling of state-church affairs with brutal candor: "Authentic dialogue [between church and state] must respect the convictions of believers and ensure the rights of the citizens and also the normal conditions for the activity of the church as a religious community to which the vast majority of Poles belong. We are aware that this dialogue cannot be easy, because it takes place between two concepts of the world which are diametrically opposed."[15]

His next theme was also politically delicate. John Paul had originally planned to devote a day of his trip to the miners and workers of the industrial region of Silesia, a locale that would provide a suitable background to a rumination on the value of labor and the worker's place in society. But the party had barred him from going there—presumably because Gierek, who had spent much of his career there, regarded Silesia as his power base and did not wish to see the pontiff encroach upon it. So the pope extended an invitation to the workers of the region to come celebrate mass with him at Jasna Góra instead. On June 6 they came. The pope marked the occasion with a prolonged rumination on the ethics of work. Labor, he declared, was a foundation of family life and a medium of individual self-realization. Therefore, it was impossible to view work as a human activity that can be divorced from spirituality: "Dear brothers and sisters, hardworking people of Silesia, Zaglebie, and the whole of Poland, do not let yourselves be seduced by the temptation to think that man can fully find himself by denying God, erasing prayer from his life and remaining only a worker, deluding himself that what he produces can on its own fill the needs of the human heart. 'Man shall not live by bread alone.'"[16] Silesia, he said, was a "land of great work and of great prayer." This allusion to the distinctive religiosity of the Polish working class would acquire particular resonance in the years to come. But for the moment it was enough for his listeners that John Paul had chosen to offer an individualist, Christian alternative to the Marxist depiction of workers as a homogeneous "class" marching toward a bright proletarian future.

The Polish authorities soon let it be known that they were not happy. In a news conference, a Polish Foreign Ministry spokesman openly expressed surprise about the number of political references in the pope's sermons. Other officials assured reporters that the government was "generally satisfied" with the way the trip had gone.[17] But it was clear that the Communist potentates could not be unaware of the damage the pope inflicted on their legitimacy with every remark.

In fact, John Paul's language was frank but not incendiary. At no point did he question the Communist Party's right to rule; nowhere did he suggest that he would prefer an alternate political order to the one that already existed. His remarks, in short, were not the stuff of revolution. They were couched in a strictly religious format; the political implications of what he was saying derived consistently and clearly from his fundamental emphasis on the redemptive message of Christ's death and resurrection. Christ was the starting point. It has to be stressed, however, that John Paul II made it clear that the observance of religious freedom and the protection of human rights applied not only to Catholics, but to all humankind.

Should anyone have chosen to take his remarks on a purely political level, they would have noted that he was merely admonishing the state to observe and enforce the freedoms specifically granted by the constitution of the People's Republic, which guaranteed full freedom of religion and speech (though in practice these principles were honored in the breach). This insistence that the Communist regime live up to its own commitments dovetailed with the approach of the dissident movements that had emerged in East Central Europe in the wake of the Final Act of the 1975 Conference on Security and Cooperation in Europe (part of the Helsinki Accords). "We therefore welcome the fact that the Czechoslovak Soviet Socialist Republic has expressed adherence to these pacts," wrote the members of the Czechoslovak human rights group Charter 77 in their founding document, two years before John Paul's visit. "But their publication reminds us with new urgency how many fundamental civil rights for the time being are—unhappily—valid in our country only on paper."[18]

KOR and other dissident groups had said similar things before; so, indeed, had Cardinal Wojtyła himself during his years in Kraków. What made the dramatic difference now was precisely that he was saying them publicly to the nation and the world, with the full authority of the global Roman Catholic Church. Despite the best efforts of the party-controlled media to play down the visit, the pope's homilies were also being broadcast on national television. (The mass at Victory Square, on day one, marked only the second time since 1944 that national media had given airtime to a mass. The first was on the occasion of the pope's inaugural, a few months earlier.) Never before had a Communist Party in the Soviet bloc endured such a direct public challenge to its ideological and informational hegemony. And it was not only the Poles themselves but also the rest of the noncommunist world, watching via satellite, that witnessed this extraordinary public rupture.

But there was something else as well: namely, the effect that this pilgrimage had on the animal spirits of those who experienced it. There was, above all else, the plain social fact of the millions who gathered to see their beloved John Paul II— and discovered each other in the process. The Communist rulers of Poland had always practiced a shrewd strategy of atomization. Every aspect of daily life—right down to the uniform design of housing blocks—reminded the individual human being of his or her subordination to the collective. Any larger public event had to be orchestrated, down to its smallest detail, according to the dictates of the party: its language, its symbols, its content. For nine days in June 1979, by contrast, Poles encountered each other in a setting from which the party and its doctrines were as good as absent. No one had ordered them to be there; whether they came at all was entirely up to them.

And it turned out, millions of them—a visible and undeniable plurality—were determined to show up. For nine days running, John Paul II drew crowds numbering in the hundreds of thousands at each of his events. The roads, the meadows, and the cities were awash in a sea of people no matter where he went. Poles—among them quite a few nonbelievers—were determined to share in his pilgrimage. The mere fact of doing so was a liberating experience. "Those very people who are ordinarily frustrated and aggressive in shop lines metamorphosed into a cheerful and happy collectivity," observed the dissident Adam Michnik.[19] "Despite the enormous crowds, there was no hysteria or tumult in the field," one American correspondent wrote wonderingly.[20]

The lack of hysteria and tumult presumably also had to do with something else: a taste, however modest, of actual power. Since 1944 the party had hammered into people's brains that it was the only force capable of organizing social life in a manner that ensured justice and prosperity for all. According to Marxist-Leninist theory, the revolution ceded the control of society to the dictatorship of the proletariat, a small but enlightened avant-garde whose insight into the laws of dialectical materialism earned it the right to govern in the name of all. Those Poles born into the postwar order had never been exposed to an alternative. But seeing, as they say, is believing. And now Poles saw that they could organize their affairs—in this case, the biggest and most complex social event in the history of the People's Republic—on their own. The lay volunteers who guided the crowds, managed transportation, and provided most of the logistical underpinnings for the papal visit pulled the whole thing off with nary a complaint. In the wake of John Paul's visit, this theme would assume far-reaching significance. It is one thing to theorize about self-governance. It is quite another to practice it. "It was the first assembly that wasn't ordered by the state," one woman who attended John Paul II's mass on Victory Square later recalled. "Earlier there had been all sorts of marches that were organized by the government and protected by the militia. Here the militia wasn't even needed."[21] The party had always presented itself as indispensable; now Poles saw that they could get along just fine without it. "For nine days the state virtually ceased to exist . . . ," wrote historian Timothy Garton Ash. "Everyone saw that Poland is not a communist country—just a communist state."[22]

The greatest emotional test of the trip was still ahead. On June 6, John Paul II returned to his old diocese of Kraków, the place where he had spent most of his adult life, honed his vocation as a priest, and built his extended pastoral family. The government was taking no chances. Having kept the police presence at previous venues relatively discreet, the authorities now sent dozens of militia vans ostentatiously through the main streets of the city. This had to be regarded as a calculated insult by people who had just succeeded in maintaining exemplary order amid enormous crowds attending the pope's masses and rallies. University students greeted the security forces with whistles and jeers. A tightly meshed system of checkpoints around the city screened out anyone who could not produce tickets for the pope's events.

The people of the city shrugged it all off. Whereas the crowds in Warsaw had greeted the pontiff with respectful calm, Krakówvians gave him a rapturous welcome as the papal vehicle, illuminated by spotlights, ferried him into the city from the meadow on the outskirts where his helicopter had landed. People gathered on rooftops or massed on balconies to get a glimpse of him on his way to Wawel Castle. "I especially greet you," the pope said upon his arrival in a message addressed to the people of Kraków. "You are so close to me. Because of the separation to which the Lord has called me, I feel even closer to you." But local media carried only brief excerpts of his remarks. In contrast to earlier stages of the journey, when local media had provided relatively detailed coverage of the pope's stops, Kraków television and radio restricted themselves to a few brief reports of John Paul's doings in the city. The state-run media were still trying to minimize the impact of the visit.

His main appearance the next day had particular resonance for a country that had known not only the horrors of Stalinism but also the terror of the Nazis. He visited Auschwitz, the city not far from Kraków whose name had become shorthand for the evils of totalitarianism. He knelt before the memorial to the victims of the Holocaust, declaring, "I couldn't not come here." He seized upon the occasion for a strong and unmistakable repudiation of anti-Semitism, presaging the efforts to overcome the church's centuries of support for enmity toward Jews that later become a major theme of his papacy. Some 2,000 Jews had lived in his hometown of Wadowice before the year 1939, but nearly all of them—including some of his childhood friends—had been murdered in the Holocaust, making it an intensely personal and immediate issue for him.

His remarks at the death camp also directly indicted the present, in terms that were definitely not calculated to please the Communist Party. "Is it enough to put a man in a different uniform and arm him with the apparatus of violence?" he asked. "Is it not enough to impose on him an ideology in which human rights are subjected to the demands of the system so as in practice not to exist at all?" Visibly exhausted, he then departed once again from his prepared text to proclaim: "Never, never again war. Only peace, only peace."[23] On many occasions during his pilgrimage, the pope had unmistakably but indirectly made the case for change. Here, once more, he emphasized that the cause of change should never be used to justify violence. It was a point he drove home more subtly the next day, when he celebrated mass for the students of Kraków—only a few hundred of whom fitted into the small church, while 30,000 others waited on the streets outside. He understood their desire for change, he hinted, but asked them to be "temperate" in how they pursued it. This, too, was a bit of advice that informed future struggles.[24]

The biggest crowd of all showed up on the last day of his pilgrimage, when an estimated 3 million people—in a country of 35 million—showed up on a field outside of Kraków to bid him good-bye. "When we are strong with the Spirit of God, we are also strong with faith in man. . . . There is therefore no need to fear." By pronouncing the words, he demonstrated that he lived by the same credo. He had shown that he was not afraid to touch upon delicate topics and repeatedly invoked the people's right to choose their own government as they saw fit. He balanced that frankness with a persistent invocation of the spirit of nonviolence, and the crowds who heard him responded with an orderly calm. Nothing could have been more ominous for the future of the Communist regime. Fear held the Soviet empire together, and the Poles, inspired by a Polish leader who lived in Rome, had declared an end to fear.

In his homily, he spoke again of his love for the city and his country. As he closed, he told them: "I beg you once again to accept the whole of the spiritual legacy which goes by the name 'Poland.' . . . I beg you never to lose your trust. Do not be defeated; do not be discouraged; do not on your own cut yourselves off from the roots from which we have our origins . . . and never lose your spiritual freedom, with which He makes a human being free."[25]

In his nine-day visit, the pope gave twelve sermons and a host of smaller speeches. He was greeted and cheered by an estimated 11 million Poles, a third of the country's population. State-owned television tried to broadcast his open-air masses without showing the pope himself, but the party's efforts at censorship were negated not least by the sheer number of those who chose to receive his message in person. This was the real Poland, not the party.

That revelation was the product of myriad acts of courage—all reinforced and amplified by John Paul II himself in consonance with his fundamental philosophy of Christian humanism. At every turn during his visit, he seized the chance to stress the centrality of human rights and basic liberties (particularly, of course, religious freedom). In June 1979, armed with his moral authority as the leader of 757 million Catholics, he preached a rejuvenating belief in Christ that ran counter to everything the Soviet system stood for. Along the way, he elaborated upon the simple idea that he had first aired in the speech he had held upon accession to the papal throne: "Be not afraid."

One could claim, with ample justification, that Poland was a special case. The combination of Catholic piety and nationalist tradition was unique; no other country in Eastern or Central Europe could claim anything like it. So perhaps the effect was isolated. "As much as the visit of John Paul II to Poland must reinvigorate and reinspire the Catholic Church in Poland, it does not threaten the political order of the nation or of Eastern Europe," commented the *New York Times*.[26] How could you possibly challenge the entrenched power of the Polish Communist Party and its Kremlin backers with a few statements of principle? This was an eminently sound, reasonable, and commonsensical summation of the state of affairs. The fact of the matter, though, is that the course of human events sometimes stubbornly defies common sense.

16

Back to the Future

The regime in Warsaw was, of course, deeply entrenched. It had enjoyed thirty-five years of unchallenged rule. It was Stalin himself, backed by the full force of the Red Army and the Soviet secret police, who had installed the Polish Communists in power in 1944. (A Soviet citizen and Red Army general, Marshal Konstantin Rokossovsky, even served as the Polish minister of defense for a few years.) The Kremlin's careful engineering of the new administration in Poland was part of a broader, carefully conceived strategy for the Soviet domination of East Central Europe that had been tacitly endorsed by the Western Allies at Yalta. So the Sovietization of the countries in the region followed a clear and uniform plan; there was very little that was spontaneous or ad hoc about the process. Because the Polish Communists and their colleagues elsewhere took direct orders from their bosses in Moscow, all of them followed the same clearly articulated policy line; Stalin did not tolerate factional disputes among his proxies.

The contrast between this story of Communist rule in Poland and its Afghan equivalent could not have been starker. The Afghan Communists rose to power in their slapdash coup of April 1978 thanks to the improvisational initiative of Hafizullah Amin, who wasn't even the head of his own party. President Mohammed Daoud's arrest of other Communist leaders had prompted Amin to activate his far-flung network of contacts in the militia and the security services in a reactive strike against Daoud's government. As a result, the coup's success owed far more to Daoud's own weaknesses than to any careful preparation by the People's

Democratic Party of Afghanistan (PDPA). Nor did the newly victorious Afghan Communists have a clearly thought-out strategy for the path ahead. For the PDPA leader, Nur Mohammed Taraki, his sudden release from prison and his ascent to the position of head of state were equally unexpected.

The same off-the-cuff style applied to the PDPA's headlong implementation of its radical reform program. The Communists tried to push through rapid land reform in a country where there were virtually no formalized deeds or cadastral surveys, virtually ensuring chaos.[1] They abolished mortgages and other traditional debt relationships without providing a new system of financing to replace them. And they vowed to open up their new institutions to women, an innovation that struck many ordinary Afghans as an affront to Islamic values. (The new PDPA rulers reinforced this sense that they had little respect for religion by replacing the old flag, with its prominent green stripe symbolizing the centrality of Islam, with a new revolutionary flag in Bolshevik red that had no space for religious imagery.) These ill-considered measures predictably sparked widespread resistance within conservative Afghan society.

The April 1978 coup was neither planned nor desired by the men in Moscow; they learned about it from news reports. They had little choice but to acquiesce. As the new regime in Kabul settled into place, its Soviet sponsors watched in consternation as the Afghan leaders recklessly pushed their agenda on a reluctant populace. For all of President Daoud's faults, no one in Moscow had seen any reason to depose him, precisely because the Soviet party leaders were aware of the instability that might result. One reason for their anxiety was the deep, crippling split within the PDPA. They knew only too well how the radical faction, the Khalq (or "Masses") group led by Taraki and Amin, despised the moderate members of Parcham (the "Banner"), exemplified by Babrak Karmal. Karmal was a Soviet favorite because he expounded a gradualist reform approach, which seemed less likely to tip the country over into chaos. Unfortunately, Karmal had taken a negligible role in the April 1978 coup, and he and his associates were soon marginalized by the country's new leaders. But the men in the Kremlin could hardly afford to write off Taraki and Amin. They had already invested far too much in the place.

Events soon tested that commitment. Taraki and Amin desperately tried to stanch the growing signs of rebellion. They received and wooed delegations of tribal leaders, assuring them of the government's good intentions. At every possible opportunity, they stressed their respect for Islam. But revolts continued to flare up around the country.[2]

Then, in March 1979, came the biggest explosion to date. So far the uprisings around the country had been confined to rural areas. Then, suddenly, a series of small revolts in neighboring villages tipped off a full-scale rebellion in the western city of Herat, the country's third largest. On March 15, a mob launched an attack on government offices and security forces. Rioters also stormed the main military base, forcing the inexperienced young garrison commander to pull out his forces. For nearly a week, communications with the central government were completely cut, and anarchy reigned in the streets. This was the first time that the communists in Kabul had lost control of one of the country's biggest cities.[3]

Many of the rebels were, like other Afghans, angry at the various manifestations of the "godlessness" of the new regime. But there were also deeper forces at work. Herat lies just over the border from Iran, and many of the Afghans in the city and around it were Persian speakers with a long history of cultural, economic, and social ties to their western neighbor. Tens of thousands of Heratis had worked in Iran during the days of the shah's economic boom, and many of them had stayed on after the beginning of the Islamic Revolution. In the wake of the shah's downfall in January 1979, many of them returned home, bearing a message of religious militancy that galvanized their compatriots.[4] Some members of the Jamiat-e Islami, the Islamist organization headed by the Kabul University theologian Burhanuddin Rabbani, had sought refuge in Iran, and now they returned to Herat, where they made contact with sympathizers in the Afghan army—including a hard-bitten officer named Ismail Khan who defected to the rebel side during the uprising and later went on to become one of the most famous mujahideen commanders.[5] But there was no real operational coordination between him and his sympathizers across the border. The revolt caught everyone by surprise. It was a genuinely spontaneous uprising.

The Soviet advisers in the city, many of them oblivious to the culture that surrounded them, were completely wrong-footed. One minute they were strolling through the picturesque streets of the ancient city. The next they were being chased down and attacked by angry crowds screaming for the blood of the *farangi*, the foreigners. Three Russians managed to escape in their cars. A few miles away from the city, the drivers of the first two cars noticed that the third was missing. They turned around to look for him and soon found his vehicle parked next to a mud-walled village. The driver was sitting behind the wheel of his vehicle, but he was dead. The attackers had disemboweled him and filled his mouth with sand.[6] Within Herat itself, the corpses of other Soviets were paraded through the city on pikes.

Security forces, including members of the new Communist secret police, fired on the rioters, killing hundreds. But when Kabul ordered regular army troops to shoot at the mob, the soldiers turned their guns instead on the local office of the party, killing PDPA officials as well as Soviet advisers. The entire Seventeenth Division of the Afghan Army mutinied, and its officers and men joined the mujahideen. (Among its commanders was Ismail Khan, mentioned above.) The rebels helped themselves to weapons from army depots and took over government buildings. They held out for a week until the resistance was broken by air strikes and a large-scale operation by the Afghan Army to retake the city. Herat would never be the same. Many of the city's glorious ancient monuments were damaged beyond repair. Estimates of the dead range from five to twenty-five thousand; years later mass graves outside the city were still yielding the bodies of victims.

Herat was a harbinger of the war to come. The inflammatory impact of the Iranian Revolution and the involvement of homegrown Islamists like the Jamiat-e Islami signaled that Afghans were no longer looking to traditional elites for leadership; moderates were already being sidelined. The ferocity of the uprising and the extent of the force needed to quell it made it clear that this went far beyond the usual local tribal rebellion. Vladimir Bogdanov, the KGB station chief in Kabul, subsequently saw it as the ignition point of a true Afghan civil war, the start of a chain of events that would end in the Soviet intervention nine months later.

Most important of all, however, Herat marked the moment when the Russians began to be drawn directly into military involvement in Afghanistan's internal conflicts. The Afghan military proved incapable of suppressing an uprising on this scale by itself, so the Soviets had to step in. Soviet pilots ended up flying many of the sorties against the rebels in Herat. Soviet advisers—at this point numbering about three thousand in the entire country—participated in the ground attack to retake the city. The leaders in Kabul were spooked. Taraki called Moscow and asked for the dispatch of troops from the USSR to shore up his regime. He told Soviet prime minister Aleksey Kosygin that backing for his government had evaporated:

"Do you have any support among the workers, city dwellers, the petty bourgeoisie, and the white-collar workers in Herat?" Kosygin asked. "Is there still anyone on your side?"

"There's no active support on the part of the population," Taraki replied. It's almost wholly under the influence of Shiite slogans—follow not the heathens, but follow us. That's what underpins the propaganda."[7]

Taraki was right that Heratis had rejected the PDPA. But he was wrong about the degree of their organization. They were not under anyone's command—at least not enough for it to matter. Neither the Iranians nor the leaders of the anti-Soviet resistance had ordered the uprising, and it had been suppressed before they could do anything to support it. But that was about to change for good.

It was inevitable, perhaps, that Pakistan would become involved. Since their abortive attempt to topple Daoud in 1975, most of the Islamist leaders had fled there, setting up headquarters in Peshawar, the most important city in Pakistan's Pashtun tribal belt. The local people in Peshawar spoke Pashtu, a language shared by many Afghans, so many of the exiles found the place congenial. The political climate in Pakistan also worked in their favor. The Pakistani president, Muhammad Zia ul-Haq (in power since July 1977), was eager to burnish his Islamic credentials by helping the mujahideen. Needless to say, his support for the holy warriors was hardly motivated by religious altruism. He saw the rebels above all as a tool for exercising influence over the situation in Afghanistan. Like many members of the Pakistani elite, he recalled only too well Daoud's attempts to stir up Pashtun nationalist sentiment on Islamabad's side of the border. He wanted to keep the Afghan resistance divided and weak.

Other countries were also keeping an eye on events. The Chinese, eager to seize any opportunity to counter Soviet influence close to their borders, funneled money and weapons to their own proxies, the small but fanatical movement of Maoist guerrillas. Saudi Arabia, flush with oil cash and eager to further its reputation as the great patron of all Islamic causes, began to consider how it might bring its influence to bear. And in Washington, officials in the Carter White House and the Central Intelligence Agency began to see the growing conflict in Afghanistan as an opportunity to make life difficult for the Soviet Union. In July, Jimmy Carter signed an executive order authorizing the CIA to supply covert assistance to the rebels. America's assistance to the mujahideen began months before the Russians invaded.

Unbeknownst to the Americans, who had few sources of intelligence inside the country, the nature of the Afghan rebellion was already starting to evolve in significant ways. One illustration of the new dynamic came from the province of Nuristan, where by May 1979 the uprising had been going on for a full year. Many other parts of the country had experienced rebellions of their own in the meantime (Herat being merely the most spectacular), but only the denizens of the Pech Valley had succeeded in expelling government forces and holding territory under their own control for so long. The valley dwellers had achieved this under the command of their tribal leaders, the influential clan chiefs whose word was law. But already war and ideology were starting to warp the conventional ways of doing things.

In the summer of 1979, a minor Islamic cleric named Maulavi Hussain arrived in the valley. He was of little importance himself; it was what he represented that mattered. And what he represented was the novel but increasingly influential notion of Islam as a modern, revolutionary force. Once, many years earlier, Hussain had run for a seat in parliament, but his campaign had been fatally undermined by the widely shared conviction among voters that politics was not a proper role for religious leaders. In the early 1970s he had joined the country's first real Islamic activist group, the Muslim Youth Organization; later in the decade he had joined Hezb-e Islami, the "Party of Islam," the most radical of the new religious groups.

Hezbis (as they were called) were not defenders of the old order, like so many of the traditional Islamic leaders. Hezbis were not only opposed to Daoud and the Communists, but also objected to a restoration of the monarchy, since, like Khomeini, they had concluded that kings were against Quranic teaching. Unlike Khomeini, though, the Hezbis and most of the other Islamic revolutionaries in Afghanistan were Sunnis, and they had no analogue of the powerful and well-organized Shiite religious establishment to guide them. That was probably just as well. Since so many Islamic clerics in Afghanistan were pillars of the old order, the Hezbis rejected them. As the religious revolutionaries saw it, the new Islamic state would be led by righteous Muslims like themselves, beneficiaries of modern education, and not by the corrupt and ignorant members of the old clerical establishment.

To be sure, some clerics, like Hussain, cast their lot with the Islamists and were happy to use their religious authority to serve the radical cause. As soon as he had settled in with the Pech Valley rebels, Hussain informed them (according to American anthropologist David Edwards) that their uprising "could not be considered a lawful jihad because it had not been authorized and commanded by a legitimate Muslim leader operating according to religious principles. Consequently, all those who had died to this point could not be called martyrs (shahidan), and the religious reward promised to martyrs in Islam was not guaranteed to them."[8] Hussain and his fellow Hezbis canvassed the locals, handing out party identity cards and telling locals how to be proper Muslims. If men wanted to play leading roles in the jihad, for example, they had to wear beards and clean white clothing, he told them.

The villagers were not sure what to think. They still hewed to their own tribal leaders and their traditional style of combat,[9] but as the tribal militias came up against government troops armed with all the modern paraphernalia of warfare—assault rifles, armored personnel carriers, helicopter gunships—the drawbacks of the received way of doing things were becoming all too apparent. Tribal democracy was fantastically unwieldy; making any decision required hearing the opinions of representatives from every community that had dispatched fighters or contributed resources. Meetings of tribal councils typically drew hundreds of attendees and could drag on for days, noted American anthropologist David Edwards, who interviewed some of the rebellion's leading personalities. Relatives tended to fight as a group within each militia and to obey only those who stemmed from the same one.[10]

These were all serious handicaps in a struggle against an opponent whose forces obeyed an efficient operational hierarchy and followed a clear, universalistic ideology.[11] This was, perhaps, one reason the new Islamist parties, which followed a very similar principle of organization, gradually asserted themselves over more traditional habits of thought. But there was a second reason, too, and it was much more concrete. By the summer of 1979, weapons were already running short. It turned out that the tribal councils inside Afghanistan had been far too generous in handing out the few arms they had obtained from the enemy, and they soon ran out. The Islamist groups, by contrast, had carefully hoarded their guns. And because their leaders had been in Pakistan for years, they had already built up fruitful working relationships with the Pakistani military intelligence service (the Inter-Services Intelligence Directorate, or ISI) and the army. This was the key to receiving money, training, and weapons. As a result, tribal fighters increasingly found that the best way to a proper gun was to sign up with one of the new parties. Whoever received a party identity card also had good chances of acquiring a modern rifle.

And now, by the summer of 1979, another process was contributing to the ascendancy of modern political Islam over the old ways. The Communist government in Kabul meted out a harsh response to any area that fought back against its rule. Wherever the army or the secret police made their way back into a rebel zone, reprisals were sure to follow. Not all of the Nuristanis, for example, had been able to hold out against the combined forces of the government, and many had already been forced to make the humiliating trek through the mountains to the refugee camps in Pakistan. There, too, it was the Islamic political parties that offered food, housing, schooling for the children—but only to those who pledged their allegiance. This, too, undermined the traditional leaders, who, once they were in exile, found they had nothing to offer their own people.

Afghanistan may have been geographically remote, but that did not mean that it was completely isolated from events elsewhere in the Islamic world in the twentieth century. The rise of political Islam on the streets of Herat and in the gorges of Nuristan represented the culmination of decades of intellectual ferment that spanned the *umma*, the global community of believers.

The main issue that concerned Islamic thinkers during the twentieth century was how to respond to Western hegemony. For centuries after its founding, the Islamic world could rightfully claim the mantle of an advanced civilization, boasting achievements in science and culture that rivaled anything in the West. But by the end of the nineteenth century, those days had receded into the mythical past. The initiative had gone over to the Europeans, who, thanks to their superior technology and organization, had divided up much of Asia and Africa among themselves. Many Muslim intellectuals concluded that the only hope for their societies lay in adopting Western ways, accepting the imperative of modernization. Some of them embraced Western ideologies, such as Communism or radical secular nationalism.

But there were also those who soundly rejected the notion that religion was the problem. They declared that Islam held all the answers and that what ailed Muslims was precisely their own lack of faith. What was needed, these thinkers argued, was a revival and renewal of Quranic teaching, not its abolition or dilution. At the end of the nineteenth century, an uprooted Persian who called himself Sayyid Jamal ad-Din al-Afghani had wandered from country to country, spreading a political philosophy that amounted to an eclectic mix of traditional Islam and anti-imperialist modernism. He portrayed the Muslim world as crippled by political and moral corruption and argued that the *umma* could respond to the threat from West only by rediscovering the primal vitality of Islamic teaching and seeking to unify itself into a single political entity. Afghani had a profound influence on Ayatollah Muhammad Ali Shahabadi, the scholar who initiated the young Ruhollah Khomeini into the mysteries of *erfan*.

In Egypt a vigorous young thinker named Muhammad Abduh followed al-Afghani's cue. He strove, somewhat more systematically than al-Afghani, to refashion Islam into the basis for a modern ideology that could challenge the West on its own ground. He opposed certain traditions, like polygamy, as outmoded and un-Quranic, and he preached tolerance for other religions (specifically the Christian Copts of his homeland). This was a form of Islamism that did not yet suffer from the violent perversions of thought that were yet to come.

What Abduh did not provide his followers was a precise organizational recipe for achieving these ends. That job fell instead to another Egyptian, a young former schoolteacher by the name of Hassan al-Banna. Intensely opposed to the effects of British colonialism on traditional Egyptian society, Banna began to imagine a modern Muslim political party that would organize believers into an all-encompassing revivalist movement that contained a pronounced element of social activism. In 1928 he decided to give this idea concrete form by establishing an organization called the Muslim Brotherhood. The Brotherhood, perhaps the first modern Islamist group, became the most influential Islamic political vehicle of the twentieth century, and its slogan—"Islam is the solution"—laid out the contours of a project that continues today. Egypt is the largest and most culturally influential country in the Arab world, and the Brotherhood eventually spawned affiliates in all the major countries of the Middle East. For centuries, scholars from all over the Muslim world have come to Cairo to study at al-Azhar University, the Islamic world's leading academic institution. Among them were many Afghans, figures of considerable learning and stature who transmitted the new ideas of the Muslim Brothers back to their home country.

One of the most influential Islamists of the century was neither an Arab nor a Persian. Abul Ala Mawdudi was born under British colonial rule in India in 1903. Mawdudi chose a religious education, but for family reasons he ended up attending several seminaries rather than completing his studies at a single one, as was the norm. This exposure to a variety of schools, as well as his fluency in English, uniquely predisposed him to a vision of Islam that ignored parochial bounds. A talented publicist as well as a theologian, Mawdudi eventually gained control over a leading journal that he quickly turned into an outlet for his unorthodox views, which went further than just about anyone else's in depicting Islam as a force for violent social change. "Islam is a revolutionary ideology and a revolutionary practice, which aims at destroying the social order of the world totally and rebuilding it from scratch," he wrote in 1926, "and *jihad* (holy war) denotes the revolutionary struggle."[12] In this respect, he conceded, Islam bore a certain resemblance to other militant ideologies of the twentieth century, although with a crucial difference. One commentator on Mawdudi glosses his argument this way: "The Nazis and Marxists had enslaved other human beings, whereas Islam sought to free them from subjection to anything other than God."[13] It was, in any case, Mawdudi's characterization of Islam as a modern revolutionary force that would resonate powerfully among his fellow Muslims in neighboring Afghanistan. Above all else, it was his vision of something he called "the Islamic state"—a form of government that was neither secular nor monarchic and promised a return, via rule by the righteous and the implementation of sharia, to the primal community of the Prophet and his followers—that inflamed the imagination of so many of his readers across the *umma*.

Mawdudi was no mere theorist. He founded a political party, the Jamaat-e-Islami, to further his aims. The Muslim establishment in the Raj did not know what to make of him. Mawdudi did not share the prevailing belief that Indian believers should focus on creating a new Muslim-majority country of their own when independence from Britain was achieved. For him it was not enough to have a state with a Muslim citizenry; what he sought was a state in which undiluted sharia had the full force of law and sovereignty belonged to God. Anything else, he said, was *jahiliyya*, the state of ignorance that had reigned before the Quran was presented to man. Capitalism, Communism, and all non-Islamic belief systems were *taghut*, idolatry. In 1977, when Muhammad Zia ul-Haq seized power in a coup, the general essentially paid tribute to the seductive power of Mawdudi's ideas by placing himself at the head of the new Islamic sensibility that Mawdudi had spent so many years cultivating. He introduced noninterest banking, banned alcohol, and allowed religious leaders to try miscreants in sharia courts.

But it was, again, an Egyptian who gave the notion of the Islamic Party its most consequential expression. This was another Muslim Brother by the name of Sayyid Qutb. Like Banna, he was a teacher by profession, and in 1948, sponsored by the Egyptian Ministry of Education, he embarked on a study trip to the United States. He returned from his two-year stay appalled by what he had seen: shallow materialism, frantic pursuit of trivial pleasures, men and women freely mingling in public. His diatribes against American life after his return to Egypt soon cost him his job, and he found himself drawn deeper into his work for the Brotherhood, where he soon had a job running the propaganda department. At the same time, he was embarking on intensive self-study of the Quran, work that would soon bear significant literary fruit.

In 1952 a group of army officers led by Colonel Gamal Abdel Nasser overthrew the king and seized power. For a time Nasser flirted with the Brotherhood, and he even tried to recruit Qutb, one of its most prominent ideologists, into his own government. But an attempt to assassinate Nasser in 1954 gave the new president an excuse to crack down on his Islamist rivals, and he threw all of their major leaders, including Qutb, into jail. Qutb endured numerous bouts of torture during his first three years in detention, an experience that seems to have intensified his radicalism. Yet Qutb put the time to good use. He wrote two books, both of which would reverberate with unanticipated force in the Afghans' bitter struggle against an alien and atheist regime.

One of them was a commentary on the Quran, a reading that subtly articulated Qutb's vision of Islam as a powerful force for social change. The other, *Milestones*, inspired a generation of Islamist radicals with its tightly wound harangues about the apostasy of contemporary civilization and the corresponding urgency of the need for a government of God. It is a book that breathes a distinctly totalitarian spirit—and the notion of totality, which Qutb conflates with the Quranic notion of *tawhid*, pervades his argument. Islam, reflecting the all-encompassing oneness of God, is an overarching system that provides the conclusive answer to all spiritual, philosophical, and political concerns. Qutb took Mawdudi's notion of modern-day *jahiliyya*, or ignorance, and deepened it. Only those states that acknowledged the sovereignty of God and the ascendance of the laws laid down in the Quran could be considered truly Islamic—and by this measure, all of the existing governments in the Muslim world were apostate regimes, regimes that could claim no legitimacy in the name of religion. (Here he was also picking up a line of argument from the medieval theologian Ibn Taymiyyah, who had asserted that even governments that claimed to be Islamic could be resisted by force if they failed to follow proper Quranic precepts.)

The only way to restore Islam to its rightful place, Qutb concluded, was by overthrowing these governments. And the best way to do this was by establishing a small cadre of single-minded believers who would devote their lives to this cause. This was a concept that probably owed more to the Leninist notion of a revolutionary avant-garde than to original Quranic theology. But in this respect, too, Qutb was entirely of a piece with his fellow Islamic modernists, who were happy to raid their ideological rivals for any political tools that might come in handy.

No sooner had Qutb emerged from jail than the Egyptian authorities arrested him again. He never returned to freedom. In 1966 he was executed. But his ideas endured. In Iran, a religious student named Ali Khamenei translated Qutb's books into Persian, and they found wide readership among the younger generation of militant young clerics. One of the Afghans who had studied at al-Azhar in Cairo, a scholar named Burhanuddin Rabbani, translated *Mileposts* into Dari, the Afghan dialect of Persian, and distributed it to his students at the Theology Faculty of Kabul University. Later, Qutb's avid readers included the Palestinian theoretician of jihad Abdullah Azzam as well as one of Azzam's most avid students, a tall young Saudi named Osama bin Laden.

It was only in the 1970s that radical political Islam finally came into its own. Israel's devastating defeat of the combined Arab armies in the Six-Day War in 1967 humiliated Nasser and the other secular leaders who had preached the gospel of socialism and Arab unity. This was partly a generational shift, partly a genuine spiritual crisis. Around the Arabic-speaking world, *al-shahbab*—"the youth"—were rejecting the leftist-nationalist slogans of their elders in favor of the statement of

faith: "There is no God but Allah, and Mohammed is his prophet." Islam filled a
spiritual void that the secular ideologies apparently could not; nor did it suffer from
the burden of alien origins. In Egypt, university students began growing beards and
agitating for segregated campus activities.[14] Young women donned head scarves in a
demonstrative display of their contempt for secular utopias. While their elders still
preached the virtues of Karl Marx or Michel Aflaq (the architect of Baathism), this
younger generation turned to al-Banna or Mawdudi for political answers.

The Islamists found one of their first battlegrounds in Lebanon, where civil war
broke out in 1975. Here, too, Cold War rivalries combined to combustive effect in
a country where the government was dominated by a Christian minority with close
ties to France and other Western powers, while the Muslim majority—including a
big Shiite population and a significant number of Palestinian refugees—gravitated
toward Moscow as a natural "anti-imperialist" ally. The war enflamed identity politics in Lebanon, and among Muslims it accelerated a shift toward religious activism,
especially among the economically marginalized Shiites. A Lebanese Islamist who
fought in the war later explained his motivations to the writer Fawaz Gerges:

> My friends and I felt that since the 1920s our leaders had been experimenting
> with bankrupt ideologies like Arab nationalism and socialism, which failed to
> liberate Palestine and restore our dignity as Arabs and Muslims. We thought
> political Islam was the only means to undo the wrongs. We also believed that
> those Western ideologies were merely ploys to divert Muslims from their
> noble goals. Our preachers and clerics often told us that Arabs would regain
> their glory only if they reclaimed Islam and established *shariah*. Lebanon, we
> thought, should not be the monopoly of Christians.[15]

The 1970s Islamic revival in the Arab countries came to be known as the *sahwa*,
the "Awakening." One of the places where it hit the hardest was Saudi Arabia, which
was somewhat ironic. From the outside the Kingdom of Saud looked like a bastion
of conservatism, tightly wrapped in the unassailable orthodoxy of Wahhabism, the
sere version of ultrafundamentalism that the first king had officially adopted upon
his assumption of power in 1932. For all its appearances, though, the fabulous influx of 1970s oil wealth had shaken the place to its foundations. A rising generation
of young religious radicals felt that the visible presence of American oil companies
and the growing popularity of Western-style television programs were leading to a
dangerous loosening of mores. They began to find allies within the kingdom's religious establishment, where some clerics worried that the deluge of gold unleashed
by the oil bonanza was undermining their own position. Meanwhile, members of

the Muslim Brotherhood fleeing persecution in Egypt were arriving in the kingdom to teach and spread their views.

Qutb's brother Mohammed, who had also been imprisoned and tortured for his political engagement, emigrated to Saudi Arabia, where he became one of the most ardent propagators of Qutb's message. He took care, however, to censor his brother's earlier works, knowing that their revolutionary implications would trigger an allergic reaction from the paranoid Saudi authorities. As it was, Qutb's contention that all existing governments in the Islamic world were actually apostate regimes did not go down well with the Saudi royal family, whose claim to power was based on their guardianship of the holy places in Mecca and Medina.

But it was this very element that could also be turned into a point of attack, and that was what finally happened in November 1979. Many of the events of 1979 are linked with the mysterious power of anniversaries. The Communist Party in Poland feared the incendiary potential of the nine-hundreth anniversary of the martyrdom of a saint. The thirtieth anniversary of the Communist takeover in China was shrewdly exploited by Deng Xiaoping and his colleagues to reinforce the sense of a new beginning. The forty-day Islamic mourning cycle proved a crucial dynamic for the revolution in Iran—as did the millennial expectations of Khomeini's followers, whose habit of referring to him as the "imam" fanned a longing for the realm of justice promised by the reappearance of the Hidden Imam. Indeed, the Islamic calendar itself was one of the many issues that fueled the discontent of Iranian believers. The shah's decision to introduce a new, non-Islamic calendar in the mid-1970s served as yet another bit of evidence to good Shiites that the monarch was an enemy of their religion—and gave Khomeini's supporters yet another potent argument.

In the Julian calendar of the West, 1979 is not an especially evocative date. But this was not true for Muslims. In the Islamic calendar, which is based on the phases of the moon and takes as its start the Prophet's exile from Mecca in 622, the Western month of November 1979 coincides with the dawning of the new year of 1400. According to certain traditions, that is the year that the Mahdi, the Islamic messiah, is supposed to reveal himself to the faithful and usher in a new age of eternal justice. For Iranians, this is the moment when historical time and the forces of eternity coincide,[16] and this apocalyptic expectation fueled the fervor with which Khomeini was greeted as the country's new savior. Some demonstrators wondered whether he might, indeed, turn out to be the Imam of the Age himself;[17] some of the faithful even claimed to have seen his face on the moon.

In the Kingdom of Saudi Arabia, a group of provincial zealots came up with a particularly fateful reading of the Mahdi myth. Like the majority of Saudis, they were not Shiite but Sunni, and they hailed from a remote corner of the kingdom that had largely missed out on the new prosperity. In November 1979, as pilgrims were arriving for the annual hajj, the obligatory pilgrimage to Mecca, heavily armed members of the group took over the al-Masjid al-Haram, the Grand Mosque, and took thousands of pilgrims from around the world hostage. They then announced that one of their leaders, a young man named Abdullah Hamid Mohammed al-Qahtani, was the Mahdi, the long-prophesied redeemer of Islam. All Muslims, they said, were religiously obligated to obey his commands. The Saudi authorities declined to do this and immediately set about the task of clearing the mosque. It took them weeks, covertly assisted by a team of commandos lent to the kingdom by the French government, to kill or capture the hostage takers. In the end, according to official Saudi figures, 270 people—hostages, hostage takers, and members of the assault force—lost their lives. Foreign diplomats who managed to get access to local hospitals concluded that the actual death toll was much higher, closer to 1,000.[18]

The leader of the group, Juhayman al-Otaibi, was captured and executed a few weeks after the end of the siege. But his ideas would prove prophetic. He had categorically denounced the corruption of the Saudi regime and rejected the presence of infidel foreigners in a country that was supposed to be the undefiled home to Mecca and Medina, two of the three most holy places in Islam. (The third is the Dome of the Rock in Jerusalem.) A subsequent generation of Saudi radicals—Osama bin Laden among them—would not forget.[19]

The seizure of the Grand Mosque had another important consequence. It forced the Saudi royal family to confront the reality of the sense of discontent that permeated society. Their response was two-pronged. First, domestically, the government reverted to a policy of unbending conservatism in all matters even remotely associated with religion; the idea was to restore its credentials among the ultraconservative religious establishment, which had proved conspicuously unwilling to offer its support during the mosque crisis, as well as to undermine those who accused the government of slackening in its observance of Islamic mores. Second, the Saudis decided to use foreign policy as a safety valve. The regime ramped up its efforts to spread the Wahhabi creed and to further Islamic causes more generally outside the borders of the kingdom. This, they hoped, would bolster their image as defenders of the true faith and also offer opportunities for shunting off malcontents. It would be years until the full implications of this effort became clear, and nowhere would the consequences be more dramatic than in Afghanistan.

Afghanistan, of course, was not an Arab country. In many ways, given its underdevelopment and its poverty, it was peripheral to the rest of the Muslim world. It had contributed no fresh ideas, no original thought, to the great Islamic revivalist movement. Yet, thanks to the quirks of geopolitics, it was fated to become the most prominent arena for the ideas of Sunni Islamism.

Afghan political Islam did not trace its lineage to a holy city or a famous seminary. It started, instead, at Kabul University. The university, founded in the 1930s by a reformist king, had expanded steadily over the years, as the nation's leaders tried desperately to push Afghanistan forward into the modern era. Still, even by the early 1970s, when it was still the only institution of higher education in the country, it boasted a student population of merely twenty-five hundred. The foreign aid that had poured into Afghanistan in the 1950s and 1960s had given the university a host of new buildings, most of them in the stripped-down concrete modernist style typical of the period. The faculty included quite a few foreigners—not all from the East bloc—and they brought with them exposure to the great political debates in the world at large.

The university was the one place, aside from the army, where Afghans came together from all over the country. As such it was a unique melting pot, one that brought together young men and women of radically different origins. Yet the student body was also riven by deep social differences. Some of the students made it in because they came from prominent families; others managed to get through the application process by dint of sheer hard work and talent. The privileged students, knowing that their instructors would not stand up to them, took liberties with university rules and sometimes engaged in lax ethical behavior—drinking, gambling, patronizing prostitutes—that irritated the students of a more religious bent. For many students, especially those from provincial backgrounds, the confrontation with the loose ways of the modern university was a deeply alienating experience.[20]

Add to this, then, the fundamental ideological conflicts that were already beginning to tear the country apart. Many of the students were active in Communist politics, and they regarded their more religious classmates as misguided rubes. As one student at the time would later recall, Khalqis kicked soccer balls at Muslim students as they prayed, defecated in the bowls used for ritual ablutions, and ostentatiously smoked or ate near those who were observing the fast. Under Daoud, the more secular-minded students could act in the knowledge that their views enjoyed the tacit approval of the state.

In the late 1960s the Muslim students began to fight back. One of their most passionate leaders was a star student by the name of Abdur Rahim Niazi. Niazi belonged to the new generation of students who believed that Islam, far from representing a backward culture, actually offered a complete range of solutions to contemporary problems. This new cohort of activists, many of them centered on the university's Faculty of Sharia, attended lectures by professors who had attended al-Azhar University in Cairo. These men had imbibed the ideas of the Muslim Brotherhood, and propagated its ideas among their charges when they returned to Afghanistan. It was one of these professors, Burhanuddin Rabbani, who had translated Qutb's works into Dari.

In 1969, Niazi formed a group called the Muslim Youth Organization, which aimed to work toward the establishment of a true Islamic government. Taking their cue from the Egyptians, the Muslim Youth leaders organized their members into conspiratorial cells; these activists would serve as the avant-garde of the revolution that would capture the state for Islam. Afghanistan's young Islamists represented a completely new breed. Just like their Iranian counterparts, these new religious militants understood that they were engaged in a struggle for survival not only against their own dictator but also against the forces of the Left more generally, and they set out to redefine their faith in terms of a modern-day political creed. Islam, the radicals argued, was more "progressive" than Communism. Niazi wrote: "Fourteen centuries back, Islam taught a very revolutionary and logical lesson for achieving revolution. God said to do jihad in the path of God with honesty. The establishment of an Islamic government requires that kind of jihad.... Today truth has been replaced by tyranny, and the only way that has been left has been to invite the people to truth and untiring militancy in this path."[21]

What was particularly striking about the Muslim Youth was its comparative lack of traditional religious leaders. In Shiite Iran, the clergy had a long tradition of playing an independent political role, and it was the clerics—or at least some of them—who had adapted to the changing mental environment of the late twentieth century. In Afghanistan, the state had tended to co-opt the mullahs by offering them emoluments, and this had undermined their status in the eyes of many ordinary Afghans—along with the petty corruption that plagued religious notables. For all of these reasons, many Afghans tended to look with suspicion upon members of the ulama who tried to play a political role. Niazi and his generation also reproached the religious establishment for its failure to stand up to the increasingly assertive Communists.

Niazi, a smart and charismatic man who had a galvanizing influence on the nascent Islamist movement, died of cancer in 1970; it is interesting to speculate what his role might have been had he lived longer. In his place a number of other young firebrands came to the fore. One of them was the engineering student Gulbuddin Hekmatyar. He was a member of the Ghilzai tribal confederacy that had often opposed the rival Durranis, the clan that provided Afghanistan with many of its leaders right up until the death of Mohammed Daoud. He came to the university after a brief stint at the military academy. In 1972 he was jailed for killing a student Maoist during one of the perennial feuds between young Islamists and leftist radicals. For the other Islamists, this was merely tangible proof of Hekmatyar's radical credentials, and they rewarded him with a leading role in the Muslim Youth.[22]

To this day, there are those in Afghanistan who insist that Hekmatyar came to the Islamic cause only after an initial flirtation with the Communists. Hekmatyar and his colleagues deny this. What is certain, however, is that Hekmatyar envisioned Hezb-e Islami, the "Party of Islam" he founded in 1977, as just the kind of organization that Qutb had mapped out in *Milestones:* an Islamic revolutionary avant-garde based on Leninist conspiratorial principles. After Niazi's death, Rabbani had transformed the Muslim Youth Organization into a party called the Jamiat-e Islami, the "Islamic Society" (a name that mimicked the party founded by Mawdudi in Pakistan). When the group failed in its attempt to foment a coup against Daoud in 1975, Hekmatyar broke away, seizing the opportunity to create an organization that would be entirely beholden to him. Strictly hierarchical, Hezb-i Islami was supposed to represent the small, elite spear point of the violent struggle that would one day transform Afghanistan into an Islamic state.

Just as Lenin directed his choicest invective at social democrats and other moderate socialists, Hekmatyar reviled the representatives of traditional religion. His Hezbis assailed village mullahs as blockheaded traditionalists who still supported the long-deposed king and were willing to keep the secular state as long as they continued to receive their accustomed perks. The traditionalists were also accused of rejecting modern science and technology, of purveying superstition, and of clinging to local Sufi traditions of saint worship—all of which was depicted by the modernizing Islamists as a rejection of the pure, "rationalist" monotheism of the Prophet's original message.[23] Hezb-i Islami shared some of these ideas with Rabbani's Jamiat; where the two parties differed strongly was in their ethnic makeup. The Jamiat was somewhat more diverse, though Tajiks (including Rabbani and Massoud) were overrepresented among its members. Hekmatyar's organization, by contrast, consisted almost entirely of Pashtuns. As the years went by, Hezb-i Islami also gained a reputation as a much more radical group, while Jamiat tended to take a more pragmatic and inclusive line. As several Afghanistan scholars have pointed out, the social and ethnic divide between the two groups strikingly paralleled that between Khalq and Parcham, the two factions whose mutual animosity had such a crippling effect on the Afghan Communists.

Ahmed Shah Massoud, by now a hardened veteran of Islamist infighting, opted to maintain his distance from these battles. His own readings of Qutb and Mawdudi had strengthened his belief in the need for an Islamic state, and he remained a member of Jamiat, technically subordinate to Rabbani. But he had long since decided to fight his own war against the Communists, and to do it entirely on his own terms. His experience among the Nuristanis had given him valuable insights into the nature of this new war. In July 1979, at the age of twenty-five, he once again returned to his home turf in the Panjshir Valley, the place where he had launched the doomed rebellion in 1975.[24] Now, thanks to the mishaps of the Khalqi regime, the Panjshiris were much more receptive to his arguments about the anti-Islamic character of the government. But this did not necessarily make up for inadequate resources. Later Massoud told an interviewer that he began his new uprising with thirty followers, seventeen rifles of various makes, and the equivalent of $130 in cash.[25]

Massoud, however, did have several important assets that he could draw upon. One of them was the Panjshir itself. For anyone intent on fighting a guerrilla war against vastly superior forces, terrain like this is the great equalizer. About sixty miles long, the Panjshir plunges from the high passes of the Hindu Kush down to the open plains just north of the Afghan capital of Kabul. A bewildering labyrinth of canyons and gorges feed into the valley, whose steep walls make life hard for would-be invaders. Most of the valley is just wide enough to allow for a single road that winds steeply up along terrifying defiles. Here and there ledges and plateaus allow for terraces where farmers grow apricots, almonds, and wheat.

The people who live in this place inhabit a relatively self-contained world, and their spirit of fierce independence was a major resource for Massoud to draw on. In 1979, however, it was still not quite enough. Massoud and his tiny army attacked government posts where they could find them, but the Khalqis and their Soviet advisers fought back ferociously, bolstered by their jet fighters, tanks, and helicopters. Massoud and his fighters held out for forty days. By August they had had enough. Battered by government air strikes, he and his band of core followers withdrew from the valley and set off for their safe haven in Pakistan. It was a brutal journey, over the high passes and down through the mountains to Peshawar on the other side. Massoud had been wounded in the leg, and one can only imagine how he managed to make the trip. It was a small beginning, to be sure. But it was a beginning that put Massoud in a good position to exploit the situation that was soon to come.

17

The Second Revolution

The students had been planning for days. A small group of activists—including the young Mahmoud Ahmadinejad, a future president of the country—had favored going after the Soviet Embassy instead. But they had been overruled: American diplomats would be the target. Now, as the day of November 4, 1979, dawned, the young radicals gathered quietly in light autumn rain. Behind the walls they could see the buildings of the US Embassy, all designed according to the same bland architectural style that had prompted the diplomats who worked there to compare it to an American high school. The student demonstrators had issued themselves armbands that would make it easier to recognize each other in the turmoil, and they bore makeshift cards identifying them as members of their group, which they called "Muslim Students Following the Imam's Line." Their ranks included a number of women. The girls hid bolt cutters underneath their chadors, waiting for the moment to cut through the locks on the embassy gates.

The students, all zealous supporters of the revolution, were eager to strike a blow at the country they saw as the "Great Satan," the evil imperialist power that had supported the shah's regime for decades. When the signal was given, hundreds of them clambered over the walls and stormed through the gates. The US Marine guards fired tear gas into the crowd, but refrained from using the deadlier weapons they had on hand, knowing that killing any of the rioters would enflame them, perhaps triggering violent reprisals. Unimpeded, the mob surged into the compound, fanning out to the various buildings. Overwhelmed by superior numbers, the Marines surrendered. Many of the students in the crowd claimed that they were there merely to stage a nonviolent protest. But among them was a hard core of radicals who were pursuing a different mission. These young militants grabbed every American they encountered. They bound their captives' hands and blindfolded them with strips of cloth brought along especially for the purpose.

Altogether they managed to take sixty-six Americans hostage. Six others managed to evade capture. A handful of the hostages were soon released, but the rest—fifty-two altogether—would remain in captivity for the next 444 days. The experience of the hostage taking transformed America's self-image and dramatically altered the course of the Iranian Revolution.

The United States and its role in Iranian politics over the previous four decades were a central issue in the Iranian Revolution. For much of its modern history, a weak Iran had been dominated by the British and the Russians. Then, in 1953, the United States had actively supported a coup to topple the nationalist prime minister, Mohammed Mossadeq, whose move to nationalize Iran's oil resources—largely controlled until then by the British—had made him so popular among Iranians that his power threatened the shah's. Washington saw a pro-Western regime in Tehran as a vital bulwark against Soviet influence in the region. From then on, the Americans did whatever they could to prop up the shah, who was happy to reciprocate by buying enormous quantities of US weaponry and providing US intelligence with listening posts close to the border of the USSR. US experts helped to train the shah's security forces, including SAVAK, his brutal secret police. The shah's relentless program of Westernization was regarded by the Americans (and many Iranian elites) as laudable evidence of progress. Never mind that many Iranians saw the same cultural transformation—public consumption of alcohol, women in revealing dress, erotic movies—as an aggressive affront to their traditional values.

The shah regarded his alliance with the Americans as a source of his power. Khomeini saw the shah's links with Washington as a major weakness. From the very beginning, the ayatollah's harsh polemics against the Americans were a major source of his public popularity. In 1964 his campaign against the government culminated in a speech assailing the shah's proposed status-of-forces law that granted US military forces in the country immunity from Iranian law. Khomeini referred to the law as a "capitulation," a word that evoked the humiliating, quasi-colonial infringements of national sovereignty claimed by the British and other foreign powers in the nineteenth century.[1] "They have reduced the Iranian people to a level lower than that of an American dog. If someone runs over a dog belonging to an American, he will be prosecuted. Even if the shah himself were to run over a dog belonging to an American, he would be prosecuted."[2] The attack struck a nerve. Those Iranians who heard about it were thrilled that one of their religious leaders should have such temerity. For the shah, it was untenable. It was precisely these statements by Khomeini that prompted his exile.

As the revolution gathered steam in the course of 1979, the rhetoric of its leaders became increasingly laced with condemnation of US "imperialism" and "neocolonialism." These terms had been absorbed from the lexicon of the Left, but they were easily wedded to a religious discourse. The United States became the "Great Satan," while its partner, Israel, rated junior status as the "Little Satan" for its oppression of the Palestinians and its occupation of the holy places in Jerusalem. (Khomeini was an ardent supporter of the Palestinian cause from the very beginning, even using some of the religious taxes donated by his followers to finance Palestinian groups.) If someone needed to whip up emotions at a revolutionary demonstration, there was no better way to do it than to start some rousing anti-American chant.

Indeed, the US Embassy in Tehran had already been attacked once before, in mid-February 1979, just a few days after the ayatollah's return. A group of young revolutionary militiamen stormed the complex, now operating with a reduced staff, and took the ambassador and his staff captive. The ambassador managed to call up the revolutionary authorities and request assistance, and about an hour after the attack they sent in forces who ordered the gunmen to disperse. Four Americans were wounded; an Iranian waiter was killed.[3]

In those first days of the revolution, Khomeini and his allies had many other things to worry about. The economy was in shambles, numerous armed factions and guerrilla groups roamed the land, and forces sympathetic to the shah were still active. It was not the moment to start a head-on conflict with the Americans. Indeed, many within Bazargan's provisional government believed that the success of the revolution depended, to an extent, on Washington's willingness to tolerate it. Though Bazargan and his colleagues joined in the anti-American rhetoric when necessary, they tried to keep it within limits.

All this changed radically when President Carter announced, on October 22, 1979, that he was allowing the shah to come to the United States for treatment of his cancer. Carter had at first demurred, but finally relented in the face of intense lobbying from such notables as Henry Kissinger, the former national security adviser and secretary of state, and former vice president Nelson Rockefeller, who considered the shah a personal friend. US officials in Iran and Iran analysts in Washington strongly advised against receiving him. Since his departure from Iran in January, the shah had wandered the world, traveling from Egypt to Morocco to the Bahamas to Mexico. The shah's cancer had been diagnosed some five years earlier, and though his disease was kept secret from the outside world for most of that time, its effects, and the drugs he took to counter them, may well have contributed to his depression and indecisiveness during the crucial months of rising turmoil. Now his illness affected the course of events once again.

The news that the hated shah was being welcomed to the United States prompted a great surge of dark emotion among the Iranian revolutionaries. The realization that Carter had granted refuge to the deposed king confirmed what many Iranians had suspected all along: even now, months after the shah had gone, his friends in Washington were still trying to help him. There was no better proof of American perfidy.

The student activists who decided to storm the embassy in November were a genuine grassroots group, a characteristic manifestation of the revolutionary ferment sweeping across Iran at the time. It remains unclear to this day whether Khomeini himself was informed in advance of the students' plans to take over the embassy. By their own account, the students wanted to apprise Khomeini of their plans, but their spiritual leader, a radical ayatollah by the name of Mohammad Mousavi Khoeiniha, persuaded them to go ahead without doing so.

Prime Minister Bazargan and the other members of his government were appalled by the news and ordered the students to cease their occupation of the embassy complex. Bazargan and the other pragmatists had been quietly making diplomatic overtures to the Americans, hoping to restore a modicum of cooperation with Washington. They had entirely unsentimental reasons for doing so. Billions of dollars in Iranian money rested in American banks. Iran's US-made fighter planes desperately needed spare parts. Oil refineries and factories depended on foreign (which all too often meant "American") know-how to keep going. The pragmatists hoped that they could prevent a complete breakdown of relations with the Americans. That was an aim that the Carter administration undoubtedly shared. But the students refused. They had other priorities.

Khomeini himself maintained a conspicuous silence at first. Members of the provisional government—like Ebrahim Yazdi, by now foreign minister—later claimed that the revolution's supreme leader initially signaled his opposition to the takeover. He was, perhaps, subsequently swayed to change his stance by news of the huge crowds of demonstrators who soon appeared outside the embassy compound, where they chanted their approval of the students' action. Whatever the reason, that evening Khomeini went on the radio to applaud the students and denounce

the Great Satan. His announcement also signaled the start of an all-out clerical offensive against critics of theocratic rule.

At the beginning of November, just before the attack on the embassy, Bazargan
and Yazdi had traveled to Algiers for the funeral of the just-deceased Algerian
president. They seized the chance to meet with Carter's national security adviser,
Zbigniew Brzezinski, to discuss how Iran and the United States might get relations back on track (and, in particular, how to release the Iranian assets still held in
US banks). Bazargan was even photographed as he shook Brzezinski's hand—an
image that haunted him in the weeks to come. As the students paraded blindfolded
American diplomats before the cameras, exulting in their humiliation of the world's
most powerful country, those businesslike diplomatic contacts with the Americans
suddenly looked like an act of treason. Three days after the students took over the
embassy, Bazargan and his ministers resigned. It was the end of the dream of a
"moderate Islamist" politics in Iran. From this point on, the Revolutionary Council,
which had for so long acted like a parallel government, began to emerge as the center of political power in the new Islamic Republic.

The White House responded to the hostage taking with confusion. Hadn't its
own representatives just conducted talks with representatives of the same government that was now openly violating the terms of the Vienna Treaty, the international agreement that dictated the proper treatment of diplomats? The United
States demanded the immediate release of the captives.

In fact, however, the Carter administration was deeply divided over how it
should react. Carter's foreign policy was run by two men who held starkly divergent
opinions about the right ways to respond to the challenges of the age. Their differences go a long way toward explaining the vacillations of US foreign policy during
this crucial period in global history.

Brzezinski was a Cold War Democrat who had a harshly realistic approach to
foreign policy. As the son of a Polish diplomat who had emigrated to the United
States, Brzezinski had a shrewd appreciation of the threat posed by totalitarian
opponents, and he favored a hard line against Khomeini and the hostage takers.
Carter's secretary of state, Cyrus Vance, was a lawyer from a privileged background
who embodied the spirit of 1970s détente.[4] He was part of the US delegation at
the Paris peace talks with North Vietnam at the end of the 1960s, an experience he
liked to cite as evidence that it was possible to conduct dialogue with even the most
ruthless of opponents. During the hostage crisis, he often mentioned President
Truman's policy of restraint toward the Chinese Communists in 1949, who had

kept US consul Angus Ward under arrest for a year, as well as the refusal of Lyndon Johnson to use force against the North Koreans when they seized the US spy ship USS *Pueblo*. In both cases, the Americans had been released after long periods in captivity. Brzezinski worried above all about the damage that an indecisive response would do to America's international stature and accordingly favored demonstrations of resolve and the consideration of military means to end the crisis; Vance believed that the safety of the hostages was paramount and advised against anything that might provoke the Iranians. The two men's disagreements meant that Carter had a hard time uniting his administration behind a single policy line. To the outside world, the American stance appeared indecisive, at times downright schizophrenic.

The year 1979 brought one crisis after another for US diplomats. At the end of November, just a few weeks after the hostages were seized in Tehran, the young Saudi insurgents who were inspired by dreams of the impending Day of Judgment occupied the Grand Mosque in Mecca. The attack—which may have been partly inspired by the young Sunnis' desire to trump the millenarian rhetoric coming from Iran—triggered an exchange of inflammatory accusations by the United States and the revolutionary government in Tehran. The Americans, with little evidence to back up their claims, publicly depicted the mosque seizure as a Khomeini-inspired intrigue. Khomeini responded by accusing the Americans of orchestrating the whole episode as part of a systematic campaign to dishonor Islam. Muslims tended to believe the ayatollah's version, and anti-US riots broke out across the Islamic world. In Pakistan a mob stormed the US Embassy in Islamabad, burning some of the buildings and killing two Americans before they were dispersed. On December 2, another group of rioters in the Libyan capital of Tripoli burned down the US Embassy building there.

All of these crises flared up and died away. Not so the situation in Tehran. US officials had failed to foresee how the seizure of the hostages would fuel a spiral of revolutionary radicalization. It unleashed a storm of nationalist emotions that the Khomeinists skillfully exploited toward their own domestic political ends. The Carter administration kept seeking "reasonable" interlocutors who could make a deal, failing to realize that the new leaders in Tehran actually had every reason to keep the situation smoldering along. Not only did the taking of the hostages feed into the ferment inside Iran, but it also dovetailed with Khomeini's urge to spread revolution throughout the Muslim world. Defying the world's most powerful superpower enabled Khomeini to pose as a latter-day Saladin, single-handedly thwarting the evil designs of the West.

For the hostages themselves, geopolitics quickly gave way to much more mundane worries. Robert C. Ode was a State Department retiree, a former consular official who had rejoined the foreign service to fill a temporary post in the Tehran embassy. On the morning of November 4, he was helping a visitor with a visa application when he was told to leave his post because a mob had managed to get into the embassy compound. Ode and a few other officials from the consular department managed to get out of the compound and started walking toward the private residence of one of the men, but a few blocks away they were met by armed students. One of them fired a shot over the Americans' heads. The students hustled them back to the compound.

There the students tied Ode's hands behind his back, blindfolded him, and put him in a room. "I strongly protested the violation of my diplomatic immunity, but these protests were ignored," he later wrote in a day-by-day account of his captivity. Later in the day he was brought together with a group of other hostages in a different part of the building, though they were forbidden to speak with each other. Their hands were untied only when they were eating or had to go to the bathroom. "Some students attempted to talk with us, stating how they didn't hate Americans—only our U.S. Government, President Carter, etc." That first night, after a meager dinner of sandwiches, Ode and the others slept on the floor of the living room in the ambassador's residence.[5]

The days that followed brought a bewildering series of changes in location. For a while Ode and his fellow captives were held in an equipment storage area, where they slept, still with hands bound, on concrete floors. His captors confiscated Ode's personal belongings, including his wedding ring. Nine days after the hostage taking began, Ode found himself in what had been the ambassador's bedroom. He and the other hostages were forced to sit on chairs facing the wall in crepuscular darkness, since the students always kept the drapes closed. "Sitting in a chair all day long was extremely tiresome." At one point the hostages received a visit from the pope's representative—"a fat, dumpy little Italian who tapped me on the arm and clucked 'Molto buono' and 'Pazienza.'" Diplomats from the Syrian and Belgian embassies also visited. They offered no conversation, "just looked at us as though we were animals in a zoo!" On November 14, the students asked Ode and others to sign a statement asking the US government to return the shah to his homeland. (Ode noted that he was number 36 on the list of signers.)

In the weeks that followed, Ode carefully documented the mundane details of his captivity. "Venetian blinds were always closed in our room and the window was covered inside and out with newspapers." Lights were often left on in the hostages' quarters at night, making it hard to sleep, and the problem was compounded by the Iranians' penchant for all-night political demonstrations, complete with chants and speeches broadcast over loudspeakers. Armed guards stood in the hallways with assault rifles. One evening, without warning, one of Ode's roommates—the embassy's assistant air attaché—was taken away and subjected to an all-night interrogation; the next day he was taken away again, with no explanations forthcoming. For months Ode did not know whether he was dead or alive. In mid-December his captors gave Ode a razor and shaving cream, and he was able to shave off the beard he had accumulated in his first thirty-eight days of imprisonment. On December 14, his forty-first day, Ode was finally allowed to go outside for the first time. "Although I had been exercising in my rooms by pacing back and forth as much as possible, being out in the fresh air for the first time made me feel almost as though I had just gotten up from a hospital bed for the first time after a long period in the hospital!" A few days later he was able to persuade the students to return his wedding ring.

In the early hours of Christmas Day 1979, Ode's captors shook him awake. His Iranian captors told him to dress and then tied his hands and blindfolded him. He and three of his colleagues were led into the living room of the embassy residence. Their hands were untied and their blindfolds removed. Their eyes were exposed to a harsh, blinding light that filled the room. TV cameras had been set up to record the scene.

The American hostages, who were now approaching the end of their second month in captivity, had been told that they would be participating in a Christian Christmas service with priests brought in especially for the purpose. Though Ode had been expecting all the hostages to be there, only three of the others were allowed to join him. (It is possible he was chosen for this select group because he was the oldest of the captives.) The men found themselves confronting a surreal tableau. "The room had been decorated for Christmas with a tree, decorations on the walls, and a table with oranges, apples, some Christmas cookies and Kraft caramels on plates," Ode recorded. A tall man in a maroon robe turned out to be William Sloan Coffin of Riverside Memorial Church in New York, famed for his days as a high-profile protester against the Vietnam War. He sat at a piano and played a few Christmas carols for the hostages, who sang along. On the floor was a pile of Christmas cards that had been collected for the hostages by a New York radio station; Ode was allowed to take a dozen or so back to his room. And, astonishingly, there was even a meal to suit the occasion: "We were served a special dinner on Christmas—turkey, sweet potatoes (candied), cranberry jelly, cake and jello."[6]

the new regime had little interest in abiding by the norms of interna-
r. The Iranians viewed the Americans' refusal to give up the shah as
ashington aimed to sabotage the revolution (or, at minimum, prevent
revealing his American-sponsored crimes in the court of public opin-
an three decades after the revolution, Washington has yet to establish
lations with the Islamic Republic, and there is little likelihood that
ry will have an interest in doing so anytime soon. Dialogue between
mained a near impossibility (aside from the extralegal machinations of
an-Contra scandal in the 1980s or a few cursory discussions of issues of
erest, such as a brief colloquy on Afghanistan in 2001).

rgence between the two worldviews is nicely encapsulated by the failure
n Eagle Claw, the Carter administration's attempt to rescue the hostages
-operations forces in April 1980. The effort to send a helicopter-borne
deep into Iranian territory ended in disaster when the choppers ran into
ted dust storm that forced one of them to crash-land. Several others suc-
malfunctions, and the mission had to be aborted before any of those income close to Tehran. For most Americans, the sorry tale of helicopters
by a swirl of desert sand served merely to heighten the worst foreign-
iliation since the defeat in Vietnam. For Iranians, the whole story offered
proof of America's perfidy and conspiratorial intentions. (The hostages
ly released, after long and arduous negotiations between the Carter Ad-
on and the government in Tehran, on January 20, 1981, as newly elected
Ronald Reagan was giving his inauguration speech.)

as, overall, a low point in the history of US diplomacy. It was also the year
in February, the US ambassador of Kabul, Adolph Dubs, was taken hos-
ftist militants. He was killed when Afghan government forces tried to free
e last US ambassador to die on the job until the killing of J. Christopher
Washington's envoy to Libya, in the city of Benghazi in 2012.

icans still tend to think of the hostage crisis in terms of its effect on the
States. But what this version of events tends to overlook is the profound
which the story of the hostages also influenced the course of events inside
lf. The seizure of the embassy came at a critical moment. The revolution
ged down in strife between the clerics and their various domestic oppo-
homeini was growing increasingly impatient with the moderates' criticisms
lans for a constitution that followed his theory of theocratic rule. The sei-
the embassy, and the surge of public emotion it unleashed, gave him just the
e he needed.

The hostage takers were hoping to der
toward their captives. It is doubtful that this
those countries with knowledge of the Orw
a century rich in totalitarian spectacle. The
tirely new kind of government, and to some
they were also resorting, all too obviously, t
ships. The Nazis and the Soviets had both pe
of way. Was this the path that Islamic goverr
well for the future of the revolution.

The Muslim Students Following the Imam
acted according to an inchoate mixture
woolly conspiracy theories. The hostages who
about their motivations usually found it a frust
lutionaries believed not only that the United Sta
crats who were conducting warfare on Muslims
Americans were responsible for natural disasters
all of them conjured up by diabolical scientists. (
captor that Iran and America had been enemies f
American responded that the United States had ex
the Iranian breezily dismissed him: Khomeini had

The Carter White House never quite manage
nents were about, either. There were very few An
notion of what life was like inside a Shiite semina
who knew the work of Shariati or the other intellect
idea of revolution with ancient Quranic teachings. C
paranoid fanaticism of Khomeini's supporters and t
theories actually had many precedents in the history
1789 and Russia in 1917 had their share of such devel
lution, the revolutionary mind-set gained an extra boo
ality of ingrained Shiite traditions of resistance to est
psychological realities seem to have completely eluded
US foreign policy, a group whose collective Cold War ex
to contemplate the mobilizing force of religious emotio
with the conclusion that Khomeini was simply mentall
The gap between the two sides quickly became unl
saw the Iranians' blatant violation of the rules for the

evidence that
tional behavi
proof that W
the shah from
ion). More t
diplomatic r
either count
them has re
the covert Ir
common int
The dive
of Operatic
with specia
contingent
an unexpec
cumbed to
volved had
humiliated
policy hur
yet more
were final
ministrati
President
1979 v
in which,
tage by le
him—th
Stevens,
Ame
United
extent t
Iran its
had bo
nents.
of his
zure of
leverag

In theory, at least, Bazargan could have pushed back. All things considered, the prime minister had done a remarkable job of stabilizing the economy—though his government was harshly criticized by the leftists for not doing enough to help the poor. He could, theoretically, have tried to use this relative success as the capital for a future political career. He enjoyed wide backing among the moderates who wanted to see a stronger division between church and state, and he even had the qualified support of some of the leftist militia groups. But in reality, it was too late. By the time he left the office, it had become eminently clear to him where Khomeini was taking the revolution. Though many of his supporters urged him to campaign for the presidency, Bazargan declined, and he quietly faded into the background of Iranian politics. He died of a heart attack in 1995.

The downfall of Bazargan's government cleared the way for Khomeini's camp to establish their vision of a theocratic state. Ali Khamenei, the young radical who later became Khomeini's successor, once said that the Revolutionary Council had appointed Bazargan prime minister "because we had no one else, and at that time we ourselves lacked the ability."[8] Such concerns apparently no longer applied. On November 15, the Assembly of Experts—the constituent assembly that had been convened two months earlier—completed its deliberations.[9] The original draft constitution had been completely transformed. Now it made the *faqih*, the jurisprudent in chief, the centerpiece of the entire political order. It gave him power over the Revolutionary Guard, the state-controlled media, and the judiciary.[10] It also gave him control over the Guardian Council, which vets candidates for election and has veto power over decisions of parliament.[11] The draft constitution also made sharia the basis of the new legal system. With time the supreme leader received even more authority, including control over broad swaths of the economy and the ability to appoint the all-important Friday prayer leaders (who were already key figures in the polity that was emerging from the phase of revolutionary turmoil). The Shia clergy received far-reaching powers for the supervision of society.[12]

Though an Islamist of long standing, Bazargan was not a cleric, and that had made it relatively easy to dispose of him. But to those who were now determined to bring Iran under tight clerical control, the case of Grand Ayatollah Mohamed Kazem Shariatmadari, the country's top-ranking religious leader, posed a much more serious challenge. Back in 1963, when Khomeini was under intense pressure from the shah, it was Shariatmadari, Khomeini's senior both literally and clerically, who had seen to it that the younger man received the title of "ayatollah"—a status that made it virtually impossible for the shah to execute him. Some Iranians contend that Shariatmadari deserved the credit for saving Khomeini's life. By 1979, in any event, Shariatmadari was the highest-ranking cleric in Iran, and second in popularity only to Khomeini. When the revolution broke out, Shariatmadari sided with the religious opposition and supported it. But he made it clear from the start that he wanted to go back to the constitution of 1906, which had established a constitutional monarchy with a small group of clerics exercising oversight over leg-islation to ensure conformity with the principles of Islam. In the summer of 1979 he opposed the narrow path for the drafting of the constitution originally proposed by the Khomeinists. Shariatmadari gave his support instead to the opposition de-mands for an elected constitutional assembly that would have represented a broad range of views. It is a mark of his stature at the time that the leaders of the revolu-tion felt that they at least had to acknowledge his reservations and craft a compro-mise. At first Khomeini's entourage had planned for an Assembly of Experts (a con-stituent assembly) with only around forty members; at Shariatmadari's urging they expanded it to seventy-three. Though the moderates congratulated themselves on their success at forcing the change, it soon became clear that the expanded assembly would do them little good. Clerics still retained a majority in the body, and the draft they presented on November 15 reflected the predispositions of the active clergy around Khomeini. Shariatmadari and other moderates were horrified by the result.

Through the fall of 1979, Shariatmadari's conflict with the new rulers steadily intensified. Though he refrained from personal criticisms of Khomeini, he had never accepted his fellow ayatollah's theory of the "guardianship of the jurist." Shari-atmadari wanted to see a democratically elected government that would be subject to collective clerical guidance. He made a point of keeping up his contacts with the members of the secular and leftist parties, and he sided with the opposition by denouncing the torture and executions that were becoming hallmarks of the new government. His interpretations of Islamic law tended to stick to received tradi-tion—in stark contrast to the innovative activist views of Khomeini.[13] When the outlines of the new constitution began to emerge in the early fall of 1979, Shariat-madari went so far as to issue a fatwa against it, declaring to his followers that the principle of *velayat-e faqih* had no legal basis. Prompted by the ruling, his followers rioted in several cities around the country.[14]

This unrest was not spontaneous. As a long-established and widely respected *marja* (a high-ranking scholar entitled to issue authoritative legal judgments), Shar-iatmadari had a strong power base of his own, centered in his home province of Azerbaijan, and a solid organization to go with it. But he also had many followers in other parts of the country, as well as in Lebanon, Iraq, the Gulf States, and Pakistan. In March 1979, Shariatmadari's supporters had founded a new party, the Islamic

People's Republican Party (IPRP), that aimed to serve as a vehicle for his relatively moderate revolutionary principles. Shariatmadari himself, who never became a member, maintained a certain distance from the new group. It was Shariatmadari's tragedy that he never quite managed to resolve the tension between his lingering distrust of clerical involvement in politics and his own eminently political role as the most credible source of opposition to Khomeini's plans. Khomeini, of course, had no such hesitations.

With the polarization of the revolutionary camp that followed the hostage taking and the fall of the Bazargan government, Shariatmadari's options rapidly began to narrow. It became increasingly easy to characterize any opposition to Khomeini, however qualified, as opposition to the revolution overall. After the new constitution passed, with overwhelming approval, in a second referendum on December 2–3, riots broke out in Shariatmadari's hometown of Tabriz, Iran's second-largest city and the capital of the province of Azerbaijan (where most of the population were Turk-speaking Azeris). Shariatmadari himself was no separatist, but many of his followers supported the idea of greater regional autonomy for Azerbaijan, and the new constitution's strict centralism was the last straw for them. IPRP members seized control of the TV station in Tabriz and began broadcasting denunciations of the government in Tehran, which they accused of betraying the democratic ideals of the revolution. Shariatmadari refused to approve their actions, understanding only too well where they would lead.

The revolutionary leaders in Tehran responded in no uncertain terms. They sent tanks and troops. Leading the way were the new Revolutionary Guards, who retook the TV station and occupied the IPRP headquarters. Some of the leaders of the uprising were summarily shot. The government arranged for massive pro-Khomeini counterdemonstrations, and Hezbollahis fought IPRP members in the streets. With the help of the military, the Tehran government soon reestablished control over the Azerbaijani media, depriving the Shariatmadari camp of a crucial means for spreading its views.

In January 1980, under growing pressure from the regime, Shariatmadari publicly disavowed the IPRP and disappeared into house arrest, where he would remain until his death in 1986. He was ordered to refrain from making public statements and kept under guard. Some of his relatives were also imprisoned. The regime forbade other clerics from participating in his funeral prayers.

In the case of Bazargan, one might have argued that the prime minister wasn't "Islamic enough." But now the revolution had turned against leading members of the clergy. This was a shift that appeared to be justified less by citations from the

242

STRANGE REBELS

Quran than by straightforward reference to raison d'état. There were other senior members of the clergy who strongly disagreed with Khomeini's theories, but they were not threats to his role in the same way that Shariatmadari had been. Khomeini could not persuade them to be completely silent, but in their cases he did not need to challenge clerical unity quite as openly as in the case of Shariatmadari.

With Shariatmadari sidelined, Khomeini could turn to the business of eliminating his other enemies—especially the Mujahideen-e Khalq, the still-powerful Islamo-Marxist militia. The Revolutionary Guard and the Hezbollahis launched an all-out offensive against the MEK. Those MEK members who managed to survive quickly went underground and unleashed a guerrilla war against the regime that continues to this day. Other leftist groups, some of them strikingly reluctant to criticize the "anti-imperialist" Khomeini, withered as an independent force.

It was in this broader context—the continuing struggle for power and Khomeini's need to find leverage against some of his most formidable opponents—that the hostage crisis occurred. It played a key role in Khomeini's push to consolidate the revolution around his vision of the Islamic state. It now became nearly impossible for anyone to attack the imam's grand design without being branded a defender of America and Israel (and, by extension, a Satanist). As the months went by, the students began to tire of their occupation of the US Embassy, but Khomeini and his entourage insisted that they stay put. There was simply too much to be gained by the continuing humiliation of President Carter. The embassy's archives contained countless documents of American dealings with Iranian political figures, including many of the moderates who had tried to open up channels of communication with the United States after the beginning of the revolution. The presentation of these compromising discoveries in the media, usually with inconvenient context edited away, became a highly effective tool for neutralizing opponents. It was a device selectively applied. Some of the people in Khomeini's entourage had also made contact with US diplomats in the course of the revolution, but no documents incriminating them were ever made public.

Clerical rule was now firmly established, and from this point until the end of his life, Khomeini focused all of his political efforts on defending the institutions he had established. For this reason, he took to calling the chapter of Iranian history that began with the hostage taking the "Second Revolution." It has yet to end.

18

Playing Bridge

It is inevitable, perhaps, that we focus on leaders when we examine grand political and economic transitions. But they are not the only actors in these dramas. Deng Xiaoping and his colleagues triumphed precisely because they unleashed the creativity and the entrepreneurial urges of millions of Chinese. Many of them—shocking though it might be to think—were not even members of the Chinese Communist Party.

In January 1979, about the time that Deng was preparing for his trip to the United States, a young man named Rong Zhiren returned to his hometown of Guangzhou (Canton), the largest city in Guangdong Province, up the river from Hong Kong. Rong had just turned thirty, but he had relatively little in the way of concrete achievements to show for someone his age. The reason was the Great Proletarian Cultural Revolution. A central part of the Cultural Revolution was Mao's campaign against intellectualism, book learning, and the "Four Olds" (old habits, old ideas, old customs, and old culture). In 1966 he had ordered the closure of China's institutions of higher education. Over the ensuing years, 17 million students were dispatched to the countryside to learn the virtues of the simple life from the peasantry. University entrance examinations did not resume in China until the autumn of 1977. By early 1979 only 7 million students had made it back to the cities.

As the Cultural Revolution played out, the overwhelming majority of students stayed in the places where they were assigned, which usually meant wasting their best years tilling the land in remote agricultural communes. Rong did not. Sent out to the countryside in 1969, he sneaked away as soon as he had the chance. He spent the next ten years dodging the police and doing odd jobs, like drawing and tutoring. He lived with friends, moving from place to place. In December 1978, back in Guangzhou but still on the run, he heard the results of the historic Third Plenum in Beijing on the local radio. Like millions of other Chinese, he understood that something fundamentally transformative was under way—and that included an opening for entrepreneurship. "I knew this policy would last because Chinese people would want to get rich," as he later put it. In January 1979, he decided that he would be one of the first to take a chance. He applied for a business license. The bureaucratic obstacles sounded daunting: one of the requirements was a complete physical checkup to ensure that he had no infectious diseases. But it turned out to be a cinch. When Rong went through the procedure in early 1979, everything was done in just a few days. (Nowadays it takes nearly three weeks.) The Guangdong government, eager to get things going, was already trying to encourage business creation.

Rong started his business on March 18—an auspicious date because the number 18 sounds like the phrase "You'll definitely get rich" in Mandarin. Following the advice of people in the neighborhood where he had been working, he decided to open a small restaurant specializing in breakfast. The main dish he offered was classic Guangdong comfort food: congee (rice porridge) with peanuts and spareribs. He set up his restaurant—really a glorified tent on a wood frame he put together himself—at an intersection close to two high schools, assuming that he could market his cheap breakfasts to hungry students. His start-up capital was one hundred yuan (roughly sixty-five US dollars at the official highly inflated exchange rate), sixty of which he had borrowed from his girlfriend. The furniture and a big cooking pot were loaned from friends. He was nervous at first. The idea of running one's own business was frowned upon by many educated people, who regarded such things as beneath their dignity. But those worries began to fade away as he immersed himself in the daily routine of his business and the money started rolling in. Almost immediately, the restaurant was an enormous success.[1]

Some small private businesses—known as *getihu*—had existed since the Communist takeover in 1949. But they belonged to a small but beleaguered minority, continuously battered by the whims of officialdom and the ebb and flow of political campaigns. The policy that took effect in 1979 embodied an entirely different philosophy. The communiqué of the Third Plenum had specifically, if cautiously, embraced the principle of private commerce. Perhaps even more important than the party's official statements were its actions. Would-be entrepreneurs were especially heartened when the official media announced, later in 1979, that the government had asked a man named Rong Yiren (no relation to the founder of the restaurant in Guangzhou) to found a new company that was expressly designed to experiment with foreign trade and investment. He called it CITIC, the China International Trust & Investment Corporation. Rong was the scion of one of China's most famous business families, who had built their wealth on a series of textile mills in the early twentieth century. After the Communists took power in 1949, most of them fled. But Rong decided to stay, giving controlling stakes in his companies to the party and taking a job, for a time, as a vice mayor in Shanghai. During the Cultural Revolution, he had suffered the predictable persecution—including torture and public humiliation—but he had bounced back after the fall of the Gang of Four. His establishment of CITIC was specifically designed to serve as an official signal that China was open for business. Deng himself encouraged Rong to be "boldly creative."[2]

Another signal came with the officially sanctioned revival of a long-prohibited aspect of business. Advertising was one of those quirks of capitalism regarded with particular contempt by the ideological purists of Chinese Communism. Right up until the end of 1978, foreign businesspeople noted how the notion of advertising elicited conflicting emotions of disgust and curiosity among their Chinese interlocutors. Then, suddenly, in the spring of 1979, representatives of a new state-owned company called the Shanghai Advertising Company showed up at the Canton Trade Fair.[3] Foreign investors were shocked, but perhaps not completely. They had already been casting about for ways to promote their products in the Chinese media, and on March 15 the well-established Western advertising giant Ogilvy & Mather succeeded in publishing its first ad in a Shanghai newspaper (for watches from the Swiss company Rado).[4]

The message that commercial success now counted more than ideological purity quickly percolated down to officials at the lower level—and nowhere more than in Guangdong Province, home to the famous Canton trade fair. The remarkable degree of bureaucratic openness that Rong Zhiren encountered when he opened his new restaurant in Guangzhou, then Guangdong's biggest city, reflected an eagerness among the province's party elite to unleash private initiative. Already under Hua Guofeng, leading party members had begun pushing the central government to grant them wide-ranging powers over the province's economic affairs. Their eagerness to gain some vital administrative flexibility was fanned not only by their relative economic backwardness but also by proximity to Hong Kong and its turbocharged entrepreneurial culture. Despite the tightly sealed border, Guangdong and Hong Kong remained linked in a surprising number of ways. Many of the people in Hong Kong had fled there from Guangdong after the Communist takeover, and often they maintained their ties with the family members they had left behind on the mainland. A certain degree of trade between both sides continued even after 1949, both officially approved and illegal. The people on both sides of the border spoke Cantonese, the dialect ubiquitous in this part of China, rather than the lingua franca of Mandarin. Many in Guangdong could pick up radio broadcasts from the British colony. In the wake of the Third Plenum, they were less shy about listening in—and even about discussing what they heard.

Media coverage of Deng's visits overseas—not only to the United States but also to Japan and Southeast Asia—had opened up a view of the larger world, as well as driving home the painful awareness of China's own backward state. More shocks were on the way. As 1979 dawned, British diplomat Roger Garside was startled to see a New Year's Eve TV broadcast featuring a singer from the "renegade province" of Taiwan. American stars like the pop musician John Denver and comedian Bob Hope trekked to China in the course of the year. Foreign classical music orchestras also put on performances. During the Cultural Revolution, book publishing had dwindled away to a minimum, and foreign works of literature disappeared. But then, one day in 1979, literature lovers awoke to find a new edition of *Hamlet* in the bookshops. The Quran and other religious works reappeared as well.

Such changes had a monumental impact. This was a China where road maps and telephone books were still regarded as state secrets, so the act of sharing them with foreigners was a crime. The same restrictions applied to weather forecasts and the location of gasoline stations; a foreigner who managed to hail a taxi could find herself in a tricky predicament if the car's gas tank turned out to be empty. (Of course, taxis were extremely hard to find. Bicycles still predominated on the streets of Beijing.)[5] Consumer products were scarce. Cloth was rationed.

There were ways to take advantage of the new atmosphere of comparative openness, but manufacturing new products took time. So some of the first obvious changes—like opening private restaurants—came in the realm of services. Hair salons quickly widened their menu of services: suddenly, every woman seemed to be getting a permanent.

As is typical of situations where an all-powerful state begins to relax its grip, a market for the illicit emerged with startling speed. The American journalist and China scholar Orville Schell recorded his adventures in a seedy Beijing café in the company of Wang Zaomin ("Benefit-the-People Wang"), whom he described as "a soldier in the People's Liberation Army and a procurer of women." Wang styled himself a petty gangster and dressed accordingly in a fedora, a Western-style trench coat, and army pants. The girls who worked for him yearned for the precious hard currency that would give them access to Western cigarettes and magazines and dreamed of one day owning the same kind of beautiful clothes they saw in foreign fashion spreads. Wang and his charges had zero interest in politics, and they displayed little of the idealism of the intellectuals who were provoking the authorities with their writings on issues of the day. But Schell rightly refused to dismiss the denizens of Wang's back alley, noting that they were, in their way, "every bit as rebellious and subversive to the geist of the old Chinese Communist Party as their dissident compatriots." What drove them was the vague yearning for the lifestyle that the West seemed to exemplify—a world of variety and stimulation: "'Why is our life so boring when Western life is so rich?' one young woman asked me in the Peace Café, confessing that she was transfixed by what she had seen on Chinese TV when Deng Xiaoping visited the United States."[6]

Schell had visited China during the waning years of the Cultural Revolution and recalled how hard ordinary people were prepared to work to ward off even the most glancing contact (much less conversation) with visiting foreigners. Returning to China on a short trip in 1978, however, "was like entering a different country," he later wrote. The impression was intensified when he came back for a longer visit in 1979. In a Beijing mental hospital he ran into a doctor who spoke unabashedly of the teachings of Freud (a taboo topic in the days of Mao) and defied long-standing party doctrine by refusing to regard the cause of mental illness as "class oppression." A young judge's assistant interrogated him about how to find jobs and housing in the United States and then openly declared his desire to emigrate.[7]

For many Chinese, though, even remote contact with the West sufficed. TVs were still few and far between in 1979, and anyone who owned a set could count on a persistent audience of friends and neighbors. But that scarcity quickly eroded in the course of 1979 and 1980. Relaxation of the rules allowed mainlanders to order sets in Hong Kong and take delivery in the People's Republic. An even more accessible technology was the cassette-tape player—the same affordable device that had such a transformative effect on political discourse in Iran. Characteristically enough, however, the Chinese did not use their tapes to record incendiary texts or to distribute political messages. They were listening to bootleg music recordings.

They were particularly enamored of a Taiwanese pop star named Teresa Teng, a young beauty who specialized in songs of tenderness and yearning. The spirit of her music was diametrically opposed to the strident revolutionary operas held high by Jiang Qing in the Cultural Revolution years. And, indeed, befitting the hesitations of the early reform period, Teng's songs were officially banned in the People's Republic until well into the 1980s because of her associations with the renegade province. But that stopped almost no one from listening. (Some of her biggest fans were in the People's Liberation Army.)[8] Teng's new fans on the mainland knew her by her Mandarin name, Deng Li Jun—and since she had the same surname as the man who was leading China into its new era, she was soon dubbed "Little Deng."[9] Though on the face of things it might seem frivolous to compare the two of them, there was actually a deeper logic to the association. Her music, and the world of bourgeois pleasures it evoked, was one of the first everyday manifestations of Big Deng's policy of "reform and opening" (gaige kaifang).

What initially escaped the notice of many of her mainland listeners was the point that Teresa Teng was far from a purely Chinese phenomenon. In fact, she was a perfect exemplar of the accelerating trend of globalization, one that was having a particularly notable impact on the countries of East Asia. She was a household name not only in her Taiwanese homeland and Hong Kong, but also in Japan, South Korea, Malaysia, and Singapore. Her popularity throughout Southeast Asia undoubtedly had something to do with the regional presence of ethnic Chinese—many of whom would take advantage of Deng's plans to open the doors to outside investors. So Teng's gentle ballads also made a fitting, if unintentional, symbol of China's return to the global information circuit from which it had cut itself off for so long.

Popular culture produced inside the People's Republic was not really in a position to compete. Movies and music still labored under the stifling legacy of the long years in which Gang of Four leader Jiang Qing had dominated the cultural scene with her bizarrely stylized "revolutionary operas" and proletarian anthems. There was, however, one notable exception in 1979—a film called *Xiao Zi Bei*, a musical comedy known in English as *Bus Number Three*. Viewed from today's perspective, *Bus Number Three* is a bit of an oddity, the suitably awkward crystallization of a transitional moment. It tells the story of a group of young Shanghainese—a bus driver, a conductor, and various passengers, all of them bearing stylized names like "Young Green" or "Young Blue"—who are trying to find their way in the new age of Deng's Four Modernizations. It is, in part, a typically didactic bit of political propaganda (including oblique references to the pernicious influence of "remaining forces," meaning adherents of the Gang of Four) that nonetheless manages to point the way forward to a less ideological age, manifested in cheery songs that capture the comparative optimism of the moment.

The foreigners who witnessed all of this wondered whether they were watching the start of a new era or yet another of those transient phases that China had experienced so often in the past—like the Hundred Flowers campaign in the 1950s, when Mao solicited public criticism of the party's reign by calling upon society to "Let a Hundred Flowers Bloom," only to crack down violently on the critics as soon as he deemed that they had overstepped their bounds. The implications of all these 1979 experiments were radical, but it was impossible to tell how far they might go. One American businessman recalls asking his Chinese interlocutors, "Do you want capitalism?" "No," they told him, and cited models like Yugoslavia, Hungary—and East Germany, at that time regarded as one of the East bloc's most successful economies.[10] These countries, which only a tiny handful of Chinese knew firsthand, stood for the vague promise of liberalization. At this stage, it was still almost impossible to imagine a China that would tolerate a full-scale restoration of private business.

The biggest test of all, many people suspected, was to be found in the countryside, where the overwhelming majority of the Chinese lived. Under Mao's leadership, the Communists had marched to victory in 1949 precisely because they had identified their struggle with that of the peasants. The party had promised them freedom from want and corruption, the ills that have always plagued China's rural dwellers. But the transformation of private farms into "communes," collectively owned and operated, had plunged the countryside into a maelstrom of famine and suffering during the chaos of the Great Leap Forward. In the late 1970s, the ghosts of that colossal disaster still haunted the land. Reviving farming seemed an almost impossible task. Or was it?

It was early in 1979, and Production Team No. 12 was getting ready for work. The team, which called a small village in Guangdong Province home, consisted of forty-nine families who farmed forty acres of fish ponds and fields.

As recounted by American anthropologist Steven Mosher in his book *Broken Earth: The Rural Chinese*, the team had its headquarters in what had once been the village's ancestral temple, a building adorned with carvings of tigers and dragons that had been constructed seventy years earlier as the spiritual center of the community. Now, more prosaically, it combined the functions of a warehouse, meeting area, and repair shop. One wall was taken up by a long storage shed—"as out of place in the high-ceilinged hall as a chicken coop in a church," Mosher writes—containing all the team's tools (hoes, baskets, buckets, carrying poles). Tubs of dried corn stood near the door; crates and boxes lay jumbled in a corner. All the property in the building belonged to the village People's Commune, of which the team was a part. In the office space at one end of the hall hung a blackboard adorned with hooks. On the hooks hung 110 tags—one for each member of the team. Through the course of the day, the team head moved the tags around the board depending on the tasks assigned to each group of workers.[11]

At seven, well after dawn, the team leader arrived to unlock the door. By this time farmers in most parts of the world would have already been out in their fields. But the members of Production Team No. 12 saw no reason to hurry. They wandered in as the morning wore on. "Now everyone is waiting for the last stragglers to arrive," said the team leader. "And no one wants to be the first to leave for the fields. They're all afraid that that the others will sneak a few minutes more of leisure." It was around a quarter past eight by the time the farmers shouldered tools and headed slowly off to their jobs. The team head later explained why the impression of stasis was deceptive. "People aren't lazy all the time, just when they do collective labor. When they work on their private plots, they work hard. There is a saying: 'Energetic as dragons on the private plot, sluggish as worms on the public fields.'"

When Mosher asked the team leader whether it had always been like this, the man replied that "before collectivization people worked hard." He explained to the American that it now took fourteen days of work to hoe the same piece of land that once took six. "Everyone works at the same slow pace. People have learned from collectivization to do just enough to get by."[12]

And this was in Guangdong, one of China's most fertile regions. As we now know, however, not every place in the Chinese countryside was in the grip of the same stagnation witnessed by Mosher. There were a few communities where both farmers and officials were quietly testing the limits of the possible. One of the most intriguing was the village of Xiaogang, in a part of Anhui Province that had been hit especially hard by Great Leap starvation. Fengyang County had lost ninety thousand people—a quarter of its population—between 1958 and 1960.[13] In the 1950s, Xiaogang village had thirty-four households; by 1979, migration and starvation had reduced the number to eighteen.[14] In bad years, due to drought or mismanagement from above, the villagers had to sell possessions for food or borrow money for seed. The year 1978 was a bad one. Some of the families in the village were boiling poplar leaves and eating them with salt; others roasted tree bark and ground it to make flour.[15]

The peasants of Xiaogang were locked into the commune system, which forced them to cultivate collectively owned farmland. In return for their efforts, they received "work points" that could be exchanged for food.[16] One night in December 1978, the villagers decided that they could not go on. The heads of the households met after dark in the village's biggest house and made a secret deal. They drew up a contract that divided up the land of the village commune among the eighteen families and stipulated that each family would have the responsibility for tending the fields assigned to it. The villagers had vivid memories of what had happened to other families who had acted against state policy, so they also agreed that they would raise the children (until the age of eighteen) of any village leaders who were arrested or shot as a result of the agreement.

The Xiaogang villagers had no way of knowing that farmers all around China were trying to get away with similar plans. But Anhui Province was a bit different. The food situation there was so dire that some officials were willing to turn a blind eye to what the farmers were doing[17]—even while others persisted with obstruction, denying fertilizers to the experimenters.[18] The new party chief in Anhui, another victim of the Cultural Revolution, had his own ideas. Wan Li had assumed the leadership of the province in 1977, just before Deng's comeback, and he soon realized that the comeback of household contracting was the only way to make sure that people avoided starvation. He gave his official blessing to the Xiaogang experiment, as well as allowing other places to try out similar measures (always under the proviso that the peasants involved were in particularly desperate straits). Farmers were allowed to divide up the land of the commune into household plots. They were required to provide a set quota of grain to the state. The rest could be sold off in private markets.

The effects were dramatic. Grain output in Xiaogang rose sixfold in the course of the year. The per capita income of the villages went from twenty-two yuan to four hundred.[19] This was a trend that would be exceedingly hard to stop. "*Baochan daohu* ["contracting by the household"] is like a chicken pest," one peasant said. "When one family's chicken catches the disease, the whole village catches it. When one village has it, the whole country will be infected."[20] In 1979, by one estimate, 10 percent of Anhui Province was practicing the household-responsibility system. In June 1979, after paying a visit to Fengyang County to see the results for himself, Wan Li approved the expansion of the program to the entire province.[21] In the countryside, at least, the party was beginning to release its grip.

Zhao Ziyang, Wan's counterpart in Sichuan Province, took note. He had already been conducting experiments of his own, allowing state-owned enterprises to produce some goods in response to market demand and to use the resulting profits as they saw fit. Many of his own farmers still labored under threat of starvation, so he, too, began to allow them to deviate from the collective pattern. In 1978 he had begun allowing the communes to subdivide their production teams into smaller groups. He justified what he was doing as a way of "bringing individual initiative into full play." He may have actually regarded the measure as an intermediate step on the way toward full-scale revival of the household-responsibility system. In 1979 he then allowed some production teams in the province to break work groups down into individual families. The measures sparked political resistance from conservatives. (The Maoists had not vanished completely, after all.) "But Mr. Zhao is ready to risk it," wrote a group of visiting British journalists. "He endorsed setting family quotas for certain tasks such as raising silkworms, pigs and fish, on condition that the animal remain the property of the collective." That was his way of ensuring that the radicals couldn't accuse him of completely betraying the principle of collective ownership.[22]

Private interest, as it emerged, was about to prove a more powerful force than the Maoists' invocations of revolutionary purity. In August 1979, encouraged by Zhao's permissiveness, farmers in Sichuan decided to take an even more daring step. They set about dismantling Xiangyang People's Commune in Guanghan, a town about forty miles from the provincial capital of Chengdu. This effectively rejected the collectivization policies behind the Great Leap Forward, a dramatic rejection of one of Mao's signature policies. The move was so sensitive that they kept it secret, and it became publicly known only the following year.[23] Zhao Ziyang and other Sichuan officials provided them with discreet political cover.

The dissolution of the first commune was a step of far-reaching implications. The Guanghan farmers divided the assets of the commune into subunits, some of them economic (having to do with agricultural production), some of them purely administrative. This set an important precedent for a nationwide abolition of communes that would change the face of China in the next few years. In the same year that the commune in Guanghan was abolished, a Sichuan newspaper declared that the "unity of economics and politics" that lay at the heart of the People's Communes was not good and that "all unfavorable situations must be changed."[24] Decades later, the former head of the commune explained to an interviewer why the communes had become untenable. They were bureaucratically inflexible, with higher-ranking planners often ordering the commune to plant crops that were contrary to local conditions. They promoted excessive egalitarianism. And they suppressed initiative by giving the same amount of reward to each member of the commune regardless of the amount worked—what the locals referred to as "eating from one rice bowl."[25]

The success of the experiments conducted by Zhao and Wan propelled them both to the top of the career pyramid. Having won Deng's favor with his reforming zeal, Zhao became prime minister, and he played a crucial role in directing the economy during the early reform period. As for Wan Li, the peasants of Anhui immortalized him with a saying: "If you want to eat rice, look for Wan Li." Wan had the extra advantage of sharing Deng's favorite pastime. When he arrived in Beijing upon his promotion to the Politburo, Wan soon became a regular participant in Deng's biweekly bridge parties, held at his house every Wednesday and Saturday evening. The power of bridge in Deng's life was not to be underestimated. It was a game that played to his personal strengths: patience, strategic focus, and a prodigious memory.

The transformation of agriculture in 1978 and 1979 proceeded with little instigation from the top. The peasants sensed the opportunities provided by the loosening of the party's political control and pushed ahead. It was a process marked by wide regional variation; there seem to have been as many different names for agricultural reform experiments during this period as there are counties in China. It was also very much a matter of trial and error. When the politicians learned what the peasants were up to, they usually waited for evidence of success before they committed themselves unambiguously. Wan Li and Zhao Ziyang could claim credit for letting the farmers do what came naturally. When the experiments of the peasants bore fruit, Deng publicized their success, recognizing a good thing when he saw it. But he certainly could not take credit for giving farmers the idea.

The irony, as American anthropologist Stephen Mosher realized, was that Western scholars at the time regarded the Chinese as incorrigible collectivists. "Group thinking" was considered an indelible part of traditional culture that predisposed the Chinese to Communist ways. As a result, Mosher had come to the countryside expecting to discover evidence that the peasants were fundamentally satisfied with the stability and predictability furnished by the regime. According to scholarly reasoning, the Communist Party had taken power in 1949 largely due to the support of the country dwellers. It had promised to improve the lot of the peasantry, and in this it had surely succeeded. After all, hadn't the Communists brought schools and basic health care to even some of the most remote villages? Hadn't they eliminated the corruption and tyranny of the old landlords? Upon his arrival, Mosher carefully noted all the characteristics of a traditional society that skewed visibly to collective ways of doing things.

The rampant cynicism and apathy that he encountered in China's real-existing countryside thus came as something of a shock, and his account provides a fascinating chronicle of how a preconceived view can disintegrate upon contact with reality. But amid the ruins of Mao's utopian edifice, Mosher also discovered intriguing evidence of a powerful source of transformative energy: individual initiative. Though they were far from the places where the most important experiments were under way, the people in Mosher's remote Guangdong village had already picked up on the spread of the household-responsibility system, and he succeeded in capturing a nice snapshot of the spirit that, once unleashed, would soon lift hundreds of millions of people out of poverty. The old entrepreneurial mind-set of the Chinese "flared anew once opportunity presented itself," Mosher noted. When one woman heard that the party might soon allow a return to household farming, she immediately began making plans to start cultivating her own mulberry patch, planting the bushes between the rows of trees on the farm. "You can't do that now because people are careless when they work," she explained to the American. "They would step on them when they are spreading mud [as fertilizer] or picking mulberry leaves. But I'll be careful because they'll be mine."[26]

In May 1979, Tom Gorman, a Hong Kong–based American businessman, set off on another one of his trips to the Canton Trade Fair. As part of his job with a Hong Kong publisher of trade magazines, he had already made the trip to the fair several times, so he knew the routine. In the 1970s, foreigners who wanted to do business with the world's most populous country had to follow a peculiar procedure. They could enter the People's Republic only at one point, from Hong Kong. There they boarded a train at Tsim Sha Tsui Station in Kowloon, across the harbor from Hong Kong Island, marked by its splendid colonial clock tower, and headed north through lush, green, semitropical countryside to the border crossing at Lo Wu. There they disembarked and walked across the ironically named Friendship Bridge, a rudimentary wooden structure that spanned the slow-flowing Shumchun River, carrying their baggage with them. On the other side, the visitors were greeted by scowling border guards wearing uniforms adorned with the emblems of the People's Republic of China, who examined the proffered visas and granted the privilege of entry.

And so it went in that spring of 1979. Just as every time before, the guards directed Gorman to a customs waiting room where he filled out an enormous number of forms documenting every item in his possession. Officials checked the vaccination records he had brought with him. (If you didn't have all the shots required, they would administer them on the spot, so it was good to be prepared.) By now it was midday, and the next stop for Gorman and his fellow travelers was the special border-crossing restaurant, which offered a remarkably sumptuous lunch, supplemented with Qingdao beer. Lunch was followed by an obligatory nap period, in a waiting room equipped with spittoons and armchairs adorned with antimacassars.

There was little alternative. Southern China is sweltering in the summers, and there was no air-conditioning in the People's Republic. And the train from Shumchun Station to Guangzhou departed only at infrequent intervals. Looking back years later, Gorman would compare the move from frenetic Hong Kong to the sleepy post-Mao mainland "like the transition from snorkeling to wearing a diving bell." You were no longer your own master. The powers that be would let you know when you were needed.

Gorman arrived at his hotel in Guangzhou to find the familiar routine in place. At that time, the only way to do business in China was to establish contacts with one of the fourteen ministries that controlled each of the country's industrial sectors (chemicals, steel, light industry, and so on). This was easier said than done. Chinese officials were still strikingly stingy with information, another legacy of the Cultural Revolution, when association with foreigners could cost you a stint in a labor camp or worse. You could always go to the trade-fair building and seek out the people you wanted to meet (assuming that you already knew who they were), but that was no guarantee of success. Still, there was little choice. You certainly couldn't expect them to come to you.

All this explains why Gorman and the handful of other Americans at the fair sat up and took notice when the Chinese approached them with an offer: Would the Americans be interested in taking a look at an investment opportunity? It was not too far away from Guangzhou; it would require an overnight trip. The Americans said yes.

On the appointed day, they set off from Guangzhou in a van that jolted down hideous dirt roads for hours. At one point it broke down, and everyone had to get out and walk to a spot where the Chinese hosts were able to arrange for another ride. The walk was not a total loss; the little group passed by a rural private market where local farmers were hawking all manner of produce, something that none of the Americans in the group could ever remember having seen before.

Finally, after a full day's journey in the intense heat, they arrived at their destination. It turned out to be just across the border from Hong Kong—not far from the Lo Wu crossing where all foreigners made their entry into mainland China. The bewildered Americans followed their hosts to the top of a dike, where the Chinese hosts gestured at the vista spread before them. It was not clear what they were meant to look at. All that the Americans could see was the usual South China landscape: there were rice paddies, worked by peasants and their water buffalo in the time-honored manner, and duck ponds. There were few trees and here and there a modest peasant dwelling. What the Chinese were describing seemed to bear no relationship to the observable reality. This, they told the Americans, was the location of something called the Baoan Foreign Trade Base. The party had designated it as a special location for foreign investment. According to the plans under consideration, it would soon be the site of chemical factories and textile mills and manufacturing plants. And, oh yes, there would also be plenty of hotels for the foreign business-men. It was going to be a wonderful chance to make money.

The Americans thought that the Chinese were crazy. "It stretched everybody's imagination," Gorman said. "I don't think there was one of us who listened to the briefing and thought, 'Yeah that sounds feasible.' It was, emphatically, 'Come on, what are you smoking?'"

The next day, after an uncomfortable night spent in the only existing local hotel (which had no electricity or running water), the Americans attended a briefing where the Chinese unrolled blueprints that depicted acres of factories, warehouses, and other facilities. The plans betrayed an ambition that was startling. "It was re-ally hard to believe," Gorman recalled. "Nothing in China at that point happened quickly—except politics. Business and construction didn't happen on those kinds of timelines."[27]

The Baoan Foreign Trade Base was located in a village that was named, like the nearby river, Shumchun. It later became known under a different version of the name: Shenzhen. It was a place that had attracted Deng's attention at least as early as the Work Conference, when he had floated the idea that the party should "enable some regions to perform better and become more prosperous." Deng had calculated that if only 5 percent of the counties and 5 percent of the citizenry be-came "relatively prosperous," this would translate into one hundred counties and 40 million residents—the equivalent of a medium-sized country and presumably a powerful catalyst for change. Shenzhen was the first on his list of nineteen places that he targeted for early prosperity. "Obviously, he had taken notice of this place at a very early date," writes former aide Yu Guangyuan. "In his view, a major factor in Shenzhen's quest to become prosperous sooner than others was its capacity to con-duct foreign trade." During the Work Conference, in fact, Yu himself had told party officials from Guangdong of his own idea—inspired by an ad a friend had brought from Hong Kong—to construct office buildings in Shenzhen under the auspices of the Chinese Academy of Sciences (Yu's home institution) and rent them to people from Kowloon, just over the border, where soaring land prices were already driving rents into the stratosphere. Yu even envisioned simplifying border-control proce-dures for visitors from Hong Kong.[28]

Gorman and his compatriots, who had all experienced firsthand the xenophobic legacy of the Cultural Revolution years during their visits to China, could hardly be blamed for feeling skeptical. What they were not yet able to appreciate was the fact that the Chinese were deadly serious about their plans to invite overseas investors into new "special districts" that were already in planning.

Lower-level officials—especially in Guangdong—were undoubtedly keen on the idea. But this was one case where Deng could claim full credit for driving the initiative forward. He had spent his years in exile brooding over how to stimulate the Chinese economy, and he had concluded, after his return to power in the early 1970s, that his country had to tap into the global marketplace for technology, know-how, and management expertise was an indispensable precondition. His 1974 trip to United Nations headquarters in New York City had been the first to jolt him into an understanding of just how far behind China had fallen.

After his third return from political oblivion in 1977, he took a series of trips around the region that reinforced this view. His itinerary included a visit to Japan, where he witnessed firsthand the evidence of that country's extraordinary post-war rise to the pinnacle of the global economy, as well as one to Singapore, which, though far smaller in absolute terms, was also demonstrating just how powerful the East Asian formula of single-party rule and market economics could be. Just how influential these experiences were becomes clear from Deng's private comments to his speechwriting team during the 1978 Work Conference and the Third Plenum—the ones in which he gushed about the Japanese and Singaporean workers who could use their bonuses to buy houses and cars.[29]

Nor was that all. Deng and his colleagues—at least those who wanted to pay attention to the outside world—were also acutely aware of the extraordinary rise in living standards already engineered by Hong Kong and Taiwan, which (like Japan, Singapore, and South Korea) had also made strategic decisions to reject "self-sufficiency" and to actively participate in global trade. Taiwan, in particular, had reaped a variety of benefits from its "Export Processing Zones," areas with special commercial, legal, and tax regimes that were designed to entice foreign investors to take advantage of a well-trained but low-wage labor force. The Taiwanese were gambling that the shortfalls in tax and customs revenues would be balanced out by the know-how that they would acquire in management and production techniques (not to mention the extra employment). By the late 1970s their gamble was paying off to spectacular effect, and the example was not lost on their compatriots on the mainland.

But the impetus for a creative approach to foreign investment did not come only from the top. There was also some intense lobbying going on at the regional level—particularly in one of the areas that stood to gain the most from trade with the outside world. That was Guangdong Province, directly adjacent to Hong Kong. Guangzhou (or Canton) was the home of the traditional trade fair because it had a long history, dating back to imperial history, as one of the few places where foreigners were allowed to do business with Chinese. The direct proximity of Hong Kong, whose population included many Cantonese-speaking refugees from Guangdong, meant that the province still had access to an extensive web of contacts with the outside world, including the huge network of overseas Chinese. All this meant that a certain amount of illegal trade had continued even during the darkest days of Maoism. (Indeed, considering the huge and intricate possibilities for smuggling offered by the Pearl River delta, the gateway to Guangdong, it could have hardly been otherwise.) Many Guangdong residents received remittances from their relatives in Hong Kong or places more distant, and these funds were a major source of revenue for a region that had otherwise been severed from its natural trading hinterland after 1949.

Guangdong party officials knew all of this very well, and they were eager to seize upon the new talk in Beijing of opening up the country to investment. They had prevailed upon the party bureaucracy to let them open a few modest channels for trade with Hong Kong, but they were already thinking big. Their plans received a major boost in 1978, when a set of high-ranking party officials, including several from Guangdong, set off on a fact-finding trip to Western Europe that affected them in much the same way as Deng's journeys had changed him. They were impressed not only by the modern air-traffic control systems at Charles de Gaulle Airport in Paris and a modern container terminal in a German port, but also by the willingness of their hosts to expose them to new insights and by the eagerness of European businesspeople to marshal funds for investment in production facilities in China.[30]

In January 1979, just two weeks after the end of the Third Plenum, the new party boss in Guangdong, Xi Zhongxun, got approval from Beijing to start drawing up plans for "special zones" that would be opened up to foreign investment. The first zone opened shortly after that in Shekou, a corner of Shenzhen. The Chinese Merchant Steamship Company, a Hong Kong firm set up and owned by the government in Beijing, had been lobbying for a place where old ships could be taken apart for scrap, which could be sold at high profits to the resource-hungry capitalists in Hong Kong. The fact that the company in question was technically "foreign" but actually controlled by the People's Republic made the experiment that much easier to implement. "Shekou thus became the first place in China to allow foreign direct investment and the first area where decisions about a company inside China could be made by people located outside the country."[31]

Economic trends in the outside world gave the officials in Guangdong an additional incentive to open up their province to the outside world. Neighboring Hong Kong was experiencing one of the characteristic disadvantages of a surge in economic growth: a sharp rise in wages. This was rapidly eroding the colony's international competitiveness, and Hong Kong businesspeople were casting desperately around for new sources of labor. The most obvious place was just over the border.

C. K. Feng was a junior executive with Eltrinic, a small Hong Kong firm that made small electrical devices: a bug zapper, an electric can opener, snow-melting equipment for the US market. Eltrinic's production was fairly labor intensive, and the rising wages were hitting it hard. So when one of the company's bosses heard from a contact on the mainland that the Communist Party was soon going to start inviting in foreign manufacturers, Feng took notice. "I volunteered to go the mainland to open up and find workers there," he said later. "I was so concerned about the workers' shortage in Hong Kong." He first traveled to Baoan—the same spot that Gorman visited a few months later—in late 1978 and soon began plans to construct a small factory building and to transport machinery there from Hong Kong. The mainland authorities gave Feng a special Hong Kong travel permit, actually a thick book used to record a variety of data. This presumably privileged access did not seem to reduce the number of papers that had to be filled out at each crossing, however. Each time he entered China, Feng said, "It was like crossing into a different world."

In the spring of 1979, after jumping through countless bureaucratic hoops, the first Eltrinic factory opened in Shenzhen. It employed twenty local workers. (Its total workforce at the time was around seven hundred.) The first year was spent training them. The factory's intended production—heating elements for blow dryers—required a certain amount of skill, and the mainland workers were starting from scratch. None of them had ever seen a blow dryer. But they weren't fussy. "The workers produced whatever you wanted them to produce," Feng recalls. "They didn't care." Maintaining communications between the factory and headquarters in Hong Kong was no easy task. The only local telephone was located in the village administration office, and placing calls was hair-raisingly frustrating business. The villagers, however, were extremely happy. When the production line was inaugurated, they killed a dog—a much-valued local delicacy—for a banquet to celebrate the occasion. The somewhat more fastidious Hong Kongers were bemused.[32]

The founding of Feng's factory preceded the formal establishment of the Special Economic Zones (SEZ) on August 26, 1979—and that, in itself, says quite a lot about how development in China was progressing at this time. Even as Guangdong was pressing Beijing for formal latitude to manage its own affairs and attract foreign investors, the first contacts between the province and foreign investors were already being made.[33]

These areas were granted exceptional conditions to attract foreign investment, but they could also be easily quarantined from society as a whole. The latter point conveniently placated party conservatives, who worried that the populace might succumb to the corrosive effects of capitalism. Ironically, potential foreign investors shared their appreciation; to them, Deng's enclave strategy offered a vital degree of protection against political backlash from the Maoists. To be sure, the SEZs needed time to show results, but that was not a problem. Reform in China was supposed to be slow; the country had experienced tumult enough. The main thing was that the keystones of a new economy—one driven by efficiency rather than ideological correctness—had been laid. The new revolution—in its own cautious way—could begin.

No one embodied that revolution better than Rong Zhiren. The restaurant that he opened in that spring of 1979 proved a big success. Three years later, by now an affluent Guangzhou entrepreneur, he received the privilege of meeting Deng Xiaoping at a social event for Guangdong Province luminaries. The fact that a local businessman was deemed worthy of such a gathering said a great deal in itself; a few years earlier, Rong would have been imprisoned for the same activities that now gave him privileged status. Deng, he says, always remained an example. "I took heart from his three-time rise and fall," Rong says. "Deng's return [in 1977] sent me an important message." If you persevered, you had the chance to do more than survive. You might even prosper.[34]

19

Fraternal Assistance

A Communist takeover in Afghanistan would have faced formidable challenges even under the best of circumstances. In the event, when the Communists finally seized power in the coup of April 1978, they did so as a group that was riven by bitter internal divisions. The enmity between the radical Khalq ("Masses") faction and the moderate Parcham ("Banner") group did not improve after the party took control of the Afghan government. If anything, the seizure of power made matters worse. Almost from the first moment of Communist rule in Afghanistan, the fragile unity of the People's Democratic Party of Afghanistan began to splinter.

At first, Babrak Karmal, the Parcham leader, received a position as deputy prime minister in the government of the new Democratic Republic of Afghanistan. This was a grudging concession from the Khalqis, who actually held the reins of power in the administration—above all the ambitious Hafizullah Amin, the man who had orchestrated the coup while ostensibly under house arrest. Amin and his friends remembered all too well how Karmal and his Parcham colleagues had dithered over the idea of launching the coup.[1] This lack of revolutionary conviction was something that the Khalqis would never let them forget. Amin secretly ordered his network of supporters in the military, and especially in the rapidly expanding secret police, to identify all the Parcham members who carried guns. Within a few months of the April coup, Amin was busily purging the army and air force of hundreds of officers whose loyalties he deemed suspect.

In early July 1978 came the announcement that Karmal and four of his most prominent Parcham comrades (including his brother and his presumed mistress) were being sent abroad as ambassadors; Karmal was dispatched to Czechoslovakia. In August Amin dramatically upped the stakes by giving the order for the arrest of Abdul Qadir, the minister of defense, and several other leading Parchamis. They were accused of conspiracy to overthrow the government in league with an unnamed foreign power.[2] This was a remarkable turn of events. Back in 1973, Qadir had lent his military expertise to Daoud's effort to seize power, and in the April Revolution he had commanded the air forces that bombed Daoud's presidential palace. Now he had become a victim of his own success.

By the fall of 1978, it was clear to astute observers that the PDPA ruled in name only. Afghanistan was actually under the control of the Khalq. Nur Mohammed Taraki, the Khalqi leader, stood at the head of the party and the country, but those in the know—including the increasingly anxious Soviets, who had always preferred the Parchamis' more cautious approach—understood that it was his deputy, the thrusting Amin, who was busily concentrating power in his own hands.

In the course of 1979, it became increasingly clear that the government's efforts to impose its authority on the population were failing. The rebellions in Herat and the Pech Valley were only part of a bigger picture. By the spring there were large swaths of the country to which the government writ did not extend. Within the army, the tempo of desertions was accelerating; entire units defected en masse. The government in Kabul fought back as best as it could, deploying hundreds of tanks and helicopter gunships recently delivered by the Soviets. Taraki used much of this matériel in an offensive aimed at Kunar Province, where the Pech rebellion was still boiling along.

By the summer of 1979, the malaise had spread to Kabul itself. Shootings and arson attacks were commonplace. Assassinations occurred. Government troops were thin on the streets. Most of the violence involved rebels attacking representatives of the government, but some of it reflected feuding between Khalqis and Parchamis. (Many of the latter had gone into hiding.)[3] In June, government troops opened fire on a crowd of demonstrators in Kabul, killing dozens of unarmed people. In August came a mutiny at the Bala Hissar fortress on the outskirts of the capital. For a moment, until the uprising was suppressed, the very existence of the regime seemed in question. The same month, an entire infantry brigade defected to the rebels in Kunar.[4]

The factional rivalry within the ruling party was not the only problem that it faced; there was also the issue of the rising antipathy between Taraki and Amin.

The collapse of the government's authority in the countryside aggravated the rift between the president and his prime minister. It is hard to imagine that Amin, a man visibly consumed by ambition, would have been content to leave Taraki in charge over the long term. It was, after all, Amin who had organized the April coup, and from the very first day of the Khalqi regime, he had worked to expand his personal power, carefully cultivating his network of supporters throughout the military and the security services. Amin was named prime minister only in March 1979, after the revolt in Herat, but many had suspected long before then that he was the real force in the government.

Taraki, however, was no fool, and he had many powerful allies of his own—including four key leaders (predictably dubbed "the Gang of Four" by their opponents) who regarded Amin's maneuverings with intense suspicion. Though the Gang was hardly squeamish about the use of violence, they criticized the harshness of the measures Amin was employing against the rebels. In at least one place, he ordered that the villagers in rebellious districts be buried alive. The prisons and the interrogation centers of the secret police were bursting with inmates. All this provided fuel for his opponents, who were busily exploiting their own ties to the many Soviet advisers working in Kabul.

As the situation in the countryside deteriorated, these differences between the two party leaders flared into open conflict. In a Politburo meeting in Kabul in July 1979, Amin blamed Taraki for everything that was going wrong. Taraki responded by accusing his subordinate of nepotism. The collapse of the Communist experiment was bringing matters to a head.[5]

At the end of August, Taraki left Kabul to attend the Non-Aligned Summit in Havana. On his way back, he stopped over in Moscow to discuss matters with Leonid Brezhnev in the Kremlin. The Soviet leader and his colleagues had, by now, become deeply distrustful of Amin. The KGB kept careful track of the internal feuding in Kabul, and their reports on the prime minister's maneuvers added to the Russians' worries about the mounting instability. Soviet spies also blamed Amin for many of the radical policies that were intensifying popular discontent. Brezhnev warned Taraki about Amin and urged him, in veiled terms, to fire his deputy. In subsequent talks with KGB officials after the meeting, Taraki, who apparently didn't entirely understand what Brezhnev was trying to get across at first, tried to calm his hosts' fears, assuring them that he was entirely in control of events in Afghanistan. "Nothing can happen without my knowledge," he boasted to the Russians.[6]

Needless to say, this wasn't entirely true. The man who was then the chief KGB officer in Kabul, Vladamir Bogdanov, later told a story about what Amin was up to during Taraki's absence. According to Bogdanov, Amin had invited all thirty-odd members of the PDPA Central Committee into his office, one by one. Amin then asked each one whom he supported, Amin or Taraki—while Amin's nephew held a pistol to their heads.[7]

As soon as he was back in Kabul, the elderly president confronted Amin, who denied all the accusations but said that he would be happy to resign as long as the move was approved by the majority of the Central Committee. (He had already prepared for just such an eventuality, as Bogdanov's story shows.) Taraki, bolstered by the assurances of support he had received in Moscow, was undeterred. During a cabinet meeting, he announced, "There's a cancer in the party, and it needs to be cut out!" Everyone understood whom he had in mind. This cued a dramatic escalation.

Amin responded by pressing Taraki to fire the members of the "Gang of Four" he viewed as his chief enemies within the government. Taraki refused to comply—and, just to be on the safe side, he sent his four allies into hiding. Amin announced that they had been fired. Publicly, he claimed that the order for their ouster had been given by Taraki. Privately, he accused Taraki of planning to assassinate him.

The Soviets had had enough. They decided to intervene directly. On September 14, a Friday, the Soviet ambassador to Kabul, Alexander Puzanov, offered to guarantee Amin's safety if he came to the presidential palace to meet with Taraki. Amin agreed. At five thirty in the evening, he arrived at the palace in the company of four armed guards. The atmosphere was unbearably tense—just the sort of situation where a nervous trigger finger can touch off catastrophe.

Inside the palace, one of the president's bodyguards told Amin's security detail to surrender their weapons. They refused. One of Taraki's men opened fire, killing the head of Amin's bodyguard instantly and wounding another. Amin was grazed by a ricocheting bullet. He and the three surviving guards beat a hasty retreat to the nearby general-staff building.[8]

Soviet diplomats desperately tried to tamp down the crisis. A hastily dispatched delegation pleaded with Amin to restrain from retaliating, insisting that it was all just a misunderstanding. But the prime minister was not to be mollified. It was clear that, as far as he was concerned, he had just escaped an assassination attempt, and he was not about to make amends with Taraki. Although he denied seeking power for his own purposes, he made sure the Russians understood a political reality: the armed forces, he told them, no longer followed Taraki's orders. They would listen only to him.[9]

Amin was done with cohabitation; now he was determined to become the man in charge. He quickly issued orders to his followers in the military and the security apparatus, and the extent of his real power within the Afghan government soon made itself manifest. Soldiers surrounded the presidential palace and took Taraki prisoner. Amid rumors of ministerial dismissals and the mysterious shooting, news agencies reported several explosions around Kabul and noted that security forces had taken up positions around the radio station. On Saturday, the government announced that four men had been shot dead the day before; the circumstances were left unexplained. The message the next day was somewhat different: using the doublespeak preferred by Communist governments, state-controlled radio announced that Taraki had "resigned" from office because of a nervous condition. (Foreign journalists pointed out that he had appeared to be in perfectly good health during the Havana summit.) The official statements made no use of Taraki's accustomed title of "Great Leader."[10]

On Monday, September 16, Amin assumed sole power in Afghanistan—but without really giving anything away about the fate of the man he was replacing. From one moment to the next, Taraki was relegated to the Orwellian status of an unperson. Amin announced that he was assuming the posts of party general secretary and president, both jobs that had been held by Taraki until the day before, even while he retained his post as prime minister and his control over the army and security organs. The speech contained only a single elliptical reference to his predecessor: "Those people who saw their greatness in the oppression of the people have been eliminated." Perceptive observers noted that that same verb had been used to report the assassination of Daoud in the April coup of the year before.[11]

Amin clearly hoped that he could use his seizure of power to reboot the Khalqi regime. In the speech, he promised to release political prisoners who had been imprisoned "unnecessarily" (which seemed to imply that the government of which he had been an integral part was guilty of jailing innocents) and promised an end to the "personality cult" that had surrounded Taraki since the day of the August coup (a cult that existed thanks in large part to Amin's own efforts). "Industrialists and big businessmen will be given help in rebuilding the economy of the country," Amin declared. He tried to burnish his Islamic credentials by launching a program to refurbish mosques.

The Russians had to make it appear as though they were on top of the situation. Brezhnev issued a statement congratulating Afghanistan's new leader: "We express confidence that fraternal relations between the Soviet Union and revolutionary Afghanistan will be further developed successfully." But foreign news reports, recalling the bear hug that Brezhnev had publicly given Taraki in Moscow just a few days earlier, speculated that it was more likely that the Russians had been caught completely off guard by this latest turn of events. If this was true, moreover, the PDPA's patrons in the Kremlin were unlikely to be pleased. The journalists were right.[12]

In fact, the Soviets were in a state of extreme consternation. The man that they regarded as a political adventurer, an unreliable radical, had seized power. What was to be done? As it happened, they had already started planning for an Afghanistan without Amin. In September, the KGB's elite special forces unit, the Zenit group, had drawn up a blueprint for kidnapping him and taking him to the Soviet Union. Now, in the wake of Taraki's disappearance, the focus shifted. The Soviets decided to take charge of the four renegade ministers who had been dismissed by Amin just before his coup and spirit them out of the country. The KGB called it Operation Raduga (Rainbow). The four men were smuggled out of Kabul to the Soviet-operated air base at Baghram. To conceal them from Amin's forces, the men were hidden in ammunition boxes equipped with airholes and mattresses and driven in trucks to the base. From there they were flown out to the Soviet Union, where they could be kept in safety until they were needed.[13]

On October 10, Radio Kabul announced that Taraki had died of an "incurable disease." The reality, as virtually everyone suspected, was entirely different. The day before, Amin had ordered three of his security officers to enter Taraki's cell and smother him with a pillow. At the same time, he gave instructions for the expulsion of Puzanov, the Soviet ambassador, whom he believed to be plotting against him. After the shoot-out in the palace, Amin's foreign minister had made a point of telling East-bloc diplomats that the Soviets had guaranteed Amin's safety during his visit to the presidential palace—tantamount to implicating them in the attempt to kill him.[14] Puzanov emphatically denied having knowledge of any such plans. Subsequent events would make it hard to take this at face value.[15]

The news of Taraki's death incensed Leonid Brezhnev. "What kind of scum is this Amin—to strangle the man with whom he participated in the revolution?" Brezhnev fulminated to his colleagues. "Who is now at the helm of the Afghan revolution? What will people say in other countries?"[16] It was this single event, more than any other, that provoked the Soviet decision to intervene directly in Afghanistan. But the Kremlin had other reasons for its disenchantment. Soon after taking power, Amin began to signal that he was preparing to move Afghanistan away from its one-sided reliance on the USSR. He made moves to replace Soviet-trained officials with Western ones.[17] He sought meetings with US officials to sound out possibilities for cooperation.

The talks don't seem to have gone anywhere, but they set off alarm bells in Moscow. The head of the KGB foreign intelligence department, Leonid Shebarshin,

meetings he attacked Soviet policy and the activities of our specialists. Our ambassador was practically expelled from Kabul. These developments have created, on the one hand, a danger of losing the domestic achievements of the Afghan revolution, and, on the other hand, a threat to our positions in Afghanistan. Now there is no guarantee that Amin, in order to secure his personal power, would not turn to the West.[23]

Andropov had minimal evidence to back up this claim. We know little about his motivations, but it appears that he was simply using every means at his disposal to prod Brezhnev into action. Andropov and Ustinov soon brought the NATO deliberations on medium-range missiles into play as well. They began suggesting—a truly farfetched argument considering the realities—that a lack of Kremlin resolve could soon result in the Americans having the chance to station short-range missiles in Afghanistan, right up against the Soviet border.[24]

By now the Kremlin was set on direct military intervention in Afghanistan. Two days after the Politburo members signed their memo, Red Army staff troops arrived to set up an operational headquarters just inside the Soviet side of the border with Afghanistan. KGB special forces in Kabul had already started their own preparations for the invasion in early December. At three in the afternoon on Christmas Day—a date presumably chosen to ensure minimal attention in the West—the 40th Army began to send troop convoys across the border. Two days later, KGB commandos launched an assault on the presidential palace on the outskirts of Kabul.[25]

What happened there remains the subject of considerable dispute, and given the lack of reliable documentation and the chaos that reigned, we may never receive a fully objective account. But certain details emerge clearly. Amin was already virtually incapacitated by the time the Soviets began their storming of the presidential residence. The KGB had already tried to kill him a few days earlier by slipping poison into his Coca-Cola; unfortunately for the Russians, the imperialist beverage had somehow neutralized the toxins, and Amin survived the attack, though it did make him seriously ill. Ironically, it was his Soviet-supplied doctor, unaware of the plot, who tried to nurse him back to health. When the KGB troops burst into the palace—having suffered high casualties as a result of the unexpectedly stiff resistance put up by Amin's guards—they found the leader of the glorious Afghan revolution wandering the hallways in a haze. One of them tossed a grenade in his direction, killing Amin and his five-year-old son.[26] Babrak Karmal, still inside the Soviet Union at this point, was pronounced his successor.

The Soviet invasion marked a turning point in the guerrilla war. For those Afghans who had been sitting on the fence, considering their options for collaboration with the homegrown Communist government, the Soviet move dramatically clarified matters. Now there was no need for the Islamic guerrillas to argue the case that the government leaders in Kabul were the puppets of their atheist masters in faraway Moscow; now the *shuravi* (Soviets) had arrived in person, and you could see them with your own eyes. The number of mujahideen operations had actually tapered off after the summer of 1979, when a harsh government counteroffensive had exposed the guerrillas' relative weakness, including the scarcity of arms and secure logistics. But the arrival of Soviet troops galvanized the resistance. It was no longer a matter of defending Afghanistan from misguided Afghans; now the guerrillas were fighting to save the country from outsiders who were trying to take it for themselves.[27]

The visible presence of a large foreign military contingent was only part of the challenge that the occupiers faced. The Red Army's commanders and their political bosses back in the Kremlin made matters even worse by seemingly doing everything they could to stoke the anger caused by the invasion. From the very beginning, the operations conducted by the Soviet troops and their Afghan allies violated every tenet of sound counterinsurgency warfare. In retrospect, this seems rather odd, given the effectiveness of the guerrilla war that the Russians had conducted against the Nazi invaders in the USSR during World War II. But militaries, with their rigid command structures, often find it difficult to adapt to changing circumstances, and the 40th Army, the core of the Soviet force that now found itself in Afghanistan, included motorized regiments shaped by planning for a modern mechanized war against NATO in Central Europe. The military doctrine that they stood for bore little resemblance to the war that the Soviet troops now found themselves fighting.

Counterinsurgency is an approach to warfare that requires well-disciplined troops who are at least somewhat sensitive to the political context of their mission. This was far from the case in Afghanistan. According to most accounts, morale among the Red Army's conscript troops—regaled with official talk of the warm reception they would meet in their sunny and exotic destination—was relatively good at the beginning. It soon plummeted, though, as soldiers' encounters with Afghan reality demonstrated that the locals despised them as occupiers. Poorly supplied with food and creature comforts, and subjected to brutal hazing by their officers, Soviet troops took to plundering homes whenever they got the chance. Many succumbed to the lure of drugs and alcohol, exacerbating problems with discipline.

The elusive and confusing nature of guerrilla warfare complicated matters. Uneducated young Russian troopers found it impossible to distinguish friend from foe—a problem intensified by the speed with which their Afghan government allies tended to desert upon contact with the enemy. The notion of "protecting the population" seemed to be completely alien to the 40th Army's commanders, who responded to attacks on their troops with massed artillery and airpower. It was a tactic that usually killed more civilians than guerrillas, thus fanning popular support for the rebels. The mujahideen, for their part, were not above terrorizing their enemies whenever they had occasion to do so, and Soviet troops who were taken prisoner rarely survived, invariably enraging the brothers-in-arms who happened across their elaborately mutilated bodies.

There were other ways, though, in which the mujahideen bore a disconcerting resemblance to their Afghan Communist opponents. The holy warriors were also prey to internecine feuding. The two Islamist parties of Rabbani and Hekmatyar, based in Peshawar since the midseventies, soon found themselves competing with five other groups representing various tribal and religious constituencies. At times the fighting among the rebels approached the ferociousness of their attacks on the Soviets. Gun battles and assassinations were all too frequent on both sides of the borders.

The one thing that unified them, however, came into ever-sharper focus as the war went on: commitment to the cause of Islam. A number of factors contributed to this. Religion proved to be a much more powerful motivating force than, say, allegiance to the old king or the model of the secular republic embodied by the much-maligned Daoud, who had discredited the very notion through his dalliances with the Communists. The seductive notion of an "Islamic state" was one of the few political designs on offer that could compete, in clarity and emotional power, with the Communist vision.

Foreign sponsorship of the seven exile parties tended to aggravate the differences among them. General Zia insisted that Pakistan should have the final say over which Afghan factions received the money and weapons that came from the Americans and the Saudis and various other outside powers. The group that he tended to favor above all else was Hekmatyar's Hezb-e Islami, which had shown itself amenable to close cooperation with Pakistani military intelligence since many of the Afghan Islamists had gone into exile in 1973–1974. There were several reasons for this preference. Hekmatyar hewed closely to an Islamist vision that Zia and his fellow generals, who were trying to bolster Islam as a political factor at home, found appealing. In contrast to some of the more disorganized Afghan groups, the

Hezbis were under tight control and could be relied upon to carry out the orders of their leader. Finally, they were overwhelmingly Pashtun, like most of the Pakistanis who inhabited the tribal areas around Peshawar. This offered, at least in theory, the advantage of diverting potential separatist sentiments among Pashtun Pakistanis to the cause of the "holy war" in Afghanistan.

A group that received far less in the way of foreign largesse was the branch of Jamiat-e Islami that had established itself in the Panjshir Valley under the ethnic Tajik Ahmed Shah Massoud, the man who had gained notoriety with his ill-fated rebellion in the Panjshir in the summer of 1979. By that action and many others, Massoud showed that he was determined to avoid taking orders from any outside forces—particularly the Pakistanis. They reciprocated by cutting him off from the flow of resources from Washington and Riyadh.

Yet, somewhat paradoxically, it was Massoud who soon gained a reputation as one of the most effective mujahideen field commanders. Having returned to the strategically vital Panjshir soon after the invasion, he forged his men into a highly effective guerrilla force that consistently threatened Soviet supply lines and repeatedly withstood large-scale attacks. And while he, too, declared his aim to be the establishment of an Islamic state, he eschewed the dictatorial powers of an emir in favor of a comparatively democratic mechanism of consultation throughout the areas under his control that determined everything from education to tax policy.

As their casualties mounted and the political situation continued to deteriorate, the Soviets desperately tried to learn from their mistakes. Some Red Army commanders gradually implemented policies to lessen the impact of the occupation, including civil affairs projects designed to improve the lot of ordinary people. But the efforts were piecemeal, and they were almost always outweighed by the heavy-handedness of the Russians' efforts to defeat the mujahideen. Air strikes and artillery barrages directed against the guerrilla fighters invariably caused civilian casualties, increasing resentment and driving more and more people into the arms of the rebels. And then, as always, there was the atheistic nature of the Soviet system, which made it hard to convince the locals that the invaders sincerely respected Islam.

Still, the overwhelming technological and military superiority of Moscow's forces began to tell as the years went on. Perhaps the most devastating weapon in the Communist arsenal was the heavily armored helicopter gunship, the perfect vehicle for counterinsurgency warfare in rugged terrain. The Soviet General Staff also began deploying increasing numbers of highly trained and well-conditioned special forces, the *spetsnaz*, to the Afghan theater—just the sort of troops that could respond efficiently to the hit-and-run attacks staged by the guerrillas. By 1985, the year that Gorbachev came to power, the USSR's military could claim to be gaining traction in the war for control.

But it was all too late. The costs of the war were weighing on the Soviet treasury, already battered by declining productivity and sinking oil prices. Public opinion turned fairly quickly against the war, since few Russians or Ukrainians could see the logic behind sending their boys off to die in a distant conflict when the economy was in all too conspicuous decline at home. And the military edge that the occupiers had so painstakingly acquired soon evaporated when the Americans began supplying the Afghan holy warriors with Stinger shoulder-launched antiaircraft missiles, which proved shockingly effective at shooting helicopters out of the sky. Gorbachev's declared priority, upon assuming office, was to reform the economic and political system in his country. The war in Afghanistan did little to further that end, and, indeed, perhaps even stood in the way of its realization. It did not take the new Soviet leader long to declare his intention to wind down the war.

In some ways, the damage had already been done. In a country that was spending as much as one-quarter of its gross domestic product on defense even before 1979, the additional burden of maintaining up to 140,000 combat troops in a distant theater of war—including all the vast logistical and administrative resources this implied—was debilitating. We now know, thanks to sources that became public after the collapse of the Warsaw Pact, that the strains of the occupation of Afghanistan constrained Soviet policy toward Poland in 1980 and 1981. It turns out that the Kremlin's threats to quash the unrest using its own troops, as it had in Hungary in 1956 and Czechoslovakia in 1968, were a bluff. Struggling to control Afghanistan, the USSR had little military capacity to spare for a full-scale occupation of a second large country as well, and this was one of the factors that motivated Soviet leaders to pressure Polish communist leaders to deal with the problem using their own forces. In this respect, the two counterrevolutions in Afghanistan and Poland can be seen as mutually reinforcing events that contributed mightily to the collapse of the Communist system.

In some ways, Gorbachev's relaxation of censorship actually aggravated the political and psychological effects of the war. As enterprising journalists began to produce candid reporting about the conflict, details of the high casualty rate, the astonishing level of brutality, and the glaring evidence of official mismanagement and corruption emerged into the public sphere. It soon became clear that everything the state had said about the war was a lie. Afghans were not welcoming socialism; the rebels were not just a few foreign-sponsored mercenaries but represented broad swaths of their society. Victory for the "forces of progress" was not in the offing. And far more young men were dying in the war than had been officially acknowledged. Veterans of the war, known as *afgantsy*, returned home brutalized and disillusioned, often bringing with them profound problems—from combat trauma to drug addiction—of just the kind that the Soviet system, still locked in its official myth of the inherent superiority of socialism, was especially ill-equipped to confront. The war in Afghanistan did more than any other single event in the 1980s to intensify the public cynicism and apathy that had such a corrosive effect on the integrity of the Soviet system on the path to its collapse. Indeed, some of the *afgantsy* who failed to find a path back into society ended up joining organized-crime groups, and their propensity for violence contributed significantly to the gang wars that plagued Russia and other republics after 1991.

All this was still in the future as the Soviet invaders hunkered down in their positions in the waning hours of 1979. At the Lubyanka, the KGB headquarters on Dzerzhinsky Square in Moscow,[28] Andropov opted for a break with tradition. In the years before, the Soviet secret police had made a tradition of honoring operatives who lost their lives in the line of duty by hanging portraits of them in the building's corridors. But the chaotic assault on Amin's palace had taken the lives of at least one hundred members of the KGB's elite commando squad; some of them, even more embarrassingly, were casualties of friendly fire. Andropov decided that such a large number of mourning portraits would draw unwanted attention to the losses. So the deaths of the men went unremarked by their comrades. It was a fitting portent of the squalid war to come.[29]

20

Solidarity

On August 7, 1980, her bosses fired Anna Walentynowicz from her job at the Lenin Shipyard in the Polish city of Gdańsk. Walentynowicz was not a run-of-the-mill shipyard laborer. Popular among her fellow workers, she had once received a decoration as a "hero of socialist labor" for her exemplary work. But in the course of the 1970s she had evolved into a critic of the Communist system, and she eventually found herself drawn to a group of activists who were setting up an independent association they called the "Committee of Free Trade Unions." The SB, the secret police, had informed Walentynowicz's bosses of her activities. Hence her dismissal.

Early on the morning of August 14, a few young men sneaked into the Lenin Shipyard with posters calling on the workers to strike for the reinstatement of Walentynowicz and a pay rise of one thousand zlotys. Some of the shipyard workers took up the call—but just as they were about to march out of the yard, others stopped them, reminding them of what had happened ten years earlier. In 1970, workers along the Baltic coast, including those at the Lenin Shipyard, had also announced a strike. In order to elicit public support, they had decided to leave their workplaces and take to the streets to press their demands. By doing that, however, they made themselves easy targets for the government security forces that had been ordered into the affected cities. The strikers had been gunned down by the dozens. Walentynowicz's supporters vowed not to repeat that mistake. They opted to stay put.

Workers began to congregate in front of the shipyard's head office. As the swelling crowd discussed how they should go about coordinating their efforts, the shipyard's director climbed up on an excavator and began haranguing them to go back to work. Some of the men seemed to be thinking it over, and for a moment the fate of the strike hung in the balance. (Indeed, another attempt to start a strike just a few weeks earlier had fizzled.) But then a short, stocky man climbed up behind the director and tapped him on the shoulder: "'Remember me?' he said. 'I worked here for ten years, and I still feel I'm a shipyard worker. I have the confidence of the workers here. It's four years since I lost my job.'"[1]

The name of the man, an ex-shipyard electrician who had also lost his job because of his extracurricular activities as a dissident, was Lech Wałęsa. He had sneaked back into his old workplace by climbing over a wall. The workers greeted him with a cheer. Some of them recognized him from an unofficial ceremony that had been held at the shipyard gates the previous December to commemorate the dead of the 1970 protests. At the ceremony, Wałęsa had stepped forward and given a rousing speech, urging the workers to organize themselves independently in order to oppose the might of the state.

Now, back inside the shipyard, he put his own advice to work. He declared an "occupation strike," reinforcing the workers' decision to stay where they were. He took charge of the effort to set up a strike committee, and in short order it issued a set of demands that included the reinstatement of Walentynowicz and himself, pay raises, security against reprisals, and a monument to the men who had died in the 1970 crackdown. The committee's negotiations with management were broadcast over the shipyard's public address system so that everyone could hear what was happening.[2]

Even before Wałęsa spoke, Walentynowicz had made it back to the shipyard and joined the strike. The shipyard director, desperate to demonstrate his good intentions and to quell the rising protest, sent his own car to fetch her. As with Wałęsa, her return was greeted with cheers and applause. That the shipyard workers welcomed both Walentynowicz and Wałęsa back with such enthusiasm was noteworthy. Both had been explicitly singled out by management as enemies of the state. Back in an earlier day, the workers might have been inclined to shy away from someone so clearly identified by the party as an "enemy of the people."

The alliance between the workers and the opposition had evolved significantly over the previous decade. In 1968, caught up in the transformative turmoil of the Czechoslovak anti-Communist movement that came to be known as the Prague Spring, Polish students had taken to the streets, calling on the workers to join them.

The workers demurred. Two years later, when workers in the industrial belt of the Baltic went on strike, the students paid them back by standing by as the security forces cracked down with tanks and thousands of troops. Dozens of workers died.

The 1970 crackdown prompted several key members of the dissident movement in Poland to realize that this gap between laborers and intellectuals would have to be closed if there was any serious hope of creating a credible alternative to Communist rule. The crackdown of 1970 was followed by a period of relative liberalization under Communist Party leader Edward Gierek, who was eager to prove his moderate credentials to the Western governments who were giving him loans, and the dissident intellectuals gradually found ways to take advantage of the resulting space for maneuver. They circulated their publications, shared their ideas, and expanded their network of contacts.

Gierek, who had taken power in the wake of the 1970 strikes, had awakened genuine optimism among some sections of the public with his welcoming rhetoric and his new economic policies. But by the mid-1970s, the bloom was off. Prices rose, shortages deepened, and workers were being asked to increase their output. In 1976 another bout of major labor unrest flared at some of Poland's biggest factories. The Communist Party managed to quell the protests with the usual mix of force and carefully calibrated concessions. Yet something was changing. Workers were exploring possibilities for labor activism. In 1976 a group of dissidents seized the opportunity by forming the Committee to Defend the Workers (known by its Polish acronym as KOR). They worked to encourage and advise a nascent movement for independent unions that was stirring the country. Yet the ingredients for broader grassroots social organization were not yet in place.

But by the time of the strike at the Lenin Shipyard, there was a surprisingly large number of workers who shared the labor activists' skepticism about the government. The alliance had gained traction after the pope's 1979 pilgrimage. John Paul II's visit established a number of important preconditions. It gave Polish society a powerful sense of self-confidence after long years of humiliation and discord. There was also the crucial experience of self-organization on a mass scale. Party institutions had ceded the task of managing the millions of pilgrims and maintaining order to the citizens themselves, an accomplishment that turned out to be hard to forget. The millions who showed up shared in the experience of self-recognition: they realized, to their astonishment, that they had the numbers to convincingly counter the weight of the state. Together they listened to the pope proclaim his insistence on the centrality of Christ and the inviolability of individual human rights. This was a message that unified many Poles across class boundaries: students, peasants, work-ers, and even quite a few not terribly religious intellectuals.

Yet the message, for all its firmness, was couched in language that avoided the rhetoric of confrontation and insisted on the primacy of reconciliation and re-straint. This, too, was important. The pope's pilgrimage showed Poles that they could "live in the truth," rejecting the lies of the Communist regime, without resort-ing to violence. Not only that: nonviolence was a crucial precondition for the sort of cultural resistance that the pope's visit had helped to make possible. The opposition could hardly claim to present a credible alternative to Communist rule, with its em-brace of revolutionary "class warfare" and its daily practice of coercion, unless they convincingly demonstrated their allegiance to nonviolent change. The Communists were not a faceless, stereotypical "enemy." They were human beings, fellow Poles and Europeans, and they should be addressed as such, in the interest of a common humanity, and according to the values so movingly articulated by the pope.

In the course of his public conversation with Polish society, John Paul had also made a point of addressing the varied concerns of particular groups. He was par-ticularly intent on including the workers. In Jasna Góra he had celebrated mass for a congregation of some 1 million workers and miners from Upper Silesia and Za-grebie, the region from which the party had barred him during his trip. The pope's remarks outlined an image of work that dispensed with the stale invocations of class struggle: "Work must help man to become better, more mature spiritually, more re-sponsible, in order that he may realize his vocation on earth both as an unrepeatable person and in community with others."[3] He saw workers not as a social force, but as a group of individuals with shared concerns, and urged them to retain awareness of the spiritual and moral dimensions of their lives: "Do not let yourselves be seduced by the temptation to think that man can fully find himself only by denying God, erasing prayer from his life and remaining only a worker, deluding himself that what he produces can on its own fill the needs of the human heart."[4] And he noted ap-provingly that "the immense development of industry" in postwar Poland had "gone hand in hand with the building of churches, the development of parishes and the deepening and strengthening of faith."[5]

His observation was factually correct, but that did not diminish its potential to provoke. If there was one thing that Communist rulers feared more than anything else—even more than religion, in fact—it was labor unrest. The reason for this should be obvious. Communist regimes drew their legitimacy from Marxist ide-ology, and Marxism had proclaimed that world revolution would be spearheaded by the industrial working class. The working class was the avant-garde of the revolution precisely because, according to Marx, power derives from control of the mode of production. In the modern world, accordingly, industrial technology, controlled by the workers, is the ultimate source of power. Once the proletariat rose up and directed that power to its own ends, there would be no stopping it. How could the bourgeoisie go on calling the shots if the railroads and the steel factories and the coal mines no longer obeyed orders? Marx paid relatively little attention to the role of the peasantry. To be sure, peasants had some degree of revolutionary potential. They could chop the heads off a few landlords. But it was the workers who really mattered.

Yet even the history of Communism has its history of strikes. There were some within the Soviet Union itself. Workers downed tools in the Soviet Union in the 1920s, years after Bolshevik rule was firmly established. At least one strike occurred as late as 1962, in the city of Novocherkassk. They were all brutally suppressed, of course, and the heretical notion of an anti-Soviet labor movement was airbrushed out of the historical record.

The real hotbed of labor activism, however, was in East Central Europe after 1945. This made sense. Many of the workers in East Germany (at least before the ascent of Hitler), Poland, and Czechoslovakia had lived in capitalist societies where there were strong labor movements, and those who had grown up later had inherited the knowledge from their parents. The most persistent strikers were the Poles, whose workers retained a fairly rebellious streak throughout Communist rule. Usually, however, their strikes revolved around economic demands rather than political ones.

What happened in the summer of 1980 at first followed a similar pattern. By the end of the 1970s, the early optimism of Gierek's program had spent itself. The year 1979, it turned out, was not only a milestone because of the pope's visit; it was also the first year since the end of the war that Poland's national income declined, falling by 2 percent.[6] The hard-currency bill for Gierek's international borrowing spree was coming due. Poland's external debt skyrocketed; by 1980 it reached $18 billion. The borrowing policy's most tangible effects were higher prices and the continued scarcity of basic goods. The only way the government could pay off its creditors was through exports, mostly agricultural goods that were already scarce at home.

In the summer of 1980, thirteen months after the pope's visit, the workers once again began to bridle. On July 1 the government announced huge increases—from 60 to 90 percent—in the price of meat. Strikes broke out around the country. The government, which had prepared a strategy of concessions in advance, offered workers large raises and shipped in extra supplies of low-priced meat to areas of particular unrest.[7] Yet this policy of carrots was not enough to satisfy the work-ers. On July 14 they spooked the Polish Politburo by stopping work in Lublin, a strategic city on the rail line that connected East Germany with the Soviet Union. The panicked party immediately threw even more cash at the discontented laborers, which had the effect of encouraging others. Strikes flickered up and down the Baltic Coast like St. Elmo's Fire.

At the Lenin Shipyard, the director responded to Wałęsa's arrival with the usual strategy, attempting to divide the workers by proposing especially large pay raises to the older workers. Many of them accepted his offer and left the yard. Once again the strike almost collapsed. But a dedicated core of several hundred strikers remained in the yard, sustained by family members and well-wishers who handed supplies of food and drink through the surrounding fence. Under Wałęsa's leadership, the workers now expanded their agenda. They made explicitly political demands an integral part of the strike program. They insisted on legal guarantees of their right to strike, a loosening of restrictions on the media, and official recognition of their organization as a genuinely independent trade union movement.

Perhaps the most notable thing about this particular strike was its extraordi-nary sense of self-discipline. Among the strikers' first acts was a ban on the con-sumption of alcohol, which was not only maintained by the strikers themselves but quickly picked up by many organizations in the surrounding city as well. Many contemporaries considered this especially remarkable, given the ubiquity of heavy drinking habits in Communist Poland.[8] Mass took place every day at five o'clock. A portrait of John Paul II soon adorned the shipyard's main gate. These moral and religious undertones suggested that there was a bit more to this particular work stoppage than initially met the eye. That impression was borne out by the establish-ment of the Interfactory Strike Committee. From early on, emissaries from other workplaces had arrived at the shipyard to offer pledges of support and requests for cooperation. The founding of the Interfactory Strike Committee, which ultimately included dozens of delegates from all over Poland, had the effect of elevating the Lenin Shipyard protest movement from a local cause to a national one.

But what to call it? One of the members of KOR who arrived in Gdańsk to help the shipyard workers was Konrad Bielinski, an alumnus of the Student Solidarity Committee that had defended the cause of the murdered student Stanisław Pyjas three years earlier. Bielinski now began editing a daily newsletter for the strikers and their hangers-on. Calling it the *Strike Information Bulletin*, he decided to add another word that harked back to his days as a student activist: *Solidarity*.[9] Solidar-ity—of workers, and of humans in generals—was also a concept frequently invoked by Wałęsa and the other Strike Committee members. So it did not take long for the shipyard Strike Committee to seize upon the word as a fitting name for the larger independent union movement that evolved out of the strike. (Its official name was the "Independent Self-Governing Trade Union 'Solidarity.'")

Solidarity is a word that points to the moral underpinnings of the peculiar revolutionary movement that began in Gdańsk in the summer of 1980. It is worth noting that John Paul II used the same word as the title of a section in his central philosophical treatise, *Person and Act*, and though it is certainly going too far to credit him with masterminding the name of the union, it is no exaggeration at all to say that the specific character of the strike owed a great deal to the concrete experience of religious solidarity that Poles had experienced in those nine days in June the year before. Not only did the strikers in the Lenin Shipyard celebrate the pope's image and attend regular mass; they also sang hymns and patriotic songs together, just as Poles had done during the 1979 pilgrimage. Sympathizers brought flowers and food to the shipyard fence in voluntary displays of support, just as they had voluntarily organized themselves during John Paul's visit. And the Lenin Shipyard, now "occupied" by the strikers, became an oasis of free expression and thought within the Communist state, just as the pope's visit had created its own alternative spaces (such as the mass gatherings where dissident banners could be raised without fear of retribution, or the events organized entirely without the participation of the Communist Party).

To be sure, the church hesitated at first. In the early days of the strike, all too aware of the momentous implications of what the Lenin Shipyard workers were up to, none other than Cardinal Wyszyński gave a sermon in which he counseled the strikers to exercise restraint. Especially in the bowdlerized version issued by the government, his remarks appeared to stop short of guaranteeing the church's support to the strike movement. The strikers chose to ignore the possibility that a member of the clergy was trying to slow them down. This proved wise. On August 27, the Polish bishops issued a statement that specifically approved the "the right to independence both of organizations representing the workers and of organizations of self-government" and cited Vatican II's unambiguous commitment to human rights. The bishops' announcement was a direct result of John Paul II's personal involvement. He had urged the bishops to support the union and had assured them of his personal support.[10] This vote of confidence was crucial. The implicit promise of the church's institutional and diplomatic backing gave Wałęsa—who had now been chosen to lead the workers' team of negotiators in their talks with the government—a crucial boost in his subsequent round of negotiations.

What emerged from those talks was a momentous achievement, something that no one could have imagined just months before. The Polish government extended official recognition to the existence of independent, self-governing trade unions. Solidarity was "independent" because, for the first time since 1944, a large number of Poles had come together to create an organization capable of successively asserting itself against the overweening power of the Communist state. And for many, the adjective *self-governing*—an eloquent reflection of a new faith in the ability of Poles to manage their own affairs—harked back to the moment, a year earlier, when John Paul II's visit had provided a brief window of opportunity for Poles to organize their own lives.

It was, undoubtedly, the collapse of the Polish economy, and the corresponding loss of confidence in the state's ability to revive it, that fueled the Solidarity revolution. But an analysis of economic conditions alone fails to account for the timing, the content, or the forms that this revolution took. The state of the economy deteriorated sharply from 1980 to 1981. Yet, as historian Timothy Garton Ash has noted, the suicide rate among Poles dropped by almost one-third in the year after Solidarity's triumph; the annual per capita consumption of pure alcohol dropped from 8.4 liters in 1980 to 6.4 liters in 1981 (which was equivalent to the level of 1973). The rise of Solidarity clearly gave Poles a renewed sense of purpose. Ash recalls a case in which a mob tried to lynch a policeman in a provincial town. Solidarity representatives intervened. The dissident Adam Michnik, who was present, used his own experience of mistreatment at the hands of the police to persuade the mob to renounce summary justice—and they did. It was, in fact, remarkable how the Solidarity revolution managed to press its aims without recourse to violence.[11]

For sixteen months, the Communist authorities chose to endure the rise of a grassroots movement that challenged their social hegemony. The Polish Communist leaders were squeezed, on the one hand, by their masters in Moscow, who pressed them to put an end to this disturbing experiment (but who were themselves reluctant to intervene directly, since they were already busy with their deepening military involvement in Afghanistan). At the same time, Stanisław Kania, the new party leader (who had replaced Gierek after he had allowed the recognition of Solidarity), was reluctant to crack down, knowing that this would compel Western governments to turn off the flow of credits, thus aggravating Poland's economic troubles.

Then, on December 13, 1981, the party finally put an end to this remarkable cohabitation. Tanks and troops moved into position at key locations. The security services fanned out to pick up members of the opposition. General Wojciech

Jaruzelski, Kania's successor, had declared martial law in Poland. The revolution of the spirit inspired by John Paul II two years earlier was over. The attempt to establish an alternate space for a free society had failed—like all those earlier attempts to do something similar in postwar East Central Europe. Or so, at least, it seemed to many at the time.

On October 23, 1989, I noticed a surprising bit of graffiti in the men's lavatory in the central train station in the East German city of Leipzig: *Es lebe Solidarność*. Someone with a red felt-tipped pen had carefully rendered the famous Solidarity logo—the one that shows the word as a stylized crowd holding a banner aloft—on the wall of a stall.

As a budding journalist, I had come to Leipzig to report on the demonstrations that were, by then, taking place every Monday night. A few weeks earlier, East Germans had begun taking to the streets to protest the Communist government that had ruled the country since 1945. That evening I joined the demonstrators—around a quarter of a million of them—as they made their way along the ring road around the center of the city.

There were wisecracking high school students, and factory workers in blue denim suits, and necktie-wearing managers carrying briefcases, and blue-haired little old ladies. This was not the usual protest by a few earnest college kids or bookish dissidents. To be sure, there were all the chants and the banners and the interest groups that one might expect from a political event. But what gave this particular demonstration its distinctive character were the candles that many of the demonstrators carried as they marched, casting a calming glow as the immense procession moved through the evening darkness. The most prominent slogan, chanted at regular intervals, was "No Violence." (The chant became loudest and most insistent when we passed the building that housed the local headquarters of the Stasi, the East German secret police.) Given the tiny figures for church attendance in East Germany, it was extremely unlikely that the people in that massive crowd regularly participated in formal services of worship. Yet there was something in the atmosphere that could only be described as religious.

The remarkable air of festive calm had much to do with the fact that the core demonstrators had begun by meeting in churches around the city, where pastors admonished them to respect the humanity of their opponents and to exercise restraint in the face of government threats. This spirit of conciliation was extraordinary, given the messages coming out of the Communist Party. Until just a few weeks earlier, the East German state media had been calling for a "Chinese solution" to the problem of public discontent. The bloody crackdown of Tiananmen Square, when the Chinese Communist Party had dispersed thousands of student protesters by force in the center of Beijing, had taken place just five months earlier. The participants in the Monday demonstrations in Leipzig had heard the rumors that their own Communist leaders were planning to follow suit. The authorities had issued live ammunition to the troops and had ordered the hospitals to stock extra blood and plasma supplies. But on October 9, just before that night's demonstration was about to begin, the director of the Leipzig Orchestra and several other local notables persuaded three local party leaders to come out publicly against a crackdown. Together they issued a call committing the party to "peaceful dialogue." The security forces never went into action. After that the number of demonstrators swelled with each successive Monday evening.

In fact, the Leipzig tradition of regular Monday-evening "Prayers for Peace" dated back to 1982, three years after John Paul II's first pilgrimage and three years before Mikhail Gorbachev's rise to the top of the Soviet leadership. Protestant clergy at Leipzig's Church of St. Nicholas organized the prayers as a forum for the non-state-approved airing of controversial social topics, ranging from military conscription to industrial pollution. Although the human rights movement in the German Democratic Republic never assumed the same prodigious scale as its Polish counterpart, it is striking how much East German dissident activity—much of it avowedly secular and left-wing—took place under the aegis of local churches. The Prayers for Peace—which were emulated by other churches around East Germany—continued throughout the 1980s, opening up an important grassroots space for discussion of human rights issues. Among their many other activities, the pastors at the Church of St. Nicholas cultivated close ecumenical contact with their Catholic counterparts in Poland.

To anyone who experienced them, the peaceful revolutions of 1989 in East Germany and Czechoslovakia owed an obvious debt—freely acknowledged by those who engineered them—to the pioneers of the peaceful Solidarity revolution in Poland. The declaration of martial law in December 1981 seemed at first to represent the end of a chapter, another failed interlude of freedom in East Central Europe's long postwar twilight. It took time to realize that the Solidarity experiment had actually changed the balance of forces in fundamental ways. It was not merely that the State of Workers and Peasants had morphed, under General Jaruzelski's rule, into something more akin to a South American military junta; nor was it just that unleashing martial law had revealed the yawning gap between the government's claims of popular legitimacy and the demoralizing reality of its estrangement from the population. The ideological facade of Polish Communism, which had suppressed a genuine working-class movement by brute force of arms, had collapsed. All that remained was coercion.

In this light, Solidarity's apparent "failure" to take over the state presents itself in a rather different light. As some sympathetic historians have argued, the point of the trade union's existence was not to seize power, but to promote an "evolutionary revolution."[12] Polish dissident Adam Michnik noted that the form of social change embodied by Solidarity was, in fact, "self-limiting": while it aimed for the radical (and perhaps unattainable) end of self-government at all levels of society, its method for pursuing this goal was always avowedly incremental and nonconfrontational. In a revealing contrast, Michnik wrote, "The Communist authorities—admittedly, under constant and brutal pressure from Moscow—were unable to offer any sensible model of coexistence."[13]

Under martial law, Poles conspicuously refused to live in fear. They joined social resistance circles that spread information and helped the families of those who were imprisoned. Clandestine factory commissions from Solidarity continued to collect union dues and paid assistance to workers who lost their jobs or fell ill. Workers signed petitions for arrested union officials. Farmers sent food to the families of people who had been arrested, and workers reciprocated by supplying them with underground literature. Taken together, these gestures attested to the remarkable resilience of the diverse new civil society that Solidarity had helped to engender.[14]

Poles did all of this themselves. But the pope's intervention—if we can so describe his 1979 pilgrimage—provided a vital catalyst. His trip did not merely boost Polish morale. By his very presence John Paul II posed a practical political challenge to party rule, one to which the Communist system had no ready response. The pope could not be thrown in jail or overwhelmed by Red Army tanks; he could not be silenced or cajoled into a corrupting moral compromise. To Poles, he became the living exemplar of an alternate morality and the protector of the national idea. His global stature offered a promise of redress. And, of course, the millions who had welcomed John Paul in those nine days had permanently confounded the party's fundamental claim: that it represented the people. The people had seized the chance to demonstrate their true will, and they had chanted, "We want God."

Throughout Solidarity's bloodless revolution, the church was a major source of "nonconfrontational solutions," and this was not just a matter of the Vatican extending the hand of protection from Rome. Priests played an important role in calming potentially destructive emotions even as they created space for the legitimate expression of protest. The most famous example of this dynamic was Father

Jerzy Popiełuszko, an activist priest who had started his pastoral mission by ministering to steelworkers and later became closely allied with Solidarity. During the early years of martial law, he went right on assailing the party's abuses of power in his enormously popular sermons in his church in the working-class Warsaw district of Żoliborz—a phenomenon that, at the time, was entirely unique within the countries of the East bloc (combined population: 400 million). "Nowhere else from East Berlin to Vladivostok could anyone stand before ten or fifteen thousand people and use a microphone to condemn the errors of state and party," as *New York Times* reporter Michael Kaufman perceptively observed in one of his reports about Popiełuszko.[15] When Popiełuszko was murdered by the secret police in 1984, it was other priests who neutralized and salved popular anger. A quarter of a million people, including Solidarity leader Lech Wałęsa, attended Popiełuszko's funeral.

It has always been tempting to see John Paul II's first pilgrimage to Poland as a uniquely Polish event. That is understandable but somewhat inaccurate. This was a pope of a distinctly European avocation—more so, indeed, than many of the Italians in the job who had preceded him. His gift for languages had a great deal to do with it. And so, perhaps, did his intense appreciation of the artificiality of the Cold War divisions of Europe. From the first moment of his papacy, he unnerved the Soviets by identifying himself as a "Slav pope" with a particular sensitivity to his fellow believers to the East.[16] (It was, indeed, a good measure of the artificiality of the Yalta order that anyone should have regarded this as a provocation.)

He made a point of offering tangible support to the beleaguered Catholic churches inside the Soviet Union itself. Upon his election as pope, he sent his cardinal's zucchetto to a leading priest in Lithuania. He openly supported Cardinal Slipyj, the head of the Greek Catholic Church in the Ukraine, who had suffered considerable persecution at Soviet hands since his appointment to the post in 1944.

Crucially, John Paul II also gave his backing to Cardinal František Tomášek, archbishop of Prague from 1977 to 1991. Tomášek, who had spent three years in a labor camp in the early 1950s, had actively supported the Prague Spring reformist movement. Then, after the Soviet invasion that put an end to it in 1968, he fell silent. But John Paul II's pilgrimage in 1979 gave the archbishop new heart, and with the Vatican's help Tomášek became an eloquent defender of the Czechoslovak human rights organizations that began to play an increasingly influential role in the 1980s—above all Charter 77, the group whose founders included leading dissident Václav Havel. In January 1988, Tomášek publicly came out in favor of a petition calling for religious freedom that drew six hundred thousand signers (both Christians and non-).[17] The petition was an important act of resistance that set a precedent for the tumultuous events of the following year, when the Czechs (inspired by the examples of their neighbors in Poland and East Germany) succeeded in launching their own nonviolent uprising against Communist rule that came to be known as the "Velvet Revolution." Here, too, Tomášek also played a vital part, pledging the support of the church to the peaceful demonstrators who clashed with the security forces.

To be sure, John Paul II cannot be credited with masterminding everything that happened in Central Europe in 1989. The ascent to power of Mikhail Gorbachev in 1985 was, of course, a factor of enormous consequence; so, too, was the deepening economic malaise within the USSR, which weakened its ability to retain its hold over its satellites. Yet neither of these conditions determined the form that change, when it came, would take. In this respect, the nine days of John Paul II's June 1979 pilgrimage had a profound impact. We have fallen into the habit of regarding the collapse of Soviet-style Communism as inevitable: the direct consequence of a dysfunctional economic model of central planning, of the rigidity and institutionalized lies of command politics, and of the vast gap between the sublime designs of Marxist-Leninism and a reality that proved infinitely more vicious and mundane. This is simplistic. That Communism's disintegration in East Central Europe could have taken a starkly different course was demonstrated by the brief but bloody civil war in Romania during its own revolution in 1989 and the long savagery that followed in Yugoslavia during the 1990s. One of the most remarkable aspects of the 1989 revolutions in Poland, East Germany, and Czechoslovakia was how peaceful they remained—and here the pope's eloquent embodiment of the principle of nonconfrontational resistance, during his 1979 pilgrimage to Poland and subsequent visits, served as a far-reaching example. All this makes it hard to disagree with the assessment of Timothy Garton Ash: "Without the pope, there would have been no Solidarity movement; without Solidarity, there would have been no Gorbachev; without Gorbachev, there would have been no 1989."[18]

There is a great deal else to be said about the significance of John Paul II's papacy, but much of that lies outside the purview of this work. His supporters will long continue to revere him for his prodigious energy, his intense and mystical faith, his devotion to young people, and his bold acknowledgment of the church's historical responsibility for anti-Semitic teachings and the attendant revitalization of ties with the Jewish world. No other pope has pursued his pastoral mission so expansively. During his papacy, John Paul II visited 129 countries, laying the foundations for an extraordinary reglobalization of the church's mission.

His critics, of course, will denounce John Paul II precisely for his defense of church traditions and his insistence on received dogma, including his rejection of birth control, homosexuality, and women in the priesthood. The harshest verdict is likely to involve his handling of the scandal involving the widespread sexual abuse of children by priests, which has devastated the standing of the church in many of the countries where it long enjoyed privileged status. The pope's failure to ensure a full and transparent reckoning of the crimes committed by members of the priesthood must also now be reckoned as a part of his legacy.

Yet history is never one-dimensional. And if we are to arrive at a full understanding of the end phase of the Communist system in Europe, we cannot neglect the extraordinary homecoming of the newly elected Polish pope in that sweltering summer of 1979.

21

Khomeini's Children

The Islamic Revolution unquestionably succeeded in its aim of fundamentally altering Iranian society. It did away with the shah and his regime, and brought many aspects of his ambitious Westernization program to a grinding halt. The thousands of foreign specialists who once lived in the country departed, never to return. So, too, did hundreds of thousands of Iranians, most of them pillars or beneficiaries of the old regime.

Scholars tend to measure the impact of revolutions by the extent to which they affect the status of those who hold power in a particular society. By this standard, the 1979 revolution in Iran was a profoundly transformative one. It brought stark change to the ruling classes, as historian Shaul Bakhash notes.[1] Industrialists and bankers left; *bazaaris* with good contacts to ruling clerics pushed aside the elite merchants who had exploited their ties with the royal family. Many high-ranking members of SAVAK and the military who were unable to flee ended up in front of firing squads; so, too, did many officials of the shah's government, like Amir Abbas Hoveyda, the reformist ex-prime minister who refused to exploit an opportunity for escape and insisted on staying in Iran after the revolution. He paid for it with his life.

The shift was felt even within the tightly knit world of Iran's religious establishment. Well-established clerical families whose scions refused to endorse Khomeini's views on Islamic government faced precipitous decline. Grand Ayatollah Shariatmadari, who may well have saved Khomeini's life through intervention on his behalf in 1963, ended his life as a virtual outcast, his family the victims of vicious persecution by the new revolutionary regime. But there were plenty of candidates eager to fill the ensuing vacuum—most of them middle-ranking clerics, some of them former students of Khomeini, all more than willing to propagate the ideals of the new theocratic regime. The new regime did not draw only on the ranks of the clerics, though. Mohammed-Ali Rajai, for example, was a street peddler and school-teacher before he became prime minister of the Islamic Republic in 1980.[2]

Perhaps the best example of revolutionary social mobility is that of Seyyed Ali Khamenei, the current supreme leader. One of Khomeini's most devoted students, Khamenei paid for his political engagement with a series of stints in the shah's jails in the 1960s and '70s. After the revolution, he became one of the imam's key political advisers, distinguishing himself by his fanatical devotion to the principle of clerical rule. Khomeini had originally envisioned that only an ayatollah could fill the office of the supreme leader, but as he neared the end of his life, he realized that none of the likely candidates lived up to his criteria, so he pushed through a constitutional revision that lowered the bar to include mere "experts in Islamic jurisprudence." Khamenei, who duly acceded to the position of supreme leader in the wake of Khomeini's death, was acclaimed an ayatollah soon after taking office. Several of the highest-ranking clerics refused to accept Khamenei's new religious status.

This collision between political and religious principles is key to understanding the evolution of the Islamic Revolution. In his search for a workable political structure that would ensure the "guardianship of the jurists" while observing the niceties of democracy, Ayatollah Khomeini created a system of unwieldy compromises and institutionalized chaos. The 1979 constitution, which remained in force for the first decade of the Islamic Republic, welded together the incompatible notions of a popularly elected legislature and virtually unchecked executive power vested in the supreme leader.

The inherent conflict between these two views of the revolution was anything but academic. They came out into the open, sometimes to lethal effect, during the power struggle between Khomeini and Abolhassan Banisadr, who was elected president in Januarys 1980. Banisadr, who had gained renown before the revolution with a book that detailed his own socialistic theory of "Islamic economics," had a simple problem: he was not a cleric. When his aides had suggested a cleric as a candidate for the office of president, Khomeini had demurred, saying that the president should come from outside the clerical establishment. At this stage, Khomeini had no reason to doubt Banisadr's devotion to the revolution; during the shah's rule, Banisadr had established himself as an Islamist intellectual with his theoretical writings on Islam and the application of Quranic social justice to the economy. Yet once Banisadr assumed office, it quickly became clear that he, like Bazargan, had a considerably more restrained view of the clergy's proper political role than Khomeini himself. As a result, Banisadr soon found himself engaged in all-out battle with the Islamic Republican Party, which controlled parliament. His main foe was the ruthless Ayatollah Mohammed Beheshti, the chairman of the IRP and the head of the revolutionary court system.

The divide between these camps deepened as the Khomeinists unleashed a campaign to purge the new regime of the last pernicious influences of alien culture. In April 1980, Khomeini gave a speech denouncing the lingering effects of the shah's Westernizing policies. It was the signal for an all-out assault by the *hezbollahi* on universities and colleges around the country. The radical defenders of the new republic turned the campuses into battlegrounds, particularly targeting the student activist groups that provided much of the manpower for the left-wing militias that, by now, remained the only organizations capable of mustering armed resistance to the new regime. The most vicious of these groups was the People's Mujahideen, which had declared itself in opposition to the new order and succeeded in assassinating several key figures of the Khomeini government. But moderates felt the heat as well—including many who saw Banisadr as the champion of a more tolerant approach to Islamic government. In an odd borrowing from Mao's China, the leaders of the Islamic Republic called their purge "the Cultural Revolution."[3] Iran's universities were closed for three years, and thousands of scholars and leading cultural figures lost their jobs. Many responded by going into exile.

For those who remained, Banisadr gradually became the last remaining focus of opposition to the stiffening clerical regime. The fronts between the two sides hardened. His own newspaper gradually became more outspoken in its criticisms of the harsh treatment the Khomeinists meted out to their foes. When the People's Mujahideen declared their support for Banisadr, Khomeini's entourage took that as further evidence of his traitorous intentions. The president's supporters, invoking those sections of the constitution that drew on popular sovereignty, claimed his vote total as evidence of his popular mandate. Banisadr's clerical opponents, on the other hand, could point to constitutional articles that enshrined the dominance of the supreme leader, who embodied the principle of the sovereignty of God over man. This was more than the usual constitutional feud between different branches of government; it was a conflict that expressed an inherent tension between the mutually exclusive worldviews that had been uncomfortably fused under the new system.

The schism also expressed itself in defense policy. In September 1980, Saddam Hussein, who had assumed the presidency of Iraq the year before, launched a series of attacks on Iran, his major rival for regional supremacy. Saddam believed that the revolutionary turmoil had compromised Tehran's ability to defend itself, and he knew that the quality and equipment of his armed forces were superior. His assessment proved only partly correct, however. The Iranian military response eloquently demonstrated both the strengths and the weaknesses of the clerical regime. The war, which lasted for a total of eight years and ultimately claimed somewhere between 500,000 and 1.5 million lives, showed that countless Iranians were ready to defend Khomeini's state. The Iran-Iraq War gave ample display to the militant spirit unleashed by the revolution, a fervor that combined the deeply entrenched ethos of Shiite martyrology with the righteous new rhetoric of anti-imperialism.

Yet it also exposed the inherently unstable character of the Islamic Republic. Banisadr's job as president came to include leadership of the Defense Council, and he embraced his position for all that it was worth, repeatedly showing up at the battlefront to underline his solidarity with the soldiers. The clerics, however, commanded the Revolutionary Guard, which distinguished itself by its single-minded devotion to the revolutionary cause. This lack of unity among the Iranian military leaders—in stark contrast to Saddam Hussein's rigidly hierarchical, Soviet-style chain of command—did not contribute to efficient prosecution of the war and undoubtedly helped to prolong the conflict.

In the end, of course, Khomeini's regime survived the war, shored up by the wave of patriotic emotion inspired by the fighting. Saddam, too, remained in place, right up until he was toppled by the US invasion of his country in 2003. But Banisadr did not have anything like the same staying power. In 1981 his enemies in parliament succeeded in impeaching him. By the time his removal from office became official, Iran's former president was hiding in the underground in Tehran. He managed to escape the country and later established himself, now in French exile, as a leading opponent of the clerical regime. But the conflict between the branches of Iran's government, as well as the underlying trend toward power struggles among the regime's leading figures, continued.

The confusion extended to management of the economy. Here, too, the differences among competing constituencies ran deep and were aggravated by the jury-rigged quality of the Islamic Republic's institutional arrangements. Part of the problem was the paucity of religious guidance on matters relating to modern economics. The Quran, while clearly defining social justice as the centerpiece of economic life, is notably silent on issues like monetary policy, labor relations, or industrial organization. In prerevolutionary Iran, a number of theorists—including both Bazargan and Banisadr—had published elaborate treatises on the proper Islamic approach to economics that arrived at strikingly divergent conclusions. Khomeini himself had little to say on the subject—a reflection of his general contempt for materialistic thinking. His assumption seemed to be that a proper Islamic government would effortlessly dispense with the inequities of development that so characterized Iran under the shah.

In practice, of course, that proved anything but simple. The new government expropriated the banks and factories of those who opted for emigration and transformed the Pahlavi Foundation, which controlled many of the royal family's business interests, into a charitable organization devoted to the needs of the underprivileged. Such foundations, known as *bonyads*, quickly proliferated, often as cover for the business interests of the new governing class. Meanwhile, the war with Iraq bolstered state control over distribution networks. The Majlis, the popularly elected parliament, inclined toward quasi-socialist policies, favoring radical land reform and nationalization of industry. But the parliamentarians often found themselves running into resistance from the traditionalist clerics in the Council of Guardians, who, tending to regard private property as sacrosanct, canceled some of the more radical laws the legislators proposed.

Khomeini, who often indulged in scorching anticapitalist rhetoric, sided now with one view, then with the other. As historian Shaul Bakhash notes, clerics have never quite managed to achieve a consensus on the precise role of the state in economic affairs, including such crucial issues as the role to be played by private business or the extent to which the government should use policy to ensure more equitable distribution of wealth.[4] The end effect of this back-and-forth is a system in which a wide-ranging welfare state and nationalized industry awkwardly coexist with privileged interest groups, from individual politicians to institutions like the Revolutionary Guard, that hold sway over large swaths of the economy. The shah's defenders can point out, with some justice, that world leaders no longer take the trouble, as they did in the 1970s, to visit Iran for clues on how to achieve high-speed growth. Today's Iran struggles to make ends meet. Globalization and the corresponding surge of technological innovation have largely passed the country by.

Khomeini died in 1989, not long after grudgingly agreeing to a compromise that ended the Iran-Iraq War without a clear victory for either side. Within Iran, of course, his influence is all-permeating. Khomeini holds a place comparable to the one that Mao once occupied for many Chinese: he enjoys near-divine status as the founding figure of the regime, the man who liberated Iran from long years of foreign domination. The system that Khomeini bequeathed to his political heirs, this bewildering blend of traditional faith and twentieth-century modernism, still reflects the sometimes mysterious motives of its chief architect. In 1987, indeed, Khomeini actually declared that the needs of the state take precedence over the dictates of the Quran—a move that dramatized the degree to which he was capable of startling departures from orthodoxy. Khomeini's political views evolved according to the needs of the moment. He began his political career in 1963 by deriding the vote for women but extended the franchise to them during the revolution, when they had proved themselves avid supporters of the cause. For that matter, the phrase *Islamic republic* does not occur in his famous book *Islamic Government*. He once famously described Islam as a "religio-political faith."[5]

To describe the government established by the Iranian Revolution of 1979 as a reversion to medieval obscurantism is to miss many of its essential characteristics. As one historian has noted, the revolution drew its force both from the long-established institutions of the Shia clergy and from the rise of the centralized twentieth-century state; both factors are crucial to our understanding of the house that Khomeini built.[6] Scholar Ervand Abrahamian notes Khomeini's remarkable capacity for moving outside the limits of received religious wisdom. As he points out, the word *fundamentalist* evokes an image of inflexible dogmatism that does little credit to Khomeini's penchant for innovative thinking. Khomeini showed a remarkable willingness to reject many Shia traditions that he regarded as irrelevant to current political problems while freely absorbing other concepts from the non-Muslim world. "The final product," Abrahamian writes, "has less in common with conventional fundamentalism than with Third World populism, especially in Latin America."[7]

It is worth noting that the postrevolutionary government quietly chose to continue some of the modernization programs started by the shah (like the Literacy Corps).[8] Indeed, in some ways the Islamic Republic has accelerated that very process. By using the nationwide network of mosques—the most ubiquitous and deeply rooted social institution—as conduits for the transmission of government policy, the mullahs have extended the reach of the state into realms of private life that the shah never succeeded in penetrating.

In so doing, however, Khomeini's vision of "Islamic government" may have ended up doing itself a disfavor. For most of the history of Islamic Iran, the religious establishment has existed as a separate institution, distinct from and parallel to the state. The events of 1979 changed that relationship to dramatic effect. It was Khomeini's hope that clerical rule would purify the state, and thus restore truly Islamic principles to the everyday life of Iranian society. But there is an inescapable sense that the revolution has instead brought religion down to the grubby level of every-day politics. Iranian officials routinely decry the increasing apathy toward religion displayed by young people; studies suggest that mosque attendance in modern-day Iran is notably lower than in other Muslim countries.[9] All-encompassing surveil-lance by overlapping security services, the obvious corruption of many government officials, and the conspicuous failure of the regime to provide for genuine economic development have all tarnished the reputation of the holy men who now hold the responsibility for the country's administration. "A chasm has opened between pub-lic and private life," wrote historian Bakhash on the tenth anniversary of the revo-lution. "A popular saying in Tehran has it that under the Shah, Iranians prayed in private and drank in public; under the Islamic Republic, they pray in public and drink in private."[10] If anything, that chasm is much greater today than it was when Bakhash was writing.

In the end Khomeini bequeathed to the Islamic Republic not only his religion-based philosophy of government, but also a volatile legacy of institutionalized in-stability, tensions between elections and despotism, brutal factional rivalry, and rigidly centralized control. Some thirty years after its founding, the revolution has yet to fulfill its original promise. Yet the simple fact that it was able to make that promise to begin with has been remarkably influential.

On October 23, 1983, a man drove a truck packed with explosives into a mili-tary barracks in Beirut and blew himself up. The explosion killed 241 mem-bers of the United States Marine Corps who had been dispatched to the Middle East by US president Ronald Reagan as part of an international intervention in the Lebanese Civil War. It was the greatest loss of life suffered by the Marine Corps in a single day since the Battle of Iwo Jima in the spring of 1945. Another near-simul-taneous attack took the lives of 58 French paratroopers—the biggest single-day loss for a French force since the 1950s war in Algeria.

The organization that assumed responsibility for this strange new form of ter-rorism—based on the attacker's self-immolation—called itself Islamic Jihad. (The same group had already claimed responsibility for an attack on the US Embassy in Beirut that had killed 60 people earlier in the year.) Although the group's origins are somewhat mysterious, it was most likely an offshoot of Hezbollah, a militant organization of Lebanon's Shiites that had been established not long before. In mul-tinational Lebanon, the mostly rural Shiites traditionally occupied the bottom rung of the sectarian and ethnic hierarchy within the country. That began to change in the

1960s and '70s, when a charismatic Iranian-born cleric named Musa al-Sadr began to organize the Shiites into a movement to campaign for their rights. His mysterious disappearance in Libya in 1978—orchestrated by Libyan dictator Muammar al-Qaddafi—temporarily derailed Shiite aspirations. But then came the revolution in Iran.

No sooner had Khomeini made his return to Tehran than the new revolutionary regime began working to spread the message. From the very start, Khomeini believed that the revolution had pan-Islamic implications. He did not believe that it should be confined to his own country. "In general, a Muslim should not just concern himself with only a group of Muslims," he once observed. "We are all responsible to stand up to the oppression by the superpowers and discredit plans like those of Sadat and [Saudi King] Fahd." From the outside, Khomeini was often viewed as a defender of Iranian Shiism, but he did not see himself this way. He saw himself as a holy warrior who was out to defend the entire global community of Muslim believers.[11]

The revolutionary government lost no time in pursuing this role—despite the economic and political problems at home. Radio Tehran became an aggressive outlet for Iranian propaganda, broadcast around the region—a factor that played a major role after the seizure of the Grand Mosque in Saudi Arabia, when Khomeini succeeded in fomenting unrest throughout the Islamic world by accusing the Americans of orchestrating the takeover. But the new government in Tehran did not restrict its pan-Islamic support to words. As early as December 1979, the Lebanese authorities found themselves coping with an influx of Iranian guerrillas eager to help their coreligionists take the fight to Israel.[12] Ayatollah Montazeri declared that Iranian militants should have the right to enter other Islamic countries without passports or visas on the grounds that Islam "has no borders."[13]

The response to the Islamic Revolution from Muslims around the world seemed—at least at first—to justify such high-flown talk. Islamist groups sang the praises of Islam's great Iranian from Indonesia to Nigeria. (There are few Shiites in Nigeria, but in some quarters there after 1979, the word *Shia* came to serve as a synonym for those who aimed for the creation of an Islamic state.) The riots that took place from Islamabad to Tripoli in response to Iranian accusations about the Mecca mosque uprising attested to the emotive force of Khomeini's appeals to Muslims throughout the *umma*. Khomeini's former students—who were, of course, not only Iranians—helped to carry his message around the world. And the demonstrated ability of Islamic revolutionaries to overthrow a hated monarch also helped to foment a bloody but little-noted rebellion against the royal family in oil-rich Shiite provinces of Saudi Arabia. Shia Muslims constitute the majority of the population there, but the Sunni House of Saud, tightly wedded to the ultraconservative Wahhabi sect, has always regarded them as virtual heretics and discriminates against them accordingly. The Shia unrest of 1979 marked merely the first in a long series of uprisings against the central government that continue to this day.

Khomeini himself, however, focused above all on two particular areas: Palestine and Lebanon.[14] His reasons for taking up the Palestinian cause were straightforward. Unlike the Marxist revolutionaries who still dominated the Palestine Liberation Organization, Khomeini saw the Arab-Israeli conflict in primarily religious terms. For him, waging war on Israel meant fulfilling Quranic injunctions against Jewish "hypocrites" inimical to the true faith as well as the ultimate recovery of the al-Aqsa Mosque in Jerusalem, which he viewed as one of the holiest places in Islam. It was Khomeini who established the annual al-Quds (Jerusalem) Day in Iran's revolutionary calendar: every year, to this day, the Tehran regime organizes demonstrations proclaiming the religious imperative for the reconquest of Jerusalem. Starting in 1979, Palestinians (who viewed the shah as an enemy because of his alliance with Israel) actively participated in various stages of the Iranian Revolution, and Iran started providing various Palestinian groups with military training early on. Later in the 1980s, Iran became one of the main sponsors of Hamas, the Palestinian Islamist resistance group based in the Gaza Strip.

Still, the Shiite factor in Iran's revolution was not to be discounted, and few Palestinians were Shiites. But what bound the two sides together was a fondness for radical politics. The Palestinians leaned naturally to revolutionary ideology since it challenged the status quo of the Middle East, and as long as this was true, the religious differences between them and the Iranians played a subordinate role. They shared a common enemy, and that was enough to help them overlook the problems of religion.

That was not true of Lebanon, which boasted its own large, and largely underprivileged, Shiite population. The revolution was still under way in Iran when the first portraits of Ayatollah Khomeini began to appear on the walls of homes throughout the Shiite villages and shantytowns of Lebanon. The Amal militia, the military wing of al-Sadr's "Movement of the Disinherited," suddenly found itself facing competition from a new group based on the paramilitary organization that had fought for Khomeini's agenda during the revolution: Hezbollah, "the Party of God." Sadr had envisioned his movement as one that would advance the cause of justice for all Lebanese. He made an effort to bring non-Shiites into its leadership and at least attempted to transcend sectarianism. Hezbollah, formed in part by Shiites who rejected Sadr's more inclusive approach, had no such scruples. The group in its current form emerged in response to the Israeli invasion of Lebanon in 1982, when its leaders publicly declared their allegiance to Khomeini's theory of *velayat-e faqih* and pledged to transform Lebanon into an Islamic republic along Iranian lines. From the very beginning, its primary aims included the destruction of the state of Israel. Hezbollah's fanaticism and success in the Lebanese Civil War gradually allowed it to supplant the more moderate Amal—even though many Shiite clerics in the country echoed some of their Iranian counterparts by rejecting Khomeini's theory of the guardianship of the jurist.[15]

The Revolutionary Guard Corps, the Islamic army Khomeini created in parallel to the conventional military, assumed patronage of Hezbollah from the beginning in 1982. Guard instructors trained its fighters and outfitted them with weapons. Money flowed from Tehran to the shantytowns of Beirut. The Iranians also helped the new group build a media operation that has become one of the most effective means of public mobilization in Lebanon today. Over the past three decades—most notably during its 2006 war with Israel—Hezbollah has established itself as one of the most effective political and military organizations in Lebanon, and thus as a potent vehicle for the advancement of Islamist (and Iranian) agendas throughout the Middle East. It has been implicated in numerous terrorist attacks.

Perhaps the most fateful innovation that resulted from Iranian involvement in Lebanese politics was the suicide bombing. Islamic Jihad achieved such devastating success precisely because the Americans and French had not prepared defenses against attackers who were prepared to kill themselves. Oddly enough, the suicide bombing was a terrorist tactic with secular rather than religious origins; it was pioneered by secular nationalists during the Lebanese Civil War, and then used to particularly deadly effect by the People's Mujahideen (Mujahideen-e Khalq or MEK), the Islamo-Marxist militia. The MEK, which turned against Khomeini in 1980, used suicide attacks as part of its terror campaign against the leaders of the clerical system.

But it was the institutionalized use of "martyrdom" by the Islamic Republic that firmly established suicide attacks as a modus operandi for Islamic fighters. By the time of the 1983 Beirut attacks, the Iran-Iraq War had been under way for three years, and the Iranians had already had ample opportunity to demonstrate the effectiveness of "martyrdom operations" against Iraqi troops that drew on the messianic fanaticism of believers still alight with revolutionary fervor. Young troops went into battle wrapped in slogans evoking the great traumas and triumphs of Shiite belief. The rhetoric of martyrdom drew on centuries of Shiite ritual adoration for Ali and Hussein, those lodestars of the true faith who were also the victims of cosmic injustice.

Nor did Khomeini view his war with the apostate Saddam Hussein as one whose consequences would be confined merely to their two countries. He saw the fight against Iraq as part of a larger crusade to restore Muslim rule throughout the Middle East. "The road to Jerusalem lies through Baghdad" was a slogan widely used by the Iranian regime during the war. "Our revolution is not tied to Iran," Khomeini once remarked. "The Iranian people's revolution was the starting point for the great revolution of the Islamic world."[16] All the more bitter for him, then, was the ignominious stalemate with which the war finally ended. Khomeini famously equated the agreement that formally concluded the war with Iraq with a "draught of poison."

Khomeini's aspirations to global leadership of the Islamic community had broader aspects as well. One was to establish Islam as a powerful alternative to the ideologies that then dominated global politics. Odd Arne Westad, a leading historian of the Cold War, observes that the Iranian Revolution marked the moment when the United States was jolted by the realization that "communism was no longer the only comprehensive, modern ideology that confronted American power." Ironically, the events in Iran brought a similarly rude awakening to the Russians. Khomeini's revolution presented a serious challenge to the Marxist theory of Third World revolutions. In this reading, "clerical reaction" was supposed to be just another way station on the path to the dictatorship of the proletariat. Yet this was clearly not what had happened in Iran.[17]

Indeed, after the collapse of the Soviet Union and the philosophy that inspired it, political Islam remained essentially the only universalist ideology that could pose serious competition to the American and European ideals of liberal democracy in the Middle East.[18] Khomeini's fatwa against the British writer Salman Rushdie, which condemned him to death for allegedly slandering the prophet in his novel *The Satanic Verses*, can be viewed in this same context of Iran's ideological rivalry with the West. The death sentence pronounced on Rushdie by the ayatollah was a transparent attempt to snatch back the mantle of leadership from various Sunni governments the Iranians depicted as too cowardly (and too craven to the United States) to defend the honor of Islam. Somewhat paradoxically, when the United States launched its post-9/11 wars in Afghanistan and Iraq, one effect was to greatly expand Iranian influence in the region by eliminating two of the regional competitors that Tehran despised most of all: the secular regime of Saddam Hussein and the ultraconservative Sunni government of the Taliban. Nonetheless, today the Islamic Republic remains one of the few foreign regimes that American politicians of all ideological stripes can reliably vilify at little cost to themselves.

But Khomeini's revolution had another legacy that was even more consequential. This was its impact on the centuries-old rivalry between the Shiite and Sunni
branches of Islam. Before 1979 the intra-Muslim divide figured little in global politics. After 1979 it was impossible to avoid. That the Shiites had succeeded before
any other Muslim nation in restoring the sovereignty of God was an extraordinary
turn of events that some Sunni believers came to regard as something akin to a calculated affront. Some scholars argue that the motives for the seizure of the Grand
Mosque in 1979 included the desire among some Sunni upstarts to show that they,
too, could topple an unjust monarch and establish a truly Islamic state.

The implications of the newfound political self-awareness among hitherto down-
trodden Shiite minorities rippled across South Asia. Iranian support for the Shiite
mujahideen fighting the Soviet occupiers in Afghanistan boosted the power of the
Hazara ethnic minority, shocking a largely Sunni population that had long regarded
Hazaras as second-class citizens. One of Khomeini's students was a Pakistani who
returned to his homeland to found the first Shiite political organization in that
largely Sunni country, contributing to decades of sectarian violence there. Khomeini's first foreign minister, Ebrahim Yazdi, met with Syrian dictator Hafez al-Assad
already in September 1979, establishing a close relationship between Tehran and
the Assad dynasty that endures to this day—despite the Syrian government's harsh
suppression of its Sunni Muslim majority. (A mere 15 percent of the Syrian population belongs to the Alawi sect, but that group includes the Assads and much of the
Syrian ruling elite among its members. Alawi beliefs, regarded as heterodox by most
Sunnis, have much in common with Shia Islam.) And the Sunni secularist Saddam
Hussein, who was worried about the restiveness of his own Iraqi Shiites even before
the revolution in Iran, saw Khomeini's ascendance as yet another reason to tighten
control over the Shiite believers that constituted the majority of his population. It
was, perhaps, inevitable that Tehran would become the main protector of the Shiite
resistance groups, such as the Dawa Party and the Supreme Council for the Islamic
Revolution in Iraq, that later played a prominent role in governing the country after
the US invasion of Iraq in 2003.

For decades after the collapse of the Ottoman Empire and the end of the caliphate in 1924, Islam was mostly a passive force, acted upon rather than putting forth
programs of its own. It was left to others to craft new ideologies for the future:
nation-state monarchies, pan-Arab nationalism, Baathism. But it is Khomeini who
really deserves the credit for returning Islam to the forefront of the global political
stage. It was he who converted his Islamic utopia into reality, and it was he who
went further than anyone else in his efforts to transplant the primal community of

the Prophet into the ministries and militias of a modern nation-state. After Khomeini, the Islamists did not just talk. They acted.

The most potent legacy of the Islamic Revolution in Iran was simply to show that it could be done. To be sure, that achievement has been greatly harmed by evidence of deeply entrenched corruption, economic anemia, and brutal authoritarianism of the regime Khomeini founded. Yet even in the twenty-first century, it is possible to encounter non-Iranian Muslims, Shiite as well as Sunni, who reflexively applaud the mullahs in Tehran for standing up to the United States and the West. This was a card that Khomeini had already learned to play by the end of 1979—often happily deploying a neo-Marxist vocabulary of "anti-imperialism" and "revolutionary struggle" that owed little to orthodox Islam. His pupils are legion. For all of its failures, Khomeini's dream retains its power to seduce.

22

Jihad

In November 1989, the eyes of the world were fixed on the astonishing torrent of images emerging from East Central Europe, where the Communist system implanted by the Red Army after 1945 was falling apart. So the global media took little note of a brief spasm of violence in Pakistan's North-West Frontier Province. The war in neighboring Afghanistan was about to enter its tenth year. The Soviet forces had left, but their proxy, the former secret police chief Mohammed Najibullah, still held precarious sway in Kabul. Since assuming the presidency in 1986, he had made a number of overtures to the opposition, even promising the introduction of sharia law. But the holy warriors, who regarded him as a creation of the Russians, still wanted him dead. And so the war continued.

By now the war had transformed the fortunes of Peshawar, the regional capital. The city had languished throughout most of the seventies in a provincial drowse, but the Soviet invasion had swiftly transformed it into the focal point of the anti-Communist jihad. There had been a time, not that long ago, when the grand political maneuverings in the rest of Pakistan, so far removed in culture and outlook from the tribal areas, took place as if beyond a distant horizon. Now, in this strange new era, the entire world had arrived in Peshawar to fight one of the great set pieces of the Cold War. It was not just that the Pakistani intelligence service, the Inter-Services Intelligence (ISI) directorate, used the city for the safe houses and logistical facilities of the rebel groups it chose to support. The diplomats and spies of countless nations also descended upon Peshawar to dispense weapons and advice and jockey for vital information. Their ranks included both operatives from the CIA, whose agreements with the ISI banned them from traveling into Afghanistan itself, and agents from the East-bloc countries, desperate to neutralize the enemies of socialism and harvest intelligence that might prove of use to Moscow. It was also in Peshawar that Muslims from around the world, drawn by earnest faith or a yearning for adventure, gathered to support the holy war against the godless Russians. Add the fact that Peshawar was also the main conduit for weapons supplies to the Afghan guerrillas, with all the shadowy flows of finance this entailed, and the result made for a combustible mix.

On the evening of November 24, a Palestinian Islamic scholar named Abdullah Azzam was on his way to Friday prayers at his preferred mosque in the center of the city. Accompanied by his two sons and the offspring of a slain mujahideen commander, Azzam stepped out of his car. At that moment a huge blast shook the street. The car vanished; only a tiny fragment of it remained after the explosion. Azzam's younger son was catapulted into the air, his body landing three hundred feet away. The other two boys were shredded by the blast, their body parts scattered across trees and power lines. "As for Sheikh Abdullah Azzam himself, his body was found resting against a wall, totally intact and not at all disfigured, except that some blood was seen seeping from his mouth," wrote one sympathizer who claimed to have seen the body immediately after the attack. Azzam was buried in the same Peshawar cemetery that became the final resting place of many of the holy warriors who fought in the Afghan war.[1]

His killing came as an enormous shock to those who had devoted their lives to the Afghan jihad, for Azzam had played a crucial role in fusing that struggle with global Muslim politics. Born in 1941 in the West Bank town of Jenin, he had come of age in the most intense phase of the Palestinians' war against Israel. In striking contrast to so many of his contemporaries, however, Azzam had rejected revolutionary Marxism or secular nationalism. He found the answer in a deeply conservative reading of Islam. He studied sharia in Syria for a few years in the 1960s. Like so many others of his generation, he was deeply demoralized by Israel's crushing victory in the war of 1967. Drawn to activism, he moved to Jordan, where he joined the Palestinian chapter of the Muslim Brotherhood. Later he continued his studies of Islamic law at Cairo's prestigious al-Azhar University, where he built up his contacts with like-minded Islamists. By the end of the 1970s, he was lecturing at King Abdul Aziz University in Jeddah in Saudi Arabia.

The outbreak of the war in Afghanistan galvanized him. In 1979 he issued a religious ruling, a fatwa, in support of the mujahideen entitled *Defense of the Muslim*

Lands, the First Obligation After Faith. He called upon Muslims to pay heed to the example of Afghanistan. Here, he said, was an Islamic nation whose pure devotion to the faith sustained a blazing jihad against the world's great atheist superpower. In rational terms, it made no sense at all. How did impoverished tribesmen dare to take on the Soviet Union's vast army, bristling with modern weapons? Yet the Afghans continued to fight on, even though they were clearly outgunned. This was a story, Azzam insisted, that could only fire the imagination of the truly pious: "The battles in Afghanistan . . . have reached a level of intensity, the likes of which have not been witnessed in the mountain ranges of Hindu Kush, nor in recent Islamic history." The stated goal of the Afghan mujahideen, he noted, was the creation of an Islamic state—a fact that stood in refreshing contrast to the official Palestinian liberation movement, which, as he saw it, had been appropriated by a dispiriting variety of political camps, including Communists, nationalists, and even some re-formist Muslims. None of them, he noted sadly, shared his Islamist priorities.

He took care to point out another salient difference between the two struggles. The Palestinian cause had become entangled in Cold War maneuverings. By accept-ing support from the USSR, the Palestinians had subjected themselves to forces over which they had no control: "The situation has become a game in the hands of the great powers." This submission to an atheist ally, moreover, betrayed the Pales-tinians' Muslim identity. The Afghans, by contrast, "refuse help from any disbeliev-ing country." (This was not strictly true even at the time that Azzam was writing: Jimmy Carter had signed the first presidential order stipulating covert support to the Afghan rebels in the summer of 1979, and though Azzam could not have known this particular detail, he would have been aware of the Americans' involvement. The fact of American support did become a complicating factor for radical Islamists as the Afghan jihad went on; they were forced to rely on "lesser of two evil" arguments to rationalize US participation. But many of them refused to have anything to do with the Americans in the field.)

Azzam noted another vital difference between Palestine and Afghanistan. It had to do with geography. The Palestinians confronted an Israeli enemy that had the power to keep their borders tightly closed and to monitor any movements across them. Afghanistan, by contrast, boasted eighteen hundred miles of open borders that were impossible to control, as well as many isolated tribes that resisted ma-nipulation from the outside.[2] Afghanistan's remoteness made it a safe haven for an Islamic state. Azzam may have been influenced in this thinking by leftist theories of guerrilla warfare, which were much in vogue in the 1970s—perhaps even by Mao's theory of the Communist "base area," which, once firmly established, could serve as the political and military launching pad for a broader insurrection against the strong points of capitalist society.

In any case, it was extraordinary to see a Palestinian activist in the 1980s publicly relegate his own people's struggle to the back burner while giving priority to the struggle of non-Arab Muslims in an entirely peripheral country. For Azzam, it was not the particular concerns of individual peoples that mattered so much as the fate of the *umma* as a whole. Like Sayyid Qutb, he believed strongly in the notion of an irreconcilable "clash of civilizations" between the community of Muslims and the non-Muslim world.

Azzam did not stop there. Following the lead of some earlier Islamist theoreticians (notably Mawdudi), he declared support for the Afghan jihad to be an individual religious obligation (*fard ayn*) for every Muslim around the world. In so doing, he effectively elevated the pursuit of a holy war to the status of a "pillar of the faith," on a par with the five core practices of Islam that are incumbent upon every believer. This went much further than the rulings of traditional Islamic scholars, who argued instead that assisting the Afghan jihad was a *fard kifaya*—a collective religious obligation that could be fulfilled if the community as a whole gave weapons, money, and other forms of support to the struggle; individual believers, in other words, weren't expected to go and do the fighting themselves. For Azzam, by contrast, prosecuting the jihad against Islam's enemies had become a central religious duty. Azzam's contrary fatwa lent crucial religious legitimacy to the new spirit of militancy that was coursing around the Islamic world as a result of the great revivalist movement of the 1960s and 1970s.[3]

His ideas were hugely influential. His writings and lectures were passionate and persuasive and characterized by a strong mystical bent that entranced his followers. (He spoke at great length about the miracles of the jihad: how birds suddenly taking wing gave warning of imminent Soviet attacks and how the bodies of slain mujahideen gave off a smell like perfume.) He used his extensive network of international contacts to distribute pamphlets and video recordings of his sermons. Many young Sunni Muslims who embraced the Islamist call to action viewed his instructions as a guide.[4]

Azzam himself strongly stressed practical results as well as theory. In 1980, seeking to get closer to the action in Afghanistan, he accepted a teaching position at the International Islamic University in the Pakistani capital of Islamabad. The name of the institution was entirely appropriate to a man who had devoted his life to the creation of a global movement in pursuit of an Islamic state. Within months, however, Azzam relocated to Peshawar, where he could lend more concrete support to the mujahideen cause. His connections now came in handy. He could call on wealthy do-nors throughout the Gulf. He could draw on organizational advice from a range of militants around the Middle East. And his cosmopolitan teaching career had given him contact both with established Islamists (like the family of Sayyid Qutb, whom he greatly admired) as well as with the younger generation of would-be jihadis.

This new generation included Osama bin Laden, a well-born Saudi whom Azzam probably met during his teaching stint in Jeddah and who joined him in Peshawar not long after the start of the war. Azzam decided that he and his follow-ers could best support the Afghan jihad by setting up an organization to coordinate the flow of weapons, funds, and fighters. He called it the Services Office (Maktab-al Khadamat). The MAK became a significant logistical hub for much of the private support for the mujahideen coming in from the Arab world (though the bulk of government money from Saudi Arabia and other Muslim governments continued to flow to the Pakistani government, which worked hard to maintain a monopoly over funding to the mujahideen). It was the MAK that provided the most impor-tant organizational base for Bin Laden's al-Qaeda.

It was Azzam and his ideological heirs—of whom Bin Laden was but one—who can be credited with transforming the local Afghan jihad into a truly global one. Azzam ultimately traveled to dozens of countries (including the United States) on his fund-raising trips, and everywhere he went he sowed the seeds for his vi-sion of a worldwide revolutionary struggle for an Islamic state. During the 1980s, thousands of fighters from around the Muslim world passed through his training camps and traveled to Afghan battlefields with his help. Their military contribution to the jihad was relatively limited; they were often regarded with contempt by the Afghans, who tended to see them as arrogant and out of touch. It was in their own homelands that the so-called Afghan Arabs and the other foreign veterans of the Afghan conflict arguably had their greatest impact.

The mujahideen struggle against the Soviets—a struggle that ultimately ended with a humiliating retreat for the forces of Moscow—filled Muslims around the world with pride. This glorious victory seemed to many a confirmation of what the Islamists had been arguing all along: with God's help, anything is possible. (The Quran is replete with verses promising victory to those who are faithful to God.) The triumph of the Afghan jihad inspired Muslims in a general way, but it gave particular impetus to the more militant strains of Islamist thought. The full psycho-logical impact is hard to quantify, of course.

One of the most concrete effects can be seen in the later journeys of the non-Afghans who personally participated in the war against the Soviets. Garlanded by their participation in the glamorous Afghan jihad, the Afghan Arabs and their fellow Islamist internationalists personally embodied the message of armed resistance to the infidels and the apostates. Not for nothing would Afghanistan in the 1980s come to be known as the "University of Jihad."

Inevitably, however, Azzam's very success as a leader and religious thinker inspired competition. Another Arab who made the pilgrimage to Peshawar was Ayman al-Zawahiri, who arrived in Pakistan in 1985. Trained as a doctor and a religious scholar, he was an alumnus of the Muslim Brotherhood who had been imprisoned after the killing of Anwar Sadat in 1981. Though professing eagerness to help the Afghans in their jihad against the Soviets, he spent much of his time in Pakistan on Egyptian affairs. He soon became the leader of a new group of Egyptian radicals that dubbed itself the Egyptian Islamic Jihad. Azzam was soon complaining to his associates that the Egyptians were gaining influence over his protégé Bin Laden, who was already becoming a lodestar of the jihadi movement.[5] There is much speculation, indeed, that Zawahiri and his confederates orchestrated the killing of Azzam as part of a plot to take over control of his organization.

But the nascent al-Qaeda and Egyptian Islamic Jihad were not the only ones bent on extending the Afghan war to the rest of the world. Another group of Egyptian radicals, mercilessly persecuted by the government at home, set up operations in Peshawar and in the eastern Afghan city of Jalalabad in the mid-1980s. This was al-Gamaa al-Islamia, the Islamic Group, which had engineered the assassination of Sadat. One of the group's most prominent figures in its exile was Mohammed Shawki Islambouli, the brother of Sadat's killer. Its religious leader was Sheikh Omar Abdel-Rahman, known as the "blind sheikh," who had also studied under Azzam and ultimately played a key role in the MAK after Azzam's death. He established close relations with Bin Laden and Hekmatyar. In 1990 Abdel-Rahmen traveled to the United States, where his preaching inspired a group of young Muslim radicals to bomb the World Trade Center in 1993.[6] Later in the 1990s, al-Gamaa al-Islamia launched a series of assassinations and terrorist attacks across Egypt that culminated in the Luxor attack of 1997, in which the group's operatives massacred 62 people (mostly foreign tourists).

After Azzam's death, Bin Laden and Zawahiri—the latter often characterized, with some justification, as the "brains" of al-Qaeda—presided over a remarkable expansion of global jihadist aspirations. Afghanistan-trained holy warriors dispersed to the four winds. They fought in Bosnia and Chechnya and lent support to the Islamist regime in the Sudan (where members of the Islamist camp had first joined the cabinet back in 1979). Muslim Filipinos returned home from the training camps in Afghanistan to found a revolutionary jihadi organization of their own, which they called Abu Sayyaf.

In Indonesia a veteran of the Afghan jihad named Jaffar Umar Thalib founded Laskar Jihad, a terror group that aimed to form an Islamic state in a far-flung corner of that sprawling country.[7] Another Indonesian by the name of Riduan Isamuddin arrived in Afghanistan in 1988, where he also sought close ties to Bin Laden. Under the nom de guerre of Hambali, he later gained notoriety for his work as the operations chief of the Jemaah Islamiah, Indonesia's most prominent militant Islamist organization. Aspiring to create a caliphate unifying the Muslim populations of Southeast Asia, he orchestrated a series of terrorist attacks that included the notorious Bali nightclub bombing of 2002, which took the lives of 202 people. Veterans of the conflict in Afghanistan also played an incendiary role in the brutal Algerian civil war that scourged that country in the 1990s, after the secular government annulled the results of an election won by Islamists. As many as 200,000 Algerians died in the fighting, which dragged on for years.

In Central Asia, still other alumni of the "University of Jihad" joined forces with the Islamists in the former Central Asian republic of Tajikistan, fighting on their side against ex-Communist secularists in another bloody civil war that tore that country apart in the 1990s. One of the men who participated on the Islamist side in that conflict went by the nom du guerre of Juma Namangani. Born in the Soviet Central Asian republic of Uzbekistan, he had fought in an elite paratrooper unit on Moscow's side during the war in Afghanistan. The experience had radicalized him, transforming him into a zealous holy warrior. He was among the founders of the Islamic Movement of Uzbekistan, arguably the first transnational Islamist guerrilla group to emerge from the former USSR. His soldiers fought on al-Qaeda's side in post-9/11 Afghanistan. In this way, too, Moscow's 1979 intervention in Afghanistan unleashed surprising demons.

The mujahideen victory in 1989, when the last of the Kremlin's troops finally vacated Afghanistan, did not actually end the war. The departure of the occupiers was followed by a surprisingly long struggle against Moscow's last client leader in Kabul, the wily Mohammed Najibullah. Through a combination of shrewd maneuvering and cynical pandering to religious sentiment, he managed to keep his government alive longer than just about anyone had predicted—all the way up to 1992, thus outlasting even the USSR itself. He achieved this partly by playing on the divisions among the various Peshawar-based resistance groups, a rancorous bunch even at the best of times. But not even Najibullah could keep this up indefinitely.

It soon proved that the mujahideen were far more effective at fighting a guerrilla war against a vastly superior enemy than they were at governing their own country. Their failure had much to do with the immense destruction visited on the country by the Communist governments in Kabul and the Soviet invaders. But it was also a result of the determined attack on traditional society and its elites orchestrated by the Islamists, who undermined existing institutions wherever they had the opportunity. US historian Barnett Rubin writes that, for the first time in Afghan history, political parties succeeded in penetrating into even the most remote corners of society.[8] Despite the allegedly universalist creeds they professed, these parties all too often turned out to be vehicles for the personal ambitions of their leaders, so they had little of value to offer when it came to filling the power vacuum they had helped to create.

No sooner had the holy warriors entered Kabul than their squabbling segued into open warfare. The old vendetta between Ahmed Shah Massoud and Gulbuddin Hekmatyar, the two pioneers of the Islamist insurgency of 1979, occupied a central role in this drama. Massoud had spent the war years fending off Soviet attacks and patiently building up his alternate government in the Panjshir Valley. Hekmatyar, who did not receive as much as he had hoped for from the power-sharing arrangement agreed upon by the seven mujahideen parties, had spent years hoarding his weaponry. Now he unleashed it on his rivals within the resistance. During the years of Soviet occupation and the Najibullah regime, Afghanistan had retained at least had some semblance of centralized government. But now that broke down completely, condemning the country to a vicious internecine conflict that continued, at various levels of intensity, right up to the US intervention in the fall of 2001.

From this environment emerged the fundamentalist group that promoted its own brand of post-1979 Afghan Islamism: the Taliban. Actively supported by the Pakistani military and intelligence services (just like Hekmatyar and Massoud in the 1970s), the Taliban exploited the squabbling among the various established jihadi groups to startling effect. Within a relatively short time, the Taliban had established itself as the dominant power in the land, imposing its own sere brand of "Islamic justice" on a citizenry exhausted by years of war. His followers declared Taliban leader Mullah Omar to be the "Amir al-Momineen," the commander of the faithful. He was also hailed as such by Osama bin Laden, who had returned from a sojourn in Islamist-controlled Sudan to seek a safe haven for al-Qaeda. It was, of course, from Taliban-controlled Afghanistan that Bin Laden launched the terror operation that led to the horrors of 9/11 and the consequences that derived from it. Gulbuddin Hekmatyar, who at first opposed the Taliban, returned to Afghanistan from Iranian exile after 9/11 and allied himself with Bin Laden. But it was, more than anyone, Ahmed Shah Massoud, the leader of the Panjshir Valley insurgency, who showed what could be achieved by a charismatic Sunni warlord who was capable of combining the thinking of revolutionary Islam and the art of insurgency. Of all the jihadis, it was above all Massoud who achieved the greatest successes on the battlefield—despite the relatively modest logistical support that he received from the Pakistanis and their paymasters in the West. It was Massoud who perfected the use of sophisticated intelligence work, raids at enemy weak points, and exploitation of the possibilities of modern media as tools in the religious war against a superpower. Throughout the struggle, his movement remained relatively moderate in its aims and never succumbed to the vision of the West as inherently inimical to the Prophet's cause. The new generation of Islamic radicals, above all Osama bin Laden and the Taliban, could not tolerate such a rival. Yet they never quite succeeded in subduing him by military means. And so it was that Bin Laden resolved to have Massoud assassinated, an effort that finally bore fruit two days before the attacks of September 11. The apprentice had supplanted his master, and the twenty-first century is still living with the consequences.

23

"The Lady's Not for Turning"

In October 1980 members of the British Conservative Party gathered in the seaside town of Brighton for the annual Conservative Party conference. Margaret Thatcher's government had completed its first seventeen months in office, and the results so far were catastrophic. In the first year of her term, the inflation rate had doubled. Unemployment had soared to 2 million, a level last seen during the Great Depression.[1] Manufacturing output ultimately dropped by 16 percent over the course of the year 1980.[2] The moderates who still dominated her cabinet—the "wets"—had become increasingly overt in their denunciation of what they described as the "dogmas" of monetarist theory. There was, in short, little evidence of the economic revival that the prime minister had promised. The conference delegates were spooked.

The reasons for this seemed clear enough to everyone. Thatcher's chancellor of the Exchequer, Geoffrey Howe, had pursued a harsh new counterinflationary course that depended on restricting the money supply, keeping interest rates high, and cutting public expenditures. The Keynesian ideas that had governed economic thinking in Britain throughout the postwar period had operated under the assumption that the most desirable policy goal was full employment. You could achieve it, Keynes had suggested, through judicious "demand management," various measures to stimulate consumption through fiscal and monetary policy. Thatcher and Howe threw this notion out the window. They were prepared to tolerate a certain degree of pain as the price of wringing inflation out of the economy. But not even they had quite planned for this.

Resistance from the miners' unions had pressured Ted Heath into the so-called "U-turn" of 1972, when he backed away from the free-market principles enshrined in the party's 1970 election manifesto. It was that reversal that later spurred Keith Joseph into his quixotic campaign for a market-oriented conservatism two years later. For Thatcher, who was serving in Heath's cabinet at the time, the U-turn was nothing less than an act of moral weakness, a shameful capitulation. Heath had caved, betraying the collective interests of the nation to the vocal demands of a radical minority. Now she wanted to show that she was made of sterner stuff, and she chose Brighton to do it.

The trade unions were there, too, and their activists were demonstrating loudly outside the hall. But Thatcher—a politician who always seemed to draw energy from the protestations of her opponents—was unperturbed. "No policy which puts at risk the defeat of inflation—however great its short-term attraction—can be right," she told the delegates.[3] She knew that many members of her own party were not entirely convinced. But she was happy to disabuse the weak-kneed: "You turn if you want to. The lady's not for turning." The reference behind the line was somewhat obscure: her speechwriter, Ronnie Millar, was playing off the title of a 1940s play.[4]

But you didn't have to spot the allusion to get the message. She was showing that she was determined to proceed with the course she had set no matter what the potential political cost—a hugely significant psychological watershed. It was aimed not only at the British public as a whole, but also at those within her own party who still clung to the hope that the old postwar consensus could be maintained. This was the moment, British journalist Simon Jenkins observed, when Thatcher forged her political brand as the woman who knew what medicine the nation needed and wasn't afraid to administer it whatever the pain. She had many more battles to fight in the years ahead, but the 1980 conference marked the point when she conclusively shook off the legacy of Heath and emerged as the prime minister who would dominate British political life for decades to come.[5] From now on, Britons would either love her or hate her, but there was no mistaking what she stood for.

She used the next few months to drive home the point. In January 1981, she began to purge her cabinet of the dissenters. The minister of state for the arts, Norman St. John Stevas, who had ascribed to himself the role of unofficial court jester—breezily referring to the prime minister as the "leaderene," for example—was summarily fired. (Thatcher said that he had "turned indiscretion into a political principle.")[6] Perhaps most important, economist Alan Walters, who played a critical role in the economic debates that were yet to come, received an appointment as her personal economic adviser.

Another emblematic moment came in 1981, when Thatcher and Howe presented a budget that reaffirmed their dogged commitment to the fight against inflation. (Howe, not a man given to hyperbole, called it "the most unpopular budget in history.")[7] Brutally deflationary, it stipulated even more cuts in public spending despite the continuing high level of joblessness. It was the most radical expression of Howe's harsh monetarist medicine yet. A few weeks before the budget debuted, 364 of Britain's leading academic economists published a letter in the *Times*, that venerable establishment mouthpiece, denouncing the government's course and proclaiming that "there is no basis in economic theory or supporting evidence" for its policies. The budget was followed, in the summer of 1981, by riots that broke out in inner cities across Great Britain. Elusive growth and mounting unemployment—as high as 60 percent in some communities—seemed to leave little room for radical experiments. Later in the year, Thatcher launched her first full-fledged cabinet reshuffle. Several of the wets were shifted or moved out of the cabinet altogether, with the effect of increasing Thatcher's dominance over economic policy.

With her evangelical zeal, Thatcher had already succeeded in shifting fundamental public assumptions about the state and its relationship to the economy. Yet it is noteworthy that, by 1981, some of her most enthusiastic defenders among the ranks of the economic liberals, like CPS stalwart Alfred Sherman, were falling away. They accused her of failing to tackle the truly daunting challenges, including the state's ownership and control of the "commanding heights" of the economy or the continuing power of the unions. But the accusation missed the point. Thatcher was, and remained, a politician. She had an extremely astute sense of the possible, and she was not yet prepared to race ahead of public opinion on every front.

Fittingly enough, it was politics that saved her. On April 2, 1982, Argentine forces invaded and occupied the Falkland Islands, a tiny British colonial possession in the South Atlantic whose population numbered in the hundreds. Thatcher capitalized on the opportunity. Refusing to negotiate with the military junta in Buenos Aires unless it withdrew its forces, and resisting considerable diplomatic pressure (even from her treasured American allies), she dispatched a naval task force that defeated the Argentines after a short but vicious war and restored British control over the islands. After long years of decline, the victory gave a much-needed jolt to national self-confidence. The first signs of economic growth were also beginning to make themselves felt. Thatcher's determination was rewarded by the electorate. In the general election of 1983—greatly helped by a hopelessly divided and ineffective opposition—she achieved a decisive victory (a 144-seat majority in the House of Commons) that allowed her to move ahead with her most ambitious projects.

It is her second term that is often described as the period of "heroic Thatcherism." Perhaps its most significant legacy was her battle with the powerful and militant National Union of Mineworkers, which went on strike in 1984 to protest the closure of unprofitable mines and determined to insist on its prerogatives as a major participant in economic decision making. An equally determined Thatcher had spent years preparing for the showdown—her government stockpiled coal at key sites and equipped the police for the riots that were sure to come. The strike ended in 1985 with a humiliating defeat for the union that transformed industrial relations in Britain.

Thatcher's efforts to sell off state-owned assets also finally came to fruition in the mid-1980s. The privatization of British Gas and British Telecom brought billions in revenue into state coffers and tipped the balance away from government control of the "commanding heights."

For all her radicalism, it is important to keep in mind some of the things that Margaret Thatcher did not do. She did not return her country to a Victorian version of laissez-faire economic policy and social Darwinist ethics, nor did she move Britain back to the 1920s and 1930s. She neither dismembered the welfare state nor gutted the modern machinery of regulation. So Milton Friedman's admiring remark that she was just another "nineteenth-century liberal" is not entirely on the mark. Nor, indeed, was she the first, or the most famous, to make the arguments or institute the policies. During her first prime ministerial campaign, she was known to cite the Australians, the New Zealanders, and the Scandinavians who had already started comparable reforms in their own countries. And Ronald Reagan, of course, later lent the considerable authority of his office to similar arguments about the moral and practical superiority of free markets.

Nonetheless, it is hard to overplay the significance of her achievements. Thatcher was certainly not an intellectual in the conventional sense of the word, but she was an extremely intelligent woman with an intense appreciation of the power of ideas. The comparison with Ronald Reagan is illuminating. Reagan was not a man who participated in think-tank discussions or engaged in polemics about texts. Thatcher once brandished her heavily annotated copy of Keynes's *White Paper* in a Commons debate; Reagan would have never gone to the trouble. What distinguished Thatcher from her opponents—some of whom could claim far more literary or philosophical credentials than she—was her often ruthless determination to follow through on the beliefs that she held. Her most insightful biographer, John Campbell, marvels at her capacity for "aggression." It was the force of her drive to realize her radically conservative ideas that made her unique.

So it is wrong to regard her first months in power merely as the modest prelude of more important events yet to come. The year 1979 itself was a radical point of departure. Her election victory itself represented the first major blow against the British postwar consensus, and this was a rupture that she largely achieved in her first year in office, even if this is sometimes overshadowed by the magnitude of what was to follow.[8]

To be sure, some of the ideas that figured in her first year were not entirely unfamiliar to British political discourse. Denis Healey, Callaghan's chancellor of the Exchequer, had already launched modestly monetarist policies before 1979. Even earlier, Ted Heath had won the 1970 election with a manifesto that gave a strong foretaste of Thatcher's program, even if he ultimately failed to follow through. At the time of Heath's win, there was also a palpable sense that British public opinion was not quite ready to accept the dramatic change of course embodied by the free-market prescriptions authored by Heath's supporters. Heath's election victory in 1970 had been completely unexpected, so it was hard to see it as a watershed that represented a new mandate for change. In 1979, by contrast, it was not just a Labour government but the very notion of socialism that had been decisively rejected by the electorate.[9]

Thatcher herself saw the assault on the assumptions behind the postwar consensus as the core of her undertaking. In a memo she drafted for her speech to the Conservative Party conference in October 1979, six months after assuming power, she wrote, "We are now tackling a range of problems which have been neglected for years. We are starting to ask the awkward questions people prefer to ignore. We are re-shaping attitudes. This is every bit as important as the laws we pass."[10] The psychological impact of her efforts continues to be felt. Indeed, she successfully dispatched many of the political and economic assumptions considered self-evident by the British political class in the 1960s and 1970s. As Thatcherite economist Tim Congdon notes, the whole notion of "incomes policy" as a means of controlling inflation—once part and parcel of everyday political discourse in Britain—has gone the way of the dinosaurs.[11] Jim Prior conceded, in his otherwise combative memoir, that this was true. When Thatcher boasted to him early in her administration that the Conservative government had "killed off the myth that wages could be controlled by anything other than the market," he reacted at first with astonishment. "However, I think that as things have turned out, she was right and I was wrong."[12]

To focus on this particular point might seem a bit abstruse at first sight. But the destruction of incomes policy was a crucial element of Thatcher's broader assault on Keynesian assumptions of demand management and full employment. It was the election of 1979 that marked the end of that era. The policies she aimed to implement had been foreshadowed by politicians before her, but their failure to address the deep structural flaws created by fifty years of collectivist economic philosophies ensured that Thatcher's success could be achieved only at what Thatcher sympathizer Richard Cockett conceded was "an almost impossibly high cost."[13]

As the 1980s continued, growth and productivity rebounded dramatically. Inflation drained away. A new culture of entrepreneurship took hold. Before Thatcher, many businesspeople aspired to escape Britain's crushing regulations and its draconian tax rates. Thanks to Thatcher's efforts, particularly the extensive program of deregulation that came to be known as the "Big Bang," London established anew its status as one of the world's financial capitals. The abolition of exchange controls that had so exercised Thatcher and Howe during their first year in office paved the way for a surge of foreign investment into the UK.

The international comparison is particularly illuminating. In 1979 UK per capita output had fallen to around 86–90 percent of that in France or Germany. By 2007 Britain's level was 1 to 6 percent higher than theirs.[14] The United Kingdom can no longer be considered the "sick man of Europe." And with the rejuvenation of the British economy came a dramatic reordering of the political landscape as well.

Thatcher was lucky in her adversaries. Perhaps the toughest of her electoral opponents was the one she defeated first, James Callaghan. A shrewd veteran of the British political game, Callaghan might well have managed to prolong his term in office had it not been for the Winter of Discontent, which demolished his self-proclaimed standing as the man who could coax the unions to behave reasonably. His departure unleashed forces within the Labour Party that tore it apart for the next decade and a half. The left wing, led by Thatcher's old Oxford classmate Tony Benn, revolted against Callaghan's moderate course and persistently undermined his successor, Michael Foot, who tried unsuccessfully to unify the party. In the 1983 general election, when Thatcher was riding high after her victory in the Falklands, Labour published a seven-hundred-page election manifesto that called for Britain's withdrawal from the European Economic Community, unilateral nuclear disarmament, and the renationalization of the industries privatized by the Conservative government. Thanks to its quixotically leftist policies, the manifesto was quickly (and prophetically) dubbed "the longest suicide note in history." The

Liberal-SDP Alliance, formed in part by moderate defectors from Labour, benefited from the party's self-immolation, but never quite managed to establish itself as a credible alternative to Thatcher's reign and ultimately fragmented the forces of opposition to her, thus cementing her rule.

Foot's successor, Neil Kinnock, was a more serious contender to national leadership, but he, too, was hampered by his party's resistance to change. Thatcher's resounding defeat of the miners rebounded on Labour itself, which had drawn much of its power from the trade union movement and had correspondingly identified itself with the miners' cause (even if Kinnock made a point of denouncing their violence and often undemocratic tactics). The comparative weakness of the unions after the failure of the miners' strike and the defection of many workers to the Conservative camp made Labour's hard times even harder. The Thatcher era altered the very nature of the British economy, shifting productive forces away from manufacturing and toward services. This also dictated a painful evolution in Labour's role and ideology. It was John Smith, the man who followed Kinnock as leader, who in 1993 finally persuaded their party to do away with the block vote (the union voting quota) at Labour Party conferences, and thus effectively ended Labour's self-image as a party defined above all by its allegiance to the working class.[15]

In the end, it turned out that the one person most dangerous to Thatcher was Thatcher herself. Her domineering style offended many within her own party over the years, and her urge to govern past her own cabinet ultimately deprived her of colleagues willing to call her out on some of her more ill-advised policies. In this way, her self-assured approach to government gradually became one of her greatest liabilities.

She succeeded in imposing her will on her cabinet colleagues and other Tory grandees as long as she could claim the loyalty of British voters. But it was within just a few years of her reelection in 1987 that her government's approval rating began to slip. Perhaps the most consequential factor in this decline was her plan to push through a drastic reform of local government taxation. The UK had traditionally financed local government through property taxes, known as the "rates." Thatcher resolved to replace them with an individual tax she called the "community charge" (dubbed by its critics the "poll tax"). Many Britons viewed the plan as an ill-concealed attempt to shift the burden of taxation from property owners onto the less advantaged. The poll tax prompted intense and widespread opposition that resulted in serious domestic unrest, culminating in a major riot in central London in March 1990. Few in her entourage, cowed by her determination to proceed, were willing to offer open criticisms of the policy.

The prime minister also stumbled over the similarly contentious issue of Europe. Her chancellor of the Exchequer, Nigel Lawson, and her foreign minister, the ex-chancellor Geoffrey Howe, believed that the UK could shape EU policy to its own advantage only by participating actively in the process of European integration; standing entirely outside of that process was impossible, they insisted, given the UK's reliance on trade with the European market. But Thatcher's intense national pride made her skeptical about allowing Britain to merge too deeply with the European Community—a stance compounded by her instinctive distrust of Europeans' presumed socialist proclivities. Lawson and Howe did manage to press Thatcher to allow the pound sterling to join the European Exchange Rate Mechanism, a system of managed exchange rates for all the EC's currencies that might ultimately serve as a prelude to a common currency. But when Thatcher persisted in publicly denigrating the notion of financial coordination with Europe, and thus undermining the very policy she had pledged to undertake, the rift between her and the two men deepened. Lawson ultimately felt compelled to resign over the issue in July 1989, while Howe accepted a transfer to a new job as deputy prime minister, a move that amounted to a humiliating demotion.

For Howe, the final straw came a year later, when Thatcher's increasing animosity toward the European question prompted her to issue a momentous rebuke. Responding to a statement by European Commission president Jacques Delors about the need for a European single market and deeper political integration, she told the House of Commons that she had a simple answer: "No, no, no." On November 1, 1990, Howe then surprised everyone by announcing his resignation, citing his differences with Thatcher on Europe. He was, as it happened, the last member of the original 1979 cabinet to leave the government. It was, fittingly enough, the departure of this diehard loyalist, a man who had so long suffered from the prime minister's overbearing manner, that precipitated her downfall.

At first Thatcher's entourage tried to paper over the break by assuring the press that Howe merely disagreed with the style of the prime minister's policies on Europe, not their substance. Howe responded by standing up in the House of Commons and coolly elucidating his reasons for his rupture with the prime minister—a devastating challenge to her authority that brought into the open all the simmering resentments within the party. Thatcher's diminished popularity due to the poll tax was compounded by rising inflation and the onset of a new recession; all this, combined with Howe's open questioning of her leadership abilities, suddenly rendered her politically vulnerable. Michael Heseltine, a cabinet heavyweight who had long been known to covet Thatcher's job, seized the opportunity to challenge her leadership of the Conservative Party. She won the first round of the internal party vote, but by such a slim margin that she was ultimately forced to concede that she had lost the confidence of her own Tory colleagues. The Iron Lady was compelled to resign—victim of an extraordinary parliamentary drama that few would have considered possible even just a month before.[16]

Her political legacy remained enormously consequential nonetheless. Her successor, John Major, backed down on the poll tax and promised a "compassionate conservatism" that would rub off some of the harder edges of Thatcher's policies. Yet the basic vector of his governing philosophy remained true to hers. He continued with the privatization of state-owned companies like British Rail and pursued efforts to make government more responsive to market forces. This was an acknowledgment of the reality that her efforts had kicked off a long period of economic growth and a climate that promoted the growth of new businesses. It was this legacy that prompted Labour strategist Peter Mandelson to utter a famous provocation: "We are all Thatcherites now."[17]

The figure who best exemplifies Margaret Thatcher's transformation of British politics is Tony Blair. Born to a generation that came of political age under Thatcher's premiership, Blair operated under assumptions dramatically different from those of his Labour forbears—and, indeed, from those held by Keynesian Tories like Harold Macmillan, who had assailed the privatizers of the 1990s for "selling off the family silver." The shift in the Labour mind-set amounted to an acknowledgment that the party could no longer expect to win votes by proposing the old Keynesian policies of public spending and nationalization to "the broad mass of the newly affluent electorate," as Richard Cockett writes. Thatcher had irrevocably shifted the center of gravity on economic policy. Cockett compares Labour's transformation to the process the Conservatives had been forced to endure in the period from 1945 to 1951, when they had jettisoned their old free-market policies in order to appeal to voters who hewed to the attractive new vision of a comprehensive welfare state. In the period from 1987 to 1992, the Labour Party was similarly forced to discard of many of its old collectivist dogmas to accommodate voters who were now living in the world that Thatcher had built.[18]

To be sure, the Thatcher era had its shadow side. The number of those living in poverty increased from 5 million in 1979 to 14.1 million in 1992. The gap between rich and poor widened: in 1979 the top 10 percent of the population measured by incomes held 20.1 percent of the wealth; by 1992 the figure had risen to 26.1 percent. Over the same period, the amount of national wealth held by the poorest 10 percent fell from 4.3 percent to 2.9 percent. The real incomes of the bottom

10 percent dropped by 18 percent over the same period, while those of the top 10 percent increased by 61 percent.[19] Unemployment, which peaked at 3.3 million in 1984, left lasting scars. It should come as little surprise that the 1980s were haunted by periodic episodes of social unrest: the 1981 riots, the miners' strike, the anti–poll tax disturbances of 1989–1990.

Thatcher's supporters respond that the strong medicine she administered was painful but urgently needed. Since the economic recovery of the late Thatcher years, they say, the country has registered strong and persistent growth. "Thatcherism can best be summed up in the statistics showing that, in the 1980s, manufacturing productivity rose faster in Britain than in any other industrial country," writes Tim Congdon.[20] Employment began to rise again during her third term in office, and by the end of the century, British joblessness was lower than in most European countries. One might also observe that revolutions (even conservative ones like Thatcher's) are invariably divisive.

It is also worth noting that some of the intellectual architects of the Thatcher counterrevolution believed that she did not go far enough. There were some at the promarket think tanks, the Institute for Economic Affairs and the Center for Policy Studies, who continued to insist that Thatcher had dodged some of the greatest challenges of the 1980s. They believed, in particular, that Thatcher signally failed when she refused to take on the daunting task of reforming the public-sector bureaucracies, the places where the real power of the state resided. Without doing this, they contended, the economic liberals "could never achieve that fundamental shift in power from the State to the individual that had been at the core of the economic liberal agenda since the 1940s," Cockett notes. To them, accordingly, the Thatcher Revolution was only a partial success.[21]

Journalist Simon Jenkins echoes this critique. Government spending as a share of the gross domestic product actually increased during her administration—evidence, he says, that her antistatist ethos was more rhetoric than reality. This was particularly true at the local level. Contrary to her decentralizing instincts, she ended up increasing London's power over many organs of provincial and municipal government—precisely, he argues, because local governments were so often dominated by socialist sympathizers who opposed her policies.

There is undoubtedly a measure of truth to this. Yet it is important to recall that Thatcher was not a libertarian. Those of her supporters who wanted to see her privatize the National Health Service, for example, were probably deluded (though she did try to make it more responsive to market incentives). Thatcher's primary aim was not to destroy the welfare state. It was to restore the primacy of the "vigorous virtues" in British life, to destroy the culture of dependency fostered by socialism, and to open up greater space for individual self-reliance and private initiative. In this, Thatcher's defenders say, she resoundingly succeeded. She did it, above all, by transforming the terms of reference of British politics—with consequences that continue to be felt in the country to this day. Whatever one's political views, no one can dispute that Margaret Thatcher left Britain a fundamentally different place from the one she encountered upon her assumption of office in 1979.

I n September 1989, Poland's economy faced a desperate situation. The country was wallowing in debt, both domestic and foreign. Its industrial capacity was 90 percent state owned. These publicly owned enterprises never fired anyone, but neither did they produce goods that anyone wanted to buy. Bankruptcy was unheard of. The Polish currency, the zloty, suffered from hyperinflation at rates of more than 600 percent.[22] The finance minister of the country's newly installed democratic government, Leszek Balcerowicz, set out to turn things around. He formed a commission staffed by some of Poland's leading economists as well as the American Jeffrey Sachs.

On October 6, Balcerowicz unveiled his new program. It gave private businesses the ability to participate in Poland's foreign trade, which until then had been entirely monopolized by the government, and made the zloty convertible (though only inside the country). Private foreign investors were invited to come into the country and put their money into new businesses. A new law on banking prohibited the central bank from financing the budget deficit; another allowed state-owned companies to go bankrupt. A special tax was imposed on wage hikes. The Balcerowicz Plan also cut state subsidies on energy. Perhaps most important of all, it freed prices for many consumer goods.

It was an approach that came to be known as "shock therapy." As the name implies, the treatment involved was not entirely gentle. Prices jumped, and unemployment soared to 20 percent. Yet it did not take long for signs of a new economic life to appear. Inflation, an abiding feature of Polish economic life, disappeared. The zloty went from being a symbol of dysfunction to a stable currency that has helped to fuel a persistent economic boom. Polish entrepreneurs have founded hundreds of thousands of companies that have produced millions of jobs. The Polish economy is today one of the most dynamic in the European Union.

The experts can fight over whether these measures were doctrinally "Thatcherite." What is beyond dispute, however, is that Thatcher's political example loomed large in the minds of the economist-politicians who engineered the plan and saw it through. Unlike the British prime minister he described as his "hero," Balcerowicz managed to stay in office only two years. But he remains a strong advocate of her economic philosophy.

Thatcherism had a remarkable and largely unappreciated impact on economic thinking around the world, and as such it has been a major factor in the global market revolution that has transformed the world in the years since she ruled Britain. Entirely in keeping with her self-image as a political crusader, her influence has been far less theoretical than practical.

The reasons for this are simple. In the 1980s and 1990s, many countries around the world found themselves in positions comparable to that of the United Kingdom in the late 1970s. Under the well-meaning influence of "development economics" in the 1950s and 1960s, developing countries had assumed that state-led modernization, public ownership of industry, and aggressive government intervention were the only ways to kick-start growth. The results, in far too many cases, were inefficiency, corruption, and chronic inflation.

The main intellectual alternative to the reigning consensus in global economics emerged from the so-called Chicago School, a term that was first applied in the 1950s to a group of free-market economists who came together at the University of Chicago. Their most famous theoretician was Milton Friedman, a founding member of the Mont Pèlerin society and a gifted polemicist for the cause of economic liberalism. The Chicago School did not content itself with merely generating ideas. It also turned out an enormously influential crop of international economists who later played direct roles in the process of economic reform in their home countries.[23] Friedman and his colleagues did much to prepare the way for Thatcher's economic counterrevolution by promoting the new thinking during the 1970s. Friedman's Nobel Prize in 1976 (coming two years after the one received by Friedrich von Hayek, who also taught for a time at Chicago) signaled the shift in thinking that was already under way.

Thatcher's impact, however, was different. She was not an academic but a practical politician, the leader of one of the world's most important economies. It was also important that she was precisely not an American. For all of their periodic obsessions with New Deal corporatism and Keynesian fine-tuning, the Americans had always remained committed to a fundamentally liberal economic philosophy— even if the US-trained development economists often did not seem to regard it as suitable for foreign conditions. In 1979, however, Thatcher and her team had confronted a set of real-world conditions that seemed painfully familiar to many reformers around the world in the 1990s: high inflation, a bloated state sector, waning productivity, and a collectivist mind-set that assumed the need for a government intervention on myriad levels and crowded out entrepreneurship and wealth creation.

All of this helps to explain why Thatcherism proved to be such a spur to the worldwide forces of neoliberal orthodoxy, the market revolution that helped to spur globalization. The newly liberated countries of Eastern Europe looked to Thatcher, not Reagan, as their economic lodestar. And that was only logical, since their problems—a lopsided public sector, a crushing bureaucratic apparatus, a deeply entrenched collectivist ethos, and a long-suppressed spirit of entrepreneurship—were so similar to the conditions faced by Thatcher and her team in the 1980s. The same applied to economies that "emerged" elsewhere, including upstarts like Brazil or Turkey that, unlike the East Asian nations, rejected the authoritarian assumptions of postwar "development economics" and adopted economic reforms more compatible with progress toward democratic rule.

Thatcherism had no greater consequence than in India, where the early-1990s reformer Manmohan Singh and his followers referred to her legacy, directly and indirectly, as they cut away a choking bureaucracy to release the wealth-creating potential of the world's largest democracy. What an irony it would be if, one day, we recall Thatcher less for her role as the reformer of a sclerotic Britain than as the inspiration for India's transformation into one of the world's economic giants.

Americans tend to believe that the values of their economic system require no elucidation, so they have never really seen the need to disseminate coherent arguments for free-market ideology. Thatcher's supporters, emerging from a political environment where collectivist ideas dominated for so long, did. In the 1980s, operating like good evangelical missionaries of the nineteenth century, they took their model of the free-market think tanks and internationalized it. Anthony Fisher, the founder of the Institute for Economic Affairs,[24] was invited in 1975 to run the Fraser Institute in Vancouver, Canada. The experiment was a success, and in 1977 he set up another one, called the International Center for Economic Policy Studies. The Center for Independent Studies followed in Australia at the end of the decade.

Building on these first cautious efforts, Fisher in 1981 then established the Atlas Economic Research Foundation, which served as the core of an international network of other free-market research centers modeled on the IEA. Within the course of the next decade, Atlas took credit for founding seventy-eight institutes around the world (thirty-nine of them in Latin America) and close ties with another eighty-eight. By the time the Berlin Wall fell in 1989, these institutes had spawned a global community of economic thinkers schooled in Hayekian principles, many of whom soon fanned out into the countries of the former Soviet bloc to argue the virtues of capitalism.[25]

"What happened under Ms. Thatcher was an eye-opener, a revelation," said Palaniappan Chidambaram, who served as India's finance minister for a while during the 1990s. "After all, we had gotten our Fabian socialism from Britain."[26] Bolivian president Gonzalo Sanchez de Lozada cited Thatcher—along with the rise of the East Asian tigers and the reforms of Deng Xiaoping—as the precedent for the program of market-oriented reform that began in 1985.[27] In Brazil in the 1990s, President Fernando Henrique Cardoso embarked on a privatization program that, measured by the value of the assets sold, amounted to twice the size of what Britain had done under Thatcher.[28] Even continental Europe found it impossible to resist the positive impact of Thatcher's privatization program. From 1985 to 2000, European governments sold off some $100 billion worth of state assets, including national champions such as Lufthansa, Volkswagen, Renault, Elf, and the Italian oil company ENI.[29]

But Thatcherism, even in its economic guise, was never just a theory about economics. Thatcher, as a clearly identifiable global brand, became the face of the market counterrevolution that swept the world. By the early 1990s, "Thatcherism" had already become identified, in places ranging from Latin America to Eastern Europe, with a particular set of policy choices.[30] The Soviet military newspaper *Krasnaya Zvezda* had nicknamed her the "Iron Lady" even before she became prime minister, and it was a label that she was happy to appropriate to herself. And it as the "Iron Lady" that she is mentioned in the movie *Platform*, Chinese director Jia Zhang Ke's marvelous paean to the early reform period in China. Thatcher's mission excited intense emotions among both opponents and fans. Her polarizing effect was precisely what made her such an extraordinary agent of change. Even today, decades after her term in office, her name still has a unique capacity to provoke dispute, debate, or outright rejection. There are very few politicians who can claim the same.

24

Socialism with Chinese Characteristics

The economic liberalization that began in China in 1979 had an almost immediate impact. Political economists often cite the success of China's market-oriented transformation as evidence of the advantages of gradual economic reform. Actually, though, the early changes unleashed the productive potential of ordinary people with astonishing speed. This was especially true in the countryside, where the overwhelming majority of the Chinese lived. By October 1981, 45 percent of the agricultural production teams in China had gone over to the household-responsibility system. By the end of 1983, 98 percent of all the teams in the country (equaling 94 percent of the farming households) had adopted the new approach.[1] Hundreds of millions of people were directly affected. If anything qualifies as economic "shock therapy," surely this was it. But it was a form of therapy that was warmly welcomed by its intended patients.

To be sure, these farmers did not actually own the land they were working. But they could do much of their work as if they did. No longer did peasants have to obey the strictures imposed upon them by distant bureaucrats. Production of grain soared by stunning margins in the space of just a few years. This reflected, perhaps, the priorities established by China's central planners, who for years had emphasized grain to the virtual exclusion of all other crops. But there were other dramatic manifestations of the new policy. Now farmers could grow whatever made sense under their own economic and climatic conditions. Suddenly, a whole range of other foodstuffs, long neglected, became available in the private markets that proliferated across China. Farmers in Guangdong now grew sugarcane in addition to rice. Northerners cultivated not only wheat but also cabbage and eggplant, mushrooms and beets. "Sideline occupations" like fish farming increased the range of available products and boosted farmers' revenues. Favored meats like pork or goose, once an unthinkable luxury for most Chinese, became widely available. Within the course of a single decade, China transformed itself from a country where millions of its citizens lived on the verge of starvation to one where its citizens could easily feed themselves and still have plenty of food left over for export.

Du Runsheng—a leading reformer who first proposed returning to the household-responsibility system back in 1978, when it still seemed nearly unthinkable—watched with satisfaction as peasants took advantage of the new freedoms offered by the reforms in the countryside. In 1982 he toured a farming region in Fujian Province.[2] He visited a private poultry business that was producing 1.2 million chickens per year. The founding capital of the company was the modest sum of 28,000 yuan, contributed by the fourteen original shareholders. Nearby was a state farm that had built its own chicken hatchery, using several hundred thousand yuan in state funds. It produced only 500,000 chickens per year.[3] This sort of productivity gap was characteristic, and it soon doomed the state's overall control of agriculture.

The unloved People's Communes, the rural cooperatives established by Mao in the Great Leap Forward, melted away like spring snow in the course of a few short years, following the pattern established in Sichuan Province in 1979. Farmers focused on cultivating the agricultural land that was split off from the old collective farms, while the new "townships"—the village administrations that emerged from the old communes—became something akin to business incubators, spinning off their old assets into new public-private companies. These were the Town and Village Enterprises (TVEs) that produced everything from bicycles to bathtubs, giving an enormous boost to prosperity in rural communities. This enormous engine of rural job creation lifted hundreds of millions of people out of poverty, and as such it may well qualify as the biggest employment scheme in human history. Foreigners sometimes cited the TVEs as a triumph of Communist Party statism, since their property formally belonged to the townships. But it is probably more accurate to say that the local officials who controlled the companies disposed of their assets just as if they owned them; in fact, therefore, the TVEs were private in all but name.[4] In any case, the dissolution of the communes paved the way for an astonishing flowering of grassroots commerce.

The Special Economic Zones took longer to have an impact. But this lay in the nature of their economic mission. The SEZs—modeled on the "Export Processing Zones" in other countries—were at first aimed entirely at production for foreign markets. (For a while in 1979–1980, they were officially referred to as "Special Export Zones.") As overseas investors piled in, the amount of goods manufactured in the zones steadily climbed. Local governments benefited in the form of taxes and administrative fees, while local people drew attractive wages—both of which stimulated further growth. Initially, though, relatively little of the SEZ production found its way into the domestic Chinese market.

Deng and other Chinese leaders had made a point of setting up the SEZs in relatively undeveloped areas, far from the People's Republic of China's existing industrial centers. This was entirely intentional: the aim was to buffer possible ideological contagion stemming from the influx of foreigners. The first zones accordingly started with very little in the way of infrastructure. Shenzhen had just five miles of paved road in 1979. Its entire public transportation network at the time consisted of a dozen buses and cars for a population of some three hundred thousand. As a result, it took some time before the capacity of the zone could be ramped up. Most of the population persisted in farming or fishing for years after the zone was established.[5] High fences were erected around all of the zones to ensure that dangerous ideas did not percolate through to adjacent counties.[6]

This gradually changed as the reform process continued. Deng—with his characteristic farsightedness—envisioned the SEZs not only as conduits for foreign investment but also as channels for the transmission of modern management techniques and new technologies. As the zones prospered and expanded, they increasingly fulfilled both roles. Hong Kong investors who set up hotels, for example, went to great pains to train their mainland staff to international standards of cleanliness and service. Local people who could afford it flocked to the restaurants, giving local entrepreneurs incentives to follow suit by embracing similar standards in their own businesses. A similar process of osmosis applied to manufacturing. Although foreign investors usually ran their own factories, they needed plenty of local staffers to keep the assembly lines running. Countless Chinese middle managers who learned their jobs on the shop floors in SEZs later went on to apply what they had learned to businesses of their own.

In the first years, the contribution made by the zones to China's foreign exchange earnings was relatively modest—even though this was one of the stated reasons for establishing them. Foreign-owned firms were allowed to operate in the zones only as of September 1983. The overwhelming majority of Chinese had little contact with them. The number of people who worked in the zones in the first five years was relatively insignificant, and most of the goods produced were designated for export, so ordinary Chinese had little inkling of what was going on there.[7]

Yet growth in Shenzhen, in particular, was fast. From 1981 to 1984, the local economy expanded by an astonishing 75 percent per year. Between 1981 and 1993, the Chinese economy grew at an annual rate of 9.6 percent; Shenzhen's growth during the same period was an extraordinary 40 percent.[8] Chinese began to use the terms *Shenzhen speed* and *Shenzhen efficiency* as benchmarks for development. Later in the decade, the government in Beijing began to speak of the Special Economic Zones as "laboratories" for economic reform, and that political signal spurred a new influx of foreign investment. Outside capital now began to flood in, much of it from Hong Kong.[9] The initial capital investments in infrastructure in the zones had come from the state, but now the authorities increasingly left that to the private sector.

The zones remained controversial for many years. It was perhaps to be expected that, when the conservative backlash against economic liberalization came, it was intimately connected with the zones. Reports of corruption—the inevitable side effect of a system that "quarantined" islands of capitalism from the rest of a still Communist country—gave the opponents of reform just the ammunition they needed. One of the most famous scandals involved Hainan Island, which received special status as an open trade zone early in the 1980s. A cabal of businessmen and local officials exploited ambiguities in the regulations to import large quantities of cars and consumer goods at artificially low prices, which they then resold on the mainland at an enormous profit. (The total amount of the goods involved was valued at $1.5 billion.)[10] Such cases fueled the calls for what was called "readjustment," policies to establish the priority of planning and rein in "uncontrolled" growth.

The foes of Deng's reforms soon even included some of his erstwhile allies. One of the most prominent opponents of economic reform was Chen Yun, the party heavyweight who had buoyed up the Deng camp at the 1978 conferences with his clarion calls for a reckoning with the Maoists. As liberalization accelerated on the economic front in the early 1980s, however, Chen's Communist instincts asserted themselves with full force, and he found himself bucking plans to give greater freedom to the private sector, which he associated with exploitation and inequality. Chen Yun—widely admired for his rectitude and apparent incorruptibility—belonged, along with Deng, to the elite group of party elders (sometimes referred to as the "Eight Immortals") who had suffered from Mao's persecutions in the 1960s and 1970s. These were men who were willing to tolerate a certain degree of economic experimentation but who also worried that wide-ranging reforms would undermine Communist Party rule itself. Opposition from such prominent quarters compelled reformers to tread carefully. When describing their aspirations, they preferred to avoid the phrase *market economy*. Their preferred euphemism was *commodity economy*.

It is easy to look askance at the enemies of reform from the vantage point of today, when the extraordinary power and prosperity that Deng's course has brought to China are manifest. But this outcome was not quite so clear to observers in the 1980s. The transfiguration of the economy brought unheralded opportunities, but it also produced dislocation, turmoil, and dizzying social change. While some sectors of the economy boomed, others collapsed, requiring huge injections of investment from the state in order to prevent mass layoffs; unemployment went up sharply in some parts of the country nonetheless. The rising prosperity of the industrial areas along the coasts attracted huge numbers of job-seeking immigrants from the interior, setting off what would ultimately become the largest peacetime migration in history. The rise of a new class of business owners and managers transformed the social hierarchy. The Communist Party was at first unsure whether to welcome them into its ranks or to hold them at arm's length.

In keeping with the demands of a new economy, the country's legal system had to be completely reengineered. Growing numbers of foreigners appeared on the streets, and knowledge of the outside world proliferated. Blue and gray Mao suits gave way to a diverse global wardrobe. Western fast food changed eating habits. Until the end of the 1970s, the average Chinese had dreamed of the Four Big Things: a sewing machine, a bicycle, a wristwatch, and a radio. In the 1980s, the list went upmarket. Now the aspirational possessions were a refrigerator, a TV set, a rice cooker, and a washing machine.

The career of Hu Yaobang offers a case study in the challenges that China faced when it came to reconciling its peculiar mix of economic liberalization and political immobility. Hu—the man who had brought up the sensitive issue of agricultural reform at the 1978 Central Party Work Conference, like a "finger pushing through a paper window"—enjoyed a steep ascent in the early years of the reform period. He was among the most determined supporters of economic reform. As the Communist Party organization chief in the late 1970s, he had also pushed aggressively for the rehabilitation of countless victims of the Cultural Revolution. It was an effort that had earned him not only plenty of moral credibility but also a bank vault's worth of valuable political capital that he could draw upon in the years to come.

In 1980, thanks to Deng's patronage, Hu became general secretary of the party and also attained membership in the Politburo Standing Committee, the small group of men who effectively ran China. Hu's record as an arch-reformer cemented his status as Deng's most important deputy. Hu pushed hard for economic liberalization and personally oversaw measures that gave industrial enterprises more autonomy and allowed them to retain more profits for themselves. He also presided over agricultural reforms that extended the term farmers were allowed to rent land from the state, thus reinforcing the principle of private initiative. His term also saw an expansion of the Special Economic Zones to encompass even greater areas along the coast.

But Hu's success also contained the seeds of his own destruction. His mercurial personality alienated Deng and created friction with fellow reformer Zhao Ziyang. In the mid-1980s, meanwhile, the release of entrepreneurial energies meant that the economy began to overheat. The gradual abolition of price controls on certain goods—the inevitable consequence of the shift away from a centrally planned economy—meant that inflation soared. Inequality deepened. Officials as well as members of the new business class often proved unwilling to wait for wealth, and corruption rose correspondingly. And Hu's insistence on the need for political reform to accompany economic restructuring went decidedly too far for a Communist Party leadership that was growing nervous about its hold on power in a tumultuous period of change. In 1987 he was forced to resign his post as general secretary of the party and retired, disappearing into the limbo that invariably envelops all Chinese leaders who fall into official disfavor.

Then came the news, in April 1989, that Hu had died of a heart attack. The party leadership initially balked at affording him a state funeral but soon relented—perhaps recalling the Tiananmen Incident of 1976, when similar reluctance to acknowledge the death of Zhou Enlai had prompted popular demonstrations against the Maoists. If so, those fears proved legitimate. In 1989, just as had been the case with Zhou, the perception of a posthumous party snub angered Hu's supporters, and soon groups of students were using his death as a rallying point for protests against corruption and rising inflation. The students believed that the best way to remedy such social ills was to curb the power of the party by establishing more democratic institutions (though the protesters were often vague about how this was to be accomplished in practice).

The party, which had rather different ideas on this score, harshly condemned the protests, which prompted them to spread beyond Beijing to dozens of other cities around China. In some places, workers joined the students, setting off alarm bells in the minds of party leaders who were especially sensitive to the ideological threat posed by anti-Communist proletarians. Some of the students camped out on Tiananmen Square started a hunger strike to press their demands for more democracy. Various party stalwarts paid visits to the students, warning them to desist. The visitors included, toward the end, Zhao Ziyang himself, who pleaded with them to put an end to the protests. Mikhail Gorbachev came to Beijing, and his example inflamed the malcontents: why couldn't China implement its own brand of perestroika?

How it all ended is known. In the early hours of June 4, 1989, the Communist Party declared martial law and sent in the troops. We may never know the precise casualties, but it seems safe to say that hundreds of people were killed in central Beijing that day. Even more obscure is the outcome in dozens of other Chinese cities where similar protests were suppressed at the same time. The chairman of the Central Military Commission, the man who issued the command for the crackdown, was none other than Deng Xiaoping. In 1977 those who yearned for an end to Maoist turmoil had greeted Deng's return to power by hanging up small bottles over Beijing's streets, a play on his name (*xiaoping* can mean "small bottle"). In 1989 students confined to their dormitory buildings smashed bottles as an expression of their anger and frustration.[11]

Deng was not shy about giving the order. Later, in an address to People's Liberation Army troops, he hailed the party's actions in the most uncompromising terms:

> We ... face a rebellious clique and a large number of the dregs of society, who want to topple our country and overthrow our party. This is the essence of the problem. ... They have two main slogans: One is to topple the Communist Party, and the other is to overthrow the socialist system. Their goal is to establish a totally Western-dependent bourgeois republic. The people want to combat corruption. This, of course, we accept. We should also take the so-called anticorruption slogans raised by people with ulterior motives as good advice and accept them accordingly. Of course, these slogans are just a front: The heart of these slogans is to topple the Communist Party and overthrow the socialist system.[12]

Rarely has Deng revealed his fundamental assumptions as clearly as he did in this passage. He had not spent his adult life anchoring Communist Party rule to see it dismantled by student radicals. At the same time, however, Deng moved to ensure that the course of economic reform would continue. This reassurance was crucial.

Notably, Deng never repeated his 1978 flirtations with the prodemocracy movement. He named his program "socialism with Chinese characteristics," and he seemed quite sincere in this. It all depends, perhaps, on one's definition of socialism. For Deng, the word seemed to mean, above all, a system that could unify a notoriously fractious country; it did not refer to Maoist-style egalitarianism, the radical leveling of all differences. To the end of his life, Deng adamantly insisted that he opposed "capitalism." And when the liberals began to express their longing for more democracy in the late 1980s, Deng issued a pitiless rejection. Some of his closest associates were brutally scapegoated, stripped of their posts and packed off into political neverland. Zhao Ziyang, the only Politburo member to vote against a military solution to the student protests, and who had visited the students in Tiananmen Square shortly before the crackdown, was stripped of his posts and relegated to house arrest.

The conservatives, whose influence had been rising even before Tiananmen, set out to brake China's rush to the market. They lowered growth targets, tightened financial controls, and pushed for greater budget discipline. They even announced a moratorium on the construction of high-end office buildings and hotels. At a party conference in late 1989, Premier Li Peng declared that party controls over all matters ideological would be intensified.[13] The SEZs, again, were at the forefront of the debate. The new emphasis on "patriotic education" and the ban on anything that smacked of "bourgeois liberalization" did not square well with the cosmopolitan allure of a place like Shenzhen. For a time, Deng was willing to concede ground to them. But he was not willing to backtrack completely.

Chen Yun seemed to have won the argument. He had always regarded the zones as "birdcages," places where the rapacious spirit of capitalism could be exploited even as it was kept in safe quarantine. (It was Chen who had argued, when the first special zones were established, that "you have to be careful about opening the window—the flies and the mosquitoes will come in.") His defense of planning and his critique of market mechanisms dominated the public discussion. The conservatives held sway over the media. Some of Deng's key allies deserted him. This time, it seemed, Deng had exhausted his political capital. He was already in semiretirement. Another comeback appeared improbable.[14]

But then, in the winter of 1992, Deng announced that he intended to set off on a vacation in the sunny South. His special train stopped first in Shanghai, Chen Yun's hometown. It was Chen's memories of the 1920s and 1930s, when Shanghai's economy was dominated by the foreign companies that retained imperial-era concessions there, that made him a staunch opponent of so-called comprador capitalism. In 1979 there had been talk of including Shanghai in the original group of Special Economic Zones, but Chen had quashed the idea. By the late 1980s, senior party officials were discussing plans to transform the Pudong district of Shanghai into a special zone designed to attract financial companies, alluding to the city's prewar role as China's banking center (a function that had since been assumed by Hong Kong). Chen continued to resist. But on his 1992 visit, Deng pressed the idea again, arguing that improved conditions for foreign banks could help to push economic development. His arguments were largely ignored by the national media—evidence, perhaps, that some in the party were already anticipating his retirement from the scene. If such expectations existed, they were soon to prove premature.

Deng's train then pressed on to Guangdong Province. In Shenzhen he met with a rousing welcome from local party officials, who understood, quite accurately, that their own political fortunes were intimately connected with his. Deng toured factories and met with their workers, who gave him glowing accounts of the improved living standards and chances for mobility that Shenzhen offered. Deng viewed the zone's first skyscrapers and inspected what had become, by now, its exemplary roads and port facilities. Shenzhen was producing goods to market around the world. It was also home to the first stock exchange in the People's Republic of China, a remarkable sign of the spread of market norms. By this time, Hong Kong investors were employing 3 million mainland workers in the zone—three times more than in Hong Kong itself.[15] The vast majority of these workers came from somewhere else in China, extraordinary evidence of social mobility in a country that had, for decades, tied people to their places of birth. As evidence of this shift, most Shenzheners spoke Mandarin, the national version of Chinese, unlike most Guangdong natives, who speak the local dialect of Cantonese.

There were many problems, too—precisely the issues that had made Shenzhen and the other SEZs targets of the opposition to reform. There were stories of drug use, prostitution, and widespread corruption. The fifty-mile fence between Shenzhen and the rest of the mainland served to prevent the capitalist mind-set from infecting China as a whole.[16]

But this was not what Deng chose to dwell upon during his visit. In speech after speech, he drew attention to the achievements of Shenzhen and the extraordinary speed of its development. At one point he recalled an early visit to the region: "I came to Guangdong in 1984. At that point, rural reform had been going for a few years, urban reform was just starting, and the special zones were taking their first steps. Eight years have gone by and I would never have believed that on this visit I would find that Shenzhen and Zhuhai special zones had developed so fast. Having seen it, my confidence has increased."[17]

At first Deng's speeches received coverage only from the Guangdong media, which celebrated his support for the province's success. Guangdongers knew that Deng had played a crucial role in giving provincial government relative freedom from Beijing's interference to push ahead with the economic experiments that had now borne such spectacular fruit. But the national media remained silent. Gradually, however, Deng's sympathizers gained traction. It was only several weeks after his trip that most Chinese began to learn of Deng's pilgrimage to Guangdong and to hear for themselves his forceful arguments in favor of continued opening to the world. The images of Shenzhen's soaring towers and turbocharged factories resolved the hesitations of many party members who had been wondering whether the march toward the market was a good idea. Deng's 1992 trip—which came to be known as the *nanxun*, the "Southern Tour"—galvanized the economic reformers and enabled them to gain a crucial edge over their opponents. It also dramatized the extent to which the Special Economic Zones had become the frontier of China's market experiment. The Chinese never looked back.

The reforms that Deng and his party comrades unleashed in 1979 have been described as the largest poverty-reduction program in human history. This is just. Over the past three decades, China's embrace of markets has lifted hundreds of millions of people out of impoverishment. As one of Deng's biographers notes, China's trade with the world totaled less than $10 billion in 1978. Over the next three decades, it expanded a hundredfold.[18]

This has not gone unnoticed in the rest of the world. China's success has been a major factor in the global "market revolution" and the rejection of collectivist approaches to economic development. To be sure, the Chinese model has retained a large role for the state; the government still steers many investment decisions through the vast Communist Party bureaucracy and the state-dominated financial sector. Yet for many of those around the world who admire China's success, it is precisely the rejection of state planning that is most worth emulating. China's runaway growth—9 percent per year—represented yet another persuasive argument for the power of markets and the failures of central planning. "Having become accustomed to being harangued by the Chinese for their lack of Marxist ideological purity, Third World socialists watched in disbelief as in the 1980s China itself embraced the market with almost pornographic enthusiasm," writes historian Odd Arne Westad. The fact that the Chinese managed to adopt this market-driven system while rejecting the accoutrements of democracy and retaining one-party control made it even more attractive to many countries where the elites were not prepared to relinquish their privileged political status.[19]

In this respect, it seems safe to say that it was Deng Xiaoping, the man who devoted his life to the ideals of Communism, who has done more than any other individual to ensure its demise as an idea.

EPILOGUE: THE PROBLEM WITH PROGRESS

In January 1888, Sidney Webb made an appearance before the Sunday Lecture Society in London. The society was the brainchild of T. H. Huxley, a dogged defender of Darwin's theory of evolution and a firm believer in the enlightenment of the working classes; they were supposed to constitute the primary audience for the lectures. Webb was a charter member of the Fabian Society, which had been founded four years earlier with the aim of persuading Britons to embrace social democracy. It was on just this subject that Webb had been invited to speak. He entitled his presentation "The Progress of Socialism."

Even today it makes for a lively read. Though Webb harshly criticized the many social ills of Victorian society, the program he presented was stirringly redolent of the strong belief in scientific and technological progress that characterized his age. "The tide of European Socialism is rolling in upon us like a flood," he proclaimed. The course of history, the development of industry, the recent discoveries in biology (meaning, presumably, Darwinism)—all these things attested to the truth of the socialist idea. "There is no resting place for stationary Toryism in the scientific universe," he told his audience. "The whole history of the human race cries out against the old-fashioned Individualism."

History was driven primarily by economics: "The student of history finds that the great world moves, like the poet's snake, on its belly." Moreover, Webb contended, all economic trends were moving clearly in the direction of collective or public ownership. As proof of this, he led his listeners to a long catalog of all the social and economic functions that were once performed by "private capitalists" but had since been taken over by various levels of government. The list, which goes on for a good three pages, spanned such disparate activities as surveying, coinage and

339

regulation of the currency, "the provision of weights and measures," and shipbuilding. Webb lovingly enumerated all the areas that had come to be regulated or otherwise controlled by the state. If this trend toward government control continued,
he concluded, private property was on the way out—and this was as it should be.
Public ownership of the means of production was the only effective way to raise
the "material condition of the great mass of the people." The technological and social advance of history inevitably led toward the embrace of socialism; socialism
and progress, indeed, were interchangeable. Webb concluded on a suitably uplifting
note: "The road may be dark and steep, for we are still weak, but the Torch of Science is in our hands: in front is the glow of morning, and we know that it leads to
the mountain top where dwells the Spirit of the Dawn."[1]

With remarkable brevity, Webb's Sunday lecture concisely anticipated one of
the most powerful strains in the political thought of the century to come. He and
his wife, Beatrice, went on to transform the Fabian Society into an institution that
paved the way for the triumph of social democratic ideas in early-twentieth-century Britain; they have been described as the "godparents of the Labour Party." The
Webbs were not Marxists; they were opposed to class warfare, though they viewed
it as unavoidable if the condition of the working class was not bettered by the
kind of gradual measures they promoted. Yet, like many other relatively moderate
"progressives" of the twentieth century, they still felt deep sympathy for decidedly
more radical visions. In 1935, after visiting the Soviet Union, they published a book
entitled *A New Civilization?* that concluded that Stalin's Russia was a model for
the kind of collectivist society that ultimately awaited us all. The Webbs, in short,
shared their beliefs in the desirability and inevitability of state-led modernization
with many other twentieth-century reformers.

Sidney and Beatrice Webb are rightly celebrated today as progenitors of the
modern welfare state; Clement Attlee's post-1945 vision of the "New Jerusalem" can
trace its origins directly to them. The modern-day observer will see much in their
thinking that is heroic—but also a great deal that is almost frighteningly naive. We
no longer share that faith in the unconditional goodness of technological and scientific progress that characterized so many members of the educated elite in the early
twentieth century. To be sure, the overwhelming majority of the earth's population
today lives under conditions that would have been barely imaginable on a comparable scale just a hundred years earlier. Yet we are also only too aware of the price
that humankind has had to pay for these achievements: mass slaughter, traumatic
social turmoil, ecological damage on a vast scale.

The idea of progress carries within it the seeds of arrogance. The engineers of social and material advancement can easily succumb to the certainty that their program is scientific, inevitable, indisputable—that progress is, essentially, an end unto itself. But this is true only as long as an overwhelming majority of people within a particular society are willing to accept this vision. The story of 1979 can be seen as the story of those who rejected it.

To be sure, they sometimes did so simply to defend their economic or social status—out of "class interests," as the Marxists would put it. But the cautionary tale of 1979 should also serve to warn us that the reactions of societies, classes, or individuals to technological and economic challenges cannot be reduced solely to technology and economics. Simple impoverishment is a poor guide to political stability; there are many poor countries that never experience revolutions. The economic slowdown of mid-1978 in Iran was not as severe as the one that occurred two years earlier—but 1976 passed with nary a hint of social disturbances, while the shallower recession that followed inspired a full-scale revolt.[2] Meanwhile, social inequality in contemporary China is close to the levels that plagued Iran in the last decades of the shah's rule—yet this does not necessarily mean that systemic collapse is just around the corner. Because Communist rule in Poland and the rest of Eastern Europe in the 1980s literally bankrupted itself, we tend to regard the 1989 anti-Communist revolts as inevitable. Yet identical systems in North Korea and Cuba endured for decades more—the former by virtue of a continued and unstinting commitment to brute force and ideological uniformity, the latter thanks to a combination of sophisticated oppression and tactical economic reforms.

Economic determinism is not particularly good at explaining why events happen precisely when they do, why people are willing to sacrifice their lives and livelihoods for their beliefs, or why the ideas of one powerless priest can bring an entire nation to its feet and a ruler to his knees. Economics certainly shapes politics, but politics is ultimately a category unto itself. And we cannot understand political dynamics without recourse to the ideas that motivate people to action.

No one demonstrated this better than Margaret Thatcher, who set out to dismantle a philosophy of government that owed a great deal to the Webbs and their ilk. Some of her more blinkered opponents liked to depict her as a defender of class interests, a willing tool in the hands of conniving capitalists. But it is precisely Thatcher's 1979 electoral victory that shows why this interpretation falls short. The Britons who chose her in that election were not voting for monetarism or stock market deregulation. They were motivated by more general concerns. The majority embraced Thatcher's argument that Britain was in a state of terminal decline and that it could be stopped only by limiting the reach of the state. More specifically, voters opted for Thatcher as a way of rejecting the most obvious manifestation of that decline: the overweening power of the unions, viewed by many late-1970s Britons as a kind of unelected government that was contrary to the very spirit of the democratic system. There were undoubtedly many who also believed that Thatcher's promised revival of entrepreneurship and personal responsibility would benefit them economically. But polling from the period convincingly shows that those who voted Tory did so based on a broader understanding of the country's problems. Thatcher appealed to voters precisely because she promised a corrective to the expansion of the state, an end to a postwar consensus that was now seen as more stifling than emancipatory. She appealed to their sense of agency and freedom rather than treating them as cogs in the impersonal machine of progress. In so doing, she demonstrated that the "old-fashioned Individualism" derided by Sidney Webb was perhaps not so old-fashioned after all.

Of course, it is much easier to indulge in individualism when you know that you can visit a doctor for free, count on regular payments from the state in the event of unemployment, and receive a guaranteed pension when you retire. For all her determination to change the way Britain worked, Thatcher showed little inclination to return to the laissez-faire world of the Victorians. She understood very well that certain innovations of the postwar welfare state—above all the entitlement programs that Britons had come to regard as their birthright—were there to stay, and she did little to challenge them in any fundamental way. As a true counter-revolutionary, she acknowledged some of the achievements of the revolution that preceded her. But in stark contrast to the Tory "wets"—the true conservatives in the Conservative Party—she did not shirk from confrontation on the fronts where she spotted opportunities for radical change. Margaret Thatcher was not a technocrat. She defined her politics through values, ideals, and moral categories. Some commentators have taken issue with her self-description as a "conviction politician," but there can be little question that she saw herself this way.

Thatcherism is often defined as an economic credo, but there was a great deal more to it than that. Though this point tends to be glossed over by commentators, Thatcher was a woman of strong religious beliefs. Her personal Christianity owed a great deal, of course, to her strict Methodist upbringing. (Contrary to some accounts, however, her father was not a fundamentalist, but a thoroughly modern believer who accepted the teachings of science and even conceded a significant role to the state in the fight for social justice.)[3] That she went over to the Church of

England later in life changes some of the details in this picture, perhaps, but not its substance. Her belief in individual responsibility and the primacy of personal freedom had its roots in a spiritual stance rather than an economic theory.

We tend to forget that modern politics has its roots in religion. For most of human history, the rulers of society have called upon the realm of the supernatural to legitimize their ascendancy. The notion of politics as a distinct and secular sphere of human activity has a rather shallow pedigree. Though the roots of this idea are much older, it is really only since the Enlightenment that politics has established itself as a business involving only human beings. Try as it might, though, even modern political movements have never quite managed to shrug off their scriptural and spiritual origins.[4] The Abrahamic religions—Judaism, Christianity, and Islam—shared the belief that history is the product of a single and unified divine being that is pushing humanity forward toward a particular end; once that end is reached, history will end, and a community of purity and justice will be established for eternity. The European religious wars in the wake of the Reformation, and especially the English Civil War in the seventeenth century, showed how millennial longings for justice and equality gave rise to organizations that had remarkable similarities to twentieth-century revolutionary movements. The syntheses of Marxism and religion attempted by Ali Shariati and the theorists of Catholic liberation theology in the 1970s show that Marx's thinking was, in a deeper sense, more congenial to Abrahamic prophecy than he might have been willing to acknowledge.

So perhaps it should come as little surprise that those who defined themselves as the militant avant-garde of "material progress" should have met with particularly bitter resistance from the forces of organized religion. For many twentieth-century modernizers, the proper "progressive" was an atheist, someone who rejected supernatural explanations of events in favor of a "scientific," materialist analysis of history. Religion, in this reading, was a backward superstition, its defenders the cynical allies of the propertied classes. "Law, morality, religion, are to [the proletarian] so many bourgeois prejudices, behind which lurk in ambush just as many bourgeois interests," Marx and Engels wrote in *The Communist Manifesto*.[5] Marxists had a near-religious confidence in their own ability to transcend superstition—an attitude so infectious that even traditional monarchs like the shah of Iran felt compelled to design his reforms so that they echoed Communist models.

Religious thinkers had one response: man does not live by bread alone. Though the Iranian Revolution was fueled by many economic concerns, its ultimate impulse was a moral one. The Westernized intellectuals had failed to provide a satisfactory answer to the fundamental dilemma of identity that Iranians felt themselves to be facing. Khomeini offered a clear and brutal response: "Yes, we are reactionaries, and you are enlightened intellectuals: You intellectuals do not want us to go back 1400 years. You, who want freedom, freedom for everything, the freedom of parties, you who want all the freedoms, you intellectuals: freedom that will corrupt our youth, freedom that will pave the way for the oppressor, freedom that will drag our nation to the bottom."[6]

To be sure, Khomeini and his revolutionary supporters among the clergy strove to outflank the "enlightened intellectuals" by redefining Islam as the more "progressive" force. (Both Shariati and Mawdudi served as sources of inspiration in this case.) Yet the extraordinary intensity of the popular joy and rage that Khomeini was able to summon in his campaign to sweep away the world's most powerful monarch drew its energy from the profound anxiety of people who felt that their most cherished values were under direct attack from those who claimed to be improving the material conditions of their existence.

Religious reactions can assume radically different forms. To Khomeini, the only viable response to the shah's rule was revolution—and violence was an essential ingredient of the process by which the revolutionaries were supposed to purge society of secular excess. John Paul II came at the problem from a radically different perspective. His personal experience of twentieth-century totalitarianism at its most vicious—Nazism and Stalinism—led him to embrace an approach to resistance that minimized the possibility of violence. His first encyclical, *Redemptor Hominis*, expressly addressed "the subject of development and progress [that] is on everybody's lips and appears in the columns of all the newspapers and other publications in all the languages of the modern world." For all its virtues, the pontiff warned, material progress always contains the potential to become an end unto itself—to lose sight of the individual lives it aspires to improve: "Man cannot relinquish himself or the place in the visible world that belongs to him; he cannot become the slave of things, the slave of economic systems, the slave of production, the slave of his own products. A civilization purely materialistic in outline condemns man to such slavery, even if at times, no doubt, this occurs contrary to the intentions and the very premises of its pioneers."[7]

"A civilization purely materialistic in outline" sounds very much, of course, like the Soviet Communism that John Paul II was striving to resist. It is clear that he regarded such a system as an absolute evil to be opposed. Yet that recognition did not justify absolute means. The strategy of cultural resistance—the construction of alternate society, of "living in truth"—implied the same quality of "self-restraint" that later provided the basis for the "self-limiting revolution" of Solidarity and 1989.

It is striking, indeed, that the most influential nonviolent activist movements of the twentieth century—notably Mahatma Gandhi's struggle for independence from the British Empire and Martin Luther King's civil rights campaign (both of which drew, in their turn, on the writings of that Christian anarchist Leo Tolstoy)—had overtly religious origins. Their legacy can be traced in the 1980s through such diverse events as the uprisings against dictatorship in South Korea, the 1986 "People's Power" revolution in the Philippines, and the "velvet revolutions" in East Central Europe.

Progress is often presented by its proponents as the only rational course. For much of the twentieth century, radical progressives were convinced that they were armed with the truth. But the fact of the matter is that people do not always want to do the allegedly reasonable thing—especially if it runs counter to the cherished sources of identity that give meaning to their lives. This is what made the events of that year so hard to fathom for many secular radicals. The Iraqi dissident, ex-Trotskyite, and self-described atheist Kanan Makiya still recalls how he and his fellow left-wing radicals were blindsided by the Islamic Revolution. "Here we had these forces that we thought we had confined to the dustbins of history that reappeared and turned out to have nothing to do with what we had always expected," he says. "The working classes were nowhere to be seen. All the categories through which we had viewed the world had fallen apart."[8] The Tudeh, once the most powerful Communist Party in its region, effectively ceased to exist after the Iranian Revolution—a decade before the collapse of the Soviet Union put an end to real-existing socialism elsewhere. The dream of the brotherhood of man was a powerful one, but it could not compete, in the final analysis, with the brotherhood of believers.

The man who started the Arab Spring was not an Islamist. On December 17, 2010, a twenty-six-year-old street vendor in Tunisia, a high school graduate with an income of some $140 a month, changed the course of history. That day Mohammed Bouazizi went to a local government office in his hometown of Sidi Bouzid to register a protest against the police who had confiscated his vegetable cart. The official in charge refused to see him or acknowledge his complaints. Bouazizi doused himself with gasoline and set himself alight.[9]

Bouazizi's death touched off a revolution in his home country that quickly found emulators across the Arab world. In Tunisia itself, the protesters who took to the streets in empathy with Bouazizi's frustrations brought down the country's long-entrenched president. In Egypt millions of other demonstrators challenged

President Hosni Mubarak—and won. Yemenis successfully dislodged their leader, Libyans toppled the regime of Muammar al-Qaddafi, and Syrians rose up against the government of Bashar al-Assad. The unrest spanned, to varying degrees, Bahrain, Jordan, Morocco, Saudi Arabia, and Kuwait. Each uprising was different. Economic and political factors worked to unique effect in each country. Yet common to all of these rebellions was an essentially moral impulse: the urge to fight against the corruption and injustice that spring from long years of dictatorial rule.

The Arab Spring caught the world—not to mention many of the people directly affected by it—completely off guard. But one of the most surprising things about it was, at least initially, the comparatively subdued role of political Islam. Islamist movements exist in all of the countries affected by the Arab revolutions, yet religious activists were relatively inconspicuous in the early stages of upheaval. The demands of the people in the vanguard of change in the Middle East in 2010 and 2011 were remarkably similar to those protesting dictatorship in other parts of the world. Demonstrators proclaimed their desires for an end to tyranny, for free elections and freedom of speech, for an end to corruption, for transparent institutions and good governance, for impartial courts and strong parliaments. They did not call—at least at first—for the implementation of the sharia, for rule by the *ulama* or a jihadi avant-garde, for God's sovereignty to override that of the people. For the crowds demonstrating on the streets of Cairo, Tunis, Damascus, and Manama, Islam—to paraphrase the famous Islamist slogan—was not necessarily the answer. Many members of the younger generation of activists claimed to see their salvation in parliamentary democracy rather than the precepts of Quranic government.

Yet the ghost of 1979 has still managed to haunt the Arab Spring. The Iranian precedent has come to seem particularly ominous in the case of Egypt, the country that gave the Arab world its most prominent revivalist movement, the Muslim Brotherhood. The Brotherhood's success in the first free presidential and parliamentary elections since Mubarak's downfall was, for many Egyptians, the logical outcome of the revolution; for many others, it represented nothing less than a betrayal of the cause.

Most striking of all, perhaps, is the extent to which Egyptians have not turned to Iran, the first Islamic Republic, for inspiration. History is probably to blame. In 1979 there was no precedent for an Islamic revolution; no one knew what it would look like or what course it would take. By 2010, however, the revolutionaries in Egypt could look back on three decades of Islamist experiments around the world. Few of them wanted to emulate Iran, where the initial euphoria associated with Khomeini's experiment had long since degenerated into stagnant authoritarianism, a vicious, bureaucratic dictatorship with a frozen economy. Most Egyptians, of course, are Sunnis, so many of them might be inclined to seek examples closer to their own version of Islam. But the precedents established so far are hardly inspiring. Endless intra-Muslim civil war in Afghanistan after the victory over the Soviets, including the Neanderthal interval of Taliban rule, did not make for an attractive model, either. Nearly a decade after the 9/11 attacks, the attractions of al-Qaeda-style apocalyptic nihilism—certainly always somewhat exaggerated—had almost entirely evaporated.

There were also examples closer to home. Indigenous Egyptian groups like al-Gama'a al-Islamiyya, led by Omar Abdel-Rahman (the "blind sheikh"), and Islamic Jihad, controlled since the beginning of the 1990s by Bin Laden's ally Ayman al-Zawahiri, both indulged in long campaigns of assassination and terror inside the country. In particular, al-Gama'a al-Islamiyya's 1990s campaign to destabilize the national economy by targeting foreign tourists proved deeply alienating to ordinary Egyptians desperate to find jobs and sustenance. In 1997 members of the group dressed as policemen staged a brutal attack on tourists at a temple complex in Luxor, killing fifty-eight foreigners and four Egyptians. The popular backlash against the act was so intense that the group ultimately found itself compelled to forswear violence altogether.

Still, it would be premature to claim that the lure of political Islam has faded altogether. To the contrary, there are many indications around the Muslim world that believers still yearn for a political order that will give place of honor to religious values. Jihadis still exist, and they will for many years. But there is reason to believe that their ideas will meet with greater competition from within the community of believers in the years to come. There are signs of a great intellectual ferment beginning to get under way within Islam. Just like Khomeini and Qutb, the theorists of al-Qaeda and its sympathizers have conspicuously avoided mapping out the details of the state they are trying to achieve—betraying an otherworldly utopianism that hardly looks compelling in a world filled with many far more attractive alternatives. The newer generation of Islamic activists seems less inclined to leave all the details up to the fanatics who claim to know what's better for them.

Some of the most interesting examples of this dynamic come from the very country that pioneered Islamic revolution: Iran. Even as the regime there has concentrated power within an ever-narrowing elite, excluding even many former members of Khomeini's entourage, the institutional order bequeathed by the revolution has continued to offer at least the possibility of self-correction through elections. Again and again, Iranian voters have used their right to vote to express their desires for liberalization and reform, and again and again the governing elite has fought to thwart those desires by whatever means it can. The most dramatic example to date came with the 2009 presidential election, when alleged government vote-fixing in favor of the incumbent, Mahmoud Ahmadinejad, triggered popular protests that brought thousands of mostly young Iranians into the streets.

The main candidate opposing Ahmadinejad, Mir-Hossein Mousavi, hardly qualified as a dissident; he was a well-established stalwart of the regime, a former prime minister of the Islamic Republic. Originally a sympathizer of Shariati (and an admirer of Che Guevara), during the revolution he quickly gravitated to Khomeini, and in 1979 he joined forces with Ayatollah Beheshti to found the Islamic Republican Party. It would be hard to find someone with more impeccable insider qualifications, and, indeed, Mousavi's campaign program was hardly the stuff of all-out counterrevolution. He promised a few modest correctives to the existing system, including an expansion of women's rights. (Among his supporters was Mohsen Sazegara, the young idealist who joined Khomeini from Chicago in the fall of 1978. Like many former Iranian revolutionaries, he has now become a reformist.)

Yet the huge protests that followed his defeat dramatized the yawning gap between the expectations of many Iranians and the increasingly isolated circle of people at the top of the regime. (Many of those who chose to defy the regime were less active supporters of Mousavi than people determined to see that their votes were respected.) It was no accident that the protesters chose the color green—the traditional emblem of Islam—as the insignia of their movement. The protesters who took to the streets in what have been described as the biggest demonstrations in Iran since 1979 called not for a secular polity, but rather for the fulfillment of what they described as authentic Islamic values of tolerance and social justice. At the same time, their dominant slogan—"Where is my vote?"—spoke to democratic norms, not religious ones. Many of the postelection protesters did call for a fundamental, even revolutionary, transformation of the Islamic Republic—demonstrating that Mousavi was, to some extent, a figurehead of widespread longing for much more radical change. But strikingly few of them called for the use of force to achieve that aim. In fact, the emphasis on nonviolence has been one of the salient characteristics of the Green Movement.

This grassroots demand for a true melding of democracy and Islam within the country that gave the world the very concept of "Islamic Revolution" underlines a fundamental incongruity. For centuries Shiite clerics had remained independent of Iranian state power, a position that gave them immense political legitimacy and spiritual authority. But having captured the state in an attempt to assert the sovereignty of God, they effectively transformed themselves into just another set of worldly rulers—a point noted by commentators at the time of the 2009 protests. "What is ironic is that instead of empowering the clerical establishment, [the revolution] made the clerical establishment a puppet of the government," the Iranian-born scholar Mehdi Khalaji told a reporter in 2009. "So, the clerical establishment has lost its independence, its social popularity, and so on; and instead, the government, in 30 years, has been transformed into a military-economic-religious complex."[10] By politicizing religion, the mullahs have transformed religion into mere politics.

If Iran were to make the transition from the present regime to a new form of government that could unite Islamic values and genuine democracy, it could once again assume its place as a model for the Muslim world. Just as the revolution in 1979 redefined Muslim global attitudes, so the Green Movement points the way forward for a model of truly democratic Islam. In this context, contemporary Iranian religious thinkers like Abdulkarim Soroush and Mohammed Mojtahed Shabestari—both closely linked with Iranian reformists—are already shaping political debates within the Islamic world.

The Green Movement also suggests that a secular future is not the only alternative to militant Islamism. It is probably unrealistic to expect that the solution to Islamic extremism lies in a complete rejection of religious politics and a full-fledged embrace of secularism. There is little indication that Islam is losing its attraction as a religion—just the opposite, in fact. In many parts of the world (including the United States), it is the fastest-growing faith. The challenge lies in reconciling Islam's powerful ethical demands with the values of democracy and human rights. There are many indications that many Muslims are already in search of just such a synthesis. True renewal can come only from within.

In the late 1970s, the act of crossing the border at Lo Wu, between Hong Kong and mainland China, meant moving from one mental universe to a completely different one. Today it has become a matter of everyday routine. The watchtowers along the border are empty. There is still a fence along the Hong Kong side of the border to prevent unwanted immigration, but it presents no barrier to the tens of thousands of travelers who pass through the crossing point every day—many of them regular commuters (even including schoolchildren) equipped with electronic identification cards that allow them to cross through special gateways with minimal delays. The Chinese border guard who examines your visa when you cross over occupies a cubicle adorned with a button that allows you to rate the quality of his performance. The whole facility is a model of twenty-first-century efficiency—a world away from the bureaucratic somnolence that reigned here thirty years before.

The border guard hands you your passport, and you step across onto the mainland—or, to be more precise, the city of Shenzhen, which introduces itself as a warren of neon-lit shops offering everything from knock-off designer goods to toy helicopters to Mont Blanc fountain pens, all of it on sale right there in the same sprawling immigration building. Much of what you see was made here. Today, by one estimate, Shenzhen and the surrounding Pearl River delta boast a larger manufacturing workforce than the entire United States. Its factories churn out everything from exercise equipment to iPods; by 2005 Shenzhen boasted the world's fourth-busiest port and one of its biggest stock exchanges. As you roam the city, you will marvel at the traffic jams, the infectious energy of the bustling crowds, the immense shopping centers selling the latest cell phones and computers. Within an hour's drive of this place are factories that can turn out just about any electronic component you can imagine as quickly as you want to have it.[11]

Don't forget to stop in at the Diwang Mansion skyscraper. (The last time I visited, it was still Shenzhen's tallest building. But this is a city where no record stays intact for long, so that status can't be taken for granted.) Buy a ticket and take the elevator to the observation deck on its highest floor, the sixty-ninth. As you step out of the elevator, walk to the windows and take in the view. Skyscrapers, apartment towers, and factories march toward the horizon as far as the eye can see, lost in the haze toward the provincial capital of Guangzhou (a.k.a. Canton). Buried under the buildings somewhere down there—probably in the vicinity of the central railroad station—are the rice paddies that American investor Tom Gorman saw when he visited the spot in 1979.

The view isn't the only attraction, though. You can also admire the sixty-ninth floor's exhibits, which are devoted as much to Shenzhen's sister city, Hong Kong, as Shenzhen itself (there's a mock-up of a famous Hong Kong street, for example). You can't quite escape the impression that the organizers felt that Shenzhen's startlingly brief history, as amazing as it is, simply doesn't provide enough content for the entire floor. A time line on the wall compares major events in the lives of the two cities. Hong Kong's starts in the year 1842 and wanders along solo through the rest of the nineteenth century and most of the twentieth. The height of the line follows the growth of the city's population, and so it rises steadily but slowly for 160 years. There's a downward bump during World War II, when Japanese occupation drove many Hong Kongers away to the mainland, and then a dramatic rebound in the postwar period. Photos and text cluster at various points along the line, commemorating everything from the founding of the People's Republic of China to the international fame of Bruce Lee in the 1970s. Still no Shenzhen, though.

Shenzhen's visual history begins only in the year 1979. The population curve is sharp: an ascent of Everest compared with Hong Kong's gentle upward slope. The key moments in Shenzhen's chronology turn on factory openings and the inauguration of big buildings. The drama of the story comes less from some particular cultural or political accomplishment than from the sheer velocity of growth. Shenzhen's population has still not quite caught up with Hong Kong's by the end of the exhibition. But Hong Kong's line has long since flattened out, whereas Shenzhen's continues to climb. Hong Kong may be around for a while yet, the exhibition implies, but the future no longer belongs to it.

Walk around the corner, though, and you come across a remarkable sight: Deng Xiaoping and Margaret Thatcher are having a chat. The two life-size wax figures—Thatcher's hair a bit too red—sit in armchairs against a backdrop photomontage: Beijing's Forbidden City behind Deng's head, Hong Kong behind Thatcher's. Two pots of tea sit on the table between them.

A plaque in front of the tableau explains that it commemorates the 1984 Sino-British Joint Declaration, when the two leaders finally agreed on the terms for Hong Kong's return to Chinese sovereignty in 1997. In 1898 the British signed a lease with the imperial government in Beijing that gave London control over the New Territories, directly to the north of Hong Kong Island and Kowloon, for ninety-nine years. By the time the lease approached its renewal date, it was clear that the era of colonialism had passed and that the Chinese government was no longer willing to consider an extension of the arrangement. And if Britain could no longer control the New Territories, it could no longer hope to hang on to Hong Kong proper, either. It was time for colonial rule to end.

But there is, of course, a deeper logic to the visual union of Thatcher and Deng—though it is not mentioned on the commemorative plaque. It was these two figures who did more to promote the market-driven globalization of the late twentieth century than just about anyone else. Their ideological origins could not have been further apart—Deng the devoted Communist, Thatcher the dedicated Cold Warrior—but their rhetoric was often strikingly similar. Both spoke obsessively of the need to create wealth before it could be distributed. ("Socialism is not poverty," as Deng used to say.) Both stressed the importance of proper incentives for performance. Both argued that a certain degree of inequality had to be tolerated. Both insisted that the state should withdraw from realms better left to the market. (And both, at various moments, sought the council of free-market economist Milton Friedman.)

They had different approaches, obviously. It was Thatcher who became the global embodiment of the Anglo-Saxon ideals of political freedom and unfettered markets. Deng's admirers enshrined him as the embodiment of what came to be known by outsiders as the "Beijing Consensus" (a phrase that Beijing officials are reluctant to use). It was an approach that married openness to internal and external market forces with the strength of the authoritarian state. In the Chinese model, a surge of private entrepreneurship—especially on the town and village level—went hand in hand with tight political control and an activist state-investment role. The result is a remarkable melding of public and private. The percentage of economic assets now in private hands in China actually exceeds that in some European countries. Yet the Chinese Communist Party still runs the banking sector, retaining decisive authority when it comes to determining who gets loans and what they are used for. The Chinese themselves often evince confusion about where the private sector ends and the public one begins.

China's success is often treated as something unique, an extraordinary outlier the likes of which the world has never seen. This is not entirely true. As the experience of 1979 and the early reform period demonstrates, China's economic reforms drew heavily on the experience (and, indeed, the investment capital) of its East Asian neighbors. Almost from the start, China received advanced technological know-how and substantial investment from Japan. Practical experience in manufacturing and considerable amounts of cash came from Hong Kong. Taiwan's history of post–World War II land reform offered a vital precedent for the mainland's efforts to boost private farming, and its experiments with export processing zones in the 1960s and 1970s spurred Deng's interest in the Special Economic Zones. Taiwan, Singapore, and South Korea all showed just how effective the combination of dictatorship and market-oriented economic development could be. There is little that Deng and his comrades did in the late 1970s and 1980s that had not been done by these countries before them; what was most radical about the Chinese Communist reformers was their willingness to imagine how a similar program of reforms could be translated into the context of a communized society. In this sense, the "Beijing Consensus" can be more accurately described as the "East Asian Model." The real pathbreaker for all of these countries, indeed, was Meiji-era Japan, the first of the non-Western nations to embark on a conscious program of Western-style economic and technological modernization. (It was this precedent, by the way, that Deng repeatedly invoked in the late 1970s and early 1980s.)

What really makes China unique, indeed, is its scale. In 2011, Chinese gross domestic product per capita was around five thousand dollars, far behind that in these smaller, more advanced Asian economies. But because of its enormous population, the People's Republic only needs to boost that number a bit in order to become the world's biggest economy.

Deng and his colleagues changed China. The China they created cannot help but transform the world. The world does not catch cold when Singapore sneezes. And this is not just a matter of economics. China's rise also has a direct effect on resource consumption, on geopolitics, on the environment. So we must all care whether China gets it right.

China's triumph has been extraordinary. Yet the Chinese Communist Party remains strikingly insecure about its success, reacting with extraordinary speed and sensitivity to even the mildest signs of dissent. The leaders of the party insist that their policies meet with the overwhelming approval of their citizens. And this could well be the case (though it is hard to tell one way or the other in a country that has neither elections nor free media). Yet the CCP continues to respond to even the most minor challenges to its power with striking obsessiveness. The amount of money allocated to internal security has now surpassed the budget for external defense.[12] Such behavior is not exactly the sign of a government that knows it enjoys the affection of its citizens. The Chinese state employs tens of thousands of people to scour the Internet for allegedly seditious content (which, in practice, often consists of reporting documenting the malfeasance of party functionaries). The Chinese Communist Party's system for censoring Web content and influencing online opinions is regarded by experts as the most extensive and sophisticated operation of its kind anywhere in the world.

Less well known to the outside world is the extent to which the party has systematically studied the failure of Communist rule in Eastern Europe.[13] Interestingly, the Polish example has figured prominently in this effort. This is partly a matter of timing. The early years of China's economic reforms were roughly contemporaneous with the first flowering of Solidarity. But it is also true that the Polish example combined two factors that the party of Deng Xiaoping continues to follow with particular alertness. One is labor activism. The party tracks every strike and independent labor movement with extraordinary care, and it responds to them with a highly sophisticated divide-and-rule strategy, buying off some organizers while coercing others.[14] At the same time, the party has gradually but notably expanded the legal space available for bargaining and legal recourse involving labor issues. There is clearly a recognition that China's further economic development depends on ensuring a certain degree of flexibility toward workers' demands for greater social justice. The second factor that worries party leaders, intriguingly, is religion. This might come as a surprise to those outsiders who tend to regard the Chinese as a ruthlessly practical people. But this is a simplification. The Communist Party knows, first, that religion can be a powerful source of organized opposition to central rule. One historical example that looms large in party thinking is the

Taiping Rebellion, the mid-nineteenth-century uprising triggered by the members of an unorthodox Christian cult whose leader—reminiscent of the organizer of the seizure of the Grand Mosque in 1979—declared himself to be the younger brother of Jesus Christ. The rebellion turned into a civil war that took millions of lives. A more recent case is represented by Falun Gong, the twentieth-century amalgam of native Buddhist and Daoist teachings that ultimately turned into the best-organized mass opposition movement to Communist rule since 1949 before it was brutally suppressed in 1999.

Official anxiety about religion is reflected not only in the party's continued persecution of Falun Gong but also in its efforts to ensure state control of other confessions. Tibetan Buddhism, for obvious reasons, is particularly high on the list. But so too, rather oddly, is Roman Catholicism, a faith that claims only about 13 million believers in China. The refusal of the People's Republic to establish diplomatic relations with the Holy See has much to do with the history of Christian missionary movements as collaborators with Western colonial movements, but it also owes a great deal to Beijing's sharp awareness of the role played by the Catholic Church in the collapse of Eastern European Communism. Once again, while secular Westerners tend to discount the political role of religion, this is a mistake that Communists are less inclined to make.

Chinese Communist Party leaders take political history very seriously. It is not only the challenge of organized faith that worries them. They are also extremely sensitive to the disruptive potential of "crises of prosperity" of the kind that—to name but one example—brought down the shah in 1979. (The CCP has not restricted its analysis of the weaknesses of one-party rule to Communist Eastern Europe at the end of the 1980s; its studies also encompass places as varied as Indonesia, Mexico, Taiwan, and Japan.)[15] As the example of 1970s Iran demonstrates, rapid economic growth can be profoundly destabilizing. As people watch society change before their eyes, old values can appear outmoded or inadequate. Sudden prosperity, as welcome as it is, can bring in its wake nagging ethical, political, and even metaphysical questions—especially if one of the results of development is a dramatic uptick in the gap between rich and poor. And, indeed, one striking trait of economic reform in China since 1979 has been a stark increase in inequality, a feature that distinguishes it dramatically from the other East Asian tigers. In terms of wealth distribution, in fact, contemporary China is much more similar to Brazil, Mexico, or Indonesia than to Taiwan or South Korea.[16]

So it is not a surprise that the Chinese Communist Party has taken measures to fill the resulting "meaning gap." In the wake of the 1989 Tiananmen Square massacre, Deng Xiaoping and his comrades tried to compensate for the loss of faith in Marxist-Leninist dogma by playing up patriotism and pride in the glories of the Chinese past. The party's propaganda campaign intensified an already existent nationalist trend, particularly among young people, that may prove hard to manage in the years to come. (Extreme nationalism was also one of the by-products of the "late modernization" of Meiji Japan and late-nineteenth-century Germany—and in neither case was it an experience that ended well for the world.) In the twenty-first century, the powers that be in Beijing have also experimented with a revival of traditional Confucian values, with particular emphasis on the Great Sage's message of respect for authority. But this, too, could potentially backfire: Confucius had minimal tolerance for corrupt or self-serving public officials—a concern shared by many of the Internet critics of the present regime.

It is striking that many of those who lived through it in China depict the turn-around of 1979 in moral terms rather than strictly economic ones. Even if the Communist Party continued to preserve its prerogatives, the rejection of the principle that ideology was more important than everything else amounted to a widening of personal freedom that most Chinese regarded with relief. "[The year] 1979 is very important for me," one Chinese journalist told me. "It's a watershed. Before that we were living in the Cultural Revolution movement and class struggle. After 1979 there was one word: *humanity*."[17] The creative energy of millions of Chinese people unleashed by the reforms of 1979 has produced remarkable achievements. How sustainable those achievements will prove in the end depends to a large extent on the Communist Party's ability to respect the humanity of its citizens.

As I strolled around Kabul on a clear, chilly afternoon in January 2002, I happened upon a place called the Behzad Book Store. At that particular moment, a few months after the collapse of the Taliban regime, the Afghan capital was enjoying a moment of peace and hope in the future; everywhere, it seemed, people were starting new businesses, expressing a longing for prosperity so long thwarted by years of war. But it was really the past that caught my eye. I was surprised to see so much surviving evidence of the period of relative prosperity that Afghanistan had experienced in the 1960s and 1970s. The cars on the street included a disproportionate number of Volkswagen Beetles and fat Chevrolets so familiar from my far-away American childhood. (Some of them still had their eight-track tape players.) The magazine that I worked for had rented a place for its employees to live in, and the ranch-style house, with its shag carpeting and tubular aluminum light fixtures, evoked exactly the same period. When US Marines reopened the long-dormant US Embassy, they

found stacks of intact vinyl records in the basement—Billy Joel and the Eagles—
and a perfectly good turntable to play them with.

The best time capsule of all, though, turned out to be the Behzad Book Store,
which had managed to save much of its inventory through the years of Taliban
rule. (Some of it, the owners told me, they had preserved by burying it.) Its shelves
were like the strata of an archaeological dig: each layer revealed more clues to Afghanistan's overly eventful recent past. There were thick academic tomes on economics and sociology, in a variety of languages, brought in by the well-meaning
development economists and missionary socialists of the 1960s and early 1970s.
There were well-thumbed paperback best sellers—such as Alvin Toffler's porten-
tous *Future Shock*, another artifact from my junior high years—in English, German, and French, left behind by the tourists and aid workers who had crowded into
the country in the years when they were still welcome. There was a Communist-
era propaganda pamphlet entitled *CIA Agents Expose Their Crimes*, published in
1984, in which captured rebels confessed to their sins against the state. And there
was even a crudely printed booklet, green letters on a fading yellow paper cover, of
Mawdudi's *Fundamentals of Islam*, translated into Russian. It was, evidently, part of
the mujahideen's information war, targeting the Red Army troops who hailed from
the Muslim republics of Soviet Central Asia.

The most poignant relics of them all, though, were the postcards. The bookstore
had a whole wall of them, each one a tiny window onto a happier time. They were
produced by Afghans inside their own country—an achievement that seemed almost unimaginable in 2002—in the days when peddling such things to tourists offered plenty of scope for profit. There were wide-angle views of Kabul that showed
a picturesque, well-watered metropolis thick with trees. There were inviting pictures of exotic mosques and archeological sites. There was a snapshot of the pool at
the Intercontinental Hotel, one light-skinned visitor in the foreground enjoying the
turquoise water with the nonchalance of his oblivious present.

There was one image that has haunted me ever since. It showed a glamorous
woman sitting on the grass, her knees bent. Her loose, flowing dress was all folkloric
swirls, purple and black, a fusion of 1970s psychedelia and ethnic chic. Her head
was uncovered, and a cigarette dangled from one casual hand.

I wondered about her fate. Had she somehow managed to survive the Soviet
invasion, the antioccupation jihad, the civil war among the victorious mujahideen,
the triumph of the Taliban? Had she stayed inside Afghanistan, or had she been
forced to live her life in one of those huge refugee camps in Pakistan? Had she

perhaps joined the hundreds of thousands of Afghans who succeeded in fleeing to the United States, or Germany, or Eastern Europe, and started a new life there? Or was she now, invisibly aged, passing by the shop as I stood there, hidden away beneath one of the light-blue burkas that seemingly all the women in Kabul were wearing in early 2002? And, if so, how would she feel about being forced to live her life under wraps? It was such a stark contrast to the moment depicted in the photo, when many women could still stroll the streets with uncovered heads. By the time of the early twenty-first century, the women who might have taken her place were mostly confined to their homes and frequently prohibited from holding jobs. It was hard to imagine burka-clad women smoking cigarettes.[18]

And it wasn't just her. Her Afghanistan had vanished as well. The tourists who had once provided a market for these postcards were long gone, and the photographers and publishers who had manufactured and sold these images had vanished, too. The hotels had shut, and the archaeological sites had become too dangerous to visit. The domestic textile industry that had once hoped to expand its markets through advertising had been consumed by decades of war and impoverishment. It was almost impossible to reconcile the Kabul in the postcards with the city that surrounded me, a place of dusty riverbeds, amputees on every corner, and miles of skeletal ruins, rocketed into dust during the 1990s civil war.

All images can lie, of course, and it would be easy to dismiss the cigarette-smoking model as an outlier, a solipsistic stand-in for a superficial program of Westernization with no organic connection to the surrounding society. But this is lazy. The Afghanistan she stood for was real. She may have belonged to a minority, but it was unquestionably a growing minority that many wanted to join. Afghanistan's path was never preordained.

It was this modest encounter with pre-1979 Afghanistan that started the train of thought that led to this book. Though the vision presented by the model in the postcard might have seemed like ancient history, it had actually existed within my own lifetime. This Westernizing, secular, hedonistic Afghanistan was not a phantom; it represented a genuine dream for many Afghans who either left the country after the Soviet invasion (among them, Akbar Ayazi, the young Kabul radio announcer, who now lives in the United States) or who, in the early 1990s, sided with the post-Communist Najibullah regime against the encroaching forces of the Islamic rebels who were determined to wipe it out forever. These traces of the past stand for an option snuffed out, a line of development that proved too weak to survive the successive blows of Communist rule, the Soviet invasion, and the harsh backlash of the mujahideen. In Afghanistan, secular modernization was a road that was not only not taken, but dynamited out of existence. We may not see anything like it return for generations, if at all.

Why did Afghanistan take the course that it did? I am not sure that anyone can ever give a truly satisfactory answer. To study 1979 is also to study the tyranny of chance. It is worth noting, among other things, that many of the leaders whose careers are examined in this book were the targets of assassination attempts. How would our story look if their lives had been cut short?[19] If we can gain any lesson from our examination of this watershed year, it is that history is, above all, the study of contingency—a search for an answer to the question of why certain courses were followed when others, equally attractive or potentially viable, were not. To say that historical or economic conditions predispose a country to embark on a particular path does not mean that its politicians will necessarily decide to take it. Under different conditions—if Mao had died earlier, for example—China might have chosen a much different course. Its economic experiments before the late 1970s, the speed of Deng's final ascendance, and the astounding vector of China's transformation since 1979 all suggest a potential that could have been exploited even earlier. The same is true elsewhere. What if Edward Heath had decided, as he apparently considered, to stick with free-market reforms in the early 1970s? What if Gorbachev had chosen Deng's path for the Soviet Communist Party? Why did the shah fail when Kemal Atatürk, the shaper of the secular modern Turkish state, succeeded? Historians are not in the business of speculation; they should strive to explain why paths were taken rather than not. Yet we will never understand past events with the necessary clarity unless we retain our sense of the choices that historical actors faced at the time—leaders as well as those who followed or defied them.

In the end the counterrevolutionaries were victorious, and they achieved that victory by mastering a central contradiction that resonates today: the paradox facing those who aspire to safeguard the old by creating the new. Counterrevolutionaries can be distinguished from mere conservatives. Conservatives strive to enhance the primacy of tradition as one of several options available in the political marketplace; counterrevolutionaries seek to restore values to a world that has been deeply altered by revolution. The example of 1979 reminds us that we should pay close attention whenever politicians begin to exploit the past. Khomeini invoked Islamic traditions as he struggled to build something that had never existed before, but he did so in competition with rivals who held dramatically different visions of those same traditions; once Khomeini succeeded, he ultimately folded many of the modern state institutions created by the hated shah (and utterly unknown to the Prophet) into his new Islamic Republic. One of the notable fault lines that ran between Deng and his Maoist opponents involved an argument about who would best safeguard what was called "the fine tradition of the Communist Party." The winners, led by Deng, were those who vowed to "restore" that legacy rather than to "uphold" it. Thatcher extolled the lost virtues of family, thrift, and nation even though she ended up retaining certain features of the post-1945 welfare state. Pope John Paul II largely repudiated twentieth-century Vatican realpolitik in his search for a new church that would respond more closely to the needs of his flock in an increasingly interconnected world. Massoud and his fellow holy warriors conducted their ultraconservative jihad even as they ransacked the political toolbox of twentieth-century revolution. As many leftists have learned to their chagrin, even transparently artificial paeans to cherished and embattled values can have a powerful appeal. Memories of tradition may be highly selective, but those who would mock the "naive" nostalgia of conservatives forget that the past has an authenticity with which disembodied utopias cannot easily compete.

Similarly, a look at the events of 1979 leads us to appreciate the myriad forms that counterrevolutions can assume. Deng Xiaoping changed China's course through stealth and subtlety. Khomeini and the Afghans chose the path of violent uprising, the sudden transformative release of pent-up aggression. The only certain thing is that political and economic trends do not travel in straight lines. Yet if the experiences of 1979 suggest one conclusion, it is that we should never underestimate the power of reaction.

The twenty-first century is already witnessing an astonishing rate of social change. Genetic research promises enormous improvements in health and agriculture. Urbanization, and the rising standards of living that accompany it, continues apace. The rise of the Internet and mobile telephony accelerates the circulation of knowledge, eroding the tyranny of distance and transforming our notions of privacy and community. The spread of electoral democracy, respect for basic human rights, and advances in the status of women and sexual minorities are making remarkable strides. There are those who cite evidence of deepening secularization in some parts of the Western world and East Asia as additional proof of positive social evolution.

Yet important parts of the 1979 story argue strongly against any streamlined, simplistic view of historical progress. The huge power of genetic engineering already inspires fears of "Frankenfoods" and cloning. New communications technologies empower extremists as well as democrats. "Hacktivists" use the Internet to stage guerrilla wars against governments or corporations, while those same governments and corporations are finding that cyberspace also offers wonderful opportunities for surveillance or the exploitation of private data. It is not hard to imagine how ecological depredation and the threat of climate change could spawn radical new political movements—and perhaps even millenarian faiths. It is equally possible, of course, that the confessional fervor that has left such a strong imprint on the era since 1979—the year that also saw the founding of the Moral Majority, the vehicle of evangelically inspired political activism that dramatically affected America's political culture—could suddenly ebb and give way to something else, as future generations revolt against the excesses of their predecessors. Yet this is likely only if the advocates of the new rationalism can find satisfactory answers to the nagging metaphysical questions or forge new sources of identity that fulfill deeply rooted human needs as effectively as the old faiths.

The story is still playing itself out. But as I write these words, the political experiments of 1979 continue to define our world. The woman in the Kabul postcard lives in all of us.

ACKNOWLEDGMENTS

This book has been quite a journey, and I've been aided in it by some fine scholars and journalists who have gone before me. I'm particularly indebted to a set of remarkable writers who have chronicled the lives of this story's protagonists: George Weigel on John Paul II, Baqer Moin on Ayatollah Khomeini, Ali Rahnema on Ali Shariati, John Campbell and Hugo Young on Margaret Thatcher, and Ezra Vogel on Deng Xiaoping.

I owe particular thanks to the men and women who allowed themselves to be interviewed about their own experiences: Akbar Ayazi, Adam Boniecki, Bao Pu, C. K. Feng (Feng Zhigen), Halina Bortnowska, Jeff Muir, Jim Laurie, John Dolfin, John Fraser, Kanan Makiya, Kourosh Rakhimkani, Mohammad Hassan Kakar, Mohsen Sazegara, Norman Tebbit, Qian Gang, Rong Zhiren, Simon Heffer, Thomas Barfield, Tom Gorman, and Radek Sikorski.

I have also benefited hugely from the good advice and editorial counsel of my friends and colleagues at *Foreign Policy*—above all Susan Glasser, whose journalistic skill and editorial savvy I value as much as her friendship. Blake Hounshell, Benjamin Pauker, Charles Homans, Christina Larson, and Isaac Stone Fish have all blessed me with their know-how. My indefatigable assistants, Arianne Swieca and Neha Paliwal, kept the trains running on time.

At *The New York Review of Books*, I am deeply grateful for the guidance I received from the inestimable Robert Silvers, an avatar of fine literary style and editorial good sense. I am also much obliged to Hugh Eakin and Sasha Weiss for their countless good deeds.

I owe a special debt to Scott Moyers, who helped to bring this book to life. It has been an honor and a pleasure to work with Lara Heimert of Basic Books, the best editor in the book business. My sincerest thanks also go to Andrew Wylie and Adam Eaglin. Richard Samuels, Director of the Center for International Studies at MIT, provided invaluable organizational support and access to a peerless intellectual environment. Kourosh Rakhimkani, Thomas Barfield, and Odd Arne Westad all helped enormously by sharing their thoughts on early versions of the manuscript.

Fortune smiled upon me in the form of a fellowship from MUSE Magazine, which enabled me to spend a semester teaching at the Journalism and Media Studies Center at the University of Hong Kong. I am deeply indebted to Frank Proctor of MUSE for sponsoring the fellowship and to Ying Chan, JMSC's indefatigable director, for hosting me. I am also grateful to the Center's staff and students, especially Gao Yubing, Doreen Weisenhaus, Gene Mustain, Doug Meigs, David Bandurski, Natasha Khan, Kylie Chan, Elizabeth Cheung, Ng Pando, and Celine Zhang.

During my stay in Hong Kong I greatly benefited from conversations with Liu Kin-Ming, Jean-Francois Huchet, Tom Mitchell, and Ilaria Sala.

An intrepid band of research assistants around the world provided crucial help at various stages of the project: Lukasz Krzyzanowski in Warsaw; Li Li in Hong Kong; and Nicholas van Beek and Alexis Zimberg in Washington, DC. Kristin Deasy and Hanna Trudo lent a helping hand with fact-checking. Jessica Yellin offered a much-appreciated bit of freelance proofreading.

Roderick MacFarquhar offered useful advice at a critical juncture, and Rory MacFarquhar shared helpful background about the work of his mother Emily, a remarkable correspondent who was a member of the reporting team from *The Economist* that visited China in 1979. Nancy Hearst, Barnett Rubin, Orville Schell, Ted Plafker, and George Weigel all responded graciously to requests for information. Helena Openchowski provided urgently needed assistance with Polish translation. Felix Corley helped out by pointing the way to some highly relevant documents.

I would not have been able to write this book without the intercession of Jeff Gedmin, first at Radio Free Europe / Radio Liberty, then at Legatum. I am deeply grateful to Jeff for continuing to believe in me.

I continue to treasure the experience of working with the fine journalists at RFE/RL, starting with the remarkable John O'Sullivan, who was also good enough to share some of his experiences of working with Margaret Thatcher. Among the colleagues who contributed insights to this book are Golnaz Esfandiari, Gregory Feifer, Akbar Ayazi, Hossein Aryan, Muhammad Tahir, and Daud Khan.

I began this project during my stint at *Newsweek*, where I had the luck to work with an unrivaled group of brilliant reporters. Several of them contributed to this book, in ways both direct and indirect. Fareed Zakaria, my editor at Newsweek

International, gave crucial encouragement and advice; a better sounding board would be hard to find. Others include Andrew Nagorski, Rod Nordland, Christopher Dickey, Jeffrey Bartholet, Akiko Kashiwagi, Kay Itoi, Hideko Takayama, Fred Guterl, George Wehrfritz, Marcus Mabry, Nisid Hajari, Tony Emerson, Mark Miller, Vladimir Volkov, and Maziar Bahari. Melinda Liu, that paragon of the Beijing press corps, shared valuable advice and useful contacts.

Finally, I must thank a number of good friends who provided moral support, occasional psychotherapy, and miscellaneous practical assistance. At the top of the list is Anne Applebaum, who has helped me in so many ways that I have now lost count. I also want to make special mention of Edward Lucas and Cristina Odone, whose friendship and advice were invaluable. Others include Andrew Solomon, Ann Kjellberg, Dexter Filkins, Diane Zeleny, Benjamin Seiver, Bill Putnam, Deborah Scroggins, Dominic Ziegler, Gwen Robinson, Liz Hunt, Jeff Kingston, Jill Dougherty, Mark Lilla, Melinda Haring, Paul and Kukula Glastris, Steve LeVine and Nurilda Nurlybaeva, and Kenneth Cukier. Suzanne Black deserves a special mention for her tireless financial management.

I'm also obligated to the noble volunteers at the Brewster Ladies' Library in Brewster, Massachusetts, and the team at the public library in Bethesda, Maryland. I'm also happy to acknowledge the contribution of the staff and patrons of the Hot Chocolate Sparrow in Orleans, Massachusetts, and the Tastee Diner in Bethesda.

Finally, a special note of love and thanks goes to Ted Caryl, who is not only the best brother imaginable, but also a great banker in the bargain. And, finally, I come to my long-suffering family: Natasha, Timothy, and Alexandra. You endured my many absences and kept me going when the going got tough. I owe you a debt I can never adequately repay. I hope that you will accept this book, nonetheless, as an emblem of my love.

NOTES

PROLOGUE

1. *Keeping Faith: Memoirs of a President,* Jimmy Carter, 458.

2. *The End and the Beginning: Pope John Paul II—the Victory of Freedom, the Last Years, the Legacy,* George Weigel, 182.

3. *The Anatomy of Thatcherism,* Shirley Robin Letwin, 33–34.

4. "Teng's Cryptic Remark," Bill Roeder, *Newsweek,* December 18, 1978.

5. *The Turban for the Crown: The Islamic Revolution in Iran,* Said Amir Arjomand, 205.

6. *Restless Empire: China and the World Since 1750,* Odd Arne Westad, 378.

7. "Speech to Conservative Rally in Cardiff," April 16, 1979. http://www.margaret thatcher.org/document/104011.

CHAPTER 1: MALAISE

1. *How We Got Here: The 70s, the Decade That Brought You Modern Life (for Better or Worse),* David Frum, 10–11.

2. *Pivotal Decade: How the United States Traded Factories for Finance in the Seventies,* Judith Stein, xi.

3. *The Shock of the Global: The 1970s in Perspective,* edited by Niall Ferguson et al., 53.

4. "Malaise," Charles Maier, in ibid., 45.

5. *The Global Cold War: Third World Interventions and the Making of Our Times,* Odd Arne Westad, 334.

6. *The Battle for Britain: Thatcher and the New Liberals,* Stephen Haseler, 144.

7. "Iceland Preparing to Take IMF Loan," *London Telegraph,* October 12, 2008, http://pimpinturtle.com/2008/10/12/iceland-preparing-to-take-imf-loan.aspx.

8. "Iceland Requests $2Bn Bail-Out from IMF," David Ibison, *Financial Times,* October 24, 2008, http://www.ft.com/intl/cms/s/0/9e812fb4-a1da-11dd-a32f-000077b07658.html#axzz1Rk2KrIQX.

9. *The Necessity for Choice: Prospects of American Foreign Policy,* Henry Kissinger (Chatto & Windus, London, 1960), quoted in Westad, *Global Cold War,* 411.

10. See, for example, *The New Industrial State*, John Kenneth Galbraith.

11. "Malaise," Maier, in *Shock of the Global*, edited by Ferguson et al., 45.

12. *Shock of the Global*, edited by Ferguson et al., 84–85.

13. "The Workers," Alex Pravda, in *Poland: Genesis of a Revolution*, edited by Abraham Brumberg, 69.

14. "Karol Wojtyła, the Pope: Complications for Comrades of the Polish United Workers' Party," Marcin Zaremba. *Cold War History* 5, no. 3 (August 2005).

15. "The Pope in Poland: A Test for Communism; The Pope's Visit Tests Polish Communism," Peter Osnos, *Washington Post*, May 27, 1979.

16. *KOR: A History of the Workers' Defense Committee in Poland, 1976–1981*, Jan Józef Lipski, 176.

17. "Zbigniew Brzezinski and the Helsinki Final Act," Patrick G. Vaughan, in *The Crisis of Detente in Europe: From Helsinki to Gorbachev, 1975–1985*, edited by Leopoldo Nuti, 19.

18. Ibid., 20.

19. *Mao's Last Revolution*, Roderick MacFarquhar and Michael Schoenhals, 10.

CHAPTER 2: DRAGON YEAR

1. *Heaven Cracks, Earth Shakes: The Tangshan Earthquake and the Death of Mao's China*, James Palmer, 160.

2. *Deng Xiaoping and the Cultural Revolution: A Daughter Recalls the Critical Years*, Deng Rong, 428.

3. The name originally came from Mao, who had coined it when admonishing them not to engage in conspiracies. Aside from Jiang, the other three members of the group were Wang Hongwen, Zhang Chunqiao, and Yao Wenyuan.

4. *Deng Xiaoping and the Transformation of China*, Ezra Vogel, 40.

5. *Heaven Cracks, Earth Shakes*, Palmer, 189, 191.

6. *Deng Xiaoping and the Transformation of China*, Vogel, 26–27.

7. Ibid., 29.

8. Ibid.

9. Ibid., 32.

10. Ibid., 60.

11. Deng did not coin the phrase. It is actually an old Sichuanese proverb.

12. *The Deng Xiaoping Era: An Inquiry into the Fate of Chinese Socialism, 1978–1994*, Maurice Meisner, 82.

13. "Deng's Legacy," *MacNeil Lehrer Report (Online News Hour)*, February 25, 1997.

CHAPTER 3: "A WILD BUT WELCOMING STATE OF ANARCHY"

1. http://www.richardgregory.org.uk/history/hippie-trail-03.htm.

2. Interview with Tom Ricks, CNN, October 29, 2009, http://edition.cnn.com/TRANSCRIPTS/0910/29/ampr.01.html.

3. *An Historical Guide to Kabul*, Nancy Hatch Dupree.

4. *Afghanistan: A Cultural and Political History*, Thomas Barfield, 321. Barfield notes that there were two localized uprisings in the intervening period: the Safi rebellion of 1946 and an uprising over taxes in Kandahar in 1959. Both were short-lived affairs that were resolved as soon as the underlying grievances were addressed.

5. *The Fragmentation of Afghanistan: State Formation and Collapse in the International System*, Barnett Rubin, 65 (Pakistan edition).

6. *Afghanistan*, Barfield, 221.

7. *Fragmentation of Afghanistan*, Rubin, 70.

8. Ibid., 43.

9. Ibid., 39.

10. Ibid., 44.

CHAPTER 4: THE EMPEROR AS REVOLUTIONARY

1. *Shah of Shahs*, Ryszard Kapuściński, 56.

2. *The Turban for the Crown: The Islamic Revolution in Iran*, Said Amir Arjomand, 106–107.

3. *Iran Between Two Revolutions*, Ervand Abrahamian, 470.

4. *Daughter of Persia*, Farman Farmaian, 262–263.

5. *Occidentosis: A Plague from the West*, Jalal Al-i Ahmad, 34.

6. *Turban for the Crown*, Arjomand, 110.

7. Ibid., 85.

8. "A Persian Night of Kings, Queens, Sheiks, Sultans, and Diamonds," Charlotte Curtis, *New York Times*, October 15, 1971.

9. *The Persian Puzzle: The Conflict Between Iran and America*, Kenneth M. Pollack, 108.

10. *Turban for the Crown*, Arjomand, 11.

11. *Social Origins of the Iranian Revolution*, Misagh Parsa, 183.

CHAPTER 5: TORY INSURRECTIONISTS

1. Journalist Richard Vinen points out that the number of days lost in the industrial unrest of 1978–1979 was far smaller than the comparable figure in the General Strike of 1926. But this is a bit beside the point. Even for those who didn't experience an immediate impact, it was still hard to escape a growing impression that the United Kingdom was descending into industrial anarchy. *Thatcher's Britain*, Vinen, 96–97.

2. http://www.margaretthatcher.org/document/103924.

3. Richard Vinen in *Financial Times*, January 6, 2012, http://www.ft.com/intl/cms/s/0/f140504a-3714–11e1-b74100144feabdco.html#axzz23YMXCoxm.

4. "Commission on Social Justice: Beveridge's Appeal for an Attack on Five Giant Evils: The Beveridge Report Turned Its Author into a Hero—'The People's William,'" Nicholas Timmins, *Independent*, October 25, 1994, http://www.independent.co.uk/news/uk/commission-on-social-justice-beveridges-appeal-for-an-attack-on-five-giant-evils-the-beveridge-report-turned-its-author-into-a-hero—the-peoples-william-nicholas-timmins-reports-1444837.html.

5. *The Commanding Heights: The Battle for the World Economy*, Daniel Yergin and Joseph Stanislaw.

6. http://www.bbc.co.uk/history/worldwars/wwtwo/election_01.shtml.

7. *The Audit of War*, Correlli Barnett, 31–32.

8. http://www.politicsresources.net/area/uk/man/lab45.htm.

9. *Commanding Heights*, Yergin and Stanislaw, 22–23.

10. Ibid., 5.

11. *Keynes, the Keynesians, and Monetarism*, Tim Congdon, 2.

12. Labour Party general secretary Morgan Phillips famously remarked that "socialism in Britain owed more to Methodism than Marx."

13. http://new.gbgm-umc.org/umhistory/wesley/sermons/50/.

14. http://new.gbgm-umc.org/umhistory/wesley/sermons/92/.

15. *Margaret Thatcher, Volume One: The Grocery's Daughter*, John Campbell, 29.

16. Ibid., 57.

17. Richard Cockett, *Thinking the Unthinkable*, 167.

18. *One of Us: Life of Margaret Thatcher*, Hugo Young, 58.

19. *Margaret Thatcher, Volume One: The Grocery's Daughter*, John Campbell, 184.

20. Ibid., 179–180.

21. Ibid., 186.

22. Ibid., 186–187.

23. *Pistols at Dawn: Two Hundred Years of Political Rivalry from Pitt & Fox to Blair & Brown*, John Campbell, 336–337.

CHAPTER 6: A DREAM OF REDEMPTION

1. "A Foreign Pope," *Time*, October 30, 1978, http://www.time.com/time/magazine/article/0,9171,912229,00.html.

2. *Man from a Far Country: An Informal Portrait of Pope John Paul II*, Mary Craig, 14–15.

3. "Karol Wojtyła, the Pope: Complications for Comrades of the Polish United Workers' Party," Marcin Zaremba, 325. *Cold War History* 5, no. 3 (August 2005).

4. *The End and the Beginning: Pope John Paul II—the Victory of Freedom, the Last Years, the Legacy*, George Weigel, 100.

5. *John Paul II: Man of History*, Edward Stourton, 60.

6. *Witness to Hope: The Biography of John Paul II, 1920–2005*, George Weigel, 73.

7. http://www.allthingsbeautiful.com/all_things_beautiful/2006/03/pope_john_paul_.html.

8. *Witness to Hope*, Weigel, 130.

9. http://www.vatican.va/archive/hist_councils/ii_vatican_council/documents/vat-ii_cons_19651207_gaudium-et-spes_en.html.

10. *Witness to Hope*, Weigel, 188–193.

11. Ibid., 195.

12. *The Sword and the Shield: The Mitrokhin Archive and the Secret History of the KGB*, Christopher Andrew and Vasili Mitrokhin, 509.

13. *Man from a Far Country*, Craig, 24–25.

14. Ibid., 29.

15. *Sword and Shield*, Andrew and Mitrokhin, 512.

16. "A Pope for All the People," *Economist*, October 21, 1978.

17. "Progress or Threat," chapter 16 of *Redemptor Hominis*, Pope John Paul II, http://www.vatican.va/edocs/ENG0218/__PH.HTM#$2U.

18. *Wizyta Jana Pawła II w Polsce 1979: Dokumenty KC PZPR i MSW*, edited by Andrzej Friszke and Marcin Zaremba, 84.

19. *Sword and Shield*, Andrew and Mitrokhin, 509.

20. "Karol Wojtyła, the Pope," Zaremba, 325.

21. "Poland: Saintly Hint," *Economist*, December 30, 1978.

CHAPTER 7: THE IMAM

1. *Inside Iran: Life Under Khomeini's Regime*, John Simpson.
2. *Iran Between Two Revolutions*, Ervand Abrahamian, 531–532.
3. *Khomeini: Life of the Ayatollah*, Baqer Moin, 10.
4. Vladimir Lenin's devotion to revolution was sparked by the execution of his brother for a political offense when he was a young man.
5. *Khomeini*, Moin, 21.
6. *Creating an Islamic State: Khomeini and the Making of the New Iran*, Vanessa Martin, 35.
7. "The Shah and the Marja's Power," Manal Lufti, *al-Sharq Alawsat*, February 20, 2009.
8. *Pioneers of Islamic Revival*, Ali Rahnema, 80–81.
9. *Iran Between Two Revolutions*, Abrahamian, 425.
10. *The Turban for the Crown: The Islamic Revolution in Iran*, Said Amir Arjomand, 85.
11. *The Reign of the Ayatollahs: Iran and the Islamic Revolution*, Shaul Bakhash, 24–27.
12. Ibid., 28. See also *Turban for the Crown*, Arjomand, 86.
13. *Reign of the Ayatollahs*, Bakhash, 30.
14. Ibid., 34.
15. Ibid.
16. *Khomeini*, Moin, 52.
17. *Reign of the Ayatollahs*, Bakhash, 32–33.
18. Ibid., 38.
19. *Islam and Revolution: Writings and Declarations of Imam Khomeini (1941–1980)*, translated and annotated by Hamid Algar, 204–205.
20. *Turban for the Crown*, Arjomand, 96.
21. Ibid., 101.
22. *The Unthinkable Revolution in Iran*, Charles Kurzman, 27–28.

CHAPTER 8: WITH A GUN IN THE HAND

1. *Before Taliban: Genealogies of the Afghan Jihad*, David B. Edwards, 47.
2. Of course, one can always make the case that the United States ended up betraying (or at least qualifying) its own ideals by allying itself with anticommunist tyrants around the world—people Washington's propaganda often portrayed as "democrats" when they were no such thing. Yet there were also many cases when US presidents criticized their authoritarian allies for violating the precepts of good behavior—as when Kennedy urged the shah toward reform in the early 1960s.
3. *The Great Gamble: The Soviet War in Afghanistan*, Gregory Feifer, 21.
4. *Before Taliban*, Edwards, 128.
5. Ibid., 134–135.
6. Ibid., 139.
7. *Ghost Wars: The Secret History of the CIA, Afghanistan, and Bin Laden, from the Soviet Invasion to September 10, 2001*, Steve Coll, 114.
8. *Ghost Wars*, Steve Coll, 116.

CHAPTER 9: THE PROPHET'S PROLETARIAT

1. Author's interview with Mohsen Sazegara, Washington, DC, Jan. 7, 2010.

2. *The Turban for the Crown: The Islamic Revolution in Iran*, Said Amir Arjomand, 106–108.

3. Author's interview with Mohsen Sazegara, Jan. 7, 2010.

4. *Iran Between Two Revolutions*, Ervand Abrahamian, 464.

5. This stand against Osman, who was not related to the Prophet, also identified Abu Zarr as a prototypical Shiite, since Shiites believe that the proper line of succession to Muhammad runs through his descendants rather than his companions.

6. "In Paris at the height of the Algerian and Cuban revolutions, he immersed himself in student politics as well as radical political philosophy." Ibid., 465.

7. For a more detailed discussion of these Islamist thinkers, see Chapter 16.

8. *An Islamic Utopian: A Political Biography of Ali Shariati*, Ali Rahnema, 226.

9. Ibid., 325–326.

CHAPTER 10: TRUTH FROM FACTS

1. *Deng Xiaoping Shakes the World*, Yu Guangyuan, 21.

2. *Deng Xiaoping and the Transformation of China*, Ezra F. Vogel, 193.

3. Ezra Vogel, *Deng Xiaoping and the Transformation of China*, 103–109.

4. "The 1979 Truth Criterion Controversy," Michael Schoenhals. *The Chinese Quarterly*, no. 126 (June 1991).

5. *The Deng Xiaoping Era: An Inquiry into the Fate of Chinese Socialism, 1978–1994*, Maurice Meisner, 91.

6. Ibid.

7. *The China Reader: The Reform Era*, edited by Orville Schell and David Shambaugh, 158.

8. *Coming Alive! China After Mao*, Roger Garside, 212.

9. "China's Winds of Change," David Butler, Holger Jensen, and Lars-Erik Nelson.

10. *Coming Alive!*, Garside, 220–221.

11. Ibid., 219.

12. Ibid., 221.

13. Ibid., 215.

14. *Deng Xiaoping Shakes the World: An Eyewitness Account of China's Party Work Conference and the Third Plenum (November–December 1978)*, Yu Guangyuan, 21.

15. *Deng Xiaoping and the Transformation of China*, Vogel, 233.

16. Ibid.

17. *How the Farmers Changed China: Power of the People*, Kate Xiao Zhou, 53–54.

18. *Deng Xiaoping Shakes the World*, Yu, 52.

19. Ibid., 44, 46.

20. *Deng Xiaoping and the Transformation of China*, Vogel, 234.

21. Ibid., 234–235.

22. Hu Yaobang, who made those daring remarks about agriculture at the conference, also worked with Yu on the final version of Deng's speech.

23. *Deng Xiaoping Shakes the World*, Yu, 13.

24. Ibid., 136.

25. Ibid., 187.

26. Ibid., 132.

27. Ibid., 130, 133.

28. *The Soviet Regional Dilemma: Planning, People, and Natural Resources,* Jan Åke Dellenbrant, 99.

29. *Deng Xiaoping and the Transformation of China,* Vogel, 246.

30. "Communiqué of the Third Plenary Session of the 11th CPC Central Committee," Beijing Review.com.cn, October 10, 2008, http://www.bjreview.com.cn/special/third_plenum_17thcpc/txt/2008–10/10/content_156226_5.htm.

CHAPTER 11: THE BLOOD OF THE MARTYRS

1. *Iran Between Two Revolutions,* Ervand Abrahamian, 501.

2. Ibid.

3. Ibid., 506–507.

4. Ibid., 501.

5. Ibid., 510.

6. *The Reign of the Ayatollahs: Iran and the Islamic Revolution,* Shaul Bakhash, 47.

7. Ibid., 48.

8. *Daughter of Persia,* Sattareh Farman Farmaian, 311.

9. *Reign of the Ayatollahs,* Bakhash, 51.

10. *Daughter of Persia,* Farmaian, 321.

11. "Iran: The Shah Takes His Leave," *Time,* January 29, 1979, http://www.time.com/time/magazine/article/0,9171,912319–1,00.html.

12. The man who made the announcement was dead by the end of the year, a victim of the factional fighting that consumed the revolution.

13. *The Turban for the Crown: The Islamic Revolution in Iran,* Said Amir Arjomand, 104.

14. 14. Vanessa Martin, *Creating an Islamic State: Khomeini and the Making of a New Iran,* 103–115.

15. Ibid., 98–99.

16. *Reign of the Ayatollahs,* Bakhash, 38–39.

17. "Islamic Government," section 3 in *Islam and Revolution: Writings and Declarations of Imam Khomeini (1941–1980),* translated and annotated by Hamid Algar, 114–115.

18. *Reign of the Ayatollahs,* Bakhash, 73.

19. *Turban for the Crown,* Arjomand, 149.

20. Ibid., 134–135.

21. He spent the next twelve years organizing resistance to the Islamic Republic from French exile. In 1991 he was stabbed to death in his home by three assassins. One of them, released from prison in 2010, was received as a hero by Iranian officials upon his return to the country.

22. *Reign of the Ayatollahs,* Bakhash, 53–55.

23. *Modern Iran: Roots and Results of Revolution,* Nikki R. Keddie, 245.

24. *The Persian Puzzle: The Conflict Between Iran and America,* Kenneth Pollack, 150.

25. *Reign of the Ayatollahs,* Bakhash, 55.

26. The vote was boycotted by the leftist parties, the National Front, Bazargan's party, the Kurds, and Shariatmadari's followers. Twenty million Iranians participated. See *Persian Puzzle,* Pollack, 152.

27. *Turban for the Crown,* Arjomand, 136.

28. *Reign of the Ayatollahs*, Bakhash, 74.

29. Ibid., 79.

30. *Turban for the Crown*, Arjomand, 136.

31. *Creating an Islamic State: Khomeini and the Making of a New Iran*, Vanessa Martin, 167.

32. *Modern Iran*, Keddie, 247.

33. This body is sometimes known as the "First Assembly of Experts" to distinguish it from the second, unrelated, government body created in 1984.

34. *Reign of the Ayatollahs*, Bakhash, 80–82.

CHAPTER 12: THE LADY

1. Author's interview with Norman Tebbit, London, May 16, 2012.

2. "Speech to Conservative Rally in Cardiff," April 16, 1979, http://www.margaretthatcher.org/speeches/displaydocument.asp?docid=104011.

3. "Speech to Conservative Rally in Bolton," May 1, 1979, http://www.margaretthatcher.org/document/104065.

4. "Speech to Conservative Rally in Finchley," May 2, 1979, http://www.margaretthatcher.org/document/104072.

5. *The Collected Works of Friedrich August Hayek: The Fortunes of Liberalism*, Friedrich A. von Hayek, 238.

6. "Statement of Aims," https://www.montpelerin.org/montpelerin/mpsGoals.html.

7. *Collected Works of Hayek*, von Hayek, 14.

8. *Thinking the Unthinkable: Think-Tanks and the Economic Counter-Revolution, 1931–1983*, Richard Cockett, 122.

9. Ibid., 124.

10. Ibid., 131.

11. Ibid., 135.

12. Ibid., 141, 148–155.

13. Ibid., 157.

14. http://www.pbs.org/wgbh/commandingheights/shared/minitextlo/prof_keithjoseph.html.

15. *Thinking the Unthinkable*, Cockett, 237.

16. "The Battlefield of Ideas," Vernon Bogdanor, *New Statesman*, October 29, 2009, http://www.newstatesman.com/education/2009/11/universities-social-ideas.

17. "Monetarism Is Not Enough," Keith Joseph, April 5, 1976, http://www.margaretthatcher.org/document/110796.

CHAPTER 13: THRICE BANISHED, THRICE RESTORED

1. *Deing Xiaoping and the Transformation of China*, Ezra Vogel, 282.

2. Ibid., 342.

3. "The New China," Angus Deming, *Newsweek*, February 5, 1979.

4. "Fun and Fantasy for Teng at LBJ Space Center: Teng Underlines Positive, Finesses U.S. Problems; Accentuating the Positive, for Now," Jay Mathews, *Washington Post*, February 3, 1979.

5. "The New China," Deming.

6. *Restless Empire: China and the World Since 1750*, Odd Arne Westad, 373.

7. *Deng Xiaoping: Portrait of a Chinese Statesman*, David Shambaugh, 61–62.

8. *Coming Alive! China After Mao*, Roger Garside, 255.

9. *China's War with Vietnam, 1979: Issues, Decisions, and Implications*, King C. Chen, 151.

10. *The Deng Xiaoping Era: An Inquiry into the Fate of Chinese Socialism, 1978–1994*, Maurice Meisner, 109.

11. "The Fifth Modernization," Wei Jingsheng, 171–172, in *The China Reader: The Reform Era*, edited by Orville Schell and David Shambaugh.

12. *Sowing the Seeds of Democracy in China: Political Reform in the Deng Xiaoping Era*, Merle Goldman, 55.

13. *Deng Xiaoping Era*, Meisner, 109.

14. Ibid., 121.

15. *Selected Works of Deng Xiaoping (1975–1982)*, Deng Xiaoping, 1984.

16. *Deng Xiaoping Era*, Meisner, 11–12.

CHAPTER 14: THE EVANGELIST

1. "Sir Larry Lamb: Obituary," *Telegraph*, May 20, 2000, http://www.telegraph.co.uk/news/obituaries/1366801/Sir-Larry-Lamb.html.

2. *Seasons in the Sun: The Battle for Britain, 1974–1979*, Dominic Sandbrook, 796–797.

3. Ibid., 797–799, 805.

4. Ibid., 797–799.

5. Author's interview with Simon Heffer, January 9, 2012.

6. *Margaret Thatcher*, vol. 2, *The Iron Lady*, John Campbell, 2.

7. *The Anatomy of Thatcherism*, Shirley Robin Letwin, 89–91.

8. *Mrs. Thatcher's First Year*, Hugh Stephenson, 12.

9. "Thatcher: Key Tests After a Bold Start; Thatcher's Boldness Surprises Britain in First 100 Days; News Analysis," Leonard Downie Jr., *Washington Post* Foreign Service, August 12, 1979.

10. *The Anatomy of Thatcherism*, Letwin, 39–41.

11. Ibid., 126–127.

12. *One of Us: Life of Margaret Thatcher*, Hugo Young, 149.

13. *Margaret Thatcher*, Campbell, 2:22.

14. *Thatcher and Sons: A Revolution in Three Acts*, Simon Jenkins, 54.

15. *One of Us*, Young, 149.

16. "John Sergeant: The Day Margaret Thatcher and I Made History," John Sergeant, *Daily Telegraph*, May 1, 2009, http://www.telegraph.co.uk/news/politics/margaret-thatcher/5258306/John-Sergeant-The-day-Margaret-Thatcher-and-I-made-history.html.

17. *One of Us*, Young, 137–138.

18. As cited in *Thatcher and Sons*, Jenkins, 47.

19. Ibid., 52.

20. Ibid., 56.

21. *A Balance of Power*, James Prior, 138.

22. Ibid., 111.

23. *One of Us*, Young, 150.

24. *Balance of Power*, Prior, 119.

25. Ibid., 122.

26. *Thatcher and Sons*, Jenkins, 59.

27. The Thatcherites, for their part, complained bitterly about presumed obstruction to their policies by the left-wing BBC.

28. "Ideological Change in the British Conservative Party," Ivor Crewe and Donald D. Searing, 376, as seen in "Thatcher and the British Election of 1979: Taxes, Nationalization, and Unions Run Amok," Matthew Greeson, *Colgate Academic Review* 4, no. 3 (2012), http://commons.colgate.edu/cgi/viewcontent.cgi?article=1060andcontext=car.

29. "Popular Versus Elite Views of Privatization: The Case of Britain," Ian McAllister and Donley T. Studlar, 157.

30. *Thatcher and Sons*, Jenkins, 151.

CHAPTER 15: ELEVEN MILLION PEOPLE

1. There is some evidence, indeed, that the pope picked Mexico as the destination of his first overseas pilgrimage precisely as a sort of challenge to the Polish government. If the pontiff could enjoy a warm welcome in a country with a long and virulent history of official anticlericalism, how would Poland look by comparison if it refused him?

2. Interview with Adam Boniecki, Warsaw, October 5, 2011.

3. *The End and the Beginning: Pope John Paul II—the Victory of Freedom, the Last Years, the Legacy*, George Weigel, 110.

4. *Der Papst, die Polen und die Freiheit*, http://www.ardmediathek.de/ard/servlet/content/3517136?documentId=7047176.

5. "Poland: Preliminary Thunder," *Economist*, May 5, 1979.

6. *The Polish Revolution: Solidarity*, Timothy Garton Ash, 280.

7. *Witness to Hope*, George Weigel, 305.

8. Ibid., 1.

9. "Homily of His Holiness John Paul II, Victory Square, Warsaw," June 2, 1979, http://www.vatican.va/holy_father/john_paul_ii/homilies/1979/documents/hf_jp-ii_hom_19790602_polonia-varsavia_en.html.

10. *Der Papst, die Polen und die Freiheit*, http://www.ardmediathek.de/ard/servlet/content/3517136?documentId=7047176.

11. "Everything Changed After John Paul's Speech in Warsaw," Norman Webster, *The Gazette* (Montreal), July 19, 2009.

12. "Pope Urges Rights for Fellow Slavs; Pope Voices Concern for Christians in Eastern Europe, Addresses Fate of Christians in Eastern Europe," Michael Getler, *Washington Post*, June 4, 1979.

13. "Can You Hear Me?," *Economist*, June 9, 1979.

14. "Homily for the Pilgrims from Lower Silesia and Silesia," Częstochowa, June 5, 1979, http://www.vatican.va/holy_father/john_paul_ii/homilies/1979/documents/hf_jp-ii_hom_19790605_polonia-jasna-gora-slesia_en.html.

15. "Homily for the Workers from Silesia and Zaglebie," Częstochowa, June 6, 1979, http://www.vatican.va/holy_father/john_paul_ii/homilies/1979/documents/hf_jp-ii_hom_19790606_polonia-jasna-gora-operai_en.html.

16. Ibid.

17. "Poland Indicates Irritation About Pope's Comments," Peter Osnos and Michael Getler, *Washington Post*, June 6, 1979.

18. http://libpro.cts.cuni.cz/charta/docs/declaration_of_charter_77.pdf.

19. "A Lesson in Dignity," in *Letters from Prison, and Other Essays*, Adam Michnik, 160.

20. "Pope Urges Rights for Fellow Slavs," Getler.

21. *Der Papst, die Polen und die Freiheit*, interview with Grażyna Oziemska, http://www.ardmediathek.de/ard/servlet/content/3517136?documentId=7047176.

22. *The Polish Revolution: Solidarity*, Timothy Garton Ash, 32.

23. "Pontiff Honors Victims of Nazis; Pope Commemorates Nazis' Victims at Auschwitz," Peter Osnos, *Washington Post*, June 7, 2011.

24. *Washington Post*, June 9, 2011.

25. *Washington Post*, June 10, 2011.

26. *New York Times*, June 5, 1979, quoted in *End and the Beginning*, Weigel, 915.

CHAPTER 16: BACK TO THE FUTURE

1. *Afghanistan: A New History*, Martin Ewans, 140.

2. "Revolution in Afghanistan," Fred Halliday.

3. *Revolution Unending: Afghanistan, 1979 to the Present*, Giles Dorronsoro, 98–104.

4. *The Tragedy of Afghanistan: A First-Hand Account*, Raja Anwar, 156.

5. *Islam and Resistance in Afghanistan*, Olivier Roy, 108.

6. *The Great Gamble: The Soviet War in Afghanistan*, Gregory Feifer, 30.

7. Ibid., 31.

8. *Before Taliban: Genealogies of the Afghan Jihad*, David B. Edwards, 154.

9. One source cited by David Edwards estimated 80 percent of locals supported tribal unity, 15 to 20 percent the government, and less than 5 percent the Islamic parties.

10. Ibid., 154.

11. *Islam and Resistance*, Roy, 108.

12. *The Turban for the Crown: The Islamic Revolution in Iran*, Said Amir Arjomand, 104.

13. *The Battle for God: Fundamentalism in Judaism, Christianity, and Islam*, Karen Armstrong, 238.

14. Ibid., 294–298.

15. *Journey of the Jihadist: Inside Muslim Militancy*, Fawaz Gerges, 63–64.

16. *Turban for the Crown*, Arjomand, 99.

17. Ibid., 101.

18. *The Siege of Mecca: The Forgotten Uprising in Islam's Holiest Shrine and the Birth of al-Qaeda*, Yaroslav Trofimov, 224–225.

19. The best account of the mosque takeover, which I have relied on heavily here, is provided by Yaroslav Trofimov's book *Siege of Mecca*.

20. *Before Taliban*, Edwards.

21. Ibid., 212.

22. *Ghost Wars: The Secret History of the CIA, Afghanistan, and Bin Laden, from the Soviet Invasion to September 10, 2001*, Steve Coll, 113.

23. *Before Taliban*, Edwards, 249–252.

24. *Ghost Wars*, Coll, 114.

25. "Guerrillas Use Cease-Fire to Rearm," William Branigin, *Washington Post*, October 18, 1983.

CHAPTER 17: THE SECOND REVOLUTION

1. I say "quasi-colonial" because Iran was not formally the colony of any foreign powers—though many Iranians undoubtedly felt that way.

2. *The Eagle and the Lion: The Tragedy of American-Iranian Relations*, James A. Bill, 159–160, http://lawrecord.com/files/34_Rutgers_L_Rec_39.pdf.

3. "U.S. Embassy Stormed by Tehran Mob," Nicholas Cumming-Bruce, *Guardian*, February 15, 1979, http://century.guardian.co.uk/1970–1979/Story/0,,106889,00.html.

4. *Guests of the Ayatollah: The Iran Hostage Crisis, the First Battle in America's War with Militant Islam*, Mark Bowden, 212.

5. "Iran Hostage's Diary: Robert C. Ode, Nov. 4, 1979, Through July 8, 1980," http://www.jimmycarterlibrary.gov/documents/r_ode/Ode_pages1thru50.pdf.

6. Ibid.

7. *Guests of the Ayatollah*, Bowden, 183.

8. *The Reign of the Ayatollahs: Iran and the Islamic Revolution*, Shaul Bakhash, 65.

9. Again, this body should not be confused with the later government organization created in the course of another round of constitutional reform in 1984. See Chapter 11.

10. Only men were eligible, needless to say (which is odd, since there are female clerics).

11. "Iran's Politics: The Supreme Leader," Karim Sadjapour, in *The Iran Primer: Power, Politics, and U.S. Policy*, 12.

12. *Reign of the Ayatollahs*, Bakhash, 83.

13. *Modern Iran: Roots and Results of Revolution*, Nikki R. Keddie, 195.

14. Ibid., 249.

CHAPTER 18: PLAYING BRIDGE

1. Author's interview with Rong Zhiren, Guangzhou, April 9, 2010.

2. "Rong Yiren, a Chinese Billionaire, Dies at 89," David Barboza, *New York Times*, October 28, 2005, http://www.nytimes.com/2005/10/28/obituaries/28rong.html?fta=y.

3. Author's interview with Tom Gorman, Hong Kong, March 10, 2010.

4. http://www.creativebrief.com/blog/2011/07/15/market-leader-interview-graham-fink-ogilvy-china/.

5. Author's interview with Jeff Muir, Hong Kong, May 5, 2010.

6. *"Watch Out for the Foreign Guests!" China Encounters the West*, Orville Schell, 54–55.

7. Ibid., 22–23.

8. Author's interview with Qian Gang, Hong Kong, May 10, 2010.

9. "Teresa Teng, Singer, 40, Dies; Famed in Asia for Love Songs," Sheryl WuDunn, *New York Times*, May 10, 1995, http://www.nytimes.com/1995/05/10/obituaries/teresa-teng-singer-40-dies-famed-in-asia-for-love-songs.html.

10. Interview with Muir.

11. *Broken Earth: The Rural Chinese*, Steven W. Mosher, 37–38.

12. Ibid., 40.

13. "Xiaogang Village, Birthplace of Rural Reform, Moves On," Wang Ke, China.org. cn, December 15, 2008, http://www.china.org.cn/china/features/content_16955209.htm.

14. *How the Farmers Changed China: Power of the People,* by Kate Xiao Zhou, 56.

15. "Xiaogang Village, Birthplace of Rural Reform, Moves On," Ke.

16. Ibid.

17. "Farmers Who Provided the Spark," Raymond Li, *South China Morning Post,* November 17, 2008.

18. *How the Farmers Changed China,* Zhou, 53–54.

19. "Xiaogang Village, Birthplace of Rural Reform, Moves On," Ke.

20. *How the Farmers Changed China,* Zhou, 53–54.

21. http://mengwah.wordpress.com/2011/03/31/3-1-reforming-the-agricultural-sector-contract-responsibility-system/.

22. "China in the 1980s," *Economist,* December 29, 1979.

23. *Hungry Ghosts,* Jasper Becker, 262.

24. *Agrarian Radicalism in China, 1968–1981,* David Zweig, 180. See also "Summary of Experiences in Rural Economic Restructuring in Experimental Counties in Guanghan, Qionglai, and Xindu Counties of Sichuan Province," Gui Yuwen, *Jingji Guanli,* April 15, 1982 (in *China Report: Economic Affairs* 238, Foreign Broadcast Information Service, June 9, 1982).

25. Interview with Zhong Taiyin, *The China Boom Project,* Asia Society, http://china-boom.asiasociety.org/bio/detail/219.

26. *Broken Earth,* Mosher, 44.

27. Author's interview with Tom Gorman, Hong Kong, March 10, 2010.

28. *Deng Xiaoping Shakes the World: An Eyewitness Account of China's Party Work Conference and the Third Plenum (November–December 1978),* Yu Guangyuan, 204–205.

29. Ibid., 188.

30. *Deng Xiaoping and the Transformation of China,* Ezra Vogel, 221–223.

31. Ibid., 397.

32. Interview with C. K. Feng, April 8, 2010.

33. *Deng Xiaoping Shakes the World,* Yu, 399.

34. Author's interview with Rong Zhiren, Guangzhow, April 9, 2010.

CHAPTER 19: FRATERNAL ASSISTANCE

1. Karmal had actually been offered a cabinet post under President Daoud, who was eager to see the Parchamis shore up his government, but had declined.

2. "Revolution in Afghanistan," Fred Halliday, 41.

3. *The Great Gamble: The Soviet War in Afghanistan,* Gregory Feifer, 19.

4. Ibid., 33.

5. *Afghanistan: The Soviet Invasion and the Afghan Response, 1979–1982,* M. Hassan Kakar, 36.

6. *Great Gamble,* Feifer, 42.

7. Ibid., 42–43.

8. Ibid., 46–47. Compare the account in *Afghanistan,* Kakar, 39.

9. *The Global Cold War: Third World Interventions and the Making of Our Times,* Odd Arne Westad, 313.

10. Barry Shlachter, Associated Press, September 17, 1979.

11. Ibid.

12. "Foes 'Eliminated,' Afghan Leader Says," Stuart Auerbach, *Washington Post*, September 18, 1979.

13. *Great Gamble*, Feifer, 52–53. One of the Afghans involved in the operation, Said Mohammed Guliabzoi, disputes the Soviet account of events, saying that he stayed in the country to coordinate the resistance to Amin. Ibid., 56.

14. *Global Cold War*, Westad, 313.

15. "Concerning the Situation in 'A': New Russian Evidence on the Soviet Intervention in Afghanistan," Odd Arne Westad, *Cold War International History Project Bulletin*, 130, http://www.wilsoncenter.org/sites/default/files/e-dossier_4.pdf. See also *Global Cold War*, Westad, 311.

16. *Failed Empire*, Zubok, 262.

17. *Afghanistan*, Kakar, 42 (see "Stumbling Toward War").

18. "Concerning the Situation in 'A,'" Westad, 128.

19. *Global Cold War*, Westad, 315.

20. *Great Gamble*, Feifer, 13.

21. Ibid., 43.

22. *Global Cold War*, Westad, 318.

23. Ibid., 319.

24. *Failed Empire*, Zubok, 263.

25. *Global Cold War*, Westad, 321ff.

26. *Great Gamble*, Feifer, 77–78.

27. *Global Cold War*, Westad, 326.

28. Now known once again by its prerevolutionary name, Lubyanka Square.

29. *KGB in Afghanistan*, Mitrokhin, 95.

CHAPTER 20: SOLIDARITY

1. *The Polish Revolution: Solidarity*, Timothy Garton Ash, 43.

2. Ibid.

3. *Pilgrim to Poland: John Paul II*, compiled by the Daughters of St. Paul, 182.

4. Ibid., 185.

5. Ibid., 184–185.

6. *The Polish Revolution: Solidarity*, Ash, 35; *From Solidarity to Martial Law: The Polish Crisis of 1980–1981—a Documentary History*, edited by Andrzej Paczkowski and Malcolm Byrne, xxxi.

7. *From Solidarity to Martial Law*, edited by Paczkowski and Byrne, xxxix.

8. In Andrzej Wajda's marvelous film account of the Solidarity movement, *Man of Marble* (1980), the cynical journalist sent to Gdańsk to collect compromising material on the strikers soon discovers, to his horror, that there is not a drop of booze to be found in the city.

9. *KOR: A History of the Workers' Defense Committee in Poland, 1976–1981*, Jan Józef Lipski, 176.

10. *The Sword and the Shield: The Mitrokhin Archive and the Secret History of the KGB*, Christopher Andrew and Vasili Mitrokhin, 515. The Vatican II reference comes from *The Polish Revolution: Solidarity*, Ash.

11. *The Polish Revolution: Solidarity*, Ash, 294.

12. Ibid., 276.

13. "In Search of Lost Meaning," in *In Search of Lost Meaning: The New Eastern Europe*, Adam Michnik, 28–29.

14. *The Polish Revolution: Solidarity*, Ash, 304.

15. *Witness to Hope: The Biography of Pope John Paul II, 1920–2005*, George Weigel, 460.

16. *The End and the Beginning: Pope John Paul II—the Victory of Freedom, the Last Years, the Legacy*, George Weigel, 113.

17. "Obituary: Cardinal Frantisek Tomasek," Felix Corley, *Independent*, August 5, 1992, http://www.independent.co.uk/news/people/obituary-cardinal-frantisek-tomasek-1538238.html.

18. "The Inspiration for a Workers' Revolution," Michael Dobbs, *Washington Post*, April 3, 2005, http://www.washingtonpost.com/wp-dyn/articles/A22109–2005Apr2.html.

CHAPTER 21: KHOMEINI'S CHILDREN

1. "The Islamic Republic of Iran, 1979–1989," Shaul Bakhash, 58.

2. Ibid., 59.

3. Yet another example, it would seem, of conservatives borrowing from the radical left.

4. "The Islamic Republic of Iran, 1979–1989," Shaul Bakhash.

5. *Khomeini: Life of the Ayatollah*, Baqer Moin, 247.

6. *The Turban for the Crown: The Islamic Revolution in Iran*, Said Amir Arjomand, 5.

7. *Khomeinism: Essays on the Islamic Republic*, Ervand Abrahamian, http://www.escholarship.org/editions/view?docId=ft6c6006wp;query=20iran;brand=ucpress.

8. *The Reign of the Ayatollahs: Iran and the Islamic Revolution*, Shaul Bakhash, 36.

9. See "Religious Participation Among Muslims: Iranian Exceptionalism," Gunes Murat Tezcur, Taghi Azadarmaki, and Mehri Bahar, in *Critique: Critical Middle Eastern Studies 15*, no. 3 (2006): 217–232, http://web.clas.ufl.edu/users/kenwald/pos6292/Tezcur%20et%20all%20Critique%202006.pdf.

10. "Islamic Republic of Iran," Bakhash, 55–56.

11. *1979: The Year That Shaped the Modern Middle East*, David W. Lesch, 119.

12. Ibid., 162–163.

13. "Islamic Republic of Iran," Bakhash, 57.

14. *1979*, Lesch, 161, quoting "Conceptual Sources of the Post-Revolutionary Iranian Behavior Toward the Arab World," Mahmood Sariolghalam, in *Iran and the Arab World*, Hooshab Amirahmadi and Nader Entessar, 22.

15. *Creating an Islamic State: Khomeini and the Making of a New Iran*, Vanessa Martin, 193.

16. "Islamic Republic of Iran," Bakhash, 57.

17. *The Global Cold War: Third World Interventions and the Making of Our Times*, Odd Arne Westad, 299.

18. For all their grand global aspirations, the Chinese do not believe that their culture applies to anyone but the Chinese and show little evidence of wishing to impose it on alien races.

CHAPTER 22: JIHAD

1. *Defense of Muslim Lands*, Sheikh Abdullah Azzam, xix–xx.

2. Ibid., 16–17.

3. Azzam, it should be noted, was a fully qualified religious scholar—something that could not even remotely be said of Osama bin Laden, though this did not stop him from issuing legal rulings.

4. *The Looming Tower: Al-Qaeda and the Road to 9/11*, Lawrence Wright, 95–96.

5. Ibid., 130.

6. "Blowback from the Afghan Battlefield," Tim Weiner, *New York Times*, March 13, 1994.

7. "Terrorism Havens: Indonesia," Council on Foreign Relations, 2005, http://www.cfr.org/indonesia/terrorism-havens-indonesia/p9361.

8. *The Fragmentation of Afghanistan: State Formation and Collapse in the International System*, Barnett Rubin, 227.

CHAPTER 23: "THE LADY'S NOT FOR TURNING"

1. In the early 1930s, joblessness reached 3 million (about 30 percent).

2. *Britain Under Thatcher*, Anthony Seldon and Daniel Collings, 14.

3. "The Lady's Not for Turning," Margaret Thatcher, *Guardian*, April 29, 2007, http://www.guardian.co.uk/politics/2007/apr/30/conservatives.uk.

4. *The Lady's Not for Burning*, Christopher Fry (1948).

5. "Strength in the Face of Adversity," Simon Jenkins, *Guardian*, April 30, 2007, http://www.guardian.co.uk/politics/2007/apr/30/conservatives.uk2.

6. *Britain Under Thatcher*, Seldon and Collings, 15.

7. *Thatcher and Sons: A Revolution in Three Acts*, Simon Jenkins, 61.

8. *One of Us: Life of Margaret Thatcher*, Hugo Young, 107.

9. Ibid., 136.

10. "The First Few Months" (Thatcher's notes for a conference speech, October 3, 1979), http://www.margaretthatcher.org/document/899D539506F54F5FBBBB75AD5B018C94.pdf.

11. *Keynes, the Keynesians, and Monetarism*, Tim Congdon, 8.

12. *A Balance of Power*, James Prior, 121.

13. *Thinking the Unthinkable: Think-Tanks and the Economic Counter-Revolution, 1931–1983*, Richard Cockett, 287.

14. "It Is Time for Britain's Economy to Buck Up," Samuel Brittan, *Financial Times*, July 7, 2011.

15. *Thinking the Unthinkable*, Cockett, 323.

16. *Margaret Thatcher*, John Campbell, 2:709–710.

17. Imitation is the sincerest form of flattery, and it is worth noting that the British Left took a page from Thatcher's playbook in the 1980s and 1990s by founding its own think tanks modeled on those that fueled the market "counterrevolution." Richard Cockett cites Martin Jacques's Demos, which, he says, "owes much of its inspiration to the working methods of the IEA, and in particular the work of Arthur Seldon." *Thinking the Unthinkable*, Cockett, 328.

18. Ibid., 322.

19. *Thatcher and Thatcherism*, edited by Eric J. Evans, 139.

20. *National Review*, Tim Congdon, 1993.

21. *Thinking the Unthinkable*, Cockett, 324.

22. "Balcerowicz Plan: 20 Years On," *Warsaw Voice*, December 16, 2009, http://www.warsawvoice.pl/WVpage/pages/article.php/21501/article.

23. Chicago School economists engineered the free-market economic reform program implemented by General Augusto Pinochet in Chile in 1973 (after the bloody coup in which he toppled his predecessor as president, Salvador Allende). The program was a resounding success that strongly influenced many other governments around Latin America—though those who implemented similar policies often thankfully did so in tandem with political liberalization as well.

24. *Thinking the Unthinkable*, Cockett, 306.

25. Ibid., 307.

26. *The Commanding Heights: The Battle for the World Economy*, Daniel Yergin and Joseph Stanislaw, 219.

27. Ibid., 233.

28. Ibid., 258.

29. *Margaret Thatcher*, Campbell, 2:625.

30. *National Review*, Congdon, 1993.

CHAPTER 24: SOCIALISM WITH CHINESE CHARACTERISTICS

1. "Crossing the River While Feeling the Rocks: Land-Tenure Reform in China," John W. Bruce and Zongmin Li, International Food Policy Research Institute, Washington, DC, 2009, http://www.ifpri.org/publication/crossing-river-while-feeling-rocks.

2. Fujian was also home to the Xiamen Special Economic Zone, the only SEZ created in 1979 that was outside of Guangdong Province.

3. "The Course of China's Rural Reform," Du Runsheng, International Food Policy Research Institute, 2006, 6, http://www.ifpri.org/sites/default/files/publications/oc52.pdf.

4. *Capitalism with Chinese Characteristics*, Huang Yasheng, 50–100.

5. *Special Economic Zones and the Economic Transition in China*, Wei Ge, 47.

6. Ibid., 49.

7. Ibid., 47.

8. Ibid., 68.

9. Ibid., 75.

10. *The Search for Modern China*, Jonathan Spence, 715–716.

11. "'Two Faces' of Deng Xiaoping," Bao Tong, Radio Free Asia, December 29, 2008.

12. "June 9 Speech to Martial Law Units," Deng Xiaoping, http://tsquare.tv/chronology/Deng.html.

13. *Deng Xiaoping and the Transformation of China*, Ezra Vogel, 659–660.

14. Ibid.

15. "Deng's Last Campaign," Roderick MacFarquhar, *New York Review of Books*, December 17, 1992.

16. Ibid.

17. Ibid.

18. *Deng Xiaoping and the Transformation of China*, Vogel, 697.

19. *The Global Cold War: Third World Interventions and the Making of Our Times*, Odd Arne Westad, 362.

EPILOGUE

1. *The Progress of Socialism: A Lecture by Sidney Webb, LL.B.* (Modern Press, London, 1890), http://archive.org/details/progressofsocialoowebbuoft.

2. *The Unthinkable Revolution in Iran*, Charles Kurzman, 99.

3. See "The Religious Mind of Mrs. Thatcher," Antonio E. Weiss. www.margaretthatcher.org/document/112748.

4. See *The Final Revolution: The Resistance Church and the Collapse of Communism*, George Weigel.

5. *The Communist Manifesto*, Marxists Internet Archive, 20, http://www.marxists.org/archive/marx/works/download/pdf/Manifesto.pdf.

6. Khomeini, "Speech at Feyziyeh Theological School," August 24, 1979; in *Anti-American Terrorism and the Middle East: A Documentary Reader*, Barry Rubin and Judith Colp Rubin, 34. Oxford University Press, USA, 2004.

7. "What Is Man Afraid Of?," *Redemptor Hominis*, John Paul II, http://www.vatican.va/edocs/ENG0218/__PG.HTM#$2Q.

8. Kanan Makiya, interview with the author, Cambridge, MA, September 29, 2009.

9. "Mohammed Bouazizi: The Dutiful Son Whose Death Changed Tunisia's Fate," Peter Beaumont, *Guardian*, January 20, 2011, http://www.guardian.co.uk/world/2011/jan/20/tunisian-fruit-seller-mohammed-bouazizi.

10. "A Shi'ite Victory That Subverted Shi'ite Tradition," Jeffrey Donovan, Radio Free Europe/Radio Liberty, February 10, 2009.

11. For a more detailed exploration of modern Shenzhen, see *Postcards from Tomorrow Square: Reports from China*, James Fallows.

12. "China Internal Security Spending Jumps Past Army Budget," Chris Buckley, Reuters, March 5, 2011, http://www.reuters.com/article/2011/03/05/china-unrest-idUSTOE72400920110305.

13. *Marketing Dictatorship: Propaganda and Thought Work in Contemporary China*, Anne-Marie Brady, 2.

14. See especially "Arise, Slaves, Arise!," in *Out of Mao's Shadow: The Struggle for the Soul of a New China*, Philip P. Pan, 113–146.

15. For a detailed description of these Chinese studies, see *China's Communist Party: Atrophy and Adaptation*, David Shambaugh.

16. *Creating Wealth and Poverty in Postsocialist China*, edited by Deborah S. Davis and Wang Feng, 6.

17. One much-noted novel from the early reform period, by the writer Dai Hou Ying, was entitled simply *Human*.

18. It is, of course, possible that the model in question was a foreigner. Even so, I argue her worth as a symbol of the secular future to which many Afghans genuinely aspired in the 1970s.

19. The post-2001 history of Afghanistan would probably have taken a dramatically different course had Ahmad Shah Massoud not fallen victim to al-Qaeda suicide bombers in September 2001. (This was after the KGB and his rivals among the mujahideen had repeatedly attempted to kill him during the 1980s.) Of the other leaders treated in this book, Deng Xiaoping, true to his extraordinary talent for survival, probably leads the pack in number of attacks survived; fanatical Maoists, who never forgave him for his heresy, repeatedly tried to kill him. John Paul II survived the 1981 attempt on his life by the Turkish assassin Mehmet

Ali Ağca (under circumstances that remain the subject of some dispute). The shah considered executing Khomeini during his arrest in 1964, but was dissuaded when senior clerics awarded Khomeini the title of "ayatollah," thus making it politically unfeasible for the shah to lay a hand on him. Finally, Margaret Thatcher survived a bomb planted in her hotel by Irish Republican terrorists during the Conservative Party conference in Brighton in 1984.

BIBLIOGRAPHY

Afghanistan: A Cultural and Political History, Thomas Barfield. Princeton University Press, Princeton, NJ, 2010.

Afghanistan: A New History, Martin Ewans. Curzon Press, London, 2001.

Afghanistan: The Soviet Invasion and the Afghan Response, 1979–1982, Mohammad Hassan Kakar. University of California Press, Berkeley and Los Angeles, 1995.

After Khomeini: Iran Under His Successors, Said Amir Arjomand. Oxford University Press, Oxford, 2009.

Agrarian Radicalism in China, 1968–1981, David Zweig. Harvard University Press, Cambridge, MA, 1989.

All the Shah's Men: An American Coup and the Roots of Middle East Terror, Stephen Kinzer. Wiley & Sons, Hoboken, NJ, 2008 (original ed., 2003).

The Anatomy of Thatcherism, Shirley Robin Letwin. Transaction, New Brunswick, NJ, 1993.

The Audit of War, Correlli Barnett. Pan, London, 2001.

A Balance of Power, James Prior. Hamish Hamilton, London, 1986.

A Failed Empire: The Soviet Union in the Cold War from Stalin to Gorbachev, Vladislav N. Zubok. University of North Carolina Press, Chapel Hill, 2008.

The Battle for Britain: Thatcher and the New Liberals, Stephen Haseler. I. B. Tauris, London, 1989.

The Battle for God: Fundamentalism in Judaism, Christianity, and Islam, Karen Armstrong. HarperCollins, London, 2000.

Before Taliban: Genealogies of the Afghan Jihad, David B. Edwards. University of California Press, Berkeley and Los Angeles, 2002.

Britain Under Thatcher, Anthony Seldon and Daniel Collings. Pearson Education, Harlow, UK, 2000.

Broken Earth: The Rural Chinese, Steven W. Mosher. Free Press, New York, 1983.

Burying Mao: Chinese Politics in the Age of Deng Xiaoping, Richard Baum. Princeton University Press, Princeton, NJ, 1994.

Capitalism and Freedom: Fortieth Anniversary Edition, Milton Friedman. University of Chicago Press, Chicago, 1962.

Capitalism with Chinese Characteristics, Huang Yasheng. Cambridge University Press, New York, 2008.

The Case of the Gang of Four, with First Translations of Teng Hsiao-Ping's "Three Poisonous Weeds," Chi Hsin. Cosmos Books, Hong Kong, 1977.

China and the Legacy of Deng Xiaoping: From Communist Revolution to Capitalist Evolution, Michael E. Marti. Brassey's, Dulles, VA, 2002.

China Guidebook: 1980/81 Edition, Arne J. de Keijzer and Frederic M. Kaplan. Eurasia Press, New York, 1980.

The China Reader: The Reform Era, edited by Orville Schell and David Shambaugh. Vintage Books, New York, 1999.

China's Communist Party: Atrophy and Adaptation, David Shambaugh. University of California Press, Berkeley, 2009.

China's War with Vietnam, 1979: Issues, Decisions, and Implications, King C. Chen. Hoover Institution Press, Stanford, CA, 1987.

"China's Winds of Change," David Butler, Holger Jensen, and Lars-Erik Nelson. *Newsweek*, December 11, 1978.

The Church and the Left, Adam Michnik. University of Chicago Press, Chicago, 1993.

The Collected Works of Friedrich August Hayek: The Fortunes of Liberalism, Friedrich A. von Hayek. University of Chicago Press, Chicago, 1992.

Coming Alive! China After Mao, Roger Garside. Andre Deutsch, London, 1981.

The Commanding Heights: The Battle for the World Economy, Daniel Yergin and Joseph Stanislaw. Simon & Schuster, New York, 1998.

Creating an Islamic State: Khomeini and the Making of a New Iran, Vanessa Martin. I. B. Tauris, London, 2007.

Creating Wealth and Poverty in Postsocialist China, edited by Deborah S. Davis and Feng Wang. Stanford University Press. Palo Alto, CA, 2008.

The Crisis of Detente in Europe: From Helsinki to Gorbachev, 1975–1985, edited by Leopoldo Nuti. Routledge, London, 2008.

Daughter of Persia, Sattareh Farman Farmaian. Bantam Press, London, 1992.

Defense of Muslim Lands, Sheikh Abdullah Azzam. 2nd ed. Azzam Publications, London, 2002.

Deng: A Political Biography, Benjamin Yang. East Gate Books, Armonk, NY, 1998.

Deng Xiaoping: Chronicle of an Empire, Ruan Ming, translated and edited by Nancy Liu, Peter Rand, and Lawrence R. Sullivan. Westview Press, Boulder, CO, 1994.

Deng Xiaoping: My Father, Deng Maomao. Basic Books, New York, 1995.

Deng Xiaoping: Portrait of a Chinese Statesman, David Shambaugh. Oxford University Press, New York, 1995.

Deng Xiaoping and the Chinese Revolution: A Political Biography, David S. G. Goodman. Routledge, New York, 1994.

Deng Xiaoping and the Cultural Revolution: A Daughter Recalls the Critical Years, Deng Rong. Doubleday, New York, 2005.

Deng Xiaoping and the Making of Modern China, Richard Evans. Penguin Books, New York, 1995.

Deng Xiaoping and the Transformation of China, Ezra Vogel. Belknap Press of Harvard University Press, Cambridge, MA, 2011.

The Deng Xiaoping Era: An Inquiry into the Fate of Chinese Socialism, 1978–1994, Maurice Meisner. Hill and Wang, New York, 1996.

Deng Xiaoping Shakes the World: An Eyewitness Account of China's Party Work Conference and the Third Plenum (November–December 1978), Yu Guangyuan, edited by Ezra Vogel and Steven I. Levine. EastBridge, Norwalk, CT, 2004.

The Downing Street Years, Margaret Thatcher. HarperCollins, London, 1993.

The End and the Beginning: Pope John Paul II—the Victory of Freedom, the Last Years, the Legacy, George Weigel. Doubleday, New York, 2010.

"Everything Changed After John Paul's Speech in Warsaw," Norman Webster, *The Gazette,* July 19, 2009.

The Fall of the Shah, Fereydoun Hoveyda. Wyndham Books, New York, 1980.

The Final Revolution: The Resistance Church and the Collapse of Communism, George Weigel. Oxford University Press, Oxford, 1992.

The Fragmentation of Afghanistan: State Formation and Collapse in the International System, Barnett Rubin. Yale University Press, New Haven, CT, 2002.

From Solidarity to Martial Law: The Polish Crisis of 1980–1981—a Documentary History, edited by Andrzej Paczkowski and Malcolm Byrne. Central European University Press, Budapest and New York, 2007.

Full Circle: A Homecoming to Free Poland, Radek Sikorski. Simon & Schuster, New York, 1997.

Ghost Wars: The Secret History of the CIA, Afghanistan, and Bin Laden, from the Soviet Invasion to September 10, 2001, Steve Coll. Penguin Books, New York, 2004.

The Global Cold War: Third World Interventions and the Making of Our Times, Odd Arne Westad. Cambridge University Press, Cambridge, 2007.

Globalized Islam: The Search for a New Ummah, Olivier Roy. CERI Series in Comparative Politics and International Studies. Columbia University Press, New York, 2004.

The Great Gamble: The Soviet War in Afghanistan, Gregory Feifer. HarperCollins, New York, 2009.

Guests of the Ayatollah: The Iran Hostage Crisis, the First Battle in America's War with Militant Islam, Mark Bowden. Grove Press, New York, 2006.

Heaven Cracks, Earth Shakes: The Tangshan Earthquake and the Death of Mao's China, James Palmer. Basic Books, New York, 2012.

An Historical Guide to Kabul, Nancy Hatch Dupree. 2nd ed. Afghan Tourist Organization, Kabul, 1972.

How the Farmers Changed China: Power of the People, Kate Xiao Zhou. Westview Press, Boulder, CO, 1996.

How We Got Here: The 70's, the Decade That Brought You Modern Life (for Better or Worse), David Frum. Basic Books, New York, 2000.

Hungry Ghosts, Jasper Becker. Henry Holt, New York, 1996.

"Ideological Change in the British Conservative Party," Ivor Crewe and Donald D. Searing. *American Political Science Review* (1988).

In Search of Lost Meaning: The New Eastern Europe, Adam Michnik. University of California Press, Berkeley and Los Angeles, 2011.

Inside Iran: Life Under Khomeini's Regime, John Simpson. St. Martin's Press, New York, 1988.

Iran and the Arab World, Hooshab Amirahmadi and Nader Entessar. St. Martin's Press, New York, 1993.

Iran Between Two Revolutions, Ervand Abrahamian. Princeton University Press, Princeton, NJ, 1982.

"Iran Hostage's Diary: Robert C. Ode, Nov. 4, 1979, Through July 8, 1980," *http://www.jimmycarterlibrary.gov/documents/r_ode/Ode_pages1thru50.pdf*.

"Iran's Politics: The Supreme Leader," Karim Sadjapour. In *The Iran Primer: Power, Politics, and U.S. Policy*. Institute of Peace Press, Washington, DC, 2010.

Islam and Resistance in Afghanistan, Olivier Roy. Cambridge University Press, Cambridge, 1986.

Islam and Revolution: Writings and Declarations of Imam Khomeini (1941–1980), translated and annotated by Hamid Algar. Mizan Press, Berkeley, CA, 1981.

"The Islamic Republic of Iran, 1979–1989," Shaul Bakhash. *Wilson Quarterly* (Autumn 1989).

An Islamic Utopian: A Political Biography of Ali Shari'ati, Ali Rahnema. I. B. Tauris, London, 2000.

It Seemed Like Nothing Happened, Peter N. Carroll. Rutgers University Press, New Brunswick, NJ, 1982.

John Maynard Keynes, 1883–1946: Economist, Philosopher, Statesman, Robert Skidelsky. Pan Books, London, 2003.

John Paul II: Man of History, Edward Stourton. Hodder & Stoughton, London, 2006.

Journey of the Jihadist: Inside Muslim Militancy, Fawaz Gerges. Harcourt, Boston, 2007.

"Karol Wojtyła, the Pope: Complications for Comrades of the Polish United Workers' Party," Marcin Zaremba. *Cold War History* 5, no. 3 (August 2005).

Keeping Faith: Memoirs of a President, Jimmy Carter. Bantam Books, New York, 1982.

Keynes, the Keynesians, and Monetarism, Tim Congdon. Edward Elgar, Cheltenham, UK, 2007.

"The KGB in Afghanistan," Vasiliy Mitrikhin, 98. Cold War International History Project, Working Paper #40, Woodrow Wilson International Center for International Scholars, Washington, DC, 2002, http://www.wilsoncenter.org/sites/default/files/WP40-english.pdf.

Khomeini: Life of the Ayatollah, Baqer Moin. Thomas Dunne Books, New York, 1999.

KOR: A History of the Workers' Defense Committee in Poland, 1976–1981, Jan Józef Lipski. University of California Press, Berkeley and Los Angeles, 1985.

Letters from Prison, and Other Essays, Adam Michnik. University of California Press, Berkeley and Los Angeles, 1987.

A Life with Karol: My Forty-Year Friendship with the Man Who Became Pope, Stanislaw Dzwisz. Doubleday, New York, 2008.

The Little Green Book: Sayings of the Ayatollah Khomeini, Political, Philosophical, Social, and Religious. Bantam Books, New York, 1980.

The Longest War: Inside the Enduring Conflict Between America and al-Qaeda, Peter Bergen. Free Press, New York, 2011.

The Looming Tower: Al-Qaeda and the Road to 9/11, Lawrence Wright. Alfred A. Knopf, New York, 2006.

Man from a Far Country: An Informal Portrait of Pope John Paul II, Mary Craig. William Morrow, New York, 1979.

The Man in the Mirror—a True Inside Story of the Revolution: Love and Treachery in Iran, Carole Jerome. Unwin Hyman, London, 1987.

Mao: A Life, Phillip Short. Henry Holt, New York, 2000.

Mao's Last Revolution, Roderick MacFarquhar and Michael Schoenhals. Belknap Press of Harvard University Press, Cambridge, MA, 2008.

Margaret Thatcher. Vol. 1, *The Grocer's Daughter*, John Campbell. Pimlico, London, 2001.

Margaret Thatcher. Vol. 2, *The Iron Lady*, John Campbell. Vintage Books, London, 2008.

Marketing Dictatorship: Propaganda and Thought Work in Contemporary China, Anne-Marie Brady. Rowman & Littlefield Publishers, Lanham, MD, 2009.

Milestones, Sayyid Qutb. Islamic Book Service, New Delhi, 2001.

Modern Iran: Roots and Results of Revolution, Nikki R. Keddie. Yale University Press, New Haven, CT, 2003.

Mrs. Thatcher's First Year, Hugh Stephenson. Jill Norman, London, 1980.

"The New China," Angus Deming. *Newsweek*, February 5, 1979.

The New Industrial State, John Kenneth Galbraith. Princeton University Press, Princeton, NJ, 1968.

1979: The Year That Shaped the Modern Middle East, David W. Lesch. Westview Press, Boulder, CO, 2001.

"The 1979 Truth Criterion Controversy," Michael Schoenhals. *China Quarterly*, no. 126 (June 1991): 243–268.

Nixonland, Rick Perlstein. Scribner, New York, 2008.

Occidentosis: A Plague from the West, Jalal Al-i Ahmad. Mizan Press, Berkeley, CA, 1984.

One of Us: Life of Margaret Thatcher, Hugo Young. 2nd rev. ed. Pan Books, London, 1993.

One Step Ahead in China: Guangdong Under Reform, Ezra Vogel. Harvard University Press, Cambridge, MA, 1989.

Out of Mao's Shadow: The Struggle for the Soul of a New China, Philip P. Pan. Simon & Schuster, New York, 2008.

The Passion of Poland: From Solidarity Through the State of War, Lawrence Weschler. Pantheon Books, New York, 1982.

People or Monsters? and Other Stories and Reportage from China After Mao, Liu Binyan. Indiana University Press, Bloomington, 1983.

The Persian Puzzle: The Conflict Between Iran and America, Kenneth M. Pollack. Random House, New York, 2005.

Pilgrim to Poland: John Paul II, compiled by the Daughters of St. Paul. St. Paul Editions, Boston, 1979.

Pioneers of Islamic Revival, Ali Rahnema. Zed Books, London, 2006.

Pistols at Dawn: Two Hundred Years of Political Rivalry from Pitt & Fox to Blair & Brown, John Campbell. Vintage, London, 2010.

Pivotal Decade: How the United States Traded Factories for Finance in the Seventies, Judith Stein. Yale University Press, New Haven, CT, 2011.

Poland: Genesis of a Revolution, edited by Abraham Brumberg. Vintage Books, New York, 1983.

Policy Implementation in Post-Mao China, edited by David M. Lampton. University of California Press, Berkeley and Los Angeles, 1987.

The Polish Revolution: Solidarity, Timothy Garton Ash. Yale University Press, New Haven, CT, 2002 (original ed., Jonathan Cape, London, 1983).

Politics of Disillusionment: The Chinese Communist Party Under Deng Xiaoping, 1978–1989, His-Sheng Ch'I. M.E. Sharpe, Armonk, NY, 1991.

"Popular Versus Elite View of Privatization: The Case of Privatization," Ian McAllister and Donley T. Studlar. *Journal of Public Policy* (1989).

Postcards from Tomorrow Square: Reports from China, James Fallows. Vintage Books, New York, 2008.

The Power of Symbols Against the Symbols of Power: The Rise of Solidarity and the Fall of State Socialism in Poland, Jan Kubik. Pennsylvania State University Press, University Park, 1994.

The President, the Pope, and the Prime Minister: Three Who Changed the World, John O'Sullivan. Regnery, Washington, DC, 2006.

The Priest and the King: An Eyewitness Account of the Iranian Revolution, Desmond Harney. I. B. Tauris, London, 1998.

Prisoner of the State: The Secret Journal of Premier Zhao Ziyang, Zhao Ziyang, Bao Pu, Renee Chiang, and Adi Ignatius. Simon & Schuster, New York, 2009.

The Reign of the Ayatollahs: Iran and the Islamic Revolution, Shaul Bakhash. I. B. Tauris, London, 1985.

"The Religious Mind of Mrs. Thatcher," Antonio E. Weiss, http://www.margaretthatcher.org/document/112748.

Restless Empire: China and the World Since 1750, Odd Arne Westad. Basic Books, New York, 2012.

"Revolution in Afghanistan," Fred Halliday. *New Left Review* 1, no. 112 (1978).

Revolution 1989: The Fall of the Soviet Empire, Victor Sebestyen. Pantheon Books, New York, 2009.

Revolution Unending: Afghanistan, 1979 to the Present, Giles Dorronsoro. Columbia University Press, New York, 2005.

The Road to Serfdom, Text and Documents: The Definitive Edition. In vol. 2 of *The Collected Works of F. A. Hayek*, edited by Bruce Caldwell. University of Chicago Press, Chicago, 2007.

"Rural Guangdong's 'Second Economy,' 1962–1974," John P. Burns. *China Quarterly* 88 (1981): 629–644.

The Search for Modern China, Jonathan D. Spence. W. W. Norton, New York, 1991.

Seasons in the Sun: The Battle for Britain, 1974–1979, Dominic Sandbrook. Allen Lane, London, 2012.

Selected Works of Deng Xiaoping (1975–1982), Deng Xiaoping. Foreign Languages Press, Beijing, 1984.

Seventies: The Sights, Sounds, and Ideas of a Brilliant Decade, Howard Sounes. Simon & Schuster, London, 2006.

The Shah, Abbas Milani. Palgrave Macmillan, New York, 2011.

Shah of Shahs, Ryszard Kapuściński. Penguin Books, London, 1985.

The Shock of the Global: The 1970s in Perspective, edited by Niall Ferguson, Charles S. Maier, Erez Manela, and Daniel J. Sargent. Belknap Press of Harvard University Press, Cambridge, MA, 2010.

The Siege of Mecca: The Forgotten Uprising in Islam's Holiest Shrine and the Birth of al-Qaeda, Yaroslav Trofimov. Doubleday, New York, 2007.

Social Origins of the Iranian Revolution, Misagh Parsa. Rutgers University Press, New Brunswick, NJ, 1989.

The Soviet Regional Dilemma: Planning, People, and Natural Resources, Jan Åke Dellenbrant. M. E. Sharpe, Armonk, NY, 1986.

Sowing the Seeds of Democracy in China: Political Reform in the Deng Xiaoping Era, Merle Goldman. Harvard University Press, Cambridge, MA, 1994.

Special Economic Zones and the Economic Transition in China, Wei Ge. World Scientific Publishing, Singapore, 1999.

"Speech to Conservative Rally in Cardiff," Margaret Thatcher, April 16, 1979, http://www.margaretthatcher.org/document/104011.

The Spirit of Solidarity, Józef Tischner. Harper and Row, San Francisco, 1984.

Strange Days Indeed: The 1970s, the Golden Days of Paranoia, Francis Wheen. PublicAffairs, New York, 2010.

The Sword and the Shield: The Mitrokhin Archive and the Secret History of the KGB, Christopher Andrew and Vasili Mitrokhin. Basic Books, New York, 1999.

"Teng's Cryptic Remark," Bill Roeder. *Newsweek,* December 18, 1978.

Thatcher and Sons: A Revolution in Three Acts, Simon Jenkins. Penguin, London, 1997.

Thatcher and Thatcherism, edited by Eric J. Evans. Routledge, London, 1997.

Thatcher's Britain, Richard Vinen. Simon & Schuster, London, 2009.

Thatcher's People: An Insider's Account of the Politics, the Power, and the Personalities, John Ranelagh. HarperCollins, London, 1992.

Theology of Discontent: The Ideological Foundation of the Islamic Revolution in Iran, Hamid Dabashi. Transaction, New Brunswick, NJ, 2005.

Thinking the Unthinkable: Think-Tanks and the Economic Counter-Revolution, 1931–1983, Richard Cockett. HarperCollins, London, 1995.

To Get Rich Is Glorious: China in the '80s, Orville Schell. Mentor, New York, 1986 (original ed., 1984).

The Tragedy of Afghanistan: A First-Hand Account, Raja Anwar. Verso, London, 1988.

The Turban for the Crown: The Islamic Revolution in Iran, Said Amir Arjomand. Oxford University Press, New York and London, 1988.

The Unthinkable Revolution in Iran, Charles Kurzman. Harvard University Press, Cambridge, MA, 1994.

"Watch Out for the Foreign Guests!": China Encounters the West,* Orville Schell. Pantheon Books, New York, 1980.

Witness to Hope: The Biography of Pope John Paul II, 1920–2005, George Weigel. Harper Perennial, New York, 2001.

Wizyta Jana Pawła II w Polsce 1979: Dokumenty KC PZPR i MSW, edited by Andrzej Friszke and Marcin Zaremba. Biblioteka Więzi, Warsaw, 2005.

INDEX

PELICAN BOOKS

THE ANCIENT CIVILIZATIONS
OF PERU

John Alden Mason was born in Philadelphia in 1885
and was educated at the Universities of Pennsylvania
and California. In 1917 he was appointed Assistant
Curator of Mexican and South American Archaeology
in the Field Museum of Natural History in Chicago,
which he left in 1924 to take up an almost similar post
at the American Museum of Natural History in New
York. He was Curator of the American Section in the
University of Pennsylvania Museum from 1926 to
1955, when he was appointed Curator Emeritus there;
he held this post until his death in November 1967. In
addition to his Ph.D. he was an Hon.Litt.D.

He went on research expeditions to Texas, New
Mexico, Utah, Arizona, California, Canada, Mexico,
Guatemala, Puerto Rico, Colombia, and Panama. He
held office in the Society for American Archaeology, the Eastern States Archaeological Federation,
the American Association for the Advancement of
Science, and the American Anthropological Association, and he edited *American Anthropologist* from 1945
to 1948. He was a member of the Institute of Andean
Research and editor for the New World Archaeological
Foundation of Provo, Utah. Much of his work on
anthropology has been published. His special interests
included archaeology, languages and the ethnology and
folklore of American Indians.

THE ANCIENT
CIVILIZATIONS OF PERU

*

J. Alden Mason

REVISED EDITION

PENGUIN BOOKS

Penguin Books Ltd, Harmondsworth,
Middlesex, England
Penguin Books, 625 Madison Avenue,
New York, New York 10022, U.S.A.
Penguin Books Australia Ltd, Ringwood,
Victoria, Australia
Penguin Books Canada Limited, 2801 John Street,
Markham, Ontario, Canada L3R 1B4
Penguin Books (N.Z.) Ltd, 182–190 Wairau Road,
Auckland 10, New Zealand

First published 1957
Reprinted 1961
Reprinted with revisions 1964
Revised edition published 1968
Reprinted 1971, 1973, 1975, 1978

Printed in the United States of America by
The Murray Printing Company, Westford, Massachusetts

CONTENTS

PART FOUR

Arts and Crafts

LIST OF TEXT FIGURES

MAPS

TABLE

LIST OF PLATES

PREFACE

IN 1527 a small party of men, Spaniards, gathered on a tiny island in the Pacific off the coast of what is now southern Colombia. In those days sea voyages were no pleasure jaunts. The cramped quarters on the small ships, the stinking water, the monotonous diet of stale food, offered no attractions and barely tolerable conditions for the hardiest of adventurers. These had been several months on the slow voyage of exploration south from Panama where rumours were constantly heard from the Indians of a civilized empire, rich in gold, to the south. But so far the men had seen little but hardships, hunger, and sudden death; most of them were disaffected and mutinous. Now the ship for which they had been waiting had arrived from Panama. The Governor's orders to abandon the expedition and return to Panama were received by most with joy. They, proud Spaniards who had come seeking gold and Indian slaves to wait on them, were in rags, subsisting on the shellfish and crabs that they caught on the shores. Enough of this! There was little wealth or luxury in Panama, but at least the basic necessities of food, shelter, and clothing were not missing.

But for one valiant soul the fleshpots of Panama had no appeal above that of the call of the unknown to action. Francisco Pizarro had not come so far in hopes of imitating Cortés to be turned back by hunger, thirst, wetness, and other such trivial bodily inconveniences. On the sand of the little island he drew a line. 'Behind you,' he said to the men, 'lie ease, pleasure – and poverty; before you, toil, hunger, death, but also Peru and its gold. I go south; who goes with me?' And he stepped over the line. One by one, thirteen other brave fellows followed him, to give their names to history as the fourteen stalwarts of Gallo.

For history certainly records no more sturdy and obstinate persistence towards a distant goal in the face of seemingly insuperable obstacles, and no more incredible example of the success of a patently foolhardy venture. For these fourteen tenacious ones were the vanguard of the 'army' of less than two hundred men who were to conquer an empire of several millions.[1]

But such, for over four centuries, has been the lure of Peru. Colonists and administrators followed Pizarro, seekers for the silver, gold, copper, tin, and other metals that the land yielded,

1. Prescott, 1847.

xi

producers of quinine, coca, and, very recently, oil, exporters of guano, of alpaca wool, and, still later, chinchillas. But not only came those who sought wealth in Peru, but also those who, attracted by its great range of nature, longed to study its flora and fauna, its geology and geography, and to report them to the scientific world. Alexander von Humboldt came, Sir Clements Markham, Darwin and Wallace, to mention only a few of the most prominent.

Inca gold now no longer lures the conqueror, but Inca – and pre-Inca – ruins attract the tourist. The Inca armies and the splendour of Cuzco are gone, but the great pyramids of adobe still tower over the desert sands, and the Quechua Indian still guides his llamas through the narrow-walled Inca streets of Cuzco. In a few short hours the aeroplane carries the tourist from Panama to Lima, over the seas that took many months for Pizarro and his little boats. And in even less time it wafts him from the warmth of arid sea-level Lima over the snow-capped Andes to the cool heights of Cuzco. *Vámonos.*

INTRODUCTION

THE history of pre-Conquest Peru, of the Inca and their predecessors – most of the latter nameless and unknown – emanates
from sources of two different types. That of the Inca depends
primarily on the chroniclers, mainly Spanish, who wrote down,
soon after the Conquest, their observations and recollections, and
especially the reports of former customs, beliefs, and traditions
that they secured from living natives. Later students have based
many studies and monographs on these often contradictory
accounts. For earlier unrecorded times we must rely upon the
work and reports of archaeologists.

Digging in Peru – treasure-hunting for gold ornaments – began
with the Conquest; *sub rosa* this still continues. The by-products
of fascinating and exotic art objects soon began to grace the
cabinets of wealthy men in Peru and Europe. Later, many foreign
travellers visited the imposing archaeological sites and described
them; and toward the close of the last century professional archaeologists began to dig with a view more to learning about the past
peoples than to enriching museum collections. The Germans
were leaders in this; the first really scientific excavation in Peru, in
which the objects characteristic of certain periods were differen-
tiated by noting their relative depths and superpositions, was
made at Pachacamac in 1896 by the late great dean of Peruvian
archaeologists, Max Uhle, for the University Museum, Philadelphia (Uhle, 1903). To-day this is the method and goal of all
professional archaeological expeditions; art objects of exhibitable
value are rare by-products.

The spectacular discovery of Machu Picchu in 1911 by Hiram
Bingham awoke popular interest in ancient Peru. Bingham was
soon followed by Philip A. Means, who in 1931 published his
Ancient Civilizations of the Andes, for many years the classic in
English on the subject. About the same time Wendell C. Bennett
began his researches in Peru; his accidental death at the age of
forty-eight in 1953 robbed Peruvian archaeology of probably its
most promising student. The dean of native Peruvianists, Julio C.
Tello, made his epochal discoveries at Paracas in 1927. But it was
not until 1937, with the founding of the Institute of Andean
Research by eight American universities and scientific institutions, that archaeological research in Peru took a sudden upswing.

INTRODUCTION

Eight field expeditions to South America were supported in 1941–2, and in 1945–8 six of these institutions collaborated in a thorough archaeological study of the Virú Valley, one of the smaller coastal valleys of northern Peru. The results of all these researches have since been published. About the same time, in 1946, appeared the modern classic of reference, *The Andean Civilizations*, with thirty-four articles by recognized authorities (Steward, Editor, 1946).

Since the appearance of the present book in 1957 (some parts of which were written several years earlier) our knowledge of Peruvian archaeology has increased greatly. Expeditions from many countries in addition to the United States have dug there, including the Japanese, who excavated mainly at Kotosh (Ishida *et al.*, 1960; Izuria and Sono, 1963). A number of young Peruvian, Ecuadorian, and Bolivian archaeologists have begun to investigate their countries' past. Many reports have been issued, and some radiocarbon dates secured. The latter are relatively few and have not altered the overall picture. There is still considerable difference and disagreement in the chronologies preferred by some of the best authorities.

The Peruvian government has continued researches at Chavín, Pachacamac, Ancón, Chancay, and some other sites, and restorations at the former two. The greatest development has been in the pre-ceramic era, with the discovery of a large number of sites. The majority of these have been in the coastal valleys, even in some that are to-day waterless. However, one in the highlands, in a cave at Lauricocha (Cardich, 1960), afforded the oldest radiocarbon date, 7566 B.C. This, like some later coastal sites, was pre-agricultural. The earlier of the horticultural sites on the coast lack maize, the later ones have it. It is now felt quite certain that maize came to Peru from Mexico. At a somewhat later period, about 900–800 B.C., an improved type of maize was introduced. Some of the coastal sites have well-made projectile points, much superior to the simple flaked cobbles made at Huaca Prieta (p. 34). A good number of textiles have also been found, as well as other plant foods. Very recently some sites of about 3800–3000 B.C., earlier than Huaca Prieta, have been discovered (Engel, 1960). These have small subterranean houses but seem to lack cotton, suggesting that Asiatic cotton was introduced about 3000 B.C. to hybridize with the wild lintless native cotton.

Of maximum importance also are recent discoveries in Ecuador, which not only strongly suggest maritime trade with Mexico about the beginning of the Christian era, but also very early (3000 B.C.) trans-Pacific contact, specifically with Japan (Estrada and Meggers, 1961, 1962, Meggers, Evans and Estrada, 1965).

In the highlands, studies of the last decade have laid great stress on Chavín and its art horizon. Close resemblances are noted with Mexico, even before the classic Chavín period; parallels with Mexican Olmec are especially strong. Even the stirrup-spout, so characteristic of the Peruvian north coast, may be a Mexican influence.

The spread of the Chavín horizon on a later level has also been traced more widely, to Early Paracas and Nazca on the southern coast and to Ayacucho in the highlands. On a still later horizon it is coming to be believed that the spread of the Tiahuanaco art style was the result of a military conquest, emanating from Huari, now generally spelt 'Wari' in archaeological literature.

Some ten years ago I wrote 'So dynamic is the state of our knowledge – or lack of knowledge – of Peruvian archaeology, that no book can be published at present with any claim to finality; the picture may be altered decidedly by the time it appears on the book shelves'. This is not quite so true now. Compared with Egypt, Mesopotamia, Greece, and Rome, Peruvian archaeology is still in its infancy; it lags behind Mexico. Many important sites are practically uninvestigated; others will be discovered. There are still relatively few radiocarbon dates, and some of these are incompatible. But the picture is now fairly well in focus.

It has not been possible to revise this book completely and to bring it fully up to date in this edition. Changes from the last (1964) edition are minimal, and almost entirely in Part 2 (pp. 11–37). Most of the more important works that have been published in the last decade have been added to the Bibliography.

J. ALDEN MASON

Philadelphia,
August 1966

ACKNOWLEDGEMENTS

I AM much indebted to my friends the American Peruvianists the late Dr Alfred L. Kroeber, Dr Alfred Kidder 2nd, Dr John Howland Rowe, and Dr Junius Bird, as well as to my colleague Dr Linton Satterthwaite, all of whom read parts of the typescript of this book and made valuable criticisms and suggestions. It must not be assumed, however, that they approve of everything herein, and certainly on some of the more controversial points they are not in entire accord.

I wish also to thank the late Dr Paul Rivet, of the University of Paris Institute of Ethnology, for permission to reproduce Figures 3, 4, 5, and 6; and the Servicio Aerofotográfico Nacional Peruano for permission to reproduce Plates 3, 5A, 6, 9A, and 15A.

Especial appreciation, however, is expressed to the Wenner-Gren Foundation for Anthropological Research, New York, for the grant which enabled me to visit Peru in 1952 and to make the personal acquaintance of the country, its archaeological sites, and its archaeologists, that is indispensable for a work of this type.

Most of the Peruvian handicraft herein illustrated is in the University Museum, University of Pennsylvania, Philadelphia; the photographs are the work of the late Reuben Goldberg, Museum photographer. Most of the photographs of archaeological sites were taken by the author; a few are the work of Sr Abraham Guillén of the Museo Etnográfico, Lima, and a very few are from miscellaneous sources.

PART ONE

THE BACKGROUND

*

Chapter 1

THE ENVIRONMENT

THE native Peruvian, though ignorant of all but his immediate surroundings, might well boast of being a resident of no mean country. For few regions in the world embrace such contrasts of environment, from sea-level to the maximum habitable altitudes, from utterly leafless deserts to the lushest tropical forests, from regions of constant warmth to those of eternal ice and snow. And probably in no other place in the world can the transition be made in so short a space. While the other great early civilizations of the Old World developed in areas of relatively homogeneous altitude and climate, the Peruvian people had to cope with the greatest possible variety. Doubtless this climatic contrast had much to do with encouraging the development of Peruvian civilization.

The great Andean cordillera[1] is the heart of Peru, as of the other nations of western South America. In a past geological age the earth's crust buckled diastrophically, creating a great ridge to the east and a submarine trough to the west so that in only about two hundred miles the surface rises from some twenty thousand feet below sea-level to twenty thousand above. Only in Bolivia is the highland much over a hundred miles in width. The continental divide is close to the Pacific Ocean, in places only about sixty miles (100 km.) from it. On the east side the land rapidly descends to almost sea-level, from which the slow-flowing rivers, affluents of the great Amazon, meander some

1. See Appendix, page 276, for Spanish and Quechua words.

THE ANCIENT CIVILIZATIONS OF PERU

three thousand miles to the Atlantic. Even the old Inca capital, Cuzco, is on the Amazon drainage. The rivers to the Pacific naturally are all small and short.

Geographers to-day divide Peru into three radically different climatic areas: the low arid coast, the cool or cold highlands, and the lush, tropical, humid eastern lowlands or *montaña*. The latter, however, is Peruvian only from a political point of view. Geographically it belongs to the Amazonian basin – and we shall not be concerned with it; the old Peruvian civilization never penetrated it deeply, though deriving many valuable tropical products from the nearest parts of it.

Northward from southern Chile, parallel to the coast, sweeps the great Peru or Humboldt Current, bringing cold water far to the north, water that averages some 5° F. (2·8° C.) colder than other waters of the same latitude. It used to be thought that this cold water came from the Antarctic, but now it is believed to be due to upwelling in certain places of the cold water from the abysmal depths of the trough parallel to the coast. Cooled by it, the winds drop their excess moisture at sea, and deposit no rain on the coast. The sun shines constantly through diffused clouds, but in the winter (June–November) heavy fogs are frequent. The normal precipitation increases towards the north. Southern Peru and northern Chile form the region of greatest aridity in the western hemisphere; here years pass without a drop of rain, and there is no visible plant life. At some places in the Atacama desert no rainfall has ever been recorded.

In northern coastal Peru there are occasional rains. In cycles a counter current, locally known as *El Niño* (the boy), flowing south over the cold Peru current, nullifies the effect of the latter, and brings heavy rain to the northern coast. Several times in a century, as for instance in 1925, the rains are torrential and terribly destructive to a country where the entire pattern of existence is based on the absence of rain. Even in the great capital city of Lima there is no apparent provision for carrying off rainwater. Then the desert springs to life, with a tremendous increase in both flora and small fauna. But normally it is a waste of rocky hills and wind-blown sand, without a leaf, not even of cactus. According to the Köppen system, the climate is symbolized as 'BWhn' (warm, desert, foggy). The coastal temperature is about 7° F. (4° C.) below that normal for this latitude.

Normally, on the coast there is naturally little native flora or fauna, except in the river valleys, but the cool sea teems with life – fish, octopus, and sea mammals. This is due to the large amount of nutriment in the cold bottom waters brought to the surface by the Peru current. It is one of the world's great fishing grounds – except in the time of El Niño. For this reason there are also enormous numbers of sea birds who nest on the islands off the coast and have deposited there great thick beds of excrement known as *guano* which for years furnished the world with fertilizing material. When the Niño strikes they fly elsewhere or die of starvation, as do quantities of carnivorous marine animals. Naturally also, then, the fishermen and their families have to tighten their belts.

But as one traverses the coast highway, through interminable uninhabited wastes of sand, suddenly one enters lush green fields of corn, cotton, and rice. Here is a river valley, bringing life-giving water from the mountains. The transition is sudden; above the highest irrigation ditch is absolute arid desert; below it, all is verdant. There are about forty-four of these small streams in present-day political Peru, of which about thirty-one are permanent, the others flowing only in the rainy season in the mountains. About twenty-five of these are of archaeological importance. Owing to the flatness of the terrain and the spread of the irrigation ditches, however, the width of the cultivated valleys is considerable. Here are the modern coastal towns, and here were the villages of the natives from time immemorial.

But the flat coastal strip is quite narrow, and only a few miles from the beach begin the foothills of the majestic Andes. As one traverses one of the roads into the interior, following one of the streams, wild plants begin to appear, at first widely scattered, a stunted cactus thirsting for moisture, then another, and finally, at a considerable altitude, one is surrounded by trees and grass. For altitude is of much more importance in Peru than latitude, and typical Peru is highland.

Much of central Peru is uncultivable, the snow-clad mountains being too high for agriculture or habitation, and rocky steep slopes. But the intermontane valleys are fertile and well watered. The climate is designated as 'Cwb', cool summer mesothermal savanna with winter dry season, the rainy season being from October to May, the warmer 'summer'. (Being south of the equator, 'winter' and 'summer' are naturally reversed.) The annual temperature range, however, is relatively slight, tending towards cool, though freezing temperatures are rare, except in the highest plateaus.

In far northern Peru the highlands are more of the Ecuador type, with greater rainfall and leafy expanses known as *páramos*, but throughout most of the country they are grassy grazing lands known as *punas*. Much of the region is unforested, and pasture for the herds of llamas and alpacas. There is at present little wild life, but the guinea-pig and similar small animals supply the natives with occasional meat.

Hemmed in between high mountain ranges are six major basins which probably contain the larger part of the habitable area of highland Peru, charming great valleys of from eight to eleven thousand feet (2400–3400 m.) altitude, fertile, wooded, with ever-running streams and grassy fields (in the summer rainy season), and numerous towns and villages. These are, from north to south, Cajamarca, Callejón de Huaylas, Huánuco, Mantaro, Cuzco, and Titicaca. The largest and best known of these are Huaylas, Cuzco, and Titicaca.

The Callejón de Huaylas is the most thickly populated and one of the largest of these, some 125 miles long and 25 wide (200 by 40 km.). It contains a number of towns, the largest of which is Huaraz. Nestling between the great Sierra Blanca and the Sierra Negra, it is looked down upon by majestic Huascarán (22,180 ft or 6761 m.). Through it flows the Huaraz River which, cutting through the Sierra Negra and thenceforth known as the Santa, empties into the Pacific in northern Peru, irrigating a large coastal area, the largest of the coastal rivers. Most of the other basins – all except Titicaca – are on the Amazon drainage.

The Cuzco basin, with an average elevation of 11,200 ft (3414 m.), is of course the best known of all, the seat of the Inca Empire.

The highest and most remarkable, however, is the basin of Titicaca in which lies Lake Titicaca, the highest navigable water in the world, 12,506 ft (3812 m.). Even more remarkable than the lake is the relatively large steamboat that traverses it. Fabricated in England, the parts were carried by ship and railroad to the lake and there assembled. Of very irregular shore line, the maximum length of the lake is 130 miles, the width 41 (208 by 66 km.). It is on no drainage system, the excess water flowing south to the marshes of Lake Poopo and then evaporating in the sands. The basin is divided between Peru and Bolivia and contains the great early archaeological site of Tiahuanaco, actually in Bolivia.

The Bolivian *altiplano* surrounding the Titicaca basin – which is a little warmer – is a chill, dreary, treeless *puna*, averaging 13,000 ft (3962 m.) in altitude. Geographers call it a tundra, or cold desert. Too high for corn cultivation, the main dependence is on potatoes, and on the other native plants quinoa and oca. But here is the homeland of the llama and the alpaca, and of their herders, the Aymara Indians.

Chapter 2

PHYSIQUE AND LANGUAGE

No human characteristic is so constant and changes so slowly as the physical type. Though the culture may change radically owing to foreign influence, the physique remains practically unaltered provided that there is no admixture of genes or radical change in the environment. It may be assumed that the present Indians of Peru, who form, according to the 1940 census, about forty per cent of the population, are physically practically identical with their ancestors of four centuries ago.

In early days the dwellers on the coast were probably of a slightly different type from those in the highlands, but the spread of the Inca in the fifteenth century resulted in a more homogeneous native type. At any rate, the modern highland Quechua Indian, descendant of the Inca, may be taken as physically representative of his ancestors.

The Quechua body build is massive, the head short, the face medium short. The stature is also rather low. The mesorrhine (medium broad) nose is often arched and the cheekbones are salient; the forehead is low, and the hairline, coming down quite low on the forehead, makes it appear still lower. The eyebrow ridges are only moderately developed, and the eyes are not deeply set. The length and shape of the nose, together with the beardless face, lend a very characteristic appearance to the Quechua Indian. The chest, shoulders, and hips in both sexes are well developed.[1]

The Quechua are rather short, averaging apparently 5 ft 2½ in. (158·7 cm.) for the men, 4 ft 9½ in. (146·3 cm.) for the women. This is somewhat below the average for South American Indians.

The cephalic index is 80·79, which puts them just into the brachycephalic (broad-headed) class. They are thus a little

---

1. Steggerda, 1950, from Eickstedt, 1934.

below the mean for South American Indians. The nose is mesorrhine, with a mean nasal index of 82.

The highland Peruvians have been described as of 'dark brown', 'coppery', 'dark olive', or 'olive grey' complexion. The eyes are 'chestnut' or 'maroon', with yellowish sclera. The head hair is black, straight, and abundant, seldom turning grey. As usual with American Indians, the face and body hair are very scant.

The outstanding characteristic of the Indians of the Andean highlands is the large size of the upper torso, doubtless related to the unusual size of the lungs. The shoulders are naturally broad, but the thighs and forearms are reported to be short.

Life in high altitudes such as are found in the altiplano of Peru and Bolivia, where the oxygen atmosphere may be only half or less of that at sea-level, requires profound adaptation and bodily changes on the part of persons accustomed to lower altitudes. This applies equally to foreigners and to Peruvians from the sea-coast. Often several months are needed before the stranger becomes acclimatized, and similar acclimatization is required for those who descend from the highlands to the coast. The altitude also affects procreation, and both humans and animals often remain sterile for a long time after moving to the highlands. Yet the tourist, gasping for breath at the slightest exertion, sees the native boys engaged in vigorous sports just as at home; skiing is enjoyed at an altitude of 17,000 ft (5100 m.), and Peruvian aviators from the highlands can ascend to 24,000 ft (7200 m.) without feeling any ill effects from lack of oxygen masks. The highest recorded habitation is at 17,400 ft (5300 m.).

The highland natives whose ancestors have always lived in that region have developed a body build adapted to the oxygen deficiency. This of course applies especially to the Quechua and Aymara Indians. The torso and the lung capacity are much greater than among low-altitude peoples. Monge speaks of the 'remarkable thoracic development and great extension of the chest', 'the very high total capacity of the lungs', and 'the great size of the altitude lung'.[1]

There are equally great differences in the blood, for the cor-

1. Monge, 1953.

puscles must be able to absorb oxygen quickly. The blood volume is almost two quarts or litres greater, and there are many more red-blood cells and more haemoglobin; the amount of the latter is almost double that of sea-level dwellers. The red-blood count is about eight millions, as compared with five millions for the average white person from low altitudes. Also the heart-rate tends to be markedly slow. Adaptation to this blood pattern is of course what produces acclimatization for the newcomer to the highlands.

Studies on the metabolism of the Indians of Peru indicate that, despite the high altitudes, they have metabolic rates well within the limits of those for North American whites of to-day. This applies equally well for both highland and coast. In this respect they differ from almost all other American Indian groups studied, whose metabolic rates are appreciably higher.

When, only a decade or so ago, the distinction in blood groups O, A, B, and AB was discovered, it was thought that these would afford conclusive data on racial migrations and mixtures; these hopes were not fulfilled when it was found that practically all peoples are mixtures of all four; the differences are in their proportions. More recently another set of types, known as M, MN, and N, independent of the O, A, B, AB grouping, was determined. A few American Indian groups consist of only O type; most of them are mixtures. M is of high, N of low, frequency in America. The frequency of the O group is very high almost everywhere. The Peruvians and Ecuadorians seem to follow this general pattern.

The linguistic condition of pre-imperial Peru will never be known; the languages were never written down and almost all have become extinct. There were doubtless some languages that belonged to independent families, related to no other, and certainly many different related languages and dialects. The Inca made their language the official idiom of their empire, and it was widely spoken as a second language. The Spanish adopted it as a second official and written tongue and ignored the local languages. Most of the latter were gradually displaced by Quechua during the seventeenth and eighteenth centuries; a few survived until the nineteenth, and one, Muchik, was spoken until a few decades ago. Two more in the southern highlands, Uru and Atacameño, will disappear soon; only Aymara and Cauqui, in addition to Quechua, will continue to be spoken for some time.[1]

Quechua, spoken to-day by the majority of Peruvian Indians, is the lineal descendant of the Inca language, and has probably altered but slightly. It is a typical American Indian language, functioning on entirely different grammatical principles from European languages, almost all of which belong to one linguistic family, the Indo-European, and have a very similar grammatical pattern. Like all American Indian languages, Quechua has a much more complex grammar, but one strictly conformable to rules.

A few words have been adopted into English from Inca or Quechua, mainly names of native plants, animals, and features, such as llama, condor, guanaco, puma, chinchilla; coca, quinine, guano, pampa. The term 'jerked' meat comes from Quechua *charqui*, through Spanish. Another interesting adoption is French *lagniappe*, from Spanish *la ñapa*, *la yapa*, from Quechua *yapa*, 'overweight'.

1. Mason, 1950.

PART TWO

THE HISTORY OF PERUVIAN CULTURE

*

THE historical viewpoint of a few generations ago is epitomized by statements of eminent historians and essayists to the effect that history is the record of the lives of a few great men, that there is no history apart from biography. History consisted of reigns, campaigns, dates. Fortunately this attitude is gone, and modern historians pay more attention – though still not enough – to the more vital point of the development of culture, to the progress of the common people.

But even if the older point of view were still regnant, it could not be followed for aboriginal America. It is dependent on written records, which are wanting in this continent. Legends and traditions, written down at the time of the Spanish conquest, give some true historical data on the preceding few centuries, but before that historical personages are unknown; in the essential democracy of native America the individual rarely was of great importance anyway. The little that is known of Peruvian history from such traditions pertains to the later Inca empire, and is to be found elsewhere herein.

Throughout the world, the history of pre-literate times and regions is reconstructed on the basis of archaeological investigations, the interpretation of the data obtained by excavating from the ground the remains and traces of former peoples. These may be graves or tombs dug in the earth, edifices covered over by drifting dirt or by the accumulations of later occupations, or debris left by successive habitation. In the Old World the results of archaeological work may be tied in with, or corroborated or contradicted by, written records for several millennia before the present; in America there is generally no such corroborative material, and the archaeological results supply the only data.

In the last half-century archaeology has developed a true scientific technique. No longer do professional archaeologists merely abstract intriguing objects from the ground or uncover buildings without much thought as to their context. Today the location of every object is marked and its spatial relationship to every other one observed. Excavations proceed downward by thin levels, and the changes in the nature of the objects found in each stratum are noted. The associations of objects in and out of graves are recorded, and so their respective ages and the characteristics of the artefacts of each period are determined. When one of these is found as a trade object in another region the respective chronologies can be tied up. Especially important is the lowly potsherd, often neglected by the amateur archaeologist. Pottery is nearly as indestructible as stone, and the possible variations in technique, shape, and especially in decoration are almost infinite. So the potsherd has naturally become the archaeologist's main and standard criterion of cultural periods, and often has supplied the distinctive names for them.

Chronology and Absolute Dating

Until very recently, all dates for the archaeology of preliterate civilizations were subjective estimates without any accurate basis, and the guesses of equally good authorities often differed greatly; they were based on such features as accumulation of debris or overburden, magnitude of cultural change, and similar factors for which there are no standard criteria. Historical records on the other hand can, after long study and comparison, afford rather accurate results; Egyptologists, for instance, feel quite certain of dates as remote as 2000 B.C. within an error of ten years.

Within the last very few years a more perfect tool for the relatively accurate dating of archaeological remains has been developed by the analysis of radioactive carbon, the isotope Carbon 14. These studies were first begun by W. F. Libby of the University of Chicago in 1946, and now (1966) have progressed so far that the dates of many hundreds of archaeological or glacial-age objects of crucial importance from a chronological point of view have been announced.

It is unnecessary here to go into the details of the study and the process, interesting *per se* as these may be. Carbon 14 is formed in the upper atmosphere by the impact of cosmic ray neutrons on atmospheric nitrogen. Like all unstable radioactive substances it disintegrates at a regular rate, having a half-life of 5730 years.[1] That is to say, half of any given amount of Carbon 14 will disintegrate in 5730 years, half of the remainder in the next 5730 years, and so on until all is gone; thus there is none left in Carboniferous-Age cold. Carbon 14 therefore forms a tiny fraction, less than one millionth, of all organic carbon. Careful investigation has indicated that this carbon isotope exists in this standard tiny percentage everywhere in the atmosphere, and has thus existed at least throughout human history. Since all living organisms, vegetable or animal, constantly ingest carbon from the atmosphere, it follows that they all, throughout their lives, contain the same small fraction of this isotope. At the organism's death it ceases to ingest Carbon 14 to replace that which continues to disintegrate. Obviously, then, a measurement of the radioactivity of any organic substance, wood, peat, bone, shell, cloth, etc., will provide data from which the number of years since its death can be calculated within a known margin of error.[2]

Tests on objects of known absolute or comparative ages have convinced both physicists and archaeologists that properly made tests on suitable organic objects will yield reliable results within a small margin of error. Unfortunately, and as should be quite obvious, there is great danger of contamination from present-day organic materials which, naturally, would greatly affect the results; however, the error is always towards less age. Objects to be tested should be gathered and carried with this specific purpose in mind, and many objects of crucial chronological

1. New (1962) revised calculation.
2. See Broecker, W. S., and J. L. Kulp, 'The Radiocarbon Method of Age Determination', *American Antiquity*, XXII, pp. 1–11, July 1956. Also Aitken, M. J., *Physics and Archaeology*, pp. 88–117. New York and London, 1961.

importance were not so treated. To procure a reliable date, several tests should be made on the same material, and the results should be very close; many of the dates secured up to the present are the results of one test, and often on material exposed to contamination. (A considerable amount of material is needed for the test, and this is destroyed in the process.) Generally, therefore, if a date reached by a radiocarbon test seems entirely unreasonable to the archaeological expert, and out of line with adjacent dates, he may decline to accept it and insist on awaiting the corroborative or contradictory results of other tests.

Eras and Periods

It is coming to be realized that, except for minor deviations, practically all of the great ancient civilizations of the world developed along more or less the same lines.[1] A fortunately situated people, on a hunting-and-gathering plane of economy, developed or adopted agriculture. With the increased and assured food-supply that this brought, they became more sedentary and multiplied greatly. While the food-supply was ample the leisure time between harvest and sowing permitted the development of arts and crafts, social and religious institutions, and other concomitants of culture, which culminated in a relatively peaceful 'Golden Age'. Then pressure of population and the resultant competition for the means of food production resulted in violent conflicts between adjacent groups, and mastery by a few of them. Finally one of the latter, impelled by the lust for power rather than by real need for economic security – although generally offering the latter as an excuse – achieved power control over all others within its sphere, establishing an empire. Names such as 'Formative', 'Florescent', 'Fusion', 'Militarist' have been applied to these developmental periods.

While most historians and archaeologists will agree to the above general outline, when it comes to applying it to specific regions, the sequential phases of culture to be placed in each division, and the specific cultural items employed as criteria for

1. Steward, 1948, 1949a.

14

such classification, there will be great differences in personal opinion and violent disagreement. Considerable Procrustean bed-fitting must be employed to force local divergences into any general scheme.

Even for a single-culture area such as Peru, no such system of cultural development can be proposed that will fit all regions and satisfy all authorities. Except in the rare instances of sudden change, as by military conquest, the slow development of civilization will not permit the assignment of a definite beginning or an ending to a cultural period. 'Cultural lag' in one region will place a cultural phase later in time than a similar cultural phase in another area; thus in any synchronized developmental scheme there is considerable overlap.

Practically every Peruvianist who has published on the general subject in the last ten years has accepted and used this concept of evolutionary cultural periods, and the differences in opinion regarding the criteria for each and the archaeological and cultural phases composing each are not great, but there is yet no standard terminology. For instance, the Wari-Tiahuanaco period is termed by some 'Expansionist', by others 'Fusion'; the Moche or Mochica period is 'Florescent' or 'Mastercrafts-men'. Some combine the Chimú and Inca periods; some eliminate the Cultist period and consider it a phase of the later 'Formative' or 'Experimenter'.

The developmental and evolutionary scheme must therefore be thought of as little more than a generalized skeleton, but it seems the most cogent method for the simple presentation of an undocumented culture history. It is most strictly applicable to the Peruvian coastal regions, especially the northern and central ones, the best known; its application to the highland cultures, less well known in their earlier phases, is largely presumptive, but not refuted.

The archaeological chronological chart on pages 16-17 is therefore given without any claim to finality. The only certainty about it is that it will be changed in some degree within a very few years, as more excavation is done and especially as more radiocarbon dates are determined. Peruvian archaeological knowledge is in such a dynamic state at present that no two such

Eras	Dates	Periods	Northern Coast	Central Coast	Southern Coast	Northern Highlands
		Colonial	Spanish	Spanish	Spanish	Spanish
	A.D. 1532					
		Imperialist	Inca	Inca	Inca	Inca
CLIMATIC	A.D. 1440					
		Urbanist	Chimú	Chancay black-on-white	Ica	Late Huamachuco
	A.D. 1000					
		Expansionist	Epigonal	Tiahuanaco 'Epigonal'	Nazca Wari	Wilkawain
	A.D. 600					
FLORESCENT		Florescent	Moche Late Gallinazo	Interlocking Early Lima	Nazca	Recuay
	A.D. 200					
DEVELOPMENTAL		Experimental	Early Gallinazo Salinar	Chancay white-on-red	Paracas Necropolis	Huaraz
	300 B.C.					
		Cultist	Cupisnique Late Guañape	Early Ancón, Supe Cerro Sechín	Paracas Cavernas Ocucaje	Chavín Kotosh
	850 B.C.					
		Formative	Early Guañape			
	1250 B.C.					Early
INCIPIENT		Early Agricultural	Huaca Prieta	Asia		Kotosh
	4000 B.C.					
		Pre-agricultural		Lomas		Lauricocha
	9000 B.C.					

PERIODS IN PERU

Central Highlands	Southern Highlands	Cultural Development (Especially applicable to the North Coast)
Spanish	Spanish	The Spanish under Pizarro conquer the Inca empire; the Colonial Period begins
Inca	Inca	The Incas ride to power, conquer all others, and establish a military empire
Early Inca	Colla	Local autonomy with large population centres were a characteristic feature in some area. Clear-cut regional styles in ceramics
Wari	Decadent Tiahuanaco	Apparently a period starting with conquest and political or social unification, breaking down into one of disruption or decadence
	Tiahuanaco	Handicraft reaches its apogee, as do engineering, architecture, and other social features
Chanapata	Early Tiahuanaco Pucara Chiripa	Many new techniques indicate a very dynamic period
		Cultural progress continues. Certain elements common to almost all regions suggest a widespread religious cult—that of Chavin
		Corn and pottery are introduced. Great technical progress is made in all crafts
		Simple agriculture, combined with fishing, hunting, and wild-plant-food gathering
		Hunting, fishing, and wild-plant-food gathering

charts drawn up by any two Peruvianists would agree in all respects, especially as to period names and dates. Some of them object to any presentation by universal culture periods on the ground that this is fully applicable to only one region, the northern coast, the data on the other regions being not so full. Probably some compromising has had to be done herein, but the data have not been controverted. The greatest difference in opinion concerns the dates.

Some Peruvianists prefer another system, an expansion of the formerly accepted division into Early, Middle, and Late, based on the three 'horizon' pottery styles that imply pan-Peruvian influences. John H. Rowe suggests such a classification, the approximate correlation of which with the system herein employed, with his preferred dates would be:

Late Horizon (Inca)	A.D. 1476–1534	Imperialist Period
Late Intermediate Period	A.D. 1100–1476	Urbanist Period
Middle Horizon (Tiahuanaco)	A.D. 800–1100	Expansionist Period
Early Intermediate Period	A.D. 150–800	Experimental and Florescent Periods
Early Horizon (Chavín)	700 B.C.–A.D. 150	Cultist Period
Initial Period	1400–700 B.C.	Formative Period

Chapter 3

THE INCIPIENT ERA

c. 9000–1250 B.C

THE history of Peru begins, of course, not with Pizarro nor with the first Inca, but with man's – and woman's – first invasion of the soil that was later to become the Republic of Peru. This was, according to the best modern consensus, over ten thousand years ago. He was a hunter of the wild game and a gatherer of the wild produce of land and sea, doubtless a man of simple culture. In physical type he may have differed somewhat from the modern Indian. For over five thousand years the improvement was slow; then he discovered or invented agriculture and life became easier, but it was another thousand years or more before he had mastered that art, the prerequisite of civilization. We therefore divide the Incipient Era into two periods, the Pre-agricultural, and the Early Agricultural.

Peruvianists see four important events in the very early history of Peru and are inclined to date coastal archaeological sites on the basis of their culture in order of increasing age, as pre-pottery (*c.* 1250 B.C.), pre-maize corn (*c.* 1400 B.C.), pre-cotton (*c.* 3000 B.C.), and pre-agriculture (*c.* 4000 B.C.).

Pre-Agricultural Hunting and Gathering Period
c. 9000–4000 B.C

Until a very few years age the history of this long period in Peru was purely hypothetical; no site had been excavated and published. Of course they are not obvious; early man left few imperishable objects around his camps, and the latter had to be changed frequently to follow the game and the ripening wild plant foods. Recently, however, several archaeologists have centred their researches on this topic and a number of very early dwelling sites have been discovered and excavated and a few of them published. Most of these are on the coast, a few in the highlands.

Cultural progress in this long period was slow, and possibly never rose much if at all above that of the present aborigines of Tierra del Fuego. It is quite possible that in those days the highland peoples were in the cultural van, the coastal fishermen backward and peripheral. There is some evidence that at this period the precipitation in the highlands was greater than at present, with a consequent larger amount of vegetation and game.

ORIGINS

The problem of the origin of the Andean peoples and of their high civilizations is of course basically one phase of the question of the origin of the American Indian and of his varied cultures. The American anthropological 'Monroe Doctrine' of a few decades ago, holding that all the ancestors of all aboriginal Americans developed their cultures without any influence from the Old World, is no longer unquestioned; there are too many apparently trans-Pacific cultural resemblances to be explained away. But other alternative or subsidiary hypotheses open up an equal number of problems. Whatever other elements – if any – there may be in the Andean populations, the great bulk of the blood is that of Asiatic Protomongoloids, and the major part of the high culture was developed *in situ* from primitive original elements. This is the standard theory today.

Man did not originate in America. There are not – and never have been – in that continent any of his nearest relatives, the anthropoid apes. No remains of early and primitive human species have been found here, nothing but *Homo sapiens*, and apparently none that could not be duplicated today in some American Indian group. And none has been found of an age anywhere near approaching that of paleolithic man in Europe and Asia, probably nothing older than the latter part of the last glacial period. America was the 'New World' not only to medieval Europe but to mankind.

A detailed discussion of this question need not concern us here. The American Indian physical type is fundamentally similar to the Asiatic and obviously a sub-group of the latter. His ancestors must have emigrated from Asia, and probably via Bering Strait in late glacial times.

The time of this migration to America is not known with any accuracy, but recent radiocarbon dates afford approximate data. Sandals found in a cave in Oregon appear to be about 9000 years old, a relatively short time after that ascribed to the melting of the last great ice-cap in northern Wisconsin, 11,000 years ago, and but little before the occupation of a cave near the southernmost tip of South America, to which an age of 8639 years is ascribed, about 6700 B.C.[1]

Transoceanic migrations to America have always been a favourite creed of those with the will to believe, but until quite recently anathema to all reputable American anthropologists; they still are to many or most. No theory of trans-Atlantic migration – or even of influence – has ever received any consideration from scientists of repute; it is supported by no credible evidence.

However, ignoring the mythical 'Lost Continent of Mu', evidences of trans-Pacific contacts are strong enough to be convincing to many good anthropologists. Their time, extent, route, nature, and effect are still so little known that no cogent, comprehensive picture of them has yet been proposed. But there are many curious and close resemblances in cultural elements between several regions in mainland America and Polynesia, Melanesia, and south-eastern Asia that are difficult to account for on other grounds than historical contact.[2] The evidence seems to indicate voyages across the Pacific at several different times or on several different horizons, some of them surprisingly early, but mostly relatively late, and to and from several different regions.

1. Recent radiocarbon determinations have suggested enormous increases in the age of man in America, such as to more than 38,000 years at Louisville in north-central Texas, and to 29,500 years on Santa Rosa Island, southern California. Unfortunately, the validity of these dates is still under discussion. (Krieger, 1964).
2. Ekholm, 1950, 1964.

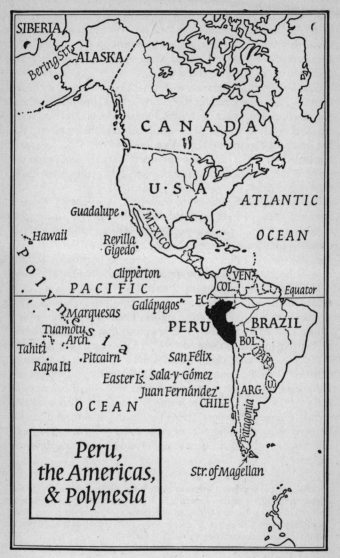

SIBERIA

Bering Str.

ALASKA

CANADA

U·S·A

ATLANTIC

OCEAN

Guadalupe

Hawaii

Revilla
Gigedo

MEXICO

Clipperton

P
O
L
Y
N
e
s
i
a

PACIFIC

VEN.

COL.

EC.

Equator

Galápagos

Marquesas

Tuamotus
Arch.

Tahiti

Rapa Iti

Pitcairn

Easter Is.

PERU

BRAZIL

BOL.

San Félix

Sala-y-Gómez

Juan Fernández

CHILE

ARG.

PAR.

U.

Patagonia

OCEAN

Str. of Magellan

Peru,
the Americas,
& Polynesia

In fine, the resemblances between certain cultural features in America and in Polynesia, Melanesia, Indonesia, or south-eastern Asia are too great and too close to be all explained away as parallel developments. It is altogether likely that certain elements of Oriental origin were introduced from time to time over a long period into America, but their effect on the general American cultural pattern was apparently relatively unimportant. Similarly, some American cultural traits may have been carried to Polynesia, Malaya, or south-eastern Asia.

Aboriginal American cultivated cotton has recently been indicated to the satisfaction of botanists to be a hybrid between Asiatic cultivated and American wild cotton. Cotton was present in early agricultural, pre-ceramic horizons of coastal Peru. Carriage by human hands across the Pacific at this early period would appear to be the only explanation. The other agricultural products found in this earliest Peruvian agricultural horizon, beans, and cucurbits (squashes and gourds), are also of widespread occurrence in both the Old and New Worlds.

On the coast of Chile characteristic stone implements have been found which must have come from Easter Island.

The pan-pipes of Peru and of early China show some astonishing similarities, such as use in pairs, connected by string, with alternate notes of the scale on alternate instruments.

In both regions a narcotic is chewed, betel-nut in the Pacific, coca in the Andean region, and the alkaloid is released by mixing the quid with lime. The gourd containers and the lime spatulas are of the same basic forms.

Bark cloth is made of the same or a similar bark by a very cognate process in Polynesia and South America, and the product has a very similar appearance. In both regions feather mosaics were important and had a very like appearance, made by analogous processes.

Some close resemblances are found in weaving. Especially interesting in both regions are the several processes of resist dyeing, by which the cloth, or the yarn from which it is woven, is tightly bound or otherwise protected before dyeing, so that certain portions remain undyed.

The sweet potato, a plant of unquestioned American origin,

was found by the earliest European explorers under cultivation in Polynesia where it was known by the same name as in Peru, *kumara*.

In Nuclear America gold ornaments were cast by a very complicated technique known as the lost wax process, which was also the one employed by European medieval goldsmiths, as well as recently – or today – in India.

One of the most interesting and significant discoveries in the field of transpacific relations is a most recent one.[1] Pottery of an unusual type, unknown elsewhere, was dug up in a small area on the coast of Ecuador. Radiocarbon tests indicated an age of 3000–2500 B.C., which is over a thousand years earlier than Guañape, the oldest known pottery on the Peruvian coast. Moreover it is ceramics of a high quality, sophisticated, not experimental, and much superior to the relatively crude Guañape ware. Also it was associated with a non-agricultural people who lived principally upon shellfish. In shapes, decoration, and other peculiarities, the pottery shows many points of resemblance to Middle Jomon ceramics which was the ware in vogue in Japan in 3000–2000 B.C. The evidence seems convincing to some Peruvian specialists. Apparently, however, this group of shipwrecked Jomon Japanese fishermen had no permanent effect or influence on the culture of the natives of Ecuador.

Whatever cultural influences possible trans-Pacific voyages and migrations may have had, they had little effect on the blood or physical type, which is predominantly Protomongoloid. Anthropologists are pretty well agreed that America was populated by peoples of this type who came via Alaska during a favourable time toward the end of the last glacial period when so much water was tied up in the ice-caps that the sea-level was lowered some three hundred feet, making a broad isthmus at what is now Bering Strait.[2] Despite the great ice-cap elsewhere, the geological evidence is that the region of the Strait and of the Mackenzie River Valley was unglaciated. Gradually the migrants spread south, filtering through Panama and reaching Patagonia

1. Estrada and Meggers, 1961; Meggers, Evans, and Estrada, 1965; Meggers and Evans, 1966.
2. See Sellards, 1952, Wormington, 1949, 1953, and Macgowan, 1950.

after many centuries or several millennia. They were a marginal or peripheral people, hunters, fishermen, and food-gatherers, in a primitive hunting stage of culture, a stone age, with a poorly developed technology.

Recently some archaeologists have suggested, on grounds of their absence at some very ancient sites, that the oldest inhabitants of America had a 'Pre-projectile-point' lithic culture and were unable to make pressure-flaked spearheads.[1] The present evidence for this is weaker in South than in North America.[2]

The oldest traces of man so far found in South America have been in the Andean highlands, the highlands of east Brazil, and in southern Patagonia; none has yet been discovered in the forested region, though it must be remembered that the latter area is still slightly known, and difficult of exploration.

Four discoveries of human remains are of outstanding importance. In 1844 the Danish explorer Lund excavated a number of caves in the Lagoa Santa region in the state of Minas Geraes, Brazil, and secured eight human skulls and other remains, in association with the bones of the great ground sloth and other extinct animals, and in an approximately equal state of fossilization.[3] The skulls are definitely archaic, having the lowest known average cranial index in South America, 71·7, and showing some non-Mongoloid characteristics. In 1933, renewed investigations in this region produced another cranium of similar type, known as the Confins skull, associated with the bones of mastodon, great ground sloth, and horse.[4] This skull had the lowest of all these cranial indices, 69·1. A series of eleven crania from rock shelters near Paltacalo[5] in southern Ecuador have almost exactly the same low cranial index, 71·4, and other archaic characteristics similar to those of Lagoa Santa; though these skulls seem to be only a part of a larger group, the overall average was certainly very dolichocranic. Also, at Punin in Ecuador,[6] a skull showing Australoid-Melanesoid physical characteristics in a much higher

1. Krieger, 1964.　　　　　　　2. Bird, 1965.
3. Lutken, 1884; Ten Kate, 1885.
4. Walter, *et al.*, 1937.
5. Rivet, 1908.
6. Sullivan and Hellman, 1925.

degree than expectable among American Indians was found close to a Quaternary fossiliferous bed in 1923.

We have seen that the Lagoa Santa and Confins remains were found in association with the bones of the extinct great ground sloth, horse, and mastodon. In Palli Aike cave near the Straits of Magellan, Bird found long-headed human skulls and artefacts associated with bones of the sloth and the horse, which latter was extinct in America at the time of Columbus. This cave is given a radiocarbon age of about 8600 years. The one measurable skull is long-headed and somewhat resembles the Lagoa Santa type.[1] The condition of the remains of a mastodon found near Quito in Ecuador suggests that it had served as a meal for men of that time.[2] In 1952, prominent United States archaeologists, invited to the site, witnessed the excavation of a mammoth skeleton in indubitable association with stone projectile points and knives in the Valley of Mexico.[3] However, these evidences of man's contemporaneity with extinct animals are no proof of great antiquity, for all the data indicate that the animals survived in America to a much later time than formerly believed.

And so our primitive aborigines finally reached Peru after their ancestors' long journey from Alaska. They probably lived in small kin groups, knew how to make fire, and flint knives, scrapers, and projectile points by pressure flaking, and how to cut and shape bone into awls and other implements. They hunted with spear and spear-thrower, for it would be many millennia before the bow and arrow would be introduced or invented. The virtual universality of certain traits in America indicates that they believed in supernatural beings and witchcraft, had shamans or medicine men who cured illness by sucking out the pernicious object, and believed in the evil influence of menstruating women, sequestering them, with special emphasis on the pubescent girl. On this primitive basis the American civilizations of Mexico and Peru were built.

For many thousands of years there was no major change in the

1. Bird, 1938.   2. Uhle, 1928.
3. Aveleyra Arroyo de Anda, 1952. A second mammoth was later discovered at this site of Santa Isabel Iztapan. See Aveleyra in *American Antiquity*, vol. 22, pp. 12–28, 1956.

life of the people. They became adapted to their varied environments and developed their various cultures to fit these. Except for elaboration of their social and religious life, some of the more backward living American aborigines never got much further, still remaining in a hunting, fishing, and food-gathering economy.

Agriculture is the basis of all civilization. On a hunting plane there are seasons of plethora and seasons of want. Domiciles often have to be temporary in order to follow the migrating game. The man's time is rather fully occupied in the search for food. A communal pattern of life is almost necessary, for the lucky hunter cannot deny his hungry neighbours food, or his family will starve the next time his luck is bad, so there is no incentive for the industrious man to labour any harder than the lazy one. The farmer, on the other hand, settles on his land, builds his permanent house, plants his tubers and seeds, and then has some leisure time before the crop matures. After harvest is in, he has even more leisure until the next planting season, and this he can spend in intellectual and cultural pursuits, in building temples and taking part in ceremonies, in creative art and all other elements of civilization.

Although most of the great early civilizations, Mesopotamia, Egypt, Mexico, Peru, reached their apogees in arid regions under the influence of irrigation, nevertheless the most ratiocinative of modern agronomists believe that the origins of agriculture must have been in clearings at the edge of wooded regions, especially in temperate mountain valleys.

Some six thousand years ago at a reasonable estimate, some of the American Indians began to plant tubers and seeds around their houses instead of merely gathering them from wild occurrences. The idea is a perfectly natural one that might have presented itself to any people, and possibly it occurred to several independent groups at more or less the same time; on the other hand, the suggestion may have come from across the Pacific. The labour in gathering the crop was much less, and soon the natives found out that by eliminating the weeds, and by cultivation, fertilization, and other agricultural methods the yield could be greatly increased. Soon, too, they realized that some individual plants were more vigorous than others and afforded a better crop;

they began to save and plant the roots and seeds of these superior plants and their quality began to improve. Naturally each group tended to plant first the crops that they were familiar with as native wild food plants, but also adopted those of neighbouring areas, especially if the latter were superior. The best of these soon spread to the limit of their natural environment, and ultimately, by long cultivation and selection and slow evolution, types developed adapted to environments much different from those tolerated by their wild ancestors. Botanists believe that several millennia of such cultivation and selection were required for native American food plants to have developed from their original wild forms to the varieties cultivated at the time of the Conquest.

The three great American food products, corn (maize), beans, and squash, thus eventually spread over the greater part of North and South America, in a great many varieties adapted to various climates. Some botanists believe that the American food plants that are known in only one species, such as corn, sweet potatoes, chilli peppers, peanuts, manioc, and tobacco, had a single centre of domestication, while those that exist in several species, such as squash, beans, tomato, and cotton, were independently developed from different wild ancestors in several different regions – or possibly one of the forms was introduced from abroad. Further, almost every region had its own local plant foods of limited distribution, plants that tolerate only a special environment, or, possibly, ones of rather recent domestication. Most of these are found in Middle America and Peru, the two great and earliest centres of plant domestication.

Maize or corn, which became the great staple food of much of aboriginal America and a great world crop, is generally admitted to be the most domesticated of all plants, without known wild relatives, and incapable of self-propagation. The origin of corn has been hotly disputed for years, and the best agronomists held conflicting opinions. Only a few years ago one of the best of them could write that the original home of maize was a greater puzzle than ever before.[1] Archaeologists had discovered very primitive types of corn, tiny ears with highly developed glumes, pop-

1. Sauer, 1950b.

corns, and pod corns, but not an extreme type of pod corn. Such corn, found in Bat Cave, New Mexico, has been given a radiocarbon age of 5605 years (i.e. 3650 B.C.), with a plus or minus possible error of 290 years.

The situation had been greatly clarified, however, by the recent and sensational discovery of maize pollen in drill cores in the Valley of Mexico from a depth of over 200 ft (over 60 m.). On the basis of currently accepted glacial chronology, this is at least 60,000 years old. The corn must have been a wild variety, the ancestor of modern corn. This discovery has impelled Mangelsdorf[1] to announce the following conclusions as established: maize is undoubtedly an American plant; its ancestor was wild maize. This was a popcorn, and a form of pod corn, but not the extreme type known today. It had at least one centre of origin in Middle America. Later it hybridized with Tripsacum or teosinte to produce new types.

More than one hundred food plants were cultivated by the American Indian, of which, of course, each region possessed only a part; Peru, with over thirty of them, was probably in the forefront. (See pages 76, 141.) Of these, only very few, such as gourds, cotton, sweet potatoes, possibly plantains, peanuts, and coconuts, have close enough relatives in the Old World to suggest importation (and the sweet potato almost certainly was of American origin); the great majority have no foreign congeners, but rather close wild relatives in America.

In the older discarded theories of cultural evolution the pastoral stage was presumed to have preceded the agricultural economic one. However this may hold for the Old World – and even there it is generally discredited today – it does not fit America at all. Only in Peru were there large animals susceptible of domestication, the llama and alpaca, native to the highlands. Whether plants or animals were domesticated first in this highland region is a moot question, without any present evidence; possibly they were always, as today, contemporary. At any rate, the llama and alpaca have both played a most important part in Peruvian native economy since very early cultural history. The bones of a llama were found in an early agricultural level in the

1. Mangelsdorf, 1954.

Virú Valley; the domesticated animal must have been brought to the coast from his native highlands. However, this was a long time – probably at least a millennium – after the earliest agriculture on the Peruvian coast.

On the Peruvian coast there are evidences of camp sites indicating that men visited that region at least 10,500 years ago[1], but the earliest preagricultural settlements have an age of about 7000 B.C. These were in what is now uninhabitable desert, but precipitation was probably a little greater in earlier days. In certain parts of the central coast the fogs carried enough moisture in the winter to nourish plant life that sprang up in the 'fog meadows' called *lomas*. Due probably to alteration in the Peru Current, the lomas thrived in larger quantity and at lower altitude than at present. Groups of men then came, probably from the highlands, and made their rude winter camps there, gathering seeds and other vegetal foods such as wild potatoes that grew there, and hunting snails, lizards, birds, and occasional deer and guanaco. There was slight dependence on the sea, which was often at some distance. Milling stones were made to grind seeds to flour, but hunting implements are uncommon. It is questionable whether the bottle gourd *lagenaria* was cultivated or gathered wild; certainly nothing else was grown. Pottery and cotton were lacking.

Different camps were made every winter so that cultural development may be traced for 4500 years with slow and slight change. Five periods are distinguished. There was increased reliance on gathering. In the earliest period the flaked tools resembled those at Lauricocha (q.v.). There is no clear evidence of pressure flaking; cobble tools are common.

About 2500–2000 B.C. the lomas dried up, probably owing to some change in the Peru Current, and the dwellers had to leave. They apparently moved to the shore where the sea provided the primary food source, but then they began to raise cotton, and probably beans, squash, and gourds on small garden plots. This horticulture forced them to establish permanent villages and thus to initiate civilization.

1. Lanning, 1963, 1965.

Cave and cliff-shelters have always been more or less permanent residences of primitive hunters, so it is to be expected that
the best archeological record of the most ancient human life in
Peru would be found in a cave. That of Lauricocha in the northern
highlands near Huánuco at 3–4000 metres elevation gave a
continuous history from 10,000 years ago to the Colonial period.[1]
The lowest stratum, which yielded seven human burials, gave a
radiocarbon age of 9525 years or 7566 B.C.; the occupation may be
roughly dated at 8000–6000 B.C. The cave dwellers were hunters,
subsisting principally on highland deer which they probably
killed with spears and spearthrowers. They had a rather crude
lithic industry, with many flakes, fewer points and scrapers.
Horizon 2, probably about 6000–3000 B.C., shows an improvement in the manufacture of flint tools with excellent pressure
flaking. The inhabitants ate fewer deer, but more of the cameloids
– llama, vicuña, and guanaco. Horizon 3 is estimated to be about
3000–1000 B.C.; this is presumably in the Early Agricultural
period, but no evidence of horticulture was preserved. Like the
earlier periods it was preceramic, lacking pottery, and is characterized by implements of bone. Horizon 4 was certainly agricultural as it contains Chavinoid (q.v.) potsherds. Period 5 and last
is recent.

A number of preagricultural and preceramic sites are now
known from the highlands. The early hunters lived well, if
simply; apparently there was ample game for them.

Early Agricultural Period
c. 4000–1250 B.C.

Even a hunting and gathering people is seldom truly nomadic;
it has certain preferred places for residence. And seacoast dwellers,
near a sea yielding ample quantities of marine food, fish, shellfish, and marine mammals, could build and inhabit large and
rather crowded permanent settlements, with their ceremonial
centres and personnel. Such were the early villages on the coast of
Peru by 4000 B.C. or earlier, at first preceramic and preagricultural.

1. Cardich, 1959, 1960, 1964.

Apparently in the fifth millennium B.C. the people became plant-conscious and began to plant and cultivate seeds and tubers. It is believed by some good agronomists that agriculture in western South America was an influence from the Amazonian forests. The earliest cultivated plants were apparently gourds, with lima beans nearly as early, followed by squash and peanuts. Cotton appeared about 3000 B.C. The cotton and gourds were used primarily for fishing nets. With little doubt, women did the cultivation on small garden plots near swampy places in the river valleys; a family's garden plot might be at some distance from the home.

By the third millennium B.C. plant domestication had reached its maturity, and took a sudden advance with the introduction of maize corn, which apparently reached the Peruvian coast about 1400 B.C. There is no question now that corn originated in Mexico. At first, however, it was merely another plant food.

Our information on the Early Agricultural period comes mainly from the coast since objects of organic materials are so much better preserved there; one important highland site is now well known, however. Actually most of our data come from two sites, Huaca Prieta[1] and Asia,[2] for, although some fifty pre-pottery and pre-maize sites are now known on the Peruvian coast, these two are the most fully reported. While differing considerably in time and details, that at Huaca Prieta at the mouth of the Chicama Valley may be considered typical. It was carefully examined by Junius Bird in 1946, and it affords our best – and a very good – picture of life on the Peru coast in this remote period.

A sample of charcoal taken from the lowest level of the Huaca Prieta mound and resting on bedrock was analysed by the radiocarbon method and ascribed an age of 4298, plus or minus 230, years. This date is acceptable to Dr Bird, who further calculates that the age is probably between 4320 and 4528, the latter being the radiocarbon maximum age. This would mean that the sample dated from between 2370 and 2578 B.C.[3]

At that remote time, conditions at the mouth of the Chicama Valley were probably somewhat different from the present. Probably the river carried more water and there were lagoons

1. Bird, 1948a, 1948b.   2. Engel, 1963.   3. Bird, 1951.

and swamps, more lush vegetation, a larger area available for agriculture, and consequent greater amount of animal life, especially of birds.

The people lived, like the Indians of the eastern coast of the United States, by an economy that included fishing and wild-plant gathering together with simple agriculture. The population, although sparse, was probably about the maximum that could be supported under these conditions. Probably the major part of the dietary consisted of fish caught in nets, as the place was not well adapted to hand-line fishing; the latter practice was known, however, as indicated by the discovery of small fish-hooks of shell or thorn, suitable only for small fresh-water fish. Hunting, either for sea mammals or land animals, played a very minor part in the economy, for no weapons whatever were found, nor any remains of land animals; a few bones of sea lion, por-poise, and sea birds indicate that these were occasionally eaten, if not hunted. Since land game was still hunted in the later Moche period, it could hardly have disappeared; apparently, except for the simple agriculture, the orientation was exclusively toward the sea. The dietary was mainly maritime – fish, mussels, clams, crabs, and even sea-urchins and starfish. It is very inter-esting that the mussels were of a deep-water variety rarely found in less than fifteen to twenty feet of water, indicating that the men must have been good swimmers.

Wild plants provided additional food in the form of roots of the cattail, tubers of a rush and a sedge, and several native wild fruits.

The agricultural complex of course is of especial interest. Corn or maize, later to become the staple food, is missing, and most of the cultivated plant foods discovered in the excavations are of world-wide occurrence; several varieties of beans, bottle gourds, squash, chilli pepper, achira (canna), and cotton were cultivated. It is not impossible, of course, that some of these grew wild.

The cotton is apparently the 26-chromosome *Gossypium bar-badense* variety, believed to be an Asiatic-American hybrid. The beans are of at least three varieties, and the cucurbits, consisting of both *Lagenaria* and *Cucurbita*, are of considerable interest.[1] The

1. Whitaker and Bird, 1949.

former is represented by *Lagenaria siceraria*, the bottle gourd, which was used for a number of purposes in addition to – or possibly not including – food, as ladles, containers, and floats for fish-nets. It is practically identical with the bottle gourds found in Polynesia and may have been introduced from there. The cucurbita are *ficifolia* and *moschata*, squashes presumed to be of American origin.

Food was apparently cooked with the aid of small hot stones, possibly by dropping them into containers of water together with the food, as was done by most of the Indians in the United States.

The houses were small, single-room, and semi-subterranean, the walls lined with small boulders or cobblestones. In another Early Agricultural site, where stone was less accessible, they were composed of rectangular adobe bricks. The roofs were made of timbers and whale bones resting on posts. The very oldest graves were merely dug in the ground, but slightly later they were small chambers, lined and capped with small boulders.

The paucity of handicraft found in the excavations illustrates the simplicity of the life. Pottery was absolutely absent as were all ground stone tools, and knives and projectile points made by pressure flaking. The absence of the latter is most surprising, for the technique of pressure flaking is one of great antiquity in the Old World, and the most beautiful pressure-flaked tools ever made in America, the so-called 'Yuma' points of the western United States, are given a radiocarbon age of about 7500 years; the Huaca Prieta artefacts are of paleolithic type.

The only tool made of bone that was found was a small awl, and the sole wooden artefact a paddle-shaped stick, probably used for digging. There were no beads or other ornaments, and only a half-dozen of the thousand of objects found, such as fragments of easily decorated gourds, showed any attempt at ornamentation, and these were very crude; the people obviously were not aesthetically inclined.

'Cloth' was made of pounded bark, a rather surprising feature, for this is an element of the culture of the tropical forest region, not of the Andean. As might be expected, mats and baskets were made of twined rushes and reeds. But probably the most interesting manufactures were the woven cloths, of which about three thousand fragments were found.

Wool was unknown – here, at least – at this time, and practically all the textiles were of cotton, a very few of bast – some local plant fibre. About three-quarters of them were made by twining, a very old process of wide distribution. Netting, looping, and coiling, used in the manufacture of wide-meshed fish-nets and bags, accounted for most of the remainder, but nevertheless there were a number of pieces of true weaving.

The twined cloths may have been made without even a frame, with merely warp strands hanging from a stick. The weft was not continuous; it crossed the warps only once and was then knotted at the selvedge. Designs of birds and serpents were neatly woven in twined fabrics by means of floating warps.

The woven fabrics are obviously examples of very early and primitive weaving. Though a true loom was necessary, it probably had no heddle, the picking of the warps being done entirely by hand. All the cloths are quite small, almost never more than eight inches (20 cm.) in width and about double that in length. Every piece is in some way combined with twining, sometimes twined rows between woven areas, or other variations. Sometimes, as with the twined cloths, the wefts are short yarns that cross the fabric only once. The warps outnumber the wefts so that the cloth is of the 'warp-faced' type, with the warps prominent on the surface. Sometimes short sections of warp were left free or floating on the surface, creating designs. Blue was the only colour found.

The over-all picture of this very early sedentary Peruvian population is therefore that of a simple, peaceful people living in a small cultivable oasis by the sea, fishing, raising a few food crops, living in small, simple, non-masonry houses, and making the objects necessary for their economic and household life, with slight attention to art. The occupation of Huaca Prieta ceased about 1200 B.C.

Naturally, the date for the beginnings of horticulture, when native plants began to be cultivated, is difficult to determine. Cotton was introduced about 3000 B.C. on the coast of Peru, corn about 1400 B.C., and pottery about 1200 B.C., but some habitation sites at Chilca on the southern coast give ages of some 3800 and even *c.* 5000 B.C.[1] and contain evidence of beans of several varieties and gourds; doubtless they were grown there. The site is ordinarily very arid but the neighbouring stream-bed would have permitted floodland farming. Chilca was a village of probably 100 families and 500 population, three kilometers from the sea which supplied the greater part of the dietary in the form of shellfish and crustaceans, fish, marine mammals, turtles, and birds.

The houses were small and of beehive shape, partly sub-terranean, made of cane and thatched with junco grass, sometimes braced with whale ribe; they are the earliest artificial shelters so far found in Peru. The cane and junco grass indicate that there were marshes nearby in occupation days. Utensils and posses-sions – at least those that have survived for more than five millennia – are simple: stone mortars and *manos*, knives and projectile points, implements of bone, shell beads, awls, axes, pins, needles, fish-hooks, spears and lances. Mats and twined bags were made, and gourd dishes. There were hides, wool, and yarn of vicuña.

Another early agricultural village that has been well published[2] is at Asia in the Omas River Valley, about 100 km. south of Lima. Asia is a typical late preceramic occupation site, dated by radio-carbon at 1225 B.C., and presumed to date from just before the introduction of pottery. The inhabitants were fishermen, gatherers, hunters, and farmers. Cotton and beans were found in the lowest occupation level; cucurbits and pepper were also cultivated. Horticulture was probably by flood-farming. Fish were caught with both hooks and nets, shellfish gathered and sea mammals captured. The occupation site was an architectural compound with walls of fieldstone and mud. A rectangular house lay in the centre. Many fabrics and bags of cotton were made, mostly twined, weaving being rare, and with loomed designs.

Doubtless the most ambitious and productive of important results of the expeditions of the past decade has been that of the Japanese[3] archeological investigations and excavations at Kotosh in 1960–62. Kotosh is on the eastern slope of the Andes in the

1. Donnan, 1964. 2. Engel, 1963. 3. Isumi and Sono, 1963.

northern highlands, 5 km. from Huánaco. A large mound that covered – and resulted from – the debris of an old temple was entirely excavated. Few dates are given but possibly 2000 B.C.–A.D. 500 might be a good guess for the occupation period. Six periods are recognized, the first three preceding Chavín and the first two falling within the time of the Early Agricultural period.

In the first period neither pottery nor evidences of agriculture were found and both may have been wanting. The second period gave no evidence of cultivated crops (such are seldom preserved in the highlands) nor of milling stones. However, plenty of potsherds were found. These are of high-grade sophisticated wares, by no means primitive, and of many types, evidently the result of a long developmental period. They most resemble wares from the neighbouring forests to the east, thus strengthening the theory that much of Andean culture came originally from the Amazonian region. The most surprising feature, however, is the radiocarbon date, 3500 years old, or 1850 B.C., making it some 600 years older than the much cruder pottery of the not-so-distant Guañape. Could the influence have taken so long to reach there?

Surprising also is the size and elaboration of the early temple which, although undated, probably is older than 2000 B.C. It predated by centuries edifices of similar complexity in Mesoamerica.

No proof of agriculture was found at Kotosh in the early periods, and no metates or manos, but it is altogether likely that horticulture was practised, since it had been pursued for possibly several thousand years on the coast. Small objects of stone, bone, and clay were well made.

Chapter 4

THE DEVELOPMENTAL ERA

c. 1250 B.C.–A.D. 200

AT least a millennium seems to have elapsed between the later stages of the simple potteryless farmers of Huaca Prieta and the time when Peru practically reached its apogee of culture and most of the techniques had been perfected. This era might properly be termed 'Developmental'.

Almost all our data on this epoch refer to the coastal people, mainly in the north, and the adjacent northern highlands, as it is in these regions that the most intensive archaeological studies have been made, and only towards the end of the era that any contemporary sites from the central and southern highlands are known. This is more likely due to the better state of preservation of coast materials than to any great difference in cultural level.

During this era there was a gradual change – on the coast at least – from a subsistence economy based mainly on sea food to one with the main dependence on agriculture. The population increased slowly but there were no large centres; the village was apparently the political unit. It was a time of early cultural development.

Probably for centuries the two ways of life, maritime and agricultural, competed in the settlements on the coast of Peru. As both methods and yield improved, horticulture instead of maritime products became the primary source of nutrition, acreage increased, and probably the man soon became the farmer. He found the distance too far from his seacoast town home to his country fields, and moved his habitation to his farm. The total population became larger with intensive agriculture, but more dispersed. The large littoral towns were eventually abandoned. Later, with further improvement in horticultural technique, large towns again sprang up, but these were at some distance inland in the river valleys, not on the coast.

Intensive agriculture began with the introduction of maize corn on the coast about 1400 B.C., and received an impetus with the introduction of an improved variety of corn at about the end of the Formative period, 900–800 B.C. For some time fields were watered by floodland farming, but soon extensive irrigation works were constructed. This, naturally, could not be done until responsible governments were established, able to apportion labour and land and compel obedience to decisions.

The era divides naturally into three periods, 'Formative', 'Cultist' and 'Experimental'.

The Formative period begins with the introduction of pottery and ends with the beginnings of Chavín influence which introduce the Cultist period. The Experimental period then takes us up to the time of the great early high cultures.

The Formative Period
c. 1250–850 B.C.

The long-occupied mound at Huaca Prieta in the Chicama Valley, the best-known site of the maizeless, potteryless, early farmers, was abandoned before the culture of its habitants had improved greatly, and the best data for the ensuing period come from excavations in the Virú Valley, a little to the south, where also is found a less-known site of the Early Agricultural Period, Cerro Prieto.[1] The period is also sometimes termed Guañape, from the near-by little fishing village of that name, where sites of this archaeological period were discovered and excavated.

Plain pottery, both black and red, was found in the earliest Guañape levels, but it is believed that the two colours were merely due to inefficient control of firing. While of a poor quality and lacking decoration, the ceramic could hardly be termed experimental, and, while doubtless of local manufacture, it is doubtful if it was a local invention, though this is not impossible. It was, of course, hand-modelled and probably built up by the coiling process. In the later periods other and better pottery types were developed and soon displaced this inferior form.

1. Strong and Evans, 1952.

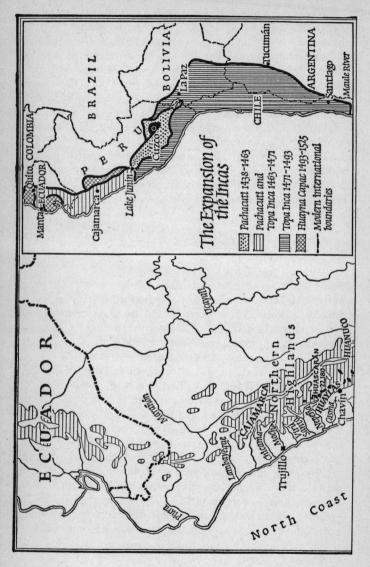

The Expansion of
the Incas

Pachacuti 1438-1463
Pachacuti and
Topa Inca 1463-1471
Topa Inca 1471-1493
Huayna Capac 1493-1525
Modern International
boundaries

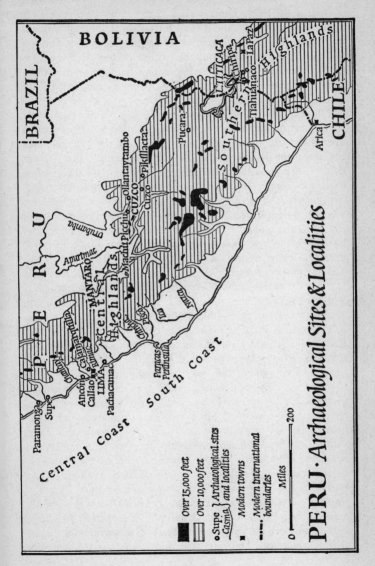

BRAZIL

BOLIVIA

PERU

P E R U

TITICACA

Chiripa
Tiahuanaco · La Paz

Southern Highlands

CHILE

Arica

Paramonga
Supe
Anc ón
Callao · Cajamarquilla
LIMA Rimac
Pachacamac

Chunin

MANTARO

Central Highlands

Apurimac

Urubamba

Machu Picchu
Ollantaytambo
CUZCO · Pikillaclta
Cuzco

Pucará

Pachas Peninsula

Nazca

South Coast

Central Coast

○ Supe ⎱ Archaeological sites
  Casma ⎰ and localities

■ Modern towns

·—·—· Modern international
       boundaries

⬛ over 15,000 feet
▥ over 10,000 feet

Miles
0 _____ 200

PERU · Archaeological Sites & Localities

41

Guañape pottery, dated at 1200–1000 B.C., is the first ceramic on the Peruvian coast, and is of such relatively poor quality that it was believed to be the primitive prototype of later coastal wares. Such it may have been, but the earliest pottery at Kotosh (p. 37), six or eight centuries earlier, is of a far superior and more sophisticated type, and it is strange that its example had not spread to the coast much sooner.

The earliest Guañape vessels were apparently exclusively utilitarian and show no decoration. But what an improvement over the gourd vessels that were apparently the only previous containers for liquids! Cooking could now be done directly over the fire. The sea still produced the greater part of the dietary, but more and more dependence was coming to be placed on farming. Toward the end of the last period, about 1400 B.C., maize corn was introduced. This earliest corn was a primitive type with small ears, probably a popcorn but definitely not a pod corn. Nevertheless it was corn, and capable of developing – as it did – into one of the world's most important food plants. But for a long time it was merely another vegetal food, and the life of the people was little changed. Most of the dwellings were still semi-subterranean, but – in some places at least – they were lined with cylindrical adobe bricks instead of by cobblestones and water-worn boulders.

Throughout the long Guañape period, which is divided into Early, Middle, and Late, the culture continued to develop and improve, both at the type site in the Virú Valley and in contemporary sites in adjacent valleys. Weaving improved, and entirely woven fabrics appeared, although twined ones continued to be made; some entirely new weaving techniques are found. Several other new types of objects, both utilitarian and ornamental, weaving implements, stone bowls, bone snuff tablets and snuff tubes, beads of bone, shell and stone, pottery stamps and figurines, and jet mirrors now appeared, indicating quite a cultural advance and a development of aesthetic feeling. A few burials of this period have been found, accompanied by a few simple objects as funerary offerings. The bodies were either fully extended or placed in a seated position with outstretched legs.

Religious ceremonialism with sacred places evidently played an important role, since at Aspero, in Supe, a rude structure which probably served this purpose has been discovered. It consists of one large and two small rooms, connected by doors; the low walls are of natural stones laid in mud plaster and the floors are of clay. A platform occupies the centre of the main room. Here were found llama bones and corn, both probably imported from the highlands. Sacrificed llamas were also found in a rude temple in the Virú Valley.

The Guañape period was a long one. On the basis of radiocarbon analysis, the beginning, with the appearance of the earliest pottery, is calculated to have been about 3200 years ago, that is, about 1250 B.C. The radiocarbon age for the end of the period, with the introduction of the first high-grade ceramics, the beginning of Cupisnique, is about 2800 years, or about 850 B.C. The period, therefore, apparently lasted about 400 years.

Like the Early Agricultural period, the Formative is known mainly from the north coast, the Early Guañape. We still know almost nothing of highland life and culture at this time because of the lack of preservation of organic objects. Presumably animal husbandry and horticulture were both fairly well advanced. However we have seen (p. 37) that at Kotosh three periods preceded the Cultist, and that in the second, about 1850 B.C., excellent pottery was found. The next, of Formative age, about 1000 B.C., has typical Formative-type ceramics, and definite cultivation of corn, uncertain at an earlier date. Apparently the adoption of the bow and the sling both postdate that of pottery.

The Cultist Period
c. 850–300 B.C.

The so-called Cultist period brought a great and rather sudden cultural advance. By some Peruvianists it is counted as beginning with the introduction of pottery and maize, and therefore including the transitional Guañape period with its rather crude ceramics. But the era truly begins with the highly developed and characteristic Chavín de Huántar horizon style, and with its aspect on the northern coast, the Cupisnique; it is so regarded herein.

The Chavín was the first of several 'horizon styles' that, at widely separated periods, were of the greatest importance in Peru and had very widespread influence. The other later ones, the Wari-Tiahuanaco and the Inca, were pan-Peruvian, affecting all parts of the land and, at least as far as the Inca were concerned, spread by population movements. The Chavín influence never reached the southern highlands and was very attenuated in the central highlands and the southern coast. It was primarily an art style, probably spread by the vogue of a new religious cult.

While the Wari-Tiahuanaco and Inca periods have always been accepted as major epochs in Peruvian archaeology, the Chavín period and its importance have been recognized only within the last forty years, mainly owing to the researches and concepts of the great dean of Peruvianists, the late Dr Julio C. Tello.[1] Wherever found stratigraphically, Chavín underlies the remains of all others of the higher cultural periods.

Chavín takes its name from the site of Chavín de Huántar in the northern highlands on the east side of the continental divide on a small tributary of the Marañon River, just across the divide from the Callejón de Huaylas. It is not a large site, and Peruvianists believe that it was only one of several ceremonial centres of the Chavín cult. But at any rate it is the most important of the few known typical sites, and the largest one on which detailed reports exist. However, nothing but very superficial excavations have yet been made there.

The land available for agriculture in the small valley surrounding Chavín is limited and could never have supported a large population; it was not the centre of a populous district. Nevertheless, a considerable body of men must have been occupied for a long time in its construction. Although it contains many rooms, they were not well suited for habitation, and the buildings were almost certainly not residential; they may well be compared with the stone buildings of the Maya of Middle America, composing a ceremonial centre.

The complex covers a considerable area.[2] For a space of over eight hundred feet (250 m.) square, the surface is completely landscaped, with a sunken court, raised platforms, terraces, plazas, and stone edifices, oriented to the cardinal points, prin-

1. Tello, 1929, 1943.   2. Bennett, 1944.

cipally east-west. Though there are a number of buildings, one, known as the Castle (*Castillo*), far exceeds the others in size and importance. Fortunately it is – or until recently was – rather well preserved, for it is unique – much the largest of the few known similar structures of this ancient period. In this highland region old buildings were neither torn apart by lush tropical vegetation as were the Maya structures, nor covered with drifting sands as in the Near East.

For one of the earliest-known large stone edifices in Peru, the Castillo is remarkably advanced architecture, and there can be no question that a long period of architectural development in masonry lay behind it somewhere. The plan is complex and it must have been built from the first stone with the finished structure in mind, if not according to a drawn plan or a model. It consists of three floors – more than were built at any later period in Peru – all of dry stone masonry. The building even contains a system of ventilating shafts, both vertical and horizontal, so efficient that it is said they still provide fresh air for the interior rooms – surely the work of no amateur masons. However, the walls are massive and thick, faced with selected split stones, and filled with rubble. The outer walls are faced with large rectangular dressed stones laid in courses of various widths, alternately thick and thin.

The Castillo is an immense complex building, large and square, about 245 by 235 ft (75 by 72 m.). It is still about 45 ft (13 m.) high at one corner. The outer walls are slightly battered, i.e. slope inwards towards the top, where also they are set slightly back in several narrow terraces. Originally there was a row of large projecting carved heads, inserted in the walls by means of tenons, which encircled the building below a decorated cornice; a few of these heads still remain. The interior consists of a maze of walls, galleries, rooms, stairs, ramps, and ventilating shafts on three floors. The rooms and galleries are rather low, about six feet (1·8 m.) high, the galleries only about a yard or metre wide, the rooms from about six to sixteen feet (2–4·5 m.). There are no external windows or doorways except for the main entrance to the first floor, reached by a stairway of admirably cut rectangular blocks (Plate 1A).

Figure 1. *Drawing of the Raimundi Chavín sculptured stone monument*

46

The edifice is massive as well as immense; the rooms and galleries are of less cubic area than the walls and other masonry. They are dark, without any lighting. Great broad slabs form the ceiling of the room below and the floor of that above, and the roof slabs are covered with earth which formed the foundation for several small rectangular masonry houses that were built upon them. In one of the galleries a large, tall vertical carved stone known as the Lanzón was discovered (Plate 36).

The status of archaeology in Peru and the immense amount of work that remains to be done there may be judged from the fact that this great, significant, and almost unique edifice has never been carefully studied. No detailed plan exists; in fact many of the rooms and galleries have never been entered, for many – or most – of them have never been cleared of the stones and debris with which they were apparently filled in ancient unrecorded times. Sad to report, such studies may now have become impossible or prohibitively expensive, since the structures were largely covered by a great landslide only a few years ago, in 1945.[1]

Though overshadowed by the Castillo, the Chavín de Huántar complex consists of many more features such as plazas, platforms, terraces, and mounds. The mounds, and apparently also the platforms, seem, like the Castillo, to be masonry constructions, honeycombed by galleries.

Chavín influence extended quite a distance to the north, since several little-known sites, such as Kuntur Wasi and Pacopampa in the Department of Cajamarca, show rather definite Chavín characteristics in architecture and sculpture.

Kotosh in the northern highlands is the archaeological site most often compared with Chavín. It is much older (p. 37), with three periods before the one equated in time with Chavín. This period (Kotosh-Chavín) contains 'typical classic Chavín pottery of superb quality'. This ceramic had a short vogue, appearing and disappearing suddenly. As in all highland sites, data on agriculture are difficult to secure, but some metates and manos were found, and other evidences of corn cultivation. In the later post-Formative periods good work in metallurgy, principally in copper, is

1. It is now (1956) being cleared by the national Dirección de Arqueología.

found, good textiles and pottery vessels. The masonry and sculpture, however, cannot compare with those of Chavín de Huántar.

However, the Chavín horizon is best known in its manifestations on the northern coast where sites and cemeteries of the period have been excavated, affording better data on the life of this time than can be secured at the highland sites. The phase best known is that of the Cupisnique graves in the Chicama Valley, but edifices and graves in the Casma, Nepeña, Virú, and Lambayeque Valleys, the debris in the lower levels in shell-heaps at Ancón and Supe,[1] and certain other sites from Piura to Lima show Chavín traits. Chavín influence also seems to be present at the earliest known sites on the southern coast, those of Paracas Cavernas and Ocucaje,[2] showing the widespread ramifications of this culture. The resemblance is seen in the ceramics, in shape, decorative technique, and motifs. Some Chavinist enthusiasts see these influences extending to Ecuador, Bolivia (Tiahuanaco), Argentina (Barreales), and northern Chile (Pichalo), but these are not accepted by the best authorities. In some places, such as Cerro Blanco and Punkurí in the Nepeña Valley, and Moxeke and Pallca in Casma Valley, the resemblances are seen in masonry temples or terraced pyramids; in the others they are recognized in the pottery and other grave furniture.

The coastal Chavinoid architectural sites were recently discovered and are not well known. None has been well excavated or described, and of most of them little is known. Several, especially Cerro Blanco in the Nepeña Valley, have mud-covered walls painted with Chavinoid designs in several colours.

A very important site which has been the cause of much dispute among archaeologists is Cerro Sechín in the Casma Valley. The unusual and striking feature is a line of erect, large, flat, unshaped stone slabs carved with large human figures and human heads in outline or low relief. The poses are rather dynamic and naturalistic, and they have been compared with the 'dancing' figures at Monte Alban, Mexico. The art, however, is very different from the Chavín-Cupisnique style. Though ap-

1. Willey and Corbett, 1954.   2. Kroeber, 1953.

48

parently on the Chavín horizon – probably, in fact, a little earlier – Cerro Sechín seems to be a sub-culture *sui generis*, like nothing else yet known.

The Southern coast boasts of no great masonry or adobe structures to attract attention. The stupendous masonry ruins of the Peruvian highlands and the immense adobe pyramids of the north coast have always been famous, but the ancient civilizations of the south coast, in the valleys of Pisco, Ica, and Nazca, without any impressive structures, were almost unknown until the present century. The cemeteries of the Nazca period with their extraordinary polychrome pottery were discovered by Max Uhle in 1901, those of Paracas with their even more splendid textiles by Julio C. Tello in 1925. In this region it can almost truly be said that it never rains, and the objects buried with the dead in the desert sands are incredibly well preserved. All surface indications of these cemeteries have long since been covered or erased by the drifting sands, and they are found today only by the spade of the archaeologist or the probe of the native treasure-hunter.

The Paracas Peninsula, lying about eleven miles (18 km.) south of the port of Pisco, is the seaward extension of a line of low sandy hills known as Cerro Colorado. The red sand is absolutely bare of all vegetation, not a leaf, not a living thing; no stream enters the ocean near by. The nearest human habitation is several miles away where wells tap underground water and a few sedges line the beach. It is the epitome of loneliness and desolation. Yet beneath these sands are found the desiccated bodies of a people unknown to history, together with some of the most magnificent cloths that the world has ever seen. Today their bones lie scattered on the surface, and the winds alternately cover and uncover fragments of the coarser fabrics, discarded by the diggers, still soft and strong after nearly two millennia. For the 'mummies' have been removed from the discovered cemeteries, and either carefully preserved by archaeologists, or rifled and only the presumably saleable goods kept by native *huaqueros*.

Two types of burials, known as Paracas Cavernas, and Paracas Necropolis,[1] were found in this region by Julio C. Tello

1. Carrion Cachot, 1949.

THE ANCIENT CIVILIZATIONS OF PERU

between 1925 and 1930. They differ greatly in nature and in contents, Cavernas being characterized by a remarkable type of polychrome incised pottery and textiles of average quality, Necropolis by magnificent cloths and simple unpainted pottery. The former shows some Chavín elements; the latter is obviously related to the Nazca culture, demonstrably later by stratigraphic proof. The great diversity of Paracas Cavernas pottery shapes, the occasional use of negative-painted designs, and the post-fired painting strongly suggest a dynamic experimental stage rather than a static standardized one. Cavernas has therefore always been considered the older and has been assigned to the Cultist period, Necropolis to the Experimental.

Paracas Cavernas was so named because the bodies are found in communal bottle-shape chambers excavated in the rock at the foot of vertical shafts, at a depth of approximately twenty feet (6 or 7 m.). Many of the tombs also have a stone-lined upper chamber at the surface. As many as fifty-five bodies were found in one of these sepulchres, of both sexes and all ages. The heads were artificially deformed, and a large proportion of them had been trephined. The bodies were wrapped in coarse cotton cloths and accompanied by mortuary offerings. It has been suggested that the tombs might have been family vaults. The considerable variation in the quality and quantity of the grave goods placed with the dead suggests a similar difference in economic conditions during life.

Paracas Cavernas pottery is of superior type and very distinctive; good collections and even single vessels are rare outside of Peru. A Chavín-Cupisnique influence is noticeable; incised lines delimit the designs and the coloured areas, and the feline motif with characteristic elements is common.[1] The pastel colours are, however, rich and polychrome, red, green, yellow, and dark brown; the polychrome pottery set the pattern that was further accentuated in the later Nazca period. The pigments are thick, glossy, and resinous, like a mastic. They were applied after firing and are disintegrated by damp earth. The majority of the decorative designs are highly conventionalized and stylized biomorphic, producing a distinctive art of high quality.

1. Kroeber, 1953.

The variation in form is very great and there cannot be said to be any standard or predominating forms. Simple-silhouette vessels such as bowls and ollas are probably most common, and double-spouted vessels with bridge handle are frequent, though not the stirrup-spout. There are a number of effigy forms, but these are not so realistic as those of Moche or Salinar. Unique are double-bottom bowls with a rattling pellet between.

The textiles are well made but far inferior to those of the neighbouring Paracas Necropolis. The gauzes are especially outstanding. As would be expected for an early culture, the single-element techniques such as netting, knotting, knitting, twining, and plaiting are especially prominent, though brocade, weft-patterns, embroidery, and painted cloth were made. Cotton, wool, fibre, and human hair were used in weaving.

The fabrics found at Paracas Cavernas indicate that the costume was of the usual coast pattern, including loincloths, waistbands, shirts, shawls, turbans, head-bands, and bags with straps. Doubtless more and heavier clothing was worn in the highlands. The people made and used baskets and mats. Bone flutes and clay pan-pipes are preserved, but it is likely that the latter were funerary replicas of the more common pipes of reeds. Among the most characteristic objects of the culture are gourds decorated with pyrographic burnt designs. The craftsmen knew how to make ornaments of thin gold but silver was apparently not yet known, though objects of pure copper have been found.

The type site of Paracas Cavernas is the only one so far found of its nature, and the peculiar shape of the graves was doubtless due to the local conditions, a hard surface stratum overlying softer rock. Graves containing pottery of similar type, and obviously of similar culture, are found fifty to eighty miles further south at Ocucaje and several other sites in the Ica Valley, but these are rectangular tombs in the sand. The bodies were obviously brought to Paracas for interment either because the sites had some sacred importance or on account of the preservatory aridity of the regions which, lacking water, are unsuited for human habitation. It may have been the local custom to carry the dead to seaside cemeteries.

The nature of the Chavín horizon has long been a mooted

point. The native Peruvianists have thought of it as a cultural entity, possibly even a pre-Incaic empire, at any rate a 'civilization'. Tello, its principal protagonist, thought that it was brought to the coast by a migration from the Andes, and that it originated in the Amazon region. Larco Hoyle believes that it began with the Cupisnique people on the northern coast and was carried by them to Chavín de Huántar and other highland parts. The opinion of United States Peruvianists, as formulated in a masterly paper by Gordon Willey,[1] is that it was not a homogeneous culture, but the expression of a widespread and rapidly diffused religious cult.

While these sites on the Chavín horizon show a basic cultural similarity, they differ considerably in detail, more than would be expected of a homogeneous culture. The common possession, the determinant feature of Chavín, is a similar art style. This emphasizes a feline – jaguar or puma – treated in a characteristic stylistic manner. It is, epitomized by Willey, 'a matter of line, of composition, of emphasis. It is the curvilinear forms, the massive heads, the intricately disposed small heads, the locked and curved fangs, the claw feet, the prominent nostrils, and the eccentric eyes.'

Presumably this feline being was a deity whose cult, with its characteristic stylized representation, spread over the region of Chavín influence. Apparently it carried with it no technological concomitants, and almost certainly was carried by no proselytizing crusaders, at any rate by no vanquishing ones. The Chavín *tradition*, however, persisted almost throughout all of Peruvian history; the feline element in art – and probably in religion – was a strong feature in both the Nazca and Moche regions and periods, in the Wari-Tiahuanaco pan-Peruvian horizon, and even later.

The radiocarbon date for the beginning of the Cupisnique period is 848 B.C. with a plus or minus error of 167 years. The ending lacks a definite radiocarbon test and two equally respected Peruvianists estimate it as 500 and as 100 B.C.; a mean of 300 B.C. is here accepted.

Although the earliest, the Chavín is generally regarded as the

1. Willey, 1951b.

greatest art style evolved in Peru. It is unfortunate that examples
are not many and known to few but Peruvianists. It is seen to best
effect in the stone carvings, either in the round or in relief. The
figures are mainly feline, human, and monstrous or demoniacal,
though the condor, snake, and some other animals are depicted.
Far from being naturalistic and pictorial, the art is decidedly
stylized, conventionalized, and symbolical. The effect is massive
and strong, and sometimes even dreadful. The lines are almost
always curvilinear. Many of the details on the figures are
extraneous from a naturalistic point of view, and evidently
symbolical (Plate 37A). Considerable resemblance to the
art of the Olmec of south-eastern Mexico has been pointed
out.

Our picture of life on the Chavín horizon is afforded by excavations and grave contents in sites of this period on the
northern coast; needless to say it must have differed considerably
in detail – though probably not greatly in general nature or
quality – in the ecologically different highland region. There
were also considerable differences between the cultures of the
various sites of the Chavín period, and between the temporal subdivisions of this horizon, though on a rather uniform basis.
Future researches will differentiate and characterize these subdivisions.

Agriculture had improved immeasurably and now was the
main source of food supply; fishing, hunting, and wild-food
gathering were of less importance. About 900–800 B.C. an improved variety of corn had been introduced to assume its place as
the staple food, and the beans and gourds of the earlier population
were now relegated to minor roles. With the superior corn came
also warty squashes, avocados, and manioc or yucca. And, of even
more importance, with these improved agricultural conditions
came the post-harvest leisure time that horticulture affords, time
in which to develop and improve technology, art, and the higher
aspects of culture. Sea food, however, continued to be of importance here – as it is yet – as evidenced by the large shell-heaps and
middens containing refuse of this period, middens, by the way,
from which come many of the archaeological objects that afford
us the data for reconstruction of the life.

Some llamas had been brought down from the highlands, but their herding probably had not yet become an important element of native life. The dog may have been introduced at this time, but it is not certain; strange to say, there is no evidence of his presence in this region at any earlier period.

The locations of the habitation sites of this period on the edges of the fertile areas at the mouths of the rivers imply that agricultural engineering was still in an incipient stage. Irrigation and drainage were primitive, and doubtless much of the watered land was swampy or overgrown with brush or weeds. The cultivable area was not great, nor was the population.

The houses of the people were apparently small, one-room, rectangular structures with thatched gable roofs. It is doubtful whether they were grouped in the settlements according to any plan with regular streets. They stood on raised stone-faced platforms, but the walls were generally of mud, made into conical adobe (sun-dried) bricks. These were laid with the flat end to the outer surface, the interstices filled with mud, and a smooth mud plaster given to the wall faces. In some places the walls were apparently made of stone, probably where suitable stone was easily available.

Religion had obviously reached an advanced, formalized stage, for the larger and more elaborate buildings were presumably temples. While conical adobes were much used in the construction of these, stone masonry is also common, the stones being set in a kind of mortar. These temples are well planned and built, quite large, with numerous rooms, platforms, and steps. The smooth plastered walls are adorned with frescoes in polychrome, or decorated with clay relief or incised designs.

The religious aspect is also present in the treatment of the dead. The Peruvian pattern that prevailed from earliest to latest agricultural times was followed. The dead were interred in the arid desert in relatively deep graves, and provided with mortuary offerings, presumably for their use in the after-world; at Cupisnique these included jewellery and other ornaments, and pottery vessels containing food and drink. Coastal graves were almost always deep in Peru, because the desert sands were easily excavated and because the people wished to place their dead below the reach of dampness from the occasional rains. The Cupisnique graves, however, were relatively shallow. The dead were interred, probably in their best clothing and with their favourite ornaments, in horizontal position, the limbs generally flexed. Most commonly the bones were covered with a red powder or pigment, probably cinnabar, a practice that is found sporadically in America from here to Maine and which suggests that the burials were secondary, i.e. that the bodies were not placed in their final graves until the flesh had decayed. The Cupisnique graves lay at depths from $2\frac{1}{2}$ to 6 ft (80 c. to 2 m.), and neither the graves nor the bodies seem to have been oriented to any particular direction. Much of the grave furniture was ornamented with theistic symbols, especially the ubiquitous Chavín feline. However, the Cupisnique graves seem not to be typical of the period. Those in other coastal sites of the Chavín horizon contain little grave furniture and few pottery vessels, and little or no food placed in them. Owing to their comparatively great age and to the greater amount of precipitation in this northern coastal region, textiles and other objects made of perishable organic substances are rarely preserved. However, the middens at Ancón and Supe preserve such perishable objects as nets, bags, baskets, mats, gourds, and textile clothing of the Chavín horizon.

The Cupisnique, and probably all other men of the northern coast on this horizon, apparently ordinarily wore nothing but a loincloth and cap; the attire of the women is not known. Bone ear-ornaments and finger rings, bracelets, wristlets, crowns, and necklaces of stone beads were worn by one or the other or by both sexes, as well as feather headdresses and capes. Stamps found in the graves suggest that the body was decorated with paint. As frequently in later periods in Peru, skull deformation was a common practice.

The potters of the Chavín horizon had reached a high plane both as craftsmen and as artists, but the industry was still too new to have achieved technical excellence. Naturally each region or site had its specific types, and within these the fashions varied from generation to generation. From the type site of

Chavín only potsherds are known, but they are of technically good quality. They represent simple shapes, mainly open bowls with thickened rims, but vessels with stirrup spouts, so characteristic of the coast, seem to be lacking. The ware is polished red, black, or brown, or combinations of them. Decoration is mainly by incised lines, with a little low relief and modelling but no true painting. Very similar potsherds have been found in the lowest levels at the shell-heaps of Ancón and Supe.

The best-known ceramic of this period is that from the Cupisnique graves of the Chicama Valley; it bears but slight resemblance to the pottery of Chavín. These vessels are, of course, mortuary furniture, the utilitarian ware being less attractive. Cupisnique pottery was not discovered until 1939, and is poorly represented in all museums outside of Peru. Although giving an impression of technical mastery, it both looks and is heavy, with thick walls. The control of the firing had not been perfected and the vessels were baked at a low temperature with a reducing atmosphere so that the surface is black, brown, or red. Toward the end of the period a few vessels of lighter colour appear. The most common shape, at any rate among the mortuary furniture, is the stirrup-spouted jar, a form that is very characteristic of Peru and which retained its vogue in the northern coastal region throughout Peruvian history (Plate 23). Two curving tubes rise from the quasi-spherical body of the vessel and coalesce into one vertical tubular spout, thus serving as a handle. The body of the vessel is altered into effigy shape or decorated.

Since dark surfaces do not lend themselves to painted decoration it is not surprising that there is little of the latter in Cupisnique ceramics. However, the beginnings of painting are seen in the occasional colouring of the designs enclosed within incised lines.

Some Cupisnique pottery vessels are said to bear impressions of moulds or even to be entirely mould-made, a process that became common in the later Moche[1] period. Quantity production

---

1. American Peruvianists prefer the new term 'Moche' to the old standard 'Mochica'. We do not know if they spoke Mochica, the language in use here in Colonial days, but we do know that they erected the structures at Moche.

at such an early cultural stage would not be expected and would indicate a surprisingly rapid advance in technique.

The decorations are on the whole simple, generally curvilinear geometric, but the feline, the determinant art element of the horizon, is frequent. Effigy vessels were modelled or moulded in the form of animals, plants, human beings, and even houses. A human portrait jar and a nursing mother are outstanding individual pieces.

In the Cupisnique graves only enough textiles have been preserved to assure us that weaving was practised, but better-preserved examples found elsewhere show that, while by no means all techniques later found were known, the art had progressed greatly over the simple fabrics of Huaca Prieta. The use of the heddle is indicated. Tapestry and embroidery were made, as well as plain weaves, a lace-like gauze, and gingham, all embellished with fringes and tassels. All seem to have been of cotton.

Although no metal objects of the Chavín period have been excavated under controlled conditions, three groups of gold ornaments are known which, judging from their art style and other circumstances, are ascribed to this horizon.[1] Two of these came from graves at Chongoyape; the provenance of the third is unknown. One of these groups apparently consisted of a man's, another of a woman's ornaments. They are probably the oldest known examples of metallurgy in America. Some are of pure gold, one is seventy-four per cent silver, and the others consist of a large proportion of gold, a small proportion of silver, and a little copper; the three metals were probably not intentionally mixed. Most of them were made of thin hammered gold, for casting, later the principal metallurgical technique, had apparently not yet been invented. The techniques employed, however, demonstrate the rapid advance of the goldsmith's art, for they include hammering, embossing, annealing, welding, soldering, strap joining, incising, champlevé, cut-out designs, and the manufacture of bimetallic objects. One pin has a gold head and a silver shaft.

For all that we know to the contrary, metallurgy and all the

1. Lothrop, 1941, 1951a.

above goldsmithing techniques may have been invented in this northern coastal Peruvian region – or they may have been introduced from we know not where. The discovery that gold and silver nuggets are soft and can be cold-hammered into thin plates must have been the first discovery; the various methods of decorating these sheets followed quickly. Later the use of heat was discovered, and metallurgy was on its way to the heights of technique and art that it later attained.

The Chavín-horizon gold ornaments are really dainty and exquisite and include a large range of objects, pendants of many different types, tweezers, staff-heads, crowns, ear and nose ornaments, cuffs, pins, plaques and disks, gorgets, ear-spools, spoons, and beads. Some human or animal figures in the round are naturalistic, but the more common repoussé ornamentation is either geometric or very conventionalized naturalistic, including elements that are typical of Chavín stone carving, especially the feline motif. Strange to say, much of the gold was painted with coloured pigments.

The Cultist-horizon peoples were also master artisans in minor media such as semi-precious stones, bone, shell, and wood. Beads, pendants, rings, combs, and similar ornaments were made of turquoise, quartz, lapiz lazuli, and other hard stones – a protracted task for a people without metal implements – as well as of bone and shell. Pyrite and jet provided materials for polished mirrors.

Among the utilitarian objects made on this horizon may be mentioned hammer-stones, club-heads, grooved stones, projectile points, mortars, pestles, bowls and boxes of stone, awls, spatulas, needles, daggers, spoons, and spear-throwers of bone or wood (or both), nets and netted bags, twined baskets, mats of *totora* reed, carved gourd containers, and clubs and boxes of wood. An object of *chonta* palm wood, found at Ancón and claimed to be a bow, is of considerable interest as showing the possible use of this weapon at this early period; in the United States its first appearance seems to have been at a much later time. Nevertheless, the Cultist hunter and warrior certainly relied much more on the spear and spear-thrower.

Large sculpture in stone was an important culture element in the highlands but unknown on the coast, except at the site of Cerro Sechín which, as we have seen, is rather a cultural anomaly, possibly of an earlier period.

The over-all picture of life on the Cultist level, the earliest Peruvian culture that could be considered a civilization, as illustrated on the north Peruvian coast, the only region from which we have sufficient data, is that of a simple sedentary people whose activities were still devoted mainly to acquiring the means of existence, food, and shelter. Nevertheless, the leisure time afforded through their main dependence on agriculture permitted the community erection of temples and other religious structures. A religious cult in which a feline deity, puma or jaguar, played the most prominent role was the common element, for otherwise the small villages apparently had no political bond, and the local cultural variations from valley to valley were considerable. Both trade and warfare were apparently of little importance. The small settlements were probably based mainly on blood relationship. Ancestor-worship and the cult of the dead had apparently hardly begun the vogue that they later reached in Peru.

It has been suggested that such great structures as Chavín de Huántar were shrines to which pilgrimages were made from a large surrounding region, and centres in which the entire population gathered on definite occasions for ceremonial celebrations and for markets. This is a Peruvian – and a nuclear American – cultural pattern of long standing, as exemplified, for instance, by the great pan-Peruvian shrine at Pachacamac, and today by the great annual *romería* at Copacabana, Bolivia. It was probably at these times that the assembled multitudes built – or at least assembled the great amount of materials necessary for – the immense structures and edifices. A small number of trained architects and masons could then work during the long intervening periods, while the great body of the people, returning to their villages, disseminated the new cultural developments – together with the gossip – that they had learned during their pilgrimage.

The Experimental Period

c. 300 B.C.–A.D. 200

The term 'Experimental' aptly characterizes the period between the 'Cultist' (Chavín-Cupisnique) and the 'Florescent' periods. It was a time of development, of improvement, of invention. In fact, the Experimental might be considered the earlier, incipient, developmental phase of the full-blown Florescent which, without any sudden break, followed it. As is inevitable in such cases, it is a question of personal opinion as to when the first ended and the second began, and whether a transitional phase should be placed in one or in the other.

Cultures on the Experimental horizon are found in almost all parts of Peru, being the earliest known in some regions, though certainly not actually the first. However, as in the earlier periods, almost all our data come from the coastal peoples. No outstanding civilization, culture, art, or technique characterizes the period, and the local phases are little known and of interest to few but archaeologists. The period lacked any over-all unity.

It must constantly be kept in mind that all these peoples and cultures of early Peru are unknown to history. Archaeologists separate the main periods and give designating terms to them, generally the modern name of the region with some temporally qualifying adjective, but we do not know what name the people applied to themselves or what their neighbours called them, what language they spoke, what their gods and chiefs were named, what inventions they contributed to mankind or what evils they perpetrated on their neighbours. For there are no written records and no traditions.

The Cultist art with its emphasis on the Chavín feline, the one unifying bond of that period, suddenly disappeared, and with it all traces of former cultural homogeneity. Probably the religious cult waned, and possibly former unifying pilgrimages were abandoned. Apparently the people became more locally minded, and each valley began to develop the local characteristics that it had begun in the Cultist period. All, however, were on practically the same cultural plane, with many common elements. Among these were two horizon styles of pottery decoration, traits that must have spread from centres. For the greater part of the period the characteristic pottery decoration of most regions was of designs painted in white on a red surface, and this has been employed as a term for this sub-period in several of the areas: 'Chancay White-on-Red' on the central coast, and 'Huaraz White-on-Red' in the northern highlands; the white-on-red style is also found on the northern coast, where it is known as Salinar. Towards the end of the period negative-painted pottery appeared in these three regions, as well as on the southern coast.

White-on-red ware is unattractive. The shapes are simple, bowls and cups with flaring sides and rims, and bottle shapes being the commonest forms. There are few effigies and no stirrup-spouts, though double spouts are found. The decoration is usually of simple rectilinear geometric designs with rather thick straight lines, parallel, hatched, or cross-hatched, dots, and circles; pictorial designs are missing, and incising and modelling rare. In a variant type of this ware either the entire vessel or large zones of it are painted white.

Although the break between the Cultist and the Experimental periods is a rather sharp one, it was apparently cultural rather than political in nature. In only one place the Cultist tradition apparently lasted into and through this period, for the Chavín feline appears again in the Moche art of the following Florescent period, though practically missing in the intervening Salinar culture of the Moche region. A very few unusual and untypical designs on Salinar bone spatulas are the only Experimental period objects that betray any Chavín influence.

A comprehensive description of the culture of the period is difficult because of the great degree of local variation. It was a period of development and experiment; archaeologically this is best seen in the technology. On the whole, although the technology is superior, the art and the aesthetic feeling are not equal to those of the preceding Cultist period.

Information on the culture of the Experimental period is derived from graves, cemeteries, from refuse deposits of dwellings, and from fortresses and shrines, the first three mainly from coastal sites, the latter two from the highlands.

As in the former periods, the coastal settlements were on the margins of the river valleys or on the coast. While there was still great dependence on sea food, the progress in agriculture had been great; irrigation was practised and a number of new culti-vated plants had been introduced. Among the latter were the frijol bean, quinoa, and several other plants known only in Peru. Terraces were built to utilize better the small amount of irrigable land available. Coca, the narcotic plant of the highlands – of the greatest cultural importance in later times as today – was grown or known, and chicha, the beer made of corn, seems to have been made. Meat was apparently preserved by drying, and grain was stored. Llamas were common in the highlands and well known on the coast. Some edifices were of stone masonry but most were of adobe, the latter being of different shapes in the three main sections of the coast: northern, central, and southern.

In socio-political matters there seems to have been little change from the preceding period. The groups continued small, and the basic social cluster was probably still the family, without any marked political or religious unity. There is little evidence of any class distinctions, the pattern being essentially democratic. Though more attention was paid than formerly to the dead, com-munity religion seems to have been of slight importance.

The local phases of the culture of this period that are best known are, as usual, those on the coast, owing both to the better preservation of the materials and to the greater amount of archaeological excavation that has been done there. Best known of all, probably, are the cultural phases of the northern coast, especially the Salinar and the Gallinazo cultures.

Salinar is a recently discovered culture, first found by Rafael Larco Hoyle in 1941,[1] since which time several hundred graves have been excavated in several large cemeteries in the Chicama Valley. Burials at Puerto Moorin in the Virú Valley are obviously closely related culturally, and it is likely that careful search would reveal similar but slightly variant cultural remains in other valleys of the northern coast. As commonly, the cemeteries were

1. Larco Hoyle, 1944, 1945d, 1946.

placed in the desert hills bordering the cultivated areas. Strati-graphical observations prove that the Salinar followed the Cupisnique (Cultist) and preceded the Moche (Florescent) periods. It takes its name from the small place in the upper Chicama Valley where the largest cemetery was found.

The Salinar people cultivated corn, squash, and gourds in addition to several plants unknown outside of Peru, and gathered shellfish and other local animal life. No house remains are known, but an effigy pottery vessel affords an illustration of one, and other pots give some idea of the costume of the people. The houses were apparently rectangular, with an open front and a sloping roof. Some clothing in addition to a loincloth was certainly worn, and the use of a cap was common. The hair was cut, though not short, and ornaments in the form of ear and nose pendants, finger rings, bead necklaces, and bracelets were worn. Skull deformation was practised, and apparently also tattooing.

Many pottery vessels of distinctive types were found in the graves; these, of course, were mortuary offerings, and the utili-tarian ware is not well known. Most of these have a red paste and surface. This red colour indicates a great technical advance, for the vessels must have been fired in a very hot 'oxydizing' fire in-stead of in the relatively low-temperature 'reducing' fire that produced the black or dark Cupisnique ceramics. Possibly the kiln had now been invented; at any rate, temperature control had improved greatly. A small minority of vessels have the dark colour of Cupisnique pottery.

The paste of Salinar pottery is superior, with more even tempering than in Cupisnique ceramics. Jars with vertical spouts and ribbon handles are common, handleless vessels being rare. The white colouring was apparently applied with a brush on the untreated surface, without the basic slip that later became almost universal. The eyes are treated in an unusual characteristic style, and the details of the facial expression are especially notable. Appliqué relief is slight and low.

The 'stirrup' jar with tubular spouts continued to be the most common shape; the body of the vessel was either modelled in effigy form, or decorated with incising, painting, or relief, or both.

The effigy vessels, at least, were made in moulds; humans, animals, birds, plants, and other objects are portrayed. The incised and painted designs are simple and geometric. The beginnings of painted pottery, later to become almost universal in Peru, are here seen. This represented another important step in cultural advance. The colouring is generally white, but a little red paint was also employed. The pictorial representations are slightly stylized, lacking the perfect realism that the later Moche pottery in this region achieved. A few of the effigy vessels are erotic, though none depict practices of perversion. This is significant in view of the slight interest in sex generally characteristic of aboriginal American art and religion, and of its importance in the later Moche ceramics.

Not enough of Salinar fabrics have been preserved to afford much information on the subject of textiles. Bone spatulas bear incised designs that connect them with Cupisnique art motifs. Fewer Salinar gold ornaments have been found than from the Cultist period and no new techniques are known, except possibly gold-copper alloy, but there is no reason to think that the goldsmith's art had deteriorated.

The better care for the dead indicates a belief in the after-life, and probably early phases of the cult of ancestor-worship which later became of maximum cultural importance. The bodies were interred wrapped in or covered with textiles, and provided with pottery vessels and gourds containing food and drink. They wore their ornaments, and a piece of beaten gold was often put in the mouth. Dogs were sometimes placed at the feet, together with pieces of chalk, quartz, and other stones, generally of a white colour. Red powder (cinnabar?) was found in most of the graves. The body was almost always laid at full length, on the right side, in elliptical graves covered with great stone slabs. No exact orientation was observed in the making of the graves, but most of the dead had the head in a westerly direction.

Large stone sculpture was apparently unknown.

On the north coast the Salinar culture was succeeded in the latter part of this period by a slightly different and more developed phase, the Gallinazo. This was probably the result of a highland influence on the Salinar people. Gallinazo is so named from a site in the Virú Valley where the culture was first identified and where it appears in strongest form. Some, believing that the culture originated in this valley, and disliking the name Gallinazo (Vulture), term it the Virú Culture.[1] Its characteristic pottery type, decorated with negative painting (see page 266), is found in some other valleys of the north coast. This negative painting is typical of the Callejón de Huaylas in the northern highlands, especially of Recuay, in the next period, and is doubtless related to, and possibly an influence from, the cultures of highland Ecuador and southern Colombia, where this technique was in great favour. Since it is also found in the Paracas Cavernas pottery on the south coast and, a little more frequently, on the central coast, it is a quasi-'horizon style', diagnostic of this time.

The Gallinazo was a period of probably several centuries duration, in the Virú Valley at least.[2] Civilization had progressed greatly and was only slightly inferior to that of the Moche in the next great period. The communities were well organized so that large pyramids, doubtless religious structures, were built of adobe bricks which were formed in moulds made of cane. Intensive agriculture, produced by irrigation, was the basis of life. Llamas seem to have been plentiful. Fishing and hunting were now of slight importance, with little dependence on the sea. Weaving was highly developed, as was metallurgy.

When first identified, the Gallinazo culture was believed to be of a much later date, following the Moche period, but the stratigraphy of recent excavation indicates its earlier position.

The pattern of economic life in the central and southern coastal regions probably differed but slightly from that of the Salinar and Gallinazo peoples, but information is scanty. Excavations at Cerro de Trinidad and Baños de Boza in the Chancay Valley show a period characterized by a rather unattractive type of pottery painted in white on the red paste; for this and other reasons it is correlated with the Salinar period. The painting is generally rude, careless, simple, and geometric; effigy vessels are rare. In fact, throughout Peruvian history, the ceramics of the central coast were aesthetically much inferior to those of the northern and southern coasts. The other objects found in the

1. Larco Hoyle, 1945a.   2. Strong and Evans, 1952.

graves differ only in minor details from those of Salinar, and include gold, cloth, pottery figurines, pan-pipes, and spindle whorls. The bodies are generally flexed in graves covered with poles, though some are covered with stone vaults.

Remains of edifices of some type, made of large hemispherical adobe bricks, are found in this region.

On the south coast the cultures of this period centre in the valleys of Pisco, Ica, and Nazca. Since rainfall, even in the mountains, is deficient in this region, the rivers are not large, though they may have carried more water in earlier days.

At Paracas, just south of Pisco, Tello discovered in 1927, close to the Cavernas tombs, a burial area of very different type and known as the Necropolis, already briefly mentioned. This was surrounded by a stone wall and contained 429 'mummy' bundles. Most of these – mainly the smaller and poorer ones – are still unopened in the Archaeological Museum in Lima. The bundles are large and of conical shape, the largest about five feet (1·5 m.) high and wide, the body having been wrapped in quantities of cloth. While probably no embalming process was employed, the viscera were apparently removed and the body allowed to dry naturally in the arid sand.

The Necropolis, a large enclosure in the midst of semi-subterranean houses and refuse-pits, was evidently a cemetery for a special class and differed in many respects from the Cavernas. The bodies were all of elderly men, probably chiefs or priests. The skulls were deformed, but in a different manner from those in the Cavernas vaults; none of them was trephined. The bodies were well preserved, in contrast to those in the Cavernas.

The nude body was placed in a seated position in a basket, and long cotton cloths wound around him. These shrouds of cotton cloth are not so well preserved as the woollen textiles, but are remarkable for their size. Whereas cloths wider than about four feet, the span of a weaver's arms, are practically unknown elsewhere in Peru, these are sometimes thirteen feet (3·9 m.) in width and eighty-four feet (25·5 m.) in length.[1] The wide loom may have been manipulated by several women. Many of the bundles

1. O'Neale, 1936.

showed that they had been completely wrapped and finished several times by adding new layers, probably at several successive ceremonial occasions.

Tucked into the bundle were articles of clothing, generally new and unworn, as well as ornaments, weapons, food, pottery vessels, pet animals, industrial materials, and similar objects. Miniature clothing, feather fans, ornaments of sheet gold, smooth sticks or batons, gourds, and a few pottery vessels were among these objects. Among the food placed for the dead were corn, beans, peanuts, yucca, and sweet potatoes. The four standard articles of clothing were cloak or mantle, short cape, skirt, and headband, but in the richer bundles many other articles were added such as small ponchos, kilts, turbans and other headgear, veils, and slings; these were mainly of llama or vicuña wool and very well preserved. Of the magnificent mantles we will speak later. As many as one hundred and fifty articles of clothing and other offerings were placed with the larger bundles.

The pottery of Paracas Necropolis – always our best criterion – differs considerably from that of the Cavernas, with thin walls, of a light colour and without painted decoration, the shapes of the mortuary ware variant but relatively simple, with some effigy shapes and biomorphic relief. The goldsmiths in this region seem not to have yet learned the technique of casting, but work of a high aesthetic and technical quality was done in ornaments of thin beaten gold with repoussé ornamentation.

But it was in the field of textiles that the Paracas craftsman excelled; the name 'Paracas' means to the archaeologist and the artist magnificent cloths. This renown is due to their large size, their wonderful state of preservation – some of them being practically as soft and brilliant as the day they were woven, and the harmonious beauty of their colouring. The techniques employed are few – mainly embroidery, and finer work was done in other periods, but for general over-all superb effect, Paracas Necropolis textiles rank with the world's best.

The magnificent Paracas mantles must be seen to be appreciated, for no description can do justice to them. They are large, averaging four and a half by eight feet (1·3 by 2·5 m.). The background is a loosely woven wool or cotton cloth on which are embroidered figures in wool in soft harmonious polychrome tones. Four to six colours were generally employed, and both the colours and the figures themselves bear an obvious close relationship to those on Nazca pottery. The embroidered figures are small and repeated many times in various colour combinations, in horizontal and vertical bands, or in chequerboard pattern. Anthropomorphic animal deities, probably mythological beings, with stylistic animal characteristics, more naturalistic animals, and occasionally geometric motifs are employed. Fish and bird deities seem to be the most popular. The workmanship is perfect, and the effect, both macroscopic and microscopic, is colourful, and – to us – exotic (Plate 49).

These magnificent textiles seem to have been made purely for mortuary purposes. The amount of work on them is marvellous, for some are almost completely covered with a veneering of embroidery, meticulously done. The stitching closely follows the weave, each stitch enveloping one warp or weft strand.

The occupation sites, the towns, of the people who buried their dead in the Paracas Necropolis have yet to be found; they may have been those of the population of the Pisco Valley, whose habitation sites seem not to have been discovered yet. The Necropolis cemetery was obviously for men of high rank who were probably brought there from some distance, as the region of the cemetery is absolutely unsuited for human existence, at least at present.

The fact that the temporal relations of the two cultures of Paracas are still a question for discussion well illustrates the present uncertainty on many vital points of Peruvian archaeology. The reports from Dr Strong's 1952 expedition indicate that in the Nazca region the refuse of that period is underlain by, in places, ten to thirteen feet (3 to 4 m.) of deposits containing pottery and textiles of both Paracas types intermingled, together with some other types heretofore unknown. This would suggest the contemporaneity of the two Paracas cultures. Most Peruvianists, however, remain unconvinced and, on other grounds, believe in the greater antiquity of the Cavernas phase.

The cultures of the highlands in the Experimental period are far less known than those on the coast, largely owing to the fact that the objects are much less well preserved, and – as a natural concomitant – much less excavation has been done there. In the northern highlands little more is known than the type of pottery, rather rude and painted with white geometric designs on the red surface; the type site is at Huaraz in the Callejón de Huaylas. The houses were semi-subterranean. The white-on-red is a horizon ceramic style linked with Salinar on the north coast and with Chancay white-on-red on the central coast, but it is missing in the south and in the central highlands.

At Chanapata, near Cuzco, excavations in 1941 revealed the occupation sites of a pre-Incaic population.[1] While only its precedence to the Inca is certain, for cultural and other reasons it is generally assigned to the Experimental horizon. Chronologically it hangs in the air, without identified antecedents or descendants. It was certainly pre-Wari-Tiahuanaco and presumably relatively early, showing some Chavín influence, though probably not as early as the latter.

The culture of the place and period was incomparably inferior to that of the Inca who later made this region the cultural centre of South America. Masonry of plain uncut field stones was employed in semi-subterranean houses and in the walls of agricultural terraces. Very little attention was paid to the dead, who were buried in unlined pits in refuse-heaps, apparently without any mortuary offerings. Metal seems to have been unknown – at least none was found – but implements and ornaments were made of stone and bone.

The pottery is *sui generis*, slightly known, and of no aesthetic or technical interest. It is mainly either incised polished black or painted white on red, with a little red on white. Flaring bowls, plates, ollas, and bottles are the typical shapes. Most of the decoration is incised, but punctate designs and appliqué are also found. Most of the decorative designs are rectilinear geometric, but some biomorphic motifs were employed, especially a feline which, however, is stylistically very different from the Chavín cat.

In the southern highlands also a site has been discovered and excavated which is ascribed to this period; in this case strati-

1. Rowe, 1944.

graphy indicates that it was pre-Tiahuanaco in age. This is at Chiripa on the Bolivian side of Lake Titicaca and therefore not far from Tiahuanaco.[1] Probably, as in all such cases, the unknown people who lived there also occupied similar settlements throughout this region, but only one small site in addition to Chiripa has been discovered so far. Here the village was composed of fourteen rectangular houses in a circle surrounding a central court. The lower part of the walls was made of small stones embedded in clay, the upper part of rectangular, sun-dried, large mud bricks (adobes), and the roofs were apparently thatched. The walls had two unique and interesting features: they were double and the space between them was utilized for storage, very much as cupboards in some modern houses. However, they were apparently used as storage bins for food, and access was through windows in the interior walls instead of doors. Even more interesting are long narrow slots left in the wall masonry at the door jambs; undoubtedly sliding doors fitted into these.

Agricultural terraces with masonry supporting walls were used in this region also at this time. The dead were interred in stone-lined box graves under the floors of the rooms. The depth of the refuse deposits indicates that the site was occupied for a very long time.

Chiripa ceramics are rather rude, with simple geometric designs painted, generally in broad lines or bands, in yellow on a red slip; the painted areas are sometimes outlined by incised lines, a technique found also in Chavín and Cupisnique, Paracas Cavernas and Ocucaje, and in the neighbouring and slightly later Pucara. A feline figure made in appliqué relief is a frequent element. The most common shape is a bowl with flat base and straight vertical sides. The utilitarian objects found include stone mortars, hammers and similar tools, bolas, bone needles, awls, spear-throwers, chisels, daggers, knives, etc. A few objects of pure copper have been found.

In the southern highlands, resemblances in ceramics and some other features indicate that the Experimental Chiripa culture developed into several later phases, among them the Pucara and

1. Bennett, 1936.

the Early Tiahuanaco. All three of these are now (1966) considered as pertaining to the Experimental period.

Pucara is a site in the Department of Puno, Peru, between Cuzco and Lake Titicaca; the architecture, ceramics, and sculpture are characteristic and unique.[1] As is the case with all the Peruvian cultures up to at least this time, we know nothing of the history of the people who lived there, not even their name or language. Inca traditions do not mention them; our knowledge is restricted to the data derived from digging, and the deductions made therefrom.

Pucara has the basic elements of the earlier and neighbouring Chiripa plus a strong influence of the Tiahuanaco region. The structure excavated by Alfred Kidder II, built of very good masonry of dressed stone with some use of adobe, was almost certainly a temple. A sunken central court is surrounded by walls forming a horseshoe-shaped group of small rooms. In this central court four burial vaults, made of dressed stone blocks and entered by means of a doorway and steps, were found. Each of these vaults contained a stone altar.

Stone sculpture is a characteristic element of Pucara. This is much better made than the stone carving of the northern highlands. Human and animal figures are found, as well as carved stelae and slabs (Plate 18B). The pottery, in form and motif, is of Tiahuanacan type, with wide-mouth bowls and goblets predominating. These, however, are painted in yellow and black on a red slip with the outlines incised. Many of the vessels are further decorated with a large feline head in high relief, the body in flat profile. The ceramic has some resemblance to the earlier Chiripa, and a little to the Early Tiahuanaco.

Probably contemporary with Pucara was Early Tiahuanaco. This is little more than a pottery type which was found principally in the lowest stratigraphical cuts at Tiahuanaco; it differs markedly from Classic Tiahuanaco in shape and design. It occurs in the refuse-heaps of dwelling sites which probably stood on the site of Tiahuanaco before this was made into a great ceremonial centre. No architecture or sculpture has been identified as belonging to this period, though a few statues in Bolivia

1. Kidder, 1943, 1948.

that bear some resemblance to Pucara are assigned to the Early Tiahuanaco culture and period. In addition to pottery fragments many implements of stone, bone, copper, and other similar materials were found in the excavations.

Early Tiahuanaco has a small area of distribution. Decanters and bowls are the most frequent of the few simple shapes. The painted decoration is either red on buff, or polychrome with black, white, red, brown, orange, and yellow, the designs mainly rectilinear geometric, but with some animal motifs. There is little or no modelling but a little incised decoration. The surface is highly polished.

The general picture of the Experimental period is one of small discrete local groups, on more or less the same cultural plane, but without any political or religious bond, and with considerable local variation. The emphasis was on agriculture, and on the development and improvement of techniques in economic life and in handicrafts. Formalized religion apparently played a small role in native life at this time; shrines and temples seem to have been few.

As before remarked, the division between the preparatory Experimental and the full-blown Florescent periods is a vague, indefinite one, for the transition was slow, even, and unbroken, and intermediate phases may be placed in one or the other, according to the opinion of the individual. Diagnostic pottery styles evolved into others: White-on-Red into Interlocking at Chancay and Pachacamac, Chiripa into Pucara and Early Tiahuanaco. Most of these later phases could be placed in either period, and Pucara and Early Tiahuanaco, as well as Paracas Necropolis, are now generally placed in this Experimental period.

The length of this Experimental period is a most controversial question, and the estimates vary greatly. According to the chronological scheme adopted herein, it lasted about five centuries, from c. 300 B.C. to A.D. 200. Other 'guess-dates' are from 400 B.C. to A.D. 400, a period of eight hundred years.

Chapter 5

THE FLORESCENT ERA

c. A.D. 200–600

By the close of the Developmental Era and the Experimental period, an epoch represented by Salinar and Early Gallinazo on the north coast, and by Paracas on the south coast, Peruvian civilization, at least as expressed in technology – weaving ceramics, metallurgy and other handicrafts – had passed its adolescence and was prepared to enter the classic stage. The crafts had a firm basis, and most of the techniques had been developed. Later periods saw a refinement of these, a great increase in quantity production, a florescence of art, a development of social institutions and civic patterns, but little change in economic or technical methods. In fact, the apogee of the latter was certainly reached in these times.

This era is therefore termed 'Florescent' because in it Peruvian culture, as represented in economy, technology, and art, flourished to achieve its maximum. It was a relatively long era, probably encompassing much of the first millennium of the Christian epoch. It consists of only one period, the Florescent. As generally believed by archaeologists, it was a period of about four centuries, during which the Peruvian cultures attained and retained a high level of excellence. There was no uniformity, no ubiquitous 'horizon style' to tie the various regions together. As in the preceding periods, we know nothing historically of the various peoples, their languages or wars; all our data have been supplied by the spade and trowel of the archaeologist.

These excavations indicate that, for a period of several centuries, artefacts and handicraft of a technical and artistic quality that was not later surpassed were made in most parts of Peru, but especially on the coast. The period ends, not with any catastrophic war, as did most Old World eras, and not with any 'dark age' of cultural retrogression, but with the appearance of the

73

Wari-Tiahuanaco 'horizon style', a pan-Peruvian influence, which affords a convenient time-marker. The many peoples with their minor variant cultures continued their lives untrammelled except for adopting and adapting to their cultural patterns the Wari-Tiahuanaco art style.

The period was characterized by admirable craftsmanship in textiles, ceramics, metallurgy, and minor arts, by high development of art styles, and, in most places, by the erection of massive architectural structures. Agricultural techniques, the basis of existence, were highly advanced with their concomitants of extensive agricultural engineering features.

Dwelling-houses were now relatively comfortable, permanent structures of adobe bricks or stone, and immense public works, temples and forts, were built in most regions, except the south coast. Skull deformation was a general practice, and trephining was very common, especially on the south coast.

Religion had apparently become highly developed, theocratic, and organized with a priesthood and a pantheon in which anthropomorphic deities, especially a feline, were prominent. Nature- and ancestor-worship seem to have been rather universal, as were human sacrifices and the taking of trophy heads. Worship was probably largely by ritualistic ceremonies and dances.

The increase in population must have been great, but competition was not so great as not to afford plenty of leisure time which the various groups utilized in cultural development according to the local pattern, in rest and relaxation, and in improvements in technology.

No cultural remains of this period have yet been identified in the central highlands, later to become the cultural centre of Peru in the Inca period, but in both the northern and southern highlands there were culture centres that are ascribed to this horizon. Apparently, however, the major civilizations continued to be on the coast. In addition to this fact, the objects there are much better preserved, and consequently much more excavation has been done there, both by native *huaqueros* and by archaeologists.

In this period flourished the two native cultures that have probably furnished the major part of the outstanding Peruvian ceramic art products that today grace the museums of the world and awake the admiration of artists and craftsmen: the Moche of the northern coast, and the Nazca of the southern coast.

The Moche culture has been known, mainly by its extraordinarily naturalistic ceramics, for a long time, but it was formerly termed Proto-Chimú or Early Chimú, since it preceded the historically known Chimú empire in the same region. The civilization centred in the valleys of Chicama, Moche, Virú, and Santa, and also extended southward to Nepeña and Casma, and northward to Pacasmayo. It had almost certainly been extended by military conquest. The irrigable areas of these valleys were utilized for agriculture while the temples and the great graveyards from which quantities of exquisite pottery and other artefacts have been extracted were placed on the desert edges of the cultivated fields; this was generally true of the villages also.

Moche culture – at least as far as ceramics are concerned – developed out of Cupisnique without being affected by Salinar and Gallinazo, cultures of lesser geographical and historical extent. Its beginnings went back into the Experimental period.

Terrestrial wild animal life was still present but was probably of slight economic importance to the Moche, though they took as much advantage of it as possible, using nets, javelins and spear-throwers, and blow-guns. Judging by the scenes depicted on the pottery, however, hunting had largely become a sport of the privileged classes. The domesticated llama and guinea-pig provided most of the meat diet. Naturally, sea food, in the shape of fish, shellfish, and even sea lions, was a welcome addition to the vegetable diet, and its procurement was an important, though doubtless unspecialized, industry. Small one-man boats or *balsas*, probably identical with those used today, were made of *totora* reed. Men ventured in these a considerable distance to sea, to fish with lines and hooks without barbs, or with harpoons, or to spread their nets supported by gourds. Large *balsas* holding several persons, like those used today on Lake Titicaca, were apparently also made.

The basis of existence, however, was agriculture, and this had been brought to technical perfection. Irrigation works, most of them now long since abandoned but a few still in use, watered almost every possible acre of land and doubtless supported a much larger population than live in these valleys at present. In some places, however, potentially fertile land seems to have been unused, indicating that the population had not reached its maximum and that the pressure of population was not very great. Aqueducts and canals were made in every valley, some of them immense engineering projects that required not only an enormous amount of labour to carry out but a high degree of knowledge and experience to plan. Thus La Cumbre canal, still in use today, conducts water from the headwaters of the Chicama River to near the mouth, a distance of about 75 miles (113 km.). Aqueducts were built to carry these irrigation canals across intersecting ravines. The aqueduct at Ascope, also in the Chicama Valley, is one of the great engineering triumphs of ancient Peru nearly a mile (1400 m.) long, fifty feet (15 m.) high, and has a cubic content of over a million cubic yards (785,000 cu. m.) of earth.

By this time all the known Peruvian food plants had been brought under cultivation and developed to practically their final stage of perfection. The major crops were corn (maize), beans, peanuts, potatoes, sweet potatoes, chilli peppers, yucca (manioc), pumpkins, gourds, cotton, and coca, as well as avocado, tuna, granadilla, chirimoya, guanábana, tumbo, papaya, pineapple, and the lesser-known pacai, lúcuma, jiquima, yacón, achira, pepino, quinoa, oca, mashua, lupin, ulluco, and cañahua. Some of these were unknown previously. The latter six are not found on the coast but restricted to the highlands. The fermented beer, chicha, was made from corn, probably exactly as it still is today. Guano fertilizer was employed, and the agricultural tools, the digging stick and the hoe, were the same as those used by the Inca many centuries later.

Our information on the Moche culture is rather fuller than that on other civilizations of this early period because, in addition to the many actual objects found in the graves, the very naturalistic modelled pottery, and the dynamic scenes painted on some of it, afford much data on many phases of native life.

Civic planning was not yet a cultural feature, and the Moche villages were groups of houses arranged haphazardly. The houses, judging by pottery models of them as well as by the actual remains, were rather small but consisted of several rectangular rooms. Some were built on terraces and some had open patios. The roofs were gabled and thatched with straw, supported by wooden posts and with opening for smoke and ventilation. The walls were of large rectangular adobe bricks made in moulds, the surface frequently decorated with arabesques, but the lower foundations were generally of rough stone.

The Moche erected enormous temples, the most impressive of these being the great twin pyramids at Moche, not far from the present city of Trujillo; they are locally known today as the 'Huaca del Sol' (Temple of the Sun) and the 'Huaca de la Luna' (Temple of the Moon). Both consist of terraced platforms, and the larger, that of the Sun, is surmounted by a terraced pyramid, all solidly built of adobe bricks in astronomical numbers. The Huaca del Sol is the most stupendous structure on the coast. The base platform measures 750 by 450 ft (228 by 136 m.) and is 60 ft (18 m.) high, rising in five terraces. A causeway 20 ft (6 m.) wide and nearly 300 ft (90 m.) long leads to the north end, and a stepped pyramid 340 ft (103 m.) square and 75 ft (23 m.) high surmounts the southern end of the platform. It has been estimated to contain 130 million adobe bricks. The Huaca de la Luna lacks the pyramid and the platform is smaller, 260 by 195 ft (80 by 60 m.), and 70 ft (21 m.) high. On the top are remains of a few rooms whose walls bear traces of frescoes painted in black, white, red, yellow, blue, pink, and brown in typical Moche design motifs (Plates 1B, 2A).

Smaller isolated pyramids of adobe bricks are found at most of the other Moche sites; some of them are decorated with arabesques in clay relief. Murals painted in colour and showing human figures very similar to those found on painted Moche pottery vessels have recently been uncovered at Pañamarca. These great sub-structures certainly served as foundations for temples, traces of some of which still remain. Other large structures are presumed to have been forts since they are located in strategic places, are often surrounded by walls, and are entered by narrow, steep stairs. Roads of a standard width of 33 ft (9·8 m.) seem to date from this period, and platforms at intervals along them suggest that the later Inca pattern of relay messengers was already in vogue.

The effigy figures on the pottery vessels as well as the objects found in the graves give us a good picture of dress and adornment in the Moche period. As among most early peoples – and as in nature – the male was much more gaily attired than the female. Women generally wore nothing but a long shirt and simple ear pendants. Presumably, when at work, the ordinary man wore only a loincloth, but the effigy figures of men, doubtless garbed in their 'Sunday best', show a great development of clothing and ornament, probably distinctive of rank or occupation. In addition to the ubiquitous breechcloth, they wore undershirts and underskirts beneath the more ornate shirts and skirts. All were, of course, rectangular pieces of woven cloth, never cut or tailored, which were fastened around the waist by woven belts. The headdresses were very varied, some just simple turbans, others very large and sumptuously decorated; the latter apparently varied according to, and indicated, rank or office. Doubtless bright-coloured feathers, and apparently even stuffed birds and ornaments of gold and silver were attached to them. Ear and nose ornaments, necklaces and finger rings were probably more or less standard adornment for any man of any social position; they were made of precious metals, semi-precious stones, shell, bone, or almost any other suitable substance.

Apparently the Moche wore no foot coverings, but painted their feet and lower legs in a fashion that recalls boots, and also sometimes painted the face and body with designs that apparently indicated rank or occupation. There is no evidence of tattooing, however.

The effigy pottery vessels indicate that amputation, bonesetting, and circumcision were practised by the Moche, and that diseases were treated by the almost universal American Indian custom of sucking out the tangible object believed to be the cause of the illness.

Owing to the occasional, though rare, heavy rains in this northern coastal region, and also the amount of saltpetre in the soil, very few Moche textiles have survived even sufficiently to afford a good idea of the techniques, though the effigies and painted scenes on the ceramics indicate that it was a highly developed industry, and possibly even made on a quantity-production level. Probably it was on the same high level of competence as in the other regions on this horizon, with the exception of the south coast, where the work was especially good. All the usual techniques such as tapestry, embroidery, brocade, gingham, and twill were known. Plain weaves made of cotton predominate, and wool fibre seems to have been rare.

Considerable progress had been made in metallurgy and Moche goldsmiths were capable craftsmen. Embossed ornaments of thin gold were still in the majority but casting (doubtless by the *cire per due* process), soldering, annealing, and gilding were common practices. Bronze was still unknown, but other alloys of gold, silver, and copper were made. As in the Old World Bronze Age, the Moche made heavy implements of solid copper; elsewhere in Peru at this time all metals served mainly ornamental purposes (Plates 62, 63).

Gourds were artistically decorated, and the graves contain many art, as well as utilitarian, objects of carved wood, shell, and bone, inlaid shell mosaics, stone club-heads and axes, staff-heads, baskets, and many other objects. Musical instruments of a number of types have been found: percussion instruments such as drums and tambourines, rattles, clappers, and gongs; trumpets; and several of variable tones, such as flutes and pan-pipes.

But it is in the field of ceramics that the Moche excelled as artists and craftsmen; the perfection of their realistic modelling has nowhere been exceeded, and rarely equalled. Quantities of tastefully moulded vessels were buried with the dead, and today large groups of them grace many museums and private collections. Specialists divide Moche pottery into five periods, two formative, two climactic, and one decadent under pressure from the Wari Tiahuanaco culture. Though made in moulds, duplicates are rare. The shapes are simple and few, but with countless variations, the stirrup-spout vase being most characteristic. In most of these the body may be modified into almost every conceivable form, humans engaged in many activities, animals, vegetables, and objects such as houses and boats. Deformation, mutilations, punishments, and captives are portrayed. Erotic

scenes – elsewhere in America a rare art element – are characteristic, and modern collector's items. The acme of realism was
achieved in the so-called portrait vases, so lifelike that they doubtless were representations of definite individuals (Plates 24, 25).

Only single figures are ordinarily represented in this ceramic
modelling, which is representational rather than symbolic.
Posture and expression are admirably portrayed. The technical
craftsmanship is excellent also, the vessels being painted in red
or black on a cream slip, well baked and polished; black vessels
are rare.

In a second group of stirrup-spouted vessels the upper part is
plain but the body painted with realistic scenes such as war, hunting, fishing, and ceremonial or diplomatic gatherings. Here the
representation is of groups of persons, always shown in profile,
and in rapid dynamic action, generally running. While very
much stylized and not approaching the modelled relief in realism,
they afford much data on the life of this early time, of which we
have not the slightest historical or traditional record, and which
could be secured in no other way. The ceramics have been aptly
termed a picture-book of the culture (Figure 2).

There is considerable evidence – though still not enough to be
convincing to most students – that the Moche had developed
some system of 'writing' or, let us say, non-verbal communication.[1] It was certainly not alphabetic, phonetic, syllabic, or probably even pictographic, and probably most nearly resembled in
kind the *quipu* of later periods. The message, however, was apparently incised on lima beans and could be interpreted only by
a special class of persons trained in such decipherment. How
standardized were the ideograms we have no means of knowing.
They were probably limited to factual data; no philosophical discussions could have been thus transmitted. And probably the
reader had to be familiar with the idiosyncrasies of the writer.

Data on this question are derived almost exclusively from
scenes on the painted vessels which show runners with a certain
type of attire, probably messengers, in dynamic attitudes, carrying small bags. Other vessels portray beans painted in dozens of
different designs, and still others are modelled in the form of

1. Larco Hoyle, 1942, 1943.

persons, again with standardized characteristics and attire, who seem to be studying the beans; these men are presumably the decoders. Similarly, apparently painted beans on Nazca vessels suggest that the latter people may possibly also have had the same or a similar custom.

The picture of the Moche afforded us by the archaeologists is that of a dynamic, almost aggressive, people, far along the road to civilization. They had evidently passed beyond the simple democratic stage and had evolved a status society in which a small aristocratic class directed or commanded the life and labour of the masses. There was also great division of labour and specialization of occupation and crafts. While we cannot be sure whether a potter or goldsmith, for instance, worked at his craft the year round or only in the agricultural off-season, there were probably priests, physicians, and similar full-time practitioners who did no farming. There may have been a slave class, and there almost certainly were aristocratic, noble, or regal classes. In the pottery effigy vessels and paintings, definite attire, accoutrements, paraphernalia, or symbols indicate the various classes and crafts, and these are often shown in zoomorphic form, such as birds, centipedes, or dragon-flies for messengers, foxes for savants, jaguars for men in authority.

The great differences in the quality of the costumes worn by different personages in the pottery effigies indicate differences in social status, as do grave contents. The paintings show certain persons on raised platforms under arbours receiving obeisances of others, or carried in litters; these obviously were leaders or rulers. They also sit at higher levels at meals. Servants are often depicted as lizards. Since there seems to have been no differentiation between secular, military, and religious leadership, it is rather obvious that the political system approached a theocracy. Strict authority is also shown by effigies of persons who have evidently undergone punishment, such as mutilation, or scenes depicting execution or stoning.

Warriors seem to have been especially highly honoured, which indicates an aggressive or militaristic pattern, for effigies of warriors in full panoply are especially frequent; they carry maces, battle-axes, spears and spear-throwers, and shields. Conquest of neighbouring peoples had probably already begun. Prisoners are depicted as nude with ropes around their necks, but even here class distinction lifts its ugly head, for some prisoners, probably war captives, are shown carried in litters. Though if some observers might prefer to consider them wounded enemies, borne off by primitive Red Cross stretcher-bearers to a first-aid dressing station, none can deny it, though such was not the aboriginal pattern!

The Moche world was obviously man's, and women definitely

Figure 2. *Drawing of a scene from a Moche pottery vessel. Chief in house receiving captives borne in litters*

occupied an inferior position. No women are ever shown in scenes of ceremonies, but only engaged in domestic tasks.

The authoritarian pattern of the Moche, when applied to the large population with leisure time in the agricultural off-season, naturally resulted in immense public works such as the great engineering irrigation features, and especially in the enormous temple pyramids.

Whether by military conquest or not, at the end of the period the Moche culture succumbed to pressure from the all-pervading highland Tiahuanaco influence from Wari which, however, dominated no farther north than Chicama. After several centuries the Moche tradition was carried on by the Chimu (q.v.).

Culturally and economically, the life of the inhabitants of the central coast valleys probably differed little from that of the Moche, but, since their products were not outstanding, less attention has been paid to them, though considerable excavation has been done in this region, especially at the great cemetery at Ancón and the famous temple at Pachacamac. No effigy vessels or painted scenes give information on the life of the people. As in the northern region, immense pyramids of adobe were built, evidence of community activity under direction or authority. Handicraft was good but not impressive. Ceramics were aesthetically unimportant as compared with the products of the north and south coasts. The sequential temporal phases are generally known by the pottery types characteristic of them, of interest and importance to few but professional archaeologists.

The valleys of Chancay, Rimac, and Lurin fall together culturally – and probably historically – and are considered as forming the Central Coast culture. The valleys of Supe, Paramonga, and Huarmey to the north are also generally included in this group, but are not so typical, nor so well known for the early periods.

Little is known of cultural developments except the changes in the ceramic types that characterized them and by which the sub-periods are known. Following the Chancay White-on-Red of the Experimental period, the Intermediate, Interlocking, and Early Lima periods are distinguished. The not-very-well-chosen name 'Interlocking' was selected because the most frequent decorative motif is a very conventionalized fish, obviously adapted from textile design, repeated in an interlocked pattern and painted in black and white on a red base. The change from White-on-Red pottery to Interlocking was one of fashion, for the change was gradual, and intermediate forms are found; it was obviously not accompanied by a change in population. The Interlocking style is generally ascribed to the Florescent period. The immense adobe pyramid of Pachacamac was probably begun in this period, since Interlocking is the earliest major ceramic type found there; the great site of Cajamarquilla close to Lima may have been begun at about the same time. At Pachacamac Interlocking is associated with a type of negative-painted ware.

Early Lima is a slightly later pottery style found at the type site of Nievería near Cajamarquilla, at Pachacamac, and at other sites in the Lima region. The shapes are more graceful, with some life forms, and the painted decoration more pleasing, predominantly white on a dark red surface. Spheroid pitchers with short vertical spouts are especially common (Plate 29B).

While the stratigraphical evidence in the Nazca Valley, more than a hundred miles south-east of Paracas, indicates clearly that the Paracas cultures preceded the Nazca and possibly gave birth to the latter, the temporal difference cannot be great. Paracas textiles show demoniacal figures very similar to those on Nazca ceramics. It is likely that the Paracas Necropolis culture was contemporary with the earliest phase (A) of Nazca, though regional differences exist, as would be expected.

The Nazca culture was unknown until 1901 when it was discovered by the old master of Peruvian archaeology, Max Uhle. Before that time only five of the beautiful Nazca polychrome pottery vessels, of unidentified provenance, were known in museums. A decade later practically all the graveyards had been almost completely looted and all great museums boasted of large collections of Nazca ceramics.

While of coastal type of culture, the Nazca were not a littoral people. The fertile valleys in this region are some fifty miles inland, the intervening area being occupied by a desolate arid range of hills and sand in which the rivers disappear.

Until 1952 no extensive excavations had been made in the Nazca region, except by treasure hunters, and practically nothing was known except the association of grave contents. Brief reports have clarified the picture greatly.

The Nazca culture developed directly out of the Paracas, apparently without change of population. The evolution may have taken place in the Nazca region where Nazca sites are underlain by ten feet (3 m.), at times, of typical Paracas refuse, with intermediate stages. No large structures were built of adobe and there was no stone masonry of this period, but small houses were built with adobe walls. While there were no known large towns, the houses tended to cluster in small village-like groups. Also prominent natural features were covered with adobes, making small pyramids and terraces. The adobes used in construction were variable in size and form, from conical to pancake shape, and were combined with wattle-and-daub to build the houses. There was apparently great building activity in the earliest Nazca period.

Owing to the absence of effigy vessels and painted scenes, our knowledge of Nazca life and customs is far less than that of the

Moche, its northern contemporary. But the general picture seems to be one of a sedentary democratic people without marked class distinctions or authoritarianism, possibly without an established religion. There is less difference in the 'richness' or poverty of the graves, and women seem to be on an equality with men in this respect. The apparent absence of great public works, of extensive engineering features, and of temple pyramids implies a lack of authoritarian leadership. Instead, the leisure time of the people seems to have been spent in individual production, especially in the making of quantities of perfect, exquisite textiles and pottery vessels. This seems to indicate a strong cult of ancestor-worship. Cloths on which an incredible amount of labour was spent were made especially for funerary offerings and interred with the dead. The orientation seems to have been towards individualized religion rather than towards community participation, dictation, coercion, and aggression.

The Nazca graves are generally bottle-shaped with a shaft running down to a chamber which may be at a depth of anywhere between close to the surface and fifteen feet (4·5 m.). Many of the skulls show longitudinal deformation, and the bodies give evidence of the practice of tattooing. The flexed bodies were wrapped with cloths which are well preserved and of excellent quality, though not equalling the exquisite products of Paracas. Many beautiful polychrome pottery vessels and other objects of mortuary furniture were placed in the graves.

'Lovely' best describes Nazca ceramics. The shapes are few and usually simple with little relief, though some effigy modelling is found; in contrast to Moche, the emphasis is on polychrome painting with polished surface (Plate 28). As many as eleven soft harmonious pastel colours may be employed on one vessel: black, white, violet, grey, flesh-colour, and two shades each of red, yellow, and brown; the absence of blue and green is noteworthy. The motifs seem to fall into two main categories, naturalistic biomorphic and mythological. The former are repeated figures of birds, fish, insects, vegetal products, and similar objects. They are obvious yet stylized, naturalistic but not realistic or pictorial. Other designs depict monstrous or anthropomorphic animals, presumably deities, in which the characteristic features are emphasized; one of the most frequent of these is a feline. Bowls are the commonest forms, also spheroid vessels with two short vertical spouts connected by a bridge.

Nazca ceramic styles are seen in four sequential stages, Early, Middle, Late, and Nazca-Wari, though the differences are not clear cut and the criteria rather subjective. Early types tended to be simple, often with repetitions of natural objects such as vegetables, birds, or fish. Vessels of the Middle period became more abstract and symbolic, the natural motifs more conventionalized or anthropomorphic. In the late period effigy forms became more common, the anthropomorphic designs more complicated. Vessels of the Nazca-Wari late period were a little decadent with more careless workmanship, as well as characteristic period shapes such as tall cups or beakers.

Nazca textiles are lovely and admirable. Progress is shown by the larger number of techniques; in fact, practically every one of the many Peruvian textile processes was known to the Nazca weaver; no important one was later invented. Embroidery, tapestry, brocade, gauze, and warp or weft patterns were the most common. Painted cloths are also found. Three-dimensional needle-knitting was popular. Wool, imported from the highlands, was more used than the native cotton. As with the ceramics, the range of colours was enormous and amazing. As many as 190 tints on the scale in seven main colours have been identified in early Nazca fabrics, though some of these may be due to differential fading. The design motifs also bear some resemblance to those on the pottery vessels.

Metallurgy, on the other hand, was retarded, being far less developed than in the Moche region. Only gold was known, and the people seem to have been ignorant of – or untrained in – the technique of casting. Dainty ornaments were made, however, by the old process of hammering the metal into thin sheets, cutting it into graceful shapes, and decorating it with embossed or repoussé designs.

The taking of human heads – probably from enemies in combat – was a striking element of Nazca culture. These are depicted in ceramic and textile designs and have also been found in the tombs, flattened, painted, and attached to slings for carrying.

The largest Nazca site, or most thickly occupied area, the putative 'capital', is at Cahuachi on the lower-middle Nazca River
just before it enters the first gorge in the sterile hills. The word
'enormous' is applied to it, but its actual area is not on record.
Just at the gorge is a remarkable site known as 'La Estaquería',
Spanish for 'the place of stakes'. This has been aptly termed a
'wooden Stonehenge'. On a level sandy area quantities of trunks
of trees, *algarrobo* and *huarango*, have been planted in orderly
rows and masses. The greater number are in a quadrangle of
twelve rows of twenty posts each, about seven feet (2 m.) apart
and there are lines of posts, and a few posts of much larger size
adjacent. Although the aligned posts are merely columns, most
of the single ones have forked tops and almost certainly supported a roof or canopy. The wood is still hard and firm – and
after at least a half, and probably a full millennium or more! For
the structure is clearly pre-Spanish, and the surrounding graves
are of Nazca period. Presumably they are late, probably Nazca-
Wari, but they may be much older; there is no evidence (Plate 8B).

In the absence of any written records or historical traditions
we can know little or nothing of the degree of scientific knowledge of the more ancient peoples of Peru, such as, for instance,
their knowledge of astronomy. But celestial phenomena have
always been of the greatest importance to early peoples, especially to farming folk who needed to know the progress of the
seasons, irrespective of the vagaries of the weather, in order to
plan their times for planting and harvest. The surprisingly accurate astronomical and calendrical knowledge of the Maya is
revealed to us almost in its entirety mainly by one old book or
codex that luckily escaped the holocausts of the Spanish Conquest. Although the Peruvians were apparently not so calendrically minded as the Mesoamericans, it is likely that all the more
highly cultured peoples of America were not much inferior to the
Maya in their astronomical erudition, and were far better informed than is generally credited.

Just as, in a number of other regions, the orientation of
edifices and other structures has thrown some light on the astronomical knowledge of their builders, so in the Nazca region the
ancient peoples left on their land tangible and intelligible evi-

dences of their interest in and knowledge of this subject. This has been one of the most interesting, surprising, and unique discoveries of recent years in Peruvian archaeology, and a direct result of aeroplane observations.[1]

In the Nazca region, at some distance from the sea, and mainly on both sides of the Palpa Valley, is a stretch of tableland, free of the sand that envelops the coastal region, and covered with small broken stones. It is about forty miles in length, a mile or more in width. Rain is unknown and the sunshine is practically eternal. Locally it is called a *pampa*, though not a blade of vegetation can be seen. The changelessness of the region is incredible. Marks furrowed on the surface several years ago look as though they had been made the day before; a bit of paper lost by a previous expedition seems to have just been dropped.

The small stones that cover the surface probably contain iron, and the suns of many millennia have formed a dark patina on their upper faces. These stones were removed from certain areas by the ancient peoples and piled at the edges of these places, leaving designs in the lighter-coloured sand and gravel below. Long straight narrow lines radiate from hills, mounds, and other strategic points. Many lines are parallel; others cross and crisscross. Large rectilinear trapezoidal spaces were also cleared, and there are furthermore a number of spirals, and large figures of animals (Plate 9A). These latter give clear proof of the identity of their makers, if more evidence were needed other than the region and the occasional fragments of typical Nazca pottery found on the surface, looking as though the vessel had just been broken. For the great figures on the surface of the land, probably representing divinities, are in the same art style as those on the surface of the potsherds, typically Nazca.

These figures, it must be remembered, are very large and made on flat ground. There is no near-by elevation and they can be seen to good advantage only from the air, from an aeroplane or balloon. Doubtless they were made to be seen by celestial deities. Their delineation, however, brings up some intriguing suggestions and possibilities. How were they made so perfect without being seen in proper perspective? The makers must have

1. Reiche, 1949; Kosok and Reiche, 1947, 1949.

known much about proportions. Could they have worked from a small model on a grid?

The lines and figures are now being carefully studied and measured, but no final definitive report on them has yet been issued. Some of the straight lines, at least, seem to verify the presumptive hypothesis that they were astronomical, pointing towards solstitial and equinoctial points, or towards other important rising or setting places. As such, they could have served as a farmer's almanac or calendar, indicating the seasons. The problem is a very difficult one, owing to the great number of such lines. However, the measurements of the lines apparently indicate the linear standards of these people. A report from Miss Maria Reiche is to the effect that, from one centre ten feet (3 m.) square, twenty-three straight lines radiate; two are solstitial lines, one equinoctial. Most of them are 595 feet (182 m.) long. Some lines are found of half or quarter this standard. Another frequent measurement, perhaps another standard, is eighty-five feet (26 m.).

Throughout the early periods, information concerning the Peruvian highlands is far less than that concerning the coast, largely because, on account of the rains, objects of organic materials are not preserved, and therefore little digging has been done by natives. Scientifically controlled excavations have also been fewer than on the coast. The little evidence seems to indicate that the culture in the two regions was about equally high, though naturally the economic life differed considerably. Less is known, of course, about the cultural evolutionary development. The sequential phases are placed in the several periods mainly on the basis of the coastal evolutionary periods with which they seem to correspond in time. This is admittedly unproved.

In the northern highlands, toward the end of the Experimental period, the interesting ceramic technique of negative painting was introduced and later came into great vogue. This also is considered a horizon style, since it was known in all the coastal cultures. It became of maximum importance, however, in the northern region, especially in the northern highlands where it is the characteristic ware of the Recuay culture, generally assigned to the Florescent period. This Recuay ware, one of the better-known types of Peruvian pottery, is of many varied shapes, many of them modelled life-forms somewhat similar, though much inferior, to Moche pottery. The surfaces are often decorated with very stylized rectilinear animal designs, in which the jaguar predominates. There is also another type of Recuay ware, known as Recuay B, painted in positive designs; this seems to be on the whole later than the negative-painted Recuay A (Plate 29A).

The vertical extent of the architecture that was a characteristic of this region in earlier days probably continued into this period, that is to say, two- and three-storey temples with heavy slab roofs, and subterranean houses and galleries with as many as two storeys underground, built mainly of stone slabs and entered by vertical shafts. Stone sculpture, missing on the coast, is also very characteristic of this region and period. The figures are probably those of deities, but are decidedly ungraceful and archaistic, being massive, and columnar or ovoid, with low relief and vestigial limbs. There are also carved slabs and lintels in a rather different art style.[1] Ornaments and tools of copper have been found in the graves, but of course textiles and other objects of organic materials have long since disappeared.

Strange to say, no important site of this period has yet been identified in the central highlands. Such sites must of course exist, and remain to be discovered or identified.

An horizon art style dominates and characterizes this period. This style apparently emanated from the highlands and is best typified at the great site of Tiahuanaco, from which it takes its name. The influence, probably that of a religious cult that had its centre at Tiahuanaco, spread to almost all parts of Peru and is obvious in the art styles of the various regions. It thus recapitulates the influence of the much earlier Chavín cult. It apparently originated and reached its apogee in the highlands in the earlier part of this period; later it reached the coast, where the style is sometimes known as 'Epigonal'. For reasons to be explained later, this horizon art style is now known as 'Wari-Tiahuanaco'. The horizon is often termed the 'Middle Period'. The classic Tiahuanaco of the highlands apparently did not develop from

1. Schaedel, 1948b, 1948c.

the 'Early Tiahuanaco' of that region; the styles are considerably different.

While a Tiahuanaco or 'Megalithic' Empire is no longer generally credited, some loose political force probably accompanied the spread of the Tiahuanaco cult. At any rate it seems to have been a period of unrest, with an increase in expansion, aggression, and conquest, and some warfare between neighbouring local groups. This was probably a result of a strengthening of political organization and more centralized power within the groups. It was apparently not due to population pressure, for there seems to be some evidence of a decrease in population, at least on the coast, although it was still large.

The Tiahuanaco influence, while strong, was not an engulfing or permanent one. The local regions retained their individualities, and, towards the end of the period, the rather uniform art style disappeared, like a fashion, and the local cultures re-emerged as quite separate entities, each with its own peculiarities.

TIAHUANACO

Mystery and glamour have always hung about the ruins of Tiahuanaco (Plate 10). It has been claimed to be of immense age, the place of origin of all American, if not of all world, civilizations.[1] Some fanatics even have it originally on an island, then sunk beneath the Pacific, and finally uplifted, together with the Andes, intact to its present height! Even solid scholars have until recently believed it the seat of a great forgotten Megalithic Empire. Discarding all such theories, silly or plausible, enough of mystery remains to intrigue and puzzle the unimaginative archaeologist.

Tiahuanaco lies at a height of about 13,000 ft (c 4000 m.), an altitude exceeded by few Alpine peaks and by only a very few in the United States; it is thirteen miles (21 km.) south-east of Lake Titicaca, the world's highest navigable lake (12,506 ft). Bleak, chilly, a practically treeless *puna*, too high for intensive agriculture, it is the last place in the world to expect a great stupendous archaeological site. No wonder many mystics have felt sure

1. Posnansky, 1946.

that the climate and environment must have been much less rigorous when it was in its prime. No credible traditions refer to it. Today the scattered families of Aymara Indians pasture their llamas and alpacas and raise their potatoes in the more fertile parts of the region – a stolid, taciturn people with no high degree of culture. Did their ancestors quarry, transport, and erect these massive stone blocks so perfectly cut and fitted?

The major structures occupy about a sixth of a square mile (1475 by 3275 ft or 450 by 1000 metres), and consist of four principal units and a number of minor ones. Tiahuanaco is a unique site. While, as usual in the highlands, no adobe was employed in the constructions and all the ruins are of stone, there are few walls, and none of any height. It was obviously an important ceremonial site rather than an occupied town, and bears considerable superficial resemblance to Carnac, with long lines of megalithic monuments, though, of course, much more carefully carved. The masonry, in fact, is among the most skilful in the Andean region, as well as among the most megalithic.

The largest unit, known as the Acapana, is a terraced pyramid about 50 ft (15 m.) high, originally faced with stone. Of irregular ground plan, it is roughly 690 ft (210 m.) on each side. The remains of a large reservoir with an overflow canal, and foundations for houses, suggest that it might have been a place of refuge in case of attack.

The Calasasaya is a large square area about 445 by 425 ft (135 by 130 m.) delimited by upright monoliths which apparently originally formed part of a continuous wall. The interior is raised, and within this is a sunken court entered by a megalithic stairway. Associated with the Calasasaya is the most famous monument at Tiahuanaco, the great monolithic gateway known as the 'Gateway of the Sun' (Plate 10B). This enormous sculpture, carved of a single block of andesite, is about ten feet (3 m.) high, twelve and a half feet (3·75 m.) wide, and is estimated to weigh about ten tons. A man can easily pass through the rectangular doorway cut in the centre, above which is a low frieze in typical Tiahuanaco style. In this, a large central figure, certainly a god and possibly Viracocha, is flanked by forty-eight small rectangular figures, running toward him. It is one of the archaeological wonders of America. For centuries broken and askew, it was restored to proper position in 1908.

Two smaller enclosures are the Palacio and one termed Puma Puncu; the latter is another platform structure. Both of these contain large stone slabs and blocks, well dressed and fitted, some of them estimated to weigh more than one hundred tons. Smaller broken monolithic gateways are also common. A few well-built subterranean chambers have been found.

Both basalt and sandstone were used in the construction of Tiahuanaco, and the nearest quarries of the latter are three miles (5 km.) from the site. The stone-work is unusually well done, with smooth faces, the great blocks perfectly fitted together. They are sometimes held together more firmly by notches, or – something new and unique in Peruvian masonry – by copper cramps. T-shaped depressions were cut into adjacent sides of two stone blocks where copper objects made to fit were hammered in.

Tiahuanaco is also famed for its great human statuary. The largest of these was unknown until 1932 when it was discovered by the American Peruvianist Wendell C. Bennett[1] in the course of his excavations; it was carried to La Paz and erected in a plaza there. This tall forbidding figure of red sandstone is over twenty-four feet (7·3 m.) in height, and from forty-two to fifty inches (1·05 to 1.27 m.) in width and thickness. The low-relief art is symmetrical, stiff, and very characteristic of the site and period (Plate 11).

It has been suggested that the site was a great ceremonial centre, to which came a large part of the population of the region on regular rare pilgrimages, at which times they worked, under expert supervision, on the constructions; this implies a well-organized and regulated society with limitless manpower, approaching that of the later Inca. The structures were apparently still uncompleted when work on them ceased.

Few excavations have been done at Tiahuanaco or in its general region. Though textiles are not preserved here, those of this period and type found on the coast suggest that the art was on a high plane, especially in the making of tapestries. Much of

1. Bennett, 1934.

the stone carving in relief is in textile motifs. High-class work was done in gold, silver, and especially in copper.

The classic Tiahuanaco pottery of the great period is most characteristic and a great art. It is a painted, not a modelled style, with relatively few and simple shapes and very diagnostic designs. A goblet with flaring sides is probably the most characteristic shape, next a container made in the shape of a puma or llama, with relief head; bowls and vases of various proportions are common. The designs are, like the Nazca, in many tints and highly burnished, with rich, blending colours, prevailingly dark; black, white, yellow, grey, and brown are the commonest. The most characteristic design is the puma, always shown in profile, but this is very much stylized and conventionalized; condors are frequent, as also are purely geometric elements (Plates 27, 30B).

Almost nothing is known of the daily life of the people of Tiahuanaco, but it probably differed only slightly from that of the highland peoples of later periods; they doubtless grew potatoes and other highland food crops, and bred and used llamas and alpacas.

The tangible evidence of the influence is in the art style of textiles and ceramics. Practically everywhere in Peru – except apparently, strange to say, in the Cuzco region – the local art styles, especially as expressed on pottery, became modified by the adoption of elements obviously related to those found at Tiahuanaco.

In most Peruvian archaeological sites of this period are found flat-based, flaring-sided goblets and bowls painted in four or more colours and highly polished. The motifs are also those of Tiahuanaco: stylized geometric profile pumas, condors, and other figures; the same unmistakable elements are found in the textiles. Every region, naturally, had its characteristic style, its ways of employing these elements and of combining them with the existing local styles.

In the absence of reliable radiocarbon dates, estimates of the date and length of the Classic Tiahuanaco phase vary greatly from the A.D. 200–600 accorded it herein. Some good authorities place it much later, such as A.D. 800–1000.

Lest the reader, who may have thought of all pre-Columbian Peruvians as Inca, be surprised at the number of apparently independent and unique cultures in prehistoric Peru, it may be stated that possibly as many other cultures still remain to be discovered. Relatively few scientific archaeological excavations have been made in Peru, and large parts of the country are practically unknown archaeologically because the paucity of saleable objects that might be recovered has not tempted natives to dig. Future excavations in new sites may be expected to reveal many new cultures, each with its specific type of architecture, ceramics, and other artefacts. Doubtless their languages, religions, and social customs were equally different; of these we will never know anything. The economic basis of life, however, was probably practically the same throughout the highlands at any given time; the same is true of the coast.

Chapter 6

THE CLIMACTIC ERA

c. A.D. 600–1532

THE Climactic Era comprises the final periods of Peruvian culture history. Material culture had reached its maximum development, and probably government also. The pattern of life was urban, militaristic, probably socialistic. Most of the groups and tribes were probably united into a few large nations or empires between which there was violent competition if not war. Beginning with the Expansionist period preceding the Urbanist period with a few such large nations, it closed with the Imperialist period of the all-embracing Inca empire. A final Colonial period, following the Spanish Conquest, might be added.

The Expansionist Period

c. A.D. 600–1000

Tiahuanaco style is found in its classic form only in the area of Tiahuanaco itself; the phases from the coast and the northern highlands are in a slightly different, evolved, but readily recognizable style, and presumed to date from a somewhat later period. It was long surmised that this later coastal Tiahuanaco style must have spread from some focus in the highlands nearer the coast than Tiahuanaco itself; recent studies have suggested that this may have been the site of Wari, and, to indicate this, archaeologists today refer to the Wari-Tiahuanaco influence or style.

The present status of archaeological research in Peru is well exemplified by Huari or Wari. Though mentioned by Cieza de León in 1554 as a pre-Inca site, under the name of Vinaque, it was forgotten until rediscovered by Tello in 1931; only in the last decade has it been investigated.[1] Wari is a large site in the pro-

1. Bennett, 1953a; Rowe, Collier, and Willey, 1950.

vince of Huanta, department of Ayacucho. The ruins may cover as much as four square miles, with quantities of walled enclosures and the remains of buildings and houses. Some of the walls tower to a height of twenty-five feet (7 to 8 metres). All are of masonry made of rude field stones laid in mud and originally faced with mud plaster. The buildings seem to lack both doors and windows and, in this respect, as well as in the type of masonry and general appearance, the site bears much superficial resemblance to Pikillacta, near Cuzco. Only a very little cut stone was used here, in great contrast to Tiahuanaco. A number of carved stone statues, however, have been found; these resemble those of Tiahuanaco more closely than any others, but there is considerable difference. Obviously here was a great residential city, not mainly a ceremonial site.

As usual, it is the ceramics that afford the clue to the temporal placing of Wari. There are a number of types, covering a considerable time period, but two groups of polychrome ware bear a very close resemblance to Coast Tiahuanaco pottery, and to the Late Nazca Wari type, presumed to date from the Tiahuanaco period. Probably, therefore, the Tiahuanaco influence spread to the coast from Wari. Logically, however, large cities like Wari and Pikillacta should belong in the next, Urbanist, period.

The best picture of the Expansionist Wari-Tihuanaco-horizon period is, as usual, secured from the coastal sites where the preservation of material objects is best, and where cemeteries are found. No great edifices were erected, but use of the older ones continued. Excellent textiles of wool and cotton continued to be made, and the tapestries of this period are the finest ever made in Peru; that had become the most popular technique, but many others were known and practised. Some new metallurgical methods, such as silverplating, had been developed.

Wari-Tiahuanaco influence, as evidenced mainly by the horizon art style, is found in all the coastal areas as far north as Chicama (but not in Lambayeque), especially at Chicama, Moche, Virú, Supe, Chancay, Ancón, Nievería, Pachacamac, Cañete, Chincha, Ica, and Nazca. The impact on the peaceful Nazca culture was strong, practically absorbing it, while it affected only slightly the vigorous Moche who soon threw it off and re-established their own pattern.

Archaeologists divide the Coast Tiahuanaco or 'Middle' period into two sub-periods, 'A' and 'B', characterized by pottery styles. 'A' is the Wari-Tihuanaco-influenced polychrome style, generally known on the coast as 'Epigonal'. At Ancón it is known as 'Middle Ancón I'. Each site had its particular modification of this ware. The shapes of coastal Tiahuanaco vessels, however, differ much from those of the highlands; only the goblet and the cup are similar, and vessels with long upright spouts, especially double-spouts, are common. Epigonal pottery is very well made, highly polychrome, with rather elaborate designs (Plate 31A).

The influence of Tiahuanaco ceased with the Epigonal style, for the succeeding 'B' style, known to Peruvianists as 'Black-White-Red', is very different; local variations of it are known as 'Middle Ancón II' and 'Late Ancón I'. The latter is a quasi-horizon style, found over much of northern Peru. It has no congeners, however, in the central and southern highlands. The ware is definitely decadent, softer, unpolished, with simple, poorly executed designs in fewer colours. The shapes are also simple with little if any modelling in life-forms, and the painted decoration is almost exclusively geometric (Plate 31B).

The influence has not been definitely recognized in the central highland, Cuzco, region, but can hardly fail to have been present. As we have seen, the site of Pikillacta near Cuzco, of still unidentified period, bears some resemblance to Wari, definitely of the Tiahuanaco period.

In the northern highlands are small sites in the Chavín architectural tradition but assigned to this period because of the associated ceramics. Wilkawaín, near Huaraz, the most important of these, consists of a stone temple and a number of other one- and two-storey stone houses.[1] The temple is a small replica of the Castillo at Chavín, with three floors, interior staircases, ramps, galleries, rooms, and ventilation shafts; there are seven rooms on each floor. The great roof slabs are placed sloping so as to form a gable roof, but this is covered with dirt and stones to form a sort

1. Bennett, 1944.

of dome. The temple measures about thirty-five by fifty-two feet (10·7 by 15·6 m.). It is much less known even than Chavín, and few of the rooms have been entered, for most of them are filled with stones and other debris which must have been brought there for this purpose. The principal rooms are large, measuring more than seven by twenty-two feet (2·25 by 6·8 m.), and over six feet (1·8 m.) high.

A very distinctive pottery type of which more should be known is what is called the Marañon style. The characteristic shape is a tripod plate, rather flattish and supported on three long conical feet. This form, so common in Mexico and Central America, is otherwise practically unknown in Peru. Shallow bowls are also found, both types painted on the interior in rather fine lines of reddish tints, generally curvilinear, and depicting demoniacal animals as well as geometric elements. The ware is often also termed Middle Huamachuco, as it is found also in the far northern highlands, near Huamachuco and Cajabamba.

In the southern highlands, following classical Tiahuanaco times and the Middle Period, the ceramics became poorer, just as on the coast, and are known as Decadent Tiahuanaco. The designs are carelessly made, the colours fewer, and dull. The classical Tiahuanaco design elements are retained but employed separately, independently, and not as parts of complete designs, such as pumas.

The four centuries here allowed for the Expansionist period, A.D. 600 to 1000, is longer and earlier than that accorded it by good authorities of another school of thought, A.D. 900 to 1200.

The Urbanist Period

c. A.D. 1000–1440

Toward the end of the Expansionist period whatever unity or homogeneity of culture the highland influence from Wari or Tiahuanaco might have produced began to lessen, and local differentiation soon eliminated practically all traces of it. The populations had now probably reached their maxima, civic organizations were well developed, and contentions for land, power, and dominance began. Fortified refuge places were built.

Villages probably contended for mastery and formed alliances and coalitions which in turn fought for domination until at last a few large commonwealths of considerable extent emerged. This was the pattern in many other parts of the world at similar stages of development, but in other times.

These minor nations might well be likened to medieval kingdoms; they set the pattern for the Inca empire that soon conquered and consolidated all of them. For, contrary to the usual American Indian democratic proclivity, there was apparently great stress on social stratification, with noble and aristocratic classes, and reverence for the chief, leader, or 'king'.

Most of our data for this period, both historical and archaeological, refer to the coastal peoples, especially to the Chimú of the northern coast, for the big fertile irrigated river valleys there supported a large concentration of population, whereas in the highland regions, more uniformly watered, the people probably remained somewhat more rural. Nevertheless, even in the highlands, this seems to have been a period when the natives tended to gather into large urban centres, with city planning. It has therefore sometimes been termed the 'City Builder Period'.

Owing to the heavier rainfall on the north coast and the consequent larger size of the irrigated valleys with their greater populations, the largest and most important of the 'kingdoms', that of Chimú, developed on that coast and controlled a great area from Piura in the north to Paramonga in the south (Plates 5B, 6). There is little doubt that military conquest extended the sway of the Chimú north to the Lambayeque and Piura Valleys, and south at least to Casma (Plate 5A). Every valley had its urban centre, but the capital of the Chimú was Chanchán, in the environs of the present city of Trujillo.[1] Chanchán is a stupendous site – and sight. The ruins cover about six square miles, filled – the major part at least – with great tall boundary walls, smaller house walls, streets, reservoirs, pyramids, and other edifices and features expected of a great metropolitan centre. All are built of large rectangular adobe bricks. The occasional torrential rains have eroded the tops of the great walls and covered their bases, but they still tower to a height of some thirty feet (9 m.). When

1. Holstein, 1927.

the lower walls are cleared of the earth that covers and protects them, many of them are found to be covered with arabesque decorations in low relief and probably made by impressions of moulds (Plate 4). The designs are of small, identical repeated motifs, in rows, and apparently derived from textile designs, mainly geometric, but also with conventionalized animals. When cleared – and unless protected – these arabesques, of course, are ruined in the next heavy rain. There are also some wall paintings.

Today the great city is deserted except for the occasional tourist's car traversing the narrow, humpy streets. For the city was planned like a modern one with long straight streets meeting at right angles. The visitor blessed with imagination can visualize them teeming with busy people, the gable-roofed houses full of the domestic sounds of women and children. The aboriginal population is estimated to have been about 50,000. In those days the city was probably green with trees, but today, the irrigation ditches filled up, not a tree grows for miles around.

The city was apparently composed of ten large units, generally rectangular, each, probably, the locale or ward of a clan or some other social group, and the domain of a sub-chief. Each unit is surrounded by one or more great high walls, within which is a gridiron of streets with many small houses, large pyramids – probably for temples, reservoirs, gardens, and cemeteries. In between the wards there were apparently irrigated and cultivated areas, marshes, cemeteries, and some isolated small structures. Some of the units are said to be as large as 1100 by 1600 ft (355 by 480 m.), or about forty acres (Plates 2B, 3).

Similar, though smaller, cities are found in each of the valleys; typical larger ones are Pacatnamú (Pacasmayo) and Purgatorio in the northern valleys. Each had its planned streets, houses, pyramid temples, reservoirs, and similar civic features. It was an urban period, and we may conceive that there were many of the facilities, functions and functionaries, and utilities of a modern city, such as jails, magistrates, and possibly even police and traffic laws!

In the absence of any wheeled vehicles, or any methods of transportation except the backs of llamas and men and women, provisioning, disposal of garbage and refuse, and similar municipal problems must have been difficult in such large and crowded population centres. Trade and commerce were doubtless slowed by the probable lack of any standard currency. The slight evidence also indicates the absence of any formalized religion.

The Chimú culture was, in its later phases, contemporary with the Inca, and indeed persisted throughout the Inca empire so that some authorities consider the late Chimú period to have lasted until A.D. 1600. The history of the later days of the Chimú empire, and traditions of earlier times, were therefore well known at the time of the Spanish Conquest, and were written down by some of the chroniclers. Miguel Cabello de Balboa[1] recounts the traditions of the dynasty of Naymlap of the Lambayeque region, and Antonio de la Calancha[2] speaks especially of the Pacasmayo area. They portray a high culture and an aristocratic and autocratic court. The Chimú language, known as Yunga, was probably entirely distinct from the Quechua spoken by the Inca, and a few words of it are still – or until very recently were – remembered by some of the coastal fishermen, especially by those of the village of Eten, near Chiclayo.

Archaeological evidence corroborates historical tradition in indicating a strong development of political and social organization. The great cities themselves suggest such a fact; such immense concentrations of populations in orderly city blocks need a centralized and efficient government. The building of the walls, edifices, and the large adobe pyramids required organized labour under experienced supervision. The division of the cities into wards, each a town in itself with all necessary public buildings and utilities, moreover, indicates social subdivisions. Also the great variation in the size and quality of the houses suggests social classes, based on wealth or birth, and the same is indicated by the differences in the quality of the burials. Some of these are simple, with few and poor gifts, while others consist of large subterranean chambers with quantities of pottery vessels, textiles, ornaments, and similar grave furniture. These, naturally, being much younger, are found in a much better state

1. Cabello de Balboa, 1840.   2. Calancha, 1638.

of preservation than the buried objects of the preceding Moche period.

Everywhere in the Urbanist period craftsmanship had reached a high level of technical accomplishment and tended to become static and standardized; the emphasis was on quantity rather than on quality. There were few new inventions, and the art products were uninspired. Textile and painted designs were typically in orderly bands and rows, with a standard sequence of a few colours, and generally consisted of repetitions of small geometric motifs and conventionalized animals.

The Chimú produced no outstanding ceramic art. Like the Inca, it was standardized and lacked creative imagination. Similarly, it is very characteristic and easily recognized. As with Moche, it was produced in great volume, mainly in moulds, and is well represented in most large collections of Peruvian ceramics. Duplicates are common. The technique of manufacture had returned to the earlier 'reducing' process of firing, so that four-fifths of the vessels are of black ware. Few vessels are painted, and these very rudely. Most of the shapes are similar to those of the Moche, the stirrup-spout predominating, but many other Moche forms had been given up. Many vessels are effigies, depicting life-forms and activities, but far less realistically than those of the Moche. Scenic painting is gone. Very characteristic are double vessels. Each of the connected bottles has a spout, and one of them is equipped with a whistle so that when the vessel is tilted and the liquid flows from one to the other, air is forced out and a whistling sound produced (Plate 26).

Chimú pottery also retains some Coast Tiahuanaco elements, but is basically rather degenerate Moche, more stereotyped, and lacking the realistic, photographic, and imaginative quality of its greater predecessor.

For the first time on the northern coast, textiles are well preserved. Painted and tie-dye cloths, double-cloth, brocade, gauzes, and pattern weaves were the popular techniques. Metallurgy had reached a high stage of development, and copper, bronze, gold, and silver were now worked. Alloying to form bronze was a new process, as was the casting of copper and bronze. Large utilitarian copper implements such as picks, knives, and awls were made, but most of the smith's skill was still employed in fashioning ornaments. Calabashes decorated with pyrographic ornamentation were common, and feather mosaic objects are often found.

While the best known of the 'empires' of this period was the Chimú, similar large groups occupied the rest of the habitable coast to the south. The valleys of the central coast such as Chancay, Lurín, and Rímac constituted the Cuismancu empire and formed an archaeological sub-culture. Each of these and other valleys had its large urban metropolis as well as some smaller ones. Pachacamac with its great famous temple pyramid was one of these; another of the largest was Cajamarquilla, a great ancient site a short distance up the river from the city of Lima. Cajamarquilla cannot compare with Chanchan in size, nor do the adobe walls tower as high, but the large congested area of house walls, streets, and raised temple (?) sites gives the visitor a memorable impression (Plate 7). All are built of puddled mud.

The great pyramid temple of Pachacamac overshadows the city in the Lurín Valley and was a famous shrine in Inca and pre-Inca days. So great was the veneration for Pachacamac and his shrine that the Inca permitted a continuation of his worship together with that of the Sun, and at the time of the Spanish Conquest Pachacamac was the Mecca of Peru. Pizarro, learning of it on his way to Cuzco in 1533, and desiring to seize the golden treasure reported to be there, dispatched his brother Fernando thither. Fernando destroyed the idol of the god, but most of the treasure had been hidden; a part was recovered. Pachacamac was also the scene of the first scientific archaeological work in Peru, and the first excavation of the old dean of Peruvianists, Dr Max Uhle, on an expedition for the University Museum of Philadelphia. By careful excavations, Uhle distinguished graves of the Inca period from earlier ones, and determined the types of artefacts diagnostic of the several periods.[1] Uhle's work was continued by the great Peruvian archaeologist Dr Julio C. Tello, and a part of the ruins of the Inca period have been restored, making the site, within easy reach of Lima, one of the 'must' sites for the tourist to Peru.

1. Uhle, 1903.

The Cuismancu empire is not so well known historically – or rather by tradition – as the Chimú, and, although the excavations at Ancón, Pachacamac, and other sites are famous, the artefacts are also not so well known. The great aboriginal cemetery at Ancón, only an hour's ride from Lima and now being developed as a suburban watering-place, has been dug in for centuries, first by native looters and later by archaeologists, and is still yielding quantities of 'mummies' to the spades of government scientists.[1]

Life on the central coast in this period was doubtless much like that in the Chimú region, and the handicraft was basically similar, though differing in detail from place to place and time to time. Most characteristic and diagnostic, as usual, is the pottery. The most striking and interesting of these styles is the Chancay Black-on-White, especially typical of the site of Chancay but also known as Late Ancón II. The ware is thin, porous, hard-baked, and red, covered with a creamy white slip on which are painted designs in boldly contrasting sepia. The shapes are generally simple-silhouette, especially large, tall, oval vessels with small orifices, and bowls. Very large pottery human figures are also characteristic. The designs are most frequently geometric, straight or wavy lines, cross-hatching, or fields of dots, but small animals or birds in a textile pattern are also found (Plate 32).

According to the chronicles, a small empire, the Chuquimancu, occupied the Mala, Chilca, and Cañete Valleys, but these are not so well known archaeologically, and they apparently did not compose a cultural entity. Nor is much known of their history.

The lesser rainfall and consequent smaller valleys on the south coast did not permit such large populations as farther to the north, but the inhabitants of the irrigated valleys were doubtless more urbanized than in the preceding periods. These valleys, Chincha, Pisco, Ica, and Nazca, composed the Chincha empire of the period immediately preceding their conquest by the Inca. The regions constitutes an archaeological entity that is known as the Ica culture. While no great cities are known,

1. Reiss and Stübel, 1880–7.

smaller sites, such as La Centinela and Tambo de Mora in Chincha Valley, and Tambo Colorado in Pisco Valley, are remarkable for their extraordinary preservation in this almost totally rainless region. Tambo Colorado in particular is the best-preserved adobe ruin in Peru; little is missing except the roofs. Many of the walls and especially the niches still preserve their original red and yellow paint. It was doubtless an administrative centre with storehouses and quarters for couriers and troops as well as for permanent officers, and was built either in the late Ica or the Inca period (Plate 8A).

Archaeologists divide the Ica period into four subdivisions, based on pottery styles. The ceramics differ radically from both Chancay and Chimú, and almost as much from their Nazca predecessor, although there was no break between Nazca and Ica. Gone are the polychrome vessels with their large naturalistic and demoniacal decorations. There is even less modelling in naturalistic or effigy shapes, and the forms have become limited to a few characteristic shapes such as bowls with relatively straight converging sides and almost flat bottoms, and spheroid vessels with small orifices. In the earliest (Epigonal, Early Ica) period, designs were rudely painted Wari-Tiahuanaco elements, but soon the very characteristic Ica type of decoration developed, the vessel being practically covered – the upper part at least – with rows and bands of repeated small elements, geometric motifs or small conventionalized birds or fish, painted in black, white, and red, evidently in imitation of textile patterns (Plate 30A). The cloths show similar styles, mainly in tapestry, embroidery, and weft-pattern weaves.

In all coastal cultures, toward the end of the Urbanist period, Inca influence became strong, as is especially seen in the manufacture of pottery vessels of typical and characteristic Inca shape, such as the pointed-base aryballus, in local styles of paste and decoration.

South of the Nazca region the rainfall, the rivers, and the inhabited areas are even smaller, and the culture of the aboriginal population was apparently lower. Not much is known of the archaeology of this region, but around Arequipa a type of pottery, apparently on a late horizon, is found which is believed to be more closely connected with the people and the culture of the Atacama region of Chile than with the Peruvian cultures to the north (Plate 33).

The Urbanist period is far less well marked or well known in the highlands than on the coast, as has been noted before. Since the inhabited areas were not restricted to irrigated river valleys, the populations were naturally not so dense or concentrated, and capital cities would not be expected. Nevertheless the ruins of a number of large ones exist. In the northern highlands few excavations of this period have been made and there are few if any traditions. The pottery is not very distinctive, some of it being painted with red and black designs on a white slip, some decorated with incised, punched, or appliqué designs. The period here is known as Late Huamachuco. No large cities are reported. In the southern highlands and Bolivia this seems to have been the period when the high masonry *chullpas*, burial towers made of admirable masonry, were built (Plate 16B). This culture, known as Colla, was one of the first to be conquered by the Inca, which may explain the apparent lack of Urbanist remains. Both here and in the northern highlands all trace of Wari-Tiahuanaco influence seems to have disappeared by this time.

Toward the end of this period the highland peoples came into the ascendancy with the rise of the Inca in the central highlands. The history of the next short period, the Imperialist – really no more than a subdivision of the Urbanist – is the history of the Inca.

While the historical accounts of the chroniclers recount the early history of the Inca, such as might be considered as falling in the Urbanist period, these are obviously largely mythological and unreliable, and differ greatly. Archaeologically almost nothing is known of the origin and early history of the Inca, or of the central highlands in the days preceding the inception of the Inca empire by the emperor Pachacuti about the year 1445.

That there were large cities in the central highlands before the Inca period is indicated by some ruins such as that of the large unique city of Pikillacta, not far from Cuzco. Evidently not built by Inca, the nature of the city is still unknown, but it covers a great area with terraces with retaining walls, streets, and the walls of countless houses. Strangely, these seem to have been made without either doors or windows and were probably entered through the roofs, now gone. All the walls are built of natural field stones. Evidence of occupation is apparently absent.

A few sites that are ascribed to the Early Inca period have been excavated, and are presumed to cover the period A.D. 1200–1440. But the masonry, ceramics, and metallurgy are rather crude and bear slight resemblance to those of the Inca period.

The Urbanist period was not one of the longer ones, but nevertheless the estimates of the time-span vary greatly. Some good authorities grant it only 138 years (A.D. 1300–1438), instead of the 440 years (A.D. 1000–1440) allowed it here.

The Imperialist Period

A.D. 1440–1532

Historically, this is the Inca period, the only one known to the average reader. Like the Aztec in Mexico, the Inca were a small militaristic group that came to power late, conquered surrounding groups, and established one of the most extraordinary empires in the world.

Herein the Inca culture is treated in greater detail, both because data on it, derived from the accounts of the chroniclers of the time of the Spanish Conquest, afford more information than on any other people, and because their culture may be considered as typical of that of other peoples in Peru at this period.

Inca influence extended all over Peru as the various other culture groups were conquered – and possibly even a little before. In this period typically Inca objects are found in all regions, or blends of Inca and local styles.

The Inca is the third great horizon pottery style in Peru. Like the others, it appears suddenly in full vigour, as if it had developed elsewhere, but no developmental or proto-Inca types are known; it has all the marks of being in a late stage of ceramic evolution. Conservatism, and lack of imagination, invention, and initiative, are apparent; it is chaste and sedate. The shapes are simple and limited to rather few which are unmistakably Inca and restricted to this period. Foremost is the so-called aryballus for containing and carrying liquids – probably chicha; this has a pointed base and a knob around which, presumably, the carrying strap or rope was wound. The aryballus varies from a few inches to a yard in height. Other typical shapes are a plate with a handle of bird-head or hoof form, a cylindrical goblet, and kylix-footed vessels. The decoration is almost always painted, in small repeated geometric designs in panels, bands, or zones. Seldom are any life-forms used, and then they are small and highly conventionalized; the animals represented are themselves small, such as insects. The colours are few and sombre, mainly black, white, and red. Technically the ware is excellent, hard baked and highly polished (Plates 34, 35).

During the empire, Inca pottery was used throughout the land, either imported, locally manufactured in typical pattern, or adapted to local patterns. In the Ica region, many Late Ica II vessels of typical Inca shapes were decorated with Ica motifs. And in the Chimú area typical Inca shapes were made in the characteristic Chimú black-ware technique.

PART THREE

THE INCA

*

Chapter 7

HISTORY

As already noted, except for mnemonic devices such as the *quipu*, which served only as a reminder to the trained and informed recorder, Inca history was purely traditional until the Spanish chroniclers, soon after the Conquest, wrote down the legends. Like such 'history' everywhere, the earliest events are very largely mythological and entirely unreliable, while the latest ones are quite detailed and probably relatively authentic; the middle period is a mixture.

Peru is the one place in America where, as commonly in the Mediterranean region, history was recounted in terms of royal reigns. The Inca remembered the names of their divine emperors, and the traditional list is generally accepted as accurate:

1. Manco Capac (*c*. A.D. 1200)
2. Sinchi Roca
3. Lloque Yupanqui
4. Mayta Capac
5. Capac Yupanqui
6. Inca Roca
7. Yahuar Huacac
8. Viracocha Inca
9. Pachacuti Inca Yupanqui (1438–71)
10. Topa Inca Yupanqui (1471–93)
11. Huayana Capac (1493–1525)
12. Huascar (1525–32)
13. Atahuallpa (1532–3)

Of the above thirteen emperors, the first five belonged to the Lower Cuzco moiety (see page 177), the others to the Upper division. The first eight were local and of slight importance, with few reliable historical records. The first, Manco Capac, was a quasi-mythological character who may be dated about A.D. 1200. Inca history really begins with the accession of the great emperor Pachacuti, the ninth in succession, whose installation has been calculated, probably fairly accurately, as A.D. 1438. It was with Pachacuti that the great expansion of the Inca empire began.

The Legendary Empire

Manco Capac was a demigod who was considered the founder of the Inca dynasty. He was turned to stone, but the dried bodies or mummies of the next ten emperors – or at least bodies that were claimed and believed to be theirs – were preserved in Cuzco until the time of Pizarro.

The Spanish chroniclers recount several different and mutually contradictory legends of Manco Capac and of the origins of the Inca dynasty and empire, all of them containing supernatural elements. The best known of these is somewhat as follows:

About 18 miles south-east of Cuzco, at a place called Paccari Tampu ('Dawn Tavern'), is a hill known as Tampu-Tocco ('Tavern Hole'), in which there were three openings.[1] From these openings emerged the founders of the empire, the ancestors of some of the Inca *ayllus* ('clans'; see page 174) from the side holes, Manco Capac and his brothers and sisters from the central or 'Splendid Opening'. His three brothers were named Ayar Auca, Ayar Cachi, and Ayar Uchu; the four sisters Mama Ocllo, Mama Huaco, Mama Cora, and Mama Raua; Manco Capac himself was then known as Ayar Manco.

The eight assumed leadership of the ten ayllus that had come out of the side holes, and led them towards the valley of Cuzco.

1. The word *tocco* is translated 'window' by some, 'cave mouth' by others. Three 'windows' in a wall at Machu Picchu are identified by Bingham as the traditional site; others consider the reference to be to natural small caves in a hill.

The exodus occupied a number of years, for the migrants paused for a year or two in several villages on the way, in one of which Sinchi Roca, the second emperor, was born to Manco Capac and his eldest sister, Mama Ocllo. Also *en route* Manco succeeded in getting rid of his three brothers. Cachi was a husky fellow and the others feared him. He climbed to the top of the hill of Huanacauri (which Inca boys also had to climb in their puberty tests), and from there threw sling-stones with such force that he created new ravines. So they sent him back to the origin hole to fetch the sacred llama, and another man went back to help him and to wall him up in the hole – where he is yet. Uchu remained at Huanacauri where he turned to stone, the *huaca*[1] of the shrine there. Auca went on to Cuzco where he became the stone field-guardian huaca of the city. That left only Manco.

Manco and his sisters continued on to the valley of Cuzco where they tested the ground with a golden staff. Finding the soil a little to the east of modern Cuzco to be fertile, they decided to settle there. The valley, of course, was inhabited, but the Inca were the chosen people of the Sun, and wanted their land of corn and llamas. The several small tribes or ayllus in the region were attacked and driven out. The amazonian Mama Huaco killed one man with a bola stone, cut out his lungs and inflated them, which horrid sight frightened the rest away. Then Manco and his four sisters built their first houses on the site of the later Coricancha, and Temple of the Sun.

Naturally several versions of the origin myth, differing considerably in details, were recorded by the Spanish. Garcilaso gives a rather different story in which Manco Capac and his sister were created by the Sun on an island in Lake Titicaca. Manco was a culture hero rather than a conqueror, and he and Mama Ocllo taught the people industries and arts and gathered them together to found Cuzco.

Manco Capac may have been a purely mythological character, invented in later years to give paternity and supernatural origin to the real quasi-historical founder of the Inca empire, Sinchi Roca.

1. Sacred object or place. See page 209. Pronounced 'waca', which phonetic but non-standard form will be used herein.

Garcilaso de la Vega is one of the most famous of the many Spanish chroniclers who wrote down the Inca legends, and his version was followed by many of his successors and accepted by many modern writers (see 'Sources', page 273). Thus Means[1] adopts the Garcilassan accounts. According to this, the Emperor Sinchi Roca began the expansion of the Inca empire, Lloque Yupanqui extended it to Lake Titicaca, Mayta Capac reached Tiahuanaco and the headwaters of the coastal rivers, and Capac Yupanqui conquered some of the coastal peoples.

Garcilaso's account is not supported by most of the earlier chroniclers, and the modern opinion is against its acceptance and inclined to believe that it was not until the reign of Yahuar Huacac that the expansion of the empire began. Even regarding this time the various accounts are rather contradictory.

If the account of Garcilaso is to be credited, the predecessors of Pachacuti had already conquered and incorporated in the Inca empire a large part of Peru and Bolivia, and yet we find, in the time of Viracocha Inca, the Inca waging a life-and-death struggle with their rivals for ascendancy, the Chanca, Lupaca, and Colla, Cuzco besieged, and Emperor Pachacuti beginning his great conquests in the close vicinity of Cuzco. Garcilaso's accounts seem to be hardly compatible with these facts, and it appears more likely that the pre-Pachacuti wars were local ones, without permanent subjugation by the Inca of any enemy people.

The historical accounts of Pedro Sarmiento de Gamboa and of the Jesuit Father Bernabé Cobo seem to be more logical and reliable, and are supported by a number of the other chroniclers. They are accepted in general by the modern authority Rowe[2] instead of the Garcilaso-Means version, and are here adopted, with the understanding that they are not presented with any claim to exactitude or finality.

According to the versions here accepted, during the reigns of the first eight Inca emperors, Manco Capac to Viracocha Inca, the Inca did not extend their sway or political influence beyond the immediate region of Cuzco. There were many independent small groups in this area, probably physically identical with the Inca, speaking slightly variant dialects or varieties of the same

1. Means, 1931.   2. Rowe, 1946.

114

language, and enjoying very much the same culture, economic and non-material. That is to say, at this time the Inca were but one of a number of equally unimportant groups in their habitat. They were constantly in competition and often at war with their neighbours, but no group had any thought of establishing permanent hegemony over the others; the imperial concept had not yet developed. The victor in inter-tribal or inter-city wars looted the vanquished and possibly imposed a tribute on them, and then let them alone until, possibly, they again acquired enough power to become a menace. The traditions of the Inca record no defeats suffered, but such set-backs are readily forgotten; only victories are remembered. All of the great empires of antiquity had a similar rise from unimportance among the obscure. Possibly the Inca custom of hereditary succession for their leaders had something to do with their later rise; it is not known whether the neighbouring groups followed a similar pattern or not.

Sinchi Roca, second emperor and son of Manco Capac and his sister Mama Ocllo, was probably an historical character, but the legends say little about him. He was not warlike and made no military campaigns, adding nothing to the Inca dominions. He succeeded Manco Capac by his father's nomination. There is disagreement among the chroniclers as to whether or not he followed his father's example of marrying his sister. His son, Lloque Yupanqui, succeeded him; Lloque is said to mean 'left-handed'. Lloque Yupanqui had an elder brother; why in this case Manco Capac's rule of primogeniture was not followed is a question. Like his father he did nothing of historical importance and performed no military exploits. According to the legend, he had no children in spite of his advanced age. Like the early biblical patriarchs, they lived to a really ripe old age in that period; Sarmiento has all the early emperors living to an age of over one hundred! So they got old Lloque Yupanqui another wife – not his sister, it seems – and by her he had a son, Mayta Capac.

Mayta Capac was a strong character like his great-grandfather, Manco Capac, and so fabulous myths grew up about him, as in the case of Manco Capac. A vigorous three-month baby, he was born with a full set of teeth. At the age of one year he was as big as an average eight-year-old, and at two years he was fighting with big lads. When only a few years older he got into a quarrel with some boys of the Alcahuiza group, the nearest neighbours of the Inca, which developed into a full-scale battle and finally into a war in which, of course, the Inca were victorious. Still in early childhood, Mayta Capac gave a good account of himself in these battles, and so went through the maturity rites at that tender age. Like most kindly fathers, Lloque Yupanqui could not understand his belligerent brat and chided him, fearing that he would involve his family and people in disaster. However, the Inca were quite ready for a fight at any time and gave Mayta Capac enthusiastic support, especially after Lloque Yupanqui died and Mayta became emperor. Garcilaso makes him the first great conqueror, who subdued the country from Lake Titicaca to the headwaters of the coastal rivers, but later historical events, as well as the testimony of earlier and more reliable chroniclers, do not support this claim, and it is more probable that the wars under Mayta Capac did not extend more than a few miles beyond Cuzco and had few results beyond the taking of booty, the imposition of tribute, and the cultivation of hostility.

The chroniclers are in even greater disagreement than usual regarding the identity of Mayta Capac's *coya* or principal wife, no less than five different women being named; only one writer states that he married his sister. He followed the precedent of his father in making an inspection tour of his entire realm immediately after his inauguration, which custom was followed by all his successors. He also, according to one of the chroniclers, legitimized the great body of soothsayers, medicine men, and the like who had hitherto been accustomed to practise clandestinely their age-old professions.

The fifth emperor, Capac Yupanqui, was appointed by his father Mayta Capac just before his death. He also, apparently, was not the eldest son, but was selected because his older brother was ugly. Though his annals are short and simple, he is reported to have been the first emperor who made conquests beyond the valley of Cuzco, though these were only a dozen miles away.

Inca Roca, his son, also waged war with neighbouring peoples and subjugated some groups within twenty miles south of Cuzco.

For the greater part, however, he preferred the flesh-pots of Cuzco and idleness therein.

Inca Roca begat a number of legitimate – or, let us say, royal – sons, among whom Titu Cusi Hualpa and Vicaquirao left their marks on Peruvian history. The former succeeded to the throne under a new name, Yahuar Huacac, 'He Who Weeps Blood', for the origin of which name a legend – doubtless apocryphal except, possibly, in skeleton – was told.

Titu Cusi Hualpa's mother, Mama Micay, was a beautiful Huayllaca woman who, it was said, had first been promised to the chief of a neighbouring group, the Ayamarca. As this promise was broken, the Ayamarca went to war with the Huayllaca and were besting them. As the price of peace the Huayllaca agreed to deliver Mama Micay's child to the Ayamarca. Inducing Inca Roca to send the boy, then about eight years old, to a neighbouring town, he was seized and taken to the chief of the Ayamarca, the rejected suitor of his mother. With indignation beyond his years Titu Cusi Hualpa wept tears of blood and threatened a curse upon his captors if he were injured. It was several years before he was returned to his father, Inca Roca, the Inca 'emperor', which illustrates the slight power of the Inca in those days.

That Yahuar Huacac was chosen emperor is strange, for he seems to have been quite unsuited for the post, unenterprising and even cowardly. His brother (cousin, according to some accounts) Vicaquirao apparently was much more capable, as well as likeable. He led some campaigns against the groups south and east of Cuzco, and probably for the first time consolidated and organized these near-by regions as integral parts of the Inca empire. Another brother or cousin, Apo Mayta, is mentioned as a successful general; according to other accounts, Apu Mayta was merely another name for Vicaquirao.

Most of the chroniclers agree – for the first time – regarding the name and identity of the *coya* or queen of Yahuar Huacac; she was not his sister, indicating that at that time sister marriage was at least not a rule.

Hatun Tupac Inca, the eighth emperor, more commonly known by his later name of Viracocha Inca, was the most famous of the sons of Yahuar Huacac; on accession to the throne he assumed his new name in honour of Viracocha, the Creator, his reputed divine ancestor, who had appeared to him in a vision in his youth.

Viracocha was apparently the first true imperialist, the first emperor who planned permanent rule over foreign non-Inca peoples. Up until his time neighbouring groups had been conquered, but no garrisons had been placed among them, no Inca officials put over them; they were left alone, and eventually were again attacked and defeated. Viracocha began making them integral parts of his realm. With his experienced and efficient generals Vicaquirao and Apo Mayta he began a series of systematic conquests. He had passed his prime, however, before he had extended the empire more than some twenty-five miles around Cuzco. The larger expansion, more aptly compared with an explosion, began toward the end of his reign, and was animated by his even more capable and imperialistically minded son, Pachacuti.

Peru had by this time reached the economic and cultural stage when it was ripe for imperialism; it was in the air and in the cards. The Inca were but one of three or four rival strong groups in the Andean region, each about equally ready to progress towards imperialism and to gain ascendancy over the others. It was one of those times when the course of history depended on the outcome of a battle or two, and the latter largely upon the quality of leadership. The Inca under Pachacuti and Viracocha's generals had the experience and were the victors.

First it might be well to introduce some of the *dramatis personae*. Aged Emperor Viracocha's favourite child was the natural son Urco, or Urcon, whom he nominated as his successor, much to the disgust of the eldest royal son Inca Roca and the generals. The latter preferred the virile third royal son Cusi Inca Yupanqui, later known to Peruvian history as the great conqueror emperor Pachacuti.

Two Aymara-speaking groups of the Lake Titicaca region far to the south-east of Cuzco were then, with the Inca, the strong nations of the area. These were the Lupaca and the Colla. With that fatuous short-sightedness that has ever induced a people to solicit the aid of a more foreign and potentially more dangerous group in order to overcome a more closely related rival, each hoped for Inca aid to subdue the other. So did the Tlaxcaltec join with Cortés to crush the Aztec; so do today (1966) Chinese Nationalists seek Western aid to overcome the Communists; so would almost any nation today ally with beings from Mars to defeat its pet terrestrial enemy. Anyway, Emperor Viracocha formed an alliance with the Lupaca. The Colla, however, learning of this, attacked the Lupaca before Viracocha could send aid, but were defeated in a great battle at Paucarcolla; that eliminated them from the race for hegemony.

Immediately to the west of Cuzco were the Quechua, and to the west of the latter the Chanca, in the province of Andahuaylas. The Quechua, as the name suggests, were of the same blood, language, and culture as the Inca, and enjoyed friendly relations with the latter; the Chanca were a rather different people, and old enemies of the Quechua-Inca. In the early part of Viracocha's reign the Chanca had overcome the Quechua and established suzerainty over them, so that the Inca and Chanca territories were contiguous; they could not long remain so without conflict. Emperor Viracocha had strengthened his position by cultivating friendship with the Quechua and by taking his queen from that region.

Finally, towards the end of Viracocha's reign, the Chanca felt strong enough to attack, hoping that Inca leadership would be weak. They advanced on Cuzco with such a large army that many of the leaders, including Viracocha himself and his son and heir-apparent Urcon, believed the cause to be lost, and barricaded themselves in a fortress in Caquia-Xaquixahuana, which they believed could be defended better than the city. However, the two royal sons, Roca and Cusi Yupanqui, refused to yield and, together with the old generals Vicaquirao and Apo Mayta and a band of other last-ditchers, planned a desperate defence of Cuzco; Cusi Yupanqui was the leader. The Chanca attack was finally repulsed by resistance so heroic that the defenders believed that the stones of the battlefield must have turned into men to aid them; Cusi Inca Yupanqui had some of them taken and placed in the city's shrines as sacred *wacas*. After their repulse from the city, the Chanca were defeated in several other battles and disappeared as rivals to Inca power.

About this time, apparently, Viracocha died and was succeeded by his son, Inca Urcon, half-brother of Cusi Inca Yupanqui. His reign was short, however, for Cusi Yupanqui refused to recognize him, had himself enthroned in his place, and ordered Urcon's name removed from the official list of emperors. Cusi Yupanqui took the new name of Pachacuti, by which he is known to history, the first of the really great Inca emperors.

There are, of course, several different versions of the story of the accession of Pachacuti. According to Sarmiento he twice journeyed to Xaquixahuana to offer the spoils of the Chanca war to Emperor Viracocha, but his father kept insisting that his favourite son and nominee Urcon should receive them. Pachacuti finally, on the generals' urging, took the throne, without his father's consent or approval. The latter never again resided in Cuzco, which he had deserted.

The death of Viracocha Inca marks the close of the Middle period and of the legendary era of Inca history. Up until this time the many chroniclers have been in great disagreement, few details can be given as incontrovertible, and in most cases the truth is beyond assurance. With the advent of the next emperor, Pachacuti, all the major and more reliable authorities are in virtual agreement.

The Historical Empire

In addition to being a conqueror, Pachacuti was evidently a great civic planner. So many great works are ascribed to him that he seems to have been a minor culture hero, getting credit for many things done about this time. It is said that he made the city plan of Cuzco and erected many of the important public buildings there, especially enriching the Temple of the Sun, in which he placed the bodies of his seven imperial predecessors. To increase the size of the city and to give its inhabitants more land he obliterated all the villages for about a six-mile radius, and sent their populations to occupy other more distant areas.

The cyclopean agricultural terraces in the Cuzco region are ascribed to his initiative and direction, as well as the gnomon towers erected on the Cuzco skyline to determine the solstices, or at least to indicate the times for agricultural activities. Some of these accomplishments he probably completed before setting out for his conquests, or in his rest periods between campaigns; most of them he probably planned and left to be carried out by subordinates during his absences.

The great British South Americanist, Sir Clements Markham, has called Pachacuti 'the greatest man that the aboriginal race of America has produced', to which encomium the great American Peruvianist, Philip Means, gives his enthusiastic approval. He demonstrated his stature not only in accomplishments but in intellect.

The great and sudden expansion of the Inca empire is one of the marvels of history. It effectually began with the inauguration of Emperor Pachacuti, generally dated at 1438, was almost at its maximum at the time of the death of his son, Topa Inca, in 1493, and ended in 1532 with the conquest by Pizarro, just a little less than a century after its beginning. In little more than fifty years father and son extended Inca domination from northern Ecuador to central Chile, a coastal distance of close to 3000 miles, and an area of about 350,000 square miles. Possibly one must look to Philip and Alexander for analogous careers. Though some of the tribes offered vigorous resistance that delayed their conquest, nowhere did the Inca armies meet any nation that was able to compete with them; even the strong Chimu 'kingdom' of the north Peru coast was no match for them. Pachacuti and Topa Inca rank with Alexander, Genghis Khan, and Napoleon as among the world's great conquerors. It was apparently the conqueror's thirst for aggrandizement and power that provoked the Inca conquests; no enemy threatened them, neither did they need additional territory for economic reasons.

Apparently, Pachacuti assembled the Inca forces with intent to bring all neighbouring peoples under his control. Those that did not submit at once and pay homage to him were attacked. The first victims were groups within about twenty miles of Cuzco. These old hereditary enemies were apparently not treated with the leniency that attended later conquests at greater distances; it seems that there were old scores to be settled. According to Sarmiento, all except children and old women were killed. The first groups thus to feel the weight of the new Inca power were the Ayamarca, the Cuyo, and the towns of Ollantaytambo, Cugma, Huata, Huancara, and Toguaro.

The next campaigns took Pachacuti to the lower Urubamba Valley and Vilcapampa to the north; then he turned west to Vilcas and Soras, beyond the Quechua and Chanca country. Next came the near-by provinces to the south, Aymara, Omasayo, Cotapampa, and Chilque, and soon almost all the mountain provinces for a considerable area surrounding Cuzco had been subjugated. Pachacuti then turned his interests towards the more distant north, and sent general Capac Yupanqui, his brother, to conduct a campaign through Angara, Huanca, and Tarma, which were added to the realm. As was a frequent Inca custom, the general bore the same name as a former emperor, which practice must have been the cause for much of the disagreement among the Spanish chroniclers, and for the confusion among their commentators.

The Inca armies consisted largely of troops recruited or drafted from conquered tribes or nations; the Inca themselves were too few to supply the great forces required. The allies generally fought well, though not so desperately as the Inca themselves. A large body of Chanca warriors, recently subjugated by the Inca, therefore formed a part of Capac Yupanqui's army. These were under the command of their former chief who had been for some time a prisoner or hostage in Cuzco, for it was the imperial policy to put the foreign troops under the command of one of their own people. The Chanca so distinguished themselves in their first battle that invidious comparisons were made between them and the Inca. According to Sarmiento, when Pachacuti heard of this he feared that the Chanca might become intransigent, and so ordered Capac Yupanqui to have their leaders killed. Anco Ayllo, the Chanca leader, was secretly informed of this command and deserted and fled with all his followers to the forested jungles of the eastern Andes. Capac Yupanqui followed but was unable to overtake them.

Capac Yupanqui had been given strict orders by his brother Pachacuti not to march beyond Yanamayo but to establish there the boundary markers of the empire. But in pursuit of the Chanca he progressed beyond the limit, to the province of Cajamarca. Finding it populous and wealthy he completed its conquest and brought back to Cuzco a great booty and the sons of the vanquished rulers. Pachacuti had him executed there, ostensibly for disobedience to orders and for letting the Chanca escape. Capac Yupanqui, however, had apparently been boastful and had bragged that his conquests were greater than his brother's; the latter was jealous and also fearful that Capac Yupanqui would aspire to the throne and would start a rebellion, supported by his great army.

The practice of *mitima* was probably adopted about this time. To forestall rebellion in conquered regions the inhabitants were transferred *en masse* to other parts of the empire, their places being taken by peasants who had been longer under Inca rule, their spirit of independence broken.

Pachacuti next turned his attention to the region of Lake Titicaca where the Inca's old rivals, the Lupaca, were fomenting trouble and had induced some towns to revolt. The emperor soon quelled the rebellious villages and then continued on to crush the Lupaca nation on the south-western shore of Lake Titicaca; he also proceeded a little way around the south end of the lake. His next campaign was against the Chumpivilca, not far south of Cuzco, who had somehow until then escaped in the conquest of the rest of this near-by region.

Pachacuti was by this time getting along in years and had begun more and more to rely on his equally capable son Topa Inca, and to permit the young man to lead some expeditions, which the latter handled most creditably. Between them they carried the Inca empire practically to its maximum extent, and in a space of about thirty years, c. 1463 to 1493, increased its area by about a thousand per cent.

According to Sarmiento, Topa Inca Yupanqui had two brothers, considerably older, who had conducted successful campaigns against the Colla, a strong Aymara-speaking group of the Titicaca highlands who were frequently in revolt. In fact, the boy was born while Pachacuti and his two elder sons were engaged in quelling one of these revolts. For some reason, Pachacuti immediately decided to make him his successor. The boy was kept rather secluded until he was about fifteen years old, when the old emperor officially announced him as the next ruler. The two elder sons continued the subjugation of the Colla while Pachacuti devoted his attention more to the building of magnificent palaces and other edifices in the environs of Cuzco, and to the celebration of religious ceremonies.

The first great campaign of Prince Topa Inca was far to the north. He marched through the northern mountain provinces of Peru, consolidating those conquered by his father Pachacuti and continuing to the borders of Ecuador. No nations of any great importance or strength then existed in northern highland Peru, but in Ecuador were several of relatively high culture, approaching that of the Inca themselves, as evidenced both by historical traditions and by more recent archaeological studies. Most important were the Quitu, who occupied the region surrounding the city of Quito, the capital of modern Ecuador.

Several other groups of relatively high culture but of less political importance lay between Quito and northern Peru. First to be met by the Inca armies, advancing from the south, were the Cañari. Finally conquered, after valiant resistance, the Cañari became and remained a loyal portion of the Inca empire. As in all conquered territory, the country was reorganized on the Inca pattern, and temples, forts, palaces, and roads were built. Topa Inca took a great liking to Ecuador – with which preference future emperors concurred, probably because of the less arid countryside – and it is reported that he especially favoured this region with many edifices and other constructions of the best quality. He also organized a personal bodyguard of Cañari warriors.

After the reorganization and consolidation of the Cañari region, and the assembling of a large army, the campaign was pushed farther northward to the borders of the land of the Panzaleo, through areas of somewhat lower cultural scale. Then the customary conciliatory messages were sent to the chief of Quito, inviting him to join the pan-Andean co-prosperity sphere, which meant, of course, to yield to Inca arms and domination – or else.

The Quiteños were a proud people, accustomed to dominance, not subservience, and the 'king' returned the indicated answer. The war was long and bitter, but Quito finally fell.

During the course of the war with Quito, Topa Inca made an expedition to the coast in the region of Manta and Huancavilca. Here he was told of some islands, well populated and rich in gold, far off the coast, to which traders sailed in large rafts with masts and sails. Curious and covetous, he is reported to have prepared a great expedition with a flotilla of rafts and many men, sailed to the islands, and taken possession of them, bringing back some 'Indian prisoners, black in colour, much gold and silver, a seat of brass, and the hides of animals like horses', according to Father Cabello. One's imagination immediately recurs to the Galápagos Islands, and Sarmiento de Gamboa specifically identifies the legendary islands with the Galápagos, which he 'discovered' in 1567. There is no evidence of the former existence of peoples of any high culture on these islands, and until the present it has always been believed that they had never been seen by men until Spanish days. However, in January 1953, Thor Heyerdahl found potsherds in James Bay and in two valleys on Santiago Island, and on Black Beach on Floreana Island. The pottery was mainly plain except for some pieces with toads in relief. It could not be identified with any well-known ware, but showed some resemblance to pottery from the Chimú region or the Ecuador coast. The carved stone statue that Mr Heyerdahl went to investigate turned out to be very recent.

The fall of Quito left but one important independent nation in Peru and Ecuador, that of the old highly cultured Chimú on the north coast of Peru (page 100). Like most old civilizations, their vigour had apparently been sapped by years of peace and comfort, and they were ill-prepared to cope with the virility of the conquering Inca hordes. The frontiers of Chimú territory towards Cuzco had been fortified by such works as the great fortress of Paramonga, but the Inca advanced from the north, taking the Chimú on the flank. The struggle, probably about the year 1470, was short and uneven; the Chimú ruler wished to fight on to death, but his counsellors realized the hopelessness of the cause and induced him to surrender before many had been slain.

After subjugating the Chimú, Topa Inca Yupanqui continued down the coast, imposing Inca rule on all the coastal valleys, probably then independent states, to about the latitude of present Lima. The sons of the Chimú and other rulers were sent to Cuzco to be indoctrinated with Inca ideology and to serve as hostages for their fathers' good behaviour; the government was reorganized according to Inca pattern, but otherwise the life of the conquered people was altered little if any. In a second campaign, the coastal valleys as far south as Nazca were incorporated into the empire.

Of the history of these coastal peoples – at any rate of those to the south of the Chimú – we know historically nothing; they are known only by their archaeological remains. They may have spoken a dialect of Inca – or a language closely related to the Inca – or some quite unknown language; Inca Quechua had apparently replaced the earlier language by the time of the Spanish conquest.

Pachacuti had now been emperor for thirty-three years and was getting old (Sarmiento says one hundred and twenty-five!). For some years he had left the military aggrandizement of the Empire to his virile son, and had devoted his attention to internal affairs. In 1471 he abdicated in favour of his son Topa Inca Yupanqui, and a few years later he died.

The Indians of the tropical forests on the eastern slope of the mountains were a mild threat to the peace of the empire. Not that they offered any great danger, but they undoubtedly frequently provoked border troubles. Topa Inca decided to put them under control, or at least to teach them the fear of Inca might. One may suspect that the campaigns somewhat resembled those of British regimental commanders against Indians in the American colonies. Anyway, Topa Inca conducted such campaigns in the upper Madre de Dios River by way of Paucartambo. The legends speak of a great army descending the river in an immense flotilla of canoes.

Apparently, before the forest campaign was finished, or the wild tribes completely subdued – possibly a Sisyphean task – a revolt broke out in the region of Lake Titicaca. The Colla and Lupaca, Aymara-speaking groups that had formerly been rivals of the Inca for hegemony, were again restive under Inca rule, and awaiting an opportunity to regain their independence. The absence of the emperor and his armies in the deep forests seemed to present this opportunity, especially since a deserter reported to them that the Inca army had met defeat, the emperor killed. The Pacasa and Omasuyu, other Aymara-speaking nations, joined the Lupaca and Colla, but the revolt was not a pan-Aymara one, since some Aymara groups, not yet brought under Inca rule, did not partake, and some others, already conquered, remained loyal.

There could hardly be a better illustration of the extraordinary organization of the empire than the fact that the Inca armies were able and prepared to transfer operations quickly from the tropical forests, close to sea-level, to heights of 12,000 ft, and to wage a successful campaign there. Overcoming a stubborn resistance, they captured the hill of Pucara, which had been fortified, and then proceeded to invest the entire province of the Colla. Another battle was fought with the Pacasa and Lupaca at the Desaguadero River, south of Lake Titicaca, in which the Inca armies were again victorious, and the rebellion was quelled.

By this time the lust for power had apparently taken full possession of the Inca, and Topa Inca Yupanqui longed to have every region known to him under his sway. His next campaign was eastward into Bolivia, and the highlands of this region were soon added to the empire. Northern Chile came next, and in a series of campaigns this country was subjugated as far as the Maule River where, at the modern town of Constitución, Topa Yupanqui decided to place the southernmost limit of the empire; it was never extended farther.

Doubtless the practical difficulties of conducting a campaign at such a great distance from the base were very great; the problems of administration would have been equally difficult if the conquests had been carried farther southward. Moreover, the forested region could have had little appeal to the Inca. Primarily, however, it was almost certainly the fierce resistance of the indomitable Araucanian Indians that stopped the Inca advance. Physically and temperamentally they much resemble the Indians of the Great Plains of the United States, especially in their zeal for independence. They fought the Spanish with equal vigour, both in early days and in subsequent frequent revolts, and they were not completely pacified until 1883. Today they still occupy a large part of their former region, a fine, upstanding, vigorous people.

The Araucanians in the northern part of their territory were pushed southward and their lands were taken over by the Inca, but as the density of the people increased, their resistance strengthened until at last the Inca ceased their offensive, consolidated their gains, and set their boundary.

After one more small expedition into the eastern forests Topa Inca Yupanqui ended his military career, one that ranks with those of the greatest of conquerors. He, too, was now getting old, and he retired to Cuzco to oversee the organization and consolidation of his realm, and to enjoy the comforts of the imperial court, not the least welcome of which was, of course, his large seraglio.

One of Topa Inca Yupanqui's great accomplishments, apart from his conquests, seems to have been the building of the great fortress of Sacsahuamán protecting Cuzco, or, at least, the great enlargement of the immense work (see page 163 and Plates 15A and B). In his declining years he had a palace built for himself on the plain of Chita, to which he retired, gravely ill. Soon after naming his son Titu Cusi Hualpa or Huayna Capac as his successor he died about the year 1493 – the year after the landfall of Columbus – after a reign of some twenty-two years.

The introduction of several other customs or regulations of the later days of the empire are ascribed to Topa Inca Yupanqui. Apparently he was the first to have a census made of the entire empire, and to set up the pyramidal decimal system of administrative officials through which the population statistics were kept accurate and current. To do this he deposed all the old hereditary chiefs and replaced them by the appointed *curacas* (page 178). The introduction of the tripartite division of land and labour is also credited to him, as well as that of the 'Chosen Women'. He apparently also inaugurated the *yanacona* class of servants (page 184). All these are explained later.

Practically all the chroniclers agree that Topa Inca Yupanqui's queen was his own sister, Mama Ocllo. This practice must have been a permitted custom for some time, and it has been ascribed by some of the chroniclers to some earlier emperors, but this was apparently the first unquestionable case, and set the pattern for later emperors. Sarmiento says that Topa Inca Yupanqui was eighty-five years old at the time of his death, also that he left two royal sons, sixty natural ones, and thirty daughters. Of his royal sons he chose Titu Cusi Hualpa, better known by his official later title of Huayna Capac, as his successor.

Although the reign of Huayna Capac was a long and successful one, and though he brought the empire to its maximum extent, the apogee of Inca greatness probably passed with the death of Topa Inca Yupanqui. Considerable unrest filled the reign of his son. With the slow means of communication and transportation then available, the empire was too great to be successfully administered from one centre by one man, a quasi-divine being without whose sanction hardly anything could be done.

Early in the reign of Huayna Capac began those dynastic troubles of succession that were to become so acute with his sons. He was very young at the time of accession, as was evidenced by the title that he assumed then, meaning 'The Young Chief Rich in Virtues'. One of his half-brothers, son of one of his father's concubines, made a claim to the throne on the grounds that it had originally been promised to him. There seems to have been some justification for this pretension, which was supported by the large body of Capac Huari's relatives and friends. Apparently, however, the dispute never developed into open strife; the majority of the court, officials, and people supported the royal son and the choice of Topa Inca Yupanqui, and the pretender's mother, who had engineered his claim, was put to death as a traitress. A somewhat similar event took place shortly after Huayna Capac's accession. As he was then very young, a regent was appointed who schemed to seize the throne. The plot was thwarted by the Governor of Chinchaysuyu, who executed the culprit and assumed his post, which he thereafter administered with honesty and efficiency.

Huayna Capac was not the great conqueror that his father was;

possibly he could have been, but there were few more worlds for him to conquer. The empire had reached almost its maximum possible extent; to the south were the indomitable Araucanians, to the east the wild tribes of the tropical forests, both of them in regions strange and uninviting to the Inca. Only to the north were peoples of rather similar culture that could be assimilated, with habitats of relatively similar nature.

After the usual several years of travels of inspection through his realm to become somewhat familiar with it and its problems of administration, a custom that had been followed by several of his predecessors, Huayna Capac set out on his first military expedition to subdue the rebellious Chachapoyas; without great difficulty he pacified these, as well as subjugating some other hitherto unconquered neighbouring tribes. He thus enlarged the empire in the provinces of Chachapoyas and Moyopampa on the edge of the tropical forests in north-eastern Peru. After returning to Cuzco, celebrating the victory, and enjoying a little rest, he made another tour of the empire, journeying to its limits in present Bolivia and Chile. Dismissing incompetent officials and promoting efficient ones, and ordering the construction of engineering works, he saw to the welfare of his people and their land.

Reports then came to him of revolts in Quito and other provinces in Ecuador. He assembled the usual great army and started northward on a campaign of pacification and conquest, taking with him two of his natural sons, one of them Atahuallpa, his favourite, who later became the emperor captured and executed by Pizarro. Huayna Capac first proceeded against the Pasto, one of the northernmost groups. In the first encounter the Inca army was routed by the Pasto through a crafty stratagem. Most of the able warriors retired before the Inca advance, leaving the women and children and a few men. Pleased at the easy occupation, the Inca armies were celebrating it when the Pasto warriors fell on them, driving the advance-guard back on the main army with great slaughter. Of course, in the end, the Pasto victory was of no advantage, for their land was soon savagely ravished.

The rest of northern Ecuador was conquered with considerable difficulty, as the inhabitants fought bravely. The most obstinate resistance was offered by the Cayambi, apparently a Cara tribe in north-eastern Ecuador. They defended several fortresses desperately and valiantly, and drove the Inca forces back several times with great losses. One of Huayna Capac's brothers, leading one attack, was killed and the emperor himself was knocked down and barely rescued. The stronghold was taken at last by a cunning manœuvre. The emperor sent a large part of his force to make a long detour of several days while he attacked openly. Giving his encircling general time to reach the rear of the fort, and at a prearranged time, he then feigned repulsion and flight; pursued by the entire garrison, the fortress was then easily taken by the army approaching from the rear. The Cayambi, now in the open, were soon annihilated by the Inca forces.

Huayna Capac set up the boundary stones indicating the northern limit of his empire at the Ancasmayo River in the land of the Pasto. It was never extended farther in that direction, and still remains the boundary between Ecuador and Colombia.

After pacifying and reorganizing highland Ecuador, the Inca turned towards the coast, where, around the Gulf of Guayaquil, were some yet unconquered tribes. These were subjugated without great difficulty, and considerable booty of emeralds, turquoise, and mother-of-pearl was taken. With this, the campaigns of conquest of Huayna Capac and of the Inca emperors came to an end. The empire had reached its maximum extent, approximately 380,000 square miles, about equal in extent to France, Belgium, Holland, Luxemburg, Switzerland, and Italy combined, or to the Atlantic Coast states of the United States. From north to south it stretched over 2500 miles (4000 km.). (See map, p. 40.)

Just before the death of Huayna Capac, about the year 1523, two interesting things happened. The empire was attacked by a foreign enemy, and the Inca had their first sight of a white man, who accompanied the invaders. The story of this Spaniard who saw Peruvians about a decade before Pizarro is not generally known to history.[1] Alejo García by name, he travelled with a band of Chiriguaná Indians from Paraguay to the eastern foot-hills of the Andes in Bolivia; he and a few companions, who probably accompanied him on the long journey, had been ship-

1. Nordenskiöld, 1917; Means, 1918b.

wrecked a few years before on the coast of Brazil. He was killed on his return to Paraguay before, unfortunately, he was able to write or recount his memoirs.

The Chiriguaná were a tribe of Guaraní-speaking Indians who made a practice, from time to time, of crossing the Paraguayan Gran Chaco to raid the eastern frontier Inca settlements of the province of Charcas in Bolivia in order to obtain bronze implements and gold and silver ornaments. Eventually they conquered some of the more primitive tribes of the eastern foothills and displaced them. While by no means threatening the existence of the great empire, they did cause some border troubles, and the Inca built several fortresses on their eastern frontier to control them. The Chiriguaná captured at least one of these, but were defeated in battle by Huayna Capac's general, Yasca.

In the year of his death, probably 1525, rumours began to reach Huayna Capac of the white men at Panama and of exploring expeditions down the coast.

With the death of Huayna Capac a schism rent the empire for the first time. He felt great affection for the region of Quito, Ecuador, and spent the final years of his life there in poor health; probably the climate, with its greater rainfall, appealed to him more than Cuzco. He had two prominent sons: Huascar, son of the queen, his sister, the legal heir; and Atahuallpa, his favourite, son of a secondary wife. Atahuallpa resided with him in Quito, Huascar in Cuzco. Huayna Capac had had as his queen an elder sister but she had borne no children and so was supplanted or supplemented by a younger sister, Ataua Ocllo, mother of Tupac Cusi Hualpa, later known as Huascar. The chroniclers differ as to the identity of Atahuallpa's mother.

According to one account, before his death Huayna Capac proposed to divide the empire, separating the 'kingdom' of Quito from the rest, and establishing Atahuallpa as its ruler; Huascar is said to have agreed to this. Sarmiento has it that a great pestilence, probably smallpox or measles, introduced by the Spanish, was then raging the country. Huayna Capac, dying of it, was asked to name his successor; he named his sons Ninan Cuyoche and Huascar, but the omens for both proved inauspicious. Before he could name another, Huayna Capac died.

The High Priest then set out to give the imperial fringe to Ninan Cuyoche, but found that he also had died. Huascar was then chosen. Sarmiento does not mention Atahuallpa in this connexion. At any rate, Huascar was installed as emperor by the High Priest in Cuzco while Atahuallpa was supported by the army and people in Ecuador.

It would almost seem that, as the Spanish believed, it was the divine plan that the great empire should be rent for the first time by civil war while the foreign invaders were planning its conquest. Had they come a decade earlier or later, the few men under Pizarro could hardly have accomplished their miraculous exploit.

It is not certain whether Atahuallpa originally intended to rebel and either to separate Ecuador from the empire or to claim the Inca throne. At first, whether sincerely or not, he seems to have given allegiance to Huascar. But the latter suspected him and maltreated the envoys that Atahuallpa sent to him, executing some of them, which act caused considerable ill feeling against him in Cuzco where the men had influential relatives. Both half-brothers then began assembling armies for the coming test of strength. Meanwhile the people of the province of Huancavilca deemed the time propitious for a revolt, but this was promptly quelled by Atahuallpa.

Huascar marched north with his army and met that of Atahuallpa at Riobamba. Like so many great battles of history better known to scholars, thousands of men died for the personal glory of their leaders. Sarmiento says that in his day the plain was still covered with their bones.

> But things like that, you know, must be
> At every famous victory.

Atahuallpa was the victor.

Huascar had another small force which caught the army of Atahuallpa resting and unwatchful after the battle, and caused it much loss, but Atahuallpa again attacked and was again victorious. Several other engagements were fought, terminating in battles at Cajamarca and Yanamarca; in all, it appears, the forces of Atahuallpa prevailed.

Atahuallpa's continued successes may probably be ascribed to the fact that he had in Ecuador his father's experienced army, as well as the best generals in the empire, Quisquis and Challcuchima. Whatever his first intentions, as soon as his armies began to register victories he gave up any thought of separating Ecuador from the rest of the empire or of offering any allegiance to Huascar, and determined to supplant him. The schism was not a national rebellion on the part of Ecuador so much as merely the following of an admired leader.

Atahuallpa journeyed south in the wake of his victorious armies, making his headquarters at Cajamarca. He was acclaimed emperor by the people through whose lands he passed, and assumed the imperial fringe of sovereignty. Success went to his head, and he apparently became very autocratic, self-conceited, vain, and cruel. Sarmiento tells a story that about this time he consulted an oracle which predicted that he would come to a violent end. Furious, he personally cut off the head of the old priest who had interpreted the prophecy, and demolished and utterly effaced the oracle and the *waca*.

Huascar set out from Cuzco with his remaining force for a last defence against the advancing enemy; he had made the most solemn sacrifices and consulted the greatest soothsayers, but most of their replies were unpropitious. The armies met at Cotabamba on the Apurimac River not far from Cuzco. Huascar's forces prevailed on the first day and he felt confident of victory when Atahuallpa's generals, Challcuchima and Quisquis, withdrew to recuperate. However, the following day his men were ambushed in a ravine, one division after another, and annihilated or captured. Challcuchima himself seized Huascar, pulling him out of his litter. Huascar's men lost heart at learning of the capture of their emperor and fled, hotly pursued by the victors, who established their new headquarters – and Huascar's prison – on the outskirts of Cuzco. Challcuchima contributed much to the flight by the crafty stratagem of having himself carried back in Huascar's litter, thus deceiving the latter's soldiers into thinking that he was their emperor, returning victorious with prisoners.

The people of Cuzco naturally feared that the city would be looted and the inhabitants slaughtered, but Atahuallpa's generals were wise administrators as well as capable warriors. They sent word that, the civil war being over, they were all one people again; there would be no reprisals. The Cuzqueños therefore came out and pledged allegiance to their new emperor, Atahuallpa. Nevertheless, several of Huascar's five principals – three generals and two high priests – were executed, and the others chastised and compelled to pull out their eyelashes and eyebrows as offerings to the new emperor. Huascar's mother blamed him for his unwise actions and slapped his face.

Atahuallpa, however, according to Sarmiento, was not so magnanimous. When he heard of his victory, receiving word at Cajamarca from his conquering generals, he ordered the entire family of Huascar, wives, children, and babies, to be killed and fastened to poles along a highway leading out of Cuzco. Huascar was compelled to watch the executions, which apparently extended even to his brothers and sisters, therefore close relatives of Atahuallpa. More than eighty of his children were thus killed, as well as most of his chief friends and supporters. Those of his concubines who had not borne him children and were not pregnant were spared.

The Spanish Conquest

The news of his victory sent by his generals to Atahuallpa in his encampment near Cajamarca reached him at just about the same time as did that of the landing of Pizarro near Tumbez in 1532. The wellnigh incredible story of the conquest of the great Inca empire by a handful of one hundred and eighty audacious Spaniards has been told in detail by Prescott, Helps, and other historians. Prescott's great work is one of the classics of history, and has doubtless been read by most educated persons. It need only be summarized here.

Atahuallpa was on the point of leaving for Cuzco to assume his imperial throne. He presumed that the Spaniards were the creator god Viracocha and his demigods returning as had been prophesied by old legends, and decided to remain where he was until they left – as Pizarro had done several years before – came to meet him, or made some other move. They came to Cajamarca. Pizarro had by this time, of course, learned all about the schism in the empire and its outcome, and realized that this source of weakness could be cultivated to suit his purposes. He urged that Huascar be brought to Cajamarca; as a matter of fact Huascar was apparently already on his way there on Atahuallpa's orders, a prisoner. Before he arrived, however, Pizarro had performed his great coup and made Atahuallpa a prisoner also. The latter, fearing that Pizarro might depose him in favour of Huascar, sent orders to kill Huascar and the other prisoners with him; this was immediately done. Huascar was then about forty years old, and had had a hectic reign of less than seven years.

Atahuallpa offered to have his cell filled with gold objects higher than a man could reach, as the price of his ransom. The area of the cell floor, according to three of the conquerors, was 25 by 15, 22 by 17, and 35 by 17 ft. The offer accepted, he dispatched messengers to all parts of the empire commanding that gold be brought to Cajamarca; soon it began to arrive, hundreds of llama loads. A large part of it, of course, came from the Temple of the Sun in Cuzco. Fabulous and wellnigh incredible though this immense quantity of gold is, apparently the room was filled to the stipulated height. Pizarro had a document drawn up to the effect that the ransom had been satisfied and paid – and there is no evidence that this callous man showed any mercy on any other occasion.

However, though officially declared free, Pizarro announced that, for the welfare of the country, Atahuallpa would remain under guard with the Spanish. His presence there became an impediment to the plans of the Spanish, and many of them began clamouring for his death. Pizarro at last consented, and the emperor was brought to trial on as many charges as could be trumped up: usurpation, the murder of Huascar, planning an uprising against the Spanish, idolatry, adultery, incest, polygamy, embezzlement, and several others. He was convicted and sentenced to be burned alive that very night in the public square of Cajamarca. A few souls were brave enough to sign a formal protest against the judgement. As the wood was about to be ignited, Atahuallpa was told that his sentence could be changed to strangulation (at that time both a Spanish and an Inca method of execution) if he would accept Christianity. He did, was baptized, and then garroted. Thus, on 29 August 1533, died the last Inca emperor.

The great heap of gold ornaments, fashioned laboriously by artistic Inca craftsmen, was melted down into bars. It is reported that it took the Indian goldsmiths a full month thus to undo their former labour, and that nine forges were employed in the process. Of the many other Peruvian gold ornaments that were sent intact to Spain not a piece is known to survive; all were melted down to bullion.

One is naturally inclined to dismiss the reports of the value of this fabulous loot as greatly exaggerated, but it must be remembered that the Crown claimed its fifth part of all such treasure, and took the indicated precautions to see that it was received; a royal treasurer accompanied expeditions to see – or try to see – that the Crown was not cheated. Moreover, we have the records of the amount of the royal fifth received in Spain. It is obvious then that the admitted value would not have been exaggerated. On the other hand there is considerable evidence – as might be expected – that the treasure was somewhat greater than reported, that some of the ransom was hidden and not reported. This was stated by some soldiers who complained that they did not get their full share of the loot, and the native *quipu* records, studied shortly after the conquest, indicate that about four per cent of the ransom was not reported or properly divided.

Various estimates of the amount of this ransom in terms of modern money have been made. In probably the most careful and reliable study, S. K. Lothrop[1] estimates that, at a valuation of $35.02 an ounce, the officially reported ransom amounted to $8,344,307.00; the purchasing value today would be many times greater. Moreover, this treasure was only one, though the most spectacular one, of a number of captures of gold and silver by the Spanish conquerors. Lothrop calculates that the loot later taken from Cuzco after the arrival of the expedition there was even greater than Atahuallpa's ransom, being worth $8,545,798.57. Also large sums were taken at Coaque, Pachacamac, and other places, which would certainly increase the total 'take' to over twenty million dollars.

1. Lothrop, 1938.

Furthermore, legends in Peru recount the credible fact that, ignorant of the exact amount required to fill Atahuallpa's cell, many more llama loads of gold ornaments were on their way to Cajamarca when word of his execution reached the native porters, whereupon they buried or otherwise hid the loads in the nearest available places. Also, on receipt of the same tragic news, the gold ornaments still remaining in temples and palaces all over the land were hidden. Much of the latter was soon found by the Spanish by judicious use of torture and other coercion, but traditions of buried and hidden treasure still abound in Peru, and labour to the amount of more than its value has been expended in the usually fruitless search for it.

The quarrels of the conquerors, abortive uprisings of the natives, and other events of Colonial Peruvian political history need not concern us here. Within a few years all the important leaders in the conquest had met violent ends by war, execution, or assassination. For forty years the Inca nobility with a few followers kept up a desultory resistance, but the last pretender to the Inca throne, Tupac Amaru, was beheaded in 1572.

The population of the Inca empire at the time of its apogee is a question on which estimates vary greatly. Means[1] estimates sixteen to thirty-two millions, with the lower number more probable, making the population double that of today. He bases this estimate on an average of five to ten persons to the family, probably much too large a number. Steward,[2] the most recent authority, estimates three and a half millions, excluding Ecuador, Colombia, and Chile.

The conquest of such an immense area by a handful of adventurers is one of the most extraordinary events of history, though it must be remembered that they were accompanied by a large army of native auxiliaries – recently conquered tribesmen and disaffected rebels. The reason, of course, was that the empire was so well organized and regimented, with all authority centred in the emperor, that, on his removal and replacement by a Spaniard, the well-geared machinery continued to function just as before. The top officials took their orders from a new man, but below the uppermost rank the *curacas* continued to

1. Means, 1931, p. 296. 2. Steward, 1949, p. 663.

execute their superiors' orders and to forward reports just as formerly. The common people farmed and lived as they always had, and, with slight change, continue to do today.

Slowly, of course, the imperial socialistic régime was altered to accord with European – and especially Spanish – sixteenth-century ideologies, though some of the old elements remain even today. The economic life was somewhat changed also, with the introduction of European cereals and other food plants, and domestic animals.

At first, the country was divided up into *encomiendas* or immense estates, and awarded – with their inhabitants – to important Spaniards as rewards for services during the conquest or later. Most of the surplus products that formerly belonged to state and church then went to the *encomendero*, whose demands constantly increased. The *yanacona* service was greatly increased to provide servants for the Spanish landlords, and quantities of Indians were drafted for very unhealthy labour in the mines. A large part of the population fled to regions then beyond Spanish control, and this, combined with the many deaths from unaccustomed diseases introduced by the Spanish, reduced the population very greatly.

The economic life of the people has bettered but slightly in the last century or two. Though no longer virtual slaves, many are in effect serfs or peons, living on the great estates of landed proprietors. Centuries of exploitation, degradation, and neglect have reduced them to a stolid, poverty-stricken people. Despite their greater freedom from regimentation and regulation, their lot is possibly less desirable than in Inca days. Since almost any change would be for the better, and since their ancient societal pattern is somewhat communal, they may present fertile ground for modern communistic ideology. Fortunately there are now national movements in the right direction.

Chapter 8

ECONOMIC LIFE

The Food Quest

By the time of the empire, wild animals, the main support of more primitive Indians, had become extremely scarce and, except for the coastal fisheries, did not figure at all in native economy. In fact, as in much of medieval Europe, private hunting was prohibited. The wild animals, however, were not kept for the sport of the nobility, but were considered state property; at intervals great public hunts were held, doubtless much enjoyed by emperor and commoner. At one of the last ones held, after the Conquest, ten thousand natives are reported to have participated, forming a ring thirty to sixty miles in circumference, and driving all the game towards the centre. Eleven thousand animals are said to have been killed and, with usual Peruvian foresight, many more, including all the females, were released to increase and perpetuate. The meat was dried for consumption and most of it distributed to the people. Each province is reported to have been divided into four areas, each of which was thus communally hunted over every fourth year.

The principal animals taken in such a hunt were deer and the wild cameloids, the guanaco and vicuña; the latter were shorn for their fine wool and then released. All predatory animals such as bears, pumas, and foxes were killed. Another method of communal hunting was to build fences and drive the animals into an area from which they could not escape. Nets and snares were used for smaller animals such as the vizcacha, a large rodent, and, in individual hunting, slings, bolas, and clubs were employed.

Wild plant food was equally unimportant. A few native plants and fruits, unknown outside of Peru, were gathered and eaten, raw or cooked, but wild plant products were useful primarily for purposes other than food, such as *ichu* grass for thatching roofs and making cordage.

As in every arid and well-populated country, fuel for cooking was a great problem; of course none could be wasted for warmth in the chilly altitudes. Centuries before Inca days the highland plateaux had been practically denuded of the few trees they contained. The farmers of the Inca period gathered all the brush and dead bushes and branches, and dried llama dung must have been the principal fuel in many regions; strange to say, this is said to burn with little odour or smoke. Naturally wooded valleys were protected by Inca laws; these areas and the tropical eastern forests produced the timber needed in house-building.

Ancient Peruvian economy was based mainly on agriculture, with considerable dependence on the herding of llamas and alpacas, especially in the southern highlands. The diet was almost exclusively vegetarian. Peru was one of the world's great centres of plant domestication, and modern agricultural economy has been tremendously enriched by Peruvian vegetables, unknown in Europe until after the Spanish Conquest. From a world point of view the most important of these was the white or 'Irish' potato. This, as well as coca, was peculiar to the Andean region. Then there were the plants that were known also in Mexico: maize or Indian corn, chilli, squash, several varieties of beans, sweet potato, tomato, peanuts, avocado, and manioc, as well as cotton and gourds, known also in the Old World (Plate 52).

On the high plateaux, up to 14,000 ft, only potatoes, together with a few other plants little known outside of Peru, quinoa, oca, ullucu, añu, mashua, lupin, and cañigua, could be grown; these were the main foods of the inhabitants of the higher altitudes. Maize, which here grows up to 11,000 ft, was the staple food for the middle heights, and the other plants mentioned above were cultivated mainly in the lower and warmer regions.

The punas, the high grassed tablelands, were – and are – naturally unsuited to agriculture but used for grazing. The cultivated fields are in the better-watered and more protected valleys. These tend to be narrow and steep, so that there is a relatively small amount of level land, and the steeper slopes were terraced with retaining walls of stone. Some valleys were so completely terraced as to be comparable with the rice-terrace valleys of Malaya; those preserved in the Urubamba Valley and at Yucay,

Pisac, and Ollantaytambo are typical. They served also to control the rapid run-off in the rainy season with its consequent damaging erosion. These great works must have been planned by engineers and built by great concentrations of manpower in a relatively short time; this suggests that it was done by *mita* labour in the later days of the empire. They were made with steps and irrigation channels. The steep terraces made irrigation easy, and this was generally practised; sometimes the nicely graded and stone-walled irrigation channels brought water for several miles (Plate 21).

Since the llama was never used – and is doubtless unsuited – as a draught animal, agricultural tools were naturally manual one-man implements; the plough was unknown. The principal tool was a strong wooden spade, *taclla*, generally called a foot-plough; breaking up the ground was hard man's work. The clods were broken up with a club consisting of a heavy stone ring on the end of a thick stick. A short hoe with a bronze blade completed the list of farming implements; the latter two were largely used by the women.

This aboriginal agricultural pattern still obtains, slightly altered, among the Quechua and Aymara of the Peruvian and Bolivian highlands. Barley, wheat, and broad beans have been added, but the potato still remains the staple crop and food. Most families own some sheep, pigs, and chickens, but oxen and horses – and consequently ploughs – are relatively rare and the mark of the well-to-do in most regions. The wooden spade and the hoe, now with iron blades, are still the principal farming tools. Some simple irrigation is practised, and some of the ancient terraces are utilized, but to nowhere near the former extent.

As in most tropical countries, the seasons are distinguished more by rainfall than by temperature. Being in the southern hemisphere, they are naturally the reverse of ours: summer, the rainy season, from December to March; the winter dry season from April to November. Ground-breaking began in the middle of the dry season, August, when the earliest corn was planted. Potatoes were put in later, just before the onset of the rainy season. A great festival preceded the first ground-breaking in the special fields devoted to the support of religion, and the labour was done to the accompaniment of singing. Husband and wife worked in pairs, each family having a long strip assigned to it. Chicha beer was provided for the workers. In Cuzco a public festival was held with sacrifices and merry-making, and the Priests of the Sun fasted from the time of planting until the appearance of the first sprouts.

The onset of the rainy season was awaited with the greatest anxiety, and if it was delayed everything possible had to be done to induce the gods, and especially the Thunder God, to send the needed rain. The people dressed in mourning and marched, weeping, through the towns. They tied up black llamas and dogs so that these would cry from hunger and thirst, and sprinkled chicha beer around them, hoping thus to appeal to the sympathies of the deities.

Throughout the rainy season the fields were tended, cultivated, weeded, and watched to keep predatory birds and animals away. If the fields could not be seen from the family house, a small hut was built from which constant watch was kept; the farmer's wife often relieved her husband at night. Despite the strict laws, human as well as animal thieves had to be guarded against.

Harvest was naturally the joyous season. The earliest maize was harvested in January, potatoes in June. The corn was picked, husked, and stored in the houses to the accompaniment of festive songs and dances and public ceremonies. Unusual ears of corn were saved and used for divination.

The symbiotic pattern of Old World agriculture – live stock, manure fertilizer, and food plants – was not so fundamental in Peru, as the llamas were too few, and much of the dung was burned as fuel. However, as today, some pulverized dried llama dung was used as fertilizer. The natives on the coast had access to the great accumulations of bird guano on the islands, and made good use of it; they also used fish heads.

Like boating, fishing was of importance only on the coast and in Lake Titicaca; in the small rivers and lakes elsewhere the fish are too few and small to play a prominent role in the native economy. Doubtless in early days, as today, some groups of

Aymara and Uru on Lake Titicaca lived mainly by fishing. Here nets of a number of different types are used, as well as the fish spear, but no hooks and lines, weirs, traps, or poisons. On the coast, naturally, fishing was very important, and provided, together with the gathering of shell-fish and the pursuit of other marine life, a large part of the native dietary. Probably almost all common types of fishing apparatus were known there.

The Peruvians were more fortunate than the rest of the aboriginal Americans in that their highland region produced large animals capable of relatively easy domestication, the American cameloids. These are of four species: the llama, alpaca, vicuña, and guanaco. The former two are relatively large and were domesticated, the latter pair smaller and wild. Even the llama and alpaca, however, are much smaller than the Old World camels, lack the hump, and have shorter necks. They have, however, the same obstinate disposition and the same habit of spitting when angry. The vicuña was hunted for its fine wool, being generally caught, sheared, and then released; the guanaco was hunted for its meat.

The llama is a little the larger, with shorter and coarser hair, generally light-coloured, sometimes black, often spotted; the alpaca has longer wool, and is generally dark brown or black. Llamas were used primarily as beasts of burden, rarely killed for their flesh, and shorn for their wool only after death; this was then used for coarse fabrics. Alpacas were raised primarily for their long and finer wool, and were shorn frequently. In general, these distinctions obtain today among the modern Quechua and Aymara.

Because of their sure-footedness, endurance, and ability to go without water, llamas make very satisfactory pack-animals; moreover they graze on the upland plateaux or punas, which are unsuited to agriculture. They will not carry a load of much over one hundred pounds, however, and are seldom ridden, as they tire and balk quickly under a man's weight. They never travel swiftly, like a horse or mule, and are almost always driven in pack-trains, covering a distance of only about nine to twelve miles (15 to 20 km.) a day. In Inca days, when most of the llamas and alpacas were the property of the state, they were driven in

(A) The Castillo, Chavin de Huántar, showing tenon heads

(B) The Huaca del Sol, Moche, nea Trujillo

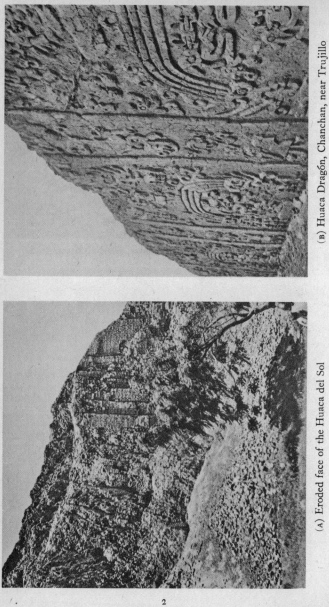

(A) Eroded face of the Huaca del Sol

(B) Huaca Dragón, Chanchan, near Trujillo

2

Air view of Chanchan, the Chimú capital, near Trujillo

Arabesques in the mud walls at Chanchan

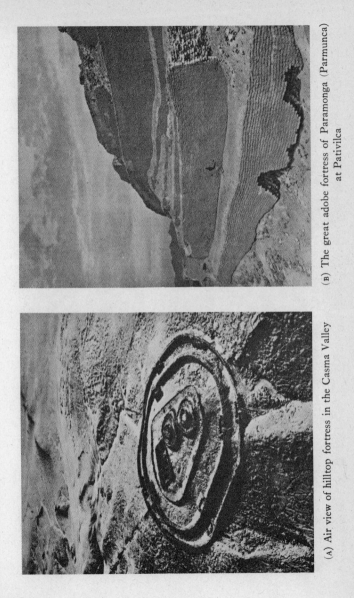

(A) Air view of hilltop fortress in the Casma Valley

(B) The great adobe fortress of Paramonga (Parmunca) at Pativilca

5

Air view of the fortress of Paramonga

The ruins of Cajamarquilla, Rimac Valley, not far from Lima

7

(A) Tambo Colorado, Pisco Valley

(B) The remarkably preserved Nazca site of La Estaqueria.
The posts probably supported a thatched arbour

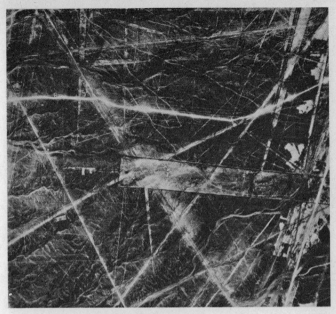

(A) Remarkable and puzzling lines and figures on the stone-covered pampa at Ingenio, Nazca region

(B) A restored *chullpa*, or charnel house, near Huaraz

(A) Tiahuanaco, Bolivia

(B) Monolithic gateway at Tiahuanaco

Great monolithic figure found (by Wendell C.
Bennett) at Tiahuanaco

(A) The Callejón de Loreto, Cuzco, with Inca high stone walls of coursed masonry on both sides

(B) The Colcompata, Cuzco. Probably built by Emperor Pachacuti, *c.* 1450

The Church of Santo Domingo, Cuzco, built on the foundations of
the Coricancha, the Inca Temple of the Sun, the curving wall of which
may be seen at the base

(A) Inca wall of coursed masonry, Cuzco

(B) The famous 'Stone of Twelve Angles' in a wall in Cuzco

(A) Air view of the great fort of Sacsahuamán, overlooking Cuzco

(B) The face of Sacsahuamán. Probably built by Emperor Pachacuti
c. 1450

(A) Wall of great Inca temple of Viracocha at Cacha (Racche)

(B) *Chullpas* (burial towers) in Bolivia

16

Ollantaytambo, a great Inca fortress or place of refuge on the Urubamba River

(A) Machu Picchu

(B) Carved stone monument, Púcara

Machu Picchu, a late Inca hillside town above the Urubamba River

(A) Tambo Machay, near Cuzco

(B) The gate of Rumicolca, near Pikillacta

(A) Ancient agricultural terraces still in use at Pisac

(B) Agricultural terraces at Pisac

Large sailing balsa, Puno, Lake Titicaca

Stirrup-spout pottery vessel, Cupisnique

(A) Moche pottery vessel showing bird deity towed on a raft

(B) Moche portrait vase, probably depicting a definite individual

Group of Moche stirrup-spout pottery vessels

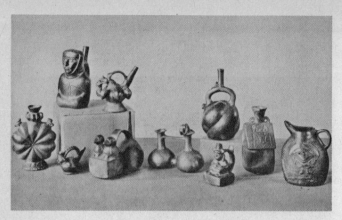

(A) Group of black-ware pottery vessels. The one at upper left is Moche, all the others Chimú

(B) Late Chimú black-ware pottery vessels

Pottery goblet of Tiahuanaco period and art

Nazca polychrome pottery; various periods

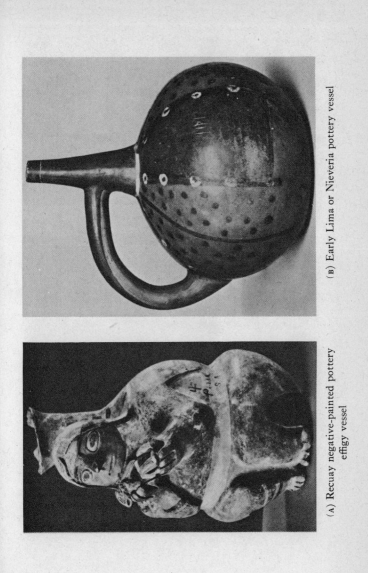

(A) Recuay negative-painted pottery effigy vessel

(B) Early Lima or Nievería pottery vessel

(A) Pottery vessels of the Ica period

(B) Pottery vessels of the Tiahuanaco period from the
Lake Titicaca region

(A) Tiahuanaco period pottery vessels from the central coast region

(B) Vessels of black-white-red ware, excavated at Pachacamac

Chancay black-on-white pottery vessels, mainly from Quintay

large trains of several hundred, and about eight drivers were needed for every hundred animals. The life-usefulness of a llama, commencing at about the age of three years, is less than ten years. Inca law made the unauthorized killing of female llamas a crime.

Besides the useful llama and alpaca, the Inca had other domesticated animals: the dog, guinea-pig, and ducks. The latter two were native animals that had been domesticated in Peru; the ancestors of the dog had probably been brought to Peru in early days, and had, of course, become specialized in type by inbreeding. It was of medium size with a pointed nose, thick body and short legs, short hair, and a curling tail. The dog was a pet and a scavenger, but was eaten by a few Andean peoples, though the custom was abhorred by the Inca.

Since few llamas and alpacas were personal property in Inca days and almost all the wild animals had been killed off, practically the only meat the average commoner got to eat was that of guinea-pigs, and every family raised them. They breed quickly, eat refuse scraps and serve as scavengers, are cleanly and harmless, and the meat is palatable. The duck was a domesticated wild variety of which little is accurately known.

The preparation of food naturally differed very greatly from coast to highland according to the staple foods of these regions. When necessary, fire was made with the wooden firedrill which, apparently, was no improvement on that used by naked savages in the Amazonian forests; the drill was twirled in the hands. Most of the culinary apparatus was equally primitive. Most food was boiled in pottery vessels directly over the fire, or roasted; soup and stew were therefore the usual results. A porridge made of quinoa or oca was one of the staple dishes. Maize corn was not boiled and then ground to a dough as in Mexico, but the dry kernels were ground to flour, as with ourselves. Among the Inca this was done in a stone mill which consisted of a thin, more or less semicircular, large and heavy stone which was rocked over the grains scattered on a flat stone. The cornmeal was cooked in various ways. Corn, however, was often or generally eaten in the ear, boiled or roasted. Leavening was unknown, as it was throughout aboriginal America, so there was no staple food resembling our bread. Salt was generally licked, not added to the food.

In the cold highlands where potatoes were the staple food these were preserved by allowing them to freeze and thaw, squeezing out the water and letting them dry. The product was (and is) called *chuñu*. Meat was kept by cutting it into thin strips, allowing it to dry, and pounding it. This dried meat was called in Quechua-Spanish *charqui*, whence comes our term 'jerked' meat. Fish and other watery foods were also dried for storage. Corn and similar relatively anhydrous products were stored either in the house or in special granaries outside.

Cooking was generally done out of doors, weather permitting, but many houses had stoves of stone or clay, much like our kitchen ranges. Two meals per day, morning and evening, were the custom.

Most serving and eating vessels, like the culinary ones, were probably of pottery, though vessels of gourd, wood, and other materials were used also, and the Inca nobility employed gold and silver.

Throughout the Andean area and from earliest times to the present the chewing of coca[1] (*Erythroxlyon coca*) has been a universal male habit. The plant is native to this area and contains the principle that is the basis of the cocaine of today. It is chewed together with lime, which liberates the alkaloid in the leaves. The latter are picked, dried, and carried in a bag. The lime is obtained from calcined shells or burnt stems of certain plants, is carried in a gourd, and applied with a spatula. The technique is very similar to the use of betel-nut in Malaya, and there may be an historical relationship (see page 23). The drug allays weariness, hunger, and thirst, and therefore has a suitable place in the life of a hard-working people. Apparently it was not greatly abused in Inca imperial days – at least not by the commoners, since its use was prohibited to them except on special occasions; we may suspect that it was a government monopoly, or else the prohibition could hardly have been effective. With the cessation of this ban, coca-chewing became the problem vice of the area, and doubtless it contributes greatly to the decadence of

1. Mortimer, 1901.

the modern Andean peoples. To a large extent, however, its use – or abuse – is a result of habitual malnutrition; it is partly a substitute for food. Better economic and social conditions would doubtless reduce its use. Naturally it was and is considered a divine plant, used in shamanism, divination, and sacrifice.

Chicha, the native beer, also has been from earliest times to the present the intoxicating beverage of much of tropical and highland South America. Since it can be made from many different vegetal materials, its use is much more widespread than that of coca. In the Andean region it is generally made of maize corn, though on the highest punas quinoa and oca are substituted. In many regions the fermenting substance is saliva, the corn being chewed, generally by women; this seems to have been the practice in the Peruvian empire. Great quantities of chicha were consumed when the ceremonial occasion called for it, and intoxication to the point of insensibility was expected of the celebrants. Unfortunately the same custom prevails to the present; the ceremonial aspect remains, in that large communal gatherings, as for fiestas, are accompanied by heavy drinking, but the attitude is more hedonistic, without so much official sanction as in earlier days.

Tobacco was rather unimportant, but used to a small extent medicinally – generally as snuff, or ritually, but never as self-indulgence. Datura was also used to a slight extent in shamanism and ritual; the seeds were ground. A snuff, *villca*, was made of ground seeds of trees of the genus *piptadenia*. It was sometimes inhaled, sometimes mixed with chicha, and gave a mild intoxicating effect.

Costume

The costume of the Inca may be taken as typical of that of all the Andean and coastal peoples; at any rate it is the only one on which we have rather full information, and in imperial days it was enforced on the conquered populations. Grave finds, and modelled and painted figures on Moche pottery vessels, give us some data on coastal garb, and we may be sure that each group and each period had its peculiarities of dress. Naturally, more and warmer clothing was worn in the highlands than on the coast. In the earliest periods the inhabitants of the former region had only wool, the latter only cotton, but at a very early time trade made both materials available everywhere. These textile fibres, wool from the highlands and cotton from the coast – especially the former – were practically state monopolies and were regularly distributed to the people. Clothing everywhere consisted of woven or knitted textiles, and these were always worn whole, never cut or tailored; they were held together by large metal pins. The garments of the common people were of rather coarse textiles.

The ubiquitous breechcloth was the man's indispensable garment, and while at work in hot weather he often wore nothing else. The strip of cloth passed between the legs, the two ends passed over and hanging from the belt to front and back. Ordinarily a sleeveless tunic, generally made of a broad piece of cloth doubled and sewn together along the edges, the bottom being left open, was also worn. This made a shirt of inverted sack shape in the fold of which a slit was made for the neck, and incomplete sewing left two holes for the arms; it reached almost to the knees. A large cloak, worn over the shoulders with two corners tied in front, completed the man's attire; sometimes this passed under one arm to leave the latter free for activity. Breechcloth, tunic, and cloak were all of cloth woven with coloured ornamentation, the latter of course varying in quality according to the man's social position. Inca sandals were of untanned llama hide, but sandals of other materials such as braided fibre are known archaeologically from some regions (Plate 57). Every man wore between his cloak and tunic a small bag in which he carried his coca leaves, amulets, and other such small personal effects; the bag filled the role of the modern man's pockets.

Hair styles varied greatly from tribe to tribe, but Inca men cut their hair, leaving it short in front, medium long behind, and confined it with either the utilitarian sling or with a narrow ornamented woven band. The Aymara Indians of the coldest *punas* wore knitted woollen caps, as do most of the highlanders today.

Women wore a one-piece dress that combined skirt and

blouse, reaching to the ankles and bound at the waist by a long, wide, woven, and ornamented sash. At the top, it reached to the neck, the upper edges fastened together over the shoulders by long pins and passing under the arms at the sides. Like all garments, this dress was a large rectangular piece of woven cloth, merely wound around the body. The analogue of the man's cloak was a large mantle, worn over the shoulders and fastened at the front with a large straight metal pin known as *topo*. These pins, of copper, silver, or gold, have large heads of various types, sometimes in the form of animal or human figures, but most commonly ending in a large, thin, circular, or semicircular disk, the sharp edges of which could be used as a knife. The women wore sandals and head-bands similar to the men's, and also a large piece of folded cloth on the head. They did not cut their hair but parted it in the middle and wore it hanging down the back; it was cut, however, as a sign of mourning.

Deformation of the head was a very common practice in ancient Peru, but, like most such customs, it varied not only from region to region but from period to period, so that it may sometimes be used as an archaeological criterion. It apparently was not the Inca fashion in imperial days, but was practised by the Aymara who preferred long heads, and by some of the earlier coastal peoples.

'War paint' was used by the Inca, and other methods of facepainting were used at other times, but apparently only on special and ceremonial occasions. Black was the mourning colour, but red and purple were used at other times. The practice was probably a universal one throughout the Andean area, but naturally little information concerning it is available. Tattooing was practised at certain times and places on the coast but there are no records of it in the highlands.

Following nature's pattern, it was the Peruvian male who decorated himself; Inca women wore only necklaces and shawlpins. Probably all men wore earplugs of some type, but the nobility, 'Inca' by birth or privilege, wore such great plugs in orifices in the ear-lobes that this class was generally referred to by the chroniclers as *Orejones*, 'Big Ears'. These insignia were up to two inches (5 cm.) in diameter, and made of various materials, those of men of higher rank being of course of gold or silver (Plate 61). Men also wore metal bracelets, the metal disks that were awarded as medals for military bravery, and necklaces made of the teeth of slain enemies. On ceremonial and festive occasions, of course, they also donned gaudy head-dresses, collars of feathers, and similar regalia.

Chapter 9

THE CYCLE OF LIFE

As among practically all peoples until recently, both birth and death rates were doubtless high in Peru; infant mortality was great. The average family was apparently about five. Babies were frequent, and always welcomed; birth control was unknown and infanticide rare. The mother performed her household duties until just before childbirth, and recommenced them very soon afterwards. The pregnant woman, for religious reasons, was not allowed to walk in the fields. She confessed her sins, prayed for a successful delivery and, together with her husband, fasted for a brief period. Experienced neighbours, especially those who had borne twins, helped her; there were no professional midwives. Immediately after delivery the mother washed both the child and herself in a near-by stream. The umbilical cord was preserved.

Until the child was old enough to walk it was kept bound in a four-legged cradle from which it was never removed. This was made so that it could equally well be rested on the ground or carried on the mother's back whenever she left the house. Two looped sticks protected the child's head so that it could be wrapped in a blanket without danger of suffocation. The mother's shawl, tied across her chest, bound the baby-carrier to her back.

The time of weaning was an important family event and marked a new stage in the child's life; a feast was held by all relatives, with drinking, dancing, and hilarity. The eldest uncle cut the baby's nails and hair, preserving them carefully, and then bestowed a name upon it, the first name it had had and which it would bear only until maturity. The relatives gave the child presents and prayed to the sun that its life might be long and lucky.

For the child of the commoner there were no schools, no formal education. There being no system of writing there was little to learn that could not be imparted by the parents in ordinary conversation, and this education by precept and example was all that the average child got. The sons of the aristocracy and of hostages of high rank resident in Cuzco, however, received some formal instruction, as did the 'Chosen Women' (page 185). As soon as they could walk, the peasant children began helping their parents and thus learning to take their places in the community.

The next important crisis in the child's life was, of course, puberty, and, as in most societies, this was an occasion for important ceremonies. Those for girls and peasant boys were relatively simple, but boys of noble birth underwent an elaborate ceremony that lasted for several weeks. The rites for boys and girls differed in that the latter were individual or familial, while those for the boys were communal and of national scope.

At the onset of first menstruation the girl's relatives were called for the usual family feast. Preceding this she fasted for three days, remaining in the house; on the third day she was permitted to eat a little raw maize. The next day her mother washed her and dressed her neatly in new clothes and white sandals to greet and wait on the relatives assembled outside. Her most important uncle then gave her the name that she would bear throughout life, and all the other relatives gave her presents.

Once a year a communal ceremony was held for all the boys who had reached puberty during the past year. They were given breechcloths and new names during rites which were doubtless simpler forms of those recorded in greater detail for sons of the royal family (page 187).

As among practically all primitive peoples – and in England until long after the Norman Conquest – there were no surnames in ancient Peru. A child was given any name that appealed to the parents, generally descriptive of some quality, or referring to animals, places, or other natural phenomena. As we have seen, a person bore several different names in various stages of his life. A child might be given the same name as that of some relative, but there was no rule. Nicknames were also sometimes applied. Among the commonest names for men were 'Strong, Happy, Liberal, Tobacco, Crystal, Hawk, Condor, Jaguar'; for women: 'Pure, Star, Gold, Egg, Coca'. Those of noble blood

25

SESTA CALLE
CORO·TASQVE

edad de doze años

uvan asup yalacumurida *enesta*

Figure 3. *Twelve-year-old girl fetching firewood, spinning
as she goes, and driving llamas*

often had several names, some of them being honorific and titles of rank.

In most primitive school-less societies marriage takes place and the individual is considered an adult at an early age, soon after puberty; such would be expected in ancient Peru. The chroniclers who mention this point are not in agreement, but it is difficult to credit the statement of Garcilaso that the men were twenty-four or more years old before they married, the girls eighteen to twenty. Cobo makes the ages much earlier, which seems more likely. At any rate, a person was not considered a full-fledged adult until he married, started a new household, and became subject to the laws regarding public labour. Since, as in most societies, especially martial ones, the adult male death-rate was higher, with a consequent surplus of women, polygyny was permitted or even favoured, but this was a privilege mainly of the aristocracy and the wealthy; the commoner had to be content with one wife. Even if marriage had not been practically required by Inca regulations, the economic pattern was such that there was no place for bachelors or spinsters; everyone was – or had been – married. Unlike most primitive societies, the state took cognizance of the marriage and sanctioned it; legal divorce was unknown, so far as the first or real wife was concerned.

The formal engagement was a function of the state. At intervals all the marriageable boys and girls were assembled and placed in two rows in the presence of the Governor. The betrothals had certainly been arranged beforehand with the approval of parents and children. Each lad chose his lassie. Only in case of rivalry for a girl's hand did the official adjudicate and decide; then the loser made a second choice. When all were paired, the Governor presented each boy with his bride-to-be, in the name of the emperor. Since travel was not permitted, marriage was of necessity within the local community.

The families of the bride and groom thereupon made preparations for the wedding which was celebrated with the feasting, drinking, dancing, and merriment which throughout the world accompany these joyous occasions. In some regions the young groom was expected to bring wood and straw and otherwise serve his parents-in-law-to-be for several days before the ceremony. There are also frequent but indefinite references by the chroniclers to a period of trial marriage, in some places at least, but it is difficult to see how this was arranged, unless it was practised before the formal betrothal.

In the Cuzco region the boy and his family went to the bride's home where her family formally presented her to him. He put a woollen sandal on her right foot if she were a virgin, one of grass if not. Then they all returned to the house of the groom where the girl gave him a tunic of fine wool, a man's head-band, and a metal ornament of a certain type, all of which he donned. After the usual Petronius-like precepts and admonitions, ubiquitous on such occasions, the customary presents to the couple, and the final feast, they were considered man and wife. There was no religious sanction for the marriage; no priest participated. According to some authorities, the state presented to each of the parties two complete sets of clothing, one for ordinary use, one for festive occasions. The boy retained the *topo* of land that had been assigned to his father for him; the girl's half-*topo* reverted to the common lands.

Incest restrictions were not so great as among ourselves. They were few for men of top rank; the last several emperors married their full sisters, and nobles were allowed to wed their half-sisters. Among the commoners, marriage was permitted with a first cousin, but prohibited for closer relationships.

Polygyny was, as before noted, permitted or even encouraged, and a man's wealth and prestige, in the absence of money, was largely indicated by the number of his wives. But in the nature of things this could be a perquisite of only a few men, who were, naturally, the aristocracy. The emperor bestowed concubines on his favourites and his victorious generals. He himself had, of course, the largest seraglio. Some of the emperors may even have out-Solomoned Solomon, for Cieza de Leon says that none of them had less than seven hundred. However, the usual exaggeration may be suspected here.

Peruvian polygyny, however, differed from most other types in that there was only one real wife, always the first one. She received state sanction, was officially betrothed, ruled over the other subsidiary wives or concubines, and could not be divorced.

If she died, the man might take another primary wife, but might not elevate one of the secondary ones to that rank. On the other hand a widow might not remarry except to her husband's brother – the old practice of the levirate, common to a number of peoples. Widows received state support.

Subsidiary wives were acquired in a number of ways besides as gifts from the emperor. In addition to inheriting the wives of his dead brother, a man inherited his father's wives who had borne no children. He also usually took over his nurses and his foster-mother; the latter might be dismissed after it was agreed that his obligations to her had been satisfied. Women captured in war would also come into this category. There was no marriage ceremony when a subsidiary wife was taken, and she could be divorced without any formality.

From marriage to death little interfered with the monotonous routine of the Peruvian commoner. The man tilled his fields and those of the church and the state, possibly did a tour of duty in the army or the mines, enjoyed his more or less regular trips to market, and the less regular celebrations on the occasion of one of the events in the lives of the children of the family, when he was probably allowed to get gloriously drunk with chicha beer. The woman was even more constantly busy with the care of the children, with preparing the meals, and with weaving the family clothing. Spinning and weaving occupied all the time not devoted to the other duties. Of course the regular religious ceremonies in which the entire population joined provided frequent occasions for public amusement.

The chroniclers give little data on the question of games. There were probably few organized athletic sports. We may be sure that adults gambled, for this is practically universal, and objects that are probably dice occur in archaeological collections, as well as 'boards' with regular depressions that were probably employed in some game requiring more skill. Few obvious toys have been found except, of course, dolls for little girls.

Ancestor-worship and the cult of the dead were of great importance in ancient highland Peru, and so mortuary customs were rather extensive. The practice held related groups together and prevented migration. The bodies of ancestors, dried and

PRIMERA CALLE
AVACOCVARMI

de edad de treynta y tres años

muger de tributo ßa

Figure 4. *Thirty-three-year-old woman weaving*

157

wrapped in cloths, were carefully preserved and worshipped. Naturally the funerary rites of the nobility were much more extensive than those of the commoners, as were the number of preserved bodies and the recollection of genealogies. Such was the reverence for an ancestor that, if a malicious person got possession of an adored body, he could practically dictate to the descendants.

As with us, black was the mourning colour and, at the death of a close relation, all donned black clothes for a considerable period; the nobility are said to have mourned thus for a year. Women cut their hair and covered their heads with shawls. At the funeral, food and drink were served to all who came. After a slow dance was performed to lugubrious music some of the possessions of the dead man were burned, the rest buried with the wrapped body. During the funeral no fires were made in the house.

Some of a great man's subsidiary wives and servants might be sacrificed and buried with him. The funerary ceremonies continued for eight days of processions and eulogies, and for some time after the funeral the relatives would visit the tomb and leave gifts of food, chicha, and clothing.

Burial rites were also extensive at the death of the real wife of a noble, but much less so for a concubine, or the wife of a commoner. A man continued to wear black for a year after the death of his wife and might not remarry during that time. Strangely, it is reported that a poorer man, who needed more the household help of a woman, often was not given a new wife for two years.

'Entomb' describes the Inca method of disposal of the dead much better than 'burial', for the body was usually placed in a beehive-shaped tomb above ground, generally in a rock shelter or cave, rather than interred. These tombs were made of rude stone masonry and clay or mud. The body, wrapped in textiles or skins, was placed inside in natal posture, seated knees to chin. The small doorway was securely blocked with stones (Plate 9B). In the arid highland atmosphere the bodies dried without decomposition. Food and chicha in baskets, pottery vessels or gourds, and some of the personal ornaments and implements of the dead man were placed with him.

Some of these tombs were apparently family vaults, opened from time to time for new burials. Interments are rare but not unknown, especially in the rainier eastern canyons, as at Machu Picchu. Babies were apparently sometimes buried in large pottery urns. One of the more unreliable chroniclers mentions cremation and the voluntary immolation of widows (Indian *suttee*), but no corroboratory evidence of these has been found. On the coast, the dead were at all times disposed of by interment in deep graves in the dry desert sands. Everywhere in Peru cemeteries were made in places unsuited to agriculture.

Chapter 10

PUBLIC WORKS

Architecture

PERU presents such a complex of climatic and ecological conditions that the types of architecture and habitations varied – and vary today – tremendously. The warm dry coast needed a very different type of structure than the chilly highlands, and the hot humid eastern slopes of the mountains a different type again. In the latter region wood for timber was plentiful, but it was deficient both in the highlands and on the coast; also, suitable stone was uncommon on the coast, plentiful in the highlands. Naturally, therefore, adobe was the preferred building material on the coast, stone in the highlands, wood in the eastern lowland provinces. However, houses of adobe were also common in the highlands, especially for dwellings of the farmers.

The typical house, whether of adobe or stone, was rectangular, generally of one room, and with a thatched, gabled roof, differing little from that of the countryfolk today. The masonry was generally rude, of uncut stone set in and chinked with mud. The exterior walls were – at least in houses of the better type – covered with a facing of fine mud that filled the interstices. Round buildings were very rare, but may have been much more common or usual in earlier days.

The houses were generally windowless and had no chimney, the smoke from the fire escaping through the thatch, and the single door was low and small. The occupants slept on hides or mats laid on the floor, in their daily clothes, with a blanket wrapped around them. The furniture was likewise scanty, without tables or chairs, probably nothing but a stone-and-mud stove; owing to scarcity of firewood, the fire was always small. In the room walls were niches in which implements and the household fetishes were kept. Sometimes the large room was divided into smaller ones by partitions. The doorway was generally covered by a mat or hide, probably never by a permanent swinging door. The room was devoid of all ornamentation and decoration, for the occupants, especially the men, spent almost all their daylight hours out of doors. Pegs in the walls held clothing and implements, and on the earthen floor lay the household equipment, storage jars, pots, baskets, cooking utensils, gourds, grindstone or mortar, mats, hides – and of course vermin. However squalid, nevertheless, it was probably not much less comfortable than the house of the average European peasant of the same period.

Generally an extended family – the families of children and parents – occupied several such houses arranged rectangularly around a central court or patio in which were also some storehouses and other similar constructions. Such a compound was surrounded by a wall, generally also rectangular and with a single entrance; the wall might be of stone or adobe, but often was of sod. A number of such compounds, clustered irregularly, composed a village.

The public buildings, especially those in Cuzco and of the later periods, were of course of superior construction, with good stone masonry and little use of adobe. Even the best buildings, however, were generally roofed with grass thatch. But some of the latest Inca public buildings in the Lake Titicaca and northern highland region were covered with corbelled slabs of stone, and some of them were made with windows; this architecture is unknown in the Cuzco district.

The temple-crowned stepped or terraced pyramid with external staircases was not the characteristic feature of religious architecture in the Andean region that it was in the Mexican area. It is missing in Inca architecture, but a few are found in earlier periods in the northern highlands. On the coast, however, as noted before, in the early periods, and especially on the northern coast in the Moche period, immense pyramids of adobe were built, a single great pyramid with its summit temple thus composing a ceremonial site. The great 'Temple of the Sun' at Moche has already been described (page 77). The great Pyramid of the Sun at the famous ceremonial site of Pachacamac covers about twelve acres in area and rises to a height of about 75 ft. The architectural features of the coastal pyramids, however, differ greatly.

In the later periods the ceremonial sites were no longer isolated from the centre of population but consisted of edifices and groups of buildings within the cities. Every important Inca town had its temple and priests; the great Inca ceremonial centre was the Coricancha in Cuzco, on the principal square. Now levelled, and with the monastery of Santo Domingo built upon its lower walls, the original plan and dimensions are difficult to determine, and the figures given by various chroniclers differ greatly. It consisted of one great room, the Hall of the Sun, and other smaller edifices. Rowe[1] calculates from present evidence that the main hall measured 93 by 47 ft, or 28 by 14 metres (Plate 13).

Although almost all Peruvian edifices are of one storey only, buildings of two and even three storeys are known. These are not terraced like the pueblos of the south-western United States, but the second storey is directly over the first. Stone slabs formed the ceiling of the lower room and the floor of the upper. Buildings of more than one storey were more common in pre-Inca periods in the north highlands; here subterranean houses were also found. These have walls of upright stone slabs and roofs of very large flat slabs. Some of them have rather complex plans, and subterranean houses of two floors are known.

The better built, large, and more impressive buildings and those that are best preserved today are, of course, the Inca public edifices, built by government labour and, presumably, planned by state architects. These and the master masons were full-time professionals, state-supported; the common labour was drafted. The architects, lacking paper, worked from models made of clay or stone.

Little is known of engineering instruments. The plumb-bob was certainly known and used, and probably there were instruments for obtaining levels and angles and for measuring distances. Most of the stone-working tools, hammers and axes, were of stone, but bronze chisels were also available. Most of the stone-cutting was done by stone hammers, sand abrasives, time, and

1. Rowe, 1944

'elbow grease'. Wooden and bronze crowbars were employed in moving and placing stones.

It was formerly believed that the megalithic masonry, employing immense stones of irregular size and shape, was pre-Inca in age and related to the Tiahuanaco period, while masonry of stone blocks of relatively uniform size, laid in courses, was typical of the Inca. But it is now generally agreed that both types were built by the Inca, and that almost all the great masonry edifices and structures in the Cuzco region, including Sacsahuamán, Ollantaytambo, Machu Picchu, and Cuzco itself, are of the late Inca period (Plates 12–20). These include the most stupendous megalithic masonry as well as the finest regular coursed walls, and others of uncut field stones set in clay; the latter type is known as *pirca* masonry. Cuzco itself contains examples of masonry of all these types, all built after 1440 by Pachacuti and some of his successors.

The Inca stonemasons used mainly three kinds of stone, and cut and laid them differently according to the desired purpose. Yucay limestone was used for foundations and for terrace and retaining walls; the great walls of Sacsahuaman were built of it. It was always cut into polygonal blocks. Green Sacsahuamán diorite porphyry was also employed for retaining walls where unusual solidity was desired; it also was used in polygonal form. For regular rectangular masonry, often of uniform size and laid in regular courses, the Inca used black andesite. The most important structures in Cuzco are of this stone; the nearest known quarries are nine and twenty-one miles (15 and 35 km.) distant from Cuzco.

Certainly no other archaeological structure in the two Americas gives the visitor the awesome impression of stupendousness that Sacsahuamán does. Forewarned as one may be, the sight still exceeds expectations (Plate 15).

It is now believed that Sacsahuamán was not so much a fort built to protect Cuzco as a safe place of refuge for the inhabitants of the city in case of attack. Stretching for a distance of over 1800 ft (540 m.), more than a third of a mile, the three terrace walls reach a total height of about 60 ft (18 m.). Each wall is a saw-tooth line of angles, salient and retiring. The lower wall, fronting on a flat plaza, is the highest and most impressive, with the most enormous monolithic blocks. The largest of these is reported to be 5·2 m. (17·3 ft) high, 3 m. (10 ft) broad, 2·7 m. (9 ft) thick, with well over 100 tons weight. The task of quarrying, shaping, transporting, and placing such a behemoth staggers the imagination, but it was done somehow. This great wall is pierced in three places by easily defendable entrances. On the broad highest terrace were buildings, towers, and reservoirs for the beleaguered population, but all except the foundation stones were removed by the Spanish for building their houses in Cuzco.

For the transportation of these great blocks of stone few resources except unlimited manpower were available. Fibre ropes of any desirable strength could be made, and the principle of the lever was understood, possibly even that of the windlass. Massive blocks were dragged on wooden sleds, and earthen ramps, subsequently removed, were doubtless made to assist in placing them in position. Protuberances were left on the blocks, or indentations made in them to assist in their movement.

However it was done, the fitting is so exact that, as has often been remarked, a thin blade can seldom be inserted in the crack between adjacent blocks, and there was no necessity for the use of any mortar. This does not apply, of course, to the ruder masonry made of uncut natural stones. The edges of the blocks were generally bevelled, for artistic effect.

Bonding in masonry was not regular, but corners were more carefully bonded, and some attention seems to have been given to avoidance of long weak joints. In adobe construction regular bonding, with alternate rows of headers and stretchers, was more carefully observed. The true arch was unknown, and the corbel vault was used only to roof small chambers. Stone lintels were used over doorways and windows in masonry, but a bundle of poles bound with grass rope and covered with mud plaster was used in adobe buildings.

The adobe masses used in construction varied greatly according to period and region, and are sometimes used as criteria for temporal eras. Those of the earlier periods were generally hand modelled; the later, and particularly the Inca adobes, were moulded in forms to rectangular shapes. At various periods on the coast adobes were modelled in conical, hemispherical, cobble, cube, and sugar-loaf shapes, each characteristic of a certain time and region. Inca rectangular adobe bricks average about 32 by 8 by 8 inches (80 by 20 by 20 cm.).

In masonry construction, and especially in retaining walls, only the face was carefully finished, the rear left irregular. Free-standing walls generally had rubble fill in the centre. Walls were usually battered, and doors, niches, and other openings of Inca buildings were trapezoidal, narrower at the top. Corners were especially well made, and frequently the masonry was strengthened by a tenon or some other projecting feature that locked with the adjacent stone block.

Engineering: Roads, Bridges, Irrigation

Roads, paved or unpaved, were probably an ancient element in the Andean culture pattern, but few pre-Inca roads have been archaeologically verified, and it was the Inca who brought them to a high stage of development. In this respect the Inca bore a close resemblance to the Romans; both needed roads for the rapid transport of supplies for their conquering armies and for the quick conveyance of information and orders, and both built roads to the limits of their conquered dominions. The main difference between them was that the Inca, possessing no wheeled vehicles, did not need such good paving, if any, nor such wide roads and strong bridges; also they could use steps on steep slopes. Without good roads it would have been practically impossible to conquer regions at such a great distance from the centre, Cuzco, and, following conquest, to administer them. The Spanish were strong in their admiration for the Inca roads, wrote full descriptions of them, and utilized them constantly in post-conquest days.

There were two main north-south roads, one along the coast and one through the highlands. Transverse roads connected these, and minor roads ran to every village in the empire. The coastal highway ran from Tumbez southward along the coast to Arequipa and possibly even as far as Chile, but the latter section was not well known or much used. The longer highland road began at the Ancasmayo River on the Colombian border and ran south to Cuzco and beyond to Ayavire where it bifurcated around Lake Titicaca, and then south-east to Tucuman in present north-west Argentina. From here a line extended to Coquimbo on the coast of Chile, and from there south to the present region of Santiago. Another branch ran from Tucuman to Mendoza in Argentina. A transverse road connected Tumbez with the highland road, and other highways linked Cuzco with Nazca and with Arequipa. Still other roads ran eastward to the edge of the forested regions.

The roads through the highlands were of course the greater feats of engineering because of the precipitousness of the terrain in many places. Though they followed a straight line whenever possible, as did the ideal Roman road, they zigsagged up steep slopes, where they were often replaced by steps. Of an average width of three feet (1 m.) and paved in many places, they were carried over marshy places on causeways, over streams on bridges, and occasionally through hills in tunnels; in some places they were lined with walls. The causeways were made of earth paved with stone slabs, and were sometimes fifteen or twenty feet (4·5 to 6 m) in width and three to six feet (1 to 2 m.) high.

On the coast the roads were straighter and wider, twelve to fifteen feet (3·5 to 4·5 m.). Through the sandy, trackless deserts they consisted of no more than twin lines of posts to mark the trail, but through the thickly populated irrigated valleys they were lined with walls that were often painted in designs, and with shade trees, irrigated by a stream. When crossing steep rocky terrain, of course, they were built like the highland roads.

The old Inca roads have recently been followed and recorded by an expedition under the leadership of Victor W. von Hagen.[1]

At regular intervals along these roads the Inca government built *tambos* or rest-houses. Since they were used exclusively for persons travelling on official business they can hardly be termed 'inns'. Ordinary ones were placed a day's journey apart, and larger and more elegant 'royal tambos' built in the cities on the road. Each of these latter was equipped with the special and

1. Van Hagen, 1955.

elegant accoutrements used by the emperor, awaiting the day when he might journey that way. Each tambo was furnished with a storehouse containing food and equipment, and was under the charge of local officials. 'Milestones' were set up on many of the roads at each unit of distance, which was the *topo*, about four and one-half miles (7 km.). (The same name is applied to a measurement of area, and to a shawl pin, usages already noted.)

Streams were crossed by bridges of several types, to meet diverse conditions. The smaller ones were spanned by a series of logs or by great stone slabs, supported by masonry piers, and the largest rivers by pontoon bridges, resting on floating rafts or small boats. Such a pontoon bridge apparently crossed the Desaguadero River near Lake Titicaca. The most interesting bridge, however, was the suspension bridge, generally spanning deep narrow ravines. Five great cables were stretched across and anchored firmly to beams embedded in masonry piers at either end. These cables were of braided or twisted fibre, vines, or long thin pliable twigs, and were up to sixteen inches (40 cm.) in diameter. Three formed the floor, which was flattened with crosssticks and matting or mud, and the other two served as hand railings, with other vines laced between them and the floor. The bridges sagged, and swayed in the wind, as no guy ropes were used, but were safe enough for foot travellers and llamas. Apparently the idea of hanging a level footpath from the cables, the method of modern suspension bridges, never occurred to the Inca. These bridges were repaired every year, this and their upkeep being the labour tax for the neighbouring inhabitants. Cobo describes one that he crossed at Vilcas which was two hundred feet (60 m.) long.

Where traffic was slight, a kind of breeches buoy is reported to have been employed: a suspended basket was drawn along a single cable by ropes in the hands of the bridge-tenders. On very long water crossings the passengers were ferried across on boats.

As before noted, irrigation was of the greatest importance in Peru, especially in the coastal region. Irrigation flumes and ditches were among the most admirable and important engineering features, often many miles in length, with the optimum gradient, following the contours of the hills. Over low spots they were carried on causeways, one in the Moche Valley being over fifty feet (15 m.) high. According to the nature of the terrain they were mere ditches, or stone-lined. Water was thus sometimes led to the top of a series of hillside terraces and allowed to flow over these.

Irrigation had been practised in Peru from a very early period, since at least Early Moche times. But, as in other engineering feats, the channels of the Inca exceeded others in efficiency. Smaller sluices controlled and closed by stone slabs led from the main channel to the fields. The terraces themselves, in certain areas covering the hillsides and supported by long parallel stone retaining walls, compared favourably with those of the Malayan region (Plate 21).

In Cuzco, drainage and water-supply were very efficiently handled. The streams running through the city were confined between walls, and the beds of the smaller streams were paved with stone. Water was conducted into some of the buildings by stone-lined and stone-covered conduits. In good agricultural land, streams were frequently straightened and narrowed in order to increase and preserve the arable area.

In several places the Inca built stone baths supplied by permanent running water. Relief models of newly conquered territory as well as of engineering projects, terraces, buildings, and even of towns were made for the guidance of the Inca engineers.

Transportation and Trade

Wheeled vehicles being unknown in Peru, as everywhere in America, land transportation was on the backs of men or llamas. Carrying objects balanced on the head does not seem to have been a usual practice. Small loads were ordinarily carried by wrapping them up in the mantles or cloaks and carrying this on the back, with two mantle corners tied across the chest; other objects were similarly carried with the help of ropes. The tump-line, with a carrying band across the forehead, was used in some places.

Litter-like frames were doubtless used for carrying heavier

objects, but the principal employment of the litter was for the personal transportation of the higher nobility. These litters of course varied in quality as befitted the rank of the rider; the finer ones had canopies for shade. The floor was solid, the seats portable stools. Litters were made for one or two persons, the latter facing each other. The ends of the long carrying poles rested on the shoulders of the four bearers.

Cieza de León gives a vivid description of the use of the litter by the Inca emperor.[1]

'When the Incas visited the provinces of their empire in time of peace, they travelled in great majesty, seated in rich litters fitted with loose poles of excellent wood, long and enriched with gold and silver work (Figure 5). Over the litter there were two high arches of gold set with precious stones, and long mantles fell round all sides of the litter so as to cover it completely. If the inmate did not wish to be seen, the mantles remained down, but they were raised when he got in or came out. In order that he might see the road, and have fresh air, holes were made in the curtains. Over all parts of these mantles or curtains there was rich ornamentation. On some were embroidered the sun and the moon, on others great curving serpents, and what appeared to be sticks passing across them. These were borne as insignia or arms. The litters were raised on the shoulders of the greatest and most important lords of the kingdom, and he who was employed most frequently on this duty, was held to be most honoured and in highest favour.'

In imperial days llamas were used mainly in large trains for transporting state goods and military supplies, but doubtless in earlier times and in other parts llamas were, as at present, privately owned, like the modern farmer's horses and cattle. They were never used for field cultivation or for any other activity except transport of goods (Figure 3).

While the planning of roads and bridges is a phase of engineering and is properly discussed in that section, their employment is pertinent to transportation.

In addition to the use of the roads for ordinary travel by officials, armies, and llama pack-trains, the Inca state maintained

1. Part 2, chapter 20, pp. 61–2 of Markham's translation, 1883.

Figure 5. *Inca Emperor and his wife carried in a litter*

a twenty-four-hour relay post service for the rapid transport of messages and light objects. Small shelters were built about a mile apart,[1] in pairs, one on either side of the road and each holding two young men; one of these was on constant watch, looking for an approaching runner. When one appeared, he sprang up, ran with the panting messenger a short distance while he learned the message – generally accompanied by a quipu – or received the package, and then ran on at top speed to deliver it to the man at the next post. The runner (*chasqui*) was immediately replaced by another man ready at the post. The young men had been especially trained for this service which was their labour tax or *mita;* they served for periods of fifteen days.

By this relay system a very high average speed could be maintained indefinitely. The system was continued after the conquest, and the chroniclers report that the run from Lima to Cuzco, about 420 miles over a bad road, required three days. This is about 140 miles (224 km.) per day, or an average speed of about six miles per hour; this was doubtless exceeded on better roads and in Inca days when they were carefully maintained. For instance, it is reliably reported that fresh fish was brought from the coast in two days to the emperor in Cuzco.

While considering the topic of communication, mention should be made of the smoke signals by means of which messages could be sent across the country much faster than by courier.

Transportation by water was of importance only on the coast and on large Lake Titicaca. In both regions small fishing-boats made of bundles of *totora* reeds were made. These are called 'balsas', generally translated as 'rafts', but they are boats rather than rafts; boats of probably identical type are used on Titicaca today (Plate 22). Mat sails made of parallel reeds are borne on masts. The boats on the coast were small and light, generally carrying, and capable of being carried by, one man; nevertheless the fishermen in groups took them far to sea. In southern coastal Peru they used inflated sealskins, and in northern Peru a number

1. The chroniclers differ very much in their estimates of the distance covered by each relay runner. They range from a quarter of a league to one and a half leagues. Probably the distance varied in accord with the nature of the terrain.

of empty gourds under a net; the sealskins could be kept inflated at sea by means of tubes. Dugout canoes were made in peripheral areas, when suitable timber was available, but they were apparently unknown in the highland heart of the empire.

In far northern Peru and in Ecuador, where increasing rainfall produced forests near or on the coast, much larger rafts were built of the very light balsa wood. These were apparently real rafts, made of a number – generally seven to nine – of great logs of graded length so that the prow was pointed, the stern square. The logs were bound together with rope and covered with a platform, and a mast for a sail was erected in the centre; oars were also used. Such a raft could accommodate fifty men and sail a great distance. In such a raft (page 125) Topa Inca made his legendary voyage of exploration, and the *Kon Tiki*,[1] which drifted from Peru to the Tuamotu Islands in 1947, was of similar type. Barring a typhoon, and following the favourable current and winds, there is no reason why a large raft of this type should not have reached Indonesia or even the Asiatic mainland, and there is some evidence that in earlier days long Pacific voyages were not infrequent (pages 21–25).

Since in the Inca empire there was no private business and no standard medium of exchange, there was little trade. Persons were not permitted to change their residences beyond their immediate vicinity nor to travel for pleasure far from home. Almost the only exchange of property possible was that of small handicraft, which could be traded or bartered at local markets or fairs which were held at frequent or regular intervals. Thus a provident and industrious man or family might specialize in the production of some household goods or utensils in universal demand, produce a surplus of them in spare time, and exchange these for desired objects of another nature produced by other craftsmen. Other materials available for barter were surplus goods received in the periodic public distributions. A family receiving goods not needed or desired might trade them to another family deficient in these. The inequalities caused by the rule-of-thumb distribution were thus remedied.

1. Heyerdahl, 1950.

Emperor Pachacuti is credited with having decreed three market days or holidays each month. This seems reasonable for small local markets, but there were probably also larger ones at longer intervals in the principal centres.

Chapter 11

SOCIAL ORGANIZATION

THE Inca names for family relationships suggest that theirs was not a clan system with exogamy (marriage outside the group) and descent reckoned in a single female line. As with us, the primary distinction was that of sex, though sometimes the sex of the speaker was a determining factor. The respective generations with regard to the speaker were also of considerable importance. Our own system is so ingrained in us that anything else seems unnatural and incomprehensible. Cousins called each other by the same term as that employed for 'brother' and 'sister', and there was no distinction between parallel and cross-cousins by their own generation, though they were distinguished by the former generation. A father had sons and daughters, but the mother had only children. The same terms were used for father and for father's brother (uncle), for mother and for mother's sister (aunt), but father's sister and mother's brother had independent terms. The terms for brother and for sister were different when used by a man and by a woman.

In Inca times, just as in Peru today, the basic social group of the people – apart from the immediate family – was the *ayllu*. This group, already frequently mentioned, was an enlarged or extended family, a sub-tribe; all the members of an ayllu considered themselves related – and probably normally were. The ayllu, moreover, was a community; as before noted, it owned a definite territory.

The ayllu therefore had many of the aspects of the classic 'clan', and until quite recently most writers on Inca social organization have taken it for granted that it *was* a typical clan, with all the characteristics of such, including totemism, descent in the female lines, and exogamy. Where the modern Quechua or Aymara clans differ from this pattern it was assumed that they had changed since Conquest days. A careful study of the accounts of the early chroniclers, however, indicates that the Inca ayllu lacked any totem, that descent was reckoned in the male line, and that endogamy – marriage within the group – was the common practice. With these important differences in mind, the ayllu may well be considered a clan.

It is true that some of the ayllus traced descent from animals, but others ascribed their origins to mythical persons and places; the animal ancestor was not considered taboo for diet, and no ayllu bore an animal name, although each had a name, generally that of a place or person.

The ayllu was undoubtedly the fundamental social and political group of Peru, and was of very great age, far antedating the Inca empire. Kinship was its basis and bond. Probably residence was always patrilocal; the son brought his wife to live with or near his parents. The pattern of commoner agricultural labour for the support of the chief or *sinchi* must also have been a very ancient one. The chief had considerable authority, responsibility for the acts of his clansmen, and for the avenging of wrongs done to them. Each ayllu had its communal agricultural lands, pasture-lands, and woodlands, and functioned as a unit in external relations. Each recognized a founder, a common ancestor of all members, kept his body or mummy sacred, and built a ceremonial cult around his reverence. In the four years between 1615 and 1619, a century after the Conquest, the Spanish collected 1365 mummified bodies of adored ancestors.

In imperial days non-kinship institutions were superimposed on kinship ones or developed from them; the fundamental features were retained or slightly modified and the ayllu became the smallest social unit in the Inca system. More stress was laid on community of residence than on that of kinship. With the establishment of a class of nobility and its caste marriages, strict endogamy became impossible; probably it was still enforced for commoners, but apparently it was one of the first features to disappear with the Spanish conquest.

The Inca empire replaced allegiance to a familiar local chief by reverence to a distant foreign ruler, and drafted men for distant wars in which they had no patriotic interest. This naturally had quite an effect on the attitude of the commoner. New ayllus were frequently formed, especially as a result of the resettlement programme; some were formed for the descendants of prominent and distinguished men. Each emperor began a new royal ayllu consisting of all his male descendants except his eldest royal son who would, normally and in the natural course of events, establish his own royal ayllu. There were eleven of these royal ayllus at the time of the Spanish conquest, one for each of the historically recognized emperors; five of these belonged to the Lower moiety, six to the Upper (see page 177).

Some writers have claimed that the ayllu was standardized in empire days into the *pachaca*, the 100-household unit (see page 178), and the excess population periodically siphoned off for *yanacona* and similar distant services in order to keep the number at the standard decimal figure, but there seems to be no historical basis for this claim. Furthermore, it was apparently unnecessary, since the division of the population into decimally calculated groups was for administrative purposes only, and in that respect it mattered little whether the number of persons in the group was slightly above or below standard.

Bram[1] has well summarized the salient features of the Peruvian ayllu, and the changes brought about in it by its incorporation in the Inca imperial pattern:

Previous to the conquest and incorporation of an ayllu or a group of ayllus into the empire, the Indians lived in a small and circumscribed political, social, economic, linguistic, and religious world.

(a) Politically, the native owed allegiance to a sinchi or a curaca whom, in most cases, he knew personally and who was not a stranger to his group. When his settlement was in danger and he had to defend it, the nature of such a war was obvious to him. He fought in a familiar environment and for his own cause.

(b) Social relationships within an ayllu were those of an almost unstratified community with collective landownership. The curaca and his family formed the only nobility, while the mass of commoners were all equals. The possibilities of economic and social advancement were practically non-existent, and this must have insured a considerable degree of stability in inter-personal relations.

(c) Economically, a village community was a self-supporting

1. Bram, 1941, pp. 41–44.

Pottery vessels from Tacna (left four) and Arequipa (right four)

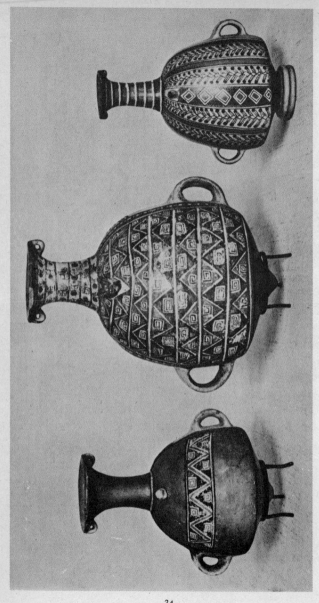

Inca pottery vessels: aryballi

34

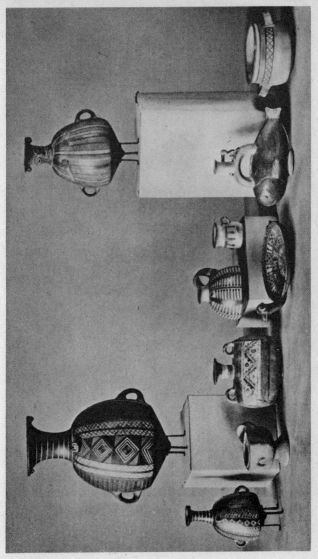

Pottery vessels of Inca type and period

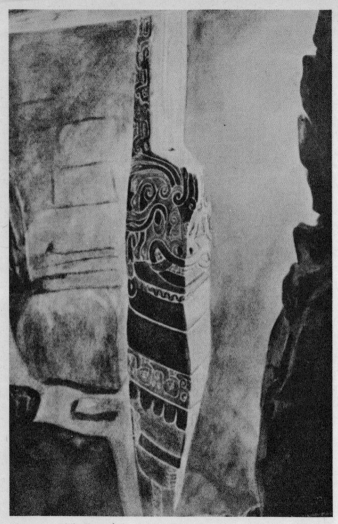

The Lanzón in the Castillo, Chavin de Huántar

(A) Stone puma, Chavin art style

(B) Inca stone bowl

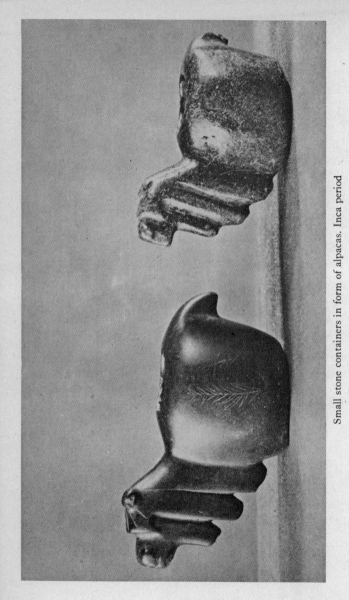

Small stone containers in form of alpacas. Inca period

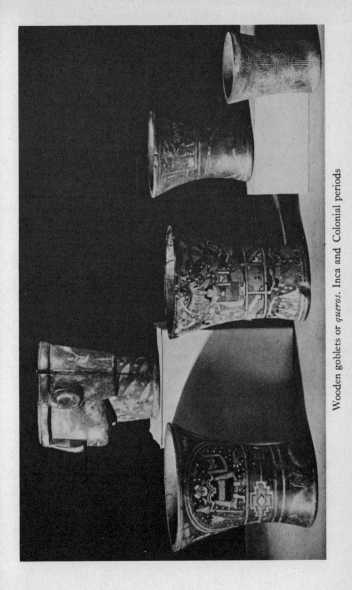

Wooden goblets or *queros*. Inca and Colonial periods

Wooden *quero* or *kero*

Bimetallic knife. Copper blade with gold bird on handle

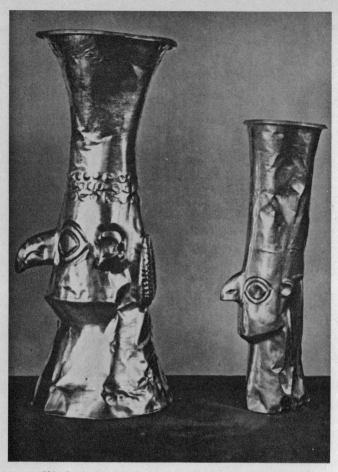

Chimú metal vases, the larger of silver, the smaller of gold

Chimú face mask of thin beaten gold

Inca silver figurine, front view

The same figurine, rear view

(A) Bone handle of spearthrower, showing man playing panpipes. Southern coast

(B) Lace-like cloth. Quintay

Painted cloth. Casma

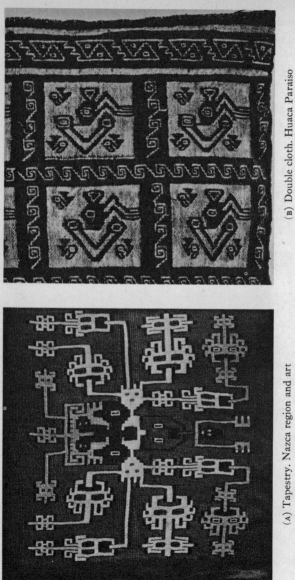

(A) Tapestry. Nazca region and art

(B) Double cloth. Huaca Paraiso

Embroidered Paracas mantle

(A) Hair-net. Pachacamac

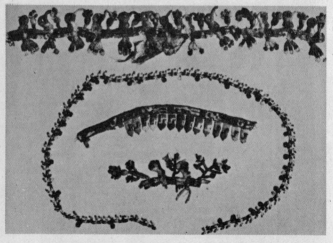

(B) Three-dimensional needle-knitted borders. Nazca region

A mummy excavated at Pachacamac

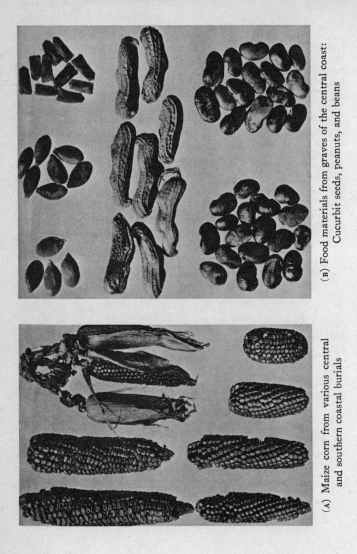

(A) Maize corn from various central and southern coastal burials

(B) Food materials from graves of the central coast: Cucurbit seeds, peanuts, and beans

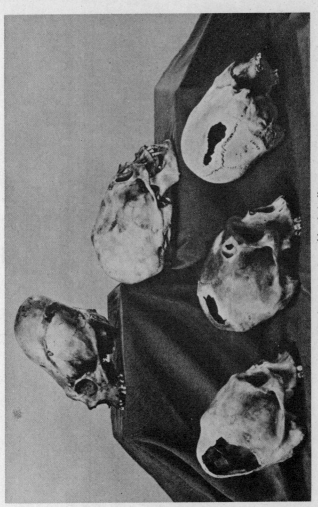

Deformed and trephined skulls

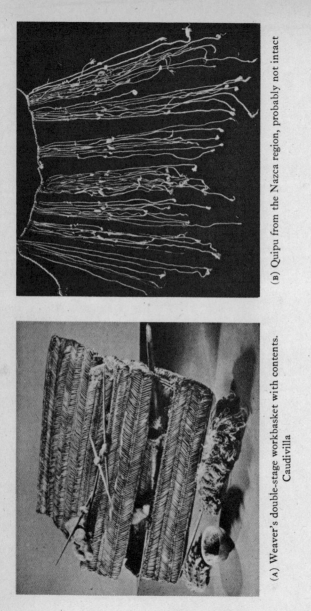

(A) Weaver's double-stage workbasket with contents. Caudivilla

(B) Quipu from the Nazca region, probably not intact

Pottery figurines from various sites of the northern and central coast

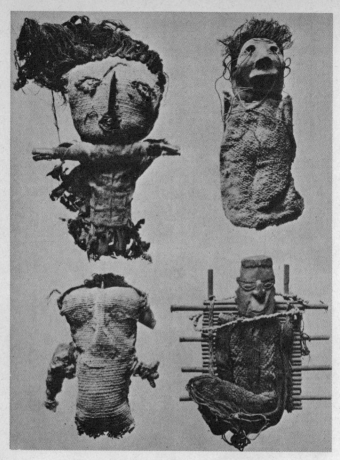

Dolls or dressed figures, from central coast sites

Ornaments, combs, and sandals, from central and southern
coastal sites

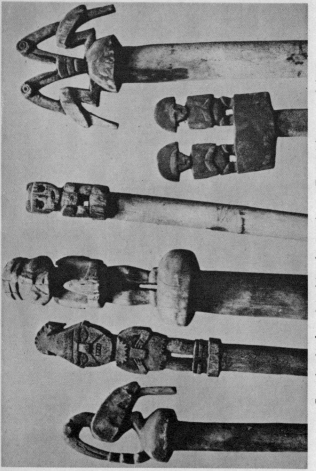

Carved ends of wooden sticks of uncertain use. From various coastal sites

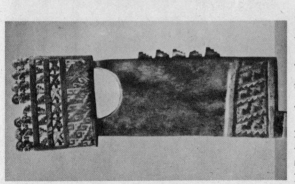

(A) Probably a handle of a painted ceremonial centre-board for raft or boat. Pisco region

(B) Weaving implements from central and southern coast sites

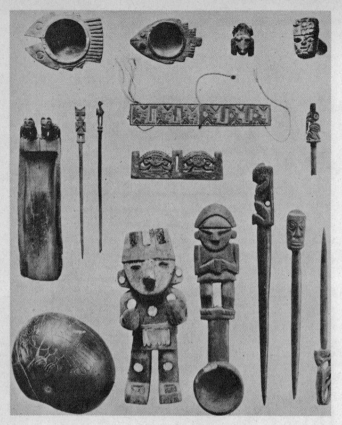

Small objects of carved wood

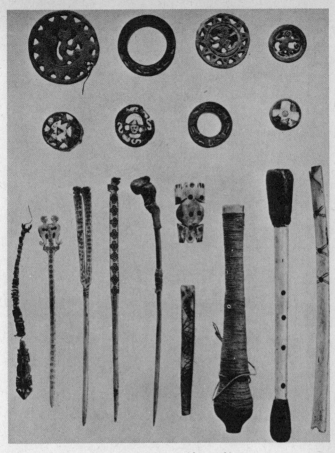

Ear ornaments, and objects of bone

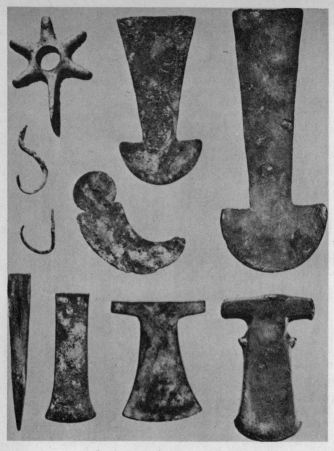

Implements of copper and bronze

Implements and ornaments of copper and silver

(A) False heads of mummy bundles. Pachacamac

(B) Mummy bundle. Pachacamac

unit, which engaged in a moderate amount of barter with neighbours. The curaca was exempt from labour in the fields, but it must have been relatively simple for a middle-sized community to support him and his family.

(d) The multiplicity of linguistic stocks in the Andean area limited the native to associations with related groups or tribes.

(e) This was even more the case in their religion. Most ayllus limited their cult to their own tutelary and totemic (*sic*) supernatural beings, and only occasionally displayed some interest in the cult of the neighbouring ayllus.

These five observations concerning the Andean ayllu-communities are literally true only of those that lived isolated and were not members of any alliances, confederacies, or feudal states. Such a state of isolation and of complete independence was not prevalent in this area. It is useful, however, for the purposes of analysis to understand first the above *simplified typical case*. Numerous changes occurred under Inca rule.

Bram then points out the great changes which incorporation in the Inca empire produced in the life of the ayllu and of the individual. They became relatively unimportant elements in a great organization instead of prominent entities in their provincial sphere. They were forced to take part in enterprises in which they had no interest, to contribute produce and labour to the support of distant projects and persons. Individuals from the village were taken to Cuzco or other distant places to be hostages, soldiers, craftsmen, servants, sacrifices, or concubines. Those that returned had broadened horizons through the experiences of travel, and introduced new points of view to the community.

The ayllus of pre-Inca Peru may have originally been grouped into two divisions or moieties, a rather common custom in primitive societies, but this dual division did not always fit into the imperial pattern and, in very populous regions, three groups were sometimes made. In general, however, there were two moieties, known as the Upper and the Lower; each ayllu belonged to one or the other. Those of the Upper moiety were given precedence over those of the Lower, and the two were rivals. They also showed a tendency toward endogamy.

The ayllus of a region, at any rate, were grouped into two – sometimes three – *saya*, or sections, and these formed a province (*guamán*). In the case of conquered peoples – the greater part of the empire – the province corresponded to a former tribe or native state; the provinces therefore differed considerably in size and number of population. Each province had its capital city, the centre for political and religious administration, and the inhabitants of each province wore some distinctive standard feature in their head-dresses.

The provinces were further grouped into one of the four quarters (*suyu*) into which the great empire was divided. Cuzco, the Inca capital, was the centre, geographically as well as politically, of all, for the division lines ran roughly north and south, east and west. The north-western quarter, Chinchasuyu, included Ecuador and northern and central Peru; the south-western, Cuntisuyu, consisted of southern Peru; to the north-east was Antisuyu, consisting largely of the eastern foothills and forests; Collasuyu to the south-east comprised the great highlands of the Aymara, the basin of Lake Titicaca, most of Bolivia, north-western highland Argentina, and northern Chile; this was the largest of the four quarters. The whole empire was appropriately called the 'Land of the Four Quarters', Tahuantinsuyu.

An Inca noble was the resident administrative official in each provincial capital, and the governors of the four quarters formed the great council of state in Cuzco; these also were Inca nobles of high rank, generally close relatives of the emperor, but their posts were not hereditary. The council reported its suggestions and opinions to the emperor for his decision and action.

Below the provincial governor were the *curacas* of four ranks, according to the number of men – or taxpayers – over whom they had charge; the latter were enumerated according to the decimal system. The curaca of lowest rank was the chief of one hundred men; he of highest rank, of ten thousand. The post of curaca was hereditary, subject to imperial approval. Over smaller groups of men, fifty and ten, were foremen of two ranks; these were commoners appointed by their curacas, and their offices were not hereditary. The two classes of leaders may cogently be compared with those in an army: corporals and sergeants over small groups, commissioned officers over progressively larger numbers. The official Inca titles of these officers of eight ranks below the emperor, listed by the chroniclers and by most other commentators, need not concern us here.

Some of the chroniclers state or imply that this system of decimal representation was a rigid one, and this has also been accepted by many writers on the Inca. But in the nature of things it would have been unworkable; the constant alteration in the numerical content of families and ayllus by births and deaths would have necessitated continual reshufflings and reclassifications. A man was presumably made the leader of a certain group, an ayllu or a saya, and given the rank called for according to the approximate number of families that his group proved to contain.

These numbers of taxpayers were determined by exact records constantly kept up to date by reports of births and deaths made by the foremen and forwarded to their superiors. The totals for major areas were recorded decimally on *quipus* and sent annually to the census office in Cuzco so that the authorities there had, at any time, an approximately correct record of population statistics for the entire empire. In these records, each individual was classified in one of a number of age-grade categories according to his physical status, from dependent babyhood to dependent senility. The chroniclers differ greatly in their reports on these groups, giving from six to twelve classes. The latter, that most generally quoted, seems unreasonable, since it makes four classes below eight years of age, years certainly of slight importance to the empire. Possibly the categories differed in different regions. The great important class, of course, was that of the *puric*, the able-bodied adult man, aged from about twenty-five to fifty years and capable of doing a hard day's work in the fields, the army, or the mines. He was the unit in the social system and represented his household. The classification applied only to male commoners, but there were probably other census records for women.

Chapter 12

POLITICAL ORGANIZATION
AND GOVERNMENT

THE Inca state was a queer blend of theocracy, monarchy, socialism, and communism, its categorization in one system or another depending mainly on definition. It has often been termed a socialistic empire,[1] for it was an aristocratic and auto-cratic socialism, not a democratic one. Land was the property of the state, and much of it was communally worked. Most of the llama herds were also state property, as also were the mines. These were almost the only 'means of production'. The state in-sured the people against hunger, exploitation, undue hardship, and all kinds of want, but regimented them rigorously and left them no choice, independence, or initiative. There were neither 'booms' nor depressions. It was the welfare state *par excellence*, toward which our modern democracies now seem to be (1966) tending. It, however, was at least efficiently administered; malfeasance, misfeasance, and nonfeasance on the part of officials were equally severely punished – or claimed to have been.

However, the Inca empire differed from the modern ideal of a socialistic welfare state in that there was a large class of nobles and priests, supported by the masses. Heavy tribute in the form of labour was demanded of the peasants, who profited very little from it.

All arable land was divided into three categories, though not into three equal parts, although fields of the three classes were necessarily close together. The produce of those of one class was for the government, of the second for the gods and religion, and of the third for the people. Although the first two were given primary consideration, their size depended on the population, for each family was first allotted just enough land to keep them

1. Baudin, 1927a, 1928; Karsten, 1949a.

comfortably fed without hunger; the balance was divided between state and church. Each year the land was reallotted by the local official – at least the communal land – and each family was given according to its current needs, the same as, or more or less than, the preceding year, according as the number of persons in the household may have increased or decreased.

The system might be termed agrarian collectivism rather than communism. Although in late days the land was considered the property of the state, i.e. of the emperor, it was controlled by the ayllu, the local clan group, communally; ayllu ownership doubtless long preceded imperial days. Probably also the pattern of lands communally cultivated for the state (formerly for the local chiefs) and for the church (formerly the local priests) was an ancient Andean one, adopted and enlarged in imperial times. Probably the greater amount of land allocated to church and state was offset, if not more than made up for, by the agricultural land produced by state enterprise, making formerly sterile acres arable by irrigation and terracing. In the periodical allocation of family fields it is reported that one *topo* (page 234) of land was assigned to each married couple, an extra strip for every son, and half a strip for each daughter.

The boundaries of the fields, especially those separating communal, state, and church properties, were well marked, and their removal was a great and almost unheard-of-crime.

On the whole, the state lands seem to have been a little larger than the others, for reasons that we will see later. State overseers constantly supervised the non-communal lands, and the common people respected their sanctity and inviolability so much that they never crossed them without repeating ritual prayers for this special purpose.

The non-communal lands were cultivated by the people *en masse* and before their own fields, those of the gods first. When time for sowing or harvesting came, the commoners were called by the officials to work the sacred fields. At the inception everyone laboured, commoners, officials, nobility, and even the emperor himself. The latter offered only a token of work, and the nobles soon followed suit, those of lowest rank labouring the longest, and soon only the peasants remaining. The emperor, or the highest official on the spot, inaugurated the work with a golden implement.

The fields were divided up by lines, a section to each family, so that the man with the most household assistance finished his job first. Like all co-operative labour, it must have been a jovial and not an onerous occasion, with plenty of chicha beer, singing, and bantering. The songs, perhaps in honour of the gods when working the church lands, or in praise of the emperor while engaged in the state fields, were appropriate to the occasion. As soon as the fields of the gods were finished, the work was repeated on the government lands, and then the people were free to cultivate their own fields. There was a communal spirit of helpfulness, and if a man was called away on state business such as military service his neighbours quietly attended to his agricultural needs.

The harvests from the state and religious fields were gathered into separate storehouses of which the government maintained two sets in each district. Other, and probably more and greater, storehouses were built at the provincial capitals and at Cuzco. For fire protection, each set consisted of a number of small buildings sufficiently separated.

The food from the religious storehouses served to support the numerous priesthood, and for sacrificial and ceremonial purposes. The government's store was drawn on for the support of the nobility and all state officials, artisan craftsmen, the army, and all other non-religious non-producers. In the latter category were the aged, infirm, and widows. The state storehouses also served as insurance against unforeseen calamities and 'acts of God' – earthquake, storms, and other causes of crop failure. The curacas were authorized to draw upon these stores in the event of such disasters and famines. In seasons of plenty, when the storehouses were too full to hold the new crop, the emperor ordered a stock dividend, distributing the food to the people so that they might eat more heartily and be more contented. In such circumstances, food from one region was sent to another where it was not grown, so that the people might enjoy a change of diet. Potatoes were never destroyed because of over-production; the gods would have been angered and would have withheld the next harvest.

In the highland grazing regions, the same triple division was applied to the herds of llamas and alpacas, as well as to the pasture-lands; both were divided into three groups for church, state, and people. In this case, because most of the wool was distributed by the government and few animals were killed except for sacrifice, the allotments to the church and state were much greater than those to the populace. Ten animals was the limit for any commoner; nobles were allowed more. The majority of the stock belonged to the government, which gathered the wool into storehouses and distributed it to the families in proportion to their size, enough to clothe all the members. In this distribution no deduction was made for the privately owned animals; the man who owned many received as much as he who owned one.

Each family made its own clothing from the wool distributed by the government, as well as making all other household equipment and tools. These, together with house, stable-storehouse, and small domestic animals, were practically the only private property.

In addition to agricultural service on state and church lands each commoner was required to perform a certain amount of other public work each year. This obligation was known as *mita*. These men provided recruits for the army, labour on the roads and bridges and in the mines, runners on the post roads, personal service for the nobles, and other public work. The number of men needed was determined, and a definite percentage of these was selected from each district. Tradition reports that thirty thousand men were thus employed in building the great fortress of Sacsahuaman. It is also said that unnecessary work was often made just for the purpose of keeping these selective-service recruits busy. Like every good army sergeant, the officials knew well that 'Satan finds some evil still for idle hands to do', and that the busy man has no time to complain or foment revolt.

There were certain districts that were exempt from this *mita* service because they provided special materials or services. Thus the Chicha made carved logs of a resinous wood to be used for sacrificial fires, the Rucana supplied the litter-bearers, and the Chumpivilca the trained dancers for the court.

Craftsmen and other skilled labourers whose work required long practice and experience were especially provided for, and were relieved from agricultural, pastoral, or the *mita* service. They were government servants, supported at public expense. Actually they were court artificers, as their handiwork was for the emperor, who distributed it as favours to the nobility. Goldsmiths, potters, woodcarvers, sculptors, and similar artisans fell into this class, as well as the *quipucamayoc* who kept accounts. These positions were generally hereditary, since the father trained his sons in his craft. But often a boy who showed special ability was chosen from the peasant class. These were the only craftsmen; otherwise there was no division of labour.

Another important group exempt from the usual labour-tax service consisted of men known as *yanacona*. These were selected in youth, removed from their ayllus with which they lost all connexion, and taken for service in other parts. In fact, some authorities believe that the craftsmen were included in the yanacona category. The status of both was hereditary. Like the 'Chosen Women' next to be mentioned, boys were selected and placed at the disposal of the emperor, who employed them in state service as pages, servants, temple attendants, supervisors, and similar offices, or gave them as rewards for faithful and efficient service to favoured nobles and warriors. Though the latter apparently often used their yanacona labour for ordinary agricultural work, nevertheless the boys were certainly selected for unusual intelligence, ability, or promise, and most of them used their positions to rise to posts of considerable importance. Many of them were sons of curacas. Their status is a little difficult to define; they can hardly be considered as slaves, but in effect they were. However, the close relationship between them and their masters gave them great opportunities to receive favours and to be placed in positions of responsibility. Some of them rose to be curacas themselves.

The Spanish conquerors took full advantage of the yanacona relationship and enlarged it greatly, drafting great numbers of young men as servants on their estates, agricultural labourers and miners; these, of course, were practically slaves with no prospects for advancement or economic improvement.

Regimentation also extended to the women. Of course almost all of them became wives and mothers of commoners and participated in their husbands' agricultural activities as well as having their own domestic ones. These, however, were the less attractive and less talented women and were known as the 'left-out girls', *hauasipascuna*, since the choice maidens were selected for public service.

A government official visited each village at intervals and classified all the girls at about the age of ten. The most beautiful and physically perfect were chosen and sent to be educated in 'convents' in the provincial capitals where they spent about four years learning 'domestic science', religion, weaving, cooking, chicha-manufacture, and similar duties. They were known as *acllacuna*, 'Chosen Women'. A few were also chosen to be sacrificed on solemn occasions; these were especially honoured and particularly proud and happy at their selection, since it assured them of an after-life of happiness and leisure.

After completing their educations, the girls were again classified. Many were given by the emperor to nobles as secondary wives. He doubtless kept the *crème de la crème* for himself. The others were consecrated to the service and homage to the Sun and became the 'Virgins of the Sun', *mamacuna*, sworn to permanent chastity. Some were attached to each shrine or 'Sun Temple', where they wove the fine textiles used in ceremonies and worn by the priests, and prepared the chicha for festivals. They had considerable resemblance to the nuns of a religious order, and were headed by a high priestess who was of the noblest birth and was considered the wife of the Sun. The 'convent' in Cuzco was of course the largest and most important, but others, presided over by a priestess of noble birth, were connected with the temple in each provincial centre.

The Emperor and the Nobility

The Inca emperor was an absolute despot but distinctly not a tyrant, using these words in their proper senses, nowadays so often confused. That is, his power was limited only by custom, but it *was* thus limited. To his subjects he was an omnipotent tribal god, merciless to their enemies, firm but just to his subjects and worshippers. The comfort and peace of his people was his primary and constant concern. He could hardly be said to have been a legal ruler, since he was above the law – his word *was* the law – but, so strong was the force of custom and precedent that he probably never violated them to satisfy personal spite.

The Inca emperor was the supreme ruler of the state and could with better reason have echoed – or anticipated – Louis XIV's claim to *be* the state. As a lineal descendant of the Sun he ruled by divine right and was worshipped and implicitly obeyed as being himself divine. He was believed to be intimately associated with the Sun, and his health affected that of the latter.

In the earlier years of the empire the emperor married the daughter of a neighbouring ruler, as among recent European royalty, but in the last three or four generations before the Conquest his person had become so exalted that none but his own sister could be considered a fit consort. Here was the *ne plus ultra* of the idea of aristocracy, of blue blood; none but a replica could be an equal. The same sentiment and ideal were in vogue among another great people of antiquity, the Egyptians; for generations the Pharaohs married their sisters. Contrary to popular folklore, in both cases this – to us – incestuous marriage seems to have produced capable, vigorous rulers. All the historic Peruvian emperors were men of unusual energy and capacity. Close inbreeding among animals has long been practised to produce superior stock, and there is no reason why the same should not be true of humans, if there is no weakness or defect in the heredity.

Like many Oriental potentates, the emperor was also allowed a large seraglio of secondary wives, generally taken from the 'Chosen Women'. These concubines were not, as is often stated, the 'Virgins of the Sun', another group of 'Chosen Women' vowed to permanent chastity. The secondary wives prepared the emperor's food, made his attire, and performed the usual domestic duties.

Naturally the emperor had a large number of offspring who belonged to the nobility and were accorded special privileges.

The descendants of each emperor in the male line formed a special royal ayllu whose duty it was to attend to the upkeep of his palace and the maintenance of his cult. For each emperor built himself a new palace which was later used as his shrine and mausoleum. At the time of the Conquest these descendants of the emperors amounted to about five hundred. This large body of aristocratic men formed a valuable court around the current living emperor, and from them he chose most of the higher officials.

There seems to have been no very definite rule for succession to the 'throne'. The emperor named his successor, always his son, and generally the most capable of his sons by the *coya*, his principal wife. The boy probably had no formal education – for who could instruct a living deity? – but was trained for his future exalted position by his parents, and learned by court example.

When the heir apparent reached puberty he was by no means exempted, as any European princeling would have been, from the fatiguing trials of the manhood ceremonies that were held annually for all the boys of the noble class who had reached that physical stage during the past year. These rites were meant to test the physical and psychological fitness of the youths for the positions of authority that they were to hold, and the Peruvians had the proper idea that the higher the rank, the greater the required capability. So the young Inca prince was given no leniency and was even treated with more than usual severity; he was expected to outdo the others in physical effort and the endurance of hardships.

When the time came for the new ruler's inauguration or installation, he fasted for three days in a house built especially for the occasion and was then invested with the royal fringe in a great public ceremony at which each noble swore allegiance. This was followed by a feast lasting for several days.

Upon his death the members of his ayllu took charge of the elaborate funerary ceremonies which were observed throughout the empire. The body was preserved in his palace by the primitive means of mummification in vogue. The entrails were removed and preserved in a special container, and the body was dried and carefully wrapped in the finest textiles. The mummy was thereafter waited upon as during life, even, it is reported, having women constantly standing at its side with fans to keep the flies away! During the greatest public ceremonies the bodies of the emperors were brought out into the sacred square of Cuzco under the care of their descendants. The mummies of all the Inca emperors were seen as late as 1559.

It was expected that the deceased emperor's favourite wives and servants would volunteer to accompany him in death, and probably each of these did his or her duty as he saw it, confident of his reward in the after-world. They were intoxicated, probably with chicha beer, during a great dance, and then strangled.

The august emperor's presence could be approached by few, and with the greatest humility by these few. Usually, in interviews, he was invisible behind a screen; a face-to-face reception was an honour accorded to only the greatest or the most favoured. No one, however, no matter what his rank or blood, could enter the chamber without removing his sandals and placing a small burden on his back to indicate his humble position. When travelling, the emperor was carried on a litter by men from the province of Rucanas who wore a special livery. His retinue on such a journey amounted to several hundred men, to clear the road and relieve the bearers. Both on account of this large number and the slow pace that his dignity required, a day's journey averaged only about twelve miles.

Other servants of the imperial court also were recruited from particular villages and regions. Garcilaso's[1] remarks upon this subject are pertinent:

The attendants for the service of the palace, such as sweepers, water-carriers, and wood-cutters, as well as cooks for the table of the courtiers (for that of the Inca himself was served by his concubines), porters, keepers of the wardrobe, warders of the treasure, gardeners, huntsmen, and all other servants holding similar positions to those in the houses of the kings and emperors, were not persons chosen by chance. But each office was filled by natives of particular villages, whose duty it was to supply faithful and efficient men in sufficient number. They were changed at

1. Garcilaso de la Vega, Part 1, Book 6, chapter 3; Vol. 2, pp. 107-8 of Markham's translation (1869-71).

certain intervals, and this was the form that the tribute took in those villages. Any negligence or inefficiency on the part of these servants was looked upon as an offence committed by their village, and for one man's fault all the inhabitants were chastised more or less severely according to the offence. If the offence was committed against the royal majesty, the village was levelled with the ground. It must not be understood that the wood-cutters went to the forest for fuel, but that they found it provided in the palace, being brought there by the vassals, as well as all other things for the royal service. And these employments were much prized among the Indians, as they enabled them to be nearer the royal person, which was an honour they most esteemed.

The villages which furnished these servants were those within six or seven leagues of the city of Cuzco, and were the first which the Inca Manco Capac ordered to be formed by the savages whom he reduced to subjection. The inhabitants of them, by his special grace and bounty, he called Incas, and they received the insignia and dress of the royal person. . . .

The emperor's clothing was of the same pattern as that of all men, but was of the finest materials, specially woven or made for him by the women of his household. His most characteristic ornament was a wide fringe, the royal insignia with which he was invested upon assuming rule. This, about four inches wide, was composed of small gold tubes from which hung red tassels. The head-dress itself was rather simple, a braid (*llautu*) wound several times around the head. He wore very large ear-plugs. The higher members of the nobility were also allowed to wear ear-plugs, head-bands, and fringes, but always of other colours and smaller or of less fine materials. The emperor wore his hair rather short.

The royal throne was a low stool of red wood, only about eight inches high and covered with a rich cloth; this was placed on a raised platform. A small, square, stiff, painted cloth pennant was the royal standard, but the emperor personally carried a war-club or mace with a star head of gold. Two similar ones on long poles were carried to flank the royal standard.

Like the simplest of his subjects, the ruler slept on the floor, on a large cotton quilt covered with woollen blankets; he ate from the most ornate containers of gold, silver, or pottery. No one else might aspire to enjoy his superior goods, so all his discards and left-overs, clothing, food, or whatnot, were carefully saved and ceremonially burnt once a year by an official. On the latter point, however, as on many others, the chroniclers differ. Garcilaso[1] says that the emperor gave his once-used clothing to another member of his family. Garcilaso's description, while probably not entirely reliable as to details, gives a good impression of certain phases of the emperor's life.

The Inca usually sat on a stool of solid gold called *tiana* ... without arms or back, and with a concave surface for the seat. It was placed on a great square board of gold. All the cups for the whole service of the house, as well for the table as for the kitchen, were, large and small, of gold and silver; and some were placed in each depot for the use of the king when travelling. This was done to avoid the necessity of carrying them about with him, and thus every royal lodging, whether on the roads or in the provinces, was fully supplied with all he required when he marched with his armies, or visited his people. . . .

There was also great store of new clothing, both for wearing and for the bed, for the Inca never put on the same dress twice, but gave it to one of his relations. All his bed clothes were woollen, woven from the wool of the vicuñas, which is so fine that, among other things belonging to that land, it has been brought over for the bed of the king, Don Philip II. These blankets were placed both under and over. They did not use mattresses, because they did not want them, for when they saw those used by the Spaniards they would not have them in their houses. They seemed to be too great a luxury, and too artificial to be in conformity with the natural life that they profess to lead.

They did not have tapestry for the walls, because they were covered with gold and silver. The dinners were very plentiful, as they were prepared for all the Inca's relations who might come to dine with the king, as well as for all the servants of the household, who were numerous. The hour for the principal meal, both for the Inca and for the people, was eight or nine in the morning. They supped before the light of day was gone, and these were their only meals. They were generally bad eaters; that is to say, they ate little. But they were not so abstemious in drinking. They

1. Garcilaso de la Vega, Part I, Book 6, chapter 1; Vol. 2, pp. 100–1 of Markham's translation (1869–71).

did not drink during the meal, but they made up for it afterwards, and their potations were continued until night. This was the custom of the rich, for the poor had only sufficient of all things, though no scarcity. They went to bed early, and got up very early to do the business of the day.

In a period of only about thirty years the Inca empire expanded from a relatively small, homogeneous state to an immense empire containing dozens of alien peoples with different languages and diverse governmental patterns. To keep these dissident elements in subjection and peace required a tremendous increase in the number of reliable administrative officials. Up until that time the Inca pattern had been to select officials from the more capable members of the royalty, blood relatives or descendants of the emperors, but now there were too few of these, and every official who showed any administrative ability was quickly advanced to a responsible position and placed among an alien group to enforce the will of the emperor. It was just as at the beginning of our recent World Wars, when a capable Navy warrant officer soon found himself a commissioned lieutenant, or a regular army sergeant a captain, drilling a company of raw recruits. It is not certain, however, whether an ordinary commoner could ever rise to the nobility.

When a former ruler or leader of one of the conquered peoples was willing to accept the new régime, he was confirmed in his position and his children were taken to Cuzco as hostages. There they were educated and indoctrinated in Inca ideology in what seems to have been the only formal school in the empire. Probably the sons of Inca nobles also attended the school, or certain classes of it. It is reported to have been, as in most modern colleges, a four-year course, the first year spent in learning the Inca language, the second in Inca religion, the third in the intricacies of the *quipu* (the knot-records) (see pages 230–31), and the fourth in Inca history. The teachers were firm believers in the pedagogical qualities of the rod, but the caning was applied to the soles of the feet. However, this phase of instruction was, by custom, limited to one application of ten blows per day.

On the father's death a son succeeded him. An able son of a former low-rank official now enjoying a high position of authority among an alien group was likewise appointed to his father's position, and in every way the Inca strove to follow their pattern of an hereditary aristocracy. The noble class was thus greatly augmented and fell into two classes, the higher and the lower aristocracy, possibly better distinguished as the royalty and the nobility.

The higher aristocracy was termed the 'Inca class' by the Spanish chroniclers; its nucleus consisted of the real old royalty, Incas by blood, descendants of the emperors in the male line. Since these were not sufficient to provide the necessary officials, the Emperor Pachacuti extended the privileges of Inca nobility to all the inhabitants of certain districts, all of whom spoke Inca as their native language and practised Inca customs; many of these were sent as officials to newly conquered distant territories. They were all given the privilege of wearing large ear-plugs, and all the other perquisites of the Inca royalty.

The lower class of nobility or aristocracy was known as the 'Curaca class' and consisted of the former independent conquered leaders who had been confirmed in their positions, and all other administrators down to those over one hundred persons.

Both the royalty and the nobility were allowed many privileges such as the use of litters, parasols, and attire somewhat resembling the emperor's, secondary wives, luxury articles, and *yanacona* servants. They were exempt from taxation and were supported by the government. Llamas and land were also awarded them for efficient service, but, in accord with the basic Inca (and usual pan-American) principle regarding land, the latter was considered as the property of the group and not of the individual. The noble might enjoy its usufruct but could not dispose of it; at his death it was similarly used by his progeny. While the nobility composed a relatively large group numerically, they formed only a tiny fraction of the entire population.

Although in Incaic Peru there was a large body of non-producers, slavery of the type of the ancient Old World despotisms was unknown; the entire class of commoner peasantry contributed equally to the support of the officials, priests, and aristocracy. There being no money, no capitalists, no private property except for the simplest and most elemental possessions, all taxation was in the form of labour service. This was accomplished by stringent rules or laws, enforced by officials, each responsible to another in a higher category until the last was the emperor himself. The laws of the emperor, moreover, were accepted by both officials and commoners as those of divinity itself and therefore just and inexorable. Disobedience and infractions were exceedingly rare, and sternly punished.

Though, theoretically, all commoners were of the same economic status, as in every society a few seem to have secured more than their share of goods, especially in the possession of llamas. There were also very poor ones who had somehow lost their ayllu affiliations and drifted to the large cities. The women of this class were probably the prostitutes, of which there was a large group in Cuzco.

In another respect also there was some economic inequality. The commoner with many children, especially boys, to help him with labour on his farm and his tax labour, was deemed richer than the man with few – or female – children.

War and Conquest

Among most American Indian peoples of relatively low cultural status, inter-group hostility and combat can hardly be dignified by the name of war. Hostility was felt towards all neighbouring groups, culminating in small semi-private war parties. It assumed a more national character with the larger sedentary groups in more thickly populated regions, and with the Inca it became the primary instrument of national policy. Warfare in Peru doubtless went through these sequential stages. In the earliest days the villages were probably constantly at enmity, the hostilities of small scope; later, the growing states, especially those on the coast such as the Chimú, probably had organized armies, but Inca warfare was of a grade that surpassed everything else in pre-Columbian America. The causes were complex, but war became a most important feature of Inca culture. While based on the primitive Andean pattern of warfare it naturally evolved practices suited to large-scale operations with immense armies.

Though some of the earlier wars, both of the Inca and of other Peruvian peoples, may have had an economic basis, economy was certainly not the primary cause of war, and it was lacking entirely in the later days of the empire. Then it was a desire for aggrandizement and increased power on the part of the emperor and the policy-makers, and an ambition to excel and to achieve glory and the advancement, perquisites, and favours that fell to the brave and victorious warrior on the part of the subordinate leaders; the common soldier was the traditional 'cannon-fodder'. Each new Inca emperor aspired to outdo his predecessor. Unlike the Aztec, annual tribute was not demanded of the conquered, though some looted spoils of victory were taken at the time of the conquest. Indeed, some conquered regions were so economically ill-favoured that their acquisition was more a liability than an asset. The nobility were already so well off that they could use little more. Neither was there the urge for captives for sacrifice that animated much of Aztec war, and the subjugated peoples were not enslaved or made to work any harder than the victors. Nevertheless, war was, on the whole, advantageous to the Inca – and probably also to the conquered peoples. The life of the people was so regimented and channelled that war presented practically the only opportunity for competition and manifestation of superiority. Moreover, in later days at least, the large organization needed by the immense forces almost required that the army be a standing one, permanently in action, and the rulers knew well that, unless busy with foreign wars, the generals might well plot revolution. Some of the wars were obviously planned to prevent peripheral enemies from stirring into revolt their recently conquered neighbours.

Doubtless among all Peruvian groups every able-bodied man was a potential warrior and had received some training in warfare since boyhood; to be incapable or inefficient was a disgrace. In the days of the Inca empire every ordinary man in the proper age-class was liable to military service, and practically all of them certainly served their terms. It is obvious that, with the size and extent of the army and the empire, most of the troops came from recently conquered peoples with little interest in subjugating others; the actual Quechua Inca of the Cuzco region were so relatively few that they served only as higher officers. The only force of 'regulars', professional soldiers, was the bodyguard of the emperor. These, of course, were a picked group; Atahuallpa executed those who broke ranks when naturally frightened by their first sight of a rearing horse. The army was subdivided according to the same decimal system that was employed with the civilian population, with the same pyramidal ranking of officers.

As with the Mediterranean, the Aztec, and most early conquering nations with large armies, Inca warfare was based on close in-fighting with hand weapons. The bow and arrow, the usual American Indian weapon in fighting as in hunting, was not employed by the mountain tribes, though of course it was known and was used by forest Indians in the Inca armies. It was little used on the coast also; in both regions suitable wood was scarce. Nor were javelins and throwing spears employed in Inca times, though they had been in earlier days. Their use lasted until the Conquest among the natives of the coast, who cast them with the help of spear-throwers; archaeologically the spear-thrower is very old in America (Plate 46A). The spears were of hard wood with fire-hardened points.

Inca battles, however, generally opened at a slight distance with the use of slings and bolas, the missile arms; these are more adapted to the open country of the Peruvian highlands. The sling was not the forked-stick-and-rubber-band weapon of the modern boy, but rather of David's Goliath-killing type. Generally of braided wool or fibre, it was up to six feet (2 m.) in length, with a wider cradle for the stone in the centre. Doubled, with both ends held in one hand, it was whirled around the head to give momentum, and then one end released, thus hurling the stone with great force and – with practice – great accuracy. The sling, constantly carried to kill or frighten away small animals or to drive domestic ones, was as ubiquitous as a modern Mexican's *machete*, and was often worn as a fillet to keep the hair back.

The bolas consisted of several stones, each fastened to the end of a cord, or thong, and the latter tied together at the other ends.

Thrown, they whirled by centrifugal force and covered a considerable area, wrapping around the victim's body or legs; this also was primarily a hunting weapon.

After the first stone-hurling, the Inca warriors closed in for hand-to-hand combat. The main arm of the common soldier was the club, generally with a doughnut-shaped stone on the end; this was often modified to a star shape with a number of points, especially in club-heads made of copper or bronze. A double-edged sword of hard wood which has given its Quechua name *macana* to this weapon was another arm; this was a heavy two-handed sword, and the wielder carried no shield. There were also various types of battle-axes and poleaxes, with blades of stone or copper. The long wooden spears had fire-hardened ends, or tips of copper or bronze.

Armour had been considerably developed among the Inca troops. Quilted cotton shirts or lengths of cloth wrapped around the body were worn. These were so efficient against native arms that the Spanish adopted the custom in preference to their heavier and hotter steel armour. Helmets of wood or plaited cane protected the head, and shields of wooden slats were worn on the back. Smaller round or rectangular shields were carried in the hand; these were generally covered with hide and decorated with some painted design or feather mosaic. Like the Roman *testudo*, a great strong cloth that could cover many men was sometimes used in siege operations.

Except for these protective devices the Inca soldier wore the usual man's costume without the cloak. Almost all wore round metal plaques which were a sort of military decoration, probably awarded by the commanding officer for valour – copper for the lowest rank, gold for the highest. There was probably no military band *per se*, but martial music was produced by small drums, trumpets, and flutes, and the fighting was accompanied by a din of shouts and curses, and possibly concerted singing of insulting songs. Each company carried a small square stiff pennant which bore the insignia of the group; this was fastened to the end of a spear.

Compared with their enemies, the Inca armies were strong and efficient, mainly because of their size and the excellently organized commissariat. Of course they were no match for fire-arms and cavalry.

Excellent discipline was observed in the Inca armies until the ranks were broken for hand-to-hand combat, from which time on there was no direction or organization. On the march, how-ever, the troops were under strict control; no deviation from the ranks was tolerated, and any foraging or molestation of non-combatants was severely punished.

Though most military operations were pitched battles in the open, the art of fortification was rather well developed. Tem-porary breastworks and trenches were apparently never used, but most important towns had hill-top forts to which the people re-tired in case of attack, and the large centres, such as Cuzco, were provided with great fortresses. These were often constructed with considerable military engineering skill, with walled terraces on the hillside, bastions, and salients. The great fortress of Sacsahuamán (Plate 15) (see page 163) overlooking Cuzco is the most noteworthy example, but many others, both in the high-lands and on the coast, remain to attest to the quality and nature of these works.

Capable and experienced generals had many military man-œuvres, strategies, and ruses up their sleeves, and the history of the Inca contains many of these. Grass was fired to demoralize an enemy army; it was led into an ambush in a ravine and over-whelmed with boulders. Retreating, apparently defeated from a battle, the Inca force would return and surprise the confident and unwary 'victors' the following dawn. The army was fre-quently divided and a large part of it kept in reserve for a surprise attack.

The great success of the Inca armies was in large measure due to the recognition of the truth of the aphorism that an army travels on its stomach. The commissariat was efficiently planned and operated. In the organized parts of the empire supplies were available in government storehouses; beyond its limits they were brought by trains of pack llamas. The storehouses were so frequent along the high-roads that the marching troops could always make their night camp at one.

Few captives, and these mainly the leaders, were brought back as prisoners of war. The emperor trod upon the conquered chiefs as a symbol of their subjection to him; they were sometimes marched through the streets of Cuzco in a triumphant victory parade. A few of the prisoners might be sacrificed, and a few of the culpable or dangerous leaders tortured, flayed, killed, or imprisoned. Heads were frequently taken as trophies, and the skull often made into a drinking-cup from which the victor drank chicha. War drums were sometimes made of the skin – and even, it is reported, of the entire body – of important defeated enemies as a particular not-to-be-forgotten insult. Necklaces were often made of the teeth of slain enemies, and flutes of their shin-bones. The absence of the frequent South American custom of cannibalism is noteworthy.

The main incentive of the warrior, however, especially of the leaders of whatever rank, was glory, honours, rewards, and advancement. The emperor was lavish in his gifts to nobles who had served him well; they were given secondary wives, fine clothing and other handicraft made by the state-supported artificers, promotion, and special privileges such as sitting on a special stool. Even for the humble common soldier there were commendatory metal plaques, gifts of clothing, and similar awards.

Pre-combat negotiation or diplomacy was a unique feature of Inca imperial militarism. Envoys invited neighbouring groups to join the empire, pointing out the advantages of alliance, the terrors of refusal. The efficient socialistic economic system was doubtless advantageous to the ordinary native, and the local rulers were generally permitted to retain their positions under the new régime. Most small groups and tribes realized the hopelessness of resistance and therefore submitted peacefully; the stronger ones generally preferred to fight against odds for their independence, almost always ineffectually.

Church and state were one in the Inca empire, and their motives, policies, and practices were practically identical with those of many other triumphant nations of the past. They firmly believed that they were the superior and master race – for hadn't they proved it both in culture and by force of arms? Like all imperialistic nations, they doubtless – and properly – felt that they could utilize the land to better advantage. Moreover, they brought the blessings of the true religion – that of the Sun – to their benighted heathen neighbours, without, however, interfering with the religious practices of these subjugated peoples.

As among most peoples before the recent atheistic ideology, the gods were importuned to lend aid, since the war was fought largely for their glory, and final victory was ascribed to divine help. In addition to ceremonies, sacrifices, fasts, and other rites to increase the sympathy and favour of their gods, an incantation was performed before the opening of hostilities to weaken the power of the enemy gods and supernatural spirits. To the accompaniment of some magical rites, such as the burning of wild birds on a fire of thorny wood, the priests prayed that the power of the enemy's supernatural aids might be weakened. Holding stones on which figures of various dangerous, noxious, and fierce animals had been painted, they marched around the fire, chanting and praying. Some black llamas which had been starved for some time were then sacrificed with the prayer that the bodies and spirit of the enemy might likewise be weakened. Black dogs were also sacrificed, and certain persons compelled to eat the meat. During these rites the participants ate only at night.

Divination, of course, played a large part in all military actions, and nothing was begun until the auguries proved auspicious. The oracles were frequently consulted, and inherently lucky days, such as that of the new moon, were always chosen. In the above-mentioned ceremony of the sacrifice of the starved black llamas, the hearts were inspected to see whether some flesh near the heart had been absorbed during the deprivation from food; the prognostication was bad if it had not.

Each fighting group carried into battle some of its portable idols, fetishes, or wacas, which served not only as moral sustainers and rallying points, like modern flags and pennons, but also lent their supernatural aid. The allies naturally carried those of their own regions and deities. As the major idols of the army, the Inca carried images or wacas representing ancestors, especially former emperors; the stones representing Manco Capac and Huanacauri were particular favourites.

The surprising success of the Inca in unifying and controlling with such relatively little belligerent unrest such a great empire, composed of many previously hostile elements, was due almost entirely to their wise policies with regard to newly conquered regions. The important elements of this programme were resettlement or colonization, and administrative reorganization.

As soon as armed resistance had ceased, a careful survey was made of the region and a census taken of its population. The survey took into account all geographical features, village sites, arable land, water supply, etc., and was recorded in clay relief models; the census noted the inhabitants by the age-grade Inca system; these were registered on *quipus*. Such data as the number of llamas were doubtless included. All these records were then forwarded to Cuzco where they were studied carefully by the emperor and his advisers who then drew up a programme. A provincial capital was chosen and official buildings erected there, and the people were moved from their protected towns and hill-top fortresses and made to settle on or near their arable fields.

Cieza de León[1] gives a vivid description of Inca resettlement practices, of which he rather approved:

Having established a governor, with garrisons of soldiers, the army then advanced, and if the new province were large, it was presently ordered that a temple of the Sun should be built, and women collected for its service, and that a palace should be erected for the lord. Tribute was collected, care being taken that too much was not exacted, and that no injustice was done in anything; but that the new subjects were made acquainted with the imperial policy, and with the art of building, of clothing themselves, and of living together in towns. And if they needed anything, care was taken to supply it, and to teach them how to sow and cultivate their lands. So thoroughly was this policy carried into effect, that we know of many places where there were no flocks originally, but where there has been abundance since they were subjugated by the Incas; and others where formerly there was no maize, but where now they have large crops. In many provinces they went about like savages, badly clothed, and barefooted, until they came under the sway of the Incas; and from

1. Cieza de León, Part II, chapter 17; pp. 49–50 of Markham's translation (1883).

that time they have worn shirts and mantles, both men and women, so that they always hold the change in their memories.

The Inca programme of resettlement and colonization was an element of the greatest importance not only for the peace of the empire, but for administrative problems in colonial days, for modern Peru, and for studies on the anthropology of Peru. For the shuffling of populations was carried to such an extent that the empire became a great melting-pot and was rapidly on its way to becoming, as was the intent of the policy, a unified homogeneous nation. Although the system had been in effect for less than a century before the time of the Conquest, by that time many of the tribes in Andean and coastal Peru had lost their identity, their language,[1] and many of their peculiar customs. The Inca language was made the official speech everywhere and quickly supplanted the native languages. This general medium of communication was a great boon to the Spanish, who quickly adopted it as a second official language, and its use has continued to spread ever since.

The extent of the resettlement programme naturally depended on the bellicosity and intransigence of the population. In some provinces the major part of the inhabitants were deported and replaced by colonists. The new settlers were brought from provinces that had been under Inca domination long enough to have lost their desire for independence and to have become rather thoroughly indoctrinated with Inca ideology and familiar with the imperial pattern of government. They were always taken from regions with similar climatic and ecological conditions. Native-born Quechuas from the Cuzco region were, of course the most desirable colonists. The new colonists were naturally scattered in villages among the newly conquered natives, and the recalcitrant elements of the latter took their places, sprinkled among the pacified population of the earlier conquered region.

These colonists were termed *mitimaes*. While under the same provincial authority as the natives, they formed favoured groups, receiving special gifts and privileges. They formed Inca garrisons whose responsibility it was to set an example to the benighted, to

1. See Mason, 1950.

convert the heathen to the true faith, and to teach the superior Quechua language to the barbarians!

Garcilaso[1] gives a good description of the Inca *mitima* practice and attitude towards it – or at least his interpretation thereof:

> The Incas transplanted Indians from one province to another for special reasons, some for the good of their vassals, and others for their own purposes and to secure their dominions from insurrections. In the course of their conquests the Incas found some provinces to be naturally fertile, but thinly populated. To these districts they sent Indians who were natives of other provinces with a similar climate. This precaution was taken that no injury might befall the settlers. On other occasions, when the inhabitants of a locality multiplied rapidly, so that their province was not large enough to hold them, they removed a certain proportion of the people to some other district. They also removed Indians from barren and sterile tracts to such as were fertile and prolific, with a view to the benefit both of those that remained and of those that went; because, being relations, they would help each other with their harvests.

As has been stated or intimated in some previous pages, Inca policy was to leave administrative matters *in statu quo ante* as much as possible, and to adapt the new régime to fit pre-existing conditions. All amenable chiefs were confirmed in their positions, made curacas and considered as nobility, their sons taken to Cuzco to serve as hostages and to be indoctrinated in Inca ideology, eventually to succeed to their fathers' positions. However, the Governor was always an Inca noble. The Inca tripartite system of land division and labour service was introduced, storehouses built, Quechua established as the official language and Sun-worship as the official religion, though no coercion was practised on the native population to compel them to abandon their old language and religion. If the people were in distress as a result of the late war, food and other supplies were brought from government storehouses in neighbouring pacified regions.

The principal portable idols or wacas of the conquered people

1. Garcilaso de la Vega, Part 1, Book 7, chapter 1; Volume 2, pp. 213 215 of Markham's translation (1869–71).

were also taken to Cuzco to be held as hostages, where they might be worshipped by visiting delegations; the sacred objects were generally accompanied to Cuzco by some of their native priests. This practice gave the native peoples a feeling of community with Cuzco as their capital instead of merely that of foreign invaders. For some reason, however, Inca costume was enforced on the conquered people, though they were allowed to retain their former head-dress, or required to adopt some other distinctive one, as an identifying symbol.

Rather similar in their melting-pot result, but in a slightly different category from the mitimaes, were some colonies of Aymara on the coast and on the warm slopes of the eastern mountains. The Aymara inhabited – and inhabit – the highest, chilliest, and most inhospitable parts of the plateau, and to permit them access to tropical or semi-tropical fruits and other desired products – as well as, probably, to enjoy occasional warmth – the Inca permitted them to establish colonies in these places. These were homogeneous enclaves, under the authority of their highland home officials. We may suspect that these Aymara were not true permanent colonists but vacationers, frequently changing residence between highland and lowland.

Law and Crime

In referring to Inca law – or, for that matter, to all Peruvian and to all pre-Colombian American law – it must be remembered that it was exclusively 'common' law, uncodified, *lex non scripta*; in the absence of any system of writing it could not have been otherwise. Since there was no private ownership of real estate, little personal property, and no private business, law was practically limited to crime and punishment. The authorities remembered the custom and precedent for punishments, and the common people also knew the sanctions. Though it can hardly be said that the emperor's wish was law, at least the laws represented his will, and their transgression was construed as disobedience to him rather than as an offence against the state or against any individual. Therefore some acts that would be considered by us as misdemeanours or even as merely sins were severely punished.

Treason and disobedience to the emperor were considered the greatest crimes.

All offences against the state, treason, theft from imperial or church fields or storehouses, burning bridges, breaking into convents, and similar crimes were punishable with death, as was murder. Capital punishment, however, could be decreed only by the highest authorities, a governor or the emperor himself, and a curaca who put any subject to death without higher official sanction was severely punished himself, even receiving the death penalty for a second offence. Capital punishment was inflicted by several methods: generally the culprit's head was bashed in with a club, but he might be thrown off a cliff, stoned to death, or hung up by the feet. Probably the choice was so that the punishment might more or less fit the crime. Imprisonment was unknown except for one delicate variety reserved for the most egregious traitor; he was placed in an underground dungeon filled with snakes and other venomous, noxious, and dangerous animals. His incarceration was necessarily a brief one. Lesser punishments were public rebuke, removal from office, banishment, torture, flogging, and the *hihuaya*, which consisted in dropping a heavy stone from a height of about three feet (1 m.) on the malefactor's back; this was often equivalent to a capital sentence.

Following their usual pattern, the Inca made openly the distinction between noble and commoner that is often made in practice in modern days. It was felt that a reprimand and loss of his emperor's approbation were worse punishment for a noble than physical castigation to a peasant. In this they probably were good judges of human nature, and anyway it was necessary to uphold the prestige of the aristocracy. On the other hand, transgressions of *noblesse oblige* were more severely punished than a similar sin by a commoner; thus, adultery with a noblewoman was a capital offence for both; the common or garden variety was punished by torture.

Extenuating circumstances were always allowed for. Killing in self-defence or slitting the throat of a wife caught *in flagrante delicto* was not murder. Intentional injuries were more severely punished than accidental ones. A lazy or improvident man might be rebuked for theft; a covetous one would be banished.

Accused persons were held under guard until their trials, which were, of course, not before a jury of their peers, but before state officials, the regular administrative officers, such as the curacas. Minor offences were judged by minor officials, important ones by higher officers; these heard testimony and the defence of the accused, called witnesses, and pronounced judgement from which there was no appeal to higher authorities. There were no lawyers, solicitors, or advocates, no fees to be paid. The only peculiarly judicial officers were the full-time governmental inspectors who regularly investigated the affairs of state officials and pressed charges against dishonest ones. On the whole, crime was rare; the static nature of the society did not provoke it, and the rigid enforcement of the laws tended to prevent it.

The government inspectors were usually of imperial blood and were considered the direct and personal representatives of the emperor, taking upon themselves one of his functions. Periodically – probably at irregular and unannounced occasions – and incognito they visited every corner of the empire.

The greatest crimes, such as treason, and all crimes committed by the royalty, were judged by the emperor in person, generally with the advice of his privy council. The penalties were severe, but the purpose was the prevention of crime rather than its punishment. A father was held equally responsible for the crime of a minor child. If a robber could prove that want drove him to the crime, the official who permitted such an abnormal and illegal situation to come to pass was also severely punished.

The guilt of an individual was often determined by divination or ordeal, such as torture. Judgement was given within a few days, five at the most. Fines, of course, were unknown. The entire village or ayllu of a great criminal was held guilty with him, and in the most heinous crimes the village was destroyed and the entire population put to death.

Chapter 13

RELIGION

PROBABLY the ancient religions of all parts of Andean Peru conformed to one general pattern but differed greatly in details and in the names of the deities. The following digest, like those of our other sections on the life of old Peru, refers particularly to the Inca or Quechua of the Cuzco district, the only region on which the data are extensive.

In empire times the religion was state-established and supported; this seems to have been the only instance in aboriginal America of an established church. But in essence it was doubtless the age-old beliefs of the Cuzco-region Quechua. There was a principal god, other gods and goddesses of greater or lesser importance, local animistic spirits or objects, and unembodied and disembodied spirits. In its later years under the empire the religion had evolved an organization in which rich ritual and ceremonialism were important. Its chief purposes were the increase or maintenance of the food-supply and the cure of the sick; spirituality, mysticism, and non-pragmatic ethics had little place in it. However, concepts of sin, confession, penance, and purification were important. Divination was one of the principal duties of the priesthood, and sacrifice to the gods was a vital element of almost every rite.

The supreme deity was the Creator. He is generally known as Viracocha, but this name was merely one of his many titles. He is said to have had no true name, but, like the great god of some other peoples, his name may have been too sacred to be spoken, and thus was unknown to the chroniclers. His form was that of man, and he was thus represented in images in temples. He was eternal and created everything, including the other deities; he was the supernatural analogue of the Inca emperor. Garcilaso was probably in error when he identified Viracocha with Pachacamac, a deity of the inhabitants of the central coast where he had a shrine, famous over all Peru, dedicated to him. Viracocha

206

was also a culture hero who taught his people how to live. After the creation he interfered little in human destinies, remaining a benign divinity in the heavens. He was therefore little worshipped, at least by the common people; the emperor and the nobles appealed to him more frequently – in time of trouble.

The Creator god was apparently a very old and fundamental deity in Peru; Means believes that he was the god worshipped at Tiahuanaco, possibly under some other non-Quechua name. Viracocha in many respects resembles the Mexican god Quetzalcoatl who was also a culture hero. According to Inca mythology, after travelling through the country instructing his people, Viracocha set off across the Pacific from the shores of Ecuador, walking on the waves. Pizarro and his men were therefore identified with the returning god, just as was Cortés in Mexico, and the white men were – and in some places are to this day – called Viracocha. In these days, when anthropologists are giving more credence than formerly to the probability of pre-Columbian trans-Pacific influences and voyages, these old American traditions of culture heroes might well be accorded new appraisals. In later years the term Viracocha seems to have been equivalent to 'Lord'; the semantic analogy with both uses of the English term is obvious.

The worship of Viracocha was apparently mainly, if not exclusively, a function of the upper classes, a philosophical rather than an animistic religion. Emperor Viracocha ascribed the defeat of the Chanca and the preservation of the Inca hegemony to his namesake god, and reanimated and encouraged his worship. He built two temples to Viracocha, the only two in Peru, one in Cuzco and another at Cacha. The latter (Plate 16A), judging by the ruins that survive, was one of the great triumphs of Peruvian architecture. The median wall, still standing in good condition, was over three hundred feet (90 m.) long and over fifty feet (15 m.) high. The lower eight feet are of excellent masonry, supporting over forty feet of adobe wall. The walls are five to six feet thick, and the building consisted of three storeys.

More important in mundane affairs than Viracocha were the sky deities – the gods and goddesses of the sun, moon, stars, and thunder, and the terraqueous goddesses, those of the earth and the sea; these were all servants of the Creator. The cult of the Earth Mother was probably the oldest, most fundamental, and most popular of all; she was the one most supplicated by the common farmer.

The Inca were sun-worshippers; the Sun, Inti, was the great deity and the progenitor of the royal dynasty. Although the priests and the Chosen Women served all the gods, the Sun was so pre-eminent that the chroniclers always referred to the women as the 'Virgins of the Sun', and to the shrines as 'Sun Temples'. The sun and the rain, together controlling the crops, tend to be the primary interest of almost every agricultural people. Though apparently generally conceived of as a man, the Sun was generally represented – as often today – by a round human face with surrounding rays. Naturally, the disk was almost always of gold, and the one in the Coricancha, the great 'Temple of the Sun' in Cuzco, was immense. One of the best-remembered tales of the Spanish Conquest is that of the Spanish soldier Sierra de Leguízano who, having received the great disk as his share of the booty, gambled it away that very night; popular tradition has it that this was the origin of the Spanish saying 'jugar el sol antes que amanezca', 'to gamble away the sun before it rises'. Sad to say, iconoclastic historical research indicates that the sun disk had then been removed, and Sierra de Leguízano's gold piece, though a great prize, was a more utilitarian object. Doubtless also Hispanic folklorists have found another origin for the proverb.

Naturally the Thunder or Weather God was the divinity of next importance; he was importuned to send the rain. The name, Illapa, connotes both thunder and lightning. He was envisaged as a man dressed in shining apparel and carrying a sling and a war club. According to one myth, his sister kept the rain in a jug which Illapa broke with his sling-shot when he yielded to earthlings' pleas for rain. As he threw, the crack of the sling was the thunderclap, the stone the thunderbolt, and the lightning was the refulgence of his glistening garments. The rain water came from the heavenly river, the Milky Way. Illapa was identified with a constellation.

The Moon, Mamaquilla, was a goddess and wife of the Sun. She was little worshipped but her functions were chiefly with reference to the calendar and the festivals and work connected therewith. The beliefs regarding eclipses of the moon paralleled others current in many places throughout the world: a serpent or puma was trying to eat the Moon Goddess, and was scared away by threats and din.

Inca star lore was extensive and, although there seems to have been no true zodiac, many of the stars and constellations were given names and apparently were considered as deities that watched over terrestrial beings and certain activities. The Morning Star, Venus, was an important figure in mythology. The Pleiades took care of seeds, and another constellation the herds; the latter was seen as a speckled llama. Other kinds of wild animals each had its star protector.

The Earth and the Sea Goddesses, Pacamama and Mamacocha, were of importance in the highlands and on the coast respectively. Their functions dealt with agriculture and fishing.

The word 'waca' (*huaca*, *guaca*) was and is of great importance in Peru. It originally meant 'sacred shrine' and is so used by the Indians today. Among the Spanish and the mestizos, however, it applies to one of the great coastal pyramids of adobe, or to any archaeological Indian grave, and the native scoundrel who makes a business of excavating aboriginal graves and selling their contents – the main source of most Peruvian collections in museums – is today known as a *huaquero*; the masculine form *huaco* is now applied to a pottery vessel from such a grave.

In ancient as in modern Peru there were thousands of wacas, ranging from great temples to hills, springs, and piles of stones. Each was believed to be – or to harbour – a spirit which might be malevolent and which should be gratified or placated by some gift or sacrifice whenever it was neared. Each native knew only those in his vicinity. One of the chroniclers lists three hundred and fifty within twenty miles of Cuzco. Springs and stones were the most numerous wacas, but hills, caves, roots, quarries, forts, bridges, palaces, prisons, houses, meeting-places, battlefields, stone field boundary-markers and field guardians, calendar markers, and other similar objects are included in the category, as well as temples, tombs, and historical or mythological sites. Mountains and hills were especially likely to be considered sacred and, generally speaking, the higher they were, the more important; all snow-capped peaks were reverenced or worshipped, and several hills around Cuzco were especially sacred, were supposed to represent deceased emperors or other persons, and played important parts in certain ceremonies.

Especially sacred was a stone on Huanacauri hill near Cuzco which was supposed to represent one of the brothers of the great Emperor Manco Capac, and which therefore was a protector of the dynasty. The city of Cuzco itself was probably considered a waca.

The wacas of the Cuzco region were thought of as lying on lines radiating from the Temple of the Sun. Three of the quarters each had nine such radiating lines; the fourth, Contisuyu, had fifteen. In the first three, the nine lines were arranged in three groups of three each, and there were from four to fifteen wacas on each line. Naturally, the lines were not perfectly straight.

Only two ceremonial directions, east and west, were recognized by the Inca; these were of course important because of the rising and setting of the sun. The wacas in the neighbourhood of Cuzco were classed according to their location in one of the four quarters into which the region was divided. These in turn corresponded to the four quarters of the empire, the two north quarters being considered as Upper Cuzco, the southern pair as Lower Cuzco. They were under the care of the royal ayllus living in those quarters.

Another type of waca called *apachita* was a sort of cairn at a dangerous or important place on a road where the traveller paused to pray for safety and strength; here he would add a stone to the pile or leave something of trivial value, such as a piece of worn-out clothing, a quid of coca, or even a handful of straw. This custom is still practised.

Almost anything strange or unusual was considered sacred and a waca: twins, persons with supernumerary digits, plants of peculiar forms. Corpses, of course. Then there were portable wacas, amulets and talismans; these might be pseudomorphs – natural stones in the shape of some object, crystals, bezoars, or any article that seemed queer.

Household fetishes, the Andean analogues of the Roman

Lares and Penates, were the guardians of the family; they were kept in niches and were inherited. Every person also had an individual fetish, the abode of his guardian spirit who was considered his twin brother or *huauqui*. Bezoars were common household fetishes; those most prized came from the vicuña, deer, guanaco, and llama, in this order.

This animistic belief in spirits of inanimate objects is widespread and wellnigh universal among primitive peoples and must have been very ancient, far pre-empire, and fundamental in the Andean area.

There were both unembodied and disembodied spirits in addition to the stationary spirits of the wacas. The minor spirits were malevolent and greatly feared. As is the situation with many societies of more logical persons, there seems to have been a confusion of belief regarding the disembodied spirits, the dead, without any realization of incompatibility. The spirits of the dead went to 'heaven' or 'hell', but nevertheless they – or some of them – might also hang around their old homes to annoy – though with a helpful purpose – the living. The dead liked to have their 'mummies' brought out to enjoy fiestas, and they expected to be given food and chicha beer now and then. The cult of the dead was very important.

'Heaven' was with the Sun, where the good enjoyed life much as on earth with a plethora of food and drink, while evil-doers went to a subterranean hell where it was always cold and there were only stones to eat. The nobility, however, were *ipso facto* guiltless; all went direct to heaven.

Properly speaking, there were no churches in ancient Peru, for almost all ceremonies were performed out of doors, and only the priests and high officials entered the temples. The great national ceremonies were enacted in one of the squares in Cuzco, to which the sacred objects were brought from the temples. The most important of these plazas was, of course, the Great Square adjacent to the imposing Temple of the Sun. This, the most sacred shrine in Peru, was a magnificent building, or group of buildings around a courtyard, and was lavishly furnished. Known as the Coricancha (Plate 13), parts of it are still preserved but so much altered by rebuilding in the upper parts that its former shape and nature are difficult to visualize. According to accounts of the time of the Conquest it consisted mainly of one great room. The roof was gabled and covered with thatch. There was only one exterior doorway. However, it served mainly as a repository for sacred objects, an altar, idols of the principal deities, and the bodies of deceased emperors. Many great religious objects of solid gold hung on the walls. Adjacent to this great room were smaller 'chapels' and shrines, and even some small independent buildings for priestly residences. The circumference of the ensemble was about twelve hundred feet.

Similar smaller Sun temples were located in all the main centres of population, especially in the provincial capitals. The more important shrines or wacas also had houses or 'temples' for the attendant priests.

The priesthood was graded into ranks very much like the secular population. At the apex was the High Priest or Pontifex Maximus, the *Villac Umu*, resident in Cuzco. He was always a brother, uncle, or other close relative of the emperor, and one of the officials of highest rank in the state. He held office for life, and presided over a council of nine other priests of high rank, each in charge of a large area. He led an exemplary life, hedged about by restrictions and taboos.

The other priests of higher rank were also of royal blood, all from the Tarpuntary ayllu, and were elected by a council of other priests, apparently for a definite term of office. The clergy of the lowest ranks were commoners and not state-supported. These lowest offices were hereditary; many of them, presumably, were local patriarchs, too old for active agricultural labour, who tended a waca.

The larger temples sheltered a considerable body of clergy, diviners, sacrificers, and servants, in addition to 'Chosen Women', and 'monks', while smaller shrines might have had only one attendant, and probably the smallest outdoor wacas had none. The principal priest at the large provincial Sun temples belonged to the imperial caste. Like the secular government, a corps of church inspectors visited the religious institutions frequently, and reported instances of malfeasance to the higher authorities.

The duties of the priests, in addition to caring for the sacred paraphernalia and participating in the regular ceremonies, were to hear confessions, make divinations, interpret oracles, make sacrifices, pray for suppliants, and cure the ill. In major temples, where there was a large group of priests, probably all specialized in one or another of these functions.

Connected with each Sun temple was a building that housed the female associates. These were not inappropriately considered by the Spanish as nuns, their quarters as a convent; it had many of the functions of one. The nature of these women and their method of selection have been mentioned before (page 185). They were of two main classes, the 'Chosen Women', *acllacuna*, and the so-called 'Virgins of the Sun', *mamacuna*. The latter formed a permanent staff and had taken vows of perpetual chastity; the 'Chosen Women' were more or less transient and were eligible to be given as secondary wives to nobles at the emperor's pleasure – or taken for himself.

No man was supposed to enter a convent, though some of the chroniclers speak of eunuchs who acted as servants and door-keepers, and also as confessors to the Virgins; this is not unlikely. These men were called monks by the chroniclers, but it is not clear whether all 'monks' were eunuchs and vice versa, or whether some non-eunuch monks had other duties.

The chroniclers differ greatly in their explanations of the roles of these women, and some certainly confused the two classes, but the true situation was probably that given above. Naturally some historians state that the Virgins of the Sun were no more than the emperor's private seraglio, and many recent writers have assumed the same. The emperor, however deified by his people, was human – and above the law. Father Cobo[1] says that, every now and then, the 'monk' (eunuch?) in charge of the convent gate would approach the emperor in the great square where he might be making a sacrifice to the Sun, would gently tug at the imperial mantle and whisper in his ear, 'Inca, on such and such a night you stole into the Sun's mansion and lay with one of his wives'. Whereat the emperor, also *sotto voce*, would answer, 'I sinned', and the guard would know that he was thereby

1. Cobo, 1890–5, Book 13, chapter 37.

absolved from neglect of duty. Any transgressor of lower rank, however, was paid the proverbial wages of sin; he was strangled and his paramour buried alive.

In the convents the women cared for the necessities of the priests, prepared their food, and wove their garments. Those in the great convent connected with the Sun Temple in Cuzco wove the imperial garments, probably the finest cloths made in Peru, which is to say about the finest in the world; it is reported that some of these textiles required a year of work to manufacture. One of the chroniclers states that the inmates of the great convent attached to the Cuzco Coricancha numbered three thousand.

As among ourselves, Inca prayers were of two kinds: personal and private, or congregational and ritualistic. The private prayers were naturally appeals for personal welfare such as health or good crops, and might be addressed to a spring, for instance, while the congregational prayers were traditional, fixed, and on a rather high aesthetic plane. Several of these prayers were preserved and recorded by some of the chroniclers. One of the most famous of these is:[1]

Viracocha, Lord of the Universe!
Whether male or female,
at any rate commander of heat and reproduction,
being one who, even with His spittle, can work sorcery.
Where art Thou?
Would that Thou wert not hidden from this son of Thine!
He may be above; He may be below;
or, perchance, abroad in space.
Where is His mighty judgement-seat?
Hear me!
He may be spread abroad among the upper waters;
or among the lower waters and their sands
He may be dwelling.
Creator of the world, Creator of man,
great among my ancestors,
before Thee my eyes fail me,
though I long to see Thee;
for, seeing Thee, knowing Thee,
learning from Thee, understanding Thee,

1. Means, 1931, p. 437, 438.

I shall be seen by Thee, and Thou wilt know me.
The Sun – the Moon; the Day – the Night; Summer – Winter;
not in vain, in orderly succession,
do they march to their destined place, to their goal.
They arrive wherever Thy royal staff Thou bearest.
Oh! Harken to me, listen to me,
let it not befall that I grow weary
and die.

Some prayers were recited, others given silently; a suppliant might ask his relatives and friends to pray for him, or might pay a priest to do so.

Fasting was an accompaniment of many religious observances. As among ourselves, it might be slight or strict, ranging from abstinence from salt and pepper to the prohibition of meat, chicha beer, and sex relations.

Confession of sin also played a prominent role in Inca religion, since sin made the gods angry and impelled them to punish the sinner by bad luck in this life and condemnation to the underworld in the next. It must be remembered that concepts and definitions of sin differ greatly according to the morals of various peoples, and Inca morals by no means paralleled ours. Offences against neighbours, such as murder and theft, were naturally condemned, but disobedience to the emperor's wishes and neglect of festivals and worship were also sinful. All misfortune, even such as congenital natal malformation, was deemed to be a punishment for sin. The sinner was disqualified from taking part in religious observances until he had confessed and purged himself. It was not necessary to confess sinful thoughts, however. An illness of the divine emperor presented quite a philosophical and theological problem; he was sickened by the sins of his subjects who cured him by their confessions and purification.

Confessions were made to the priests, generally the minor priests of either sex, in charge of local wacas. The confessor heard all the members of his ayllu; the confession was generally heard by the side of a stream. More serious sins had to be taken to priests of higher rank; the confessions were in secret, and were not to be divulged. The emperor, the royal family, and the High

THE ANCIENT CIVILIZATIONS OF PERU

Priest confessed in secret to the Sun, whose intercession they asked with Viracocha, the Creator.

Incomplete confession of sin was considered a great sin in itself, and the priest-confessor took measures, including interrogation, physical coercion, and divination, to make sure that the confession was full. When thus assured, he fixed a penance, usually a period of fasting and praying, or both. Often, it is said, the expiation was in opposite ratio to the priest's fee. After such penance, the sinner washed in a stream so that the sin might be borne away. Or he might spit into a handful of straw and throw that into the river.

The Spanish clergy of colonial days were naturally astounded at the many close analogies to their religion, which resemblance they ascribed to the machinations of the Great Deceiver, Satan.

As with most religions, sacrifice was also a most important feature among the Inca, the concept undoubtedly being that of *quid pro quo*, a gift to the god or gods in return for favours bestowed or solicited. Sacrifices had a great range, from a handful of straw left at a wayside *apachita* to human sacrifices by the High Priest in a great public ceremony in Cuzco.

Food and drink, the latter in the form of chicha beer, were regular offerings to the wacas, and to preserved bodies, especially those of the emperors. The food was burned, the chicha libation poured on the ground. Coca was, of course, a frequent offering; this was burned, either as dried leaves or as quid after chewing. Other frequent sacrificial materials were corn flour, wool, and llama fat. Sea-shells were offered to springs, generally after sowing time. If a worshipper had nothing else, he offered a few eyelashes or eyebrow hairs. Wealthier men sacrificed fine clothing, which was burned, and little gold or silver figurines, or even lumps of these metals; these were buried or hung in the temples.

However, domestic animals, llamas and guinea-pigs, were the most common sacrifices; wild animals were not ordinarily used. Llamas, being valuable animals, were rarely sacrificed by individuals – and then only by wealthy ones, but were generally from the governmental herds, offered in public ceremonies to the image of one of the deities. The priest led the llama around the figure and made it face it, recited the proper prayer, and cut the animal's throat. White llamas and alpacas were sacrificed to the Sun, brown llamas to Viracocha, and mottled ones to Thunder.

Human sacrifice was rare in Peru, at least in Inca days, in contrast to the hecatombs that Cortés encountered in Mexico. To the gods it was the most precious and most welcome offering, given on only the most sacred or most ominous occasions, such as the installation of an emperor, his illness or departure for war, or military defeat, famine, or plague. Human beings were offered to only the most important deities or shrines by priests at great communal ceremonies.

Boys and girls about ten years old were the principals – the word 'victim' is not quite appropriate – in these sacrifices. The girls were selected from the 'Chosen Women' being educated in the 'convents' (page 213); some at least of the boys were offered by their parents who were in great need. The children had to be physically perfect, and fine examples of youth. They were feasted and sometimes made drunk before the sacrifice so that they might appear before the deity contented and happy. Less often, adults were immolated. These were from a newly conquered province, brought to Cuzco to be sacrificed to the Sun in celebration of the victory. Like the children, they were outstanding physical examples.

After marching several times around the image or waca, the victims were strangled and their throats slit or, as in Mexico, the heart cut out. The priest then marked or smeared the venerated object with some of the blood, and sometimes a libation of blood was poured on the ground.

Sometimes, when a very ill man had been told by a diviner that he would certainly die, he would sacrifice one of his sons to the Sun, or to Viracocha, in the hope that thus his own life would be spared.

Most of the sacrifices were made to wacas, and at set ceremonial occasions in connexion with the seasonal calendar. For these the sacrificed objects – mainly llamas – were taken from the flocks and fields devoted to religion, some of which were allocated to every waca and from which also the attendant priests derived their support. Part of the sacrifice of an individual was also devoted to the upkeep of the personnel of the waca.

State sacrifices to Viracocha were made in the name of the wacas of the country rather than in that of the emperor.

Cuzco was of course the great centre for sacrifices as for all Inca religious ceremonies. Every morning, as it rose, the Sun was greeted with a sacrifice of some food that had been specially prepared, the rest of which served for the priests' breakfast. A fire of specially carved wood had been laid; this was kindled at sunrise and the food thrown in, while a priest recited, 'Eat this, Lord Sun, and acknowledge thy children'. Later in the day a dark-red llama was sacrificed to the Sun, together with some coca. The fragrant carved wood for the fire was supplied by the Chicha people. Another fire of this same material was kept constantly burning in a stone brazier near the Temple of the Sun, and from this all sacrificial fires had to be kindled.

On the first day of each month a preparatory ceremony was held in the presence of the emperor and his court assembled in the Great Square. One hundred selected llamas were brought in and divided among some thirty attendants, three or four to each. Every attendant had one day of the month allotted to him, and on this day he brought his animals and sacrificed them. Before the division, all the llamas had been ceremonially made to circle the images of the gods four times and had been dedicated by the High Priest to Viracocha in the name of the Sun. These animals were cut into quarters and completely burned in a large fire made of the same carved scented wood, into which coca, white corn, and ground chilli peppers were also thrown. The bones that remained were ground to a fine powder, and the priests blew a little of this into the air while they recited a short ritual. The remaining powder was stored in a neighbouring building called the 'Puma's tail'.

Calendrical Ceremonies

The major Inca public religious ceremonies were performed in the Great Square in Cuzco, and the majority of these were recurrent annual church holidays (holy-days). Most of them also were associated with agricultural events, such as with planting-time and harvest. The cult objects, such as images of the gods and bodies of deceased emperors, were brought out and venerated by the assembled populace. The current emperor and his court always attended. The ceremonies, accompanied by sacrifices, dancing, singing, recitations, and the consumption of quantities of chicha beer, were elaborate and impressive. The effect must have been, in general, very similar to a church fiesta in Peru or other parts of Latin America today, and the transition from pagan to Christian must have been effected with little change in attitude on the part of the people.

In each month at least one important annual ceremony was held, generally associated with the current agricultural activity. The chroniclers of the time of the Conquest recorded these in considerable detail. In describing these monthly ceremonies the Spanish chroniclers correlate the Inca lunar months with ours, giving one of our names to each. Such correlation is only approximate and applicable for only a short time (see pages 228–9); nevertheless it must be adopted for descriptive purposes.

December was a most important month, for then the puberty ceremonies for boys of noble rank were held; these filled not only the entire month but a part of the next one. Athletic tests and competitions took place, as well as a sham battle. Many of the other monthly ceremonies occupied many days.

Sacrifices of llamas by various methods and with details appropriate to the occasion were an important part of almost every ceremony, and on rare occasions children were sacrificed. A sacred white – probably albino – llama, which was carefully tended until he died a natural death, played an important role in some rites. Fasting and feasting, the drinking of quantities of chicha beer, and community dancing accompanied most of the more joyful ceremonies, and offerings and auguries played a large part in many. Some were followed by ceremonial baths to cleanse the partakers from evil and illness. The ceremony for the month of June was second only to that of December and was centred about the adoration of the Sun. An important feature of the solemn occasion was the making of new fire – also a vital element of Aztec ceremonialism.

Divination and Omens

Unlike the Mexicans, the Inca apparently did not recognize good and bad, lucky and unlucky days, or at any rate these were not of such transcendent importance. Their priests, instead of determining these days, made divinations to predict the future – as of course did the Mesoamericans, also – and the success or misfortune of any project. The results of these divinations and consultations of oracles were, of course, supposed to represent the will of the gods, whose wishes should be consulted before any undertaking. Divination was practised to determine any doubtful question, future or past; also unsolicited omens were constantly looked for.

For the most serious problems, such as identifying traitors, the solemn divination by fire was practised. The emperor himself often partook in this, after a fast of several days, and it was generally accompanied by the sacrifice of most valuable objects, sometimes including children. By means of this fire, communication with spirits was established. The chief practitioners, known as *yacarca*, who came from the town of Huaro near Cuzco, were most respected and feared.

This method of fire divination required considerable preparation. Fire was built in two braziers placed end to end, wood soaked in fat being used. Food and drink in dishes were placed around the fire, which was intensified by blowing through a tube with copper and silver ends. The Chief Priest, taking a quid of coca in his mouth, begged the spirits to come to the banquet in the presence of Fire, Sun, and Earth. Either the spirits of living or dead persons might be thus invoked with chanting and weeping. The flames from the holes in the braziers were considered the voices of the spirits, and the diviners heard and interpreted them, answering questions put to them. Sometimes a different spirit appeared in each brazier.

Divination by means of a llama's viscera was a more common practice and has been mentioned before. With its head held to the east by four priests, another cut open the left side and extracted the heart, lungs, and gullet, entire, connected and uncut.

If the lungs were still breathing when they were drawn out it was considered a most propitious omen. If this and other signs failed, a second and even a third trial was given, and if all proved calamitous there was great foreboding of ill luck. Another method was to inflate the lungs by blowing and to interpret the augury by the vein pattern. Important yes-or-no questions were thus decided; for ones of less importance a guinea-pig or even a bird might be used.

There were also many simpler and more easily practised methods of divination. One, like our 'she loves me . . not' daisy-petal method, involved the counting of objects for odd or even total. Pebbles, beans, corn kernels, and pellets of llama dung were among the most usual materials employed; the pebbles were generally wacas to which a magical origin had been ascribed. Llama fat and coca leaves were burned and the fire watched. Or the diviner spat into his hand and watched the spittle run down his two fingers; if the flow was equal, the augury was good, otherwise it was bad.

The movements of confined animals, particularly snakes and spiders, were watched as an augury; spider divination was especially practised in the Chinchasuyu quarter of central and northern Peru. The spider was kept in a jar, and if, on first observation, any of its legs was bent, the prognosis was bad.

While almost every waca would serve as an oracle to be consulted by divinatory practices, there were several oracles that were peculiarly such, and that were consulted on important questions by many pilgrims from all over the empire. Two of them gave their names to the rivers on which they were situated: Apo-rimac on the Apurimac River near Cuzco, and Rimac (meaning 'oracle') on the Rimac River near Lima. Probably most important, however, was the great shrine of Pachacamac, on the coast south of Lima; Huari in the Jauja Valley was another. The Apurimac oracle was a tree-trunk in a house; it was dressed in female apparel, with breasts of gold and a sash. A row of smaller figures was placed to either side. This oracle was in the charge of a priestess who may have hidden in or behind the trunk, for a Spanish prisoner heard it reply to a question put to it by Manco

Inca in 1534. The oracles seen by the Spanish were generally thickly smeared with sacrificial blood.

The soothsayers were supposed to talk directly with the spirits; they wore special garb and hair-dress, and spoke with the spirits in the dark in words that could be heard but not understood. Some of them drank chicha beer mixed with the juice of an intoxicating berry, and gave their answers after they had recovered. Diviners found missing articles, predicted future or described distant events, diagnosed diseases, determined the truth of statements, and settled all dubious questions.

Unsolicited omens were numerous and constantly watched for. A rainbow was generally an evil omen, and comets, eclipses, and meteors were especially bad, the latter foretelling the death of the emperor. The word for comet meant 'ill-luck star'; Atahuallpa gave up hope immediately when one appeared during his imprisonment by Pizarro. The sight of noxious animals, such as snakes, spiders, lizards, toads, worms, moths, or foxes, especially in the house, was a bad omen. The howling of a dog or the hooting of an owl presaged the death of a relative, and the singing of other birds foretold a quarrel. The ill luck occasioned by encountering a snake could be avoided by killing and urinating on it, and stepping on it with the left foot. Birds were made offerings of coca and told to take their ill luck to the man's enemies. Somewhat like our 'burning ears', a twitching in any part of the body, a humming sound in the ears, or a stumbling indicated that one was about to hear some news, good if the manifestation was on the person's right side, bad if on the left. If the fire flared or gave off sparks it was angry and had to be appeased by an offering of a little chicha or maize corn.

Dreams, as usual, had their standard interpretations; they were regarded as supernatural experiences and very important omens. Deities and spirits sometimes appeared to important persons in dreams. To dream of fire predicted illness; the sun, moon, a river, or a bridge foretold the death of a parent, and killing a llama meant the death of a father or brother.

When praying or otherwise addressing a deity or the emperor, a standard attitude or gesture of reverence was observed. With arms outstretched to the front, the suppliant bowed low from the hips; the arms were parallel and high, the hands open with palms outward. He next made a kissing sound and then kissed his finger-tips. A switch was held in the hands when addressing the highest deities.

Slight value was attached to ceremonial or sacred numbers. Three and four seem to have had some value, and quipus found on the coast appear to stress the importance of the number seven.

A little chicha beer was always sprinkled towards the sun, and also to the ground and to the fire, whenever natives were indulging in that drink.

Travellers always took a drink of the water when passing a spring or crossing a stream, meanwhile breathing a prayer for a safe passage.

Disease and Healing: Sorcery

Among many if not most pre-scientific peoples, as has been remarked before, no misfortune, accident, or illness just happens; it is always a result. Illness, disease, and death in particular are always caused by the ill-will of someone, by sorcery or otherwise; someone wanted it to happen. The ancient Peruvians had progressed somewhat beyond this stage, and the magic of hired sorcerers was only one of the causes of illness. A more important and more frequent cause was the supernatural ill-will of deities angered by sin or by neglect of worship, or accidental contact with inherently malevolent spirits found especially in winds and springs. Illness might also be caused by winds, and by loss of soul which could be frightened out of the body. The Inca still retained the belief, wellnigh universal in aboriginal America, that the proximate cause of illness was generally the presence in the body of some foreign object, placed there by sorcery.

Just as personal illness was considered punishment for individual sin, so public calamity was thought to be the punishment for mass or public sin.

All illness thus having a supernatural cause, it had to be treated by magical and religious means. Even when herbs and other medicines of genuine therapeutic value were employed, their effect was presumed to be magical, and there was no appreciation of their chemical nature and reactions. As outlined in preceding pages, sacrifice, prayer, penance, fasting, confession, bathing, and other similar rites were as important healing measures as pharmacy and therapeutics.

The relationship between publicly supported and recognized priests of the state religion, and curers, medicine-men, and diviners is not quite clear. Diagnosis and curing were certainly among the important functions of the priesthood, and probably priests of high rank performed these duties for the emperor and the royal family. Ordinary curers were doubtless priests of low rank, and probably many of them were laymen not supported by the church; secret sorcerers were certainly not members of the priesthood. The offices of diviner or diagnostician and curer were almost always combined.

Like the medicine-men of more uncultured peoples, the curer generally acquired his power in a vision or dream; a man who had recovered quickly from a severe illness also had unusual capabilities as a physician. In the usual vision a human spirit appeared and gave the man his power, instruments, and instructions. A sacrifice was generally made to this vision by the curer before commencing the treatment.

Different treatments were indicated according to the cause of the illness as diagnosed by the curer by divination. If the cause was a foreign object in the body, the doctor proceeded like the usual American Indian medicine-man: he sucked at the seat of the pain and produced some small object which he claimed – and probably himself believed – to have extracted. If he decided that the viscera had been displaced, he oiled the body with guinea-pig fat, massaged it, and thus restored the organs to their proper places.

If the illness was the result of neglect of worship, the doctor made a powder of corn-flour of various colours and pulverized sea-shells, and placed it in the patient's hand. The latter blew it in the direction of a waca while reciting a prayer for forgiveness. To the Sun he offered some coca, and for Viracocha he might put some bits of gold and silver on the ground. If it was the man's ancestors that were offended, he offered them some food and chicha, placing it on the tomb if possible. Then the invalid was purified by washing. This was done by the curer if the man was bedridden; if he was able to walk he went to a stream or, better, to the junction of two rivers, and washed himself with water and flour made from white corn.

Broken bones or dislocations were caused by the malevolence of the local spirit of the place where the injury occurred, and were cured by appeasing the spirit, mainly by sacrifices at the spot.

If the diagnosis indicated that a man was bewitched, that his illness was caused by sorcery and black magic, the cure, of course, had to be of the same nature, and a sorcerer was called in to counteract the evil. His treatment was akin to that used to cause the illness.

There was probably no class of professional midwives – women who did nothing or little else, though there is some disagreement on this point. However, in every neighbourhood there were doubtless women who made this an avocation. They qualified through having a vision like the male doctor, by bearing twins, or by performing a long series of rites and ceremonies; they could produce abortions. However, many women delivered unassisted.

The pharmacopoeia of ancient Peru was most extensive and probably every plant was thought to have some magical property for good or evil. Many, of course, have actual therapeutic value in the complaints for which they were used, and some have been adopted by modern medicine; many others could have had no value.

Strangely, and contrary to general belief, cinchona, from which quinine is derived, Peru's most valuable gift to the medical world, apparently was not used to any extent, if at all, in ancient Peru. The *quina-quina*, from which the name was derived, was a different tree, Peruvian balm. This queer fact is understandable when it is realized that malaria, against which cinchona is a specific, was apparently unknown in pre-conquest America, and was one of the plagues introduced from Europe.

Animal products and mineral substances were also used as *materia medica*: fresh meat, ointments from animal fats, blood, urine, bezoar stones, and ointments containing mercury, sulphur, or arsenic. Blood-letting, purges, emetics, and enemas, baths, and control of diet were also prescribed. Tobacco in the form of snuff was used for medical purposes. Embalming was rudimentary and consisted mainly in the removal of the viscera, after which the body was allowed to dry in an arid place.

Even today Bolivian native doctors known as *collahuaya* travel over a large part of South America and are everywhere welcomed by the Indians and reverenced for their medical knowledge. They carry chests of medicines.[1]

A great paleopathologist, R. L. Moodie, thus[2] characterizes ancient Peruvian surgery:

I believe it to be correct to state that no primitive or ancient race of people anywhere in the world had developed such a field of surgical knowledge as had the pre-Columbian Peruvians. Their surgical attempts are truly amazing and include amputations, excisions, trephining, bandaging, bone transplants(?), cauterizations and other less evident procedures.

The information on Peruvian surgery is mainly based on the examination of skeletal remains rather than on the statements of the chroniclers, and is pan-Peruvian in extent. In fact, in some respects the earlier peoples of the coast seem to have been superior surgeons to the Incas. Moche pottery vessels frequently depict the results of surgical operations, or even the operation itself. Probably coca was used as an anaesthetic. Forceps were employed and probably also the tourniquet. Bandaging with gauze and cotton was a frequent practice.

Some skulls show the result of operation on the frontal sinus, but the most striking – and apparently one of the most frequent – ancient Peruvian operation was that of trephination or trepanning. The percentage of trephined crania among those known is the highest anywhere in the world; the proportion seems to be greatest among the skulls from Paracas Cavernas (see page 66) (Plate 53). One skull shows five such operations. It is not definitely determined whether trephination was performed to relieve compressions – the result of fractures – or to release demons,

1. Wrigley, 1917.   2. Moodie, 1927, p. 278.

but obviously cranial fractures must have been very frequent among a warlike people who fought mainly with cast stones and clubs. The incisions might be round or rectangular, and were performed by scraping, sawing, or cutting with sharp obsidian, copper, or bronze instruments.

In all serious operations the patients were first made insensible, possibly with coca, possibly intoxicated with chicha, possibly by hypnotism. The operating-room was first cleaned and purified by the sprinkling and burning of maize corn-flour, first black, and finally white.

Malpractitioners who dealt in sorcery and black magic existed in Peru as almost everywhere and were, of course, beyond the law. When convicted of murder, not only the sorcerer but all his family were put to death. They were naturally feared and hated, but doubtless the suspects far outnumbered the few practitioners. Poison and magic were the two methods by which they worked. Poisoning needs no explanation; the practice of magic follows the same general pattern as throughout the world, that of sympathy and contagion.

A figure might be made to represent the victim, dressed in bits of his cast-off clothing or containing something belonging to him, especially some of his exuviae such as nail parings or hair; the image was then maltreated and possibly finally burned, the suffering being similarly felt by the human prototype. Or the sorcerer would take a toad, skewer the eyes and mouth shut with thorns, tie up the feet, and bury it where the victim would come into contact with it. A noose might be made of black and white wool, spun in the opposite-to-ordinary direction, and placed where the victim would catch his foot in it. By burning fat, thorns, ears of maize, and some of the enemy's hair in his corn-field the harvest could be ruined. Other tools of black magic were the ubiquitous witches'-cauldron ingredients: hairy spiders, animal heads, dried animals, roots, herbs, ointments, shells, figurines, and amulets.

Of course sorcerers could also supply love philtres and charms – all at the proper price. The ingredients, except for feathers, differed little from the above list. The charm was to be hidden in the bed or the clothes of the uncomplaisant loved one.

Chapter 14

INTELLECTUAL LIFE

Astronomy and the Calendar

IT is often asserted that the astronomical knowledge of the Peruvians was much less than that of the ancient Mexicans, and they were certainly much less astronomically and calendrically minded than the Maya. But all cultured peoples of antiquity took great interest in the celestial bodies and their recurrent periods, especially as they bore on the stages of the agricultural year. Though proof is lacking, the Inca probably knew the length of the year and that of the lunar month, and possibly also the period of Venus, with considerable accuracy.

The complexities and accuracies of the Maya calendar have been worked out mainly through studies on the surviving codices. These are entirely lacking in Peru, and the chroniclers have given us insufficient information on the Inca calendar; the Spanish immediately put their own calendar into operation, the two were fused, and the Conquest chronicles represent some of this fusion – and confusion.

The Inca were not particularly interested in dates and calendars. The basic calendar was apparently a lunar one, counted from new moon to new moon. Such a lunar calendar is all that the majority of aboriginal peoples in America had, and probably all that the Peruvian commoner ever had. They seem to have reckoned roughly, like most peoples, twelve lunar months to a year, but the twelve lunations are short of the solar year by about 10·9 days, so that in a little less than three years they were a lunar month behind. Since the ceremonies of the month were integrated with the agricultural activities pertinent to that period, and each month had a name appropriate to the activities or the festivities, it is likely that they interpolated a nameless month – or repeated the last one – when the ceremonies got too much out

228

of step with the season. The chroniclers are silent on this point; apparently they did not realize the problem.

Some more modern writers also have not realized the difficulty and have made inconsistent and irreconcilable statements. Thus Means makes each month run from about the 22nd to the 22nd (obviously based on the solstices and equinoxes), but has the full moon occur regularly on the 15th of January.[1] Others have presumed that there were twelve thirty-day months and that some months had – as with us – an extra day, or that five days were added at the end of the year, as with the Mexican-Maya calendar. This would, of course, have been entirely incompatible with a sequence of lunar periods as divisions of the solar year. In practice the lunar months and the solar year were probably not correlated exactly; the high priest and the emperor doubtless knew the discrepancy pretty accurately, and when something had to be done about it they issued an order.

The months probably began at conjunction, or, more likely, at visible new moon. It is not fully agreed which was the first month of the Inca year; it was either the one containing the June solstice or the December one. The best opinion favours the latter since it marked the beginning of the welcome rainy season.

According to one tradition, the ancient people originally timed their planting season by the blooming of a certain variety of cactus – a natural way for primitive peoples. Then the Emperor Viracocha established the twelve-month (lunation) 'annual' calendar. Finding, in a very few years, that the months and the seasons and festivals were all out of their proper relation, the Emperor Pachacuti had some towers built on the skyline by which the progress of the seasons could be accurately observed and allowed for. It is difficult to believe, however, that the discrepancy between the twelve lunar periods and the solar year was not known to all from time immemorial.

It is certain that four small masonry towers were built in rows on the skylines east and west of Cuzco, and that from a seat in the centre of the Great Square of that city the rising of the sun could be observed with relation to these towers. While a few of

1. Means, 1931, p. 382.

the chroniclers state that the solstices, and even the equinoxes, were thus observed, the evidence is against this, and apparently the sun positions thus observed merely indicated the proper times for planting.

Record-keeping: the Quipu

In spite of the Peruvians' high accomplishments in almost every phase of material culture, they never developed any system of writing – pictographic, ideographic, hieroglyphic, or alphabetic. The statement of one chronicler, Montesinos,[1] that a system of writing on leaves had once been in vogue among the Inca but had been forbidden and forgotten, is given no credence by modern scholars. However, at least one, possibly two, mnemonic devices were in use.

As before noted (page 80), many Moche pottery vessels picture runners carrying bags, together with kidney-shaped objects, generally identified as beans, that are painted with lines, dots, and similar devices. Other scenes depict persons apparently examining these objects. Larco Hoyle[2] claims that these are ideographic symbols, denoting standardized concepts; he also believes that they show close analogies with Maya glyphs. The evidence is purely archaeological, without historical verification, and conservative Peruvianists, while intrigued at the interesting suggestion, are not yet convinced of its proof.

The Inca had a highly developed mnemonic device known by the native name of *quipu*. Probably in simple form it had a long and widespread history in this region, but, like many other devices, had been perfected by the Inca for their special needs. All the extant examples of the quipu are from the dry coastal graves, but most if not all are of the Inca period (Plate 54B). As it was in constant use among the Inca, many of the chroniclers have left us descriptions and explanations of it.

The quipu consists basically of a series of strings in which knots are tied. The great variation possible in the colour and posi-

---

1. Montesinos, 1920, pp. 33, 62, 64; Bingham, 1922, pp. 308–10, *id.*, 1930, pp. 226–7.
2. Larco Hoyle, 1942, 1943.

tion of the strings, and the nature, number, and position of the knots permits its use for numerical records and mnemonic purposes. All known quipus are different and vary greatly in size and complexity; relatively few of those extant are complete, a necessity for the correct interpretation of any mathematical record.

The main cord, which was held in a horizontal position, is generally of larger size, from a few inches or centimetres to over a yard or metre in length. To this are attached from one to over one hundred pendent strings, of various colours, twists, and other modifications. They may be fastened to the main cord in groups, and subsidiary strings may be attached to them. Knots of various types and positions were tied in these pendent cords. The knots certainly have numerical values; the colours and other qualities of the strings probably signify the nature of the objects thus counted. Several of the chroniclers give interpretations for some of the colours, but the disagreement is so great that no deductions can be drawn.

Studies of quipus by several specialists[1] in this field have demonstrated clearly that the numerical records are given in a decimal arithmetical system very much like our own, with place-value. This was to be expected, since the Quechua numeral system was and is decimal, and the social system was organized on a decimal basis. A simple knot represents 'one'; digits from two to nine are denoted by longer knots in which the cord was wound or looped a given number of times before it was pulled tight. The concept of zero was understood but required no symbol; the absence of any knot in the expected position denoted zero. Place-value was indicated by distance from the main cord; the unit digits were at the farther or lower end of the string, the higher multiples – tens, hundreds, and thousands – closer to the main cord. In the known extant quipus calculations in thousands are rare, and apparently only one instance of ten thousand is known. Generally the long knots of many loops were employed only for the unit digits; multiples of the higher orders were represented by the proper number of single knots close together.

The quipu was a recording and mnemonic, not a calculating device. Its principal purpose was doubtless that of statistical

1. Locke, 1912, 1923, 1938; Nordenskiöld, 1925a, 1925b.

record; this is obvious from the statements of the chroniclers who saw them in use. Probably the majority were censuses of the population by age-classes in given districts, as well as records of domestic animals, quantities of agricultural products, and such statistics. Probably the figures could be read by any Inca *quipucamayoc* or professional quipu-interpreter, who doubtless also knew the meaning – or various meanings – of the string colours, but certainly in many or most instances some verbal information of interpretative value had to accompany a quipu (Figure 6).

However, the quipu could be, and certainly was, employed as a mnemonic device for the recitation of traditional material such as historical ballads and genealogical records. Thus, according to some of the chroniclers, the life and activities of each emperor were recorded on a quipu. Such quipus could, of course, be interpreted only by the maker or by someone fully familiar with the data.

As a result of his study of many quipus found in graves on the coast – the only extant ones – Nordenskiöld[1] comes to the conclusion that these at least were not statistical records but were used in divination and possibly for the determination of lucky and unlucky days. He argues, from his wide experience with American aborigines, that it would be absolutely contrary to American Indian psychology to place with the dead any information regarding the living, since this would give the former some control over the latter. His point is doubtless well taken, and we may be rather confident that these quipus were not current censuses. Nordenskiöld finds in these quipus an unexpected frequency of occurrence of the number seven and concludes that this must have been a sacred number. Also he derives sums and totals, many of which seem to agree, more or less closely, with the rotation periods of celestial bodies; therefore he believes these quipus to be calendrical and astronomical in nature and used in magic and divination. Although Nordenskiöld was one of the greatest Americanists, his conclusions on this point are not generally accepted by modern authorities, mainly because there are many discrepancies in his calculations that need to be explained away, and because the Inca apparently had little interest

1. Nordenskiöld, 1925a, 1925b.

Figure 6. *Quipucamayoc with quipu and counting apparatus*

in lucky and unlucky days, which were so important among the Mesoamericans. It must be kept in mind, however, that we have no historic information regarding the peoples of the coast where these quipus were buried.

It is rather certain that an abacus[1] was employed in making the calculations that were later recorded on the quipus. No example has yet been discovered archaeologically, but some chroniclers have described its use[2] and even given a picture of one (Figure 6). This seems to have been a rectangular block with twenty (5 by 4) compartments in which from one to five kernels of corn or other small objects were placed and manipulated.

Standards

Inca standards of measurement were quite accurate and exact, and in the case of at least one of them – the 'fathom', used in the measurement of land – a measure of this standard length is reported to have been kept as a criterion and official check. Small measures of length up to the fathom, about 64 inches (162 cm.), the height of an average man, were based on parts of the human body. Larger measurements of distance were based on the pace, and the unit for long distances was the *topo*, about 4½ miles (7·25 km.). Areas were also figured by the *topo*, but the areal *topo* was only an acre or so.

Standard measures for weight and volume were of much less importance, and the Inca are said to have had none for weight or for liquid volume, but dry materials, such as grain, were measured by a standard that amounted to about twenty-seven quarts (29 litres).

The weighing balance-beam was known, and possibly even the steelyard.

Music, Art, Literature

Peruvian music would probably have sounded very dissonant and cacaphonic to our ears. Probably the music of the modern Quechua and Aymara resembles it greatly, and detailed studies

1. Wassén, 1931, 1940.   2. Acosta, 1880 (1590).

have been made upon this.[1] The nature of the ancient music is deduced from the musical instruments that have been preserved. These are of two kinds, wind and percussion, for stringed instruments were practically unknown everywhere in America. Among the monotonic instruments were drums, rattles, whistles, bells, and trumpets. Flutes with finger-holes produced several tones, but of especial interest and importance is the syrinx or pan-pipe, closely resembling those of ancient China (Plate 46A). Musical instruments were made of wood, reeds, pottery, bone, shell, or metal.

The art of the Inca period was that of a pragmatic people and the last stage of a long history: it was technically excellent, under perfect control, but uninspired, aesthetically the poorest of the several major art traditions developed in Peru.

Stone sculpture was entirely missing, architectural decoration extremely rare, so that art was expressed almost exclusively in the form and embellishment of small manufactured objects, mainly in pottery, weaving, and metal-work, with minor attention to feather mosaics, woodcarving, and work in bone, shell, gourds, and other such materials.

Pottery forms were limited and of simple silhouettes, with little relief ornamentation. Colours were few and sombre, the designs almost exclusively geometric, generally repetitions of small simple figures (Plate 35). But in the decades just preceding the Spanish Conquest, some realistic painting appeared in the form of small animals, birds, and insects. There was no realistic modelling. Most of the ceramic forms, especially goblets, plates, and a pointed-base liquid-container now called an aryballus (Plate 34), were characteristic of the period.

Much the same can be said of the textiles, which are largely geometric in ornamentation with over-all designs and many small panels. Very characteristic of the period are the wooden goblets, painted in thick mastic, and called *quero*; these show scenes of human activity (Plates 39, 40). Many of them date from the Colonial period. The small figures in stone and metal are natural but lifeless and generally standardized to a few characteristic forms, such as llamas and plain human figures.

1. Harcourt and Harcourt, 1925.

Despite the fact that it was unwritten, the Inca had a considerable body of literature of high quality. For greater ease in memorizing, this traditional material was cast in metrical, poetic form. History and mythology were thus preserved in quasi-epics and sagas. Also there were religious prayers and hymns and secular poems, songs, and dramas. An example of a prayer has been given on page 214.

Very little indeed of this literature has been preserved for us, and most of that little was recorded in Spanish translation, generally much abbreviated. Most of it contained ancient religious ideology and so, together with the more purely religious literature, it was condemned or repressed by the Spanish clergy. The few preserved examples indicate lofty sentiment and beauty of expression, with many allusions to natural phenomena.

The folk literature consisted largely of love poetry and songs, and apparently differed slightly from similar material found today in the Andean region, the content and spirit of which are strongly aboriginal.

There was probably no true drama in pre-Conquest days, but merely dramatic parts of native dances with solos and choruses. The Spaniards, however, soon wrote morality plays in the Inca language, and later true dramas were composed which embodied old legends and songs. The most famous of these, which has been recorded in several old versions, is a play called 'Ollanta'. Its earliest recorded form, however, does not antedate the eighteenth century.

Presumably almost every Peruvian group had its legendary tradition of the creation of the world and of the origins of local features and institutions, and these of course differed greatly in detail if not in essence. That of the Inca is the only one preserved for us, and this doubtless existed in a number of versions with minor details. The best known of these is as follows:

The Creator, Viracocha, made the world, but it was a dark, sunless one. Then he created a population of giants by carving figures of stone and giving them life. But they displeased him, so he turned some of them back to stone – the great stone figures found at Tiahuanaco and other archaeological sites – and drowned all but two of the rest in a great flood. Before creating other beings of this same human shape he produced light by causing the sun and the moon to rise from Titicaca Island. At first the moon was the brighter, but the envious sun threw ashes in the moon's face, thus reducing its radiance. Viracocha then, at Tiahuanaco, made clay figures of all the animals and men of different nations, and decorated the latter with their assigned and traditional costumes. Putting life into them, he instructed them in their various and characteristic languages, customs, and even their ceremonies and songs, and sent them underground to emerge in the districts that they were to occupy.

Viracocha himself, with his two assistants, journeyed north to observe the results of his orders and the extent of their obedience; he travelled up the cordillera, one assistant went along the coast, and the other up the edge of the eastern forests. Since he travelled in the disguise of an old man, few of the people recognized him, and in some places greeted him with stones, an almost universal method of treating foreigners – and therefore *ipso facto* enemies – in pre-internationalistic days. At Cacha, in Canas province, he was so angered at his reception that he caused a rocky hill to ignite, which began to burn up the country. Terrified, the people beseeched his pardon and aid, whereat he extinguished the fires with a blow of his staff. On the burned hill, a volcanic cone, the Canas erected a shrine, and the Inca later built a great temple.

The Creator then proceeded to Urcos, near Cuzco, where he commanded the future population to emerge from a mountain, on which a shrine dedicated to him was later made. He visited Cuzco, and then continued north to Ecuador where, in the coastal province of Manta, he took leave of his people and, walking on the waves, disappeared across the ocean.

A NOTE ON THE NAME 'INCA'

The best terminology to employ for the people of Peru in the imperial period, for their emperor and their language, presents a difficult problem and a point on which there has been little agreement and much cause for confusion.

The native word 'Inca' designated originally a member of a

group of related families at Cuzco which became the focus of imperial expansion. Later, by imperial edict, the term was extended to include any other native speaker of the same language, Inca by privilege; the Spanish further extended the term to include any native subject of the Inca empire. However, they also applied the term specifically to the Inca *par excellence*, the emperor, just as the chief of a Scottish clan is *the* Campbell, for instance. In a language that can distinguish between *el Inca* and *los Incas* there is little room for confusion, but not so with English *the Inca*, especially with the modern tendency – advisable on the whole – of using only the singular forms of rare native proper names, such as 'the Maya', 'the Bagobo'. Some writers avoid the equivocation by calling the people 'Peruvians', surely an inadmissible term in a work such as this. Herein the people are termed 'the Inca'; the emperor is designated by that latter term.

Today the Peruvian Indians and their language – both but slightly changed from aboriginal days – are known as 'Quechua', a usage begun only a century ago. Although now standard, it is an unsuitable term, since the Quechua, being native to the region of Abancay, were originally only one of many small groups speaking the language of the Inca. Herein we refer to the pre-Spanish idiom as 'the Inca language'.

PART FOUR

ARTS AND CRAFTS

*

THE ancient Peruvians erected no Parthenons or Colosseums, they carved no Venus di Milo, they painted no masterpiece. Their architecture was characterized by massiveness rather than by beauty, remarkable for its stupendous masonry rather than for its art. Stone sculptures are rare on the coast, ponderous and severe in the highlands. It was on the smaller objects, the pottery vessels, the textiles and the metal-work, that the Peruvian artist lavished his skill and his creative art. Art was a constant element of his daily life, not an interest apart from it. However, it was as a craftsman – or craftswoman – rather than as an artist, that the Peruvian was pre-eminent. As weavers, potters, and goldsmiths they could hold their heads proudly among their peers anywhere in the world. And in the textile industry the Peruvian woman is considered by many technical experts to have been the foremost weaver of all time.

Chapter 15

TEXTILES

IT is difficult to write of Peruvian weaving in any but fulsome phrases or to avoid suspicion of exaggeration and bias. Textile experts – not merely enthusiastic archaeologists – state that the ancient Peruvians employed practically every method of textile weaving or decoration now known, with the exception of roller and block printing and several very special techniques of recent invention, and made finer products than are made today. Certain of the finer fabrics have never been equalled from a point of view of skill. Among the textiles one finds twining, twilling, braid, gingham, repp, plain weave, warp-face and weft-face or bobbin-pattern weave, warp and weft interlocking, brocade, tapestry, tubular weave, pile knot, gauze, double cloth, triple cloth, embroidery, needle-knitting, painted and resist-dye decoration, and several other special processes peculiar to Peru, probably impossible to produce by mechanical means.

In its aridity, coastal Peru much resembles Egypt. In both countries burials were made deep in places where rain is almost unknown, with consequent remarkable preservation of objects made of organic materials, such as wood and fibre. Superficially, some Peruvian fabrics resemble Coptic. Peruvian 'mummies' (Plates 51, 64), like Egyptian embalmed ones, were wrapped in quantities of cloth, probably made specifically for mortuary purposes and of especially fine quality, and were buried, often at great depths, in the barren deserts that flank the cultivated river valleys. The rare but occasional rains have damaged most of the cloths, especially in the northern coastal region, and the quantities now preserved in museums must be but a small fraction of those originally interred. Most of the textiles in collections, like most of the pottery and other grave furniture, were dug by *huaqueros*, mercenary natives who make a business of such excavation. Recent laws, making the practice illegal, have not entirely stopped this vandalism. Practically all the known Peruvian fabrics come from these coastal graves. Judging from the examples of cloths obviously woven in the highlands that have been found in these graves, it is certain that the highlanders of Peru and Bolivia wove as excellent textiles as the coastal peoples, and this may also have been true of Ecuador and Colombia.

There are three reasons why the textile art was of such importance in Peru, and therefore attained such a high degree of excellence. The cool climate of the high plateau required warm clothing, and even on the coast it was welcome protection from the chill fogs. The Peruvians had the advantage over all other American Indians in possessing wool, from the cameloid animals; thus, of the four important natural textile fibres, cotton, wool, bast, and silk, they lacked only the last. The most important bast fibre, flax, was also absent. And last, owing to their developed agricultural economy, there was plenty of leisure time between harvest and planting, leisure to be devoted to technical and artistic progress. In Peru, under the Inca empire at least, certain persons, especially some of the 'Chosen Women', spent practically their entire time at spindle and loom.

Probably throughout Peruvian history as in the later Inca period, and as generally among primitive peoples throughout the world, the women were the weavers; presumably as today they spent much of their time at the loom, and constantly spun as they walked. In addition to weaving new garments they mended old ones, re-weaving worn and torn places, much like a modern 'invisible mender', instead of darning them. Weaving new cloths for mortuary purposes consumed not a little of the time. Frequently found in Peruvian graves, probably always those of women, are work-baskets made of rushes, oblong with lids. These always contain a number of spindles, balls of cotton and wool yarn or thread, and other such small weaving implements and materials (Plate 54A).

Practically all the woven cloths were of course used for personal apparel, but some are so immense that they must have been employed as wall hangings in temples.

The development of textile techniques in Peru seems to have been a native evolutionary one, from simple beginnings. Among the earliest known Peruvian fabrics are those that were found in the excavations at Huaca Prieta (see page 34), a very early pre-ceramic site.[1] While the Huaca Prieta cloths are by no means primitive, they are much ruder than those of later periods, and made by a few simple methods.

Twining and netting are very ancient techniques the world over, possibly having developed from basket, bag, and net making, and preceding the invention of the loom. Tapestry weaving and embroidery are also very old textile arts of world-wide extent, and we would expect them to have been the next developments in Peru. Tapestry weaving requires only a rudi-mentary loom, hardly more than a frame, necessitating neither lease rods nor heddle, while embroidery might be expected to develop early from the practice of attaching objects to the surface of plain cloth. Tapestry, as expected, is very early, on the Chavín-Cupisnique horizon, in some instances combined with gauze. Embroidery, however, does not appear until the Paracas period and, if our chronological sequences are correct, was preceded at Supe by more complicated techniques such as brocade, pattern weaves, and gauze.

While twining and weaving were contemporary throughout the pre-ceramic period at Huaca Prieta, it is curious that weaving remained subordinate to twining for so long. It has been sug-gested that this implies the lack of any effective heddling device.

However, it is on the south coast that the greatest amount of material is available for study of textile art and development. In this almost perfectly arid region the state of preservation of the fabrics is remarkable. The known quantity is very great, the technical and artistic quality extraordinary. The most prolific source of fine textiles is the Paracas Necropolis, but the Nazca cemeteries have also yielded their quota.

According to radiocarbon datings, about a thousand years elapsed between the time of the last potteryless fishermen-farmers of Huaca Prieta and that of the men who deposited the burials in the Paracas Necropolis, and technology had made tremendous advances in this period. From then up to the time of Pizarro no great technical advancement was made in the textile industry. The tools used by the 'Chosen Women' who made

1. Bird, 1948a, 1948b.

Atahuallpa's vestments were practically the same as those used by the women who made the Paracas mantles: simple spindles, loom, bobbin, and weaving sword. There was no shuttle that was thrown through the warp sheds; the bobbin was passed through by hand. Probably the spindle itself often served as bobbin also.

The earliest known weavers of the southern coast, those of the Paracas period, as well as those of the later Nazca Valley, practised every important fundamental technique known in the latest periods.

There is considerable difference between the weaves and materials at Paracas Cavernas, Paracas Necropolis, and Nazca. Plain weaves are common everywhere, and plaiting common at Necropolis. Twill is missing in the early period and very rare in the middle and late ones. Tubular weaves are extremely rare but several very early ones are found. Tie-dye is missing in the early period, and pile-knotting absent entirely. Pattern weaves, brocade, and double-cloth are rare and brocade is missing at the Necropolis site. Paracas painted fabrics are the earliest known.

Wool is found in the earliest periods in this southern region, indicating regular trade with the highlands even at this time. Wool was always used for embroidery and for tapestry weft, as it was over most of Peru in all periods.

From Nazca-Paracas times on, almost all techniques were found in all regions, varying in proportion according to the prevailing fashions. In the middle periods embroidery became relatively rare, the emphasis being on tapestries, generally large and complex. From the north coast few fabrics from this period are preserved. Coast Tiahuanaco textiles are noted for their tapestries, though brocade, double cloth, and other techniques are found. The designs are of highland origin. The finest tapestries were made in this period, especially those of the Tiahuanaco horizon found at the central coast sites of Ancón and Pachacamac.

In the late periods embroidery again became prominent, but not an over-all veneer as Paracas embroidery tended to be. Double cloth, painted cloth, and resist-dye processes were in vogue also. Fabrics from the Chimú period on the north coast are now preserved, tapestry and embroidery being favoured over other techniques, these, with weft patterns, being the most common decorative weaves in the late periods on the south coast.

Much of our knowledge of Peruvian textile industry is derived from Colonial accounts of Inca weaving, though few fabrics from this period have been preserved, except on the coast. Tapestry, repp, and warp patterns were the favourite weaves, but all techniques were known. Three types of loom were used, one no wider than the span of a woman's arms, a horizontal loom mainly for blankets, and a vertical one for tapestry weaving. The first one, the backstrap loom (Figure 4, p. 157), was the one on which most textiles were woven. One loom bar was attached to a pole or tree, the other to a belt which went around the woman's waist, and supplied the needed tension. After about half of the cloth had been woven, it seems that the loom was reversed and weaving begun from the other end. As the gap between lessened. the wooden weaving tools had to be removed and the picking done by hand, the last interstice finished with a needle.

Three types of cloth were also distinguished, a coarse grade for blankets, a medium grade for ordinary apparel, and the finest fabrics. The latter was certainly tapestry, of the finest alpaca or vicuña wool; the medium class for ordinary clothing was a warp-faced cloth, with the pattern in the warp, probably made of alpaca wool. Probably llama wool was employed for the utilitarian blankets. While tapestry weave is still practised today, especially in Bolivia, warp-patterns are now almost universal; the manufacture of fine tapestries ceased soon after the Conquest.

The amount of time required to plan and weave a patterned textile is far greater than ordinarily realized. The entire ensemble has to be conceived and planned beforehand, and the order of the picking of the warps carefully calculated. Primitive craftsmen often seem to have an almost incredible ability to visualize the design that they are working on, and to calculate and memorize the steps to be followed in producing it, and it is quite possible that the Peruvian weaver had no material visual aid whatever, and certainly no very detailed or complete one. It is also possible, however, that some model, possibly painted on wood, a small woven sampler, or some other mnemonic aid was used. In a well-known painted Moche vase, showing a group of weavers, some of them seem to have by them an object showing the pattern to be reproduced in the fabric.

Fibres

Nothing is known of the beginnings of the textile industry in the Peruvian highlands, but on the coast cotton was the earliest fibre, with bast definitely of secondary importance. In early Ancón and Supe only a trace of wool was found, and on the south coast and in northern Chile the older fabrics show a much higher percentage of cotton than the later ones. Cotton, however, continued in use in all periods and regions.

Cotton occurs naturally in Peru in a slight colour range from white to reddish-brown and grey. Today the natives are said to apply different terms to cotton of six naturally different hues. These were – and still are – employed in weaving to provide contrasting colours, just as the dyed cotton was.

Linen and silk were unknown in Peru, but bast, the fibres of various plants, was used in all periods and places. It was seldom if ever employed for cloth, however, but generally for special products, such as fine hair-nets, and especially for cordage.

Wool appears early on the coast and was in constant use thereafter, especially in the highlands. The source was the native highland cameloids, the domesticated llama and alpaca, and the wild vicuña. Llama wool is coarse and generally a yellow-brown; it was employed for only the coarsest fabrics. The garments of the average person, in the highlands at least, were probably made of alpaca wool, which is finer than llama wool and white, black, or brown in colour. Most highly prized was the fine wool of the wild vicuña, which was caught in communal drives. This is very soft and long, generally of a dark-yellow colour, and in Inca times it is reported that its use was confined to the nobility. However, the finest selected alpaca wool is as fine as vicuña, and apparently in every case where a very fine textile has been closely examined by an expert, the wool has turned out to be alpaca.

The oft-quoted statement that the Peruvians spun bat wool is given no credence by modern authorities; the hair (maximum length 5 mm.) is much too short to spin into yarn. Human hair was occasionally employed for certain purposes, and probably also the wool of the viscacha, a chinchilla-like rodent. In northern Chile, textiles made of the wool of the guanaco, the small wild cameloid of the pampa, are said to have been found, but guanaco wool is probably too short for efficient use.

Dyes

The use of colouring materials certainly long preceded the manufacture of textiles, and their application to cloth was a natural extension of an age-old practice of painting. Most of the dyes were probably of vegetal origin, such as indigo (*Indigofera suffruticosa*) for blue, and a madder (*Relbunium*) for red, but products of the animal world were known, and possibly mineral colours also. The red insect cochineal (*Coccus cacti*) was cultivated for this purpose, and probably a purple colour was obtained from *Purpura* molluscs, as it was by natives of Central America. A related shellfish produced the famed Tyrian purple of classic Mediterranean days. Pigments were mixed to obtain a great variety of tones; O'Neill distinguished one hundred and ninety hues in the textiles from Paracas Necropolis, though doubtless many of these may be ascribed to differential fading. In addition, of course, there were the natural variations in the tones of cotton, white to brown, and those of llama, alpaca, and vicuña wool.

Cotton was sometimes dyed raw before the removal of the seeds; this is probably the explanation for the statement made by some observers that a blue cotton was grown. Wool was more often dyed as yarn, since dyeing tends to tangle the fibres. The dyeing of woven cloth does not seem to have been a common practice, though it must have been done at times, and was necessary in the *plangue* type of tie-dye process of decoration.

Little is known about the use of mordants to fix the colours and to make them permanent. Generally no trace of them remains today to respond to any chemical test, and it is possible that often no fixative was employed. Some tests indicate the validity of one colonial statement to the effect that alum was used; urine is a more common reagent in aboriginal South America.

Spinning

The twisting of the raw fibres into yarn or thread is the first technical process in weaving; this is termed spinning. It must be preceded, however, by some preparation of the fibres. In the case of cotton the lint has to be separated from the seeds in the boll. Whatever the fibre, it must first be cleaned and the strands placed in parallel alignment so that they will combine evenly; the latter process is known as carding.

In Peru the cotton seeds were probably torn from the lint by hand – just as they were everywhere until the invention of the cotton gin – and bits of foreign material were picked out. Wool was presumably washed to remove the dirt. Carding, for which process most peoples use some special brush- or comb-like implement, was apparently done by hand, though it has been suggested that possibly some of the one-row combs that are frequently found in graves were used for this purpose. Thus loose fluffy balls of cotton or wool with the fibres roughly parallel were obtained.

The threads and yarns spun by the pre-Columbian Peruvian women with simple hand spindles have awakened the admiration of expert authorities in this industry. 'The perfect thread is not to seek', says one.[1] 'It has been made.' 'The yarns are the best ever produced. . . . No machine yarns, however excellent, can approach their perfection.'[2] Primarily these praises refer to the fineness, though the evenness is also at least equal to that of modern machine-made yarns.

Aboriginal Peruvian cotton was not of the fine quality of modern cotton, and finer cotton threads have been hand-spun in Dacca, India (500 count), and occasionally made by machine in Manchester (420), but, considering their material, the old Peruvians made by hand extraordinarily fine cotton yarns with a count up to 250; the finest yarns made today of Peruvian cotton do not go higher than 70.

Wool cannot be spun as fine as cotton, but in the alpaca and

1. Murphy, 1912, Volume 3, p. 83.
2. Crawford, 1915, p. 77.

vicuña the Peruvians had exceptionally fine wool, and they utilized it to the full; their wool yarns were the finest and most perfect ever made. The finest worsteds made today have a count, on the industry's cotton scale, of 70 to 90; the best old Peruvian wool yarns are almost three times as fine, between 180 and 200. The finest wool tapestry weaves frequently have over two hundred weft strands to the inch, and three hundred is not very rare.

Such extremely fine threads and yarns were of course the product of years of care, experience, practice, emulation, and competition. The yarns in the oldest known textiles, those found in the Chicama Valley, are relatively coarse and uneven, evidently an early stage in the art. But progress was fast, and the fabrics in the very early Paracas period were already approaching the perfection achieved in the latest periods. In fact, some of the finest thread was made in the early periods.

The implements employed in the manufacture of these extraordinarily fine and even threads and yarns were of the simplest, a forked stick for a distaff to hold the fluffed fibre, and a plain hand spindle. In these, as in the loom, there seems to have been little improvement throughout the long history of Peruvian weaving, although in the very earliest period, as for instance in the Chicama Valley, no identifiable spindles or whorls have been found, and it is possible that plain sticks were used. However, the simple hand spindle, a straight stick with a whorl or disk on it to give momentum, was the universal spinning implement almost everywhere in the world until relatively recently, for the spinning wheel was only a few centuries old when it went the way of the whale-oil lamp. The spindle was given a whirl with the fingers, which twisted into thread or yarn the cotton or wool fibres as they were pulled out from the loose ball of fibre on the distaff. While it was twirling, the spinner's fingers teased out over-large knots of fibre to make the thread of even thickness.

Today the Peruvian Indian woman is constantly spinning as she walks when away from home, letting the spindle fall and thus providing the needed tension. The drop spindle is used today only with wool yarn; cotton is spun while seated, the spindle whirling in a gourd or bowl. The drop spindles are larger, with larger whorls, and the yarn produced is probably coarser than the cotton threads. Presumably the customs were the same in early days (Figure 3). Many of the spindles found archaeologically, of thorn or hard wood, are so small with such tiny whorls that it has been doubted whether they really served this purpose. They were probably used in spinning the finest threads and yarns, revolving in a cup and thus reducing strain and vibration.

The direction of the twist varied in different times and places. In the Inca period it was generally clockwise. However, in doubling, to produce a two-ply yarn, the direction was always opposite to that used in making the single-ply yarn, so the spinner had to be equally adept in both directions.

Single-element Techniques

True knitting and crocheting are claimed to have been unknown in ancient Peru, but somewhat similar results were obtained by other processes. Netting was of the greatest importance since earliest days, and probably long preceded loom weaving; it was a common technique at Huaca Prieta. Several other knotted and looped techniques were known. The products range from large, coarse fishing-nets and sacks to small bags and hair-nets. Lace-work falls in this category. Knotting reached its highest development in the creation of closely knotted fabrics, usually caps or hats, frequently including decorative feathers or pile. Single-element fabrics are found in all horizons, but are more common in the early ones.

Lace is often mentioned casually in articles and books on Peruvian fabrics, but no definite study of Peruvian laces seems to have been made. The delicate gauzes have a very lace-like appearance and doubtless have often been mistaken for lace. The term lace covers a number of different techniques, some single-, some multi-element, and even drawn-work. Doubtless many non-woven products of the early Peruvians, such as some hair-nets, will be found to match some of these techniques (Plates 46B, 50A).

PLAITING AND BRAIDING

Naturally the technique of making objects by twisting together three or more similar elements was not unknown to or ignored by the ancient Peruvians. The process is somewhat related to twining, except that all three elements are parallel. It was employed to some extent in almost all periods and regions, naturally mainly in the manufacture of long narrow objects such as slings, ropes, and cords, and to a lesser extent in flat bands. Even in these utilitarian objects, however, the Peruvian talent and artistic sense manifested themselves, for every possible method of decoration was applied to them, and every conceivable variation of manufacture employed. Since a long cultural history, antedating loom weaving, would be expected, it is surprising that no examples of braiding or plaiting were found at Huaca Prieta.

PILE KNOT

Several processes for giving a raised effect to fabrics were known in Peru. Loom-woven cloth was varied by pulling out weft strands to form loops like a Turkish towel, and fibre was caught in the weave in a quasi-pile technique (see page 257). But the most interesting and most attractive pile-knot technique, and the one that gives an effect most approaching that of Oriental rugs, was apparently peculiar to Peru. The piles was not woven into the fabric, but the technique was related rather to the single-element one of netting. That is, the bunches of fibre were caught in the loops of a single yarn. The pile was later trimmed off to give an even, regular surface.

Bright colours forming designs and patterns were used in these bunches of wool fibre, and the technique was employed principally on hats, head-bands, and bags. A variation of the process produced long cords of unknown purpose; the looped yarn enmeshing the pile tufts was wound around long fibre cords. The pile technique was apparently a rather late invention, and was particularly favoured in the Tiahuanaco period, in which it first appeared.

Weaving

The admirable fineness and quality of Peruvian fabrics were due to the patience, care, knowledge, and skill of the weaver, not to the quality of her apparatus, for this was of the simplest. The primitive back-strap loom was used in all periods and underwent little development from earliest to latest time; it was the implement on which the finest textiles were woven. One end was fastened to a post or tree, the other to a band round the weaver's back, by which means the desired tension was maintained. The heddle was lifted and fixed in position by hand; there was no treadle. Apparently several other types of loom were known at different times and places, for different products, but the small, one-woman, arm-span loom was the standard everywhere at all times, as it is today (Figure 4).

Apparently the weaver's only other tool was a weave sword or batten for separating the sheds more widely and for beating down the weft (Plate 59B). As the weaving proceeded, the finished cloth was wound up on the lower loom bar while the warps were unwound from the upper bar. It is believed that after about half of the cloth had been woven, the loom was reversed and weaving begun from the other end. As the gap between lessened, the wooden weaving tools had to be removed and the picking of the warps done by hand, the last interstice finished with a needle.

TWINING

Twining is the simplest, and probably the oldest method of fabric-making, and was possibly adopted from the certainly earlier processes of basket- and mat-making. While made by crossings of warp and weft, a true loom is not required, a simple frame sufficing. The intertwining of warp and weft is done by hand, a pair of weft strands being twisted around a warp element; the twisting is continuous.

Twining is certainly the oldest fabric technique in Peru. Excavations in the pre-ceramic sites of the northern Peru coast indicate that 78 per cent of the fabrics were twined, most of the remainder being single-element netted objects. The twining, however, was highly developed, the crossings being varied to produce pleasing patterns and effects.

Soon, with much greater dependence on woven textiles, twining became unimportant and disappeared from the picture almost completely.

GAUZE

Delicate lace-like gauzes in a great number of patterns were very popular in the early periods on the coast, especially at Paracas Cavernas, though they continued to be made in all periods. Pairs or more of warps are crossed or intertwined in various patterns and then fixed in position by the weft. Though the manipulation may be done with the fingers, the work is simplified by the use of a heddle. Almost all Peruvian gauzes are fancy, or combinations of plain and fancy techniques, elaborate and skilful. They are also decorated with other techniques, such as embroidery. Almost all are of cotton, a very few of wool. Developed at a very early period, gauzes are among the loveliest, most interesting, and most varied of many admirable Peruvian weaves. They somewhat resemble lace and are sometimes mistaken for it.

TAPESTRY

Tapestry is generally visualized as a large, loosely woven fabric used as a wall covering or other hanging. None of these characterizations applies to Peruvian tapestries, which are very tightly woven, of moderate size, and used for garments, pouches, and similar purposes. For, to the textile expert, tapestry is a technique, not a product, and tapestry technique is basically the same in the small exquisite Peruvian fabrics and in the great Gobelin wall hangings.

Tapestry weaving has been defined as darning or embroidery on bare warps. Though generally woven on a loom with a heddle, only a frame is needed since there is no division into warp sheds, and the weft is ordinarily not carried across the full width of the warps. The pattern is always formed by the weft. More colours can be employed than in loom pattern weaves; there is no limit to the number of colours that can be used in a fabric. Each coloured yarn is carried on a separate bobbin, and the weaver builds up the pattern bit by bit, passing the bobbin over and under the warps until the pattern calls for a new colour, then letting the old colour bobbin hang, and taking up the new one. Two methods of procedure are possible. The weaver may finish one line of weft at a time, dropping one colour bobbin and taking up the next as the design changes, or she may build up one complete coloured design before proceeding to the next. In the latter case it requires much skill to keep the weft lines even and the cloth unpuckered. Nevertheless, this seems to have been the usual technique of the Peruvian weaver when making slit 'kelim' and 'eccentric' tapestry; in the more usual interlocked weave the weft lines were carried straight across.

Gobelin tapestries portray life scenes; Peruvian ones are not pictorial but have regular patterns, generally rectilinear and frequently geometric, though more often stylized and conventionalized biomorphic. Gobelin tapestries have the backs unfinished, with loose-hanging yarn ends, but Peruvian tapestries are mostly two-faced, the two sides identical and equally well finished; the ends of the yarn are carefully tucked in and hidden between the warps so that they are never seen and never come loose. The pattern with the same colour on both sides of the cloth is the identifying criterion of tapestry; in loom pattern weaving in two colours the two are different to front and back.

Tapestry weaving is simpler than loom pattern weaving and presumably older, preceding the adoption of the heddle. It is the weave used in much primitive weaving, at least in America; Navaho blankets or rugs, Mexican serapes, and most other examples of aboriginal American weaving are done in this technique.

Tapestry seems to have been the favourite – or at least the most highly prized – Peruvian technique, especially in the Middle and the Inca periods. It was at its apogee in the Coastal Tiahuanaco or Epigonal period. The most perfect, the finest, and the loveliest

Peruvian fabrics are the tapestries; they are among the world's triumphs in the textile art (Plate 48A).

Peruvian tapestry is always made with warp of cotton and weft of wool, generally fine alpaca or vicuña wool, and the weaving is the finest and daintiest. The weft is always battened down hard so that it completely covers the warp. Gobelin tapestries are coarse, with an average of twenty wefts per inch, and the finest European tapestries seldom exceed eight-five. In Peru two hundred per inch is not uncommon, and Bird records[1] one extraordinary piece with an average of 327 and running up to 500 in some closely packed parts of the design. This is presumably of two-ply vicuña wool. The warp is of three-ply cotton, sixty-seven to the inch.

In almost every type of weaving, the Peruvians experimented and produced variations which are unknown elsewhere. One such has been termed 'sheer tapestry'. Though made by tapestry technique it has the appearance of voile, being loosely woven of singly-ply cotton crape, interlocked. A very rare variation of this is the Swedish or two-way interlock, in which the weft-locks produce a ridge on the rear side of the cloth.

In tapestry weaving, rectilinear patterns present no problem when they are diagonal, but it is obvious that vertical straight lines leave a slit between the design elements unless both wefts encircle the same dividing warp, which makes closely battened weaving impossible. Frequently the slits, especially if short, were left open – a technique known as kelim. To close them, and to eliminate this element of weakness, any one of several tricks might be employed. In the Nazca area subsidiary wefts of hard-spun, single-ply cotton, so fine that they were hidden between the wool weft, were often inserted; the term 'reinforced kelim' has been suggested for this. Another method was to interlock half or less of the weft loops across the slit. Or a vertical weft might be wound round an intervening warp strand, occasionally looping to the sides to blind in the adjacent warps. This independent weft is often of a black colour, and gives a dainty dark outline to the coloured pattern; the same black yarn is sometimes employed to outline all rectilinear design areas.

1. Bennett and Bird, 1949, p. 277.

SCAFFOLDING TECHNIQUES

The Peruvian weaver, as has been intimated before herein, was no routine labourer; she took the old-fashioned guildsman's pride in her work. Every piece was somewhat different from any other; her loom was an instrument for art expression, not merely a machine. And just as she gave thought to the intended design, and calculated the number of picks required to produce it, so she experimented with all possible manipulations of warp and weft. Often combinations of several techniques are found on one fabric. It is natural, therefore, that complicated textile processes were invented that have been found nowhere else in the world, that must be described in detail to be understood, that cannot be duplicated by mechanical means, and for which a new nomenclature must be developed. It is unnecessary to go into such detail here.

Several such techniques were performed on skeleton yarns or cords which were removed after the cloth was woven, and the fabric later strengthened and locked by the insertion of other new and additional strands.

This technique has been called 'weft scaffolding' or 'patchwork', and is found in a number of variations. One of these gave rise to the term 'patchwork'. In this the cloth was woven in solid-colour squares, but the vertical weft loops were not interlocked. When the horizontal yarns over which the warps were looped were removed, the cloth fell apart into small rectangles. These were then decorated with tie-dye designs and, since the edge loops to top and bottom were open, the fabric was pieced together again by the insertion of the horizontal yarns, doubtless with the aid of a needle.

PATTERN WEAVES

Both warp-faced and weft-faced or bobbin patterns were made by the ancient Peruvians, and the results were up to their usual high standard, but these processes were never so popular as tapestry, embroidery, and brocade; brocades are much more common than bobbin-weaves. The best examples of warp-faced textile are found in the later periods on the southern coast, and the technique continues important in Peruvian native weaving today.

The warps were always of cotton, the weft of wool or cotton. While one or two heddles may have been used, the design was probably most often made by hand-picking the warps.

One variety of warp-faced plain cloth known as repp was very common and is often considered a characteristic feature of ancient Peruvian weaving. The fewer and heavier weft strands give a ribbed appearance to the fabric.

DOUBLE CLOTH

Double cloth was a favourite weave, though a rather intricate one. Two sets of warps and wefts, each pair of the same colour, are employed, producing two layers of cloth of contrasting colours, the design being made by interlocking the cloths so that the motif appears on the reverse face in the opposite colour. This weave was popular in earlier days in the United States for home-made bedspreads.

In Peru, double cloth was employed principally for pouches where light weight and durability were essential; the pieces are never large. The weave is not very fine, never more than forty-eight to the inch, the warp and weft count always equal. Almost all are of cotton yarn, and brown and white are the colours most frequently employed. The setting up of the loom is of course rather complex, and for rapid work four heddles would be required. It is doubtful if these were employed in Peru; in this, as in all simple weaving, heddles can be dispensed with if the weaver takes the time to count the warps and pick them by hand. Rare examples of three- and even of four-layered cloths, each of a different colour, have been found in Peru (Plate 48B).

The earliest example of double cloth is from Paracas Cavernas, but the high quality of the work indicates a long developmental period somewhere; the technique became quite common in later periods in practically all areas.

On the question of clo*on of Fabrics*
from pure weaving to the ion, there is a gradual variation
makes it difficult to separa nt of objects, a gradation that
one extreme there is the draw chniques into categories. At
like a Turkish towel, a process of weft strands into loops
but producing much the same e erent in technique from,
fibres during weaving. Another p s, the insertion of pile
weaving is brocade; embroidery gives of decoration during
is applied after weaving. The tie-dye h the same effect but
either before or after weaving. nique may be used

The Turkish-towel effect is found on som tton shirts where
a loop an inch long is left between the war on certain weft
strands, producing horizontal lines of loops a regular spaced
intervals. Probably the wefts thus manipulated re passed over
a gauge or rod that was later withdrawn. The pur se was probably warmth rather than decoration, which can cer inly be said
of some shirts and shawls from northern Chile of a ter period.
Here ten-inch tufts of alpaca wool were wrapped around certain
warps during the process of weaving; the result is coarse, heavy,
and utilitarian but definitely not beautiful. Both of these processes were probably rare and of very limited temporal and geographical distribution.

BROCADE

Though brocade resembles embroidery so closely that they are
sometimes difficult to distinguish, the methods of manufacture
are entirely different. Both are decorative overlays on cloth, but
embroidery is added with a needle-like implement after the cloth
is woven, while brocade is applied during the weaving process by
means of supplementary wefts which are brought to the surface
when needed to form the pattern, and hidden under the utilitarian weft when not. Brocade must therefore always follow the
weft line, while embroidery may be sewn at any angle. One
criterion for distinction is that embroidery is always carried

through the cloth and appears e... ...nly on the reverse side,
while brocade is hidden in t... ...when not desired in the
design. Brocade wefts are ... ...and less hard-spun than
the real weft so as to cover ... ...r in patterns; they are also
inserted more loosely. ... ...at Supe; it is also common at

The earliest brocade i...
Paracas Cavernas.

Both brocade and e... ...ery were very popular in Peru, and
the former is much m... ...ommon than bobbin weave, probably
largely because mor... ...urs could be used.

EMBROIDERY

The fundam... ...al technique of embroidery has been discussed
in the precedi... section on brocade. Embroidery was both very
popular and ...traordinarily well made in Peru, especially in
some of the e...ly periods. It was done with a needle-like implement in cot...n or wool yarn, and generally on a loosely woven
cotton fabri... Unknown at Huaca Prieta, no examples have been
found at Supe, and the earliest known pieces are from Paracas
Cavernas. Later it declined in popularity as in quality, and late
embroideries are distinguishable from brocades only on careful
examination, since the stitch always follows the weft line. In fact
in all periods, free embroidery, with stitches at any angle, is
virtually unknown; it was not in accord with the aesthetic sense.
The exquisite embroidered Paracas mantles (Plate 49) have been
described earlier.

'Needleknitting'

Some of the daintiest and loveliest Peruvian sewing is done in a
technique now generally termed 'needleknitting', although other
names have been applied to it, for its exact nature was long not
understood. It has the superficial appearance of knitting, but is
actually an embroidery technique, and probably was done with
a needle. The stitch used is that known as 'buttonhole' in embroidery. While it is also employed in edge and seam bindings,

and even to ... her large fabrics, its highest and most
spectacular and ... development is in small three-
dimensional figure... must be seen to be ... as one writer has aptly remarked,
generally of birds and h... These are tiny realistic figures,
that were made independe... occasionally of other objects,
the edges of Nazca fabrics. T..a border or fringe, and sewn to
delicate and even knitting bu...ve the impression of the most
foundation of yarn or tape, compl...actually embroidered on a
always done in two-ply wool yarn, ...veneering it. The work is
loops to the inch, and in five or six brig... an average of twenty
is found in all periods in the southern an... olours. This technique
but not on the north coast; it was most co...entral Peruvian coast
highest perfection in the early periods at ...mon and brought to
(Plate 50B).

Shaped Fabrics

Tailored clothing – that is to say, garments made of cloth, cut to
desired shape and sewn together – is a relatively recent concept
in the world and one mainly due to European influence. Most
native peoples wear – and wore – their textiles uncut and just as
woven; this was probably universally true in aboriginal America.
With their highly developed textile industry, however, it is
natural that the Peruvians should have experimented with the
manufacture of fabrics woven in non-rectangular shapes, a
process today practically limited to knitting. The techniques
involved, however, are rather simple, as were the results. Most
of the shaping was achieved by making one edge of the cloth –
generally the upper edge – wider or narrower than the opposite
one.

Tubular Weaving

Weaving seamless tubular belts, ribbons, and straps was one of
the interesting accomplishments of the Peruvians; such objects
are much more easily and frequently produced – today at least –

by knitting. No technical study of th... been made, but presumably the warps were strung on ...ving as loom bars, the
weft forming a continuous spira... are generally decorated
in warp-faced technique. Som... they are perfectly tubular,
of circular cross-section, but ...ften the two sides are combined to make a thick, flat fa... ith rounded hollow edges in a
sort of double-cloth fashi... ese were used especially for the
handle bands of cloth po... es. The historical development of
tubular weaving has no... been worked out, but, as might be
expected, it apparentl... not found in the early periods but
became common and ... pular in the later ones.

Tie-and-Dye Techniques

The decoration of cloth – and of other objects – by processes that
involve the covering of certain parts so that these remain un-
affected when the object is dyed is one of widespread distribution, especially in south-eastern Asia. The best known of these is
the batik technique, by which a design is painted in wax on the
cloth which is then dyed and the wax removed, leaving the
design in white, the background in colour. This process was and
is unknown in America on cloth, though on pottery, known as
negative painting, it was sporadically widespread. The pre-
Columbian American resist-dye processes on cloth are those
known as tie-dye, in which the parts of the cloth or fibre to
remain undyed were bound with cord or some other similar relatively impermeable material. Two varieties of the technique
were practised: *plangue*, in which the finished cloth was treated
and dyed, and *ikat*, in which the yarn was tied and dyed before
being woven into cloth.

The designs that can be made on cloth by the plangue process
are necessarily simple, and the cloth is generally a loosely woven
fabric that can easily be thoroughly soaked. The most common
technique was to gather up and tie small puckers of the cloth in
regular lines. This resulted in lines of small, light-coloured, rude
squares or circles with a dark dot in the centre, on a dark background. Sometimes this was done twice with different colours.

This tie-dye process was often used in connexion with 'patch-work' weaving (see page 255).

The ikat tie-dye process was much more intricate, for the entire pattern had to be planned and calculated in advance so that the warps would be dyed in such a manner that they would form a design when woven into cloth; wefts were never dyed in this fashion. The warps were counted, grouped, and tied with impermeable cord before dyeing; they were often retouched with paint later. Relatively few examples are known, and all are limited to the late Tiahuanaco horizon of the Chimú area; however, the process is well known today in the Andean highlands and in Guatemala. It apparently appeared later than the plangue technique. Both processes are still very popular in Indonesia.

Borders and Fringes

By far the majority of Peruvian fabrics were made to be worn as garments and therefore their aesthetic effect was of maximum importance. Very rarely were edges left plain, and generally the last few inches of the cloth adjoining the border were decorated with a pattern different from the body of the textile; this was often also done in a different weaving technique. Very generally also tassels or fringes were made on the edges, either sewn on or, much more often, made during the weaving process.

Fringes were easily made from the warp loops where they encircled the loom cord or rod, and the wefts were often carried out to either side, possibly with the help of temporary warps; these warp and weft loops were either left open or treated in some decorative fashion. Another method of finishing the warp-end edges of cloth was to complete the weft weaving around the loops so that a tubular edge of very slight diameter was produced. To do this it was almost certainly necessary to remove the fabric from the loom and probably to complete the weave with the aid of a needle.

Painting and Appliqué

One of the simplest methods of decoration, whether of cloth or of any object, is by painting. Painted fabrics are found in various periods in Peru, but apparently none earlier than Paracas Necropolis. Probably most often made hastily in an emergency, they are not in keeping with the Peruvian perfectionist sense in textiles; they are common in no period. Naturally the cloths and the designs are rather large, the colours few (Plate 47). A few cloths decorated with designs made by stamps, presumably of carved wood, are known.

Fabrics covered with a mosaic of feathers are rather common and are exquisite, but the emphasis is on the overlay; they are feathers attached to a utilitarian background rather than decorated fabrics. Sometimes they are cemented to the cloth, but more often attached to cords and sewn on.

In the later periods cloth garments were decorated by the attachment of metal sequins, bangles, beads, and such extraneous ornaments.

solid bridge, and especially the stirrup-spouted ones, in which two upward-curving tubes unite in one vertical tube. The double whistling vessel is common in Peru. This consists of two bottle-shaped jars connected at the bottom. One of them has an open neck, while that of the other contains a whistle, generally combined with a naturalistic figure. When tilted so that the liquid flows from one chamber to the other, air is forced out of the whistle orifice.

In Peru, as indicated by the excavations at Huaca Prieta, the art of weaving preceded that of pottery-making. However, the earliest known Peruvian ceramic is already of good quality and must have had a long period of development behind it, possibly in some other area, near by or far away. The sequence of technical ceramic development still remains to be worked out for Peru. However, there seems to have been no important technological improvement from earliest to latest times; the Inca potter used essentially the same processes as his Guañape predecessor.

Metallurgy

Because of the technical difficulties of producing and working metals they always appear late in the histories of cultures and are marks of considerable advancement. In the Old World, copper and bronze appeared late in human history, iron even later, and all were used mainly for utilitarian objects.

Aboriginal America never achieved an iron age. Iron in a free state is almost never found except in meteorites, and the melting temperature is very difficult to attain by primitive methods. Native copper was worked by prehistoric Indians in the region of Lake Superior, and in Mexico gold and a very little copper and silver appear on a late horizon, but the Andean region was the great, and probably the earliest, centre of metallurgy in America. Gold, silver, copper, and even platinum were worked, and tin was alloyed with copper to form bronze. Very rarely lead and mercury were utilized. Most of the products, however, were ornamental rather than utilitarian.

Historically, gold was doubtless the first metal to be worked

It is easily secured in pure condition by placer mining, and can easily be fashioned into lovely untarnishable ornaments. The first gold objects in America were probably made either in Colombia or on the coast of Peru. The earliest technique was apparently that of repoussé; the gold was beaten into thin plates and tooled or hammered over forms into designs.

In the Chavín period goldsmithing had already reached a high technical and artistic plane. The next gold ornaments appear in the Salinar period on the Peruvian northern coast and the Nazca-Paracas period on the southern coast; the latter are not uncommon and of a high quality of art and technique. In these early times there seems to have been no copper or silver used, and no casting in gold.

The development of metallurgy is not of sufficient importance – nor indeed are the evolutionary details well enough known – to warrant detailed exposition here. Suffice it to say that through the centuries the casting of metal objects was developed, copper was melted and cast and mixed with tin to form bronze, and silver was also melted, beaten, and cast.

Goldsmithing was widespread, and both the quantity and the quality of the work in Ecuador, Colombia, and Panama were equal to that in Peru. Silver and bronze are not found in the northern countries, and platinum was worked only in southern Colombia and Ecuador.

The discovery of ornaments of platinum on the coast of Ecuador has astounded and intrigued modern metallurgists, for its melting point (about 1770° C. or 3218° F.) is beyond the capabilities of primitive furnaces, and it was unknown in Europe until quite late. The tiny beads and other ornaments appear to be of pure platinum but actually consist of an alloy rich in platinum with some gold and a little silver. It was worked by the process known as sintering. Small grains of platinum were mixed with a little gold dust; the gold melted under heat and soldered or welded the grains together; it was then hammered into shape.[1]

Gold was apparently secured only by placer washing in streams. The nuggets and 'dust' sometimes contain a consider-

[1]. Bergsoe, 1937; Root, 1949b.

able quantity of silver. Silver, copper, and tin were mined from pure veins or lodes; it is questionable whether the Peruvians were ever able to smelt these metals from ores, but the evidence favours the smelting of copper and silver.

In their furnaces the Indians seem to have used charcoal, but they had not invented the bellows; draught was produced by blowing through tubes, and sometimes a large number of natives were thus employed on one furnace. Another method was to build the furnace on a hillside where there was a constant updraught.

Gold, silver, and copper were all hammered into thin sheets and embossed (Plates 42-5). They react differently to cold hammering and to tempering. Cold-hammering makes copper very hard, harder than cast bronze of low tin content; this is probably the true explanation of many legends of lost arts of tempering copper. Apparently all processes of hammering, annealing, and alloying were practised in Peru to give the most desirable results. Alloying lowers the melting point of metals, and bronze was probably produced primarily for greater ease in casting rather than for greater hardness.

Gold, silver, copper, and bronze objects, and especially gold ornaments, were made by casting. The process was that known as *cire perdue* or 'lost wax', a technique known also to Old World goldsmiths; it is an open question whether it was independently invented in America. The desired ornament was modelled in wax, either with or without a core of clay or of some similar substance. This was then covered with a thick envelope of clay through which an orifice was left. After the clay had hardened, the mass was heated and the melted wax allowed to run out through the hole. Molten metal was then poured in to replace it, duplicating in metal – sometimes with a pottery core – the wax figure. The outer envelope was broken to extract the ornament, so there was no duplication or quantity production. This was the method employed in Mexico, and almost certainly also in Peru and the regions between.

Probably pure gold was the first metal to be cast in the Moche period, then silver and copper, later various alloys, and finally bronze. An alloy of gold and copper known as *tumbaga* was much used in Colombia and the Isthmian region, but to no great extent in Peru; this and bronze were the most important alloys. All South American bronzes are of the so-called alpha type, with a tin content of less than twelve per cent; they are relatively soft unless cold-hammered.

The technique of annealing or tempering was probably discovered even before casting; some metals or alloys are hardened by this process, some softened. It is uncertain whether or not welding was known, but soldering was practised from the earliest periods. No mercury or amalgam was used, but powdered copper salt was mixed with a gum and applied to the surface with heat; this reduced the salt to metal and fused the surfaces together.

Several processes of gilding were known. One was true gilding, the application of thin gold – or silver – leaf to a surface. A mould was sometimes lined with gold before the molten copper was poured into it. Much more common, at least in Colombia and the Isthmian region, was a process which is known as *mise en couleur* and was known also to Old World goldsmiths. An object was cast of an alloy of gold and copper, and the surface then treated with the juice of an acid-bearing plant which dissolved the copper. The pure gold surface could then be burnished.

Tiny beads of exquisite and dainty workmanship were cast, especially in Ecuador, and larger objects were made of two different metals such as gold and copper, gold and silver, or of two different alloys of gold of different colours (Plate 41). Gold or silver inlays were also made in base metal or other materials.

Woodcarving

Carving in wood is a practically universal craft that must have been practised by almost every American group, past or present. Owing to rapid decay, however, only under exceptional conditions have wooden objects of past civilizations been preserved; such American archaeological objects are extremely rare everywhere except in Peru. Here, as in Egypt, very arid desert conditions on the coast have permitted their preservation almost in their original state. They occur mainly in graves on the coast, but many have also been found while excavating guano on the islands off the coast; these were probably lost there during similar visits for fertilizer in pre-Columbian days.

Spades, shovels, paddles, clubs, digging-sticks, batons, and similar objects are the larger things known; very often their use is problematical. Many are ornately decorated with carving and painting. Weaving tools such as loom sticks, weaving swords, spindles, and bobbins are the commonest objects found in graves, but there are also ear ornaments, figurines, spear-throwers, and dozens of other implements and ornaments (Plates 58-60).

One of the most characteristic types of wooden objects is the kero or *quero*, a tall, flaring wooden cup of thick, hard, dark wood. While the shape was most characteristic of the Tiahuanaco period, most of the known keros date from the last days of the Inca empire, or from early colonial times. They are usually painted with pictorial scenes featuring ornately dressed human figures, and frequently these wear Spanish costumes. The bright colours are in a sort of mastic lacquer, inlaid in a modified cloisonné technique. Most of those now known have probably been preserved in Peruvian houses since the day of their manufacture (Plates 39, 40).

Miscellaneous Techniques

Feathers were favourite materials of the ancient Peruvians. Brilliant colours such as red, blue, and yellow were preferred, and feathers of the parrot and macaw probably supplied the bulk of the material; for small and delicate mosaics, humming-bird feathers were used. Naturally few of these fragile art pieces are preserved in a state approaching their pristine beauty. Feathers were applied to many things, but large mantles, collars, and the capes of head-dresses, with rich designs in feather mosaic of bright colours, are the most striking. The small feathers of uniform size were individually tied to a background fabric.

Colourful fine-grain stones taking a high polish were naturally carved into beads, pendants, and ornaments of many types. Most of these stones are extremely hard, but nevertheless the lapidary probably practised his art with little if any use of metal tools (he had only bronze at the best), but depended more on abrasives. Naturally the work was very slow. Beads tend to be small. Small stone bowls with llama effigy heads are very characteristic of the Inca period (Plate 38).

Similar objects were made of bone and shell, but each material has its specific properties; thus bone was used for awls, needles, weaving implements, and many long tools. The large spondylus shell was happily employed for roseate inlays and ornaments, while the triton and other large univalve shells were used as trumpets.

Basketry, an art in which many American Indian groups excelled, was of no artistic importance in Peru. Doubtless rather rude utilitarian basket containers were made for many purposes, but few of these have been preserved. The best known are small oblong rectangular baskets with attached lids, made of rushes or grass, which were used by women to hold their small weaving tools and balls of yarn, and which were buried with them (Plate 54A).

APPENDIX

*

Sources

IT must be constantly kept in mind that we have no first-hand sources of information on Peruvian history and customs until the Inca were overwhelmed by the Spanish in 1532. Before that time there was no system of writing; the only known records, the quipus – knotted strings – were mnemonic aids, accurate only arithmetically, the context known only to those cognizant of the subject in question. For the greater part of this pre-Columbian era our only data are those supplied by the trowel of the archaeologist and the spade of the native *huaquero* (treasure-hunter), data mainly on material culture and manufactures. Some deductions regarding social and religious life can be drawn from these – a good deal in the case of the life forms and paintings on Moche pottery – but no clues to such topics as history.

Immediately after the Spanish Conquest chroniclers began to record in Spanish their observations of Peruvian life and customs, and to interrogate informed natives regarding these and the historical traditions. These are our principal sources. They vary greatly, especially on such points as history. In appraising their value modern students take into account such factors as the circumstances under which they were written, the presumptive reliability of the native informants, the degree to which statements agree with the general picture of Peruvian life and national temperament and ideology, and especially whether several reliable chroniclers corroborate a given statement.

In English – and probably in any language – the most thorough study of Peruvian sources is *Biblioteca Andina*, by Philip Ainsworth Means,[1] one of the greatest of recent Peruvianists. Means gives full data on the lives of the many chroniclers, the circumstances of their writings, and appraisals of the value of their works. The latter, however, do not always agree with the opinions of Means' successors of to-day. In his evaluations he placed great

1. Means, 1928.

stress upon the attitudes of the writers, and contrasted two 'schools', the Toledan and the Garcilassan. The former consists of those who, like Francisco de Toledo,[1] Viceroy of Peru from 1569 to 1582, and his associate, Pedro Sarmiento de Gamboa,[2] were antagonistic to the Inca régime and who sought to prove that the Inca emperors were tyrannical usurpers who had no just claim to rule. The Garcilassan 'school' was typified by the 'Inca' Garcilaso de la Vega,[3] of royal Peruvian blood, whose point of view was naturally sympathetic towards his mother's people. Means concluded that the statements of the latter group would naturally be more reliable than those of the former, took Garcilaso as his most reliable source, and accepted his statements whenever they conflicted with those of other chroniclers assigned by Means to the Toledan school. Garcilaso's statements were also widely copied and plagiarized by later writers, and he has long enjoyed a reputation as the foremost authority. Many modern critics, however, consider Garcilaso unreliable, especially as regards pre-Conquest history and religion.[4] Garcilaso wrote his 'Royal Commentaries' long after he had returned to Spain, and based much of his historical accounts on the writings of the now discredited Jesuit Blas Valera.[5]

Both Means and Rowe, however, agree in their high opinion of Father Bernabé Cobo[6] who wrote his four-volume *Historia del Nuevo Mundo* about 1653, and, in spite of its relatively late date, this can probably be recommended as on the whole the most reliable account of Peruvian life and history. Pedro de Cieza de León's *Crónica del Perú*[7] is another of the best-known sources, and he is generally considered 'honest, conscientious, and thorough'. These above-named are the largest, most important, and best-known sources, but a large number of others were their contemporaries. Means and the great British Peruvianist, Sir Clements R. Markham, have translated a number of these sources into English.

1. Toledo, 1940; Levillier, Roberto, 1935.
2. Sarmiento de Gamboa, 1906, 1907; Ocampo, 1907.
3. Garcílaso de la Vega, 1722, 1723, 1869–71.
4. Rowe, 1945, 1946.
5. Valera, 1879.
6. Cobo, 1890–95.
7. Cieza de León, 1554, 1864, 1880, 1883, 1932.

Spelling of Native Words

The spelling of native words of a language without written or printed literature always presents a most difficult problem. All languages have sounds that are missing in another language, and for which the latter has no character. Usually these are expressed, in non-technical writing, by their nearest equivalent, or by combinations of characters, though sometimes special characters are invented – a much preferable procedure, but requiring a key for the non-cognizant. Unfortunately, every modern language has its particular pattern of orthography. English, with its irregular and illogical orthography – indicating different vowels by doubling a following consonant or by suffixing a voiceless *e*, as *filing* and *filling*, *not* and *note*, is perfectly hopeless for recording unaccustomed words and exotic sounds.

Fortunately Spanish, with which we are at present concerned, is one of the best in this respect, though lacking characters for many rather common sounds, such as English *sh*, and employing a few double characters for simple sounds, as *qu* for *k*, *hu* for *w*. Immediately after the Conquest, the Spanish in Peru began writing the Inca language, now known as Quechua, made it a second official language, and developed a standard orthography for it, as they did with Aztec, Maya, and several Guatemalan languages. This differed little from the standard Spanish of the time, employing no new characters, but a few devices such as a doubled letter for a peculiar Inca consonant of *k* type.

Today many native Peruvian archaeologists and other writers are adopting a modified system of writing Quechua, at least as regards proper names, writing *k* and *w* in the English manner in place of Spanish *qu* and *hu*, and changing a few other sounds to give a closer approximation to the proper Quechua. Thus they are coming to write and print – in scientific publications at least – Keshwa for Quechua, Wira Kocha for Viracocha, Pisaj for Pisac, etc. Newly discovered or slightly known archaeological sites that have not become standardized in Spanish spelling are ordinarily known by only the more modern phonetic form, as Kenko, Wilka Wain, Kuntur Wasi.

Of course, linguistic studies of modern Quechua employ the phonetic alphabet of the linguists, which requires special characters in printing, but certain Peruvianists are using an orthography without special characters which gives a much closer approximation to the Quechua or Inca pronunciation. Logically it might have been better to employ this spelling in the native words used herein, but since the system is new and the words not standard, in general the traditional and standard Spanish spelling has been employed.

One such modified phonetic orthography was developed by Dr John H. Rowe and used in his classic article, 'Inca Culture at the Time of the Spanish Conquest'.[1] Further study of the Inca language at the time of the Conquest led him to modify this orthography somewhat, as explained in a later article.[2] He has graciously supplied revised phonetic forms for most of the Quechua-Inca words used in the Inca section of this book, which are given below.

Dr Rowe's modified phonetic form of Quechua orthography has met with almost universal approval. The Inter-American Indianist Congress of 1954 meeting in La Paz gave the system its formal recommendation, it is already widely used in Cuzco, and the Bolivian government is considering making it an official orthography.

ll represents a palatal *l* in both Colonial Spanish and Rowe's phoneticized orthography.

A glottal stop and glottalized stop consonants are frequent in Inca-Quechua. Ignored in standard orthography, they are represented phonetically by an apostrophe ('). All Inca-Quechua words apparently beginning with a vowel actually begin with a glottal stop.

Quechua has a velar (back throat) stop in addition to *k*. They were frequently undifferentiated in classic orthography, but *q* is used phonetically for the velar stop.

Stops (*p, t, k, q*) are found as both aspirated and unaspirated. In phonetic orthography the aspirated stops are represented by a following *h*, as *ph, th, kh, qh*. This applies also to the affricative *ch* and *chh*.

Glossary of Spanish and Quechua Words

(From Spanish)

Adobe	Sun-dried mud, generally as bricks
Altiplano	High plateau, specifically that of southern Peru and Bolivia, and the Lake Titicaca region
Balsa	Raft; in this region made of reeds
Cordillera	Major mountain range

1. Rowe, 1946.   2. Rowe, 1950.

Encomienda	Assignment of Indians to a landlord
Encomendero	Landlord of an *encomienda*
Hacienda	Plantation or landed estate
Hacendado	Owner of an *hacienda*
Llano	Plain, prairie
Maotaña	Forested foothills; specifically those at the eastern base of the Andes.
Páramo	High, wet grasslands
Sierra	Mountain range

(From Quechua)

Classic Form	*Phoneticized*	
Acllacuna	'akllakuna	'Chosen Women'
Alpaca	(Aymara word)	Domestic cameloid animal
Amauta	hamawt'a	Sage, wise man
Apachita	'apachita	Sacred offering, cairn
Aquilla	'akilla	Golden goblet
Ayllu	'ayllu	Social division, 'clan'
Çanca	zankhu	Sacred bread
Charqui	chharki	Dried, 'jerked' meat
Chasqui	chazki	Relay runner
Chicha	(not Quechua)	Fermented beverage, corn beer
Chullpa	ch'ullpa	Burial vault or tower
Chuñu	ch'uñu	Desiccated potatoes
Coca	kuka	Narcotic plant
Collahuaya	qollawaya	Class of native physicians
Coya	qoya	Queen
Curaca	kuraka	Subsidiary chief
Guaman	wamani	Province, political division
Guanaco	wanaku	Wild cameloid animal
Guano	wanu	Bird or bat excrement
Hauasipascuna	hawasipaskuna	'Left-out Girls'
Hihuaya	hiwaya	A form of punishment
Huaca	wak'a	Sacred place; archaeological site
Huaco	wako	(Sp.) Archaeological vessel
Huaquero	wakero	(Sp.) Native digger; treasure-hunter
Huauqui	wawqe	Supernatural Guardian; brother
Huayara	wayara	Fertility festival
Ichu	'ichhu	Coarse grass
Inca	Inka	Inca
Llama	llama	Domesticated cameloid animal

Classic Form	*Phoneticized*	
Llautu	llawt'u	Fillet, head-band
Macana	maqana	War club
Mamacuna	mamakuna	Mother Superior
Mita	mit'a	Tax-service
Mitima(es)	mitma	Compulsory colonist, settler
Napa	napa	White (albino) llama
Oca	oqa	Cultivated tuber (*oxalis*)
Pachaca	pachaka	Political unit of 100 families
Pampa	pampa	Low-level treeless or grassy plain
Pirca	pirqa	Masonry of undressed field stones
Pucara	pukara	Fortress
Puna	puna	High-level grassy plain
Puric	pureq	Able adult man, head of household
Quechua	K'ichuwa	Quechua
Quero	qeru	Wooden goblet
Quinua	kinuwa	Cultivated amaranth (*Chenopodium*)
Quipu	khipu	Knotted record
Quipucamayoc	khipu-kamayoq	Knot-record keeper
Saya	saya	Section of a province
Sinchi	zinchi	Chief, leader
Situa	Sithuwa	Curatice festival
Suyu	suyu	Quarter of empire
Taclla	taklla	Spade *or* foot-plough
Tambo	tampu	Inn, barracks
Tocco	t'oqo	Cave mouth, window
Topo	tupu	Shawl pin; standard of measurement
Totora	t'utura	Reed, rushes
Tumbaga	(not Quechua)	Gold-copper alloy
Vicuña	wik'uña	Fine-haired wild cameloid animal
Villac Umu	Willa-'uma	High Priest
Villca	willka	A narcotic (*Piptadenia*)
Yacarca	yaqarqa	Soothsayer, diviner
Yanacuna	yanakuna	Class of servants

DEITIES

Illapa	'Illap'a	Thunder
Inti	'Inti	Sun
Mamacocha	Mamaqocha	Mother Sea

APPENDIX

Classic Form	Phoneticized	
Mamaquilla	Mama Killa	Moon
Mama sara	Mama Zara	Mother Corn
Pachamama	Pachamama	Earth Mother
Viracocha	Wiraqocha	Creator

PERSONS

Ayar Auca	'Ayar 'Awqa	Brother of Manco Capac
Ayar Cachi	'Ayar Kachi	Brother of Manco Capac
Ayar Uchu	'Ayar 'Uchu	Brother of Manco Capac
Ayar Manco	'Ayar Manku	Manco Capac
Mama Ocllo	Mama 'Oqllu	Sister of Manco Capac
Mama Huaco	Mama Waqo ('jaw')	Sister of Manco Capac
Mama Cura	Mama Qora	Sister of Manco Capac
Mama Raua	Mama Rawa	Sister of Manco Capac
Manco Capac	Manku Qhapaq	Mythical founder of Inca empire
Sinchi Roca	Zinchi Roq'a	Son of Manco Capac

MONTHS

Capac Raimi	Qhapaq raymi	December
Camay	Kamay	January
Hatun Pucuy	Hatun poqoy	February
Paucar-Huara or Pacha-Pucuy	Pawqar waray or Pacha poqoy	March
Ayrihua	'Ayriwa	April
Hatun Cuzqui	'Aymuray or Hatun kuzki	May
Yntip Raimi	'Inti raymi	June
Chahuar Huarquiz	Chawawarkiz	July
Yapaquiz	Yapakiz	August
Coya Raimi	Sithuwa or Qoya raymi	September
Uma Raimi	K'antaray or 'Uma raymi	October
Ayamarca Raimi	'Ayamarka raymi	November

REGIONS AND PLACES

Chinchasuyu	Chinchay-suyu	North-east quarter of empire
Cuntisuyu	Kunti-suyu	West quarter of empire
Collasuyu	Qolla-suyu	Southern quarter of Empire
Antisuyu	'Anti-suyu	Eastern quarter of empire
Tahuantinsuyu	Tawantin-suyu	The Inca empire
Apurimac	'Apu-rimaq	Apurimac River

Classic Form	Phoneticized	
Rimac	Rimaq	Rimac River
Paccari Tampu	Paqari Tampu	'Origin *tambo*'
Tampu-Tocco	Tampu T'oqo	'Tambo Hole' (Mythical Inca place of origin)
Huanacauri		Sacred hill near Cuzco
Coricancha	Qori-kancha	Temple of Sun in Cuzco

KEY TO BIBLIOGRAPHY

The titles, etc., of the books indicated in the following classification can be found in the bibliography on pp. 287–324

(A) *General*

BIBLIOGRAPHIES

Basadre 1938a; Dorsey; Espejo Núñez Horkheimer 1947, 1950; Markham 1907; Means 1928; Medina; Richardson and Kidder; Rivet and Créqui-Montfort; Schwab; Tello 1927.

GEOGRAPHY, ENVIRONMENT, AND ECOLOGY

Bowman 1916; Gilmore; Monge 1948; Ogilvie; Sauer 1950a; Sievers; Troll.

PHYSICAL ANTHROPOLOGY

Boyd; Candela; Eaton 1916; Eickstedt; Gonzales; Hartweg; Hrdlička 1914; Imbelloni 1946b; MacCurdy; Monge; Newman; Quevedo; Steggerda; Stewart; Stewart and Newman.

LINGUISTICS

Basadre 1938b; Carrera; González Holguín; Markham 1864; Mason 1950; Medina; Middendorf; Rivet 1952; Rivet and Créqui-Montfort; Rowe 1950; Santo Tomás; Torres Rubio; Tschudi, 1853 1891.

CULTURE SEQUENCE

Bennett 1953b; Kidder 1956, Kidder *et al.* 1963, Lumbreras Means 1917b, 1918e; Steward 1948, 1949a, 1949d; Strong 1948; Willey 1953b.

ABSOLUTE AND RADIOCARBON DATING

Bird 1951; Johnson, Frederick; Johnson, Rainey, Collier, and Flint; Kubler 1948; Libby; Rowe 1945, 1948b; Wauchope.

(B) *Pre-Inca Culture*

ANCIENT MAN IN AMERICA

Ameghino; Aveleyra Arroyo de Anda and Maldonado-Koerdell; Bird 1938, 1965; Créqui-Montfort and Rivet; Gamarra Dulanto; Hrdlička 1917; Hrdlička *et al.*; Lütken; Jennings and Norbeck; Krieger; Lanning and Hammel; Macgowan; McCown 1950, 1952; Rivet 1908; Sellards; Sullivan and Hellman; Ten Kate; Uhle 1928; Walter *et al.* Wormington.

THE ANCIENT CIVILIZATIONS OF PERU

OLD-WORLD CONTACTS

Carter; Dixon; Ekholm 1965; Estrada and Meggers Gladwin; Heine-Geldern; Heyerdahl; Hutchinson, Silow, and Stephen; Imbelloni 1934; Meggers and Evans; Meggers, Evans and Estrada; Perry; Rivet 1926; Schmidt, Wilhelm; Smith; Sullivan and Hellman.

AGRICULTURAL AND PASTORAL ORIGINS

Cook 1937; Cutler, Kelley and Bonavia; Mangelsdorf; Mangelsdorf and Reeves; Mangelsdorf and Smith Means 1918c; Sauer 1936, 1950b, 1952; Stonor and Anderson; Towle; Yacovleff and Herrera.

TRAVEL AND EXPLORATION

Bingham 1913, 1922; Bollaert; Castelnau; Enock 1907, 1912; Humboldt; Hutchinson 1873; Johnson, George R.; Kosok, 1964; Langlois 1935–6; Mason 1926a, 1952; Means 1918a; Middendorf 1893–5; Nordenskiöld 1906; Orbigny; Raimondi 1874–1913; Seler 1912; Squier 1877; Tschudi 1847, 1869; Uhle 1906c, 1906d; Wiener; Rowe 1954.

PREHISTORIC CULTURE: GENERAL

Baessler 1906b; Bastian; Bennett 1946a, 1946b; Bennett and Bird; Bird 1962; Buse; Bushnell; Canals Frau; Fuhrmann; Hewett; Horkheimer 1950a, 1950b; Joyce 1912; Kidder 1964; Lothrop *et al.* 1961; Markham 1892; Mead 1924; Means 1919a, 1931; Nordenskiöld 1946; Rivero and Tschudi; Rowe 1958, 1963; Seler 1893; Steward 1949c; Steward (Editor); Tello 1921, 1929, 1942; Thompson; Trimborn 1936; Tschudi 1891; Uhle 1910, 1926, 1935, 1939; Urteaga 1909; Valcárcel 1943–9, 1953; Von Hagen 1965; Wiesse.

ARCHAEOLOGY, GENERAL

Bennett 1945, 1948a; Bennett (Editor); Coe; Hrdlička 1911; Hutchinson 1874; Kauffmann Doig 1963a, 1965; Kidder 1942, 1956; Kroeber 1926c, 1927, 1944, 1948; Newman 1948; Nordenskiöld 1931a; Strong 1943; Uhle 1906a, 1920b; Von Hagen 1949b; Willey 1945, 1948, 1951a.

NORTH COAST

Antze; Bennett 1939, 1950; Bird 1948a, 1948b; Brown; Carrera; Collier; Ford; Ford and Willey; Harcourt 1928a, 1928b; Harth-Terré; Holstein; Horkheimer 1944; Joyce 1913a, 1913b, 1921, 1922; Kelly; Kroeber 1925a, 1926a, 1930; Kroeber and Muelle; Kutscher; Larco Herrera; Larco Hoyle 1938–9, 1941, 1942, 1943, 1944, 1945a, 1945b, 1945c, 1945d, 1946, 1948, 1965; Lilien; Lothrop 1941, 1948, 1951a, 1954; Mason 1926b, 1930; Middendorf 1892; Muelle 1936; O'Neale 1946; Posnansky 1925; Raimondi 1903; Rowe 1942, 1948b, 1948c; Schaedel 1949, 1915b, 1951c; Strong and Evans; Tello 1938, 1956; Towle 1952a; Uhle 1913a, 1920a; Von Hagen 1965; Wardle 1940; Whitaker and Bird; Willey 1947, 1953a.

KEY TO BIBLIOGRAPHY

CENTRAL COAST

Gayton; Harcourt 1922; Jijón y Caamaño 1949; Kroeber 1925b, 1926b, 1954; Lanning 1963; Lothrop 1950; Lothrop and Mahler 1957a; Muelle 1935; Patterson and Lanning Reiss and Stübel; Strong 1925; Strong and Corbett; Strong and Willey; Strong, Willey, and Corbett; Stumer; Tabio 1965; Tello and Miranda; Uhle 1903, 1908a, 1913c; Víllar Córdova 1935; Wallace; Willey 1943a, 1943b; Willey and Corbett.

SOUTH COAST

Berthon; Cañas; Carrión Cachot 1931, 1949; Doering 1927; Donnan; Engel; Gayton and Kroeber; González de la Rosa 1908; Kosok and Reiche; Kroeber 1937, 1953; Kroeber and Strong; Larrabure and Unánue; Levillier, Jean; Lothrop and Mahler 1957b; Mason 1932; Menzel; O'Neale 1932, 1935, 1936, 1937, 1942; Putman; Reiche; Root 1949a; Sawyer; Seler 1923; Squier; Stafford; Strong 1957; Tello 1917, 1928, 1959, Uhle 1913b, 1917b, 1919a, 1919b, 1922, 1924a, 1924b, 1924c, 1924d; Wardle 1939; Wendt, Kroeber, 1956; Soldi; Volcarcel 1932; Wallace 1962; Yacovleff 1931; Yacovleff and Muelle.

NORTHERN HIGHLANDS

Bandelier 1907; Bennett 1942, 1943, 1944; Casdich; Casafranca, Engel 1956; Enock 1905; Espejo Núñez; Ishida *et al.*; Izami and Sohol; Kauffmann Doig 1963b; Kinzl; Kroeber 1953; Langlois; Lathrap; Markham 1910b; McCown 1945; Polo; Raimondi; Reichlen; Schaedel 1948b, 1948c; Tello 1923, 1930, 1943, 1961; Willey 1951b.

CENTRAL HIGHLANDS

Bennett 1953a; Bingham 1911, 1912a, 1912b, 1913, 1914, 1915a, 1915b, 1916, 1922, 1930, 1948; Bonavia; Bowman 1912; Collier 1962a; Fejos; Flores Espinoza Franco Inojosa; Franco Inojosa and González; Kubler 1952; Pardo; Rowe 1944; Rowe, Collier, and Willey; Saville 1926; Tschopik, Harry; Uhle 1920c; Valcárcel 1924, 1933, 1934-5, 1939; 1946; Víllar Córdova 1923; Von Hagen 1949a; 1952a.

SOUTHERN HIGHLANDS

Ballivián; Bandelier 1905, 1910, 1911; Bennett 1934, 1936, 1948b; Casanova; Créqui-Montfort; Fung de Lanning; González de la Rosa 1910; Kidder II; Lothrop 1937; Markham 1910b; Means 1918f; Menghin; Menghin and Schroeder; Nestler; Ponce Sanginés; Posnansky 1911a, 1911b, 1913, 1914, 1946; Rowe 1956; Rydén; Schaedel 1948a; Stübel and Uhle; Tschopik, Harry, 1950; Tschopik, Marion; Uhle 1898; Valcárcel 1935.

THE ANCIENT CIVILIZATIONS OF PERU

(c) *The Inca and Their Culture*

(See also 'Sources')

GENERAL

Bingham 1917; Brindage; Hanstein; Hewett; Joyce 1912; Karsten; Krickeberg; Markham 1856, 1873, 1910a; Mead 1924; Means 1931, 1938; Murdock; Nordenskiöld 1925–7; Rowe 1946, 1948a; Tello 1937; Urteaga 1931; Verger; Von Hagen 1957.

HISTORICAL

Buchwald; Helps; Imbelloni 1946a; Kubler 1946; Lothrop 1938; Markham 1871; Means 1918b; 1932; Michkin; Nordenskiöld 1917; Prescott; Rowe 1945; Uhle 1912.

ECONOMIC LIFE, FOOD-QUEST, COSTUME, LIFE CYCLE

Baudin 1927b, 1929, 1942, 1958; Carrión Cachot 1923, 1931; Cook 1938; Eaton 1925; Harshberger; Kosok 1940–3; Montell; Torres-Luna; Uhle 1907b; Weberbauer; Yacovleff and Herrera.

ARCHITECTURE, ENGINEERING, TRANSPORTATION

Bennett 1949a; Kosok 1942; Lothrop 1932; Means 1942; Oyague y Calderón; Regal; Von Hagen 1952b.

POLITICAL AND SOCIAL ORGANIZATION

Antonio; Baudin 1927a, 1928; Belaúnde; Castaing; Cosio; Cúneo Vidal; Cunow; Eguiguren; Falcón; Joyce 1913b; Kirchhoff; Latcham; Means 1925a; Minnaert; Saavedra; Trimborn 1923–4; Tudela y Varela; Valdez de la Torre; Zurkalowski.

CRIME AND SIN

Minnaert; Trimborn 1925, 1927; Urteaga.

WAR, CONQUEST, AND COLONIZATION; WEAPONS

Bram; García y Merino; Harcourt 1928b; Means 1919c; Uhle 1907a, 1909, 1917a.

RELIGION

Ávila; Jijón y Caamaño; Lehmann-Nitsche; Métraux; Mortimer; Polo de Ondegardo 1916a, 1917a.

MEDICAL PRACTICES, SURGERY, TREPHINING

Ackerknecht (large bibliography); Lastres *et al.*; Moodie; Muñiz and McGee; Nordenskiöld 1907; Quevedo 1943; Tello 1912; Wrigley.

RECORDING, QUIPU, STANDARDS

Altieri; Bennett 1949b, 1949c; Cipriani; Guimaraes; Kreichgauer; Larco Hoyle 1942, 1943; Locke; Nordenskiöld 1921b, 1925a, 1925b, 1930; Saville 1925; Uhle 1897, 1908b; Wassém 1931, 1940.

284

LITERATURE AND MUSIC

Basadre; Garcés Bedregal; Harcourt, Raoul and Marie 1925; Izi-kowitz; Mason 1932; Mead 1903; Middendorf 1891; Mitré.

(D) *Arts and Crafts*

ART

Baessler 1902–3, 1928; Bennett 1954; Bird 1962, 1963; Dusselhoff and Linne; Doering 1936, 1952; Greslebin; Hamy; Kelemen; Kroeber 1949; Kubler 1962; Larrea; Lehmann and Doering; Mason 1931; Mead 1906, 1909, 1916a, 1917; Means 1917a, 1918d, 1921a, 1921b; Muelle and Blas; Museum of Modern Art; Posnansky 1913; Rubin de la Borbolla; Sanyen, King; Schmidt, Max; Tello 1918, 1938; Uhle 1889; Yacovleff 1932.

TECHNOLOGY: GENERAL

Bailey; Bennett and Bird 1949; Uhle, 1889–90.

TEXTILES AND WEAVING

Barnett 1909, 1910; Benners; Bird 1947, 1961; Bird and Bellinger; Crawford; Fester; Frödin and Nordenskiöld; Harcourt 1934; Harcourt, Raoul and Marie 1924b; Holmes; Joyce 1921, 1922; King; Levillier, Jean; Mead 1906, 1916b, Means 1925b, 1927, 1930a, 1930b; O'Neale; O'Neale and Clark; O'Neale and Kroeber; Osborne; Schmidt, Max 1910, 1911; Singer; Stafford; Valette; Van Stan; Wardle 1936, 1939, 1944, 1949; Yacovleff and Muelle 1934; Zimmern.

CERAMICS

Bingham 1915b; Doering 1927; Gayton and Kroeber; Harcourt 1922; Harcourt, Raoul and Marie 1924a; Joyce 1913b; Kelly; Kroeber 1925a, 1925b, 1926a, 1926b; Kroeber and Muelle; Kroeber and Strong 1924b; Lastres *et al.*; Lilien; Linné; Mason 1926b, 1932; Menzel; Posnansky 1925; Putnam; Rowe 1942; Rowe and Dawson; Sawyer; Saville 1926; Seler 1923; Strong 1925; Strong and Corbett; Valcárcel 1935; Wardle 1940; Wassermann-San Blas; Willey 1943b, 1949.

METALLURGY

Antze; Baessler 1906a; Bergsøe; Caley and Easby; Easby; Farabee; Harcourt 1928a; Heine-Geldern; Joyce 1913a; Lothrop 1937, 1941, 1950, 1951a, 1951b, 1954; Mason 1930, 1933; Mathewson; Mead 1915; Nordenskiöld 1921a; Orchard; Rivet 1924; Rivet and Arsandaux; Root; Saville 1921; Valcárcel 1930.

WOOD, STONE, FEATHERS, AND MISCELLANEOUS

Lavachery; Mason 1935; Mead 1907; Nordenskiöld 1931b; Rowe 1961; Schaede 1951a; Tello 1918; Uhle 1898, 1906b; Wardle 1948; Yacovleff.

SOURCES

Acosta; Anonymous Conqueror; Arriaga; Avendaño; Ávila; Betanzos; Cabello de Balboa; Cabral; Calancha; Castro and Ortega Morejón; Cieza de León; Cobo; Estete; Garcilaso de la Vega; Gutiérrez de Santa Clara; Jiménez de la Espada; Las Casas; Levillier, Roberto; Markham 1872, 1873; Means 1928; Molina of Cuzco; Molina of Santiago; Montesinos; Morúa; Ocampo; Oviedo y Valdés; Pachacuti-Yamqui Salcamayhua; Pizarro, Hernando; Pizarro, Pedro; Polo de Ondegardo; Poma de Ayala; Quipucamayocs; Ramos Gavilán; Relaciones Geográficas; Román y Zamora; Sancho de la Hoz; Santillán; Sarmiento de Gamboa; Tello 1939; Tito Cusi Yupanqui; Toledo; Valera; Vargas Ugarte; Vega Toral; Xérez; Zarate.

BIBLIOGRAPHY

For subject classification see Key, pp. 281–6

ACKERKNECHT, Erwin H. (1949). 'Medical Practices'. *In* Steward (Editor) 1949, pp. 621–43.

ACOSTA, Father José de (1880). *The Natural and Moral History of the Indies.* Edited by Clements R. Markham. 2 vols, nos 60, 61, Hakluyt Society, London.

(1940). *Historia natural y moral de las Indias.* Mexico.

ALTIERI, Radamés A. (1941). 'Sobre 11 antiguos Kipu peruanos', *Revista del Instituto Antropológico de la Universidad Nacional de Tucumán,* 2, 8, pp. 177–211.

AMEGHINO, Florentino (1880). *La antigüedad del hombre en el Plata,* vol. 1. Paris.

Anonymous Conqueror (1929). *The Conquest of Peru as related by a Member of the Pizarro Expedition.* New York Public Library (facsimile reproduction of the edition of 1534).

ANTONIO, Fray (1920). *Discurso sobre la descendencia y gobierno de los Incas.* Colección de Libros y Documentos referentes a la historia del Perú, Ser. 2, vol. 3, pp. 1–53.

ANTZE, Gustav (1930). 'Metallarbeiten aud dem nördlichen Peru. Ein Beitrag zur Kenntnis ihrer Formen', *Mitteilungen aus dem Museum für Völkerkunde in Hamburg,* vol. 15, pp. 1–63. Hamburg.

ARRIAGA, Pablo José de (1920) (1621). *Extirpación de la idolatría del Perú.* Col. Libs. Docs. refs. hist. Perú. Lima.

AVELEYRA ARROYO DE ANDA, Luis, and Manuel MALDONADO-KOERDELL (1952). 'Asociación de artefactos con mamut en el pleistoceno superior de la cuenca de México', *Revista Mexicana de Estudios Antropológicos,* 13, 1, pp. 3–29. Mexico.

AVENDAÑO, Hernando de (1648). *Sermones de los misterios de nuestra Santa Fe Católica, en lengua Castellana, y la general del Inca.* Lima.

ÁVILA, Father Francisco de (1873). 'A Narrative of the Errors, False Gods, and other Superstitions and Diabolical Rites in which the Indians of Huarochiri lived in Ancient Times.' Translated and edited by Clements R. Markham in *Rites and Laws of the Yncas,* pp. 122–47. Hakluyt Society, London.

(1939). 'Dämonen und Zauber im Inkareich, aus dem Khetschua übersetzt und eingeleitet von Dr. Hermann Trimborn', *Quellen und Forschungen. Geschichte der Geographie und Völkerkunde,* vol. 4. Leipzig.

AYRES, F. D. (1961). 'Rubbings from Chavín de Huántar, Peru', *American Antiquity,* vol. 27, pp. 238–45.

BAESSLER, Arthur (1902–3). *Ancient Peruvian Art.* 4 vols, Berlin and New York.

(1906a). *Altperuanische Metallgeräte.* Berlin.

(1906b). *Peruanische Mumien*. Berlin.

(1928). *L'Art précolombien*. Paris.

BAILEY, Truman (n.d.). *The Manual Industries of Peru*. Museum of Modern Art, New York.

BALLIVIAN, Manuel Vicente (1910). *Monumentos prehistóricos de Tiahuanaco*. La Paz.

BANDELIER, Adolf Francis (1905). 'The Aboriginal Ruins of Sillustani, Peru', *American Anthropologist*, VII, pp. 49–68.

(1907). *The Indians and Aboriginal Ruins near Chachapoyas, Northern Peru*. New York.

(1910). *The Islands of Titicaca and Koati*. New York.

(1911). 'The Ruins at Tiahuanaco', *American Antiquarian Society Proceedings*, XXI, pp. 218–65.

BARNETT, Anna (1909). 'Étude technologique d'un tissu péruvien', *Journal de la Société des Américanistes*, VI, pp. 265–8.

(1910). 'Étude sur la mode de fabrication des frondes péruvíennes antiques', *ibid.*, VII, pp. 117–20.

BASALRE, Jorge (1938a). *Bibliografía de la literatura quechua*. Biblioteca de Cultura Peruana, vol. 1. Paris.

(1938b). *Literatura inca (Selección de . . .)*. Biblioteca de Cultura Peruana, Primera Serie, no. 1. Paris.

BASTIAN, Adolf (1878–89). *Die Culturländer des alten America*. 3 vols., Berlin.

BAUDIN, Louis (1927a). 'Une Expérience socialiste: le Pérou des Inka', *Journal des Économistes*, LXXXVII, pp. 506–19. Paris.

(1927b). 'La Formation de l'élite et l'enseignement de l'histoire dans l'empire des Inka', *Rev. des Études Historiques*, 93rd year, pp. 107–114. Paris.

(1928). *L'Empire socialiste des Inka*. Institut d'Ethnologie, Travaux et Mémoires, vol. 5. Paris.

(1929). 'L'Organisation économique de l'empire des Incas', *Rev. de l'Amérique Latine*, XVII, pp. 385–93. Paris.

(1942). *La actualidad del sistema económico de los Incas*. Congreso Internacional de Americanistas, 27, Lima, vol. 2, pp. 175–87.

(1958). *La vida cotidiana en el tiempo do los últimos Incas*. Lima.

BELAÚNDE, Victor Andrés (1908). *El Perú antiguo y los modernos sociólogos*. Lima.

BENNERS, Ethel Ellis (1920). 'Ancient Peruvian Textiles', *Museum Journal*, University Museum, University of Pennsylvania, vol. 11, no. 3, pp. 140–7.

BENNETT, Wendell C. (1934). *Excavations at Tiahuanaco*, Anthropological Papers, American Museum of Natural History, vol. 34, pp. 359–494. New York.

(1936). *Excavations in Bolivia*, *ibid.*, vol. 35, pp. 329–507. New York.

(1939). *Archaeology of the North Coast of Peru*, *ibid.*, vol. 37, pp. 1–153. New York.

(1942). *Chavín Stone Carving.* Yale Anthropological Studies, vol. 3. New Haven, Connecticut.

(1943). 'The Position of Chavín in Andean Sequences', *Proceedings of the American Philosophical Society*, vol. 86, no. 2, pp. 323–7. Philadelphia.

(1944). *The North Highlands of Peru*, Anthropological Papers, American Museum of Natural History, vol. 39, pt 1. New York.

(1945). 'Interpretations of Andean Archeology', *Transactions of the New York Academy of Sciences*, Ser. 2, vol. 7, pp. 95–9. New York.

(1946a). 'The Andean Highlands: An Introduction'. *In* Steward (Editor) (1946), pp. 1–60.

(1946b). 'The Archeology of the Central Andes'. *Ibid.*, pp. 61–147.

(1948a). 'The Peruvian Co-tradition'. *In* Bennett (Editor) (1948), pp. 1–7.

(1948b). 'A Revised Sequence for the South Titicaca Basin'. *Ibid.*, pp. 90–2.

(1949a). 'Architecture and Engineering'. *In* Steward (Editor) (1949), p. 1–65.

(1949b). 'Numbers, Measures, Weights and Calendars'. *Ibid.*, pp. 601–10.

(1949c). 'Mnemonic and Recording Devices'. *Ibid.*, pp. 611–19.

(1950). *The Gallinazo Group, Virú Valley, Peru.* Yale University Publications in Anthropology, 43. New Haven.

(1953a). *Excavations at Wari, Ayacucho, Peru. Ibid.*, 49. New Haven.

(1953b). 'New World Culture History: South America'. In *Anthropology Today*, pp. 211–25. Chicago.

(1954). *Ancient Arts of the Andes.* Museum of Modern Art. New York.

BENNETT, Wendell C. (Editor) (1948). *A Reappraisal of Peruvian Archaeology.* Memoir 4, Society for American Archaeology. Menasha.

BENNETT, Wendel C., and Junius B. BIRD (1960 Revised edition). *Andean Culture History.* Handbook Series No. 15, American Museum of Natural History. New York.

BERGSØE, Paul (1937). *The Metallurgy and Technology of Gold and Platinum among the pre-Columbian Indians.* A, *Ingeniørvidenskabeliege Skrifter*, A, no. 44. Copenhagen.

(1938). *The Gilding Process and the Metallurgy of Copper and Lead among the pre-Columbian Indians. Ibid.*, no. 46. Copenhagen.

BERTHON, Paul (1911). *Étude sur le précolombien du Bas-Pérou.* Nouvelles archives des missions scientifiques, fascicule 4. Paris.

BETANZOS, Juan de (1880). *Suma y narración de los Incas.* Ed. Marcos Jiménez de la Espada. Biblioteca Hispano-Ultramarina, vol. 5. Madrid.

BINGHAM, Hiram (1911). 'The Ruins of Choqquequirau'. *American Anthropologist*, XII, pp. 505–25.

(1912a). 'Vitcos, the last Inca Capital', *American Antiquarian Society Proceedings*, XXII, pp. 135–96.

(1912b). 'The Discovery of Pre-historic Human Remains near Cuzco, Peru', *American Journal of Science*, XXXIII, pp. 297–305.

(1913). 'In the Wonderland of Peru', *National Geographic Magazine*, vol. 24, no. 4, pp. 387–573. Washington, D.C.

(1914). 'The Ruins of Espíritu Pampa, Peru', *American Anthropologist*, XVI, pp. 185–99.

(1915a). 'The Story of Machu Picchu', *National Geographic Magazine*, February 1915. Washington.

(1915b). 'Types of Machu Picchu Pottery', *American Anthropologist*, XVII, pp. 251–271.

(1916). 'Further Explorations in the Land of the Incas', *National Geographic Magazine*, May 1916. Washington.

(1917). *The Inca Peoples and their Culture*. International Congress of Americanists XIX, pp. 253–60. Washington.

(1922). *Inca Land*. Boston.

(1930). *Machu Picchu, a Citadel of the Inca*. New Haven.

(1948). *Lost City of the Incas*. New York.

BIRD, Junius B. (1938). 'Antiquity and Migrations of the Early Inhabitants of Patagonia', *Geographical Review*, 38, 2, pp. 250–75.

(1947). 'A Pre-Spanish Peruvian Ikat', *Bulletin, Needle and Bobbin Club*, vol. 31, nos. 1 & 2, pp. 73–7. New York.

(1948a). 'Preceramic Cultures in Chicama and Virú'. *In* Bennett (Editor) (1948), pp. 21–8.

(1948b). 'America's Oldest Farmers', *Natural History*, 57, 7, pp. 296–303, 334, 335. New York, 1948.

(1951). 'South American Radiocarbon Dates'. *In* Johnson (Editor) (1951), pp. 37–49.

(1961). 'Textile Designing and Samplers in Peru'. *In* Lothrop and others, pp. 299–316.

(1962). 'Art and Life in Ancient Peru', *Curator*, 2, pp. 145–209. New York.

(1963). 'Pre-ceramic Art from Huaca Prieta, Chicama Valley', *Nawpa Pacha* I, pp. 29–34. Berkeley.

(1965). 'The Concept of a "Pre-Projectile Point" Cultural Stage in Chile and Peru', *American Antiquity*, vol. 31, no. 2, pp. 262–70.

BIRD, Junius B., and Louisa BELLINGER (1954). *Paracas Fabrics and Nazca Needlework*. Washington.

BOLLAERT, William (1860). *Antiquarian, Ethnological, and Other Researches in New Granada, Ecuador, Peru, and Chili, with Observations on the Pre-Incarial, Incarial, and Other Monuments of Peruvian Nations*. London.

BONAVIA, Duccio (1964). *Investigaciones en la Ceja de Selva de Ayacucho*. Museo Nacional de Antropología y Arqueología. Lima.

BOWMAN, Isaiah (1912). 'A Buried Wall at Cuzco and its Relation to the Question of a Pre-Inca Race', *American Journal of Science*, XXXIV, pp. 497–509.

(1916). *The Andes of Southern Peru*. New York.

BIBLIOGRAPHY

BOYD, William C. (1950). 'Blood Groups of South American Indians. *In* Steward (Editor) (1950), pp. 91–5.

BRAM, Joseph (1941). *An Analysis of Inca Militarism.* Monographs of the American Ethnological Society, No. 4. New York.

BROWN, C. Barrington (1926). 'On Stone Implements from North-West Peru', *Man*, vol. 26, pp. 97–101. London.

BRUNDAGE, Burr C. (1963). *Empire of the Inca.* Norman, Oklahoma.

BUCHWALD, Otto von (1919). 'Los primeros Incas', *Boletín de la Sociedad Ecuatoriana de Estudios Históricos Americanos*, VII, pp. 115–121.

BUSE, H. (1962). *Peru 10,000 Años.* Lima.

BUSHNELL, G. H. S. (1949). 'Ancient Peoples of the Andes', *Science News*, no. 13, pp. 58–86. Penguin Books, Harmondsworth.

(1956). *Peru.* London.

CABELLO DE BALBOA, Miguel (1840). 'Histoire du Pérou'. Translated and edited by H. Ternaux-Compans, in *Voyages, relations, et mémoires originaux pour servir a l'histoire de la découverte de l'Amérique.* Paris.

CABRAL, Jorge (1913). *Los cronistas é historiadores de Indias y el problema de las dinastías de la monarquía peruana.* Buenos Aires.

CALANCHA, Antonio de la (1638). *Corónica moralizada del orden de San Agustín en el Perú, con sucesos egemplares en esta monarquía.* Barcelona.

CALEY, Earle R., and Dudley T. EASBY, Jr. (1959). 'The Smelting of Sulfide Ores of Copper in Pre-Conquest Peru', *American Antiquity*, vol. 25, no. 1, pp. 59–65.

CANALS FRAU, Salvador (1950). *Prehistoria de América.* Buenos Aires.

CAÑAS, Francisco (1854). *Exploración de las islas de Chincha con tres planos.* Lima.

CANDELA, P. B. (1943). 'Blood Group Tests on Tissues of Paracas Mummies', *American Journal of Physical Anthropology*, vol. 1, pp. 65–7 Philadelphia.

CARDICH, M. Agusto (1959). 'Los yacimientos de Lauricocha, Perú', *Revista del Centro Argentino de Estudios Prehistóricos.* Buenos Aires.

(1960). 'Investigaciones prehistóricas en los Andes peruanos'. *In* Matos Mendieta (Editor), pp. 89–118.

(1964). 'Lauricocha. Fundamentos para una prehistoria de los Andes Centrales', *Studia Prehistórica* III. Centro Argentino de Estudios Prehistóricos. Buenos Aires.

CARRERA FERNANDO DE LA (1939). *Arte de la lengua yunga* (1644). Publicaciones Especiales del Instituto de Antropología de la Universidad Nacional de Tucumán, no. 3. Tucumán, Argentina.

CARRIÓN CACHOT, Rebeca (1923). 'La mujer y el niño en el antiguo Perú, *Inca*, I, pp. 329–54.

(1931). 'La indumentaria en la antigua cultura de Paracas', *Wira Kocha*, vol. 1, no. 1, pp. 37–86. Lima.

(1948). 'La Cultura Chavín', *Revista Museo Nacional de Antropología y Arqueología*, vol. 2, pp. 99–172. Lima.

(1949). *Paracas, Cultural Elements*. Corporación Nacional de Turismo. Lima, Perú.

CARTER, George F. (1950). 'Plant Evidence for Early Contacts with America', *Southwestern Journal of Anthropology*, 6, 2, 161–82. Albuquerque.

(1953). 'Plants across the Pacific'. *In* 'Asia and North America; Transpacific Contacts', Memoir 9, Society for American Archaeology, pp. 62–71.

CASAFRANCA, José (1960). 'Los nuevos sitios arqueológicos Chavinoides en el Departamento de Ayacucho'. *In* Matos Mendieta (Editor), pp. 325–33.

CASANOVA, Eduardo (1942). 'Los yacimientos arqueológicos en la península de Copacabana', *Anales del Museo Argentino de Ciencias Naturales 'Bernardino Rivadavia'*, vol. 40, pp. 333–99.

CASTAING, Alphonse (1884). *Le Communisme au Pérou*. Paris.

CASTELNAU, Francis de (1852). *Expédition dans les parties centrales de l'Amérique du Sud. Troisième partie: Antiquités des Incas et autres peuples anciens*. Paris.

CASTRO, Cristóbal de, and Diego Ortega MOREJÓN (1936). *Relación y declaración del modo que este valle de Chincha y sus comarcanos se governavan . . . etc.* (1558). 'Quellen zur Kulturgeschichte des präkolumbischen Amerika', *Studien zur Kulturkunde*, vol. 3. Stuttgart.

CIEZA DE LEÓN, Pedro de (1554). *Parte primera de la chrónica del Perú, que tracta de la demarcación . . . etc.* Antwerp.

(1864). *The travels of Pedro de Cieza de León. A.D.* 1532-1550 (contained in the first part of his chronicle of Perú). Hakluyt Society, no. 33. London.

(1880). *Sefunda parte de la crónica del Perú, que trata del señorío de los Incas Yupanquis . . . etc.* Biblioteca Hispano-Ultramarina, vol. 5. Madrid.

(1883). *The Second Part of the Chronicle of Peru*. Translated and edited by Clements R. Markham. No. 68, Hakluyt Society, London.

(1932). *Parte primera de la crónica del Perú*. Edición Espasa-Calpe, Madrid. (Also many other editions.)

CIPRIANI, Lidio (1928). *Su due 'quipus' del Museo Nazionale di Antropologia e Etnologia di Firenze*. International Congress of Americanists, XXII, pt 1, pp. 471–80. Rome.

COBO, Bernabé (1890–5). *Historia del Nuevo Mundo*. Ed. Marcos Jiménez de la Espada. 4 vols, Sociedad de bibliófilos andaluces, Seville.

COE, Michael D. (1960). 'Archaeological Linkages with North and South America at La Victoria, Guatemala', *American Anthropologist*, vol. 62 pp. 363–93.

(1962). 'An Olmec Design on an Early Peruvian Vessel', *American Antiquity*, vol. 27, pp. 579–80.

COLLIER, Donald (1955). 'Cultural Chronology and Change as Reflected in the Ceramics of the Virú Valley, Peru'. *Fieldiana: Anthropology*, vol. 43. Chicago Natural History Museum, Chicago.

(1961). 'Agriculture and Civilization on the Coast of Peru'. *In The Evolution of Horticultural Systems in Native South America*, pp. 101–9. Sociedad de Ciencias Naturales La Salle, Caracas.

(1962a). 'The Central Andes', *Viking Fund Publications in Anthropology*, no. 32, pp. 165–76. New York.

(1962b). 'Archaeological Investigations in the Casma Valley', *Akten des 34 International Amerikanistenkongressen, Wien*, 1960, pp. 411–17, Vienna.

COOK, O. F. (1937). *El Perú como centro de domesticación de plantas y animales*. Imprenta del Museo Nacional, Lima.

(1938). *Campos de cultivo en andenería de los antiguos peruanos*. Translated by Federico Ponce de León. Cuzco.

COSIO, Felix (1916). *La propiedad colectiva del ayllu*. Cuzco.

CRAWFORD, M. D. C. (1915). *Peruvian Textiles*. Anthropological Papers of the American Museum of Natural History, 12, 3, pp. 52–104. New York.

(1916a). *Peruvian Fabrics. Ibid.*, 12, 4, pp. 105–91. New York.

(1916b). *The Cotton of Ancient Peru*. Boston.

(1916c). 'The Loom in the New World', American Museum of Natural History, *Journal*, XVI, pp. 381–6.

CRÉQUI-MONTFORT, Count G. de (1906a). *Fouilles de la mission scientifique française à Tiahuanaco*. International Congress of Americanists XIV, pt 2, pp. 531–51. Stuttgart.

(1906b). Fouilles dans la nécropole de Calama. *Ibid.*, pp. 551–67.

CRÉQUI-MONTFORT, Count G. de and Paul RIVET (1914a). 'L'Origine des aborigènes de Pérou et de la Bolivie', *Comptes-rendus des séances de l'Académie des Inscriptions et Belles-Lettres*, 1914, pp. 196–202. Paris.

(1914b). *L'Origine des aborigènes des hauts plateaux boliviens et péruviens*. Institut français d'anthropologie, II, p. 39.

CÚNEO VIDAL, Rómulo (1914). 'Del concepto del "Ayllu"', *Boletín de la Sociedad Geográfica de Lima*, XXX, pp. 4–9.

CUNOW, Heinrich (1896). *Diesoziale Verfassung des Inkareichs*. Stuttgart.

(1898. *Die soziale Verfassung des Inkareichs*. Brunswick.

(1930). *El sistema de parentesco peruano y las communidades gentilicias de los Incas*. Translated by María Woitscheck. Paris.

CUTLER, Hugh C. (1946). 'Races of Maize in South America', *Botanical Museum Leaflets*, vol. 12, no. 8, pp. 257–91. Harvard University, Cambridge, Mass.

DISSELHOFF, H. D., and S. LINNE (1961). *The Art of Ancient America; Civilizations of Central and South America*. New York.

DIXON, Roland B. (1933). 'Contacts with America across the Southern Pacific'. *In* Diamond Jenness, *The American Aborigines; their Origin and Antiquity, pp.* 313–53. Toronto.

DOERING, Heinrich Ubbelohde (1926). 'Tonplastik aus Nazca', *Ipek*, vol. 3, pp. 167–76.

(1936). *Old Peruvian Art*. London.

(1952). *The Art of Ancient Peru*. New York.

(1959). 'Bericht über Archäologische Feldarbeiten in Peru, II', *Ethnos*, nos. 1–2. Stockholm.

DONNAN, Christopher B. (1964). 'An Early House from Chilca, Peru', *American Antiquity*, vol. 30, no. 2, pp. 137–44.

DORSEY, George A. (1898). *A Bibliography of the Anthropology of Peru*. Field Museum of Natural History, Anthropological Series, vol. 2, no. 2. Chicago.

EASBY, Dudley T., Jr. (1955a). 'Los vasos retratos de metal del Perú: Cómo fueron elaborados?', *Revista del Museo Nacional*, vol. 24, pp. 137–53. Lima.

(1955b). 'Sahagún y los orfebres precolombinos de México', *Abales del Instituto de Antropología y Historia*, vol. 9, pp. 85–177. Mexico.

(1956a) 'Ancient American Goldsmiths', *Natural History*, vol. 65, no. 8, pp. 401–9. New York.

(1956b). 'Orfebrería y orfebres precolombinos', *Anales del Instituto de Arte Americano*, vol. 9, pp. 9–26. Buenos Aires.

(1966). 'Early Metallurgy in the New World', *Scientific American*, vol. 214, no. 4, pp. 72–8, 81.

EATON, George F. (1916). *The Collection of Osteological Material from Machu Picchu*. Memoirs, Connecticut Academy of Arts and Sciences, vol. 5. New Haven.

(1925). *Food Animals of the Peruvian Highlands*. International Congress of Americanists, XXI, pt 2, pp. 61–6. Göteborg.

EGUIGUREN, Luís A. (1914). *El ayllu peruano y su condición legal*. Lima.

EICKSTEDT, Egon F. von (1934). *Rassenkunde und Rassengeschichte der Menschheit*. Stuttgart.

EKHOLM, Gordon F. (1950). 'Is American Indian Culture Asiatic?' *Natural History*, 59, 8, pp. 344–51, 382. New York.

(1965). 'Transpacific Contacts'. *In* Jennings and Norbeck, pp. 489–510.

ENGEL, Frederic (1956). 'Curayacu, A Chavinoid Site', *Archaeology*, vol. 9, pp. 98–105.

(1957). 'Early Sites on the Peruvian Coast,' *Southwestern Journal of Anthropology*, vol. 13, pp. 54–68.

(1957b). 'Sites et établissements sans céramique dans la côte péruvienne', *Journal de la Société des Américanistes*, vol. 46, pp. 67–155. Paris.

(1957c). 'Early Sites in the Pisco Valley of Peru – Tambo Colorado', *American Antiquity*, vol. 23, pp. 34–45.

(1958). 'Algunos datos con referencia a los sitios precerámicos de la costa peruana', *Arqueológicas*, vol. 1, no. 3. Lima.

(1960). 'Un groupe humain datant de 5000 ans a Paracas, Pérou', *Journal de la Société des Américanistes*, vol. 49, pp. 7–35. Paris.

(1963a). 'A Preceramic Settlement on the Central Coast of Peru: Asia, Unit 1'. *Transactions*, vol. 53, no. 3. American Philosophical Society, Philadelphia.

(1963b). 'Notes relatives à des explorations archéologiques à Paracas', *Travaux de l'Institut Français de Études Andines*, Tomo IX. Paris.

(1964). 'El precerámico sin algodón en la costa del Perú', *XXXV Congreso Internacional de Americanistas*, vol. 3, pp. 141–52. México.

ENOCK, C. Reginald (1905). 'The Ruins of "Huánuco Viejo" or Old Huánuco', *Journal of the Royal Geographical Society*, XXVI, pp. 153–79. London.

(1907). *The Andes and the Amazon*. London.

(1912). *Peru*. London (3rd ed., improved).

ESPEJO NUÑEZ, Julio. (1964). Bibliografía arqueológica de Chavín. Lima.

ESTETE, Miguel de (1872). *The Narrative of the Journey made by … Hernando Pizarro … from the city of Caxamalca to Parcama, and thence to Xauxa*. Translated and edited by Clements R. Markham, and inserted in pp. 74–94 of his edition of Xérez. Hakluyt Society, London.

(1924). *Noticia del Perú*. Edition H. H. Urteaga and C. A. Romero. Colección de Librosy y Documentos referentes a la historia del Perú, Ser. 2, vol. 8, pp. 3–56. Lima.

ESTRADA, Emilio, and Betty J. MEGGERS (1961). 'A Complex of Traits of Probable Transpacific Origin on the Coast of Ecuador', *American Anthropologist*, vol. 63, pp. 913–39.

ESTRADA, Emilio, Betty J. MEGGERS, and Clifford EVANS (1962). 'Possible Transpacific Contact on the Coast of Ecuador', *Science*, vol. 135, no. 3501, pp. 371–2.

FALCÓN, Francisco (1918). *Relación sobre el gobierno de los Incas*. Edited by Drs Horacio H. Urteaga and Carlos A. Romero. Colección de Libros y Documentos referentes a la historia del Perú, Ser. 1, vol. II, pp. 135–76. Lima.

FARABEE, William Curtis (1921). 'The Use of Metals in Prehistoric America', *Museum Journal*, vol. 12, no. 1. Philadelphia.

FEJOS, Paul (1944). *Archaeological Explorations in the Cordillera Vilcabamba, Southeastern Peru*. Viking Fund Publications in Anthropology, no. 3. New York.

FESTER, G. A. (1954). 'Some Dyes of the Ancient South American Civilizations', *Dyestuffs*, vol. 4, no. 9. Bulletin National Aniline Division, Allied Chemical and Dye Corporation, New York.

FLORES ESPINOSA, Isabel (1960). 'Wichqana: Sitio temprano en Ayacucho'. *In* Matos Mendieta (Editor), pp. 335–44.

FORD, James Alfred (1954). 'The History of a Peruvian Valley', *Scientific American*, vol. 191, no. 2 (August), pp. 28–34.

FORD, James Alfred, and Gordon R. WILLEY (1949). *Surface Survey of the Virú Valley, Peru*. Anthropological Papers of the American Museum of Natural History, 43, 1. New York.

THE ANCIENT CIVILIZATIONS OF PERU

FRANCO INOJOSA, José María (1935–7). 'Janan Kosko', *Revista del Museo Nacional de Lima*, vol. 4, pp. 209–33; vol. 6, pp. 201–31.

FRANCO INOJOSA, José María, and Alejandro GONZÁLEZ (1936). 'Exploraciones arqueológicas en al Perú', *Revista del Museo Nacional de Lima*, vol. 5, pp. 157–83.

FRÖDIN, Otto, and Erland NORDENSKIÖLD (1918). *Über Zwirnen und Spinnen bei den Indianern Südamerikas*. Göteborg.

FUHRMANN, Ernst (1922a). *Reich der Inka*. Hagen.

(1922b). *Peru ii*. Hagen.

FUNG DE LANNING, Rosa (1959). 'Informe preliminar de las excavaciones efectuades en el Abrigo Rocoso No. 1 de Tschopik'. In *Actas y Trabajos del II Congreso Nacional de Historia del Peru*, vol. 1, pp. 253–74. Lima.

GAMARRA DULANTO, Luís (1942). 'Apuntes sobre el guano del Peru y la antigüedad del hombre en América', International Congress of Americanists, *Proceedings*, Session 27 (Lima, 1939), vol. 1, pp. 123–127.

GARCÉS BEDREGAL, Miguel (1942). 'Evolución técnica de la música peruana, gama eptafónica', *Actas y Trabajos Científicos del xxvii Congreso Internacional de Americanistas de Lima* (1939), t. 11, pp. 25–32. Lima.

GARCIA Y MERINO, Manuel (1894). 'Proyectiles primitivos de los peruanos', *Boletín de la Sociedad Geográfica de Lima*, IV, pp. 210–217.

GARCILASO DE LA VEGA (El Inca) (1722). *Historia general del Perú*, 2nd edn. Madrid.

(1723). *Primera parte de los Commentarios reales que tratan, de el origin de los Incas, reies, qve fveron del Perú, de sv idolatría, leies, y govierno, en paz, y en guerra: de svs vidas, y conquistas: y de todo lo que fue aquel imperio, y su república, antes que los Españoles pasaran á él*. 2nd edn. Madrid.

(1869–71). *The First Part of the Royal Commentaries of the Yncas*. Translated and edited by Clements R. Markham. 2 vols, nos 41, 45, Hakluyt Society, London.

GAYTON, A. H. (1927). *The Uhle Collections from Nievería*. University of California Publications in American Archaeology and Ethnology, vol. 21, pp. 305–29. Berkeley.

GAYTON, A. H., and A. L. KROEBER (1927). *The Uhle Pottery Collections from Nazca. Ibid.*, vol. 24. pp. 1–46. Berkeley.

GILMORE, RAYMOND M. (1950). 'Fauna and Ethnozoology of South America'. *In* Steward (Editor) (1950), pp. 345–464.

GLADWIN, Harold S. (1947). *Men out of Asia*. New York.

GONZÁLES, Alberto Rex (1961). 'Les squelettes des sites sans céramique de la Côte du Pérou', *Journal de la Société des Américanistes*, Tomo L. Paris.

GONZÁLEZ DE LA ROSA, Manuel (1908). 'Estudio de las antigüedades halladas bajo el huano', *Revista Histórica*, II, pp. 180–99. Lima.

BIBLIOGRAPHY

(1910). *Les Deux Tiahuanaco, leurs problèmes et leur solution.* 16th International Congress of Americanists, pp. 405–28. Vienna.

GONZÁLEZ HOLGUIN, Diego (1901). *Arte y diccionario qquechua-español.* Lima.

GRESLEBIN, Hector (1926). *El arte prehistórico peruano. Anales de la Sociedad Argentina de Estudios Geográficos,* t. II, num, 2, pp. 1–44. Buenos Aires.

GUIMARAES, Enrique de (1907). 'Algo sobre el quipu. With a Note by Max Uhle', *Revista Histórica,* II, pp. 55–65. Lima.

GUTIÉRREZ DE SANTA CLARA, Pedro (1904–10). *Historia de las guerras civiles del Perú.* Col. libs. docs. refs. hist. América, vols 2, 3, 4, 10 Madrid.

HAMY, E. T. (1897). *Galerie américaine du Musée d'Ethnographie du Trocadéro.* Paris.

HANSTEIN, Otfrid von (1925). *The World of the Incas.* Translated by Anna Barwell. London and New York.

HARCOURT, Raoul d' (1922). 'La Céramique de Cajamarquilla-Nievería'. *Journal de la Société des Américanistes de Paris,* XIV, pp. 107–18.

(1928a). *La Fabrication de certains grelots métalliques chez les Yunka.* International Congress of Americanists, XXII, pt 1, pp. 541–3. Rome.

(1928b) *Les Vêtements et les armes d'un guerrier Yunka d'après le décor d'un lécythe de la région de Trujillo. Ibid.,* pp. 545–8. Rome.

(1934). *Les Textiles anciens du Pérou et leurs techniques.* Paris.

HARCOURT, Raoul, and Marie d' (1924a). *La Céramique ancienne du Pérou.* Paris.

(1924b). *Les Tissus indiens du Vieux Pérou.* Paris.

(1925). *La Musique des Incas et ses survivances.* Paris.

HARSHBERGER, J. W. (1898). 'The Uses of Plants among the Ancient Peruvians', *Bulletin of the Free Museum of Science and Art,* vol. 1, no. 3. Philadelphia.

HARTH-TERRÉ, Emilio (1923). 'La fortaleza de Chuquimancu', *Revista arqueológica del Museo Larco-Herrera,* no. 2. Lima.

HARTWEG, Raul (1958). 'Les squelettes des sites sans céramique de la côte du Pérou', *Journal de la Société des Américanistes,* vol. 47, pp. 179–98.

HEINE-GELDERN, Robert von (1954). 'Die asiatische Herkunft der süd-amerikanischen Metalltechnik', *Paideuma,* vol. 5, pp. 347–423. Bamberg.

HELPS, Sir Arthur (1900). *The Spanish Conquest in America.* London and New York.

HEWETT, Edgar Lee (1939). *Ancient Andean Life.* New York.

HEYERDAHL, Thor (1950). *Kon-Tiki.* London.

(1952). *American Indians in the Pacific.* London.

HOLMES, William H. (1889). *Textile Fabrics of Ancient Peru.* Bureau of American Ethnology, Bulletin 7. Washington.

HOLSTEIN, Otto (1927). 'Chan-Chan: Capital of the Great Chimu', *Geographical Review*, vol. 27, pp. 36–61. New York.

HORKHEIMER, Hans (1944). *Vistas arqueológicas del Noroeste del Perú.* Trujillo.

(1947). 'Breve bibliografía sobre el Perú prehispánico', *Fénix*, no. 5, pp. 200–82. Lima.

(1950a) *El Perú prehispánico.* Lima.

(1950b). *Guía bibliográfica de los principales sítios arqueológicos del Perú.* Lima.

HRDLIČKA, Aleš (1911). *Some Results of Recent Anthropological Exploration in Peru.* Smithsonian Institution Miscellaneous Collections, vol. 56, no. 16. Washington.

(1914). *Anthropological Work in Peru in 1913, with Notes on the Pathology of the Ancient Peruvians. Ibid.*, vol. 61, no. 18. Washington.

(1917). *The Genesis of the American Indian.* 19th International Congress of Americanists, 1915, pp. 559–68. Washington.

HRDLIČKA, Aleš, W. H. HOLMES, B. WILLIS, F. E. WRIGHT, and C. N. FENNER (1912). *Early Man in South America.* Bulletin 52, Bureau of American Ethnology. Washington.

HUMBOLDT, Baron Alexander von (1810). *Vues des cordillères et monuments des peuples indigènes de l'Amérique.* Paris.

HUTCHINSON, J. B., R. A. SILOW, and S. G. STEPHEN (1947). *The Evolution of Gossypium and the Differentiation of the Cultivated Cottons.* London, New York, and Toronto.

HUTCHINSON, Thomas J. (1873). *Two Years in Peru, with Exploration of its Antiquities.* 2 vols. London.

(1874). 'Explorations amongst Ancient Burial Grounds (chiefly on the Sea-Coast Valleys) of Peru'. Royal Anthropological Institute of Great Britain and Ireland, *Journal*, vol. 3, pp. 311–26. London.

IMBELLONI, José (1934). 'Toki del Perú', *Actas y Trabajos Científicos del xxv Congreso Internacional de Americanistas de La Plata, 1932*, t. II, pp. 253–7. Buenos Aires.

(1946a). *Pachacuti ix (El Inkario Crítico).* Buenos Aires.

(1946b). 'Recientes estudios craniológicos sobre los antiguos peruanos', *Boletín bibliográfico de Antropología Americana*, vol. 7, pp. 85–99. Mexico.

ISHIDA, Eichiro, Taiji YAZAWA and others (1960). *Andes; The Report of the University of Tokyo Scientific Expedition to the Andes in 1958.* Tokyo.

IZIKOWITZ, Karl Gustav (1935). *Musical and Other Sound Instruments of the South American Indians: a Comparative Ethnographical Study.* Göteborg.

IZUMI, Seiichi, and SONO, Toshihiko (1963). *Andes 2: Excavations at Kotosh, Peru, 1960.*Tokyo.

JENNINGS, Jesse D., and NORBECK, Edward (Editors) (1964). *Prehistoric Man in the New World.* William March Rice University, Houston.

BIBLIOGRAPHY

JIJÓN Y CAAMAÑO, Jacinto (1919). *La religión del imperio de los Incas.* Quito.

(1949). *Maranga. Contribución al conocimiento de los aborígenes del valle del Rímac, Perú.* Quito.

JIMÉNEZ DE LA ESPADA, Marcos (1879). *Tres relaciones de antigüedades peruanas.* Madrid.

JOHNSON, Frederick (1951). 'Introduction to *Radiocarbon Dating*'. *In* Johnson (Editor) (1951), pp. 1–3.

JOHNSON, Frederick (Editor) (1951). *Radiocarbon Dating.* Memoirs of the Society of American Archaeology, 8. Salt Lake City.

JOHNSON, Frederick, Froelich G. RAINEY, Donald COLLIER, and Richard F. FLINT (1951). 'Radiocarbon Dating: A Summary'. *In* Johnson (Editor) (1951), pp. 58–62.

JOHNSON, GEORGE R. (1930). *Peru from the Air.* American Geographic Society, Special Publications No. 12. New York.

JOYCE, Thomas Athol (1912). *South American Archaeology.* London.

(1913a). 'Note on a Gold Beaker from Lambayeque', *Man*, XIII, pp. 65–6. London.

(1913b). 'The Clan-Ancestor in Animal Form as Depicted on the Ancient Pottery of the Peruvian Coast', *ibid.*, pp. 113–17.

(1921). 'The Peruvian Loom in the Proto-Chimu Period', *ibid.*, XXI, pp. 177–80.

(1922). 'Note on a Peruvian Loom of the Chimu Period', *ibid.*, XXII, pp. 1–2.

KARSTEN, Rafael (1949a). *A Totalitarian State of the Past: the Civilization of the Inca Empire in Ancient Peru.* Helsingfors Societas Scientarum Fennica Commentationes Humaniorum Litterarum, XVI, 1.

(1949b). *Das altperuanische Inkareich und seine Kultur.* Leipzig.

KAUFFMANN DOIG, Federico (1963a). *El Perú arquelógico.* Lima.

(1963b) *Tres étapas pre-Chavín.* Lima.

(1965). 'La cultura Chimú'. *Las grandes civilizaciones del antiguo Perú*, Tomo 4. Lima.

KELEMEN, Pál (1943). *Medieval American Art.* 2 vols. New York.

KELLEY, David H., and Duccio BONAVIA B. (1963). 'New Evidence for Pre-ceramic Maize on the Coast of Peru', *Ñawpa Pacha* I, pp. 39–42. Berkeley.

KELLY, Isabel T. (1930). *Peruvian Cumbrous Bowls.* University of California Publications in American Archaeology and Ethnology, XXIV, pp. 325–41, Berkeley, California.

KIDDER II, Alfred (1942). 'Speculations on Andean Origins', *Proceedings, 8th Pan-American Scientific Congress*, vol. 2, p. 161. Washington.

(1943). *Some Early Sites in the Northern Lake Titicaca Basin.* Papers of the Peabody Museum of Archaeology and Ethnology, Harvard University, vol. 27, no. 1. Cambridge, Mass.

(1948). 'The Position of Pucara in Titicaca Basin Archaeology'. *In* Bennett (Editor) (1948), pp. 87–9.

(1956). 'Settlement Patterns, Peru'. *In Prehistoric Settlement Patterns in the New World*. Viking Fund Publications in Anthropology, no. 23, pp. 148–55. New York.

(1964). 'South American High Cultures'. *In* Jennings and Norbeck, 1964, pp. 451–86.

KIDDER II, Alfred, Luis G. LUMBRERAS S., and David B. SMITH (1963). 'Cultural Developments in the Central Andes – Peru and Bolivia'. *In Aboriginal Cultural Development in Latin America*. Smithsonian Miscellaneous Collections, vol. 146, no. 1, pp. 89–101. Washington.

KING, Mary Elizabeth (1965). *Ancient Peruvian Textiles from the Collection of the Textile Museum, Washington, D.C.* A Museum of Primitive Art Book. New York Graphic Society, Greenwich, Conn.

KINZL, Hans (1935). 'Altindianische Siedlungsspuren im Umkreis der Cordillera Blanca'. *In* Philipp Borchers, *Die Weisse Kordillere*, pp. 262–95. Berlin.

KIRCHHOFF, Paul (1949). 'The Social and Political Organization of the Andean Peoples'. *In* Steward (1949), pp. 293–311.

KOSOK, Paul (1940–3). *The Role of Irrigation in Ancient Peru*, 8th American Scientific Congress, vol 2. Washington.

(1942) 'Extensión de la irrigación en el antiguo Perú', *Boletín de la Sociedad Geográfica de la Paz*, no. 64, pp. 30–1. La Paz, Bolivia.

(1964). *Vida, Tierra, y Agua en el antiguo Perú*. Long Island University.

KOSOK, Paul, and María REICHE (1947). 'The Mysterious Markings of Nazca', *Natural History*, vol. 56, no. 5, pp. 200–7 and 237–8. New York.

(1949). 'Ancient Drawings on the Desert of Peru', *Archaeology*, vol. 2, pp. 206–15.

KREICHGAUER, P. D. (1926–8). 'Das Rätsel der Quipus', *Anthropos*, t. XXI, pp. 618–20; t. XXIII, pp. 322–4. Wien.

KRICKEBERG, Walter (1922). 'Die Völker Sudamerikas'. In *Illustrierte Völkerkunde*, G. Buschan (Editor). Stuttgart.

KREIGER, Alex D. (1964). 'Early Man in the New World'. *In* Jennings and Norbeck, pp. 23–81, 1864.

KROEBER, A. L. (1925a). *The Uhle Pottery Collections from Moche*. University of California Publications in American Archaeology and Ethnology, vol. 21, pp. 191–234. Berkeley.

(1925b). *The Uhle Pottery Collections from Supe. Ibid.*, pp. 235–64. Berkeley.

(1926a). *Archaeological Explorations in Peru. Pt i: Ancient Pottery from Trujillo*. Field Museum of Natural History, Anthropological Memoirs, vol. 2, no. 1, pp. 1–43. Chicago, Ill.

(1926b). *The Uhle Pottery Collections from Chancay*. University of California Publications in American Archaeology and Ethnology, vol. 21, pp. 265–304. Berkeley.

(1926c). 'Cultural Stratifications in Peru', *American Anthropologist*, vol. 28, pp. 331–51.

(1927). 'Coast and Highland in Prehistoric Peru', *ibid.*, vol. 29, pp. 625–53.

(1930). *Archaeological Explorations in Peru. Pt ii: The Northern Coast.* Field Museum of Natural History, Anthropological Memoirs, vol. 2, no. 2. Chicago, Ill.

(1937). *Archaeological Explorations in Peru. Pt iv: Cañete Valley. Ibid.*, vol. 2, no. 4. Chicago, Ill.

(1944). *Peruvian Archaeology in 1942.* Viking Fund Publications in Anthropology, no. 4. New York.

(1948). 'Summary and Interpretations'. *In* Bennett (Editor) (1948), pp. 113–21.

(1949). 'Art'. *In* Steward (Editor (1949), pp. 411–92.

(1953). *Paracas Cavernas and Chavín.* University of California Publications in American Archaeology and Ethnology, vol. 40, no. 8, pp. 313–48. Berkeley and Los Angeles.

(1954). 'Proto-Lima; A Middle Period Culture of Peru'. *Fieldiana: Anthropology*, vol. 44, no. 2. Chicago Museum of Natural History, Chicago.

(1956). 'Towards Definition of the Nazca Style'. *University of California Publications in American Archaeology and Ethnology*, vol. 43. Berkeley.

(1963). 'The Methods of Peruvian Archaeology', *Nawpa Pacha* I, pp. 61–71. Berkeley.

KROEBER, A. L., and J. C. MUELLE (1942). 'Cerámica paleteada de Lambayeque', *Revista del Museo Nacional*, vol. 11, pp. 1–24. Lima.

KROEBER, A. L., and W. D. STRONG (1924a). *The Uhle Collections from Chincha.* University of California Publications in American Archaeology and Ethnology, vol. 21, pp. 1–54. Berkeley.

(1924b). *The Uhle Pottery Collections from Ica. Ibid.*, pp. 95–133. Berkeley.

KUBLER, George (1946). 'The Quechua in the Colonial World'. *In* Steward (Editor) (1946), pp. 331–410.

(1948). 'Towards Absolute Time: Guano Archaeology'. *In* Bennett (Editor) (1948), pp. 29–50.

(1952). *Cuzco; Reconstruction of the Town, and Restoration of the Monuments.* UNESCO: Museums and Monuments, III. Paris.

(1962). *The Art and Architecture of Ancient America; The Mexican, Maya, and Andean Peoples.* Pelican History of Art series, z 21. Harmondsworth.

KUTSCHER, Gerdt (1950). *Chimu; eine altindianische Hochkultur.* Berlin.

LANGLOIS, Louis (1935–6). 'De ci de là à travers le Pérou précolombien', *La Géographie*, vol. 64. pp. 297–308; vol. 65, pp. 25–38, 203–11.

(1940). 'Utcubamba, investigaciones arqueológicas en el Departamento de Amazonas (conclusión)', *Revista del Museo Nacional*, vol. 9, pp. 191–228. Lima.

LANNING, Edward P. (1963a). 'A Pre-agricultural Occupation on the Central Coast of Peru', *American Antiquity*, vol. 28, pp. 360–71.

(1963b). 'An Early Ceramic Style from Ancón, Central Coast of Peru', *Nawpa Pacha* I, pp. 47–60. Berkeley.

(1965). 'Early Man in Peru', *Scientific American*, vol. 213, no. 4, pp. 68–76.

LANNING, Edward P., and Eugene A. HAMMEL (1961). 'Early Lithic Industries in Western South America', *American Antiquity*, vol. 27, pp. 139–54.

LARCO HERRERA, Rafael (1928). *La civiltà Yunga*. International Congress of Americanists, XXII, pt 1, pp. 565–81. Rome.

LARCO HOYLE, Rafael (1938–9). *Los Mochicas*. 2 vols. Lima.

(1941). *Los Cupisniques*. Lima.

(1942). 'La escritura mochica sobre pallares', *Revista Geogràfica Americana*, Año IX, vol. 18, 93–103. Buenos Aires.

(1943), 'La escritura peruana sobre pallares', *ibid.*, Año XI, vol. 20, pp. 1–36. Buenos Aires.

(1944). *Cultura Salinar*. 20 pp. Buenos Aires.

(1945a). *La cultura Virú*. 28 pp. Buenos Aires.

(1945b). *Los Cupisniques*. 25 pp. Buenos Aires.

(1945c). *Los Mochicas*. 42 pp. Buenos Aires.

(1945d). 'La cultura Salinar. Una civilización remota del Perú preincáico', *Revista Geográfica Americana*, vol. 23, no. 141, pp. 327–36. Buenos Aires.

(1946). 'A Culture Sequence for the North Coast of Peru'. *In* Steward (Editor) (1946), pp. 149–75.

(1948). *Cronología arqueológica del norte del Perú*. Trujillo, Peru, and Buenos Aires, Argentina.

(1965). *La cerámica Vicus*. Lima.

LARRABURE Y UNÁNUE, Eugenio (1874). *Cañete, apuntes geográficos y arqueológicos*. Lima.

LARREA, Juan (1935). *Arte peruano (Colección Juan Larrea)*. Madrid.

LAS CASAS, Bishop Friar Bartolomé de (1892). *De las antiguas gentes del Perú*. Edited by Don Marcos Jiménez de la Espada. Madrid.

LASTRES, Juan, Jorge MUELLE, J. M. B. FARFÁN, y Abraham GUILLÉN (1943). *Representaciones patológicas en la cerámica peruana*. Publicaciones del Museo Nacional. Lima, Imp. del Museo Nacional.

LATCHAM, R. E. (1923). *La existencia de la propiedad en el antiguo imperio de los Incas*. Santiago.

(1927a). 'El dominio de la tierra y el sistema tributario en el antiguo imperio de los Incas', *Revista Chilena de Historia y Geografía*, LII, pp. 201–57. Santiago de Chile.

(1927b). 'The Totemism of the Ancient Andean Peoples', *Journal of the Royal Anthropological Institute*, LVII, pp. 55–87.

(1927–8). 'Los Incas, sus orígenes y sus ayllus', *Revista de la Universidad de Chile*, V, pp. 1017–1154; VI, pp. 159–233.

LATHRAP, Donald W. (1958). 'The Cultural Sequence at Yarinacocha, Eastern Peru', *American Antiquity*, vol. 23, no. 4, pp. 379–88.

LAVACHERY, H. A. (1930). 'Neuf Sculptures péruviennes en bois',

Bulletin de la Société des Américanistes de Belgique, pp. 20–5. Brussels.

LEHMANN, Walter, and Heinrich DOERING (1924). *The Art of Old Peru.* New York.

LEHMANN-NITSCHE, Robert (1928). 'Coricancha, el Templo del Sol en el Cuzco y las imágenes de su altar mayor', *Revista del Museo de La Plata*, XXXI, pp. 1–260. La Plata, Argentina.

LEVILLIER, Jean (1928). *Paracas, A Contribution to the Study of Pre-Incaic Textiles in Ancient Perú.* Paris.

LEVILLIER, Roberto (1935). *Don Francisco de Toledo, supremo organizador del Perú: su vida, su obra* (1515–1582), vol. 1. Madrid.

LIBBY, Willard F. (1952). *Radiocarbon Dating.* Chicago.

LILIEN, Rose (1950). 'Tripod Vessels from the Virú Valley', *American Antiquity*, vol. 15, no. 4, pp. 339–40. Menasha,, Wisconsin.

LINNÉ, Sigvald (1925). *The Technique of South American Ceramics.* Göteborgs Kungl Vetenskaps- och Vitterhets-Samhälles Handlingar, Fjärde följden, vol. 29, no. 5. Göteborg.

LOCKE, L. Leland (1912). 'The Ancient Quipu, a Peruvian Knot-Record', *American Anthropologist*, XIV, pp. 325–32.

— (1923). *The Ancient Quipu, a Peruvian Knot-Record.* New York.

— (1938). *Supplementary Notes on the Quipus in the American Museum of Natural History.* Anthropological Papers, American Museum of Natural History, vol. 30, pt 2, pp. 39–74. New York.

LOTHROP, Samuel Kirkland (1932). 'Aboriginal Navigation off the West Coast of South America', *Journal of the Royal Anthropological Institute*, 67, 229–56.

— (1937). 'Gold and Silver from Southern Peru and Bolivia', *ibid.*, pp. 305–25. London.

— (1938). *Inca Treasure as Depicted by Spanish Historians.* Frederick Webb Hodge Anniversary Publication Fund. Vol. 2. Los Angeles.

— (1941). 'Gold Ornaments of Chavín Style from Chongoyape, Peru', *American Antiquity*, vol. 6, no. 3, pp. 250–62. Menasha, Wisconsin.

— (1948). 'Pariñas-Chira Archaeology; A Preliminary Report'. *In* Bennett (Editor) (1948), pp. 53–65.

— (1950). 'Metalworking Tools from the Central Coast of Peru', *American Antiquity*, vol. 16, pp. 160–4.

— (1951a). 'Gold Artifacts of Chavín Style', *ibid.*, 226–40. Salt Lake City.

— (1951b). 'Peruvian Metallurgy'. In *The Civilizations of Ancient America.* Selected Papers of the XXIXth International Congress of Americanists, pp. 219–23. Chicago.

— (1954). 'A Peruvian Goldsmith's Grave', *Archaeology*, vol. 7, pp. 31–36.

LOTHROP, Samuel K., and MAHLER, Joy (1957a). *A Chancay Style Grave at Zapallan, Peru.* Papers of the Peabody Museum of Archaeology and Ethnology, Harvard University, vol. 50, no. 1. Cambridge.

— (1957b). *Late Nazca Burials in Chavina, Peru. idem*, vol. 50, no. 2.

LOTHROP, Samuel K., and others (1961). *Essays in Pre-Columbian Art and Archaeology*. Cambridge, Mass.

LUMBRERAS, S. Luis G. (1960a). 'Espacio y cultural en los Andes', *Revista del Museo Nacional*, vol. 29, pp. 222–39. Lima.

(1960b). 'Algunos problemas de arqueología peruana'. *In* Matos Mendieta (Editor), pp. 129–48.

LÜTKEN, Chr. Fr. (1884). *Des crânes et des autres ossements humains de Minas Geráes dans le Brésil Central, découverts et déterrés par le feu*. Professeur P. W. Lund. Congrès International Américaniste (Copenhagen, 1883). Pp. 40–8.

McCOWN, Theodore D. (1945). *Pre-Incaic Huamachuco: Survey and Excavations in the Northern Sierra of Peru*. University of California Publications in American Archaeology and Ethnology, vol. 39, no. 4. Berkeley.

(1950). 'The Antiquity of Man in South America'. *In* Steward (Editor) (1950), pp. 1–9.

(1952). 'Ancient Man in South America'. In *Indian Tribes of Aboriginal America*, pp. 374–9. Selected Papers of the 29th International Congress of Americanists, Chicago.

MACCURDY, George Grant (1923). 'Human Skeletal Remains from the Highlands of Peru', *American Journal of Physical Anthropology*, vol. 6, no. 3, pp. 217–329. Philadelphia.

MACGOWAN, Kenneth (1950). *Early Man in the New World*. New York.

MANGELSDORF, Paul C. (1954). 'New Evidence on the Origin and Ancestry of Maize', *American Antiquity*, 19, 4, pp. 409–10.

MANGELSDORF, P. C., and R. G. REEVES (1939). *The Origin of Indian Corn and Its Relatives*. Texas Agricultural Experimental Station, Bulletin No. 574.

(1959). 'The Origin of Corn', *Botanical Museum Leaflets*, vol. 18, no. 7, pp. 329–56. Harvard University, Cambridge, Mass.

MANGELSDORF, P. C., and C. Earle SMITH, Jr. (1949). 'New Archaeological Evidence of Evolution in Maize', *Botanical Museum Leaflets*, vol. 13, no. 8, pp. 213–47. Harvard University, Cambridge, Mass.

MARKHAM, Sir Clements Robert (1856). *Cuzco: A Journey to the Ancient Capital of Peru; with an Account of the History, Language, Literature, and Antiquities of the Incas*. London.

(1864). *Contributions toward a Grammar and Dictionary of Quichua. the Language of the Yncas of Peru*. London.

(1871). 'On the Geographical Positions of the Tribes which Formed the Empire of the Yncas', *Journal of the Royal Geographical Society*, 41, pp. 281–338. London.

(1872). *Reports on the Discovery of Peru*. Hakluyt Society, no. 47. London.

(1873). *Rites and Laws of the Incas*. Hakluyt Society, no. 48. London.

(1892). *A History of Peru*. Chicago.

(1907). *Bibliography of Peru* (1526–1907). Hakluyt Collection, Ser. 2, vol. 22, pp. 267–358. Cambridge, England.

(1910a). *The Incas of Peru*. London and New York.

(1910b). *A Comparison of the Ancient Peruvian Carvings and the Stones of Tiahuanacu and Chavín*. International Congress of Americanists, XVI, pp. 389–95. Vienna.

MASON, J. Alden (1926a). 'Dr Farabee's Last Journey', *Museum Journal*, vol. 17, no. 2, pp. 128–65. Philadelphia.

(1926b). 'Additions to the American Section', *idem.*, vol. 17, no. 3, pp. 273–93. Philadelphia.

(1930). 'A Silver Vase from Peru', *University Museum Bulletin*, vol. 1, no. 2, pp. 23, 24, 26. Philadelphia.

(1931). 'A Peruvian Painting Set', *idem*, vol. 3, no. 1, pp. 10–12. Philadelphia.

(1932). 'Peruvian Pottery Whistles', *idem*, vol. 4, no. 1, pp. 20–22. Philadelphia.

(1933). 'Gold and Copper Ornaments from Peru', *idem*, vol. 4, no. 4, pp. 94–6. Philadelphia.

(1935). 'Three Inca Wooden Cups', *idem*, vol. 5, no. 5, pp. 53–5. Philadelphia.

(1950). 'The Languages of South American Indians'. *In* Steward (Editor) (1950), pp. 157–317.

(1952). 'Peruvian Panorama', *Archaeology*, vol. 5, pp. 220–7.

MATHEWSON, C. H. (1915). 'A Metallographic Description of Some Ancient Peruvian Bronzes from Machu Picchu', *American Journal of Science*, vol. 40, no. 240.

MATOS MENDIETA, Ramiro (Editor) (1960). *Antiguo Peru, Espacio y Tiempo*, Lima.

MEAD, Charles W. (1903). *The Musical Instruments of the Incas*. Guide Leaflet No. 11, American Museum of Natural History, New York.

(1906). *The Six-Unit Design in Ancient Peruvian Cloth*. Boas Anniversary Volume, pp. 193–5. New York.

(1907). *Technique of Some South American Feather-work*. Anthropological Papers of the American Museum of Natural History, New York, 1, pt 1.

(1909). *The Fish in Ancient Peruvian Art*. Putnam Anniversary Volume, pp. 126–36. New York.

(1915). *Prehistoric Bronze in South America*. Anthropological Papers, American Museum of Natural History, vol. 12, pp. 15–52. New York.

(1916a). *Conventionalized Figures in Ancient Peruvian Art. Idem.* vol. 12, pp. 193–217. New York.

(1916b). 'Ancient Peruvian Cloths', *American Museum of Natural History Journal*, XVI, pp. 389–93.

(1917). *Peruvian Art*. Guide Leaflet No. 46, American Museum of Natural History, New York.

(1924). *Old Civilizations of Inca Land*. American Museum of Natural History, Handbook Series, No. 11, New York.

MEANS, Philip Ainsworth (1917a). *A Survey of Ancient Peruvian Art.*
Connecticut Academy of Arts and Sciences, *Transactions*, vol. 21,
pp. 315–442. New Haven.

(1917b). *Culture Sequence in the Andean Area.* International Congress
of Americanists, XIX, pp. 236–52. Washington.

(1918a). *A Glimpse of Northern Peru.* Bulletin, Pan American Union,
no. 47, pp. 333–49. Washington.

(1918b). 'A Note on the Guarani Invasions of the Inca Empire',
Geographical Review, American Geographical Society, IV, pp. 482–
484.

(1918c). 'The Domestication of the Llama', *Science*, XLVII, pp.
268–9.

(1918d). 'Realism in the Art of Ancient Peru', *Art and Archaeology*,
VI, pp. 235–46. Washington.

(1918e). 'Precolumbian Peruvian Chronology and Cultures', *Man*,
XVIII, pp. 168–9.

(1918f). 'A Note on Two Stone Objects from Southern Bolivia',
American Anthropologist, XX, pp. 245–6.

(1919a). 'La civilización precolombina de los Andes', *Boletín de la
Sociedad Ecuatoriana de Estudios Históricos Americanos*, III, pp.
213–42. Quito

(1919b). *Una nota sobre la prehistoria peruana.* Lima.

(1919c). 'Distribution and Use of Slings in Pre-Columbian America,
with Descriptive Catalogue of Ancient Peruvian Slings in the
United States National Museum', *Proceedings of the U.S. National
Museum*, vol. 55, pp. 317–49. Washington.

(1921a). 'Aspectos estético-cronológicos de las civilizaciones andinas',
Boletín de la Academia Nacional de Historia, I, pp. 195–226.

(1921b). 'Ciertos aspectos estéticos del arte antiguo del Perú', *Mercurio Peruano*, VI, pp. 215–23. Lima.

(1925a). 'A Study of Ancient Andean Social Institutions', Connecticut Academy of Arts and Sciences, *Transactions*, vol. 27, pp. 407–
469. New Haven.

(1925b). 'A Series of Ancient Andean Textiles', *Bulletin of the
Needle and Bobbin Club*, IX, pp. 3–27. New York.

(1927). 'A Group of Ancient Peruvian Fabrics', *ibid.*, XI, pp. 10–25.
New York.

(1928). 'Biblioteca Andina: Part One, the Chroniclers, or, the Writers
of the Sixteenth and Seventeenth Centuries Who Treated of the
Pre-Hispanic History and Culture of the Andean Countries', Connecticut Academy of Arts and Sciences, *Transactions*, vol. 29,
pp. 271–525. New Haven.

(1930a). *Peruvian Textiles; Examples of the Pre-Incaic Period.* New
York.

(1930b). *The Origin of Tapestry Technique in Pre-Spanish Peru.*
Metropolitan Museum Series, III, pt 1, pp. 22–37.

(1931). *Ancient Civilizations of the Andes.* New York.

(1932). *Fall of the Inca Empire and the Spanish Rule in Peru*, 1530–1780. New York.

(1938). 'The Incas, Empire Builders of the Andes', *National Geographic Magazine*, 73, pp. 225–64.

(1942). 'Pre-Spanish Navigation off the Andean Coast', *American Neptune*, 2, 2, pp. 107–26. Salem, Mass.

MEDINA, José Toribio (1930). *Bibliografía de las lenguas quechua y aymará*. Contributions, vol. 7, no. 7, Museum of the American Indian, Heye Foundation. New York.

MEGGERS, Betty J., EVANS, Clifford, and ESTRADA, Emilio (1965). 'Early Formative Period of Coastal Ecuador: The Valdivia and Machalilla Phases'. *Smithsonian Contributions to Anthropology*, vol. 1. Washington.

MEGGERS, Betty J., and EVANS, Clifford (1966). 'A Transpacific Contact in 3000 B.C.', *Scientific American*, vol. 214, no. 1, pp. 28–35.

MENGHIN, Osvaldo, F. A. (1954). 'Cultures precerámicas en Bolivia', *Runa*, vol. 6. Buenos Aires.

(1957). 'Vorgeschichte Amerikas'. In Oldenbourg's *Abriss der Weltgeschichte*. Munich.

MENGHIN, Osvaldo F. A., and SCHROEDER, Gerhard (1957). 'Un yacimiento en Ichuña (Dept. Puno, Peru) y las industrias precerámicas de los Andes centrales y septentrionales', *Acta Praehistórica* I. Buenos Aires.

MENZEL, Dorothy (1959). 'The Inca Occupation on the South Coast of Peru', *Southwestern Journal of Anthropology*, vol. 15, no. 2, pp. 125–42.

MENZEL, Dorothy, ROWE, John H., and DAWSON, Lawrence E. (1964). 'The Paracas Pottery of Ica: A Study in Style and Time', *University of California Publications in American Archaeology and Ethnology*, Vol. 50. Berkeley.

MÉTRAUX, Alfred (1949). 'Religion and Shamanism'. *In* Steward (Editor) (1949), pp. 559–99.

MIDDENDORF, E. W. (1890–2). *Die einheimischen Sprachen Perus*. 6 vols. Leipzig.

(1890a). *Das Runa-Simi oder die Keshua-Sprache*. Leipzig.

(1890b). *Wörterbuch des Runa-Simi*. Leipzig.

(1891). *Dramatische und lyrische Dichtungen der Keshua-Sprache*. Leipzig.

(1892). *Das Muchik oder die Chimu-Sprache*. Leipzig.

(1893–5). *Peru*. 3 vols. Berlin.

(1960). *El Muchik o lengua de los Chimú*. Spanish version by Federico Kauffmann Doig. Lima.

MINNAERT, Paul (1925). *Les Institutions et le droit de l'empire des Incas*. Ostende.

MISHKIN, Bernard (1946). 'The Contemporary Quechua'. *In* Steward (Editor) (1946), pp. 411–76.

THE ANCIENT CIVILIZATIONS OF PERU

Mitré, Bartolomé (1881). *Ollantay: Estudio sobre el drama Quichua.* Buenos Aires.

Molina (of Cuzco), Cristóbal de (1873). 'The Fables and Rites of the Yncas'. Translated and edited by Clements R. Markham, in *Rites and Laws of the Yncas*, pp. 1–64. Hakluyt Society, London.

— (1913), 'Relación de las fábulas y ritos de los Incas', *Revista Chilena de Historia y Geografía*, 5, pp. 117–90. Santiago de Chile.

— (1916). *Idem.* Colección de Libros y Documentos referentes a la historia del Perú, vol. 1. Lima.

Molina (of Santiago), Cristóbal de (1916). 'Relación de muchas cosas acaecidas en el Perú . . .', *idem*, vol. 1, pp. 105–90. Lima.

Monge, Carlos (1948). *Acclimatization in the Andes.* Baltimore.

— (1952). 'Physiological Anthropology of the Dwellers in America's High Plateaus'. In *Indian Tribes of Aboriginal America*, pp. 361–73. Selected Papers of the 29th International Congress of Americanists, Chicago.

— (1953). 'Biological Basis of Human Behavior'. In *Anthropology Today* pp. 127–44. Chicago.

Montell, Gösta (1925). 'Le vrai poncho, son origine postcolombienne', *Journal de la Société des Américanistes de Paris*, vol. 17, pp. 173–83.

— (1929). *Dress and Ornaments in Ancient Peru.* Göteborg.

Montesinos, Fernando (1882). *Memorias antiguas historiales y políticas del Perú.* Édition Marcos Jiménez de la Espada. Colección de libros españoles raros o curiosos, vol. 16, pp. 1–76. Madrid.

— (1906). *Anales del Perú.* 2 vols. Madrid.

— (1920). *Memorias antiguas historiales del Peru.* Translated and edited by P. A. Means. Hakluyt Society, Ser. 2, no. 48. London.

Moodie, Roy L. (1926). 'Studies in Paleopathology, xiv: A Prehistoric Surgical Bandage from Peru'. *Annals of Medical History*, vol. 8, pp. 69–72.

— (1927). 'Studies in Paleopathology, xxi: Injuries to the Head among the pre-Columbian Peruvians', *ibid.*, vol. 9, pp. 277–307.

— (1928). 'Studies in Paleo-odontology, 1: Materials for a Study of Prehistoric Dentistry in Peru', *Journal of the American Dental Association*, vol. 15, pp. 1826–50.

— (1929). 'Studies in Paleopathology, xxii: Surgery in Pre-Columbian Peru', *Annals of Medical History*, n.s., vol. 1, pp. 698–728.

Mortimer, W. Golden (1901). *Coca, the Divine Plant of the Incas.* New York.

Morúa, Martín de (1922–5). *Historia del origen y genealogía real de los reyes Incas del Perú, de sus hechos, costumbres, trajes y manera de gobierno.* Edited by H. H. Urteaga and C. A. Romero. Colección de Libros y Documentos referentes a la historia del Perú, Lima, Peru.

Muelle, Jorge C. (1935). 'Restos hallados en una tumba en Nievería', *Revista del Museo Nacional de Lima*, vol. 4, pp. 135–52.

(1936). *Los valles de Trujillo*. Lima.

MUELLE, Jorge C., and Camilo BLAS (1938). 'Muestrario de arte peruano precolombino', *Revista del Museo Nacional*, vol. 7, pp. 163–280. Lima.

MUÑIZ, Manuel Antonio, and W. J. McGEE (1895). *Primitive Trephining in Peru*. Annual Report, Bureau of American Ethnology, XVI, pp. 1–72.

MURDOCK, George Peter (1934). *Our Primitive Contemporaries*. New York.

MURPHY, William S. (1912). *The Textile Industries*. 8 vols. London.

MUSEUM OF MODERN ART (1955). 32 *Masterworks of Andean Art*. New York.

NESTLER, Julius (1910). *Die Bedeutung der Ruinenstätte von Tiahuanaco nach den Publikationen von Dr. Max Uhle and Sir Clements Markham*. 16th International Congress of Americanists (1908), pp. 395–407. Vienna.

(1913). *Beiträge zur Kenntnis der Ruinenstätte von Tiahuanaco*. Vienna.

NEWMAN, MARSHALL T. (1943). 'A Metric Study of Undeformed Indian Crania from Peru', *American Journal of Physical Anthropology*, N.S., vol. 1, pp. 21–45. Philadelphia.

(1947). *Some Indian Skeletal Material from the Central Coast of Peru*. Papers of the Peabody Museum of Archaeology and Ethnology, Harvard University, vol. 28, no. 1.

(1948). 'A Summary of the Racial History of the Peruvian Area'. *In* Bennett (Editor) (1948), pp. 16–19.

NORDENSKIÖLD, Baron Erland (1906.. 'Ethnologische und archaeologische Forschungen im Grenzgebiet zwischen Peru und Bolivia', *Zeitschrift für Ethnologie*, XXXVIII, pp. 80–99. Berlin.

(1907). 'Recettes magiques et médicales du Pérou et de la Bolivie', *Journal de la Société des Américanistes*, t. IV, pp. 153–74. Paris.

(1917). 'The Guaraní Invasion of the Inca Empire in the Sixteenth Century', *Geographical Review*, IV, pp. 103–21. American Geographical Society, New York.

(1921a). *The Copper and Bronze Ages in South America*. Comparative Ethnographical Studies, vol. 4. Göteborg.

(1921b). 'Emploi de la balance romaine en Amérique du Sud avant la conquête', *Journal de la Société des Américanistes*, t. XIII, fasc. 2, pp. 169–71. Paris.

(1922a). *Deductions Suggested by the Geographical Distribution of Some Post-Columbian Words Used by the Indians of South America*. Comparative Ethnographical Studies, vol. 5. Göteborg.

(1922b). 'La Moustiquaire est-elle indigène en Amérique du Sud?' *Journal de la Société des Américanistes*, t. XIV, pp. 119–26. Paris.

(1925a). *The Secret of the Peruvian Quipus*. Comparative Ethnographical Studies. Gothenburg (Göteborg) Museum, vol. 6, part 1. Göteborg.

(1925b). *Calculations with Years and Months in the Peruvian Quipus.* Idem, vol. 6, pt 2. Göteborg.

(1925–7). 'Peru under the Incas and After', *Peru*, t. 11. London.

(1930). 'The Ancient Peruvian System of Weights', *Man*, t. xxx, pp. 215–21. London.

(1931a). *Origin of the Indian Civilizations in South America.* Comparative Ethnographical Studies, 9. Göteborg.

(1931b). *Ancient Inca Lacquer Work.* Idem, vol. 9, pt 2, pp. 95–100. Göteborg.

(1946). *Origen de las civilizaciones indígenas en la América del Sur.* Buenos Aires.

OCAMPO, Baltasar de (1907). *Account of the Province of Vilcapampa and a Narrative of the Execution of the Inca Tupac Amaru.* Hakluyt Society, Ser. 2, no. 22, pp. 203–47.

OGILVIE, Alan Grant (1922). *Geography of the Central Andes.* American Geographic Society, Map of Hispanic America. Publication no. 1.

O'NEALE, Lila M. (1932). 'Tejidos del período primitivo de Paracas', *Revista del Museo Nacional*, vol. 1, no. 2, pp. 60–80. Lima.

(1933a). 'A Peruvian Multicolored Patchwork', *American Anthropologist*, vol. 35, pp. 87–94.

(1933b). 'Peruvian "Needleknitting" ', *ibid.*, pp. 405–30.

(1935). 'Pequeñas prendas ceremoniales de Paracas', *Revista del Museo Nacional*, vol. 4, no. 2, pp. 245–66. Lima.

(1936). 'Wide-loom Fabrics of the Early Nazca Period'. In *Essays in Anthropology, presented to A. L. Kroeber*, pp. 215–28. Berkeley.

(1937). *Archaeological Explorations in Peru. Pt. iii: Textiles of the Early Nazca Period.* Field Museum of Natural History, Anthropological Memoirs, vol. 2, no. 3, pp. 119–218. Chicago, Ill.

(1942). *Textile Periods in Ancient Peru: ii, Paracas Caverns and the Grand Necropolis.* University of California Publications in American Archaeology and Ethnology, vol. 39, pp. 143–202. Berkeley.

(1946). 'Mochica (Early Chimu) and Other Peruvian Twill Fabrics', *Southwestern Journal of Anthropology*, vol. 2, no. 3, pp. 269–94. Albuquerque.

(1949). 'Weaving'. *In* Steward (Editor) (1949), pp. 97–138.

(1954). 'Textiles'. *In* Willey and Corbett.

O'NEALE, Lila M., and Bonnie Jean CLARK (1948). *Textile Periods in Ancient Peru. iii: The Gauze Weaves.* University of California Publications in American Archaeology and Ethnology, vol. 40, no. 4, pp. 143–222. Berkeley.

O'NEALE, Lila M., and A. L. KROEBER (1930). *Textile Periods in Ancient Peru.* Idem, vol. 39, pp. 143–202. Berkeley.

O'NEALE, Lila M., and others (1949). 'Chincha Plain-Weave Cloths', *Anthropological Records*, vol. 9, no. 2. University of California, Berkeley.

ORBIGNY, Alcide d' (1876). *Voyage dans les deux Amériques.* Paris.

ORCHARD, William C. (1930). 'Peruvian Gold and Gold Plating'. *Indian Notes*, Museum of the American Indian, Heye Foundation, VII, pp. 466–74. New York.

OSBORNE, Carolyn M. (1950). 'Shaped Breechcloths from Peru', *Anthropological Records*, vol. 13, no. 2. University of California, Berkeley.

OVIEDO Y VALDÉS, Gonzalo Fernández de (1851–5). *Historia general y natural de las Indias, islas y tierra-firme del mar océano*. Edition José Amador de los Rios, 4 vols, Madrid.

OYAGUE Y CALDERÓN, Carlos (1904). 'Arquitectura incáica y construcción general', *Boletín de la Sociedad Geográfica de Lima*, XV, pp. 410–417.

PACHACUTI-YAMQUI SALCAMAYHUA, Juan de Santa Cruz (1873). *An Account of the Antiquities of Peru*. Translated and edited by Clements R. Markham in *Rites and Laws of the Yncas*, pp. 67–120. Hakluyt Society, London.

(1879). *Relación de antigüedades deste reyno del Pirú*. Edited by Marcos Jiménez de la Espada, *Tres relaciones de antigüedades peruanas*, pp. 229–328. Madrid.

PARDO, Lufs A. (1937). *Ruinas precolombinas del Cuzco*. Cuzco.

PATTERSON, Thomas C., and LANNING, Edward P. (1964). 'Changing Settlement Patterns on the Central Peruvian Coast'. *Nawpa Pacha*, No. 2, pp. 113–23. Berkeley.

PERRY, William James (1923). *The Children of the Sun*. London.

PIZARRO, Hernando (1872). 'Letter to the Royal Audience of Santo Domingo, November 1533'. In *Reports on the Discovery of Peru*, Hakluyt Society Publications, no. 47, pp. 11–127. London.

PIZARRO, Pedro (1844). *Relación del descubrimiento y conquista de los reinos del Perú, etc.* Colección de Documentos inéditos para la historia de España, vol. 5, pp. 201–388. Madrid.

(1921). *Relation of the Discovery and Conquest of the Kingdoms of Peru*. Cortes Society. Translated and edited by P. A. Means. 2 vols. New York.

POLO, José Toribio (1899). 'La piedra de Chavín', *Boletín de la Sociedad Geográfica de Lima*, IX, pp. 192–231, 262–90'

POLO DE ONDEGARDO, Juan (1873). Report by Polo de Ondegardo. 'The Rites and Laws of the Incas'. Translated and edited by Clements R. Markham. Hakluyt Society, pp. 151–71. London.

(1916a). *Los errores y supersticiones de los Indios, etc.* Colección de Libros y Documentos referentes a la historia del Perú, Ser. 1, vol. 3, pp. 1–43. Lima.

(1916b). *Relación de los fundamentos acerca del notable daño que resulta de no guardar a los Indios sus fueros*. *Idem*, pp. 45–188.

(1917a). *Relación de los adoratorios de los Indios en los cuatro caminos (zeques) que salían del Cuzco*. Edited by Drs Urteaga and Romero. Colección de Libros y Documentos referentes a la historia del Perú, IV, pp. 3–44. Lima.

THE ANCIENT CIVILIZATIONS OF PERU

(1917b). *Del linage de los Ingas y como conquistaron.* Edited by H. H. Urteaga. *Idem,* pp. 45–138. Lima.

(1940). 'Informe del Licenciado Juan Polo de Odegardo . . . sobre la perpetuidad de las encomiendas en el Perú'. *Revista Histórica,* vol. 13, pp. 125–96. Lima.

POMA DE AYALA, Felipe Guamán (1936). *Nueva corónica y buen gobierno* (*codex péruvien illustré*). Institute d'Ethnologie, Travaux et Mémoires, vol. 23. Paris.

PONCE SANGINÉS, Carlos (1961). *Informe de labores, octubre 1957 – febrero 1961. Centro de Investigaciones Arqueológicas en Tiwanaku,* Publicación no. 1. La Paz.

POSNANSKY, Arthur (1911a). *Tihuanacu y la civilización prehistórica en el altiplano andino.* La Paz.

(1911b). 'Razas y monumentos prehistóricos del altiplano andino', *Trabajos del iv Congreso Científico,* XI, pp. 2–142. Santiago

(1913). *El signo escalonado . . . con especial referencia a Tihuanacu.* Berlin

(1914). *Una metrópoli en la América del Sur.* Berlin.

(1925). *Die erotischen Keramiken der Mochicas und deren Beziehungen zu occipital deformierten Schädeln.* Festschrift zur Feier des 25-jährigen Bestehens der Frankfurter Gesellschaft für Anthropologie und Urgeschichte, pp. 67–74.

(1946). *Tihuanacu. The Cradle of American Man.* 2 vols. New York.

PRESCOTT, William Hickling (1847). *History of the Conquest of Peru.* (Many later editions.)

PUTNAM, Edward K. (1914). 'The Davenport Collection of Nazca and other Peruvian Pottery', *Proceedings of the Davenport Academy of Science,* vol. 13, pp. 17–45. Davenport.

QUEVEDO A., A. SERGIO (1941–2). 'Ensayos de antropología física. Los antiguos pobladores del Cuzco (región de Calca)', *Revista del Museo Nacional,* vol. 10. pp. 282–309. Lima.

(1943). 'La trepanación incana en la región del Cusco', *Revista Universitaria.* Cusco, 2 sem. de 1943, pp. 1–197.

Quipucamayocs (1920). *Discurso sobre la descendencia y gobierno de los Incas.* Edited by Drs Horacio H. Urteaga and Carlos A. Romero. Colección de Libros y Documentos referentes a la historia del Perú.

RAIMONDI, Antonio (1874–1913). *El Perú.* 6 vols. Lima.

(1901). 'Ruinas de Huánuco Viejo', *Boletín de la Sociedad Geográfica de Lima,* XI, pp. 397–400.

(1903). 'Enumeración de los vestigios de la antigua civilización entre Pacasmayo y la Cordillera', *ibid.,* XIII, pp. 159–71.

RAMOS GAVILÁN, Alonso (1621). *Historia del célebre santuario de Nuestra Señora de Copacabana, y sus milagros, é invención de la cruz de Carabuco.* Lima.

REGAL, Alberto (1936). *Los caminos del Inca en el antiguo Perú.* Lima.

REICHE, María (1949). *Mystery on the Desert.* Lima.

REICHLEN, Henry et Paule (1949). 'Recherches archéologiques dans les

Andes de Cajamarca. Premier rapport de la Mission Ethnologique française au Peróu septentrional', *Journal de la Société des Américanistes*, t. XXXVIII, pp. 137–74. Paris.

——— (1950). 'Rescherches archéologiques dans les Andes du Haut Utcubamba', *Journal de la Société des Américanistes*, t. XXXIX, pp. 219–46. Paris.

REISS, Wilhelm, and Alphons STÜBEL (1880–7). *The Necropolis of Ancon in Peru*. 3 vols. Berlin.

Relaciones geográficas de Indias, Perú (1881–97). 4 vols. Madrid.

RICHARDSON, Francis B., and Alfred KIDDER II (1940). 'Publicaciones estadunidenses y británicas sobre la arqueología peruana', *Boletín Bibliográfico*, Año 13, nos 1–2, pp. 13–10. Lima.

RIVERO, Mariano E., and J. D. DE TSCHUDI (1851). *Antigüedades peruabas*. 2 vols. Vienna.

RIVET, Paul (1908). 'La Race de Lagoa-Santa chez les populations précolombiennes de l'Équateur', *Bulletins et Mémoires de la Société* (1924). *L'Orfèvrerie colombienne*. International Congress d'Anthropologie de Paris, Ser. 5, vol. 9, pp. 209–74. Paris.

——— (1924). *L'Orfèvrerie colombienne*. International Congress of Americanists, Sess. 21, The Hague, pp. 15–28.

——— (1926). 'Les Malayo-Polynésiens en Amérique', *Journal de la Société des Américanistes de Paris*, 18, pp. 141–278.

——— (1952). 'Langues américaines'. *In* Meillet et Cohen, *Les Langues du monde*. Paris.

RIVET, Paul, and H. ARSANDAUX (1946). 'La Métallurgie en Amérique précolombienne', *Travaux et Mémoires de l'Institut d'Ethnologie*, vol. 39. Paris.

RIVET, Paul, and Georges DE CRÉQUI-MONTFORT (1951–3). *Bibliographie des langues armará et kičua*. 3 vols. Paris.

ROMÁN Y ZAMORA, Jerónimo (1897). *Repúblicas de Indias; idolatrías y gobierno de México y Perú antes de la conquista*. Colección de libros raros o curiosos que tratan de América, vols 14–15. Madrid.

ROOT, William C. (1949a). 'The Metallurgy of the Southern Coast of Peru', *American Antiquity*, 15, 1, pp. 10–37.

——— (1949b). 'Metallurgy'. *In* Steward (Editor) (1949), pp. 205–25.

ROWE, John Howland (1942). *A New Pottery Style from the Department of Piura, Peru*. Carnegie Institution of Washington Notes on Middle American Archaeology and Ethnology, no. 8. Washington.

——— (1944). *An Introduction to the Archaeology of Cuzco*. Papers of the Peabody Museum of Archaeology and Ethnology, Harvard University, vol. 27, no. 2. Cambridge.

——— (1945). 'Absolute Chronology in the Andean Area', *American Antiquity*, vol. 10, no. 3, pp. 265–84.

——— (1946). 'Inca Culture at the Time of the Spanish Conquest'. *In* Steward (Editor) (1946), pp. 183–330.

——— (1948a). 'On Basic Highland Culture'. *In* Bennett (Editor) (1948), p. 20.

(1948b). 'On Absolute Dating and North Coast History'. *In* Bennett (Editor) 1948), pp. 51–2.

(1948c). 'The Kingdom of Chimor', *Acta Americana*, vol. 6, no. 1, pp. 26–49. Mexico.

(1950). 'Sound Patterns in Three Inca Dialects', *International Journal of American Linguistics*, 16, pp. 137–48.

(1954). 'Max Uhle, 1856–1944, A Memoir of the Father of Peruvian Archaeology', *University of California Publications in American Archaeology and Ethnology*, vol. 46, no. 1. Berkeley.

(1956). 'Archaeological Explorations in Southern Peru, 1954–1955'. *American Antiquity*, vol. 22, no. 2, pp. 135–51.

(1958). 'Tiempo, estilo, y proceso cultural en la arqueología peruana', *Revista Universitaria del Cuzco*. Cuzco.

(1960). 'Cultural Unity and Diversification in Peruvian Archaeology', *Fifth International Congress of Anthropological and Ethnological Sciences*, pp. 627–31. Philadelphia.

(1961). 'The Chronology of Inca Wooden Cups'. *In* Lothrop and others, pp. 317–41.

(1962). *Chavín Art, An Inquiry into Its Form and Meaning*. New York.

(1963). 'Urban Settlements in Ancient Peru', *Nawpa Pacha* I, pp. 1–28. Berkeley.

ROWE, John H., Donald COLLIER, and Gordon R. WILLEY (1950). 'Reconnaissance Notes on the Site of Huari, near Ayacucho, Peru', *American Antiquity*, 16, 2, pp. 120–37. Salt Lake City.

RUBIN DE LA BORBOLLA, Daniel (1961). *Los tesoros artísticos del Peru*. Museo Nacional de Ciencias y Arte, Mexico.

RYDEN, Stig (1947). *Archaeological Researches in the Highlands of Bolivia*. Göteborg.

(1957). 'Andean Excavations I. The Tiahuanaco Era East of Lake Titicaca'. *Publication* no. 4, Ethnographical Museum of Sweden, Stockholm.

(1959). 'Andean Excavations II. Tupuraya and Cayhuasi: Two Tiahuanaco Sites', *Publication* no. 6 (*id.*).

SAAVEDRA, Bautista (1913). *El ayllu*. La Paz.

SANCHO (DE LA HOZ), Pedro (1917a). *An Account of the Conquest of Peru*. Translated and edited by P. A. Means. Cortés Society, New York.

(1917b). *Relación para S. M. de lo sucedido en la conquista y pacificación de estas provincias de la Nueva Castilla, etc.* Colección de Libros y Documentos referentes a la historia del Perú, Ser. 1, vol. 5, pp. 122–202. Lima.

SANTILLÁN, Fernando de (1879). *Relación del origen, descendencia, política y gobierno de los Incas*. Edited by Marcos Jiménez de la Espada, *Tres relaciones de antigüedades peruanas*, pp. 1–133. Madrid.

SANTO TOMÁS, Domingo de (1891). *Arte de la lengua quichua, compuesta por Domingo de Sancto Thomás, publicado de nuevo por Julio Platzmann*. Edición facsimilar. Leipzig.

SARMIENTO DE GAMBOA, Pedro (1906). *Geschichte des Inkareiches*.

BIBLIOGRAPHY

Abhandl. Königl. Gesellsch. Wissensch. Göttingen. Philologisch-historische Klasse, vol. 6, no. 4. Editor, Richard Pietschmann. Berlin.

(1907). *History of the Incas*. Translated and edited by Sir Clements R. Markham. Hakluyt Society, Ser. 2, no. 22. Cambridge.

SAUER, Carl O. (1936). 'American Agricultural Origins: A Consideration of Nature and Culture'. In *Essays in Anthropology*, presented to A. L. Kroeber, pp. 279–97. Berkeley.

(1950a). 'Geography of South America'. *In* Steward (Editor) (1950), pp. 319–44.

(1950b). 'Cultivated Plants of South and Central America'. *In* Steward (Editor) (1950), pp. 489–543.

(1952). *Agricultural Origins and Dispersions*. The American Geographical Society, New York.

SAVILLE, Marshall H. (1921). 'A Golden Breastplate from Cuzco, Peru', *Notes and Monographs*, no. 21. Museum of the American Indian, Heye Foundation, New York.

(1925). 'Balance-beam Scales in Ancient Peru'. *Indian Notes*, Museum of the American Indian, Heye Foundation, II, pp. 266–85. New York.

(1926). 'The Pottery Arybal of the Incas'. *Ibid.*, III, pp. 111–19. New York.

(1954). *The Nathan Cummings Collection of Ancient Peruvian Art*. Chicago.

(1961). 'Paracas and Nazca Iconography', *Essays in Pre-Columbian Art and Archaeology* by S. K. Lothrop and others, pp. 269–98. Cambridge, Mass.

SAWYER, Alan R. (1966). *Ancient Peruvian Ceramics; The Nathan Cummings Collection*. The Metropolitan Museum of Art, New York. New York Graphic Society, Greenwich, Conn.

SCHAEDEL, Richard P. (1948a). 'Monolithic Sculpture of the Southern Andes', *Archaeology*, vol. 1, pp. 66–73.

(1948b). 'The Callejón de Huaylas of Peru and Its Monuments', *ibid.*, vol. 1, pp. 198–202.

(1948c). 'Stone Sculpture in the Callejón de Huaylas'. *In* Bennett (Editor) (1948), pp. 66–79.

(1949). 'Uncovering a Frieze on the Peruvian Coast', *Archaeology*, vol. 2, pp. 73–5.

(1951a). 'Wooden Idols from Peru', *ibid.*, vol. 4, pp. 16–22.

(1951b). 'Mochica Murals at Pañamarca', *ibid.*, vol. 4, pp. 145–54.

(1951c). 'Major Ceremonial and Population Centers in Northern Peru', *Civilizations of Ancient America*, pp. 232–43. Selected Papers, 29th International Congress of Americanists, Chicago.

SCHMIDT, Max (1909). 'Uber altperuanische Ornamentik', *Archiv für Anthropologie*, VII, pp. 22–38. Brunswick.

(1910). 'Szenenhafte Darstellungen auf altperuanischen Geweben', *Zeitschrift für Ethnologie*, XLII, pp. 154–64. Berlin.

(1911). *Uber altperuanische Gewebe mit szenenhaften Darstellungen.* Baessler-Archiv, I, pp. 1–61. Leipzig and Berlin.

(1929). *Kunst und Kultur von Peru.* Berlin.

SCHMIDT, Wilhelm (1913). 'Kulturkreise und Kulturschichten in Südamerika', *Zeitschrift für Ethnologie*, 45, pp. 1014–1124.

(1939). *The Culture Historical Method of Ethnology.* New York.

SCHROEDER, Gerhard (1957). 'Hallazgos de artefactos de piedra en al Perú, y los problemas del poblamiento de América', *Revista del Museo Nacional*, vol. 26, pp. 290–94. Lima.

SCHWAB, Federico (1936). 'Bibliografíca de etnología peruana', *Boletín Bibliográfico*, Año 9, no. 1, pp. 1–26; no. 2, pp. 4–27. Lima.

SELER, Eduard (1893). *Peruanische Alterthümer.* Berlin.

(1912). 'Archäologische Reise in Süd- und Mittel-Amerika', *Zeitschrift für Ethnologie*, pp. 201–42.

(1923). *Die buntbemalten Gefässe von Nasca im südlichen Peru und die Hauptelemente ihrer Verzierung.* Edited by Caecilie Seler-Sachs in *Gesammelte Abhandlungen zur amerikanischen Sprach- und Altertumskunde*, IV, pp. 171–338. Berlin.

SELLARDS, E. H. (1952). *Early Man in America.* Austin, Texas.

SIEVERS, Wilhelm (1931). *Geografía de Bolivia y Perú.* Barcelona-Buenos Aires, Editorial Labor S.A., 221 pp. (Colección Labor, sección VII, no. 288.)

SINGER, Ernestine Wieder (1936). 'The Techniques of Certain Peruvian Hairnets', *Revista del Museo Nacional*, vol. 1, t. V, pp. 16–24. Lima.

SMITH, Grafton Elliot (1924). *Elephants and Ethnologists.* London.

SOLDI, P. (1956). *Chavín in Ica.* Ica.

SQUIER, E. G. (1871–2). 'Antiquities from the Huanu Islands of Peru', *Journal of the Anthropological Institute of New York*, vol. 1, pp. 47–56. New York.

(1877). *Peru. Incidents of Travel and Exploration in the Land of the Incas.* New York.

STAFFORD, Cora Elder (1941). *Paracas embroideries.* New York.

STEGGERDA. Morris (1950). 'Anthropometry of South American Indians'. *In* Steward (Editor) (1950), pp. 57–69.

STEWARD, Julian H. (1948). 'A Functional-Developmental Classification of American High Cultures'. *In* Bennett (Editor) (1948), pp. 103–4.

(1949a). 'Cultural Causality and Law: A Trial Formulation of the Development of Early Civilizations', *American Anthropologist*, 51, I, 1–27.

(1949b). 'The Native Population of South America'. *In* Steward (Editor) (1949), 655–68.

(1949c). 'The Central Andean Peoples'. *In* Steward (Editor) (1949), pp. 731–42.

(1949d). 'Andean Culture Development'. *In* Steward (Editor) (1949), pp. 753–6.

STEWARD, Julian H. (Editor) (1946). 'Handbook of South American

Indians'. Bulletin 143, Bureau of American Ethnology, Smithsonian Institution, vol. 2, *The Andean Civilizations*. Washington.

(1949). 'Handbook of South American Indians'. Bulletin 143,
Bureau of American Ethnology, vol. 5, *The Comparative Ethnology
of South American Indians*. Washington.

(1950). 'Handbook of South American Indians'. Bulletin 143, Bureau
of American Ethnology, vol. 6, *Physical Anthropology, Linguistics,
and Cultural Geography of South American Indians*. Washington.

STEWART, T. Dale (1943a). 'Skeletal Remains with Cultural Associations from the Chicama, Moche and Virú Valleys, Peru', *Proceedings*, U.S. National Museum, vol. 93, pp. 153–85. Washington.

(1943b). 'Skeletal Remains from Paracas, Peru', *American Journal of
Physical Anthropology*, N.S., vol. 1, pp. 47–61. Philadelphia.

(1950). 'Deformity, Trephining, and Mutilation in South American
Indian Skeletal Remains'. *In* Steward (Editor) (1950), pp. 43–8.

STEWART, T. D., and Marshall T. NEWMAN (1950). 'Anthropometry of
South American Indian Skeletal Remains'. *In* Steward (Editor)
(1950), pp. 19–42.

STONOR, C. R., and Edgar ANDERSON (1949). 'Maize among the Hill
Peoples of Assam', *Annals of the Missouri Botanical Garden*, 36,
pp. 355–404. St Louis.

STRONG, William Duncan (1925). *The Uhle Pottery Collections from
Ancon*. University of California Publications in American Archaeology and Ethnology, vol. 21, pp. 135–90. Berkeley.

(1943). *Cross Sections of New World Prehistory*. Smithsonian Miscellaneous Collections, 104, 2, Publication 3739. Washington.

(1948). 'Cultural Epochs and Refuse Stratigraphy in Peruvian
Archaeology'. *In* Bennett (Editor) (1948), pp. 93–102.

(1957). *Paracas, Nazca, and Tiahuanacoid Cultural Relationships in
South Coastal Peru, Memoir 13*, Society for American Archaeology.
Salt Lake City.

STRONG, William Duncan, and John M. CORBETT (1943). *A Ceramic
Sequence at Pachacamac*. Columbia Studies in Archeology
and Ethnology, Columbia University, vol. 1, pp. 27–122. New
York.

STRONG, William Duncan, and Clifford EVANS, Jr. (1952). *Cultural
Stratigraphy in the Virú Valley, Northern Peru. Idem*, vol. 4.
Columbia University Press, New York.

STRONG, William Duncan, and Gordon R. WILLEY (1943). *Archeological Notes on the Central Coast. Idem*, I, 1. New York.

STRONG, William Duncan, Gordon R. WILLEY, and John M. CORBETT
(1943). *Archeological Studies in Peru, 1941–1942. Idem*, vol. 1.
New York.

STÜBEL, A., and Max UHLE (1892). *Die Ruinenstätte von Tiahuanaco*.
Leipzig.

STUMER, Louis Michael (1953). 'Playa Grande; Primitive Elegance in
Pre-Tiahuanaco Peru', *Archaeology*, vol. 6, no. 1, pp. 42–8.

(1954). 'The Chillón Valley of Peru; Excavation and Reconnaissance, 1952–53', *Archaeology*, vol. 7, no. 3, pp. 171–8.

SULLIVAN, Louis R., and Milo HELLMAN (1925). *The Punin Calvarium.* Anthropological Papers, American Museum of Natural History, vol. 23, pt 7, pp. 309–37. New York.

TABIO, Ernesto E. (1957). 'Excavaciones en Playa Grande, costa central del Peru, 1955', *Arqueologicas*, I–I. Lima.

(1965). *Excavaciones en la costa central del Perú.* Academia de Ciencias. Habana.

TELLO, Julio C. (1912). *Prehistoric Trephining among the Yauyos of Peru.* International Congress of Americanists, XVIII, pp. 75–83. London.

(1917). *Los antiguos cimenterios del valle de Nasca.* Washington.

(1918). *El uso de las cabezas artificialmente momificadas en el antiguo arte peruano.* Lima.

(1921). *Introducción a la historia antigua del Perú.* Lima.

(1923). 'Wira Kocha', *Inca*, vol. 1, pp. 93–320, 583–606. Lima.

(1927). 'Bibliografía de antropología del Perú', *Bol. Bibl. Univer. San Marcos*, vol. 3, no. 3, pp. 31–6. Lima.

(1928). *Los descubrimientos del Museo de Arqueología Peruana en la península de Paracas.* International Congress of Americanists, XXII, pt 1, pp. 679–90. Rome.

(1929). *Antiguo Perú; primera época.* Lima.

(1930). *Andean Civilization. Some Problems of Peruvian Archeology.* International Congress of Americanists, Sess. 23 (1928), pp. 259–290. New York.

(1937). 'La civilización de los Inkas', *Letras*, no. 6, pp. 5–37. Lima.

(1938). 'Arte antiguo peruano', *Inca*, vol. 2. Lima.

(1939). *Las primeras edades del Perú por Guamán Poma.* Lima.

(1942). *Origen y desarrollo de las civilizaciones prehistóricas andinas*, Lima.

(1943). 'Discovery of the Chavín Culture in Peru', *American Antiquity*, vol. 9, pp. 135–60.

(1956). *Arqueología del Valle de Casma; Culturas Chavín, Santa o Huaylas Yunga y Sub-Chimú. Informe de los trabajos de la Expedición Arqueológica al Marañon de 1937.* Lima.

(1959). *Paracas, Primera Parte.* Lima.

(1961). *Chavín, Cultura Matrix de la Civilización Andina.* Universidad Nacional Mayor de San Marcos, Lima.

TELLO, Julio C., and Próspero MIRANDA (1923). 'Wallallo', *Inca*, I, pp. 475–549.

TEN KATE, Herman F. C. (1885). 'Sur les crânes de Lagoa-Santa', *Bulletin de la Société d'Anthropologie de Paris*, Ser. 3, vol. 8, 240–4.

THOMPSON, J. Eric (1936). *Archaeology of South America.* Field Museum of Natural History, Anthropology Leaflet No. 33. Chicago.

TITO CUSI YPUANQUI, Diego de Castro (1916). *Relación de la conquista del Perú y hechos del Inca Manco II.* Colección de Libros y Documentos referentes a la historia del Perú, vol. 2.

BIBLIOGRAPHY

TOLEDO, Francisco de (1940). *Informaciones que mandó levantar el Virrey Toledo sobre los Incas*. Ed. Roberto Levillier, *Don Francisco de Toledo, supremo organizador del Perú*, vol. 2, pp. 1–204. Buenos Aires.

TORRES-LUNA, A. (1923). 'El vestuario en la época incáica', *Revista de Arqueología*, I, pp. 50–64. Lima.

TORRES RUBIO, Father Diego de (1603). *Gramática y vocabulario en la lengua general del Perú, llamada Quichua*. Seville.

TOWLE, Margaret Ashley (1952a). 'Description and Identification of Plant Remains from Certain Sites in the Virú Valley'. *In* Strong and Evans.

(1952b). 'Plant Remains from a Peruvian Mummy Bundle', *Botanical Museum Leaflets*, vol. 15, no. 9, pp. 223–46. Harvard University, Cambridge, Mass.

1961. *The Ethnobotany of Precolumbian Peru*. Viking Fund Publications in Anthropology, No. 30. New York.

TRIMBORN, Hermann (1923–4). 'Der Kollektivismus der Inkas in Peru', *Anthropos*, XVIII, pp. 978–1001. Vienna.

(1925). 'Straftat und Sühne in Alt-Peru', *Zeitschrift für Ethnologie*, LVII, pp. 194–240. Berlin.

(1927). 'Die Gliederung der Staende im Inka-Reich', *Journal de la Société des Américanistes de Paris*, XIX, pp. 303–44.

(1936). *Quellen zur Kulturgeschichte des präkolumbischen Amerika*. Strecher und Schröder, Stuttgart.

TROLL, Von C. (1931–2). *Die geographischen Grundlagen der andinen Kulturen und des Incareiches*. Ibero-Amerikanisches Archiv, vol. 5, pp. 257–94. Berlin.

(1958). *Las culturas superiores andinas y el medio geográfico*. Instituto de Geografia de la Universidad Nacional Mayor de San Marcos. Lima.

TSCHOPIK, Harry, Jr. (1946). 'Some Notes on Rock Shelter Sites near Huancayo, Peru', *American Antiquity*, vol. 12, no. 2, pp. 73–80.

(1950). 'An Andean Ceramic Tradition in Historical Perspective', *American Antiquity*, vol. 15, no. 3, pp. 196–218.

TSCHOPIK, Marion Hutchinson (1946). *Some Notes on the Archaeology of the Department of Puno, Peru*. Papers of the Peabody Museum of American Archaeology and Ethnology, 27, 3. Cambridge.

TSCHUDI, Johann Jakob von (1847). *Travels in Peru, during the Years 1838–1842*. Translated by Thomasina Ross. London.

(1853). *Die Kechua-Sprache*. 3 vols. Vienna.

(1869). *Reisen durch Süd-Amerika*, vol. 5. Leipzig.

(1891). *Culturhistorische und sprachliche Beiträge zur Kenntniss des alten Peru*. Vienna.

TUDELA Y VARELA, Francisco (1905). *Socialismo peruano*. Lima.

UHLE, Max (1889–90). *Kultur und Industrie der südamerikanischen Völker*. 2 vols. Berlin.

(1897). 'A Modern Kipu from Cutusuma, Bolivia'. *Bulletin of the Free Museum of Science and Art*, vol. 1, no. 2, pp. 51–63. Philadelphia.

(1898). 'A Snuffing-tube from Tiahuanaco', *ibid.*, vol. 1, no. 4, pp. 159–77. Philadelphia.

(1903). *Pachacamac; Report of the William Pepper, M.D., LL.D., Peruvian Expedition of 1896*. Trans. C. Grosse. University of Pennsylvania, Department of Archaeology, Philadelphia.

(1906a). 'Los Kjoekkenmoedings del Perú', *Revista histórica*, 1, pp. 3–23. Lima.

(1906b). 'Las llamitas de piedra del Cuzco', *ibid.*, 1, pp. 388–92.

(1906c). *Bericht über die Ergebnisse meiner südamerikanischen Reisen*. International Congress of Americanists, XIV, pt 2, pp. 567–79. Stuttgart.

(1906d). *Aus meinem Bericht über die Ergebnisse meiner Reise nach Südamerika 1899–1901. Idem*, pp. 581–92.

(1907a). 'La estólica en el Perú', *Revista histórica*, II, pp. 118–28. Lima.

(1907b). 'La masca paicha del Inca', *ibid.*, pp. 227–32. Lima.

(1908a). *Ueber die Frühkulturen in der Umgebung von Lima*. International Congress of Americanists, Sess. 16, pp. 347–70. Vienna.

(1908b). *Zur Deutung der Intihuatana. Idem*, pp. 371–89.

(1909). 'Peruvian Throwing-Sticks', *American Anthropologist*, XI, pp. 624–7.

(1910). 'Tipos de civilización en el Perú', *Boletin de la Sociedad Geográfica, de Lima*.

(1912). *Los orígenes de los Incas*. Congreso Internacional de Americanistas, Sess. 17 (Buenos Aires, 1910), vol. 1, pp. 230–53.

(1913a). 'Die Ruinen von Moche', *Journal de la Société des Américanistes de Paris*, vol. 10, pp. 95–117.

(1913b). 'Zur Chronologie der alten Culturen von Ica', *ibid.*, pp. 341–367.

(1913c). 'Muschelhügel von Ancon, Peru'. International Congress of Americanists, *Proceedings*, Sess. 18 (London, 1912), pp. 22–45.

(1917a). 'Fortalezas incaicas', *Revista chilena de Historia y Geografía*. Santiago de Chile.

(1917b). *Los aborígenes de Arica*. Santiago de Chile.

(1919a). 'Fundamentos étnicos de la región de Arica y Tacna', *Boletín de la Sociedad Ecuatoriana de Estudios Históricos Americanos*, II, pp. 1–37. Quito.

(1919b). 'La arqueología de Arica y Tacna', *ibid.*, vol. 3, pp. 1–48.

(1920a). 'Apuntes sobre la prehistoria de la región de Piura', *ibid.*, vol. 4, pp. 165–7.

(1920b). 'Los principios de las antiguas civilizaciones peruanas', *ibid.*, vol. 4, no. 12, pp. 448–58.

(1920c). 'Los principios de la civilización en la sierra peruana', *ibid.*, vol. 4, nos. 13–14, pp. 44–56.

(1922). *Fundamentos étnicos y arqueología de Arica y Tacna*. 2nd edn. Quito.

(1924a). *Explorations at Chincha*. University of California Publications in American Archaeology and Ethnology, XXI, pp. 58–94.

(1924b). *Notes on Ica Valley*. Idem, pp. 121–3.

(1924c). *Notes on Sites and Graves excavated*. Idem, pp. 123–7.

(1924d). *Ancient Civilizations of Ica Valley*. Idem, pp. 128–32.

(1926). 'Los elementos constitutivos de las civilizaciones sudamericanas', *Anales de la Universidad Central. Quito, Ecuador*, vol. 36.

(1928). *Späte Mastodonten in Ecuador*. International Congress of Americanists, Sess. 23, pp. 247–58. New York.

(1935). *Die alten Kulturen Perus im Hinblick auf die Archäologie und Geschichte des amerikanischen Kontinents*. Berlin.

(1939). 'Procedencia y origen de las antiguas civilizaciones americanas', *Actas y Trabajos científicos del xxvii Congreso Internacional de Americanistas*, t. I, pp. 355–68. Lima.

URTEAGA, Horacio H. (1909). 'El antiguo Perú a la luz de la arqueología y de la crítica', *Revista histórica*, IV, pp. 200–23. Lima.

(1921). 'La organización judicial en el imperio de los Incas', *ibid.*, IX, pp. 1–50. Lima.

(1931). *El imperio incáico. En el que se incluye la historia del ayllo y familia de los Incas*. Lima.

VALCÁRCEL, Luís E. (1924). 'El Cuzco precolombiano', *Revista Universitaria del Cuzco*, no. 44.

(1930). *Metallarbeiten aus dem nördlichen Peru. Ein Beitrag zur Kenntnis ihrer Formen*. Mitteilungen aus dem Museum für Völkerkunde in Hamburg, vol. 15. Hamburg.

(1932). 'El Gato de Agua, Sus Representaciones en Pucara y Nazco', *Revista Museo Nacional de Antropología y Arqueología*, vol. 1. Lima.

(1933). 'Esculturas de Pikillajta', *Revista del Museo Nacional*, vol. 2, pp. 21–48. Lima.

(1934–5). 'Sajsawaman redescubierto', *ibid.*, vol. 3, pp. 3–36, 211–23; vol. 4, pp. 1–24, 161–203. Lima.

(1935). 'Litoesculturas y cerámica de Pukara', *ibid.*, vol. 4, no. 1, pp. 25–8.

(1939). *Sobre el origen del Cusco*. Lima.

(1943–9). *Historia de la cultura antigua del Perú*. Lima, Imprenta del Museo Nacional y del Ministerio de Educación Pública, t. 1, 2 vols. Lima.

(1946). 'Cuzco Archeology'. *In* Steward (Editor) (1946), pp. 177–82.

(1953). *Altiplano andino. Programa de historia de América*. Instituto Panamericano de Geografía e Historia, México.

VALDEZ DE LA TORRE, Carlos (1920a). 'El ayllu', *Mercurio peruano*, V, pp. 187–209. Lima.

(1920b). 'Régimen de la propiedad durante los Incas', *ibid.*, V, pp. 399–413.

VALERA, Blas (1879). *Relación de las costumbres antiguas de los naturales del Perú*. Ed. Marcos Jiménez de la Espada, *Tres relaciones de antigüedades peruanas*, pp. 135–227. Madrid.

VALETTE, M. (1913). 'Note sur la teinture de tissus précolombiens du Bas-Pérou', *Journal de la Société des Américanistes de Paris*, x, pp. 43–6.

VAN STAN, Ina (1955). 'Peruvian Domestic Fabrics from Supe; A Study of the Uhle Collection of Painted Cloths', *Notes in Anthropology*, vol. 1, no. 3. Florida State University, Tallahassee.

(1958). 'Problems in Pre-Columbian Textile Classification', *Florida State University Studies*, no. 29. Tallahasee.

VARGAS UGARTE, Rubén (1939). *Historia del Perú; Fuentes*. Lima.

VEGA TORAL, Tomás (1841–4). *Historia del reino de Quito*. Edited by Don Agustín Yerovi. 3 vols. Quito.

(1921). *La Tomebamba de los Incas*. Cuenca.

VERGER, Pierre (1950). *Indians of Peru*. New York.

VESCELIUS, Gary S., and Edward P. LANNING (1963). 'Some New Finds at San Nicolas', *Nawpa Pacha* I, pp. 43–6. Berkeley.

VILLAR CÓRDOVA, Pedro Eduardo (1923). 'Las ruinas de la provincia de Canta', *Inca*, I, pp. 1–24.

(1935). *Arqueología peruana. Las culturas prehispánicas del departamento de Lima*. Lima.

VON HAGEN, Victor Wolfgang (1949a). 'Hiram Bingham and His Lost Cities', *Archaeology*, vol. 2, pp. 40–6.

(1949b). *Guides to Peru: Cusco, Sacsahuaman, Machu Picchu, Lima, etc*. New York.

(1952a). 'The Mystery of Pisac', *Archaeology*, vol. 5, pp. 33–8.

(1952b). 'The Highways of the Inca', *ibid*., vol. 5, pp. 104–9.
Highway of the Sun, New York and Boston, 1955.

(1957). *Realm of the Incas*.

(1965). *The Desert Kingdoms of Peru*. New York Graphic Society.

WALLACE, Dwight T. (1963). 'Early Horizon Ceramics in the Cañete Valley of Peru', *Nawpa Pacha* I, pp. 35–8. Berkeley.

WALTER, H. V., A. CATHOUD, and Anibal MATTOS (1937). 'The Confins Man – A Contribution to the Study of Early Man in South America', *Early Man*, ch. 34, pp. 341–8. Philadelphia.

WARDLE, H. Newell (1936). 'Belts and Girdles of the Inca's Sacrificed Women', *Revista del Museo Nacional*, vol. 1, t. v, pp. 25–38. Lima.

(1939). 'An Ancient Paracas Mantle', *University Museum Bulletin*, vol. 7, no. 4, pp. 22–5. Philadelphia.

(1940). 'Fictile Art of the Mochicas', *ibid*., vol. 8, no. 1, pp. 15–24. Philadelphia.

(1944). 'Triple Cloth; A New Type of Ancient Peruvian Technique', *American Anthropologist*, vol. 46, pp. 416–18.

(1948). *False Heads of Peruvian Mummy-bales*. International Congress of Americanists (Seville, 1935). pp. 208–17. Madrid.

(1949). *A Rare Peruvian Tapestry Bonnet*. International Congress of Americanists (New York, 1949), pp. 216–18. New York.

BIBLIOGRAPHY

WASSÉN, Henry (1931). 'The Ancient Peruvian Abacus', *Comparative Ethnographical Studies*. Gothenburg (Göteborg) Museum, vol. 9, pp. 189–205. Göteborg.

— (1940). 'El antiguo ábaco peruano según el manuscrito de Guamán Poma', *Ethnological Studies*, no. 11, pp. 1–30. Göteborg.

WASSERMANN-SAN BLAS, B. J. (1938). *Cerámicas del antiguo Perú; de la colección Wassermann-San Blas*. Buenos Aires.

WAUCHOPE, Robert (1954). 'Implications of Radiocarbon Dates, from Middle and South America', *Middle American Research Records*, II, 2. Middle American Research Institute, Tulane University, New Orleans.

WEBERBAUER, Augusto (1945). *El mundo vegetal de los Andes peruanos*. 776 pp. Lima, Editorial Lumen.

— (1962). 'Cerrillos, An Early Paracas Site in Ica, Peru', *American Antiquity*, vol. 27, pp. 303–14.

WENDT, W. E. (1964). 'Die präkeramische Siedlung am Rio Seco, Peru', *Baessler Archiv*, n.s., Band 11, No. 2, pp. 225–75. Baessel.

WHITAKER, Thomas W., and Junius B. BIRD (1949). *Identification and Significance of the Cucurbit Materials from Huaca Prieta, Peru*. American Museum Novitates, no. 1426. American Museum of Natural History, New York.

WIENER, Charles (1880). *Pérou et Bolivie*. Paris.

WIESSE, Carlos (1913). *Las civilizaciones primitivas del Perú*. Lima.

WILLEY, Gordon R. (1943a). 'Excavations in the Chancay Valley', *Columbia Studies in Archaeology and Ethnology*, 1, 3. New York.

— (1943b). 'A Supplement to the Pottery Sequence at Ancón', *ibid.*, 1, 4. New York.

— (1945). 'Horizon Styles and Pottery Traditions in Peruvian Archaeology', *American Antiquity*, vol. 11, no. 1, pp. 49–56.

— (1947). 'A Middle Period Cemetery in Virú Valley', *Journal of the Washington Academy of Science*, vol. 37, pp. 41–7. Washington.

— (1948). 'Functional Analysis of "Horizon Styles" in Peruvian Archaeology'. *In* Bennett (Editor) (1948), pp. 8–15.

— (1949). 'Ceramics'. *In* Steward (Editor) (1949), pp. 139–204.

— (1915a). 'Peruvian Settlement and Socio-Economic Patterns', *The Civilizations of Ancient America* (Selected Papers of the XXIXth International Congress of Americanists), pp. 195–200. University of Chicago Press, Chicago.

— (1951b). 'The Chavín Problem: a Review and Critique', *Southwestern Journal of Anthropology*, 7, 2, 103–44. Albuquerque.

— (1953a). *Prehistoric Settlement Patterns in the Virú Valley, Peru*. Bulletin 155; Bureau of American Ethnology, Smithsonian Institution, Washington.

— (1953b). 'Archaeological Theories and Interpretations'. In *Anthropology Today*, pp. 387–80. Chicago.

WILLEY, Gordon R., and John N. CORBETT (1954). *Early Ancon and Early Supe Culture; Chavín Horizon Sites of the Central Peruvian*

Coast. Columbia Studies in Archaeology and Ethnology, 3. Columbia University Press, New York.

WORMINGTON, H. M. (1949). *Ancient Man in North America*. Popular Series, 4. 3rd edn. The Denver Museum of Natural History, Denver.

(1953). *Origins; Indigenous Period*. Program of the History of America, 1, 1. Instituto Panamericano de Geografía e Historia; Comisión de Historia. Mexico.

WRIGLEY, G. M. (1917). 'The Travelling Doctors of the Andes, the Callahuayas of Bolivia', *Geographical Review*, 4, 183–96.

XÉREZ, Francisco de (1872). *Reports on the Discovery of Peru*. Translated and edited by C. R. Markham. Hakluyt Society, London.

(1917). *Verdadera relación de la conquista del Perú y provincia del Cuzco llamada la Nueva-Castilla*. Colección de Libros y Documentos referentes a la historia del Perú, Ser. 1, vol. 5, pp. 1–121. Lima.

YACOVLEFF, Eugenio (1931). 'El Vencejo (*Cypselus*) en al arte decorativo de Nasca', *Wira Kocha*, vol. 1, pp. 25–35. Lima. (1932). 'Las falcónidas en el arte y en las creencias de los antiguos peruanos', *Revista del Museo Nacional*, vol. 1, no. 1, pp. 33–111. Lima.

(1933). 'Arte plumaria entre los antiguos peruanos', *ibid.*, vol. 2, pp. 137–58. Lima.

YACOVLEFF, Eugenio, and Fortunato L. HERRERA (1934–5). 'El mundo vegetal de los antiguos peruanos', *ibid.*, vol. 3, no. 3, pp. 241–322, vol. 4, no. 1, pp. 29–102. Lima.

YACOVLEFF, Eugenio, y Jorge C. MUELLE (1932). 'Una exploración en Cerro Colorado. Informe', *ibid.*, vol. 1, pp. 31–59, 81–9. Lima.

(1934). 'Un fardo funerario de Paracas', *ibid.*, vol. 3, nos 1 & 2 pp. 63–163. Lima.

ZARATE, Agustín de (1853). *Historia del descubrimiento y conquista de la provincia del Perú*. Biblioteca de Autores Españoles, vol. 26, pp. 459–574. Madrid.

ZIMMERN, Nathalie Herman (1944). 'The Tapestries of Colonial Peru', *Brooklyn Museum Journal*, 1943–4, pp. 25–52. New York.

ZURKALOWSKI, Erich (1919). 'Observaciones sobre la organización social del Perú antiguo', *Mercurio peruano*, 11, pp. 337–52, 480–95. Lima.

INDEX

325

INDEX

327

INDEX

INDEX

330

INDEX